Introductory

SEVENTH EDITION

Computer Confluence

TOMORROW'S TECHNOLOGY AND YOU

George Beekman
Michael J. Quinn
OREGON STATE UNIVERSITY

PEARSON
Prentice
Hall

Upper Saddle River, New Jersey 07458

Computer Confluence, Seventh Edition
Introductory edition
George Beekman, Michael J. Quinn

Executive Editor, Print: Stephanie L. Wall
Executive Editor, Media: Jodi McPherson
Publisher and Vice President: Natalie E. Anderson
Development Editor: Maureen Allaire Spada
Senior Project Manager, Editorial: Eileen Clark
Editorial Assistant: Alana Meyers
Senior Project Manager, Media: Cathi Profitko
Project Manager, Production: Lynne Breitfeller
Director of Marketing: Sarah Loomis
Senior Marketing Manager: Emily Knight
Marketing Manager: Sarah Davis
Associate Director, Manufacturing: Vincent Scelta
Manufacturing Buyer: Lynne Breitfeller
Manager Print Production: Christy Mahon
Design Manager: Maria Lange
Art Director and Interior/Cover Design: Blair Brown
Composition: Pre-Press Company, Inc.
Photo Research: Elaine Soares and Pre-Press Company, Inc
Printer/Binder: Courier/Kendallville
Cover Printer: Phoenix Color
Back Cover Author Photo: Scobel Wiggins

10 9 8 7 6 5 4 3 2
ISBN 0-13-152530-1

To students all over the world –

The promise of the future

lies not in technology

but in you.

—G.B.

—M.J.Q.

Brief Contents

Contents

PART 1 Approaching Computers: HARDWARE AND SOFTWARE FUNDAMENTALS

Chapter 2   Hardware Basics: Inside the Box   70

Chapter 3   Hardware Basics: Peripherals   100

Chapter 4   Software Basics: The Ghost in the Machine   138

PART 2   Using Computers: ESSENTIAL APPLICATIONS

Chapter 5   Basic Productivity Applications   176

Chapter 6   Graphics, Digital Media, and Multimedia   220

Chapter 7   Database Applications and Privacy Implications   264

PART 3   Exploring with Computers: NETWORKING AND THE INTERNET

Chapter 8   Networking and Telecommunication   302

Chapter 9   Inside the Internet and the World Wide Web   340

PART 4   Living with Computers: ISSUES AND IMPLICATIONS

Chapter 10   Computer Security and Risks   384

About this Book

Confluence

1: a **coming or flowing together**, meeting, or gathering at one point (a happy confluence of weather and scenery);

2a: the flowing together of **two or more streams**;

  b: the **place of meeting** of two streams;

  c: the **combined stream** formed by conjunction

—Merriam Webster's Collegiate Dictionary, Electronic Edition

When powerful forces come together, change is inevitable. Today we're standing at the confluence of three powerful and rapidly evolving technological forces: computers, communication networks, and electronic entertainment. The computer's digital technology is showing up in everything from telephones to televisions, and the lines that separate these machines are eroding. This digital convergence is rapidly—and radically—altering the world's economic landscape. Start-up companies and industries are emerging to ride the waves of change. Some thrive; others dive into oblivion. Meanwhile, older organizations reorganize, regroup, and redefine themselves to keep from being washed away.

Smaller computers, faster processors, smarter software, larger networks, new communication media—in the world of information technology, it seems like change is the only constant. In less than a human lifetime, this technological cascade has transformed virtually every facet of our society—and the transformation is just beginning. As old technologies merge and new technologies emerge, far-fetched predictions routinely come true. This headlong rush into the high-tech future poses a challenge for all of us: How can we extract the knowledge we need from the deluge of information? What must we understand about information technology to successfully navigate the waters of change that carry us into the future? *Computer Confluence: Tomorrow's Technology and You* is designed to aid travelers on their journey into that future.

Meeting this challenge means going far beyond knowing how to create a spreadsheet or remembering how many pages of text will fit on a CD-ROM. A deeper understanding of information technology will help you answer much more meaningful questions. How can we cope with spam? What should we do to reduce our chances of being a victim of identity theft? What should we consider when setting up a home network? Will automation result in massive, long-term unemployment? Will information technology be a tool to bring the people of the world closer together, or will it drive a permanent wedge between the rich and the poor? *Computer Confluence: Tomorrow's Technology and You* is designed to help you explore these questions. It goes beyond simply describing the latest gadgets and explains many of the benefits we derive (and risks we tolerate) when we incorporate information technology into our lives.

What Is *Computer Confluence?*

Computer Confluence presents computers and information technology on three levels:

- Explanations: *Computer Confluence* clearly explains what a computer is and what it can (and can't) do; it clearly explains the basics of information technology, from multimedia PCs to the Internet and beyond.

- Applications: *Computer Confluence* illustrates how computers and networks are—and will be—used as practical tools to solve a wide variety of problems.

■ Implications: *Computer Confluence* puts computers in a human context, illustrating how information technology affects our lives, our world, and our future.

The book consists of 11 chapters, numbered 0 through 10 in the grand tradition of computer science. Chapter 0, "Basics," provides an introduction for students who have little or no experience with PCs and the Internet. The chapter also includes an orientation to the *Computer Confluence* book, CD-ROM, and Web site.

The remaining chapters are organized into four broad sections:

1. Approaching Computers: Hardware and Software Fundamentals
2. Using Computers: Essential Applications
3. Exploring with Computers: Networking and the Internet
4. Living with Computers: Issues and Implications

In general, the book's focus flows from the concrete to the controversial and from the present to the future. Individual chapters have a similarly expanding focus. After a brief introduction, each chapter flows from basic concepts toward abstract, future-oriented questions and ideas. Most chapters raise ethical issues related to computer use and misuse. Every chapter asks readers to think about the tradeoffs associated with information technology innovations. The book provides a framework to help readers focus on their dreams and aspirations and think about ways to use information technology as a way to help them achieve their goals

About the Authors

George Beekman is an Honorary Instructor in the School of Electrical Engineering and Computer Science at Oregon State University. For more than two decades he designed and taught courses in computer literacy, interactive multimedia, computer ethics, and computer programming at OSU. An innovative computer literacy course he created more than two decades ago served as the inspiration for *Computer Confluence*. George Beekman has taught workshops in computer literacy and multimedia for students, educators, and economically disadvantaged families from the Atlantic to Alaska. He has written more than 20 books on computers, information technology, and multimedia, as well as more than 100 articles and reviews for *Macworld* and other popular publications. In his spare time he hikes and runs along forest trails and plays acoustic and electronic percussion with his band, Oyaya.

Michael J. Quinn is a Professor in the School of Electrical Engineering and Computer Science at Oregon State University. In the past two decades he has taught a wide variety courses, including computer literacy, computer programming, computer ethics, analysis of algorithms, and parallel computing. He has written four books and more than 50 peer-reviewed papers in the area of parallel computing. His fifth book, *Ethics for the Information Age*, discusses moral issues raised by the use of information technology. For recreation, he enjoys playing golf with his friends.

About this Edition

Even if you're **on the right track**, you'll get **run over** if you **just sit** on it.

—*Pat Koppman*

The pace of change threatens to make even the most successful introductory computer classes irrelevant. *Computer Confluence*, Seventh Edition, helps students and instructors deal with rapid changes by emphasizing big ideas, broad trends, and the human aspects of technology—critical concepts that tend to remain constant even while hardware and software change. Every edition of *Computer Confluence* is rewritten to reflect changes in the technological landscape. We have refined and rewritten this edition to reflect developments in information technology, changes in pedagogical methods, and feedback from readers and reviewers. We've included new features, new artwork, new issues, and a new design. The CD-ROM has been completely redesigned, too, and packed with new material to enhance and expand on material presented in the book.

We have added many new **Screen Tests** and redesigned the old ones. These multi-screen sequences show what it's like to use a particular software package to achieve a specific goal. They provide students with a glimpse of programs they might not otherwise experience. Throughout the book there's less coverage of familiar applications and more emphasis on emerging technologies and their ethical and social impact.

We've also added new *How It Works* boxes and redesigned some of the old ones so they're clearer and more visually interesting. Like the other How It Works boxes, these optional features use pictures and words to make complex topics easy to understand.

The popular Rules of Thumb boxes of the Sixth Edition have morphed into **Working Wisdom** boxes, with streamlined text and added illustrations. These boxes contain relevant and intriguing tips that can help readers produce better results and steer clear of trouble.

The future continues to slip into the present, and we've rewritten several of the Inventing the Future boxes to ensure that they continue to provide solid information about emerging technologies and promising research.

Inventing the Future boxes provide futuristic perspectives at the ends of chapters 1-10.

Crosscurrents articles are some of the best contemporary, short essays focusing on our complex relationship with technology. Topics include the erosion of personal privacy, the abuse of intellectual property laws, software reliability, and machine intelligence.

We have **enhanced the end-of-chapter material**. We have added additional multiple-choices questions to the end of each chapter, bringing the total up to 15 per chapter. There are many new projects. Many existing projects are now explained in much more detail. We have also added new discussion questions and updated the sources and resources.

Here is a chapter-by-chapter summary of highlights new to this edition.

Chapter 0, "Basics." This unique chapter addresses the most commonly reported problem of introductory computer concepts classes—the diverse backgrounds of students in those classes. Many instructors report that the majority of their new students have some PC and Internet experience. These students don't need to be told about keyboarding, using a CD-ROM, or navigating a Web site. But if these topics aren't covered, the inexperienced students are at a distinct disadvantage. The Basics Chapter is designed for those beginners, so they can fill in the gaps in their knowledge before launching into the rest of the book, the CD-ROM, and the Web site. In the Seventh Edition we have moved content from other parts of the book into this chapter. We have expanded the section on file management, with new information on file organization, types of files, file compression, and backup media. We have added two Screen Tests: "File Management with Windows" and "Exploring Hypertext Web Links." We moved most of the material on entering and editing text in a word processor from Chapter 5 to Chapter 0. We have moved material describing the advantages of online communication from Chapter 8 to Chapter 0. We streamlined the *Computer Confluence* Quick Start guide and added more visual elements to make it even easier for beginners to get the most out of this book and its supplements.

Chapter 1, This chapter's new title, "Computer Currents and Internet Waves," reflects its purpose: to provide a necessary perspective for understanding the future by emphasizing broad trends rather than historical details. This chapter places the rapid changes in computer technology and the Internet in perspective, providing a solid foundation for the chapters that follow. The Inventing the Future box that closes the chapter provides an overview of strategies for predicting the future—strategies that are applied in later chapters. The chapter opens with a timely story about Sergey Brin and Larry Page, the "Google Guys" who changed the way we all use the Web. A new "History of the Future" section describes devices that will become commonplace in the next ten years due to the continued rapid increase in computer power. The chapter closes with a new Crosscurrents article by Rodney Brooks: "Toward a Brain-Internet Link."

Chapter 2, "Hardware Basics: Inside the Box," We have rewritten How It Works 2.1 (Binary Numbers) so that it now covers binary addition. We have revised How It Works 2.4 (Memory) to clarify the distinction between RAM and ROM. The Crosscurrents article "Silicon Hogs" has been moved from Chapter 1 to Chapter 2.

Chapter 3 "Hardware Basics: Peripherals" We have updated How It Works 3.1 (Digitizing the Real World). The new two-page spread clearly illustrates the technology at the heart of digital imaging and digital audio.

Chapter 4, "Software Basics: The Ghost in the Machine." We have completely redesigned How It Works 4.1 (Executing a Program) to make the instruction execution cycle easier to understand. A new section on File Management covers organizing files and folders, file management utilities, managing files from applications, locating files, and defragmentation. We have moved the coverage of intellectual property issues from Chapter 10 to Chapter 4, and we have expanded our discussion of ethical issues related to copying intellectual property.

Chapter 5 "Basic Productivity Applications." Two new Working Wisdom boxes are designed to be of value to all readers. One focuses on creating professional-looking documents. The other discusses the development of correct spreadsheets and effective data charts.

Chapter 6, "Graphics, Digital Media, and Multimedia." A new, two-page Working Wisdom box contains practical advice for giving effective PowerPoint presentations. A new Screen Test highlights Flash animations. We have revised the Screen Test showing the creation of a CD cover using the latest version of Photoshop. We have added coverage of scalable vector graphics. A brand new How It Works box demystifies the technology that enables amateur and professional musicians to create and edit music with a computer.

Chapter 7, "Database Applications and Privacy Implications." We have revised the Screen Test to emphasize the portability of data between PCs and various handheld devices. We have added significant coverage of ethical issues related to large government databases, including the National Crime Information Center. We have also added coverage of the USA PATRIOT Act.

Chapter 8, "Networking and Telecommunication." We have added a two-page How It Works box on home networking and WiFi. We have expanded our coverage of issues related to wireless networking, including a much-revised Inventing the Future box.

Chapter 9, "Inside the Internet and the World Wide Web." We have added content focusing on issues related to Internet access, including censorship and the digital divide. Two new Screen Tests help readers understand the difference between Web search engines and Web subject directories.

Chapter 10, "Computer Security and Risks." We have added coverage of identity theft and spyware. A new Working Wisdom covers "Protecting Yourself from Identity Theft." We have created a How It Works box on firewalls and added a section focusing on the key role system administrators play in protecting a computer network. A new Inventing the Future box looks into the future of Internet security.

Throughout Computer Confluence

you'll find these special focus boxes here:

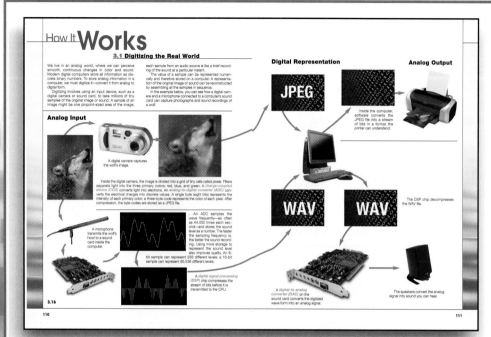

How it Works

How it Works boxes provide additional technical material on more complex topics. For classes where this kind of technical detail isn't necessary, students can skip these boxes. How It Works boxes are numbered so that instructors can create customized reading assignments by specifying which are required and which are optional.

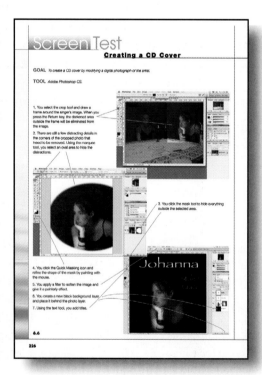

Screen Test

We have added many new **Screen Tests** and redesigned the old ones. These multi-screen sequences show what it's like to use a particular software package to achieve a specific goal. They provide students with a glimpse of programs they might not otherwise experience. Throughout the book there's less coverage of familiar applications and more emphasis on emerging technologies and their ethical and social impact.

Inventing the Future

Inventing the Future boxes provide futuristic perspectives at the end of every chapter.

Crosscurrents

Crosscurrents articles are some of the best contemporary, short essays focusing on our complex relationship with technology. Topics include the erosion of personal privacy, the abuse of intellectual property laws, software reliability, and machine intelligence.

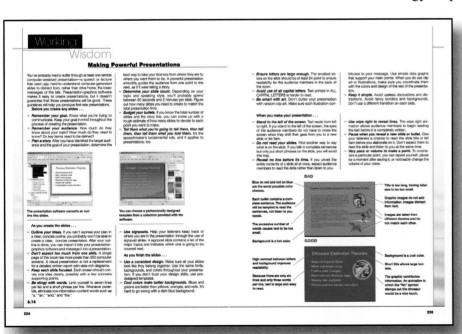

Working Wisdom

The popular Rules of Thumb boxes of the Sixth Edition have morphed into **Working Wisdom** boxes, with streamlined text and added illustrations. These boxes contain relevant and intriguing tips that can help readers produce better results and steer clear of trouble.

For the Student

If you're like most students, you aren't taking this course to read about computers—you want to use them. That's sensible. You can't really understand computers without some hands-on experience, and you'll be able to apply your computer skills to a wide variety of future projects. But it's a mistake to think that you're techno-savvy just because you can use a PDA to surf the Internet. It's important to understand how people use and abuse computer technology, because that technology has a powerful and growing impact on your life. (If you can't imagine how your life would be different without computers, read the vignette called "Living without Computers" in Chapter 1.)

Even if you have lots of computer experience, future trends are almost certain to make much of that experience obsolete—probably sooner than you think. In the next few years, computers are likely to take on entirely new forms and roles because of breakthroughs in artificial intelligence, wireless technology, security, ethics, robotics, multimedia, and cross-breeding with telephone and home entertainment technologies. If your knowledge of computers stops with a handful of PC and Internet applications, you may be standing still while the world changes around you.

When you're kayaking down an unfamiliar waterway, you need to be able to use a paddle, but it's also important to know how to read a map, a compass, and the river. *Computer Confluence*: Tomorrow's Technology and You is designed to serve as a map, compass, and book of river lore to help you ride the information waves into the future.

Computer Confluence will help you understand the important trends that will change the way you work with computers and the way computers work for you. This book discusses the promise and the problems of computer technology without overwhelming you with technobabble.

Computer Confluence is intentionally nontechnical and down to earth. Occasional ministories bring concepts and speculations to life. Illustrations and photos make abstract concepts concrete. Quotes add thought-provoking and humorous seasoning.

Whether you're a hard-core hacker or a confirmed computerphobe, there's something for you in *Computer Confluence*. Dive in!

Student CD-ROM

The Student CD-ROM has been revised and updated, with a more powerful engine, a newly designed user interface, and a wealth of new multimedia material, from new book specific Train & Assess IT content to provocative G4TechTV video clips and interactive tutorials and tests. The material on the CD is clearly keyed to corresponding sections in the book. The Web site www.computerconfluence.com is continually updated to reflect changes in the Web and the subject matter.

Companion Web Site

This text is accompanied by a Companion Web site at www.computerconfluence.com. This redesigned site brings you and your students a richer, more interactive Web experience than ever before. Features of this new site include an interactive study guide, downloadable supplements, online end-of-chapter materials, additional Internet exercises, G4TechTV videos, Web resource links such as Careers in IT, and crossword puzzles, plus Technology Updates and Bonus Chapters on the latest trends and hottest topics in information technology. All links to Web exercises will be constantly updated to ensure accuracy for students.

For the Instructor

Computer Confluence is designed to help you to provide students with the background they need to survive and prosper in a world transformed by information technology. The 7th edition comes in two forms, the Introductory Edition and the Complete Edition. The Introductory Edition covers all of the essentials in eleven chapters. The Complete Edition includes five additional chapters for classes where that coverage is important. It incorporates material that is well suited for courses in business, CIS, CS, and other subjects.

Both books include a variety of supplements and ancillary materials designed to help you enhance your students' learning experience.

OneKey
www.prenhall.com/onekey

OneKey is all you need

OneKey lets you in to the best teaching and learning resources all in one place. OneKey for *Computer Confluence* is all your students need for anywhere, anytime access to your course materials, conveniently organized by textbook chapter to reinforce and apply what they've learned in class. OneKey is all you need to plan and administer your course. All your instructor resources are in one place to maximize your effectiveness and minimize your time and effort. OneKey for convenience, simplicity, and success . . . for you and your students.

Instructor Resources

The new and improved Prentice Hall Instructor's Resource Center on DVD-ROM includes the tools you expect from a Prentice Hall Computer Concepts text, like:

- The Instructor's Manual in Word and PDF formats
- Solutions to all questions and exercises from the book and Web site
- Multiple, customizable PowerPoint slide presentations for each chapter
- Computer concepts animations
- G4TechTV videos
- Image library of all of the figures from the text

This DVD-ROM is an interactive library of assets and links. This DVD writes custom "index" pages that can be used as the foundation of a class presentation or online lecture. By navigating through this DVD, you can collect the materials that are most relevant to your interests, edit them to create powerful class lectures, copy them to your own computer's hard drive, and/or upload them to an online course-management system.

Companion Web Site

This text is accompanied by a companion Web site at www.computerconfluence.com. This redesigned site brings you and your students a richer, more interactive Web experience than ever before. Features of this new site include an interactive study guide, downloadable supplements, additional Internet exercises, G4TechTV videos, Web resource links such as Careers in IT, and crossword puzzles, plus technology updates and bonus chapters on the latest trends and hottest topics in information technology. All links to Web exercises will be constantly updated to ensure accuracy.

Companion Website

TestGen Software

TestGen is a test generator found on your instructor resource DVD that lets you view and easily edit testbank questions, transfer them to tests, and print in a variety of formats suitable to your teaching situation. The program also offers many options for organizing and displaying testbanks and tests. Powerful search and sort functions let you easily locate questions and arrange them in the order you prefer.

QuizMaster, also included in this package, allows students to take tests created with TestGen on a local area network. The QuizMaster utility built into TestGen lets instructors view student records and print a variety of reports. Building tests is easy with TestGen and exams can be easily uploaded into WebCT, Blackboard and CourseCompass.

Tools for Online Learning
Training and Assessment
www.prenhall.com/taitdemo

Computer Confluence features brand new computer-based Train & Assess IT content that reinforces the key computer concepts covered in the text. Developed specifically for *Computer Confluence*, this training enables students to enhance their knowledge in a visual and interactive computer-based environment.

Web delivered, Train & Assess IT for *Computer Confluence* presents new and updated multimedia modules and fully integrated G4TechTV clips in a fresh new graphic design. Each chapter includes a series of activities, animations and video clips that examine in depth and expand upon the material presented in the text, as well as a quiz to test the students' knowledge of the concepts covered.

Online Courseware

Now you have the freedom to personalize your own online course materials!
Prentice Hall provides the content and support you need to create and manage your own online course in WebCT, Blackboard, or Prentice Hall's own CourseCompass. Content includes lecture material, interactive exercises, e-commerce case videos, additional testing questions, and projects and animations.

CourseCompass

www.coursecompass.com

CourseCompass is a dynamic, interactive online course-management tool powered exclusively for Pearson Education by Blackboard. This exciting product allows you to teach market-leading Pearson Education content in an easy-to-use, customizable format.

Blackboard

www.prenhall.com/blackboard

Prentice Hall's abundant online content, combined with Blackboard's popular tools and interface, results in robust Web-based courses that are easy to implement, manage, and use—taking your courses to new heights in student interaction and learning.

WebCT

www.prenhall.com/webct

Course management tools within WebCT include page tracking, progress tracking, class and student management, a grade book, communication tools, a calendar, reporting tools, and more. GOLD LEVEL CUSTOMER SUPPORT, available exclusively to adopters of Prentice Hall courses, is provided free of charge upon adoption and provides you with priority assistance, training discounts, and dedicated technical support.

G4TechTV

Formed by the May, 2004 merger of G4 and TechTV, G4techTV is the one and only 24-hour television network that is plugged into every dimension of games, gear, gadgets and gigabytes. Headquartered in Los Angeles, the network features all original programming dedicated to the passions and lifestyle of the gamer generation. To learn more, log onto www.g4techtv.com or contact your local cable or satellite provider to get G4techTV in your area.

Acknowledgments

We're deeply grateful to all of the people who've come together to make *Computer Confluence* a success. Their names may not be on the cover, but their high quality work shows in every detail of this project.

We're especially thankful to Natalie Anderson, whose clear vision and personal commitment to *Computer Confluence* helped elevate the learning package to a new level of excellence. We're also grateful to Jodi McPherson, the savvy Executive Editor who worked with Natalie and the rest of the team to ensure that the project stayed on track. Thanks to Editorial Project Manager Eileen Clark, who worked on all aspects of the project, from initial book planning to coordinating the CD and Web efforts. Thanks to Jodi Bolognese for managing the massive multimedia package that accompanies this book. And thanks to Alana Meyers who quietly toiled behind the scenes, taking care of countless details.

Our most heartfelt thanks go to Maureen Allaire Spada, the editor responsible for making the first edition of this book a reality. George was delighted when Maureen agreed to rejoin the team for the sixth and seventh editions, and Mike was thrilled to find such a seasoned professional on board when he signed up. Throughout the project she rose to every challenge, redefining her role to deal with unanticipated circumstances and keep the project on schedule. Her work was consistently first-rate, timely, and thorough, and she kept her cheerful demeanor even in the most stressful situations. Just as she did with the first edition, Maureen made this book happen.

Many others brought their considerable talents to *Computer Confluence*. Blair Brown, designer, is the person most responsible for the beautiful design of the book. Lynne Breitfeller worked on all aspects of production, helping ensure that the project could make all those nearly impossible deadlines. Elaine Soares uncovered many of the new photos in this edition. Gordon Laws and the staff at Pre-Press Company, Inc. produced the final book from all of the raw materials supplied by the others listed here. Courier/Kendallville handled the printing process. The CD was rebuilt from the ground up by Bob Lalonde and his team at Bluedrop.

Back in Oregon, we had help from an amazing team of professionals. Ben Beekman served as an indispensable assistant on previous editions of *Computer Confluence*. For this edition Ben helped with manuscript development, screen shots, research, and other critical tasks. His contributions were invaluable. The same can be said of our other Oregon assistant, Scobel Wiggins. Scobel did an amazing job creating the art manuscript and art log and ensuring that all of the diverse elements of the book coordinated with each other. She also took many of the best photographs in the book and made sure that every meeting had at least a couple of good laughs in it.

All of this effort would be wasted if *Computer Confluence* didn't reach its intended audience. Thankfully, Emily Knight is a first-rate marketing manager who thoroughly understands *Computer Confluence* and the academic world it serves. We're delighted to have Emily on the *Computer Confluence* Team. Of course, Emily's work would be in vain if she didn't have Prentice Hall's amazing team of sales reps. These people work hard to bring books to professors and students, and we can't thank them enough for their efforts.

We both owe special thanks to our families, who made countless sacrifices so that we could write this book. We're especially grateful to our wives, Susan Grace Beekman and Victoria Quinn, who selflessly maintained the infrastructures of our lives while we struggled to meet the difficult deadlines of this project.

There are others who contributed to *Computer Confluence* in all kinds of ways, including critiquing chapters, answering technical questions, tracking down obscure references, guiding us through difficult decisions, and being there when we needed support. There's no room here to detail their contributions, but we want to thank the people who gave time, energy, talent, and support during the years that this book was under development, including: Naftali Anderson, Martin Erwig, Otto Gygax, Francisco Martin, Jim Folts, Jan Dymond, Johanna Beekman, Mike Johnson, Margaret Burnett, Sherry Clark, Walter Rudd, Cherri Pancake, Bruce D'Ambrosio, Bernie Feyerherm, Rajeev Pandey, Dave Stuve, Clay Cowgill, Keith Vertanen, Nicole Mahan, Gary Brent, Robert Rose, Marion Rose, Megan Slothover, Claudette Hastie-Baehrs, Melissa Hartley, Shjoobedebop, Oyaya, Breitenbush, Oregon Public Broadcasting, KLCC, Dave Trenkel, Mark Dinsmore, Sandra Bernales, and all of the editors and others who helped with previous editions of *Computer Confluence*. Thanks also to all the hardware and software companies whose cooperation made our work easier.

Reviewers of the 6th Edition

Thanks to all of the dedicated educators who reviewed the manuscript at various stages of development; *Computer Confluence* and its accompanying CD-ROM are significantly more valuable educational tools as a result of your ideas, suggestions, and constructive criticism.

Nazih Abdallah, University of Central Florida

Lancie Affonso, College of Charleston

Ita Borger-Boglin, San Antonio College

Eugenia Culham, Kwantlen University College

Joseph DeLibero, Arizona State University

Timothy Flanagan, Portland Community College, Sylvania Campus

Robert Heinrich, The Richard Stockton College of NJ

Andria Hunter, University of Toronto

Darrel Karbginsky, Chemeketa Community College

Eric Kisling, Indiana University at Bloomington

John Liefert, Middlesex Community College

Catherine Maydan, Kwantlen University College

Rebecca A. Mundy, University of Southern California

Mike Peterson, Chemeketa Community College

Jennifer Pickle, Amarillo College

Sam R. Thangiah, Slippery Rock University

Teresa Tegeler, Olney Central College

Multimedia

on the CD-ROM and the Web:

~ A **Hitchiker's Guide** to the Future

~ **Interactive tutorial** on file management

~ **Interactive tutorial** on communicating with email

~ **Instant Access** to glossary and keyword references

~ Interactive **self-study quizzes**

...and more.

 computerconfluence.com

Objectives

After you read this chapter you should be able to:

▌ Describe the basic parts of a PC and how they work together

▌ Explain the relationship between hardware and software

▌ Use a keyboard and mouse to enter and edit text

▌ Explain how files are organized within a PC

▌ Explain how the Internet extends the functionality of a PC

▌ Describe some of the risks of Internet use and how to minimize them

▌ Use a Windows PC or Macintosh to explore the *Computer Confluence* CD-ROM

▌ Use a Windows PC or Macintosh to explore the *Computer Confluence* Web site

In 1983 Steve Roberts realized he wasn't happy chained to his desk and his debts. He decided to build a new lifestyle that combined his passions—writing, adventure, computers, bicycling, learning, and networking. Six months later, he hit the road on Winnebiko, a recumbent bike equipped with a laptop and solar panel. He connected each day to the CompuServe network through pay phones, transmitting magazine articles and book chapters.

HUMAN DREAMS AND DREAM MACHINES

The obvious choices **aren't the only choices**.

—*Steve Roberts*

Years later Roberts was exploring America on BEHEMOTH (Big Electronic Human-Energized Machine . . . Only Too Heavy), a million-dollar bike with seven networked computers and wireless communication capability. Roberts pedaled 17,000 miles before pursuing a new dream: "life with no hills." He has created a pair of high-tech sailboats, *Wordplay* and *Songline*, that have allowed him and his partner Natasha to extend their technonomadic lifestyle to the ocean. "There's a *lot* of world to explore out there. Having had a taste of it, how could I spend my life in one place?"

0.1 Steve Roberts with BEHEMOTH

Basics

0.2 Vaughn Rogers

Vaughn Rogers "wasn't into computers." Computers, he thought, were useful for typing papers, but they weren't exciting. *Art* was exciting to Rogers, who had been drawing all his life.

In 1995 he went with a friend to the Computer Clubhouse, a digital playground for disadvantaged youth started by Natalie Rusk at the Museum of Science in Cambridge, Massachusetts. He saw other teens using computers to create art, edit video, and mix music. Before long, Vaughn was doing his art at the Computer Clubhouse after school.

Today, Rogers studies visual communication and animation at Katharine Gibbs College. His goal is to work in computer animation and video, using his drawing talent enhanced with computer technology. He now works as an assistant manager at the Computer Clubhouse, helping others learn to use computers to pursue their passions.

When Patricia Walsh lost her sight at 14, she almost lost sight of her dreams. She had already completed the advanced mathematics and science classes at her high school, and she wanted to go further. She learned to read and write Braille, but Braille couldn't help with the equations and formulas she needed to study. Her PC could talk using text-to-speech software, but it had nothing to say about scientific graphs and charts.

Fortunately, Walsh met John Gardner, a blind physics professor at Oregon State University. Gardner was developing tools to make math and science accessible to visually impaired people. His Tiger Tactile Graphics and Braille Embosser printed equations, formulas, and graphs as raised patterns that could be read by touch. Using this technology, Walsh could read class notes emailed by her professors. Once again she could "see" the figures that were critical to her studies.

Walsh started helping Gardner develop accessibility tools. She became a spokesperson for adaptive technology, telling others about tools that can open doors for people with disabilities. Walsh is now a computer science major at Oregon State University, where she uses the tools that she helped develop to pursue her dream. "Computers have allowed me to get in the mainstream. Now I can do what I used to love before I became blind." ∼

0.3 Patricia Walsh

Steve Roberts, Vaughn Rogers, and Patricia Walsh would be living very different lives today if they hadn't connected with computers. Their stories are interesting and inspiring, but they aren't unique. Every day computer technology changes people's lives all around the world.

Sometimes it seems like everybody uses computers. In fact, the great majority of people on our planet have never touched a computer!

Most of the people who *do* use computers have fairly limited experience and ability—typically the basics of word processing, electronic mail, and finding information on the World Wide Web. The percentage of people who can go beyond the basics and harness the power of a modern PC is relatively small.

If you're a member of this tiny community of *power users*, the next few pages aren't for you. But before you move on to Chapter 1, take a look at the "Quick Start" and "Navigating *Computer Confluence*" sections later in this chapter. You'll find tips for getting the most out of this book and the companion CD-ROM and Web site. Also, check out the thought-provoking Crosscurrents article at the end of this chapter. If you're a casual computer user, comfortable with the basic operation of a PC, a CD-ROM drive, and a Web browser, you may want to look through this chapter quickly and spend more time with the "Quick Start," "Navigating *Computer Confluence*," and Crosscurrents sections before moving on to Chapter 1, where the real story begins. (If you're not sure about your knowledge level, check out the questions at the end of the chapter. If you have trouble answering them, spend a little more time looking over this chapter before you move on.)

If you're a beginner, your experience is limited or out of date, you're uncomfortable with PC technology, or you just want to be thorough, this chapter is for you. Here you'll find the basic knowledge you'll need to bring you up to speed, so you're not struggling to catch up as you explore the rest of the book. You'll also learn what you need to know to take full advantage of the *Computer Confluence* CD-ROM and Web site. Along with this book, these resources can provide you with a rich multimedia introduction to the world of computers and information technology.

Whichever path you choose, don't wait until you're sitting in front of a computer to read *Computer Confluence*. Hands-on computer experience is important, but you won't need the computer to take advantage of this book. Wherever you are, just dive in.

Key terms in this chapter, and throughout the book, are highlighted in blue boldface and are listed at the end of each chapter. *Secondary terms* are highlighted in blue italics. Both key terms and secondary terms are defined in the glossary. In this chapter, the key terms are the ones that are critical for getting started with the Computer Confluence book, CD-ROM, and Web site; secondary terms are terms that are introduced briefly here and covered in more detail later.

0.4

PC Basics

The beginning is the **most important part** of the work.

—Plato

Computers come in all kinds of packages, from massive supercomputers to tiny computers embedded in cell phones, credit cards, and even microscopic machines and "smart" pills. But in this chapter, we'll focus on the typical desktop computer—the **personal computer**, or **PC**. We'll start with a look at the physical parts of a PC—the PC's **hardware**. This whirlwind tour will offer a quick, practical overview; you'll learn more in later chapters.

PC Hardware Basics

Hardware: the parts of a computer that **can be kicked**.

—Jeff Pesis

Modern desktop PCs don't all look alike, but under the skin, they're more alike than different. Every PC is built around a tiny *microprocessor* that controls the workings of the system. This **central processing unit**, or **CPU**, is usually housed in a box, called the *system unit* (or, more often, just "*the computer*" or "*the PC*") that serves as command central for the entire computer system. The CPU is the brains of the computer; it controls the operation of the core computer components, like its memory and ability to perform mathematical operations. Some computer components are housed in the system unit with the *CPU*; others are peripheral devices—or simply **peripherals**—external devices connected via cables to the system unit.

The system unit includes built-in **memory**, sometimes called *RAM*, and a **hard disk** for the storage and retrieval of information. The CPU uses memory for instant access to information while it's working. The built-in hard disk serves as a longer-term storage device for large quantities of information.

The PC's main hard disk is a permanent fixture in the system unit. Other types of disk drives work with *removable media*—disks that can be separated from their drives, just as an audio CD can be removed from a stereo system. The most popular types of removable media today are 5¼ inch optical discs that look like common audio CDs. A typical PC system unit includes a CD-ROM drive, a CD-RW drive, a DVD drive, or some other kind of optical drive. A **CD-ROM drive** enables the computer to read audio CDs and CD-ROMs (including the one included with this book). A **CD-RW drive** can read CDs and also write, or *burn*, information onto CD media. A **DVD drive** can read (and sometimes burn) DVD movies and high-capacity data DVDs as well as audio and data CDs. In addition to an optical drive, an older PC might also include a *disk drive* (also known as a *floppy disk drive*), which enables the computer to store small amounts of information on pocket-sized plastic-covered magnetic **disks**.

Disk drives that are included in the system unit are called *internal drives*. *External drives* can be attached to the system unit via cables. For example, a PC system might include an external hard disk for additional storage and a DVD/CD-RW drive for reading and writing CDs and reading DVDs.

Other system unit components, including the video display card, the sound card, the network interface card, and the modem, communicate with external devices, other computers, and networks.

CD-ROM drive
DVD drive
speakers
system unit
monitor
keyboard
mouse

0.5 A standard desktop PC or Mac is made up of several components, including a system unit, a monitor, speakers, a keyboard, and a mouse. The system unit typically includes an internal hard disk and an optical drive, such as a CD-ROM or DVD drive.

Using a Keyboard

Typing letters, numbers, and special characters with a computer keyboard is similar to typing on a standard typewriter keyboard. But unlike a typewriter, the computer responds by displaying the typed characters on the monitor screen at the position of the line or rectangle called the *cursor*. Some keys on the computer keyboard— *Enter*, *Delete*, the *cursor (arrow) keys*, *the function keys (f-keys)*, and others— send special commands to the computer. These keys may have different names or meanings on different computer systems. This figure shows a typical keyboard on a Windows-compatible PC. Keyboards for Macintoshes and other types of systems have a few differences but operate on the same principles.

Function keys (f-keys), labeled F1, F2, and so on, send signals to the computer that have no inherent meaning. The function of these keys depends on the software being used. F1 might mean "Save file" to one program and "Delete file" to another. In other words function keys are programmable.

Backspace on a PC tells the computer to delete the character just typed (or the one to the left of the cursor on the screen, or the currently selected data).

Control and *Alt* are modifier keys that cause nothing to happen by themselves but change the meaning of other keys. When you hold down a modifier key while pressing another key, the combination makes that other key behave differently. For example, typing S while holding down the Control key might send a command to save the current document.

Enter sends a signal telling the computer or terminal to move the cursor to the beginning of the next line on the screen. For many applications this key also "enters" the line just typed, telling the computer to process it.

Cursor (arrow) keys are used to move the cursor up, down, left, or right.

0.6

But the PC's main purpose isn't to communicate with other machines: It's there to communicate with *you*. Five common peripherals aid this human–computer interaction:

- A **keyboard** enables you to type text and numerical data into the computer's memory.
- A **mouse** enables you to point to text, graphical objects, menu commands, and other items on the screen.
- A **monitor** (or *display*) enables you to view text, numbers, and pictures stored in the computer's memory.
- **Speakers** emit music, voices, and other sounds.
- A **printer** generates printed letters, papers, transparencies, labels, and other hard copies. (The printer might be directly connected to the computer, or it might be shared by several computers on a network.)

Boxes on this page and the next page illustrate the fundamentals of a basic PC keyboard and mouse. Chapter 3 explores peripherals in more detail.

Using *a Mouse*

The mouse enables you to perform many tasks quickly that might be tedious or confusing with a keyboard. As you slide the mouse across your desktop, a pointer echoes your movements on the screen. You can click the mouse—press the button while the mouse is stationary—or drag it—move it while holding the button down. On a two-button mouse, the left button is usually used for clicking and dragging. You can use these two techniques to perform a variety of operations.

CLICKING THE MOUSE

If the pointer points to an on-screen button, clicking the mouse presses the button.

If the pointer points to a picture of a tool or object on the screen, clicking the mouse *selects* the tool or object; for example, clicking the pencil tool enables you to draw with the mouse.

If the pointer points to a part of a text document, it turns from an arrow into an *I-beam*; clicking repositions the flashing cursor.

Jack and Jill fell down and I Jill came tumbling after.

DRAGGING THE MOUSE

If you hold the button down while you drag the mouse with a selected graphic tool (like a paintbrush), you can draw by remote control.

If you drag the mouse from one point in a text document to another, you select all the text between those two points so you can modify or move it. For example, you might select a movie title so you could italicize it.

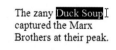

The zany Duck Soup I captured the Marx Brothers at their peak.

You can drag the mouse to select a command from a menu of choices. For example, this command enables you to locate specific documents that are stored on your computer.

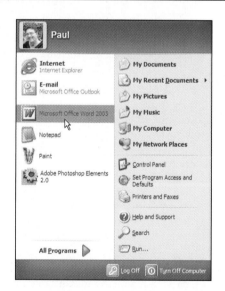

OTHER MOUSE OPERATIONS

If you double-click the mouse—click twice in rapid succession—while pointing to an on-screen object, the computer will probably open the object so you can see inside it. For example, double-clicking this *icon* representing a letter causes the letter to open.

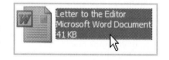

If you *right-click*—click the right mouse button—while pointing to an object, the computer will probably display a menu of choices of things you can do to the object. For example, if you right-click the letter icon, a menu appears at the pointer.

0.7

PC Software Basics

All this hardware is controlled, directly or indirectly, by the tiny CPU in the system unit. And the CPU is controlled by software—instructions that tell it what to do. *System software*, including the operating system (OS), continuously takes

> Computers can figure out **all kinds of problems**, except the things in the world that **just don't add up**.
>
> *—James Magary*

care of the behind-the-scenes details and (usually) keeps things running smoothly. The operating system also determines what your screen display looks like as you work and how you tell the computer what you want it to do. Most PCs today use some version of the *Microsoft Windows* operating system; Macintosh computers use some version of Apple's *Mac OS*.

Application programs, also called simply applications, are software tools that enable you to use a computer for specific purposes. Some applications are designed to accomplish well-defined, short-term goals. For example, the *Computer Confluence* CD-ROM includes an application that supplements and expands on the material in this book by providing interactive quizzes, animated demos, video presentations, and other multimedia material. Other applications programs have more general and open-ended goals. For example, you can use a word processing program, such as Microsoft Word, to create memos, letters, term papers, novels, textbooks, or World Wide Web pages—just about any kind of text-based document.

In the PC world, a document is a file created by an application, regardless of whether it has actually been printed. Application files and document files are different types of files. A file is a named collection of data stored on a computer disk or some other storage medium. Applications are sometimes called *executable files*, because they contain instructions that can be executed by the computer. Documents are sometimes called *data files*, because they contain passive data rather than instructions. When you type a report with the Microsoft Word application, the computer executes the Word instructions. When you save the report on the computer's hard disk, the computer creates a Word document—a data file that contains the contents of the report.

Entering, Editing, and Formatting Text

You can type and edit a word processing document using standard PC techniques and tools. As you type, your text is displayed on the screen and stored in RAM. With virtually all modern word processors, words appear on the screen almost exactly as they will appear on a printed page. This feature is often referred to as WYSIWYG—short for "what you see is what you get" and pronounced "wizzy-wig." Because of a feature called word wrap, the word processor automatically moves any words that won't fit on the current line to the next line along with the cursor.

Word processing programs—and many other types of applications—contain text editing tools for changing and rearranging the words on the screen. Most computer users are familiar with the Clipboard, which can temporarily store chunks of text and other data, making it possible to cut or copy words from one part of a document and paste them into another part of the same document or a different document. In many programs, you can achieve similar results by using drag-and-drop technology that allows you to drag a selected block of text from one location to another. Find-and-replace (search and replace) tools make it possible to make repetitive changes throughout a document.

Formatting Characters

Text formatting commands enable you to control the *format* of the document. For example, you can change the way the words will look on the page. Most modern word processors include commands for controlling the formats of individual characters and paragraphs as well as complete documents.

Most printers can print text in a variety of point sizes, typefaces, and styles that aren't possible with typewriters. Characters are measured by point size, with one point equal to $\frac{1}{72}$ inch. Most documents, including this book, use smaller point sizes for text to fit more information on each page and larger point sizes to make titles and headings stand out.

Examples of	12-point size	24-point size
Serif fonts	Times New Roman	Times New Roman
	Georgia	Georgia
	Palatino	Palatino
Sans-serif fonts	Arial Narrow	Arial Narrow
	Helvetica	Helvetica
	Univers 55	Univers 55
	Verdana	Verdana
Monospaced fonts	Courier	Courier
	Monaco	Monaco

0.8 These fonts represent only a few of the hundreds of typefaces available for personal computers and printers today.

In the language of typesetters, a **font** is a size and style of **typeface**. For example, the Helvetica typeface includes many fonts, one of which is 12-point Helvetica bold. In the PC world, many people use the terms *font* and *typeface* interchangeably.

Whatever you call them, you have hundreds of choices of typefaces. **Serif fonts**, like those in the Times family, are embellished with serifs—fine lines at the ends of the main strokes of each character. **Sans-serif fonts**, like those in the Helvetica or Verdana family, have plainer, cleaner lines. **Monospaced fonts** that mimic typewriters, like those in the Courier family, produce characters that always take up the same amount of space, no matter how skinny or fat the characters are. In contrast, **proportionally spaced fonts** enable more room for wide characters, like w's, than for narrow characters, like i's.

The Screen Test boxes on the following pages show examples of software at work. In these simple examples, we'll use a word processing application to edit and save a document containing the essay, "Why I Went to the Woods," by Thoreau. The first example uses Microsoft Word on a PC with the Microsoft Windows XP operating system. The second example, shows the same thing using Microsoft Word on a Macintosh with Mac OS X. In both examples, we'll perform the following steps:

1. Open Microsoft Word—copy the application program from the computer's hard disk into memory where it can be executed
2. Type, edit, and format the document
3. Save the document
4. Close the application

Before we begin, a reminder and a disclaimer:

The reminder: The *Screen Test* examples are designed to give you a feel for the software, not to provide how-to instructions. You can learn how to use the software using lab manuals or other books on the subject, some of which are listed in *Sources and Resources* at the ends of the chapters in this book.

The disclaimer: These examples are provided so you can compare different types of interfaces, not so you can establish a favorite. The brand of software in a particular Screen Test box isn't as important as the general concepts built into that software. One of the best things about computers is that they offer lots of different ways to do things. These examples, and others throughout the book, are designed to expose you to possibilities. Even if you have no plans to use the operating systems or applications in the examples—*especially* if you have no plans to use them—you can learn something by looking at them as a curious observer.

0.9 Software makes it possible for PCs to be put to work in homes, schools, offices, factories, and farms.

Screen Test

Using Microsoft Word with Microsoft Windows

GOAL *To create a document containing highlights from a famous essay*

TOOLS *Microsoft Word and Microsoft Windows XP*

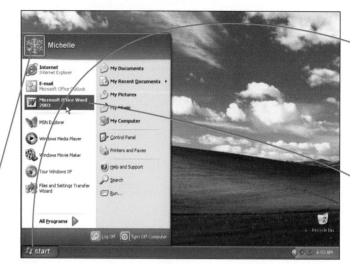

1. After your PC completes its startup process, the Windows desktop appears—a screen that includes icons representing objects used in your work.

2. You click Start in the lower-left corner of the screen. The Start menu appears, enabling you to select from the applications and documents you use most frequently.

3. You select Microsoft Word and click to open the program. The PC is now ready to work on any Word document, including your paper.

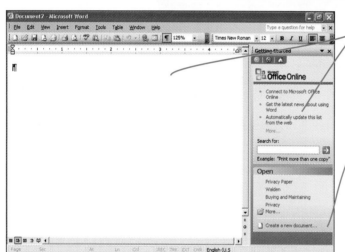

4. The Microsoft Word application opens, and you are presented with a blank document and a task pane (right) containing options that represent frequently used commands and files.

5. Because this is a new paper, you click Create a new document. You're ready to start typing the paper.

6. As you type, the top-most lines scroll out of view to make room on the screen for the new ones. The text you've entered is still in memory, even though you can't see it on the screen.

7. You can view it anytime by scrolling backward through the text using the vertical scrollbar on the right edge of the window. In this respect, a word processor document is like a modern version of an ancient paper scroll.

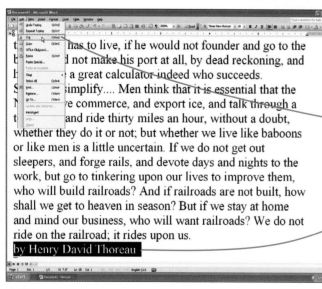

8. After you enter the text, you decide that "by Henry David Thoreau" should be at the top of the document, immediately below the title, rather than at the bottom of the document. Using the mouse, you select the author's byline. Selected text appears highlighted on the screen.

9. Choosing the Cut command from the Edit menu tells the computer to cut the selected text from the document and place it in the **Clipboard**—a special portion of temporary memory used to hold information for later use.

0.10

10. After using the mouse or arrow keys to reposition the cursor at the beginning of the document, you select the Paste command from the Edit menu. The computer places a copy of the Clipboard's contents at the insertion point; the text below the cursor moves down to make room for the inserted text.

11. To italicize the title "Walden," you select the characters to be changed and click the button labeled with an "*I*" in the toolbar.

12. You can center text by selecting it and clicking the Center button located on the toolbar.

13. You're done working with the essay for now, so you choose Save from the File menu.

14. Because you haven't saved the document before, the Save dialog box opens and prompts you for the name of the file and the location of the directory in which to store it.

15. The File menu also contains a "Print" command, allowing you to print a hard copy of the essay.

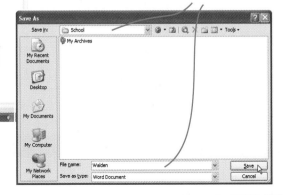

Screen Test

Using Microsoft Word with Mac OS X

GOAL *To edit a term paper*   **TOOLS** *Mac OS X and Microsoft Word*

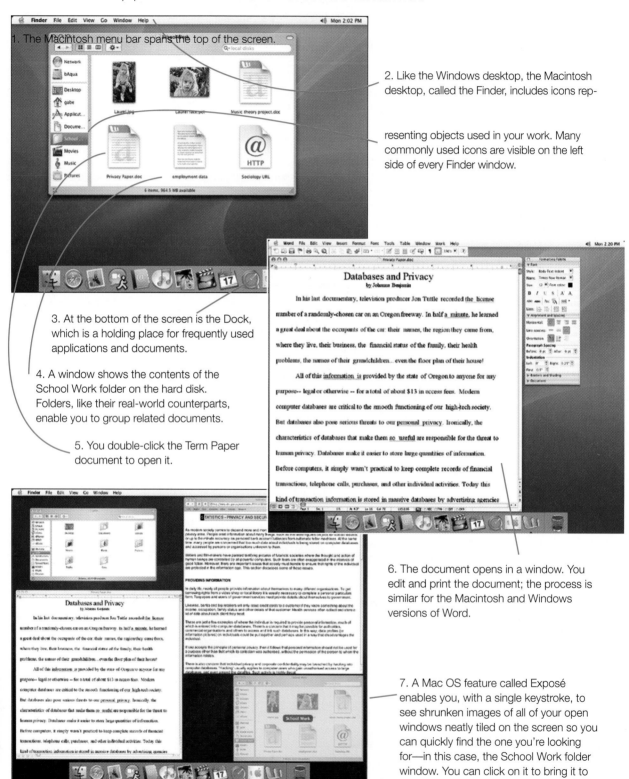

1. The Macintosh menu bar spans the top of the screen.

2. Like the Windows desktop, the Macintosh desktop, called the Finder, includes icons representing objects used in your work. Many commonly used icons are visible on the left side of every Finder window.

3. At the bottom of the screen is the Dock, which is a holding place for frequently used applications and documents.

4. A window shows the contents of the School Work folder on the hard disk. Folders, like their real-world counterparts, enable you to group related documents.

5. You double-click the Term Paper document to open it.

6. The document opens in a window. You edit and print the document; the process is similar for the Macintosh and Windows versions of Word.

7. A Mac OS feature called Exposé enables you, with a single keystroke, to see shrunken images of all of your open windows neatly tiled on the screen so you can quickly find the one you're looking for—in this case, the School Work folder window. You can click on it to bring it to the foreground.

0.11

File Management Basics

A **place** for **everything** and everything **in its place**.

—English Proverb

In Windows and the Mac OS, a file is represented by a name and an icon. It's not always easy to tell what a file contains based on its name. Most people know that it's a good idea to name files with clearly descriptive names, but some names are difficult to decipher. A filename includes an *extension*—a string of (usually) three characters that follows a period (.) at the end of the filename. The extension gives more information about the file's origin or use. For example, the name of a Windows executable file typically includes the extension *.exe*, as in *biggame.exe*. The filename of a Microsoft Word document usually ends with *.doc*, such as *termpaper.doc*. A *.pdf* extension typically designates files containing information stored in Portable Document Format, which you can view with Adobe Acrobat Reader. If a file doesn't have a visible extension in its name, you still might be able to tell what it is by looking at its icon. Most popular applications create documents with distinctive icons.

Hundreds of filename extensions exist. Fortunately, you don't need to worry about memorizing them, because the operating system usually knows which application program is associated with each extension. For example, double-clicking the icon for file *Table.xls* results in the operating system running Microsoft Excel, because it associates the *.xls* extension with Excel spreadsheets.

File Organization Basics

In the physical world, people often use file folders to organize their paper documents into meaningful collections—class documents, financial papers, receipts, and the like. Similarly, computer files can be organized into collections using **folders** (sometimes called directories). The operating system enables you to create folders, give them meaningful names, and store documents and other files inside them. When you open a folder, the

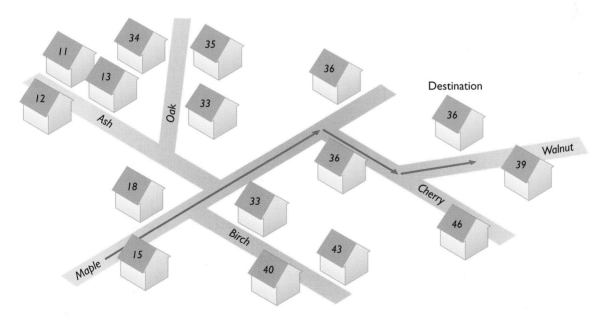

0.12 The hierarchical organization of folders is like a suburban subdivision with dead-end streets fanning out from a single road. Suppose your destination is 36 Walnut Street. You follow Maple Street to Cherry Street, Cherry Street to Walnut Street, and then you can get to 36 Walnut Street.

folder's window opens, revealing the files that it contains. You can organize folders *hierarchically*, meaning a folder can contain other folders, which in turn can contain still more folders. For example, a folder called My Documents might contain folders called My School Work, My Financial Papers, My Letters, and My Pictures. My School Work might contain folders for individual classes, each of which might be subdivided into Homework, Projects, and so on. Windows and Mac operating systems include a variety of tools for quickly navigating through nested folders to locate particular files.

In the real world, people aren't as organized as computers, and files don't always end up in the appropriate folders. Modern operating systems include Search or Find commands that can help you find files no matter where they are stored on the system. You can search for filenames, but you can also search for words or phrases inside a document. So if you don't know the name of a file, but do know some of the text in that file, you can still use the search tool to find your data.

File Compression Basics

Modern PCs support a wide range of multimedia activities. The largest files on your hard disk are probably those containing videos, songs, or images. File compression is the process of reducing the size of a file so that you can fit more files into the same amount of disk space. File decompression is the process of restoring the file to its original state. Compressing a file is like squeezing a sponge. You can fit a lot more sponges in a box if you squeeze them together. When you want to use one of the sponges, you remove it from the box, and it springs back to its original size. Letting the sponge go back to its original size is like decompressing a file.

You can perform file compression by using an application, an operating system, or another type of software program. For example, with Adobe Photoshop you can save a digital photograph by using GIF or JPEG compression to reduce its file size. Similarly, with Winamp and iTunes, you can convert standard digital music files to compressed MP3 files. You use specialized compression utility programs, such as PKZIP, WinZIP, and Stuffit, to compress almost any kind of file (or group of files). If you see a file with a *.zip* or *.sitx* extension, it needs to be decompressed before you use it in an application. File compression is especially important when working with video, audio, and multimedia files. Chapter 6 covers file compression techniques in more detail.

0.13 The CD-R disc is a popular back-up medium.

Backup Basics

Just about any computer file user can remember losing important work because of a hard disk failure, a software bug, or a computer virus that destroyed data files. It's a good idea to protect yourself against disaster by frequently backing up your data. A back-up copy is a copy of a file created as insurance against the loss of the original. It makes sense to keep back-up copies on a different device than the one that holds the original copies. Many people use disks, CD-Rs, and other back-up media to hold back-up files and save computer storage space.

A floppy disk is suitable for storing a few small documents, but not large images, music files, or videos. Most people use optical discs, including CD-Rs and DVD-Rs, to back up large media files. Blank CD-R discs cost less than floppy disks and can hold about 500 times more data. You can store a reasonable number of images, music, and/or video files on one CD-R disc. But backing up an entire hard disk on CDs or DVDs can involve many disks—and hours of tedious disk swapping. To save time, many organizations and individuals back up large hard disks using high-capacity magnetic tapes and removeable hard drives.

Screen Test

File Management with Windows

GOAL *To organize files into folders*

TOOL *Microsoft Windows*

1. Your files are scattered across your desktop; you'd like to organize them by folder. After you open the My Documents folder from the Start menu, you select all the unfiled documents (by dragging a rectangle around them) and drag them to the My Documents folder. The icons appear as transparent images in the window while you're dragging them.

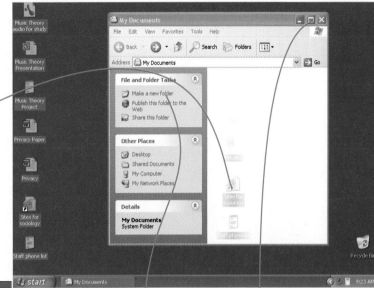

2. You click the Maximize button (the button with two overlapping windows) so that the My Documents window fills the screen.

3. You use a button in the sidebar to create two new folders named School and Work within the My Documents folder.

4. You select and drag all of the work related documents into the Work folder. The Work folder icon is highlighted when you drag the documents into it.

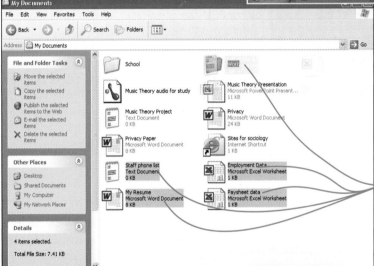

5. You create a third folder, Personal, and distribute the unsorted documents into the new folders that you've created. You click on the Folders tab at the top of the window to show the hierarchical organization of the folders on your hard drive.

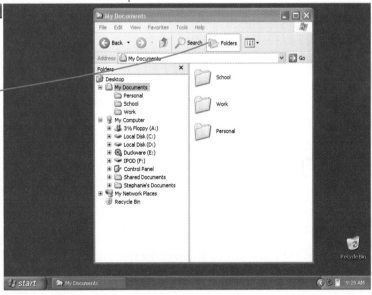

0.14

Network and Internet Basics

Networks aren't made of printed circuits, but of **people . . . . My terminal is a door** to countless, intricate pathways, leading to **untold numbers of neighbors**.

—Cliff Stoll, in The Cuckoo's Egg

Today's PCs are powerful tools that can perform a variety of tasks that go far beyond the basic word processing examples illustrated here. Later chapters explore many of these applications, from money management to multimedia. But a PC becomes even more powerful when it's connected to other computers through a network.

PC Network Basics

A computer may have a *direct connection* to a network—for example, cables might connect it to other computers, printers, and other devices in an office or student lab. These networked machines can easily and quickly share information with each other. When a computer isn't physically close to the other machines in the network, it can still communicate with those machines through a *remote access* connection. Using a *modem*, the remote computer can connect to the network through an ordinary phone line. Or you can use wireless routers.

An entire computer network can be connected to other networks through cables, wireless radio transmissions, or other means. The Internet is an elaborate network of interconnected networks—a network that is dramatically changing the way people work, play, and communicate.

0.15 Networked computers in this lab allow students to share files, send messages, and connect to the Internet.

Internet Basics

What interests me about it . . . is that it's a form of communication **unlike any other** and yet the second you start doing it **you understand it**.

—Nora Ephron, Director of You've Got Mail

There was a time, not too many years ago, when word processing was the most popular computer activity among students. For most students, the computer was little more than a high-powered typewriter. Today, a PC can be a window into the global system of interconnected networks known as the Internet, or just the *Net*.

The Internet is used by mom-and-pop businesses and multinational corporations that want to communicate with their customers, sell products, and track economic conditions; by kindergartners and college students doing research and exploration; by consumers and commuters who need access to timely information, goods, and services; and by families and friends who just want to stay in touch. Most people connect to the Internet because it gives them the power to do things that they couldn't easily do otherwise.

Using the Internet you can perform the following tasks:

- Study material designed to supplement this book, including late-breaking news, interactive study aids, and multimedia simulations that can't be printed on paper.
- Send a message to 1 or 1,001 people, around town or around the world, and receive replies almost as quickly as the recipients can read the message and type a response.
- Explore vast libraries of research material, ranging from classic scholarly works to contemporary reference works.
- Find instant answers to time-sensitive questions.
- Get medical, legal, or technical advice from a wide variety of experts.

- Listen to live radio broadcasts from around the world.
- Participate in discussions or play games with people all over the globe who share your interests; with the right equipment, you can set aside your keyboard and communicate through live audio-video links.
- Shop for obscure items, such as out-of-print books and CDs that you can't find elsewhere.
- Download free software or music clips from servers all over the world onto your computer.
- Order a custom-built computer, car, or condominium.
- Track hourly changes in the stock markets and buy and sell stocks based on those changes.
- Take a course for college credit from a school thousands of miles away.
- Publish your own writings, drawings, photos, and multimedia works so Internet users all over the world can view them.
- Start your own business and interact with clients around the world.

Every revolution has a dark side, and the Internet explosion is no exception. The Internet has plenty of worthless information, scams, and questionable activities. People who make the most of the Internet know how to separate the best of the Net from the rest of the Net. Every chapter of this book contains information that will help you understand and use the Internet wisely. In this chapter, we'll focus on the basics of the two most popular Internet applications: finding information on the World Wide Web and communicating with electronic mail.

0.16 In Seattle, Washington (top), a mother checks on her four-year-old daughter from work using Internet-link video cameras. Grassroots organizers used the Internet to mobilize support for Presidential candidate Howard Dean (center). The Internet provides up-to-date sporting news to enthusiasts and athletes (bottom).

World Wide Web Basics

The **World Wide Web (WWW)** makes the Internet accessible to people all over the planet. The *Web* is a huge portion of the Internet that includes a wealth of multimedia content accessible through simple point-and-click programs called **Web browsers**. Web browsers on PCs and other devices serve as windows to the Web's diverse information.

The World Wide Web is made up of millions of interlinked documents called **Web pages**. A Web page is typically made up of text and images, like a page in a book. A collection of related pages stored on the same computer is called a **Web site**; a typical Web site is organized around a home page that serves as an entry page and a stepping off point for other pages in the site. Each Web page has a unique address, technically referred to as a **uniform resource locator (URL)**. For example, the URL for this book's home page is **http://computerconfluence.com**. You can visit the site by typing the exact URL into the address box of your Web browser.

The Web is an example of a *hypertext* system. A typical Web page contains information, such as words and pictures, as well as connections to other Web pages. A Web browser enables you to jump from one Web page to another by clicking **hyperlinks** (often called *links*), which are words, pictures, or menu items that act as buttons.

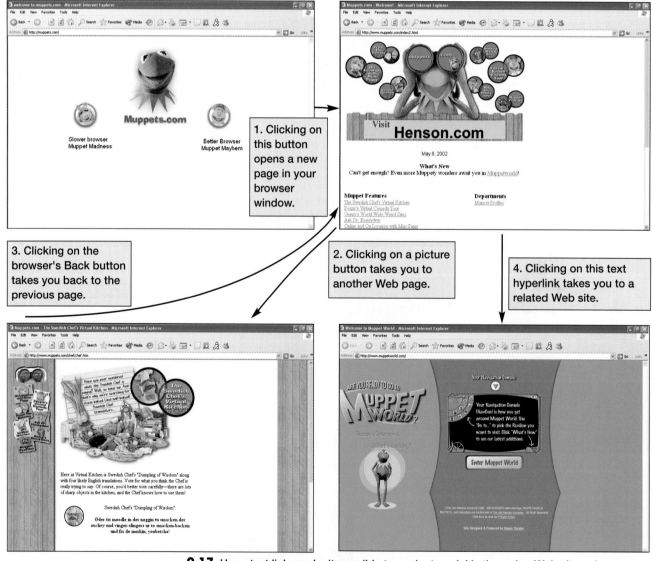

0.17 Hypertext links make it possible to navigate quickly through a Web site to locate a page containing specific information.

Hypertext systems, such as the Web, contain "pages," but they don't work like books. The author of a novel expects you to start at page one, move on to page two, and continue reading the pages in order until you have finished the last page. Hyperlinks enable you to access the pages of a hypertext system in a variety of ways, depending on your needs. For example, at the *Computer Confluence* Web site, you can select a chapter number to jump to pages related to that chapter. Within the chapter, you can click Multiple Choice to jump to a page containing practice quiz questions. Or you can click Chapter Connections to jump to a page full of hyperlinks that can take you to pages on other Web sites. These off-site pages contain articles, illustrations, audio clips, video segments, and resources created by others. They reside on computers owned by corporations, universities, libraries, institutions, and individuals around the world.

Text links are typically, but not always, underlined and displayed in a different color than standard text on the page. You can explore an amazing variety of Web pages by clicking links. But this kind of random jumping isn't without frustrations. Some links lead to cobwebs, which are Web pages that haven't been kept up to date by their owners, and dead ends—pages that have been removed or moved. Even if a link is current, it may not be reputable or accurate; because anybody can create Web pages, they don't all have the editorial integrity of trusted print media.

It can also be frustrating to try to find your way back to pages you've seen on the Web. That's why browsers have *Back* and *Forward buttons*; you can retrace your steps as often as you like. These buttons won't help, though, if you're trying to find an important page from an earlier session. Most browsers include tools for keeping personal lists of memorable sites, called *bookmarks* or *favorites*. When you run across a page worth revisiting, you can mark it with a Bookmark or Add to Favorites command. Then you can revisit that site anytime by selecting it from the list.

Web Search Basics

The World Wide Web is like a giant, loosely woven, constantly changing document created by thousands of unrelated authors and scattered about in computers all over the world. The biggest challenge for many Web users is extracting the useful information from the rest. If you're looking for a specific information resource, but you don't know where it is located on the Web, you might be able to find it using a search engine.

> The ability to **ask the right question** is more than half the battle of **finding the answer**.
>
> —*Thomas J. Watson, founder of IBM*

0.18 A search for the phrase *global warming* yields hundreds of hits on the Google search engine.

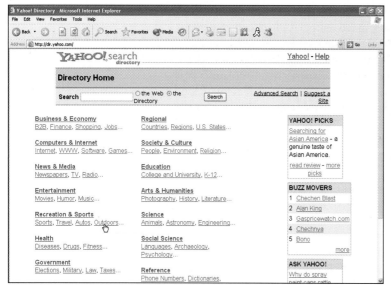

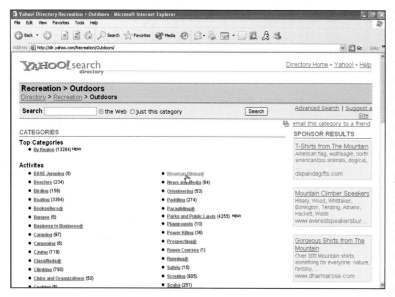

0.19 Yahoo's subject tree enables you to narrow your search by clicking categories within a subject.

A search engine is built around a database that catalogs Web locations based on content. (Databases are covered later in the book; for now, you can just think of them as indexed collections of information stored in computers.) For some search engines, researchers organize and evaluate Web sites. Other search engines use software to search the Web and catalog information automatically. The usefulness of a search engine depends in part on the information in its database. But it also depends on how easy it is for people to find what they're looking for in the database.

To find information with a typical search engine, you type a keyword or keywords into a search field, click a button, and wait a few seconds for your Web browser to display a list of *hits*—pages that contain requested keywords. A search engine can easily produce a list of hundreds or thousands of hits. Most search engines attempt to list pages in order from best to worst match, but these automatic rankings aren't always reliable.

Another popular way to use a search engine is to repeatedly narrow the search using a *directory* or *subject tree*—a hierarchical catalog of Web sites compiled by researchers. The search engine at Yahoo! is probably the best-known example. A screen presents you with a menu of subject choices. When you click a subject—say, Government—you narrow your search to that subject, and you're presented with a menu of subcategories within that subject—Military, Politics, Law, Taxes, and so on. You can continue to narrow your search by proceeding through subject menus until you reach a list of selected Web sites related to the final subject. The sites are usually rank-ordered based on estimated value. The list of Web sites on a given index page is not exhaustive; there may be hundreds of pages related to the subject that aren't included in any directory. It's simply not possible to keep a complete index of all the pages on the ever-changing Web.

Popular search engines are located on Netscape Netcenter, Yahoo!, and other Internet *portals*—Web sites designed as first-stop gateways for Internet surfers. Internet Explorer, Netscape Communicator, and other Web browsers include Search buttons that connect to popular search engines. And many large Web sites include search engines that enable you to search for site-specific information.

Email Basics

Each person on the **"Internet"** has a unique email **"address"** created by **having a squirrel** run across a computer keyboard . . . .

—*Dave Barry, humorist*

Electronic mail (also called email or *e-mail*) is the application that lures many people to the Internet for the first time. Email programs make it possible for even casual computer users to send messages to family, friends, and colleagues easily.

Because an email message can be written, addressed, sent, delivered, and answered in a matter of minutes—even if the correspondents are on opposite sides of the globe—

email has replaced air mail for rapid, routine communication in many organizations. If you send someone an email message, that person can log in and read it from a computer at home, at the office, or from anywhere in the world at any time of day. Unlike a ringing phone, email waits patiently in the mailbox until the recipient has the time to handle it, making email particularly attractive when the communication is between people in different time zones.

Closer to home, email makes it possible to replace time-consuming phone calls and meetings with more efficient online exchanges. Email conversations allow groups of people to discuss an idea for hours, days, or weeks, thus avoiding the urgency of needing to settle a complicated issue in a single session. You can send a message to a group of people on a mailing list as easily as you send the message to one person. Since an email message is digital data, you can edit it and combine it with other computer-generated documents. When you're finished, you can forward the edited message back to the original sender or to somebody else for further processing.

Details vary, but the basic concepts of email are the same for almost all systems. When you sign up for an email account—through your school, your company, or a private *Internet service provider (ISP)*—you receive a **user name** (sometimes called a *login name* or *alias*) and a storage area for messages (sometimes called a *mailbox*). Any user can send an email message to anyone else, regardless of whether the recipient is currently *logged in*—connected to the network. The message will be waiting in the recipient's *inbox* the next time that person launches his or her email program and logs in. An email message can be addressed to one person or hundreds of people. Most email messages are plain text, and don't include the kinds of formatting and graphic images found in printed documents. Messages can carry documents, pictures, multimedia files, and other computer files as *attachments*.

You can send messages to anyone on your local system or ISP by simply addressing the message to that person's user name. You can also send messages to anyone with access to Internet email, provided you know that person's Internet address. An Internet email address is made up of two parts separated by an at sign: the person's user name and the *host name*—the name of the host computer, network, or ISP address from which the user receives mail. Here's the basic form:

```
username@hostname
```

Here are a few examples of typical email addresses:

```
realgeorge999@aol.com
jandumont@engr.ucla.edu
enathab@pop3.ispchannel.com
```

Some organizations use standardized email addresses so it's easy to guess member addresses. For example, every employee at ABCXYZ Company might have an email address of the form *firstname_lastname@abcxyzco.com*. (The underscore character is sometimes used as a substitute for a space because spaces can't be embedded in email addresses). It's important to address email messages with care; they can't be delivered if even a single character is mistyped. Fortunately, most email programs include address books. So that after entering contact information once, users can look up email addresses by name and automatically address messages. Many World Wide Web sites, including Yahoo!, Excite, and search.com, offer free email search services and directories.

Many commercial Web sites offer free email accounts. Sometimes these free email services are subsidized by advertisers; sometimes they're provided to attract Web site visitors. Free email services are popular with users of public computers (for example, in libraries), people who don't receive email from their ISPs, people who want multiple email addresses not associated with their workplace, and travelers who want to check email on the road without lugging a laptop.

The example in the Screen Test shows a simple email session using Hotmail—an email service that's accessible through a standard Web browser. The concepts illustrated in the example apply to all email programs.

Screen Test

Communicating with Electronic Mail

GOAL *Catch up on your email*

TOOL *Microsoft Hotmail*

1. Hotmail is a popular email service available through the World Wide Web. When you navigate to www.hotmail.com in a Web browser, you are presented with the Hotmail logon page. Here, you enter your username and password; then you click Sign In to continue.

2. After you sign on, you are presented with the contents of your electronic inbox. This is the folder where incoming mail—email that was sent by others to you—is stored. Here, you can see a list of read and unread mail, navigate to other email folders, and delete email. You can also jump to other email tasks, such as composing a new email message of your own or managing your *contacts*—those people with which you correspond regularly.

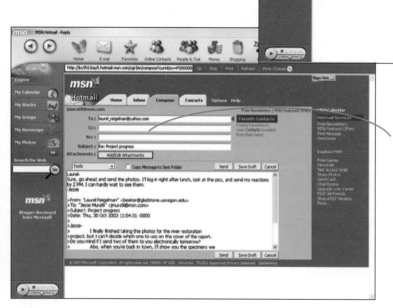

3. To open an email message, simply click the sender's name, which is highlighted as a hyperlink. The email message displays. From here, you can respond to the message, forward the message to others, delete the message, or move it to a different email folder.

0.20

Internet Security Basics

Despite its wonders, the Internet can be a dangerous place. In the same way that you should wear a seat belt and observe local laws when driving a car, you should approach the Internet understanding the security risks involved. After you connect a computer to a network or the Internet, you dramatically increase the risk that your system will be compromised in some way. But that doesn't mean that the Internet should be avoided. Rather, you just need to make sure you're taking the proper precautions.

The most common form of Internet-based security risk is probably spam, or junk mail. This is unwanted email you receive from (usually) unknown senders, such as mass mailers who are attempting to sell goods or deceive people into paying for nonexistent items. Most email programs now include *spam filters* that help keep this problem manageable, but even with a filter you're likely to spend plenty of time manually deleting spam messages.

Viruses are a more sinister email problem. Generally delivered as email attachments, viruses are executable programs designed by malicious programmers—sometimes called *hackers*—to infiltrate your system. Some viruses simply duplicate themselves and send themselves to other PCs by harvesting email addresses in your email address book; these types of viruses can slow the performance of your network, making Internet access unbearably slow. Others can delete files and folders on your system. Either way, you shouldn't open unexpected attachments from unknown senders.

Another problem on the Internet is password theft. There are low-tech methods for stealing other people's passwords: For example, someone might look over your shoulder and watch as you type a password. Hackers that can electronically monitor keystrokes and send the information over the Internet to others. A wider but related issue concerns *identity (ID) theft*. Hackers or other unscrupulous individuals can access your computer and obtain enough information about you to assume your identity. In cases of ID theft, thieves have been known to use victims' credit cards to rack up thousands of dollars in bills. To protect yourself against ID theft, you should keep personal information, including your social security number, credit card numbers, and passwords a secret while online.

Obviously, there's a lot more to Internet security. We look extensively at this issue in Chapter 10.

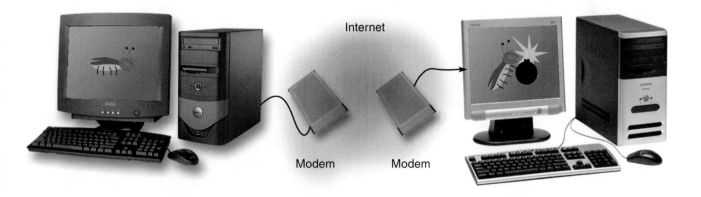

A programmer writes a tiny program—the virus—that has destructive power and can reproduce itself.

Most often, the virus is attached to a normal program; unknown to the user, the virus spreads to other software.

The virus is passed by disk or network to other users who use other computers. The virus remains dormant as it is passed on.

Depending on how it is programmed, a virus may display an unexpected message, gobble up memory, destroy data files or cause serious system errors.

0.21 How a virus spreads.

Applying the Basics

It is good to have **an end** to journey toward, but it is **the journey** that matters in the end.

—Ursula K. LeGuin, author of The Dispossessed

In a few pages, you've learned the basic concepts behind the PC and the Internet. Now it's time to apply what you've learned in a practical, hands-on way. The next few pages guide you with a few helpful rules of thumb for navigating through the remaining chapters of *Computer Confluence*. They're followed by a step by step opening session with the *Computer Confluence* CD-ROM and Web site. After you complete this quick tour, you'll be ready to dive into the heart of *Computer Confluence*, starting with Chapter 1. So what are you waiting for?

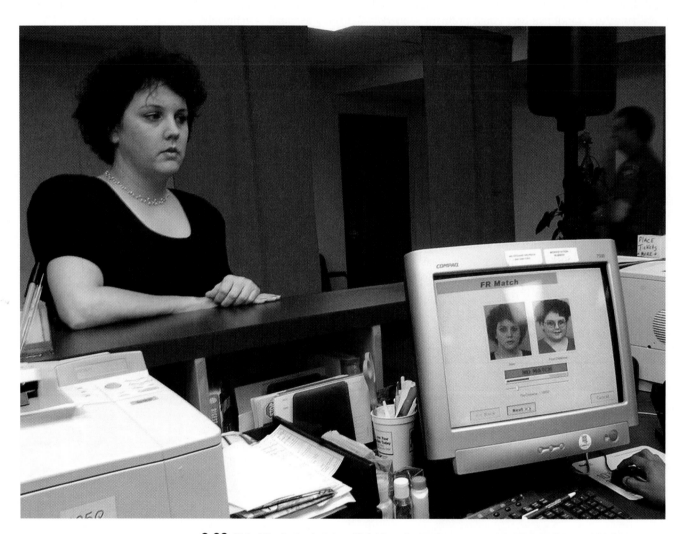

0.22 This Mississippi state official is using software to compare previous and current driver's license photos. The software makes identity theft more difficult by discouraging false driver's license applicants.

Working Wisdom

Navigating *Computer Confluence*

Here are a few pointers for exploring *Computer Confluence*. Take a minute to read these and you'll probably save hours later.

➡ **Know your boxes.** Text chapters include several types of boxes, each of which is designed to be read in a particular way.

 ● The *Screen Test* boxes show you short sequences of screens from test drives of some of today's most popular software. These boxes can be especially helpful if they cover applications you aren't learning to use firsthand. The *Computer Confluence* CD-ROM includes multimedia introductions to some of the applications featured in these boxes.

 ● *Working Wisdom* boxes (similar to this one) provide practical tips on everything from designing a publication to protecting your privacy. They bring concepts down to earth with useful suggestions that can save you time and money, and provide peace of mind.

 ● *How It Works* boxes are for readers who want—or need—to know more about what's going on under the hood. These boxes use words and pictures to take you deeper into the inner workings without getting bogged down in technical detail. The *Computer Confluence* CD-ROM includes multimedia versions of many of these boxes as well as bonus How It Works features that aren't in the text. If your course objectives and personal curiosity don't motivate you to learn how it works, that's okay; you can skip every How It Works box and still understand the rest of *Computer Confluence*.

 ● *Inventing the Future* boxes examine today's technological trends and research projects to speculate on the future of the technology and its impact on our lives. The *Computer Confluence* CD-ROM includes video clips that supplement and illustrate the ideas in many of these boxes.

 ● *Crosscurrents* boxes showcase diverse, timely, and often controversial points of view on the technology and its impact on our lives. These short essays, which close each chapter, offer perspectives from some of the most important writers and thinkers in the information technology field.

➡ **Read it and read it again.** If possible, read each chapter twice: once for the big ideas and the second time for more detailed understanding. You may also find it helpful to survey each chapter's outline in the table of contents before reading the chapter for the first time.

➡ **Don't try to memorize every term the first time through.** Throughout the text, key terms are introduced in boldface blue, and secondary terms are *italicized in blue*. Use the Key Terms list at the end of each chapter to review and the glossary to recall any forgotten terms. The CD-ROM contains an interactive cross-referenced version of the glossary so you can find any term quickly.

➡ **Don't overanalyze examples.** *Computer Confluence* is designed to help you understand concepts, not memorize keystrokes. You can learn the nuts and bolts of working with computers in labs or at home. The examples in this text may not match the applications in your lab, but the concepts are similar.

➡ **Don't get stuck.** If a concept seems unclear on the first reading, make a note and move on. Sometimes ideas make more sense after you've seen the bigger picture. If you still don't understand the concept the second time through, check the CD-ROM and the Web site for further clarification. When in doubt, ask questions.

➡ **Remember that there's more than one way to learn.** Some of us learn best by reading, others learn best by exploring interactive examples, and still others learn best by discussing ideas with others, online or in person. *Computer Confluence* offers you the opportunity to learn in all of these ways. Use the learning tools that work best for you.

➡ **Get your hands dirty.** Try the applications while you're reading about them. Your reading and lab work will reinforce each other and help solidify your newfound knowledge.

➡ **Study together.** There's plenty to discuss here, and discussion is a great way to learn.

In a hurry? Turn the page. The next page will give you a quick start—just enough information so you can start using the CD-ROM, the Web site, and related computer applications right away.

Computer Confluence Multimedia Quick Start

The first few chapters of this book provide you with a broad orientation to computers, CD-ROMs, the Internet, and related technology. In the meantime, this Quick Start provides the basics—without detailed explanations—so you can get started with the *Computer Confluence* CD-ROM and Web site right away.

Details vary from computer to computer, but the basics are generally the same. If you're working in a computer lab, you'll probably need a few additional lab instructions to supplement the steps in this Quick Start.

LAUNCHING THE *COMPUTER CONFLUENCE* CD-ROM

1. Insert the Computer Confluence CD-ROM into your computers CD-ROM drive. If your computer is set to autorun, the Computer Confluence CD-ROM will launch automatically. Simply follow the onscreen prompts to access all of the interactive content for each chapter.
2. If your computer is not set to autorun, follow these instructions:

Windows

a. From the Windows Start menu (lower-left corner of your screen) select Run.
b. Type in "X:\start.exe" (where X is the letter of your CD-ROM drive) in the Open dialog box and click "OK".

Macintosh

a. Point to the CD icon and double-click on it.
b. Double-click the Start icon in the CD window.

3. The application takes a few seconds to load into the computer's memory. When it does, a new window opens on your screen.

EXPLORING THE *COMPUTER CONFLUENCE* WEB SITE

To explore the *Computer Confluence* Web site, you'll need a Web browser and an Internet connection. Your computer probably includes one or more of these browsers: Internet Explorer, Netscape Navigator, Netscape Communicator, or America Online's Web browser.

1. Open your browser by double-clicking on the browser icon on your desktop. If you're using a modem to connect to the Internet, this will probably cause the modem to dial the appropriate number.
2. Type the URL (web address) for the Computer Confluence Companion Website into the browser address bar as shown here

and Press Enter or Return.
3. If an error message appears, click the OK button, check your typing carefully, correct any errors, and press Return or Enter again. When you type it correctly, you'll be taken to the *Computer Confluence* opening screen.
4. Bookmark this page so you can return to it easily. If you're using Internet Explorer, select Add to Favorites from the Favorites menu. If you're using Netscape Navigator or Communicator, select Add Bookmark from the Bookmark menu
5. At the *Computer Confluence* site, you can click on-screen images and menus to select the edition of the book you're using, a chapter, and activities within that chapter.

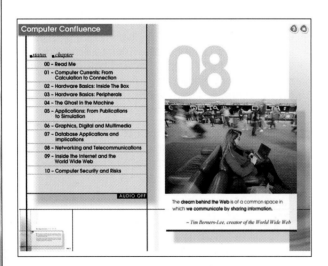

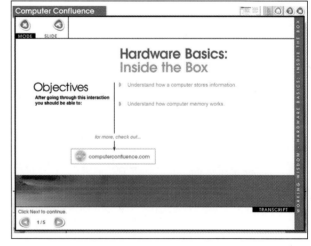

0.23

Crosscurrents

The Myth of Generation N *Simson Garfinkel*

Every chapter of this book ends with an article that explores issues related to computer technology and its impact on our lives. This essay was first published in August 2003, in MIT Technology Review. *In it Simson Garfinkel, author of* Database Nation, *raises some thought-provoking questions about the "net generation."*

For decades, social scientists and technologists have alternatively predicted the emergence of "computer kids" or a "net generation"—a cohort of children, teenagers, and young adults who have been immersed in digital technology and the digital way of thinking since their conception.

This new generation, the thinking went, would be everything that their parents weren't when it came to technology: They would know how to type, partake in electronic communications, and be able to rapidly figure out how all this stuff worked. They would be so adept at using computers that calling them "computer literate" would be an insult. They would see society as something to be mastered and hacked, not something that they need to fit inside.

Certainly, a lot of evidence supports a "net generation" effect. Although there are no reliable statistics on computer literacy, good figures do exist on Internet usage, thanks to the Pew Internet Project. According to its survey released earlier this year, 74 percent of people in the United States age 18 to 29 have Internet access, compared with 52 percent of those age 50 to 64. Among the over-65 set, Internet access plummets to just 18 percent. And in my own age group, 30 to 49, 52 percent have some kind of Net access. These figures certainly argue for the existence of a "Generation N."

But the more time I spend with the kids who should be members of Generation N—today's high school and college students—the more convinced I am that the notion of universal computer competence among young people is a myth. And the techno-laggards among us risk being relegated to second-class citizenship in a world that revolves around, and often assumes, access to information technology.

People who spend years working with computers learn how to use them; people who lack that experience, don't. I've seen 40- and 50-somethings who burn their own CDs and have phenomenal command of applications like Word, PowerPoint, and Excel. Like Generation N, they've wanted to get something done and invested the time to do it.

The difference between these old fogies and today's teens is that, for many teens today, learning to use a computer is no longer optional. The teachers in my town's high school refuse to accept papers unless they are typed on a computer. Typing itself is taught in the middle school (where they call it "keyboarding"); students who went to a less technologically progressive school system and transferred in are expected to pick up the skill on their own. Not a problem! "We all figured out how to get Napster going and download music," says a friend of mine who recently graduated from Stanford University and now works for a major investment firm. Everybody her age knows how to use a computer, she says, just like "everybody knows how to change their oil."

Experts in human–computer interaction say that the real difference between teenagers and their elders is teens' willingness to experiment with computers, combined with their acceptance of the seemingly arbitrary conventions that are endemic to contemporary computer interfaces. In other words, teens aren't worried about breaking their computers, and they're not wise enough or experienced enough to get angry at and reject poorly written programs. The teens just deal with computers, as they are forced to deal with many other aspects of their lives. These strategies, once learned and internalized, are incredibly effective for working with today's computer technology.

Likewise, today's systems are teaching their users—young and old alike—to multitask as never before. Just as their parents talked on the phone while doing math homework, today's teens browse the Web, send e-mail, and simultaneously engage in multiple chat and Instant Message sessions while allegedly working on an essay. A friend of mine has a daughter who developed a flair for language: she routinely has chat windows going in English, French, and Japanese—and both her parents are native English speakers!

But the point that seems to have escaped my friend is that everybody doesn't know how to change the oil on their car. It's not a generational thing; it's simply the result of 20 years' experience. But when you are surrounded by people who all share the same technological skills, it's easy to forget that there are others who aren't with the program (so to speak). Unfortunately, with the changes overtaking our society, today's kids who don't have tech experience and tech aptitude are going to be left behind much faster than their elders.

And that's the danger in believing that time will give us a population that's completely computer literate. Remember, the Pew study found that 26 percent of young adults do not have Internet access. An even bigger determiner than age is education: only 23 percent of people who did not graduate from high school have Internet access, compared with 82 percent of those who have graduated from college.

Certainly, more kids today are growing up wired—but millions of them are not. Meanwhile, we're rebuilding our society in ways that make things increasingly difficult for people who aren't online. For example, people who don't want to (or can't) buy their airplane tickets on the Web now typically have to wait on hold for 30 minutes with the airline or go through a travel agent and pay an agency fee—sometimes as much as $50. When I needed to renew my passport, the local post office didn't have the form: they told me to download it from the Internet.

This is a problem that won't be solved through more education or federal grants. As a society, we need to come to terms with the fact that a substantial number of people, young and old alike, will never go online. We need to figure out how we will avoid making life unbearable for them.

Discussion Questions

1. Do you think there is a difference between the way young people approach computers and the way their parents approach computers? If so, what is the difference?

2. Do you agree with the statements in the last paragraph of this essay? Why or why not?

Summary

PCs come in a variety of shapes and sizes, but they're all made up of two things: the physical parts of the computer, called hardware, and the software instructions that tell the hardware what to do. The PC's system unit contains the CPU, which controls the other components, including memory, disk drives, and monitor screens. The keyboard and mouse enable a user to communicate with the computer, which sends information back to the user through displays on the monitor.

The computer's operating system software takes care of details of the computer's operation. Application software provides specific tools for computer users. The file system contains the numerous files needed for the operating system and application software to run smoothly, and the personal files created by the computer's users. A hierarchical system of folders organizes the files, making it easier for application programs and computer users to find the files they need.

PCs can be networked to other computers using cables, radio waves, or other means. A computer can also be connected to a network through standard phone lines using a modem.

The Internet is a global network of computer networks used for education, commerce, and communication. The most popular Internet activities are exploring the World Wide Web and communicating with electronic mail.

A Web browser is a computer application that provides easy access to the World Wide Web—a wide-ranging array of multimedia information on the Internet. Web pages are interconnected by hyperlinks that make it easy to follow information trails. Search engines serve as indices for the Web, locating pages with subject matter that matches keywords.

Electronic mail (or email) enables almost instant communication among Internet users. Some email systems can be accessed through Web browsers.

The Internet is not without risks. Internet users must be prepared to deal with unsolicited (and often unsavory) email, computer viruses, identity theft, and other risks.

The *Computer Confluence* CD-ROM and companion Web site use PC multimedia and Internet technology to enhance and expand the information and ideas presented in this book.

Key Terms

(All terms introduced in this chapter will be revisited in later chapters.)

application program
  (application)...........................(p. 9)
back-up copy ....(p. 16)
back-up media ....(p. 16)
button......................................(p. 8)
CD-ROM drive..........................(p. 6)
CD-RW drive............................(p. 6)
central processing unit
  (CPU).....................................(p. 6)
click..(p. 8)
Clipboard................................(p. 9)
copy.......................................(p. 9)
cut..(p. 9)
disks.......................................(p. 6)
document................................(p. 9)
double-click............................(p. 8)
drag..(p. 8)
drag-and-drop.........................(p. 9)
DVD drive...............................(p. 6)
electronic mail (email) ....(p. 22)
file..(p. 9)
file compression ....(p. 16)

file decompression...................(p. 16)
Find.......................................(p. 16)
find-and-replace (search and
  replace) ....(p. 9)
folder ....(p. 15)
font ....(p. 10)
formatting ....(p. 9)
hard disk ....(p. 6)
hardware ....(p. 5)
hyperlink................................(p. 20)
Internet ....(p. 18)
keyboard ....(p. 7)
memory...................................(p. 6)
menu......................................(p. 8)
monitor ....(p. 7)
monospaced font ....(p. 10)
mouse ....(p. 7)
open ....(p. 8)
operating system (OS)..............(p. 9)
paste.......................................(p. 9)
peripheral...............................(p. 6)
personal computer (PC)............(p. 5)

point size ....(p. 9)
printer ....(p. 7)
proportionally spaced
  font......................................(p. 10)
sans-serif font ....(p. 10)
serif font ....(p. 10)
Search....................................(p. 16)
search engine ....(p. 21)
software ....(p. 9)
spam ....(p. 25)
speakers ....(p. 7)
typeface ....(p. 10)
uniform resource locator
  (URL) ....(p. 20)
user name...............................(p. 23)
viruses....................................(p. 25)
Web browser...........................(p. 20)
Web page ....(p. 20)
Web site ....(p. 20)
word wrap...............................(p. 9)
World Wide Web (WWW) ......(p. 20)
WYSIWYG ....(p. 9)

Interactive Activities

1. The *Computer Confluence* CD-ROM contains self-test quiz questions related to this chapter, including multiple-choice, true or false, and matching questions.

2. The *Computer Confluence* Web site, http://www.computerconfluence.com, contains self-test exercises related to this chapter. Follow the instruc-

tions for taking a quiz. After you've completed your quiz, you can email the results to your instructor.

3. The Web site also contains open-ended discussion questions called Internet Explorations. Discuss one or more of the Internet Exploration questions at the section for this chapter.

True or False

1. The majority of people in the world use computers at least occasionally.

2. A computer keyboard includes some keys that don't respond by displaying characters on the screen, but instead send special commands to the computer.

3. Windows PCs and Macintoshes use the same operating system (OS).

4. An entire computer network can be connected to other networks through cables, wireless radio transmissions, or other means.

5. Hypertext links make it easy to jump between Web pages created by different authors around the world.

6. A Web search engine is built around a database that catalogs Web locations based on content.

7. An Internet email address is made up of a user name and a host name separated by an at sign (@).

8. Web searching and email checking require different application programs on virtually all PCs.

9. Spam is a type of computer virus that attacks only email documents.

10. The Internet has become virtually risk-free within the last few years.

Multiple Choice

1. The computer's system unit typically contains the computer's "brain," called the

   a. Central processing unit
   b. Memory
   c. Peripheral
   d. Monitor
   e. Modem

2. The PC's main hard disk
   a. Is a permanent part of the system unit
   b. Is sometimes called an internal drive
   c. Can hold more information than the computer's memory
   d. Serves as a long-term storage device
   e. All of the above

3. Which of the following is not considered removable media?
   a. Disks
   b. CD-ROMs
   c. Audio CDs
   d. Hard disks
   e. DVDs

4. Which of the following is not a peripheral?
   a. A printer
   b. A mouse
   c. A CD-ROM drive
   d. A processor
   e. All of the above

5. What is a software program designed to help you accomplish a specific task called?
   a. An application
   b. An operating system
   c. A document
   d. A desktop
   e. A browser

6. Virtually all modern word processors display words on the screen almost exactly as they will appear on the printed page. What is this feature called?
   a. Electronic paper
   b. Highlighting
   c. Point-and-click interface
   d. Virtual reality
   e. WYSIWYG (what you see is what you get)

7. In Windows and the Mac OS, a file is represented by
   a. A beige folder icon
   b. A special key on the keyboard
   c. A name and an extension
   d. A link to a Web page
   e. All of the above

8. In Windows and the Mac OS, which word or phrase best describes how files and folders are organized?
   a. Democratically
   b. Hierarchically
   c. In a network
   d. In pools
   e. Randomly

9. A blank CD-R is better than a disk for backups because
   a. It costs less and it holds 500 times more information
   b. It holds 500 times more information, even though it costs 10 times more
   c. It automatically compresses the files being backed up
   d. Data files cannot be stored on disks
   e. The entire contents of a hard drive can be stored on a single CD-R

10. Which of the following does every Web site on the World Wide Web have?
    a. Hyperlinks to dozens of other Web sites
    b. Multimedia material
    c. Publicly accessible information on a particular subject
    d. A unique address called a URL
    e. All of the above

11. If you want to retrace your steps and return to the screen previously displayed in the browser window, you should use
    a. The left-arrow key
    b. The R key
    c. The browser's Back button
    d. The spacebar
    e. The Undo key

12. Which of the following enables you to narrow your search for information on the Web repeatedly?
    a. The down-arrow key
    b. The right mouse button
    c. The scrollbar
    d. An email browser
    e. A directory or subject tree

13. Which of the following can be attached to an email message?
    a. A picture
    b. A multimedia file
    c. A word processor document
    d. A computer virus
    e. All of the above

14. Which of these is definitely *not* a valid email address?
    a. http://www.computerconfluence.com
    b. beanbag_boxspring@prenhall.com
    c. president@whitehouse.gov
    d. thisisaverylongnameindeed@aol.com
    e. All of the above could be valid email addresses.

15. Which of the following is the most common use of spam?
    a. Transmitting computer viruses
    b. Identity theft
    c. Marketing unsolicited goods and services
    d. Web searches
    e. Hacking

Review Questions

1. Briefly define or describe each of the key terms listed in the Key Terms section.

2. How are hardware and software related?

3. Which computer component is the most critical to the computer's functioning, and why?

4. Which two computer components are most often used by people for getting information into PCs?

5. What is the difference between operating system software and application software?

6. How do folders allow files to be organized?

7. What is the purpose of file compression?

8. List some ways that a computer might be connected to a network.

9. What is the fundamental difference between ordinary text (such as a novel) and hypertext?

10. Give examples of ways email can change the way you communicate with other people.

11. How can you use hyperlinks to explore the World Wide Web? Give an example.

12. How can you find a site on the Web if you don't know the URL?

13. What security procedures should you follow while exploring the *Computer Confluence* Web site?

Discussion Questions

1. Spend some time exploring the *Computer Confluence* CD-ROM. What features of the software do you think will be most helpful to you? Why?

2. Spend some time exploring the *Computer Confluence* Web site, **http://www.computerconfluence.com**. What features of the site do you think will be most helpful to you? Why?

Projects

1. Keep a log of your progress as you use the *Computer Confluence* book, CD-ROM, and Web site. Make notes on which features are most helpful and which are least helpful. When you finish the book and related material, you may want to send a summary of your log to the author c/o Prentice Hall. Your notes will help make future editions of *Computer Confluence* more useful for others.

Sources and Resources

At the end of every chapter of *Computer Confluence*, you'll find an annotated list of valuable resources for learning more about the subjects covered in the chapter. Some of these resources are magazines, journals, and other periodicals with particularly good coverage of computers, the Internet, and the impact of technology on our lives. Some of the resources are books—fiction and nonfiction— that provide insights into the world of information technology. Some are films and videos that vividly portray concepts and issues related to the technology. And, of course, some are Web sites that can take you far beyond the basic ideas covered in this book. If you want to learn more, start with these sources and resources.

Multimedia

on the CD-ROM and the Web:

~ Stewart Brand on computers and the **counter-culture**

~ Interactive tutorial on embedded computers

~ Timeline on the evolution of computers

~ Instant access to **glossary** and **key term** references

~ Interactive **self-study,** quizzes

. . . and more.

 computerconfluence.com

Objectives

**After you read this chapter
you should be able to:**

▶ **Characterize what a computer is and what it does**

▶ **Describe several ways computers play a critical
role in modern life**

▶ **Discuss the circumstances and ideas that led to
the development of the modern computer**

▶ **Describe several trends in the evolution of modern
computers**

▶ **Comment on the fundamental difference between
computers and other machines**

▶ **Explain the relationship between hardware and
software**

▶ **Outline the four major types of computers in use
today and describe their principal uses**

▶ **Describe how the explosive growth of the Internet is
changing the way people use computers and
information technology**

▶ **Explain how today's information age differs from
other times in history and prehistory**

▶ **Discuss the social and ethical impact of
information technology on our society**

CHAPTER 1

Google is one of the most successful companies to spring from the World Wide Web. The Google search engine, which helps people find relevant Web pages, handles about 200 million queries a day, making it the most popular search engine in the English-speaking world. To many Web users, the term "google" is synonymous with "search." People routinely use Google to find facts, track down quotes, locate other people, and even do background checks on blind dates.

This amazing venture was launched by two entrepreneurial graduate students from opposite sides of the globe. Sergey Brin was born in Moscow in the former Soviet Union. Larry Page is the son of a computer science professor at Michigan State University. The two met while they were computer science Ph.D. students at Stanford University.

Soon after enrolling at Stanford, Page talked with his advisor, Professor Terry Winograd, about ways to improve Web search engines. Early Web search engines determined the extent to which a Web page related to a

THE GOOGLE GUYS SEARCH FOR SUCCESS

You can make money **without doing evil**.

—*From Google's mission and philosophy statement*

---

key word or phrase by counting how many times that word or phrase appeared in the Web page. Low-quality Web sites could fool these search engines by repeating a particular phrase hundreds of times. Winograd and Page had the idea of determining a Web page's relevance by the number of times *other* related Web pages linked to it.

Page teamed up with Brin and began writing the software to implement a new kind of search engine. They called it BackRub, since the reputation of one site depends on links to it from other sites. Page borrowed money and built a Web server hosting BackRub in his dorm room; Brin's dorm room became the business office. In 1998 twenty-six-year-old Page and twenty-five-year-old Brin raised $1 million and officially launched their company, renamed Google. (The name Google is a play on the huge number *googol*—a 1 followed by 100 zeroes.) At first, the start-up operated out of a garage, but in just a few months it outgrew its humble quarters. Today, Google has more than 1,000 employees, including a significant number of Ph.D.s. Ironically, Brin and Page have taken indefinite

Computer Currents and Internet Waves

The Long View

leave from their Ph.D. studies to help manage their wildly successful venture.

In April 2003, Google announced it would offer shares to the public, making Brin and Page instant billionaires. However, Google's management defied convention by establishing procedures to ensure the company could stay focused on long-term strategic investments rather than short-term profits. In their letter to potential investors, Brin and Page wrote, "Google is not a conventional company. We do not intend to become one." ～

1.1 Sergey Brin and Larry Page

Computers are so much a part of modern life that we hardly notice them. But computers are everywhere, and we'd certainly notice them if they suddenly stopped working. Imagine . . .

Living Without Computers

1.2 In a modern radio station, all the songs are stored on computer hard drives.

You wake up with the sun well above the horizon and realize your alarm clock hasn't gone off. You wonder if you've overslept. You have a big research project due today. The face of your digital wristwatch stares back at you blankly. The TV and radio are no help; you can't find a station on either one. You can't even get the time by telephone because the phone doesn't work either.

The morning newspaper is missing from your doorstep. You'll have to guess the weather forecast by looking out the window. No music to dress by this morning, as your CD player and your MP3 player refuse your requests. How about some breakfast? Your automatic coffeemaker refuses to be programmed; your microwave oven is on strike too.

You decide to go out for breakfast. Your car won't start. In fact, the only cars moving are at least 15 years old. The lines at the subway are unbelievable. People chatter nervously about the failure of the subway's computer-controlled scheduling device.

You duck into a coffee shop and find long lines of people waiting while cashiers clumsily handle transactions by hand. While you're waiting, you join the conversation that's going on around you. People seem more interested in talking to each other in person since all the usual tools of mass communication have failed.

You're down to a couple of dollars in cash, so you stop after breakfast at an automated teller machine. Why bother?

You return home to wait for the book you ordered online. You're in for a long wait; planes aren't flying because air traffic control facilities aren't working. You head for the local library to see if the book is in stock. Of course, it's going to be tough to find since the book catalog is computerized.

As you walk home, you speculate on the implications of a worldwide computer failure. How will people function in high-tech, high-rise office buildings that depend on computer systems *to control everything from elevators to humidity? Will electric power plants be able to function without computer control? What will happen to patients in computerized medical facilities? What about satellites that are kept in orbit by computer-run control systems? Will the financial infrastructure collapse without computers to process and communicate transactions? Will the world be a safer place if all computer-controlled weapons are grounded?*

Our story could go on, but the message should be clear enough by now. Computers are everywhere, and our lives are affected in all kinds of ways by their operation—and nonoperation. It's truly amazing that computers have infiltrated our lives so thoroughly in such a short time.

1.3 Computers are used to coordinate thousands of Union Pacific trains in this high-tech Omaha control room.

Computers in Perspective: An Evolving Idea

Although computers have been with us for only about five decades, these extraordinary machines are built on centuries of insight and intellectual effort.

Computing Before Computers

Consider the past and you shall **know the future**.

—Chinese Proverb

Computers grew out of a human need to quantify. Early humans were content to count with fingers, rocks, or other everyday objects. As cultures became more complex, so did their counting tools. The abacus (a type of counting tool and calculator used by the Babylonians, the Chinese, and others for thousands of years) and the Hindu-Arabic number system are examples of early calculating tools that had an immediate and profound effect on the human race. (Imagine trying to conduct business without a number system that allows for easy addition and subtraction.)

By the early nineteenth century, the capitalist culture's appetite for mathematics had outgrown its tools. People labored for hours to produce mathematical tables that were riddled with errors. An eccentric British professor named Charles Babbage invented a Difference Engine that could automatically calculate table values with the turn of a crank. But before he could actually build a working Difference Engine, Babbage tackled an even more ambitious project—the forerunner of the modern computer.

Inspired by French textile maker Joseph-Marie Charles Jacquard's automated loom, Babbage conceived of an *Analytical Engine* that could be programmed with punched cards like that loom. Babbage's design included the four basic components found in every modern computer: components for performing the basic functions of input, output, processing, and storage.

Augusta Ada King, Countess of Lovelace, the daughter of poet Lord Byron, worked for years on the project with Babbage. She is sometimes

1.4 This cart's built-in computer helps golfers navigate the course.

called the first computer programmer because she wrote a plan for using the Analytical Engine to calculate a series of Bernoulli numbers. Babbage never built the Analytical Engine. There simply wasn't enough public demand to justify the high cost. But a century later, the unfinished Analytic Engine would serve as a blueprint for the first real computers.

The Information-Processing Machine

Like the Analytical Engine, the computer is a machine that changes information from one form to another. All computers take in information called input and give out information called output, as shown here.

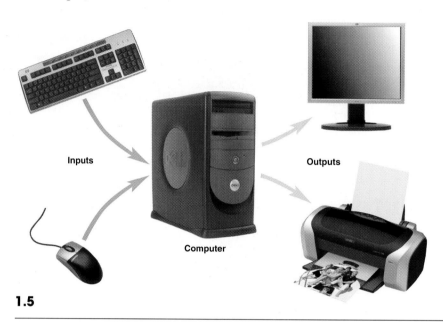

Inputs

Outputs

Computer

1.5

Because information can take many forms, the computer is an incredibly versatile tool, capable of everything from computing federal income taxes to guiding the missiles those taxes buy. For calculating taxes, the input to the computer might be numbers representing wages, other income, deductions, exemptions, and tax tables, and the output might be the number representing the taxes owed or the tax refund due. If the computer is deploying a missile, for example, the input might be satellite signals used to locate the missile and the target, and the output might be electrical signals to control the flight path of the missile. Amazingly enough, the same computer could be used to accomplish both of these tasks.

How can a machine be so versatile? The computer's flexibility isn't hidden in hardware—the physical parts of the computer system. The secret of its functionality is in its software, or programs—the instructions that tell the hardware how to transform the input data (information in a form it can read) into the necessary output.

Whether a computer is performing a simple calculation or producing a complex animation, a software program of some type controls the process from beginning to end. In effect, changing programs can turn the computer into a different tool. Because it can be programmed to perform various tasks, the typical modern computer is a general-purpose tool, not a specialized device with one use.

The First Real Computers

First we shape our tools, thereafter **they shape us**.

—*Marshall McLuhan*

Although Lady Lovelace predicted that the Analytical Engine might someday compose music, the scientists and mathematicians who designed and built the first working computers a century later had a more modest goal: to create machines capable of doing repetitive calculations. Even so, their stories are rich with drama and irony. Here are a few highlights:

- In 1939, a young German engineer named Konrad Zuse completed the first programmable, general-purpose digital computer. "I was too lazy to calculate and so I invented the computer," Zuse recalls. In 1941, Zuse and a friend asked the German government for funds to build a faster electronic computer to help crack enemy codes during World War II. The Nazi military establishment turned him down, confident that their aircraft would quickly win the war without the aid of sophisticated calculating devices.

- At about the same time, the British government was assembling a top-secret team of mathematicians and engineers to crack Nazi military codes. In 1943, the team, led by mathematician Alan Turing and others, completed Colossus, considered by many to be the first electronic digital computer. This special-purpose computer successfully broke secret codes used by the Nazis, allowing British military intelligence to eavesdrop on even the most secret German messages throughout most of the war.

- In 1939, Iowa State University professor John Atanasoff, seeking a tool to help his students solve differential equations, developed what could have been the first electronic digital computer, the Atanasoff–Berry Computer (ABC). His university neglected to patent the machine, and Atanasoff never managed to turn it into a fully operational product. The International Business Machines Corporation responded to his queries by telling him "IBM will never be interested in an electronic computing machine."

- Harvard professor Howard Aiken was more successful in financing the automatic, general-purpose calculator he was developing. Thanks to a $1 million grant from IBM, he completed the Mark I in 1944. This 51-foot-long, 8-foot-tall monster used noisy electromechanical relays to calculate five or six times faster than a person could, but it was far slower than a modern five-dollar pocket calculator.

- After consulting with Atanasoff and studying the ABC, John Mauchly teamed up with J. Presper Eckert to help the U.S. cause in World War II by constructing a machine to calculate trajectory tables for new guns. The machine was the Electronic Numerical Integrator and Computer (ENIAC), a 30-ton behemoth with 18,000 vacuum tubes that broke down, on average, once every seven minutes. When it was running, it could calculate 500 times faster than the existing electromechanical calculators—about as fast as a modern pocket calculator. It wasn't completed until two months after the end of the war, but it convinced its creators that large-scale computers were commercially feasible.

1.6 J. Presper Eckert describes the UNIVAC I computer to CBS correspondent Walter Cronkite before the 1952 presidential election (top). After counting 5 percent of the votes, UNIVAC correctly predicted that Eisenhower would win the election, but CBS cautiously chose to withhold the prediction until most of the votes were counted. In the 2000 presidential election (bottom), eager TV network officials used computer projections to predict Al Gore would win the state of Florida and the election. In fact, George W. Bush prevailed in Florida and became the 43rd President of the United States.

After the war, Mauchly and Eckert started a private company and designed the UNIVAC I, the first general-purpose commercial computer. Mauchly and Eckert were better engineers than businessmen. Razor maker Remington Rand bought them out in 1950, completed the UNIVAC I, and delivered it to the U.S. Census Bureau in 1951.

Evolution and Acceleration

Invention breeds **invention**.

—*Ralph Waldo Emerson*

Computer hardware evolved rapidly from those early days, with new technologies replacing old every few years. The first computers were big, expensive, and finicky. Only a big institution like a major bank or the U.S. government could afford a computer, not to mention the climate-controlled computing center needed to house it and the staff of technicians needed to program it and keep it running. But with all their faults, computers quickly became indispensable tools for scientists, engineers, and other professionals.

The transistor, invented in 1948, could perform the same function as vacuum tubes used in early computers by transferring electricity across a tiny resistor. Transistors were first used in a computer in 1956. Computers that used transistors were radically smaller, more reliable, and less expensive than tube-based computers. Because of improvements in software at about the same time, these machines were also much easier and faster to program and use. As a result, computers became more widely used in business, science, and engineering.

But America's fledgling space program needed computers that were even smaller and more powerful than the transistor-based machines, so researchers developed technology that enabled them to pack hundreds of transistors into a single integrated circuit on a tiny silicon chip, also called a semiconductor. By the mid-1960s, transistor-based computers were replaced by smaller, more powerful machines built around the new integrated circuits.

Integrated circuits rapidly replaced transistors for the same reasons that transistors superseded vacuum tubes:

1.7 These three devices define the first three computer generations. The vacuum tube (left) housed a few switches in a space about the size of a lightbulb. The transistor (middle) allowed engineers to pack the same circuitry in a semiconductor package that was smaller, cooler, and much more reliable. The first silicon chips packed several transistors' worth of circuitry into a speck much smaller than a single transistor.

- *Reliability.* Machines built with integrated circuits were less prone to failure than their predecessors, because the chips could be rigorously tested before installation.
- *Size.* Single chips could replace entire circuit boards containing hundreds or thousands of transistors, making it possible to build much smaller machines.
- *Speed.* Because electricity had shorter distances to travel, the smaller machines were markedly faster than their predecessors.
- *Efficiency.* Since chips were so small, they used less electrical power. As a result, they created less heat.
- *Cost.* Mass production techniques made it easy to manufacture inexpensive chips.

Just about every breakthrough in computer technology since the dawn of the computer age has presented similar advantages over the technology it replaced.

The relentless progress of the computer industry is illustrated by Moore's law. In 1965, Gordon Moore, the chairman of chipmaker Intel, predicted half-seriously that the power of a silicon chip of the same price would double about every 18 months for at least two decades. So far, Moore's prediction has been uncannily accurate, over three decades later!

The Microcomputer Revolution

Computer cost-effectiveness has risen **100 millionfold** since the late 1950s—a 100,000-fold rise in **power** times a thousandfold drop in **cost**.

—George Gilder

The inventions of the vacuum tube, the transistor, and the silicon chip had tremendous impact on our society. But none of these had a more profound effect than the invention in 1971 of the first microprocessor—the critical components of a complete computer housed on a tiny silicon chip. The development of the *microprocessor* by Intel engineers caused immediate and radical changes in the appearance, capability, and availability of computers.

The research and development costs for the first microprocessor were awesome. But once the assembly lines were in place, silicon computer chips could be mass-produced cheaply. The raw materials were certainly cheap enough; silicon, the main ingredient in beach sand, is the second most common element (after oxygen) in the Earth's crust.

U.S. companies soon flooded the marketplace with watches and pocket calculators built around inexpensive microprocessors. The economic effect was immediate: Mechanical calculators and slide rules became obsolete overnight, electronic hobbyists became wealthy entrepreneurs, and California's San Jose area gained the nickname Silicon Valley when dozens of semiconductor manufacturing companies sprouted and grew there.

1.8 Today, a single chip the size of your fingernail can contain the equivalent of millions of transistors.

1.9 The microcomputer revolution didn't just increase the number of computers in offices, it opened up entirely new possibilities for computing habitats. This police officer uses a computer to record case notes and track crime information. David Solove uses a portable computer, a digital camera, and a scanner to produce an online diary of circus life for his family and friends. The marine biologist uses a laptop computer to record research notes and analyze data in the field.

The microcomputer revolution began in the late 1970s when companies, such as Apple, Commodore, and Tandy, introduced low-cost, typewriter-sized computers as powerful as many of the room-sized computers that had come before. **Personal computers**, or **PCs**, as microcomputers have come to be known, are now common in offices, factories, homes, schools, and just about everywhere else. Because chip manufacturers have been so successful at obeying Moore's law, microcomputers have steadily increased in speed and power during the last two decades. At the same time, personal computers have taken over many tasks formerly performed by large computers, and every year people find new, innovative ways to harness these tiny, versatile workhorses.

With the rise of PCs, the era of *institutional computing* came to a close. Indeed, small computers had an even greater impact on society than their room-sized predecessors. Still, desktop computers haven't completely replaced big computers, which have also evolved. Today's world is populated with a variety of computers, each particularly well suited to specific tasks.

Computers Today: A Brief Taxonomy

An IBM electronic calculator speeds through **thousands of intricate computations** so quickly that on many complex problems, it's just like having **150 extra engineers**.

—IBM ad showing dozens of slide-rule-toting engineers in the February 1952 issue of National Geographic

Today, people work with mainframe computers, supercomputers, workstations, notebook computers, handheld computers, embedded computers, and, of course, PCs. Even though they're based on the same technology, these machines have important differences.

Mainframes and Supercomputers

Before the microcomputer revolution, most information processing was done on **mainframe computers**—room-sized machines with price tags to match. Today, large organizations, such as banks and airlines, still use mainframes for big computing jobs. But today's mainframes are smaller and cheaper than their ancestors; a typical mainframe today might be the size of a refrigerator and cost around a million U.S. dollars. These industrial-strength computers are largely invisible to the general public, because they're hidden away in climate-controlled rooms.

But the fact that you can't see them doesn't mean you don't use them. When you make an online airline reservation or deposit money in your bank account, a mainframe computer, behind the scenes, is involved in the transaction. Your travel agent and your bank teller communicate with a mainframe using a computer **terminal**—a combination keyboard and screen with little local processing power that transfers information to and from the computer. The computer might be in another room or even in another country halfway around the globe.

1.10 Computer-driven display systems are important fixtures in meeting rooms.

1.11 Terminals like the one in the photo on the left make it possible for ticket agents all over the world to send information to a single mainframe computer like the one shown on the right.

A mainframe computer can communicate with several users simultaneously through a technique called **timesharing**. For example, a timesharing system allows travel agents all over the country to make reservations using the same computer and the same flight information at the same time.

Timesharing also makes it possible for users with diverse computing needs to share expensive computing equipment. Many research scientists and engineers, for example, need more mathematical computing power than they can get from personal computers. Their computing needs might require a powerful mainframe computer. A timesharing machine can simultaneously serve the needs of scientists and engineers in different departments working on a variety of projects.

Many researchers can't get the computing power they need from a mainframe computer; traditional "big iron" simply isn't fast enough for their calculation-intensive work, such as weather forecasting, telephone network design, simulated car crash testing, oil exploration, computer animation, and medical imaging. Power users with these special requirements need access to the fastest, most powerful computers made. These superfast, superpowerful computers are called **supercomputers**. Typically, these supercomputers are constructed out of thousands of microprocessors.

1.12 The world's fastest supercomputer is the NEC Earth Simulator at the Yokohama Institute for Earth Sciences in Japan. The massively parallel computer can perform 40 trillion mathematical operations per second.

1.13 Virginia Tech's cluster of Power Mac computers, with 2,200 microprocessors, can perform more than 10 trillion mathematical operations per second. Students have nicknamed this computer, one of the world's fastest, "Big Mac."

Servers, Workstations, and PCs

For applications that serve multiple users, a high-end computer called a server—a computer designed to provide software and other resources to other computers over a network—is used. Although just about any computer can be used as a server, some computers are specifically designed with this purpose in mind. (Networks and servers are discussed later in this chapter and in later chapters.)

A workstation—a high-end desktop computer with massive computing power—is used for high-end interactive applications, such as large-scale scientific data analysis. Workstations are widely used by scientists, engineers, financial analysts, designers, and animators whose work involves intensive computations. Of course, like many computer terms, *workstation* means different things to different people. Some people refer to all desktop computers and terminals as workstations. Those who reserve the term for the most powerful desktop machines admit that the line separating workstations and high-end personal computers is fading. As workstations become less expensive and personal computers become more powerful, the line becomes as much a marketing distinction as a technical one.

Most computer users don't need the power of a scientific workstation to do their day-to-day business. A modern PC has plenty of computing power for word processing, accounting, gaming, enjoying digital music and video, and running other common applications. A personal computer, as the name implies, is almost always dedicated to serving a single user at a time.

A word about terminology: The terms *personal computer* and *PC* occasionally generate confusion because in 1981 IBM named its desktop computer the IBM Personal Computer. That's why the terms *personal computer* and *PC* often are used to describe only IBM computers or machines compatible with IBM hardware. ("The office has a network of Macs and PCs.") But in another context, PC might describe any general-purpose single-user computer. ("Every

1.14 Workstations are used by scientists, engineers, and others who need more computational power than a standard PC can deliver.

1.15 Personal computers today come in a variety of forms. Apple's iMac houses the CPU, display, and storage devices in an all-in-one design. The Dell Dimension tower on the right is a more traditional design, with the display separate from the CPU and storage.

student needs a PC to connect to the Internet.") When we refer to PCs generically in this book, we are referring to any PC, not just those that are made by or compatible with IBM's products.

Portable Computers

Two decades ago, the terms *personal computer* and *desktop computer* were interchangeable because virtually all PCs were desktop computers. Today, however, one of the fastest-growing segments of the PC market involves machines that aren't tied to the desktop. We call these devices portable computers.

Of course, *portability* is a relative term. The first "portable" computers were 20-pound suitcases with foldout keyboards and small, TV-like screens. Today, those "luggable" computers have been replaced by flat-screen, battery-powered notebook computers (sometimes called laptop computers) that are so light you can rest one on your lap while you work or carry it in a briefcase when it's closed.

Today's notebook typically weighs between 3 and 10 pounds, depending on the machine. Many laptops perform as well as desktop PCs; these heavy but powerful devices are called desktop replacements. Extra-light, ultramobile notebooks are sometimes called subnotebooks. To keep size and weight down, manufacturers often leave out some components that would be standard equipment on desktop machines. For example, some laptops don't have built-in optical drives for playing or recording CD-ROM or DVD discs. Some have expansion bays that allow these devices to be inserted one at a time. Most have several ports that allow external drives to be attached with cables. A few models can be expanded with docking stations or port replicators, which enables a user to connect the laptop to an external monitor, keyboard, mouse, and disk drives. Many mobile workers use docking stations to turn their laptops into full-featured desktop PCs when they return to their offices. Even without docking stations, a laptop can be easily connected to peripherals and networks when it's deskbound.

Handheld computers, which are often small enough to tuck into a shirt pocket, serve the needs of users who value mobility over a full-sized keyboard and screen. Docking cradles for handheld computers enable them to share information with desktop and laptop PCs. Handheld computers are sometimes called personal digital assistants (PDAs).

Size notwithstanding, most portable computers in all their variations are general-purpose computers built around microprocessors similar to those that drive desktop models. But portability comes at a price—portable computers generally cost more than

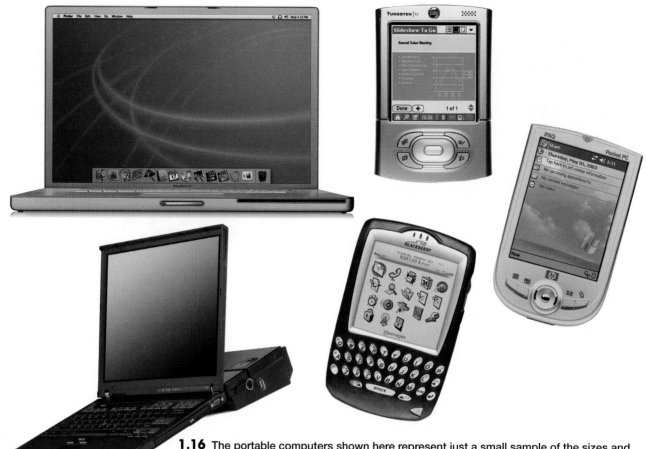

1.16 The portable computers shown here represent just a small sample of the sizes and types available today. Apple's PowerBook G4 (top left) is a full-featured desktop replacement notebook computer. The IBM ThinkPad T40 (bottom left) can be converted from a notebook to a desktop system using a docking station (pictured) or port replicator. The Palm Tungsten (top center) is a handheld computer designed to accept input via a stylus; it can synchronize wirelessly with a PC. The RIM Blackberry (bottom center) is a handheld computer designed for email communications with a tiny, thumb-operated keyboard. The Hewlett-Packard iPAQ Pocket_PC device (right) uses a version of Microsoft Windows designed for handheld computers and ships with Pocket versions of popular Office applications.

comparable desktop machines. They're also more difficult to upgrade when newer hardware components become available.

Embedded Computers and Special-Purpose Computers

Not all computers are general-purpose machines. Many are special-purpose, dedicated computers that perform specific tasks, ranging from controlling the temperature and humidity in a high-rise office building to monitoring your heart rate while you work out. Embedded computers enhance all kinds of consumer goods: wristwatches, toys, game machines, stereos, digital video recorders (DVRs), and ovens. In fact, more than 90 percent of the world's microprocessors are hidden inside common household and electronic devices! Because of embedded computers, a typical new car probably has more computing power than the salesperson's PC.

Most special-purpose computers are, at their core, similar to general-purpose personal computers. But unlike their desktop cousins, these special-purpose machines typically have their programs etched in silicon so they can't be altered. When a program is immortalized on a silicon chip, it becomes known as firmware—a hybrid of hardware and software.

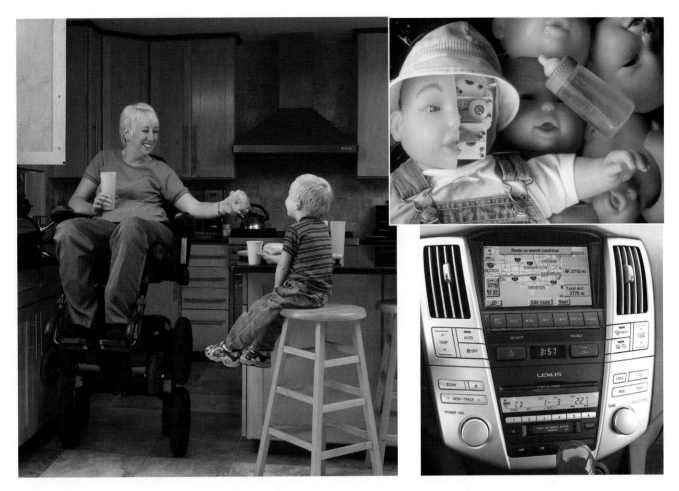

1.17 Embedded computers are so common in today's world that they're all but invisible. The Independence IBOT Transporter is an intelligent wheelchair that allows people to climb up and down stairs, "stand up" on two wheels, and even stroll on the beach. This experimental children's doll is really a robot. The dashboard computer in this car provides maps and navigation information for the driver.

Computer Connections: The Internet Revolution

We've seen how breakthroughs in various technologies have produced new types of computers. Each of these technological advances had an impact on our society as people found new ways to put computers to work. Most historians stopped counting computer generations after the microcomputer became commonplace; it was hard to imagine another breakthrough having as much impact as the tiny microprocessor. But while the world was still reeling from the impact of the microcomputer revolution, another information technology revolution was quietly building up steam: the network revolution. Today we can look back on the late 1990s as the beginning of the era of *interpersonal computing*.

> All persons are caught in an **inescapable network of mutuality**, tied in a single garment of destiny. Whatever affects **one** directly, affects **all** indirectly.
>
> —*Martin Luther King, Jr.*

The Emergence of Networks

The invention of timesharing in the 1960s allowed multiple users to connect to a single mainframe computer through individual terminals. When personal computers started

Computer Time Line

These *Time* covers symbolize changes in the way people saw and used computers as they evolved through the last half of the twentieth century. Notice that the beginning of each new "era" doesn't mean the end of the old ways of computing; today we live in a world of institutional, personal, and interpersonal computing.

1950   1975   1995

Institutional Computing Era
(Starting approximately 1950)

Characterized by a few large, expensive mainframe computers in climate-controlled rooms; controlled by experts and specialists; used mainly for data storage and calculation.

Personal Computing Era
(Starting approximately 1975)

Characterized by millions of small, inexpensive micro-computers on desktops in offices, schools, homes, factories, and almost everywhere else; controlled mostly by independent users; used mostly for document creation, data storage, and calculation.

Interpersonal Computing Era
(Starting approximately 1995)

Characterized by networks of interconnected computers in offices, homes, schools, vehicles, and almost everywhere else; controlled by users (clients) and network operators; used mostly for communication, document creation, data storage, and calculation.

1.18

replacing terminals, many users found they had all the computing power they needed on their desktops. Still, there were advantages to linking some of these computers in local area networks (LANs), sometimes simply referred to as networks. When clusters of computers were networked, they could share resources, such as storage, printers, and even processing power. Using a network, a single high-speed printer could meet the needs of an entire office. As a bonus, people could use computers to send and receive messages electronically through the networks.

The advantages of electronic communication and resource sharing were multiplied when smaller networks were joined to larger networks. Emerging telecommunication technology eventually allowed wide area networks (WANs) to span continents and oceans. A remote computer could connect to a network through standard telephone lines by using a modem—an electronic device that could translate computer data into signals compatible with the telephone system. Banks, government agencies, and other large, geographically distributed institutions gradually built information-processing systems to take advantage of long-distance networking technology. But for most computer users outside of these organizations, networking was not the norm. People saw computers as tools for doing calculations, storing data, and producing paper documents—not as communication tools. So until the late 1990s, most PCs were stand-alone devices, islands of information.

There were exceptions: A group of visionary computer scientists and engineers, with financial backing from the U.S. government, built an experimental network called ARPANET in 1969. This groundbreaking network would become the Internet—the global collection of networks that radically transformed the way the world uses computers.

The Internet Explosion

In its early years, the Internet was the domain of researchers, academics, and government officials. It wasn't designed for casual visitors; users had to know cryptic commands and codes that only a programmer could love. But in the 1990s, Internet software suddenly took giant leaps forward in usability.

Electronic mail programs first attracted nontechnical people to the Internet. Email software made it easy to send messages across the office or around the world without learning complex codes.

But the biggest changes came in the early 1990s with the development of the World Wide Web (WWW, or Web), a vast tract of the Internet accessible to just about anyone who could point to buttons on a computer screen. The Web led the Internet's transformation from a text-only environment into a multimedia landscape incorporating pictures, animation, sounds, and video. Millions of people connect to the Web each day through Web browsers—programs that, in effect, serve as navigable windows into the Web. Hypertext links on Web pages loosely tie together millions of Web pages created by diverse authors, making the Web into a massive, ever-changing global information storehouse.

Widespread email and Web use have led to astounding Internet growth in the last decade. In 1994, 3 million people were connected; early in 2003, 580 million people had Internet connections. Over 54 percent of all American households are connected to the Internet; before the first decade of the twenty-first century is over, 90 percent of U.S. households will likely be connected, making the Internet almost as universal as the television and the telephone. The United States leads the world in Internet activity, but the rest of the

It is **not proper** to think of networks as connecting computers. Rather, they connect people using computers to **mediate**. The **great success of the Internet** is not technical, but **its human impact**.

—*Dave Clark, Internet pioneer, now a senior research scientist at MIT*

1.19 This computer-generated 3-D map represents major Internet connections in the United States.

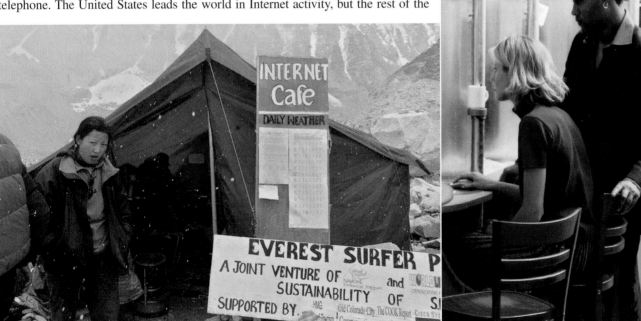

1.20 People throughout the world use "Cyber Cafés" as both access points to the Web and places to socialize.

developed world is catching up. About 39 percent of all Europeans were online in 2001, and their numbers are rising quickly. By 2006, some predict, 67 percent of Europeans will be online.

In the late 1990s, Internet users tended to be younger, better educated, and wealthier than the rest of the population. But as the Internet's population has grown, it has come to look more like the population at large. According to the U.S. Internet Council, the percentage of African-Americans and Hispanics who use the Internet is rising rapidly. More than half of all active Internet users are now female. And while there are still some areas, even in the United States, with no Internet access, those are becoming harder to find. In just about any city on Earth, you can rent time on a PC to check your email or explore the Web.

The Internet is growing faster than television, radio, or any other communication technology that came before it. This growth is largely fueled by the rapid expansion of commerce on the Web. The U.S. Internet economy generates hundreds of billions of dollars in revenues and millions of jobs each year.

The Internet has become so pervasive that many organizations have rebuilt their entire information-processing systems around Internet technology. A growing number of companies are replacing their aging mainframe-and-PC-based systems with intranets—private intraorganizational networks based on Internet technology. Intranets mimic the Internet in the ways in which they enable people to transmit, share, and store information within an organization.

Some companies, including Sun, Oracle, and Hewlett-Packard (HP), are so taken with the notion of Internet-based computing that they are developing and marketing stripped-down computers designed to function mainly as network terminals. These companies don't all agree on exactly what these boxes should include, how much they should be able to do without the aid of a server, or even what they should be called. You might hear people referring to these machines as network computers, *NCs*, or *thin clients* when they talk about network-centric machines.

Whatever they're called, all these machines share two common characteristics: They typically cost less than most PCs because they contain less hardware, and they are easier to maintain, because much of the software can be stored on a central server. Like a TV, a network computer is designed to receive information from elsewhere. But unlike a TV, an NC allows you to send and receive information; it's a two-way connection to the wired world. However, network computers

1.21 Modern video game consoles, such as the Sony PlayStation 2, allow users to connect to the Internet and play games against their friends and other people from around the globe.

are unlikely to outsell PCs any time soon, and it's likely that they may simply replace terminals in certain situations.

Network computers make economic sense in many workplaces, but most of them are not designed for use in homes. But some consumer-oriented manufacturers now sell information appliances (or Internet appliances) that enable home and office users to connect to the Internet without using a full-blown PC. (Some people use the terms *Internet appliance* and *information appliance* to refer to network computers in offices and homes; the terminology is, at this point, as fluid as the technology.) For example, Internet telephones have screens and keyboards to enable easy access to email and the Web. Set-top boxes, including modern video game consoles, such as the Sony PlayStation 2 and Microsoft Xbox, provide Internet access through television sets. Many new handheld computers provide wireless access to the Internet. And many cellular phones can display Internet data on their tiny screens. Who knows? Future homes and businesses may have dozens of devices—computers, telephones, televisions, stereos,

1.22 Millions of homes may soon be connecting to the Internet using televisions through set-top boxes such as this one.

security systems, and even kitchen appliances—continually connected to the Internet, monitoring all kinds of data that can have an impact on our lives and our livelihoods. Whatever happens, it's clear that the role the Internet is going to play in our future is increasing.

Into the Information Age

Every so often, civilization dramatically changes course. Events and ideas come together to transform radically the way people live, work, and think. Traditions fall by the wayside, common sense is turned upside down, and lives are thrown into turmoil until a new order takes hold.

It is the **business of the future** to be dangerous....The **major advances** in civilization are processes that all but **wreck** the societies in which they occur.

—*Alfred North Whitehead*

Humankind experiences a paradigm shift—a change in thinking that results in a new way of seeing the world. Major paradigm shifts take generations because individuals have trouble changing their assumptions about the way the world works.

Roughly ten thousand years ago people learned to domesticate animals and grow their own food using plows and other agricultural tools. Over the next few centuries, a paradigm shift occurred as people gave up nomadic hunter-gatherer lives to live and work on farms, exchanging goods and services in nearby towns. The agricultural age lasted until about two centuries ago, when advances in machine technology triggered what has come to be known as the Industrial Revolution.

The Industrial Revolution ushered in the industrial age. Factory work promised a higher material standard of living for a growing population, but not without a price. Families who had worked the land on sustainable farms for generations found it necessary to take low-wage factory jobs for survival. As work life became separate from home life, fathers were removed from day-to-day family life, and those mothers who didn't have to work in factories assumed the bulk of domestic responsibilities. As towns grew into cities, crime, pollution, and other urban problems grew with them.

The convergence of computer and communication technology is at the heart of another paradigm shift—the shift from an industrial economy to an information economy. In the information age, most people earn their livings working with words, numbers, and ideas.

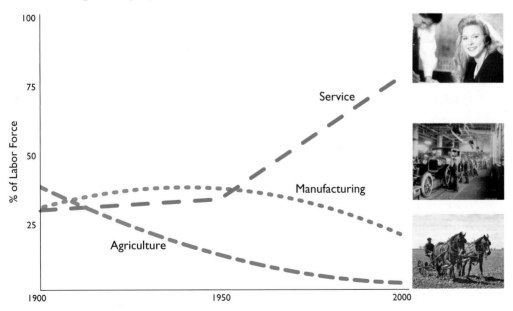

1.23 At the beginning of the twentieth century, three-quarters of American jobs were in agriculture or manufacturing. By the end of the century, three-quarters of American jobs were in the service sector. We have shifted from an industrial economy to an information-based economy.

Instead of planting corn or making shoes, most of us shuffle bits in one form or another. As we roar through the information age, we're riding a wave of social change that rivals any that came before.

Living with Computers

Just as Michelangelo's contemporaries couldn't have foreseen **abstract expressionism**, we **can't foresee** how people will use the computing medium in the future.

—*Clement Mok, in* Designing Business

1.24 Smart bombs, such as those employed in both Gulf wars, helped the U.S. armed forces target enemy installations with greater accuracy than was possible in earlier wars.

In less than a human lifetime, computers have evolved from massive, expensive, error-prone calculators, like the Mark I and ENIAC, into (mostly) dependable, versatile machines that have worked their way into just about every nook and cranny of modern society. The pioneers who created and marketed the first computers did not foresee these spectacular advances in computer technology. Thomas Watson Sr., the founding father of IBM, declared in 1943 that the world would not need more than five computers! And the early pioneers certainly couldn't have predicted the extraordinary social changes that resulted from the computer's rapid evolution. In the time of UNIVAC, who could have imagined Apple's iMac, Sony PlayStations, handheld Palm devices, smart bombs, or online shopping?

Technological breakthroughs encourage further technological change, so we can expect the rate of change to continue to increase in coming decades. In other words, the technological and social transformations of the past five decades may be dwarfed by the changes that occur over the next half-century! It's just a matter of time, and not very much time, before today's state-of-the-art PCs and Palms look as primitive as ENIAC looks to us. Similarly, today's high-tech society just hints at a future world that we haven't yet begun to imagine.

What do you really need to know about computers today? The remaining chapters of this book, along with the accompanying CD-ROM and Web site, provide answers to that question by looking at the technology on three levels: explanations, applications, and implications.

Explanations: Clarifying Technology

You don't need to be a computer scientist to coexist with computers. But your encounters with technology will make more sense if you understand a few basic computer concepts. Computers are evolving at an incredible pace, and many hardware and software details change every few years. And the Internet is evolving even faster; some suggest that one normal year is equal to several "Internet years," a phrase coined by Intel cofounder, Andy Grove. But most of the underlying concepts remain constant as computers and networks evolve. If you understand the basics, you'll find that it's a lot easier to keep up with the changes.

Applications: Computers in Action

Many people define *computer literacy* as the ability to use computers. But because computers are so versatile, you can learn no single set of skills to become computer literate in every situation. Application programs, also known simply as applications, are the software tools that enable you to use a computer for specific purposes. Many computer applications in science, government, business, and the arts are far too specialized and technical to be of use or interest to people outside the field. On the other hand, some applications are so flexible that nearly anyone can use them.

Regardless of your background or aspirations, you can almost certainly benefit from knowing a little about the following applications:

- *Word processing and desktop publishing.* Word processing is a critical skill for anyone who communicates in writing—on paper, via documents, or on the Web. Desktop-publishing software can transform written words into polished, visually exciting publications.
- *Spreadsheets and other number-crunching applications.* In business, the electronic spreadsheet is the personal computer application that pays the rent—or at least calculates it. If you work with numbers of any kind, spreadsheets and statistical software can help you turn those numbers into insights.
- *Databases.* Word processors may be the most popular stand-alone-PC productivity applications, but databases reign supreme in the world of mainframes and servers. Of course, databases are widely used on PCs, too. Even if you don't have database software on a PC, you can apply database-searching skills to find books in your library—or just about anything on the Internet.
- *Computer graphics and digital photos.* Computers make it possible to produce and manipulate all kinds of graphics, including charts, drawings, digital photographs—even realistic 3-D animation. As graphics tools become more accessible, visual communication skills become more important for all of us.
- *Digital audio, digital video, and multimedia.* Modern desktop computers make it easy to edit and manipulate audio and video, opening up creative possibilities for all kinds of people, including potential artists. Multimedia software can combine audio and video with traditional text and graphics, adding new dimensions to computer communications. Interactive multimedia documents, including those found on many Web sites, enable users to explore a variety of paths through media-rich information sources.

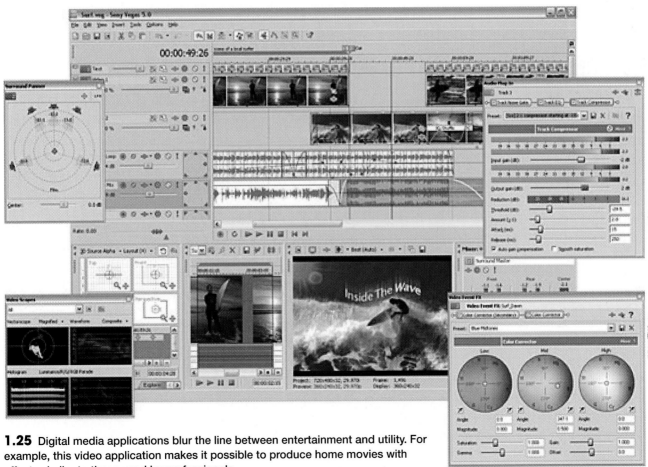

1.25 Digital media applications blur the line between entertainment and utility. For example, this video application makes it possible to produce home movies with effects similar to those used by professionals.

15th century
Gutenberg's printing press

16th century
Algebraic symbols; lead pencil

17th century
Three-color printing; Industrial Revolution

18th century
Calculus; Pascal's calculator; probability; binary arithmetic; newspapers; mailboxes

19th century
Automated loom; Difference Engine; telegraph; Boolean algebra; cathode ray tube; telephone;
typewriter; color photograph; Hollerith's data processing machine; radio; sound recordings

Early 20th century
Vacuum tube; assembly-line automated production;
analog computer; television; motion pictures

1930s
Atanasoff-Berry Computer (U.S.); Zuse's programmable mechanical computer
(Germany); electronic switching circuits implement Boolean functions

1940s
Turing's Colossus computer breaks Nazi codes; Harvard Mark 1
completed; ENIAC completed; programs stored in memory; Small-
Scale Experimental Machine (England), transistor; Orwell writes *1984*.

1950s
Computerized banking begins; IBM creates first mass-market computer; Sony introduces
transistor radio; Bell Labs builds transistorized computer; USSR launches Sputnik; U.S. forms
ARPA; integrated circuit invented

1960s
Laser invented; DEC introduces first minicomputer; Doug Engelbart patents computer mouse;
first computer crime prosecuted; software sold separately from hardware for the first time;
ARPANET created; Bell Labs develops UNIX; first person on the moon

1970s
Intel invents microprocessor; ROM invented; first home computer game; first email
message sent; microcomputer invented; Cray-1 supercomputer; Xerox PARC pioneers
graphical user interface; Apple II; spreadsheet; Pac-Man

1.26 The floodgates are open, and information technology ideas are flowing faster all the time.

11th century
Movable type, decimal number system, musical notation

12th century
Modern abacus

1980s
IBM PC; Apple Macintosh; desktop publishing; trans-Atlantic fiber-optic cable; Connection Machine massively parallel supercomputer; Internet worm cripples thousands of computers; Apple's HyperCard pioneers multimedia software

1990s
Microsoft creates de facto computing standard with Windows; handheld computers take off; computers become multimedia machines; World Wide Web introduced; United States completes GPS system; dot-com boom followed by dot-bomb bust; Linux open-source operating system introduced; Apple iMac heralds age of innovative PC designs; first full-length computer-animated feature film is released; Internet email outpaces post office volume; computer program beats world chess champion; Y2K bug captures public attention and costs businesses billions

2000s
Denial of service attacks cripple commercial Web sites; Arizona holds first Internet primary election; email viruses afflict millions of users; Microsoft found guilty of monopolistic practices but later settles with U.S. government; U.S. video game receipts eclipse movie box office receipts; 9/11 terrorist attacks result in bolstered security and compromised civil liberties; U.S. high-tech weapons demolish Iraqi defenses; Internet file-sharing frenzy fuels music industry downturn and leads to growth of legal online music stores

- *Telecommunication and networking.* A network connection is a door into a world of email, online discussion groups, Web-publishing ventures, and information sharing.
- *Artificial intelligence.* Artificial intelligence is the branch of computer science that explores the use of computers in tasks that require intelligence, imagination, and insight—tasks that have traditionally been performed by people rather than machines. Until recently, artificial intelligence was mostly an academic discipline—a field of study reserved for researchers and philosophers. But that research is paying off today with commercial applications that exhibit intelligence, from basic speech recognition to sophisticated expert systems.
- *Entertainment.* With fast processors, advanced graphics capabilities, and huge displays, computers make excellent video game systems, and because they are often connected to the Internet, it's possible for gamers to compete online with people they've never met in person. But PCs aren't just good for games; they are also used to watch DVD movies, download digital video, listen to audio CDs and digital sound files, read electronic books, and perform other tasks that help users pass time when they're not working.
- *General problem solving.* People often use computers to solve problems. Most people use software applications written by professional programmers. But some kinds of problems can't easily be solved with off-the-shelf applications; they require at least some custom programming. Programming languages aren't applications; they're tools that enable you to build and customize applications. Many computer users find that their machines become more versatile and valuable when they learn a little about programming.

Implications: Social and Ethical Issues

> True **computer literacy** is not just **knowing how** to make use of computers and **computational ideas**. It is knowing **when it is appropriate** to do so.
>
> —*Seymour Papert, in* Mindstorms

Computers and networks are transforming the world rapidly and irreversibly. Jobs that existed for hundreds of years are eliminated by automation, while new careers are built on emerging technology. Start-up businesses create new markets overnight, while older companies struggle to keep pace with "Internet time." Instant worldwide communication changes the way businesses work and challenges the role of governments. Computers routinely save lives in hospitals, keep space flights on course, and predict the weekend weather.

More than any other recent technology, the computer is responsible for profound changes in our society; we just need to imagine a world without computers to recognize their impact. Of course, computer scientists and computer engineers are not responsible for all the technological turbulence. Developments in fields as diverse as telecommunications, genetic engineering, medicine, and atomic physics contribute to the ever-increasing rate of social change. But researchers in all these fields depend on computers to produce their work.

Although it's exciting to consider the opportunities arising from advances in artificial intelligence, multimedia, robotics, and other cutting-edge technologies of the electronic revolution, it's just as important to pay attention to the potential risks. Here's a sampling of the kinds of social and ethical issues we'll confront in this book:

- *The threat to personal privacy posed by large databases and computer networks.* When you use a credit card, buy an airline ticket, place a phone call, visit your doctor, send an email message, or explore the Web, you are leaving a trail of personal information in one or more computers. Who owns that information? Is it okay for the business or organization that collected the information to share it with others or make it public? Do you have the right to check its accuracy and change it if it's wrong? Do laws protecting individual privacy rights place undue burdens on businesses and governments?

1.27 This robot security guard protects a museum from vandals and thieves. But does it threaten the jobs of human security guards?

- *The hazards of high-tech crime and the difficulty of keeping data secure.* Even if you trust the institutions and businesses that collect data about you, you can't be sure that data will remain secure in their computer systems. Computer crime is at an all-time high, and law enforcement officials are having a difficult time keeping it under control. How can society protect itself from information thieves and high-tech vandals? How can lawmakers write laws about technology that they are just beginning to understand? What kinds of personal risk do you face as a result of computer crime?

- *The difficulty of defining and protecting intellectual property in an all-digital age.* Software programs, musical recordings, videos, and books can be difficult and expensive to create. But in our digital age, all of these can easily be copied. What rights do the creators of intellectual property have? Is a teenager who copies music files from the Web a computer criminal? What about a shopkeeper who sells pirated copies of Microsoft Office for $10? Or a student who posts a clip from *The Matrix* on his Web site? Or a musician who uses a two-second sample from a Beatles song in an electronic composition?

- *The risks of failure of computer systems.* Computer software is difficult to write, because it is incredibly complex. As a result, no computer system is completely fail-safe. Computer failures routinely cause communication problems, billing errors, lost data, and other inconveniences. But they also occasionally result in power blackouts, telephone system meltdowns, weapons failure, and other potentially deadly problems. Who is responsible for loss of income—or loss of life—caused by software errors? What rights do we have when buying and using software? How can we, as a society, protect ourselves from software disasters?

1.28 What impact will computer technology have on traditional cultures that evolved for thousands of years without computers?

■ *The threat of automation and the dehumanization of work.* Computers and the Internet fueled unprecedented economic growth in the last decade of the twentieth century, producing plenty of new jobs for workers with the right skills. But the new information-based economy has cost many workers—especially older workers—their jobs and their dignity. And many workers today find that their jobs involve little more than tending to machines—and being monitored by bosses with high-tech surveillance devices. As machines replace people in the workplace, what rights do the displaced workers have? Does a worker's right to privacy outweigh an employer's right to read employee email or monitor worker actions? What is the government's role in the protection of worker rights in the high-tech workplace?

■ *The abuse of information as a tool of political and economic power.* The computer age has produced an explosion of information, and most of that information is concentrated in corporate and government computers. The emergence of low-cost personal computers and the Internet makes it possible for more people to access information and the power that comes with that information. But the majority of the people on the planet have never made a phone call, let alone used a computer. Will the information revolution leave them behind? Do information-rich people and countries have a responsibility to share technology and information with the information-poor?

■ *The dangers of dependence on complex technology.* One of the biggest news stories of 1999 was the impending threat of massive problems caused by the so-called Y2K bug—the failure of some computer programs on January 1, 2000, because those systems represented the year with only two digits. People stockpiled food and fuel, hid cash and jewels, and prepared for the possibility that the power grid would fail, leaving much of the world's population helpless and hungry. Businesses and governments spent billions of dollars repairing and replacing computer systems, and the Y2K crisis never materialized. But the Y2K scare reminded us how much we have come to depend on this far-from-foolproof technology. Are we, as a society, addicted to computer technology? Should we question new technological innovations before we embrace them? Can we build a future in which technology never takes precedence over humanity?

Today's technology raises fascinating and difficult questions. But these questions pale in comparison to the ones we'll have to deal with as the technology evolves in the coming years. Imagine . . .

History of the Future

You wake up to the sound of your bedside radio, which selects songs and news stories matching your personal interest profile. Today you're leaving on a much-anticipated foreign vacation, visiting your sister who's studying in Rome.

After a quick shower and breakfast, you're on your way to the airport. You check the gas gauge of your car. It tells you that you have a little more than a gallon of gasoline left— enough fuel to travel 137 miles. That sounds about right. Your hybrid gasoline-electric car, with a body made out of strong, lightweight composites, gets just over 100 miles per gallon. As you approach the freeway your car suggests an alternative route to avoid a traffic slowdown caused by a recent accident. You're not familiar with the alternative route, but the car gives clear directions at each intersection.

Arriving at the airport, you drive into the long-term parking area. You step out of the car near the shuttle station, remove your suitcase, lock the car, and signal it to park. The car glides off under battery power, automatically finding an empty parking space.

You wait with a few other passengers for the shuttle train to arrive. A few minutes later the electric train pulls into the station. You step into the lead car and sit down. Looking toward the front of the train, you realize that the safety testing period must be over, because the train no longer has a human operator. You pull your phone PDA from your jacket pocket, say "translate Italian" into it, and then ask "Is this the bus to Vatican City?" The phone responds, "È questo il bus alla città di Vatican?" into the tiny wireless earpiece you always wear.

The line at the airport counter is long, but moves quickly. When you get to the front of the line, a security person directs you to an acceptance station. You insert your passport into the terminal, put your hand on the scanner and put your face into a shielded enclosure. After the system confirms your identity by taking your handprint and scanning your retinas, it issues a boarding pass, baggage claim slip, and routing tag. Under the watchful eye of the security person, you attach the routing tag to your bag and place it on the conveyer belt leading to the baggage handling area.

You realize you forgot to pack your toothbrush and toothpaste. You enter the airport gift shop and ask the shop's electronic assistant kiosk to help you locate toiletries. It tells you exactly where to look and suggests a brand of toothpaste that is on sale. While you're there, you download a best-selling electronic book into your phone PDA for the trip. There is a security person at the door of the shop, but no cashier. As you leave the store, a sensor detects tiny RFID tags on the items you purchased and automatically debits your bank account. Your phone PDA tells you that $13.97 has just been deducted from your account and lets you know the current balance.

Heading toward your gate, you pass through the security screening area. You walk through an arch containing an X-ray machine that can literally see through your clothes. Thankfully, it's just a computer that is examining your naked image for hidden weapons. By law, a human may only look at the screen if the computer identifies an object that appears to be dangerous.

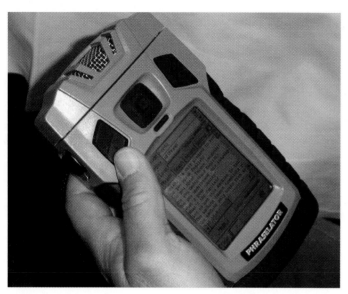

1.29 The Phraselator 2 translates English phrases into another language. About 50 different language modules exist.

The world described in the preceding scenario is not a science fiction fantasy: it's an educated guess at what a major city in 2015 might be like. Early versions of most of these devices already exist. To a great extent, these new technologies are possible because microprocessors continue to double in speed every 18 months. Between 1995 and 2005, microprocessors got about 100 times faster, enabling all sorts of new applications. Between 2005 and 2015, microprocessors will get another 100 times faster. These affordable, incredibly fast computers will vastly increase the number of automated services and help scientists and engineers create dramatic new technologies, such as strong, lightweight composite materials.

Technologies are not value neutral. New technologies affect the way we see the world around us and how we interact with other persons. For example, the availability of cell phones has changed communication patterns. Many college students carry a cell phone and routinely make calls between classes. A cell phone enables these students to spend more time maintaining relationships with friends and family members. On the other hand, they may be spending less time communicating with classmates or people they pass on the sidewalk.

In the decades to come, we will need to confront social issues arising from the progress of computer technology, such as those in the following examples:

■ *Relentless automation.* Ever-faster microprocessors enable engineers to build new automated devices. Many of these devices will be genuine conveniences. We'll have decent automatic vacuum cleaners, and quicker check-out devices will reduce the amount of time we spend waiting in lines. On the other hand, we'll be spending more of our time interacting with machines as automation continues to displace secretaries, bank tellers, cashiers, bookkeepers, and even pets.

1.30 The "Meteor" subway line of the Paris Metro is completely automated. The trains have no drivers.

■ *The death of privacy.* Governments and private companies alike are installing extensive video surveillance networks to monitor security and track lawbreakers. Computer databases are accumulating more information about you all the time, and networks are making it easier to transmit, share, and merge that information. Will these converging technologies destroy the last of our personal privacy, as some experts have suggested? Is there anything we can do about it?

■ *The blurring of reality.* Virtual reality (VR) is widely used by scientific researchers and computer gamers alike. But if VR doesn't yet live up to its name, it does suggest a future technology in which artificial environments look and feel real. Rapid developments in Internet technology are likely to lead us to shared virtual environments, ranging from shopping malls to gaming centers. Already some people are suffering from computer and Internet addictions. Will these diseases become epidemics when VR feels like real life, only better? Will unscrupulous con artists abuse VR technology? Should governments limit what's legal when just about anything is possible?

■ *The evolution of intelligence.* Artificial intelligence research is responsible for many products, including software that can read books to the blind, understand spoken words, and play world-class chess. But tomorrow's machine intelligence will make today's smartest machines look stupid. What rights will human workers have when software can do their jobs better, faster, and smarter? What rights will smart machines have in a world run by humans? Will there come a time when humans aren't smart enough to maintain control of their creations?

■ *The emergence of biodigital technology.* Today, thousands of people walk around with computer chips embedded in their bodies, helping them overcome disabilities and lead normal lives. At the same time, researchers are attempting to develop computers that use biology, rather than electronics, as their underlying technology. As the line between organism and machine blurs, what happens to our vision of ourselves? What are the limits of our creative powers, and what are our responsibilities in using those powers?

For better and for worse, we will be coexisting with computers until death do us part. As with any relationship, a little understanding can go a long way. The remaining chapters of this book will help you gain the understanding you need to survive and prosper in a world of computers.

1.31 Though somewhat controversial, cochlear implants use modern technology to help the profoundly deaf hear.

Inventing the FUTURE

Tomorrow Never Knows

It is **the unexpected** that always happens.

—*Old English proverb*

There is no denying the importance of the future. In the words of the scientist Charles F. Kettering, "We should be concerned about the future because we will have to spend the rest of our lives there." However, important or not, the future isn't easy to see.

In 1877, when Thomas Edison invented the phonograph, he thought of it as an office dictating machine and lost interest in it; recorded music did not become popular until 21 years later. When the Wright brothers offered their invention to the U.S. government and the British Royal Navy, they were told airplanes had no future in the military. A 1900 Mercedes-Benz study estimated that worldwide demand for cars would not exceed 1 million, primarily because of the limited number of available chauffeurs. In 1899, Charles B. Duell, the director of the U.S. Patent Office, said, "Everything that can be invented has been invented."

History is full of stories of people who couldn't imagine the impact of new technology. Technological advances are hard to foresee, and it is even harder to predict the impact that technology will have on society. Who could have predicted in 1950 the profound effects, both positive and negative, television would have on our world?

Computer Scientist Alan Kay has said, "The best way to predict the future is to invent it." Kay's visionary research at XEROX more than three decades ago defined many of the essential qualities of today's PCs. Of course, we can't all invent world-changing tools. But Kay says there are other ways to predict the future. For example, we can look in the research labs today to see the commercial products of the next few years. Of course, many researchers work behind carefully guarded doors, and research often takes surprising turns.

A third way is to look at products from the past and see what made them succeed. According to Kay, "There are certain things about human beings that if you remove, they wouldn't be human any more. For instance, we have to communicate with others or we're not humans. So every time someone has come up with a communications amplifier, it has succeeded the previous technology." The pen, the printing press, the telephone, the television, the PC, and the Internet are all successful communication amplifiers. What's next?

Kay says we can also predict the future by recognizing the four phases of any technology or media business: hardware, software, service, and way of life.

➡ **Hardware.** Inventors and engineers start the process by developing new hardware. But whether it's a television set, a PC, or a global communication network, the hardware is of little use without software.

➡ **Software.** The next step is software development. Television programs, sound recordings, video games, databases, and Web pages are examples of software that give value to hardware products.

➡ **Service.** Innovative hardware and clever software aren't likely to take hold unless they serve human needs. The PC industry is now in the service phase, and the companies that focus on serving their customers are generally the most successful.

➡ **Way of life.** The final phase happens when the technology becomes so entrenched that people don't think about it anymore; they only notice if it isn't there. We seldom think of pencils as technological tools. They're part of our way of life, so much so that we'd have trouble getting along without them. Similarly, the electric motor, which was once a major technological breakthrough, is now all but invisible; we use dozens of motors every day without thinking about them. Computers are clearly headed in that direction.

Kay's four phases of predicting the future don't provide a foolproof crystal ball, but they can serve as a framework for thinking about tomorrow's technology. In the remaining chapters of this book, we'll examine trends and innovations that will shape future computer hardware and software. Then we look at how this technology will serve users as it eventually disappears into our way of life ∼

1.32 The 1930 movie *Just Imagine* presented a bold, if not quite accurate, vision of the future; here Maureen O'Sullivan sits in her personal flying machine.

Toward a Brain-Internet Link *Rodney Brooks*

While we may carry a cell phone and spend hours every day in front of a computer screen, there is still a clear separation between us and our electronic tools. In this November 2003 article from Technology Review, *writer Rodney Brooks suggests that in the not-too-distant future, we may choose to let computers read our minds.*

A few weeks ago, I was brushing my teeth and trying to remember who made "La Bamba" a big hit back in the late 1950s. I knew the singer had died in a plane crash with Buddy Holly; if I'd been downstairs I would have gone straight to Google. But even if I'd had a spoken-language Internet interface in the bathroom, my mouth was full of toothpaste. I realized that what I really want is an implant in my head, directly coupled into my brain, providing a wireless Internet connection.

In my line of work, an effective brain-computer interface is a perennial vision. But I'm starting to think that by 2020 we might actually have wireless Internet interfaces that ordinary people will feel comfortable having implanted in their heads—just as ordinary people are today comfortable with going to the mall to have laser eye surgery. All the signs—early experimental successes, societal demand for improved health care, and military research thrusts—point in that direction.

Remote-controlled rats are perhaps the most stunning evidence of this trend. Last year, John Chapin and his colleagues at the State University of New York's Downstate Medical Center in Brooklyn reported installing brain implants that stimulate areas of the rat cortex where signals are normally received from the whiskers. Left/right cues from a laptop computer made the rats feel as if their whiskers had brushed into obstacles, prompting them to turn in the appropriate directions. To impel the rats up difficult inclines, a second implant stimulated pleasure centers in their brains.

This experiment was built on the 1999 efforts of Chapin and Miguel Nicolelis at Duke University that enabled rats to mentally induce a robot arm to release water. First, a computer recorded the patterns of neural firing in key areas of the rats' brains when the rodents pressed a lever that controlled the robot arm. Once the computer learned the neural pattern associated with lever-pushing, it moved the robot arm when it detected the rats merely "thinking" about doing so. In later versions of this technology, monkeys were able to control a more sophisticated robot arm as though it were their own.

Machine-neuron connections are working in people, too. Thousands of once deaf people can understand conversations thanks to cochlear implants. A tiny microphone in the ear picks up sound, and a small package of electronics translates this into direct stimulation of neurons in the cochlea. More recently, there have been reports of human trials in which comparable (though much more crude and early-stage) visual implants enabled blind patients to perceive something of their surroundings. And a handful of quadriplegic patients have neural implants that let them control computers by "thinking" about moving particular muscles.

Why am I confident that brain-Internet interfaces will become a reality? Because it's not really such a vast leap from here to a thought-activated Google search: these human-tested technologies already give us the components that we would need to directly connect the Internet to a person's brain. And because there are both medical and military pulls on related technologies. On the medical side, besides the urgency of providing physical and mental prostheses to patients with severe injuries, baby boomers are getting older, and their nervous systems are starting to fall apart. There will be increased demand for patching up deteriorating nervous subsystems, and baby boomers have always gotten what they demand. At minimum, this will drive the development of direct visual interfaces that by 2010 will help blind people as much as today's cochlear implants help deaf people.

And on the military side, direct neural control of complex machines is a long-term goal. The U.S. Defense Advanced Research Projects Agency has a brain-machine interface program aimed at creating next-generation wireless interfaces between neural systems and, initially, prosthetics and other biomedical devices.

Just as the modern laptop was inconceivable when the standard computer interface was the punch card, it's hard to imagine how a brain-Internet interface will feel. As brain-imaging technologies continue their rapid advance, we will get a better understanding of where in the brain to insert signals so that they will be meaningful—just as the control signals for the rats were inserted into neurons normally triggered by whiskers.

We still need broad advances, of course. We need algorithms that can track the behavior of brain cells as they adapt to the interface, and we'll need better understanding of brain regions that serve as centers of meaning. But we'll get there. And when we do, we won't "see" an image similar to today's Web pages. Rather, the information contained in a Web server will make us feel as though "Ritchie Valens" just popped into our heads.

Discussion Questions

1. Soldiers with thought-controlled weapons systems could have a decisive advantage over soldiers using conventional weapons. Should the United States military conduct research in thought-controlled weapons systems?

2. What would the advantages and disadvantages of a brain-Internet link be? Would you be interested in a brain-controlled computer, if it were available at a reasonable price?

Summary

While the basic idea behind a computer goes back to Charles Babbage's nineteenth-century plan for an Analytical Engine, the first real computers were developed during the 1940s. Computers have evolved at an incredible pace since those early years, becoming consistently smaller, faster, more efficient, more reliable, and less expensive. At the same time, people have devised all kinds of interesting and useful ways to put computers to use in work and play.

Computers today, like their ancestors, are data processing machines designed to transform information from one form to another. When a computer operates, the hardware accepts input data from some outside source, transforms the data by following instructions called software, and produces output that can be read by a human or by another machine.

Computers today come in all shapes and sizes, with specific types being well suited for particular jobs. Mainframe computers and supercomputers provide more power and speed than smaller desktop machines, but they are expensive to purchase and operate. Timesharing makes it possible for many users to work simultaneously at terminals connected to these large computers. At the other end of the spectrum, servers, workstations, personal computers, and a variety of portable devices provide computing power for those of us who don't need a mainframe's capabilities. Microprocessors aren't just used in general-purpose computers; they're embedded in appliances, automobiles, and a rapidly growing list of other products.

Connecting to a network enhances the value and power of a computer—it can share resources with other computers and facilitate electronic communication with other computer users. Some networks are local to a particular building or business; others connect users at remote geographic locations. The Internet is a collection of networks that connects the computers of businesses, public institutions, and individuals around the globe. Email provides hundreds of millions of people with near-instant worldwide communication capabilities. With Web browsing software, those same Internet users have access to billions of Web pages on the World Wide Web. The Web is a distributed network of interlinked multimedia documents. Although it started as a tool for scientists, researchers, and scholars, the Web has quickly become a vital center for entertainment and commerce.

Computers and information technology have changed the world rapidly and irreversibly. Our civilization is in a transition from an industrial economy to what we might call the information age, and this paradigm shift is having an impact on the way we live and work. Computers and information technology are central to this change, and we can easily list dozens of ways in which computers now make our lives easier and more productive. Personal computer applications, such as word processing, spreadsheets, graphics, multimedia, and databases, continue to grow in popularity. Emerging technologies, such as artificial intelligence, offer promise for future applications. Devices that were the stuff of science fiction novels 50 years ago are appearing on store shelves. At the same time, computers threaten our privacy, our security, and perhaps our way of life. As we rush into the information age, our future depends on computers and on our ability to understand and use them in productive, positive ways.

Key Terms

Interactive Activities

1. The *Computer Confluence* CD-ROM contains self-test quiz questions related to this chapter, including multiple-choice, true or false, and matching questions.

2. The *Computer Confluence* Web site, **http://www.computerconfluence.com**, contains self-test exercises related to this chapter. Follow the instructions for tak-ing a quiz. After you've completed your quiz, you can email the results to your instructor.

3. The Web site also contains open-ended discussion questions called Internet Explorations. Discuss one or more of the Internet exploration questions at the section for this chapter.

True or False

1. The information age began when Charles Babbage invented the Analytic Engine.

2. Because it can be programmed to perform various tasks, the typical modern computer is a general-purpose tool, not a specialized device with one use.

3. One of the first computers helped the Allies crack Nazi codes during World War II.

4. According to Moore's law, the power of a silicon chip of the same price would double about every 10 years for at least 50 years.

5. A mainframe computer is, by definition, the main computer on a network.

6. Timesharing technology allows one person to use several computers at the same time.

7. Workstations are typically more powerful than standard desktop PCs.

8. More than 90 percent of the world's microprocessors are hidden inside common household and electronic devices.

9. A local area network (LAN) is usually the best way to connect houses in a neighborhood to the Internet and to each other.

10. Computer technology, like any technology, carries significant risks to individuals and society.

Multiple Choice

1. What is the most popular search engine in the English-speaking world?
   a. Altavista
   b. Google
   c. MSN
   d. Teoma
   e. Yahoo!

2. What did Charles Babbage and Lady Augusta Lovelace conceive of and design?
   a. The first fully functional computer
   b. The first commercially produced programmable digital computer
   c. A computer-like device about a century before the first working computer was built
   d. The first personal computer
   e. The Internet

3. For which of the following do we depend on computer technology?
   a. Controlling our money and banking systems
   b. Keeping our transportation systems running smoothly
   c. Making many of our household appliances and gadgets work properly
   d. All of the above
   e. None of the above

4. PCs are extremely versatile tools because they can accept instructions from a wide variety of
   a. Hardware
   b. Software
   c. Firmware
   d. Networks
   e. Programmers

5. Many of the most important developments in the earliest days of the computer were motivated by what world event?
   a. World War I
   b. The Great Depression
   c. World War II
   d. The Vietnam War
   e. The Cold War

6. Which was the first American company to produce a commercial computer?
   a. Burroughs
   b. IBM
   c. Intel
   d. Remington Rand
   e. Texas Instruments

7. Which represents the order in which computer circuitry evolved through three generations of technology?
   a. Silicon chip, vacuum tube, transistor
   b. Vacuum tube, silicon chip, transistor
   c. Transistor, vacuum tube, silicon chip
   d. Vacuum tube, transistor, silicon chip
   e. Transistor, silicon chip, vacuum tube

8. As computers evolved, they
   a. Grew in size
   b. Became faster
   c. Consumed more electricity
   d. Became less reliable
   e. Cost more

9. What event stimulated the miniaturization of computers?
   a. The first world computer chess championship
   b. The Space Race
   c. The Korean War
   d. The Watergate scandal
   e. President Reagan's proposal to build a missile defense system.

10. When a bank clerk transfers money into your account, where is the actual transaction probably being stored?
    a. A supercomputer
    b. A mainframe computer
    c. A workstation
    d. An embedded computer
    e. A Web page

11. Some computers are able to maintain simultaneous connections to many users through a technique called
    a. Atomic operations
    b. Time warping
    c. Tunneling
    d. Parallel processing
    e. Timesharing

12. So many semiconductor companies grew up around San Jose, California, that the area became known as
    a. Silicon Valley
    b. Death Valley
    c. Orange County
    d. Disneyland
    e. Microsoftville

13. A personal digital assistant (PDA) is a handheld device that
    a. Serves as a limited input device to a PC
    b. Contains thousands of tiny transistors
    c. Is a fully functional computer designed with portability in mind
    d. Cannot be programmed to do anything more than simple calendar and address book functions
    e. Costs thousands of dollars because of its expensive circuitry

14. Several people in an office can share a printer by using a
    a. Local area network (LAN)
    b. Wide area network (WAN)
    c. Building area network (BAN)
    d. Circuit area network (CAN)
    e. None of the above

15. An intranet is
    a. A network that connects the Internet to a LAN
    b. A network that uses Internet technology for communication within an organization
    c. A network that uses LAN technology for Internet communication
    d. A wireless communication technology used mainly with handheld computers
    e. None of the above

Review Questions

1. List several ways you interact with computers in your daily life.

2. Why was the Analytical Engine never completed during Charles Babbage's lifetime?

3. How are computers today similar to those from World War II? How are they different?

4. How are hardware and software related?

5. What is the most important difference between a computer and a calculator?

6. What is the difference between a mainframe and a microcomputer? What are the advantages and disadvantages of each?

7. What kinds of computer applications require the speed and power of a supercomputer? Give some examples.

8. If current trends continue, the microprocessors of the year 2015 will be 10,000 times faster than the microprocessors of 1995. To get a feel for what it means to do something 10,000 faster, figure out how long it would take a microprocessor of 2015 to perform a task that would take a 1995 microprocessor one week.

9. What types of computers typically employ timesharing?

10. List several common personal computer applications.

11. Why is it important for people to know about and understand computers?

12. Describe some of the benefits and drawbacks of the information age.

Discussion Questions

1. What do people mean when they talk about the information age? Why is it a societal paradigm shift?

2. How do you feel about computers? Examine your positive and negative feelings.

3. What major events before the twentieth century influenced the development of the computer?

4. Suppose Charles Babbage and Lady Lovelace had been able to construct a working Analytical Engine and develop a factory for mass-producing it. How do you think the world would have reacted? How would the history of the twentieth century have been different as a result?

5. How would the world be different today if a wrinkle in time transported a state-of-the-art notebook computer, complete with software, peripherals, and manuals, onto the desk of Herbert Hoover? Adolf Hitler? Albert Einstein?

6. The automobile and the television set are two examples of technological inventions that changed our society drastically in ways that were not anticipated by their inventors. Outline several positive and negative effects of each of these two inventions. Do you think, on balance, that we are better off as a result of these machines? Why or why not? Now repeat this exercise for the computer.

7. Over a period of just a few years, digital CDs pushed vinyl LPs (long playing records) from music store racks. What were the results (both good and bad) of the "CD revolution" in music?

8. Should all students be required to take at least one computer course? Why or why not? If so, what should that course cover?

9. Computerphobia—fear or anxiety related to computers—is a common malady among people today. What do you think causes it? What, if anything, should be done about it?

10. In your opinion, which computer applications offer the most promise for making the world a better place? Which computer applications pose the most significant threats to our future well-being?

11. Some cities are installing video cameras, computers, and image-recognition software at traffic intersections to catch people who are running red lights. What are the advantages and disadvantages of installing surveillance systems at traffic intersections?

12. How much privacy are you willing to give up in airports to reduce the chance of an airplane being hijacked?

13. Suppose a company were marketing a tiny microcomputer designed to be implanted in your brain behind your right ear. The tiny device is designed to help you remember people's names. It is particularly popular among people who work with the public. You plan to have a career in sales. Would you consider getting such an implant? Why or why not? What questions would you want to have answered before you agreed to have the device implanted in your brain?

Projects

1. Start a collection of news articles, cartoons, or television segments that deal with computers. Does your collection say anything about popular attitudes toward computers?

2. The title "Inventor of the Computer" has been given to Charles Babbage (for the Analytical Engine), Konrad Zuse (for the Z1, Z2, and Z3), John Atanasoff and Clifford Berry (for the Atanasoff-Berry Computer), John Mauchly and J. Presper Eckert (for the ENIAC), and F. C. Williams, Tom Kilburn, and Geoff Tootill (for the Small-Scale Experimental Machine). Research these inventors and their machines. Draw a table comparing the features of these computing devices. Decide for yourself who deserves the title "Inventor of the Computer."

3. Make a table or graph that charts how the price of an entry-level personal computer system changed between 1990 and 2005. Go through back issues of a personal computer magazine such as *PC World*, *PC Magazine*, *Macworld*, or *Mac Addict*. Examine advertisements for personal computer systems, and record the price of entry-level systems between 1990 and 2005. Use the Consumer Price Index inflation calculator, found at **http://www.bls.gov/cpi/home.htm**, to adjust all the prices to 1990 dollars.

4. Trace computer-related articles through several years in the same news magazine, such as *Time*, *Newsweek*, *U.S. News & World Report*, or *The Economist*. Put related articles together, and look for changes or trends. What do these trends tell you about the future of computing?

5. Develop a questionnaire to try to determine people's awareness of the computers around them. You can ask them about how often they use a computer, the uses to which they put a computer, the most valuable thing a computer does for them, and so on. Once you have collected the answers, analyze them. What percentage of the people assumed you were talking about "personal computers" when you asked them about their computer use? How many of them mentioned embedded computers, such as the computers in cell phones, microwaves, clock radios, ATM machines, and automobile engines?

6. Take an inventory of all the computers you encounter in a single day. Be sure to include embedded computers, such as those in cars, appliances, entertainment equipment, and other machines. Hint: If a device has an LCD screen or LED numbers (digital numbers made out of light segments), it contains a microprocessor.

Sources and Resources

Books

Google and Other Search Engines: Visual Quickstart Guide, by Diane Poremsky (Berkeley, CA: Peachpit Press, 2004). The Google guys have built a billion dollar business out of our need to find information quickly on the Internet. Google may be the most popular search engine, but it's by no means the best tool for every search job. This handy guide demystifies the art of searching the Web. Like other books in Peachpit's popular Visual Quickstart Guide series, this little volume can help you learn by example, using simple screen sequences and clear, step-by-step instructions..

The Difference Engine: Charles Babbage and the Quest to Build the First Computer, by Doron Swade (New York: Penguin USA, 2002). This book tells the story of the design of Babbage's visionary computing machine. It also reveals the problems Babbage faced getting funding for the ill-fated project. Swade led a team that built a working model of a Difference Engine for the 1991 Babbage bicentenary.

The Difference Engine, by William Gibson and Bruce Sterling (New York: Bantam, 1992). How would the world of the nineteenth century be different if Charles and Ada had succeeded in constructing the Analytical Engine 150 years ago? This imaginative mystery novel takes place in a world where the computer revolution arrived a century early. Like other books by these two pioneers of the "cyberpunk" school of science fiction, *The Difference Engine* is dark, dense, detailed, and thought-provoking.

A History of Modern Computing, *Second Edition*, by Paul E. Ceruzzi (Cambridge, MA: MIT Press, 2003). This book traces the first 50 years of computer history, from ENIAC to Internetworked PCs. The social context of the technology is clear throughout the book.

Accidental Empires: How the Boys of Silicon Valley Make Their Millions, Battle Foreign Competition, and Still Can't Get a Date, *Revised Edition*, by Robert X. Cringely (New York: HarperBusiness, 1996). Robert X. Cringely is the pen name for *InfoWorld*'s computer-industry gossip columnist. In this opinionated, irreverent, and highly entertaining book Cringely discusses the past, present, and future of the volatile personal computer industry. When you read the humorous, colorful characterizations of the people who run this industry, you'll understand why Cringely didn't use his real name. *Triumph of the Nerds*, a 1996 PBS TV show and video based loosely on this book, lacks much of the humor and insight of the book but includes some fascinating footage of the pioneers reminiscing about the early days.

Crystal Fire: The Birth of the Information Age, by Michael Riordan and Lillian Hoddeson (New York: Norton, 1998). One of the defining moments of the information age occurred in 1947 when William Shockley and his colleagues invented the transistor. *Crystal Fire* tells the story of that earthshaking invention, clearly describing the technical and human dimensions of the story.

ENIAC: The Triumphs and Tragedies of the World's First Computer, by Scott McCartney (New York: Walker and Co., 1999). This engaging book tells the human story of two pioneers and their struggles to be recognized for their monumental achievements in those early days of computing.

Fire in the Valley: The Making of the Personal Computer, Second Edition, by Paul Freiberger and Michael Swaine (Berkeley, CA: Osborne/McGraw-Hill, 1999). This book chronicles the early years of the personal computer revolution. The text occasionally gets bogged down in details, but the photos and quotes from the early days are fascinating. The 1999 film *Pirates of Silicon Valley* is based loosely on this book.

Dave Barry in Cyberspace, by Dave Barry (New York: Ballantine Books, 1997). Dave Barry, the irreverent humor columnist, turns his wit loose on the information revolution in this hilarious little book. Here's a typical chapter title: "A Brief History of Computing from Cave Walls to Windows 95—Not That This Is Necessarily Progress." Whether you think computers are frustrating or funny, you'll probably find a few good laughs here.

Dictionary of Computer and Internet Words: An A to Z Guide to Hardware, Software, and Cyberspace, Third Edition, edited by American Heritage Dictionaries (New York: Houghton Mifflin, 2001). It sometimes seems like the computer industry makes three things: hardware, software, and jargon. Many computer terms are too new, too obscure, or too technical to appear in standard dictionaries. Fortunately, several good dictionaries specialize in computer terminology. This is one of the most comprehensive and up-to-date. It covers PC, Macintosh, and Internet terms.

In the Beginning Was the Command Line, by Neal Stephenson (New York: Avon Books, 1999). Stephenson, one of today's leading science fiction and cyberspace novelists, and "the hacker Hemingway," discusses his take on cyberculture past and present with a look at the pros and cons of the major computing platforms of the early twenty-first century. A funny and insightful read, and highly recommended to anyone pondering the role of computers in the meaning of life.

Periodicals

PC World (http://www.pcworld.com). Because the world of personal computers changes so rapidly, computer users depend on magazines to keep them up-to-date on hardware and software developments. This periodical is one of the most popular sources for keeping up with developments in the PC world. The companion Web site offers up-to-the-minute information along with archives from past issues.

PC Magazine (http://www.pcmag.com). *PC Magazine* is a popular PC periodical, containing news, reviews, and feature articles for a variety of interests.

Macworld (http://www.macworld.com). This is the premier periodical for Mac users, covering hardware, software, and Internet issues with clear, easy-to-read articles and reviews.

MacAddict (http://www.macaddict.com). This magazine for Macintosh true believers tends to be slightly more technical—and more partisan—than the more mainstream *Macworld*.

Mobile Computing & Communication (http://www.mobilecomputing.com). This is a good source of news and information on portable computing devices, from laptops to palmtops, as well as mobile phones and other traveling companions.

Pen Computing (http://www.pencomputing.com). This magazine covers pen-based computers, from tiny palm devices to full-sized tablet PCs.

Windows & .NET Magazine (http://www.winnetmag.com). Dedicated to IT professionals and systems administrators working with Microsoft's platforms, this magazine is the premier resource for Windows and the .NET technologies.

InfoWorld (http://www.infoworld.com). This magazine covers business computing, including applications for mainframes, servers, and other behind-the-scenes machines that aren't typically covered in PC-centric publications.

Wired (http://www.wired.com). This highly stylized monthly started out as "the first consumer magazine for the digital generation to track technology's impact on all facets of the human condition." Today, *Wired* devotes more pages to the business of technology and less to the impact of technology, but it's still a thought-provoking, influential magazine.

Technology Review (http://www.technologyreview.com). This relatively new periodical from MIT provides excellent coverage of technology in the labs today that will change our lives tomorrow.

Scientific American (http://www.scientificamerican.com). This old standby still provides some of the best writing on science and technology, including emerging information technologies.

Web Pages

Some of the best sources and resources on computers and information technology are on the World Wide Web. But the Web is changing quickly, and new sites are appearing every day. The *Computer Confluence* Web pages include up-to-date links to many of the best computer-related resources on the Web. To find them, open your Web browsing software, enter the address http://computerconfluence.com, follow the on-screen buttons to the table of contents, select a chapter, and click the links that interest you.

Multimedia

on the CD-ROM and the WEB:

~ Video on energy-efficient office equipment

~ A binary number **counting game**

~ **Animated** tutorials that explain how a **CPU** and memory work

~ **Instant** access to **glossary** and **keyword** references

~ Interactive **self-study** quizzes

. . . and more.

 computerconfluence.com

Objectives

After you read this chapter you should be able to:

▶ **Explain in general terms how computers store and manipulate information**

▶ **Describe the basic structure and organization of a computer**

▶ **Discuss the functions and interactions of a computer system's principal internal components**

▶ **Explain why a computer typically has different types of memory and storage devices**

As president or, as he has been called, the "emperor" of IBM, Thomas J. Watson, Sr., created a corporate culture that fostered invention and discovery. In 1914, he joined the ailing Computing-Tabulating-Recording Company (C-T-R) as a salesperson. The company specialized in counting devices that used punched cards to read and store information. Ten years later, Watson took it over, renamed it International Business Machines (IBM), and turned it into the dominant force in the information industry.

THOMAS J. WATSON, SR., AND THE EMPEROR'S NEW MACHINES

There is no invention—**only discovery**.

—*Thomas J. Watson, Sr.*

Thomas Watson has been called autocratic. He demanded unquestioning allegiance from his employees and enforced a legendary dress code that forbade even a hint of color in a shirt. But in many ways, Watson ran his company like a family, rewarding loyal employees with uncommon favors. During the Depression, he refused to lay off workers, choosing instead to stockpile surplus machines. As if to prove that good deeds don't go unrewarded, the director of the newly formed Social Security Administration bought Watson's excess stock.

One of Watson's most enduring contributions to the IBM legacy was his creation of the company's unofficial slogan "THINK." In 1911, while Watson was managing sales and advertising for the National Cash Register Company (NCR), he reportedly told coworkers, "The trouble with every one of us is that we don't think enough. Thought has been the father of every advance since time began. 'I didn't think' has cost the world millions of dollars." He then wrote the letters "THINK" on the easel behind him. Watson brought the THINK concept with him when he joined IBM forerunner C-T-R in 1914, eventually making it IBM's one-word company slogan. When IBM entered the portable computing market in the early 1990s, it used the name ThinkPad. Today, the company uses the word to brand many of its other products.

Watson provided financial backing for Howard Aiken's Mark I, the pioneering electromechanical computer developed in the early 1940s at Harvard. But he stubbornly refused to develop a commercial computer,

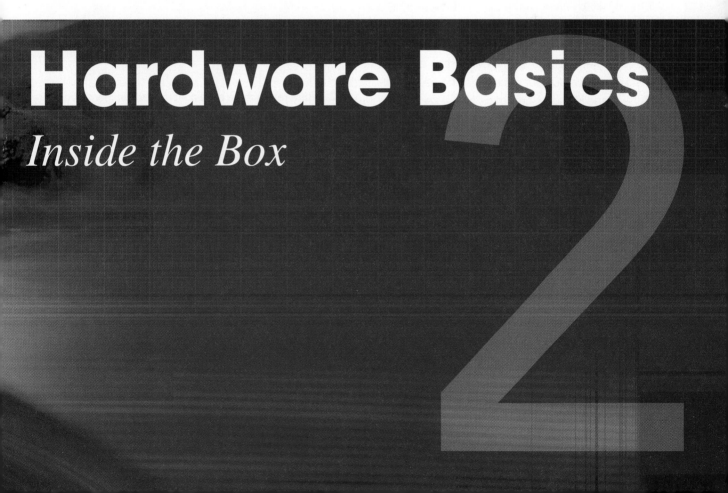

Hardware Basics

Inside the Box

2.1 Thomas J. Watson, Sr. (1874–1956)

more nimble companies, such as Compaq, Dell, Sun, and Microsoft, to seize emerging markets. Massive revenue losses forced IBM to reorganize, replace many of its leaders, and abandon the company's longstanding no-layoffs policy. Eventually, IBM even abandoned its legendary dress code, opting for a more casual image. But today, in spite of stiff competition (or perhaps because of it), IBM is again a major source of innovation in the industry, with major research projects in everything from massive supercomputers to microscopic storage devices. Thomas Watson is long gone, but invention and discovery—and even the THINK motto—are alive and well at IBM today. ～

even as UNIVAC I achieved fame and commercial contracts for the fledgling Sperry company.

Shortly after Watson retired from the helm of IBM in 1949, his son, Thomas Watson, Jr., took over. The younger Watson led IBM into the computing field with a vengeance, eventually building a computing empire that dwarfed all competitors for decades to come.

After establishing its first microcomputer as the de facto business computing standard in 1981, the conservative giant was slow to adjust to the rapid-fire changes of the 1980s and 1990s, making it possible for smaller,

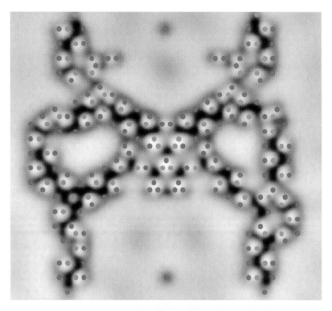

2.2 IBM researchers have constructed functional logic circuits from carbon monoxide molecules. The circuits are 260,000 times smaller than those used in the latest electronic computer chips. About 200 billion of them would fit on the top of a pencil eraser.

Computers schedule airline flights, predict the weather, play and even create music, control space stations, and keep the world's economic wheels spinning. How can one kind of machine do so many things?

To understand what really makes computers tick, you would need to devote considerable time and effort to studying computer science and computer engineering. Most of us don't need to understand every detail of a computer's inner workings any more than a parent needs to explain wave and particle physics when a child asks why the sky is blue. We can be satisfied with simpler answers, even if those answers are only approximations of the technical truth. We'll spend the next three chapters exploring answers to the question, "How do computers do what they do?"

The main text of each of these chapters provides simple, nontechnical answers and basic information. How It Works boxes use text and graphics to dig deeper into the inner workings of the computer. Depending on your course, learning style, and level of curiosity, you may read these boxes as they appear in the text, read them after you've completed the

2.3 PCs are assembled in factories such as this one owned by Dell Computer. In this chapter and the next, we'll examine the hardware components that make up a modern computer.

basic material in the chapter, or (if you don't need the technical details) bypass some or all of them. You'll find interactive multimedia versions of many of these How It Works boxes on the *Computer Confluence* CD-ROM and the *Computer Confluence* Web site, http://www.computerconfluence.com. Use the Sources and Resources section at each chapter's end for further explorations.

What Computers Do

The simple truth is that computers perform only four basic functions:

■ *Receive input.* Computers accept information from the outside world.
■ *Process information.* Computers perform arithmetic or logical (decision-making) operations on information.
■ *Produce output.* Computers communicate information to the outside world.
■ *Store information.* Computers move and store information in memory.

> Stripped of its interfaces, **a bare computer** boils down to little more than a pocket calculator that can **push its own buttons** and **remember** what it has done.
>
> —*Arnold Penzias, in* Ideas and Information

Every computer system contains hardware components—physical parts—that specialize in each of these four functions:

■ **Input devices** accept input from the outside world. The most common input devices today, of course, are keyboards and pointing devices, such as mice.
■ **Output devices** send information to the outside world. Most computers use a TV-like display, or video monitor, as their main output device, a printer to produce paper printouts, and speakers to output sounds.

■ A **microprocessor**, also called the **processor or central processing unit (CPU)**, is, in effect, the computer's "brain." The CPU processes information, performs arithmetic calculations, and makes basic decisions by comparing information values.

■ **Memory** and **storage devices** both store information, but they serve different purposes. The computer's memory (sometimes called *primary storage* or **RAM**, for **random access memory**) is used to store programs and **data** (information) that need to be instantly accessible to the CPU. Storage devices (sometimes called *secondary storage*), including hard disk drives, recordable CD and DVD drives, and tape drives, serve as long-term repositories for data. You can think of a storage device, such as a hard disk drive, as a combination input and output device because the computer sends information to the storage device (output) and later retrieves that information from it (input).

These four types of components, when combined, make up the hardware part of a computer system. Of course, the system isn't complete without software—the instructions that tell the hardware what to do. But for now, we can concentrate on hardware. In this chapter, we take a look at the central processing unit and the computer's memory; these components are at the center of all computing operations. In the next chapter, we look at the input, output, and storage devices—that is, the **peripherals** of the computer system. Because every computer hardware component is designed to transport or to transform information, we start with a little bit of information about information.

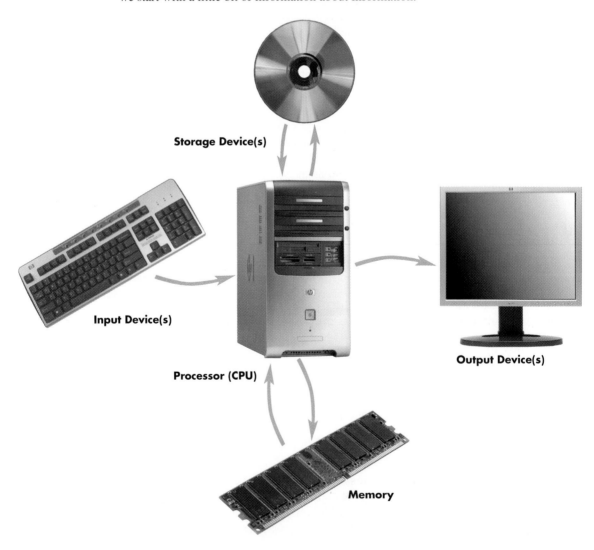

2.4 The basic components of every computer system include the central components (the CPU and memory) and various types of peripherals.

A Bit About Bits

The term information is difficult to define because it has many meanings. According to one popular definition, *information* is communication that has value because it *informs*. This distinction can be helpful for dealing with data from television, magazines, computers, and other sources. But it's not always clear and it's not absolute. As educator and author Richard Saul Wurman points out, "Everyone needs a personal measure with which to define information. What constitutes information to one person may be data to another. If it doesn't make sense to you, it doesn't qualify."

The great Information Age is really an **explosion of non-information**; it is an **explosion of data**. To deal with the increasing **onslaught of data**, it is imperative to distinguish between the two; information is **that which leads to understanding**.

—*Richard Saul Wurman, in* Information Anxiety

At the opposite extreme, one communication theory defines information as anything that can be communicated, whether it has value or not. By this definition, information comes in many forms. The words, numbers, and pictures on these pages are symbols representing information. If you underline or highlight this sentence, you're adding new information to the page. Even the sounds and pictures that emanate from a television commercial are packed with information, though it's debatable whether most of that information is useful.

Some people attempt to strictly apply the first definition to computers, claiming that computers turn raw data, which has no value in its current form, into information, which is valuable. This approach emphasizes the computer's role as a business data processing machine. But in our modern interconnected world, one computer's output is often another's input. If a computer receives a message from another computer, is the message worthless data or valuable information? And whose personal measure of value applies?

For our purposes, describing the mechanics of computers in these chapters, we lean toward the second, more subjective, approach and use the terms *data* and *information* more or less interchangeably. In later chapters, we present plenty of evidence to suggest that not all computer output has value. In the end, it is up to you to decide what the real information is.

Bit Basics

Whatever you call it, in the world of computers information is digital: This means it's made up of discrete, countable units—digits—so it can be subdivided. In many situations, people need to reduce information to simpler units to use it effectively. For example, a child trying to pronounce an unfamiliar word can sound out each letter or syllable individually before tackling the whole word.

A computer doesn't understand words, numbers, pictures, musical notes, or even letters of the alphabet. Like a young reader, a computer can't process information without dividing it into smaller units. In fact, computers can only digest information that has been broken into bits. A bit, or binary digit, is the smallest unit of information a computer can process. A bit can have one of two values: 0 and 1. You can also think of these two values as yes and no, on and off, black and white, or high and low.

If you think of the innards of a computer as a collection of microscopic on/off switches, it's easy to understand why computers process information bit by bit. Each switch stores a tiny amount of information: a signal to turn on a light, for example, or the answer to a yes/no question. (In modern integrated circuits, high and low electrical charges represent bits, but these circuits work as if they were really made up of tiny switches.)

Remember Paul Revere's famous midnight ride to warn the American colonists of the British invasion? His coconspirators used a pair of lanterns to convey a choice between two messages, "One if by land, two if by sea"—a binary choice. It's theoretically possible to send a message like this with just one lantern. But "One if by land, zero if by sea" wouldn't have worked very well unless there had been some way to know exactly when the message was being sent. With two lanterns, the first lantern could say "Here is the message" when it

How It Works

2.1 Binary Numbers

A computer's memory is made up of millions of microscopic switches that can be either "on" or "off." A single switch can represent only two symbols: 0 and 1. Still, two symbols are all a computer needs to represent numbers and perform arithmetic operations on them. Let's look at the inner workings of a calculator to see how this is done.

1. When you use a calculator, you use the keys 0–9 to type numbers. These are decimal (base ten) numbers, because there are ten different digits. The microprocessor inside the calculator actually stores the numbers as a series of 0s and 1s. These are binary (base two) numbers, because there are only two different digits.

2. Just as we use more than one decimal digit to represent numbers larger than 9, processor designers use more than one binary digit (bit) to represent numbers larger than 1. A collection of 8 bits is called a byte.

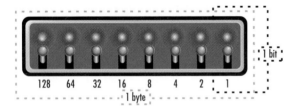

3. A byte can represent all the numbers between 0 and 255. The positional values are powers of 2, not 10. They start at 1 (the units' place) and double in value for each additional place. If all bits are 0, the value is 0; if all 8 bits are 1, the value is 255 (1 + 2 + 4 + 8 + 16 + 32 + 64 + 128).

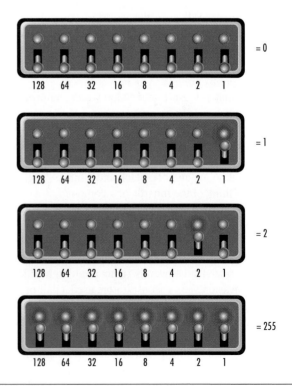

2.5

4. To represent values larger than 255, processor designers combine bytes. Two bytes, with 16 bits, can represent all the numbers from 0 to 65,535.

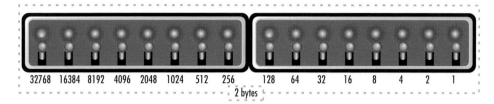

32768 16384 8192 4096 2048 1024 512 256 128 64 32 16 8 4 2 1
2 bytes

5. Adding binary numbers is much simpler than adding decimal numbers because there are fewer rules to remember. That's good news for hardware designers.

$$\begin{array}{r}0\\+0\\\hline 0\end{array}\qquad\begin{array}{r}0\\+1\\\hline 1\end{array}\qquad\begin{array}{r}1\\+0\\\hline 1\end{array}\qquad\begin{array}{r}1\\+1\\\hline 10\end{array}$$

6. Using these rules, we can compute the binary sum of twelve and ten:

$$\begin{array}{r}1100\\+1010\\\hline 10110\end{array}$$

7. The calculator transforms the sum from binary back into a decimal number displayed on the calculator's screen.

22
ON/C
MRC
M−
M+
CE
√
%
÷
7
8
9
×
4
5
6
−
1
2
3
+
0
•
=

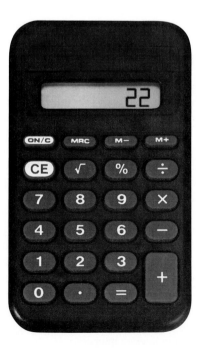

was turned on. The second lantern communicated the critical bit's worth of information: land or sea. If the revolutionaries had wanted to send a more complex message, they could have used more lanterns ("Three if by subway!").

In much the same way, a computer can process larger chunks of information by treating groups of bits as logical units. For example, a collection of 8 bits, called a byte, can represent 256 different messages ($256 = 2^8$). If you think of each bit as a light that can be either on or off, you can make different combinations of lights represent different messages. (Computer scientists usually speak in terms of 0 and 1 instead of on and off, but the concept is the same either way.) The computer has an advantage over Paul Revere in that it sees not just the number of lights turned on but also their order, so 01 (off–on) is different from 10 (on–off).

Building with Bits

2.6 The MITS Altair, the first popular personal computer, came with no keyboard or monitor. It could be programmed only by manipulating a bank of binary switches on the front panel for input. Binary patterns of lights provided the output. (Courtesy of The Computer History Museum.)

There's a **runaway market** for bits.

—*Russell Schweickart, astronaut*

What does a bit combination like 01100110 mean to the computer? There's no single answer to that question; it depends on context and convention. A string of bits can be interpreted as a number, a letter of the alphabet, or almost anything else.

Bits as Numbers

Because computers are built from switching devices that reduce all information to 0s and 1s, they represent numbers using the *binary number system,* a system that denotes all numbers with combinations of two digits. Like the 10-digit decimal system you use every day, the binary number system has clear, consistent rules for every arithmetic operation.

The people who worked with early computers had to use binary arithmetic. But today's computers include software that converts decimal numbers into binary numbers automatically, and vice versa. As a result, the computer's binary number processing is completely hidden from the user.

Bits as Codes

Today's computers work as much with text as with numbers. To make words, sentences, and paragraphs fit into the computer's binary-only circuitry, programmers have devised codes that represent each letter, digit, and special character as a unique string of bits.

The most widely used code, ASCII (an abbreviation of American Standard Code for Information Interchange, pronounced "as-kee"), represents each character as a unique 8-bit code. Out of a string of 8 bits, 256 unique ordered patterns can be made—enough to make unique codes for 26 letters (upper- and lowercase), 10 digits, and a variety of special characters.

As the world shrinks and our information needs grow, ASCII's 256 unique characters simply aren't enough. ASCII is too limited to accommodate Chinese, Greek, Hebrew, Japanese, and other languages. To facilitate multilingual computing, the computer industry is embracing Unicode, a coding scheme that supports 65,000 unique characters—more than enough for all major world languages.

Of course, today's computers work with more than characters. A group of bits can also represent colors, sounds, quantitative measurements from the environment, or just about any other kind of information that we need to process. We explore other types of information in later chapters.

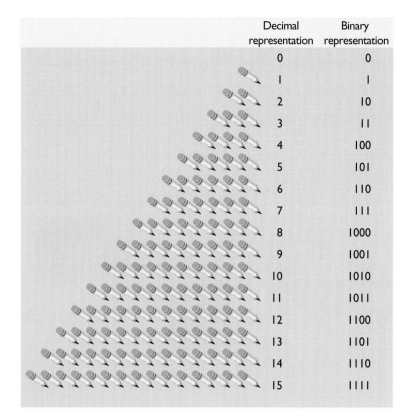

Decimal representation	Binary representation
0	0
1	1
2	10
3	11
4	100
5	101
6	110
7	111
8	1000
9	1001
10	1010
11	1011
12	1100
13	1101
14	1110
15	1111

2.7 In the binary number system, every number is represented by a unique pattern of 0s and 1s.

Character	ASCII binary code
A	01000001
B	01000010
C	01000011
D	01000100
E	01000101
F	01000110
G	01000111
H	01001000
I	01001001
J	01001010
K	01001011
L	01001100
M	01001101
N	01001110
O	01001111
P	01010000
Q	01010001
R	01010010
S	01010011
T	01010100
U	01010101
V	01010110
W	01010111
X	01011000
Y	01011001
Z	01011010
0	00110000
1	00110001
2	00110010
3	00110011
4	00110100
5	00110101
6	00110110
7	00110111
8	00111000
9	00111001

2.8 The capital letters and numeric digits are represented in the ASCII character set by 36 unique patterns of 8 bits each. (The remaining 92 ASCII bit patterns represent lowercase letters, punctuation characters, and special characters.

Bits as Instructions in Programs

So far we've dealt with the ways bits represent data. But another kind of information is just as important to the computer: the programs that tell the computer what to do with the data you give it. The computer stores programs as collections of bits, just as it stores data.

Program instructions, like characters, are represented in binary notation through the use of codes. For example, the code 01101010 might tell the computer to add two numbers. Other groups of bits—instructions in the program—contain codes that tell the computer where to find those numbers and where to store the result. You learn more about how these computer instructions work in later chapters.

Bits, Bytes, and Buzzwords

Trying to learn about computers by examining their operation at the bit level is a little like trying to learn about how people look or act by studying individual human cells; there's plenty of information there, but it's not the most efficient way to find out what you need to know. Fortunately, people can use computers without thinking about bits. Some bit-related terminology does come up in day-to-day computer work, though. Most computer users need to have at least a basic understanding of the following terms for quantifying data:

> Even the most **sophisticated** computer is really only a large, well-organized **volume of bits**.
>
> —*David Harel, in* Algorithmics: The Spirit of Computing

■ Byte: A logical group of eight bits. If you work mostly with words, you can think of a byte as one character of ASCII-encoded text.

The United States has long been at the center of the computer revolution; that's why the ASCII character set was originally designed to include only English-language characters. ASCII code numbers range from 0 to 127, but this isn't enough to handle all the characters used in the languages of Western Europe, including accents and other diacritical marks.

The Latin I character set appends 128 additional codes onto the original ASCII 128 to accommodate additional characters.

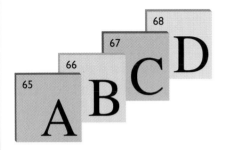

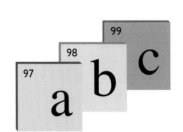

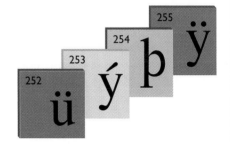

Both the ASCII and the Latin I character sets can use 8 bits—1 byte—to represent each character, but there's no room left for the characters used in languages such as Arabic, Greek, Hebrew, and Hindi, each of which has its own 50- to 150-character alphabet or syllabary. Asian languages, such as Chinese, Korean, and Japanese, present bigger challenges for computer users. Chinese alone has nearly 50,000 distinct characters, of which about 13,000 are in current use.

A character set that uses 2 bytes, or 16 bits, per character allows for 256 • 256, or 65,536 distinct codes—more than enough for all modern languages. The international standard double-byte character set called Unicode is designed to facilitate multilingual computing. In Unicode, the first 256 codes (0 through 255) are identical to the codes of the Latin I character set. The remaining codes are distributed among the writing systems of the world's other languages.

Most major new software applications and operating systems are designed to be transported to different languages. Making a software application work in different languages involves much more than translating the words. For example, some languages write from right to left or top to bottom. Pronunciation, currency symbols, dialects, and other variations often make it necessary to produce customized software for different regions even where the same language is spoken.

Computer keyboards for East Asian languages don't have one key for each character. Using phonetic input, a user types a pronunciation for a character using a Western-style keyboard and then chooses the character needed from a menu of characters that appears on the screen. The software can make some menu choices automatically based on common language-usage patterns.

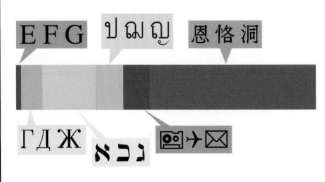

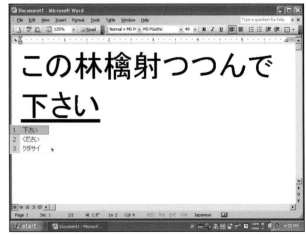

2.9

- **Kilobyte (KB or K):** About 1,000 bytes of information. For example, about 5K of storage is necessary to hold 5,000 characters of ASCII text. (Technically, 1K is 1,024 bytes because 1,024 is 2^{10}, which makes the arithmetic easier for binary-based computers. For those of us who don't think in binary, 1,000 is often close enough.)
- **Megabyte or meg (MB):** Approximately 1,000KB, or 1 million bytes.
- **Gigabyte (GB or gig):** Approximately 1,000MB, or 1 billion bytes.
- **Terabyte (TB):** Approximately 1 million MB or 1 trillion bytes. This massive unit of measurement applies to the largest storage devices commonly available today.
- **Petabyte (PB):** This astronomical value is the equivalent of 1,024 terabytes, or 1 quadrillion bytes. While it's unlikely that anyone will be able to store 1PB of data on their home PC anytime soon, we're definitely heading in that direction.

The abbreviations K, MB, GB, and PB describe the capacity of memory and storage components. You could, for example, describe a computer as having 512MB of memory (RAM) and a hard disk as having a 120GB storage capacity. The same terms are used to quantify sizes of computer files as well. A file is an organized collection of information, such as a term paper or a set of names and addresses, stored in a computer-readable form. For example, the text for this chapter is stored in a file that occupies about 169KB of space on a hard disk drive.

To add to the confusion, people often measure data transfer speed or memory size in *megabits (Mb)* rather than megabytes (MB). A megabit, as you might expect, is approximately 1,000 bits—one-eighth the size of a megabyte. When you're talking in bits and bytes, a little detail like capitalization can make a significant difference.

The Computer's Core: CPU and Memory

It may seem strange to think of automated teller machines, video game consoles, and supercomputers as bit processors. But whatever it looks like to the user, a digital computer is at its core a collection of on/off switches designed to transform information from one form to another. The user provides the computer with patterns of bits—input—and the computer follows instructions to transform that input into a different pattern of bits—output—to return to the user.

> The **microprocessor** that makes up your personal computer's central processing unit, or CPU, is the **ultimate computer brain, messenger, ringmaster,** and **boss**. All the other components— RAM, disk drives, the monitor—exist only to bridge the gap between you and the processor.
>
> —*Ron White, in* How Computers Work

The CPU: The Real Computer

The CPU, often called just the *processor*, performs the transformations of input into output. Every computer has at least one CPU to interpret and execute the instructions in each program, to perform arithmetic and logical data manipulations, and to communicate with all the other parts of the computer system indirectly through memory.

A modern *microprocessor*, or CPU, is an extraordinarily complex collection of electronic circuits. In a desktop computer, the CPU is housed along with other chips and electronic components on a circuit board. The circuit board that contains a computer's CPU is called the motherboard.

Many different kinds of CPUs are in use today; when you choose a computer, the type of CPU in the computer is an important part of the decision. Although there are many variations in design among these chips, only two factors are important to a casual computer user: compatibility and performance.

Green Computing

When compared with heavy industries, such as automobiles and energy, the computer industry is relatively easy on the environment. But the manufacture and use of computer hardware and software does have a significant environmental impact, especially now that so many of us are using the technology. Fortunately, you have some control over the environmental impact of your computing activities. Here are a few tips to help minimize your impact:

➡ *Buy green equipment*. Today's computer equipment uses relatively little energy, but as world energy resources dwindle, less is always better. Many modern computers and peripherals are specifically designed to consume less energy. Look for the Environmental Protection Agency's Energy Star certification on the package.

➡ *Use a notebook*. Portable computers use far less energy than desktop computers. They're engineered to preserve precious battery power. But if you use a laptop, keep it plugged in when you have easy access to an electrical outlet. Batteries wear out from repeated usage, and their disposal can cause environmental problems of a different sort. (If you're the kind of person who always needs to have the latest and greatest technology, a notebook isn't the best choice because notebooks are difficult or impossible to upgrade.)

➡ *Take advantage of energy-saving features*. Most modern systems can be set up to go to sleep (a sort of suspended animation state that uses just enough power to preserve RAM) and turn off the monitor or printer when idle for more than an hour or so. If your equipment has automatic energy-saving features, use them. You'll save energy and money.

➡ *Turn it off when you're away*. If you're just leaving your computer for an hour or two, you won't save much energy by turning the CPU off. But if you're

leaving it for more than a few hours and it's not on duty receiving faxes and email, you'll do the environment a favor by turning it off or putting it to sleep.

➡ *Save energy, not screens*. Your monitor is probably the biggest power guzzler in your system. A screen

2.10 Windows and Mac OS X systems have advanced energy-saver control panels that can be used to switch the monitor, hard drive, and CPU to lower-power sleep modes automatically after specified periods of inactivity.

Compatibility

Not all software is **compatible** with every CPU; that is, software written for one processor will usually not work with another. Every processor has a built-in instruction set—a vocabulary of instructions the processor can execute. CPUs in the same product family are generally designed so newer processors can process all instructions handled by earlier models. For example, chips in Intel's Pentium 4 microprocessor family are **backward compatible** with the Celeron, Pentium III, Pentium II, Pentium Pro, Pentium, 486, 386, and 286 chips

2.11 Portable computers consume far less energy than desktop models do. This one is powered by the sun using a Neptune Solar Panel.

saver can be fun to watch, but it doesn't save your screen, and it doesn't save energy, either. As long as your monitor is displaying an image, it's consuming power. Use sleep.

➡ ***Print only once***. Don't print out a rough draft just to proofread; try to get it clean on-screen. (Most people find this one hard to follow 100% of the time; some errors just don't seem to show up until you proofread a hard copy.)

➡ ***Recycle your waste products***. When you do have to reprint that 20-page report because of a missing paragraph on page 1, recycle the flawed printout. When your laser printer's toner cartridge runs dry, ship or deliver it to one of the many companies that

recycles cartridges. They may even pay you a few dollars for the empty cartridge. When your portable's battery dies, follow the manufacturer's instructions for recycling it. While you're in recycling mode, don't forget all those computer magazines and catalogs.

➡ ***Pass it on***. When you outgrow a piece of hardware or software, don't throw it away. Donate it to a school, civic organization, family member, or friend who can put it to good use.

➡ ***Send bits, not atoms***. It takes far more resources to send a letter by truck, train, or plane than to send an electronic message through the Internet. Whenever possible, use your modem instead of your printer.

that preceded it, so they can run most software written for those older CPUs. (Likewise, many of the processors designed by Advanced Micro Devices—AMD—are purposefully made to be compatible with those made by Intel.) But software written for the PowerPC family of processors used in Macintosh computers won't run on the Intel processors found in most IBM-compatible computers; the Intel processors can't understand programs written for the PowerPC CPUs. Similarly, the Macintosh PowerPC processor can't generally run Windows software.

A related issue involves the software systems that run on these hardware platforms. Programs written for Linux, a popular UNIX-like operating system, can't run on Windows, even though both operating systems can be installed on PCs powered by an Intel microprocessor. In Chapter 4, you will learn more about these issues and see how virtual machine software can often overcome incompatibility problems by translating instructions written for one CPU or software system into instructions that another can execute.

Performance

When it comes to handling information, some processors are much faster than others. Most computer applications, such as word processing, are more convenient to use on a faster machine. Many applications that use graphics or do computations, such as statistical programs, graphic

2.12 The motherboard of a typical PC contains the CPU, memory, and several other important chips and components.

design programs, and many computer games, require faster machines to produce satisfactory results.

A computer's overall performance is determined in part by the speed of its microprocessor's internal *clock*—the timing device that produces electrical pulses to synchronize the computer's operations. A computer's clock speed is measured in units called *gigahertz (GHz)*, for billions of clock cycles per second. Ads for new computer systems

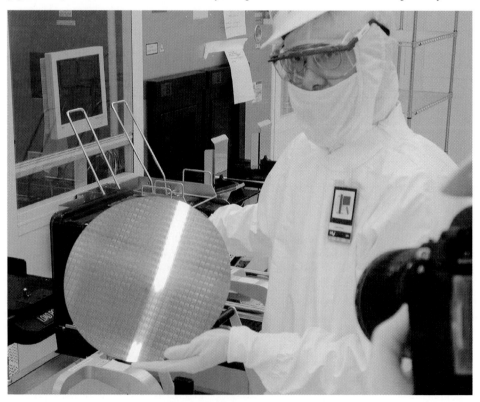

2.13 This chip specialist is examining a silicon wafer before it is sliced into many silicon chips.

2.14 The Intel Pentium-M (left) and Pentium 4 chips contain circuitry that looks like geometric patterns when magnified.

often emphasize gigahertz ratings as a measure of speed. But these numbers can be somewhat misleading; judging a computer's speed by its gigahertz rating alone is like measuring a car's speed by the engine's RPM (revolutions per minute). The PC notebook powered by a 2.4-GHz Pentium 4-M chip isn't necessarily faster than a 1.42-GHz Power Mac G4 or a 2-GHz Pentium 4 chip; in fact, for some tasks, it's actually slower. That's because much of the notebook's circuitry isn't as advanced, or speedy, as the circuitry in the other systems.

PC performance can also be limited by the **architecture** of the processor—the design that determines how individual components of the CPU are put together on the chip. For example, newer chips can manipulate more bits simultaneously than older chips can, which makes them more efficient, and therefore faster, at performing most operations. The number of bits a CPU can process at one time—typically 32 or 64—is sometimes called the CPU's *word size*. More often, though, people use the number without a label, as in "The Itanium is Intel's first mainstream 64-bit processor." Today, only high-end workstations and servers use 64-bit processors; while most PCs and Macintoshes use 32-bit processors. Some embedded and special-purpose computers still use 8- and 16-bit processors because their performance needs are smaller.

Because performance is so important, engineers and computer scientists are constantly developing techniques for speeding up a computer's ability to manipulate and move bits. One common technique for improving a computer's performance is to put more than one processor in the computer. Many personal computers, for example, have specialized subsidiary processors that take care of mathematical calculations or graphics displays, and many Macs and some PCs now employ two microprocessors to improve overall performance. This capability, **parallel processing** (sometimes called **symmetric multiprocessing** or just **multiprocessing** in the PC world), has been used in high-end servers and workstations for some time. Indeed, some of the largest servers in the world now include up to 64 or 128 processors!

Another way to improve performance on high-end server systems is simply to add more machines to the mix. This way, the processing resources of multiple servers can be grouped together in a **cluster** to improve rendering speeds in lifelike computer graphics or calculate the sums of complex financial trading computations more quickly. Google uses a cluster of more than 10,000 PCs to handle 200 million search queries a day. Server clusters are also used for reliability reasons: If one machine in a cluster shuts down because of errors, or to be serviced, the other servers can pick up the slack.

How It **Works**

The central processing unit (CPU) is the hardware component that executes the steps in a software program, performing math and moving data from one part of the system to another. The CPU contains the circuitry to perform a variety of simple tasks, called *instructions*. An individual instruction does only a tiny amount of work. A typical instruction might be "Read the contents of memory location x and add the number y to it." Most CPUs have a vocabulary of fewer than 1,000 distinct instructions.

All computer programs are composed of instructions drawn from this tiny vocabulary. The typical computer program is composed of millions of instructions, and the CPU can execute millions of instructions every second. When a program runs, the rapid-fire execution of instructions creates an illusion of motion in the same way a movie simulates motion out of a sequence of still pictures.

The typical CPU is divided into several functional units: control, arithmetic, decode, bus, and prefetch. These units work together like workers on an assembly line to complete the execution of program instructions.

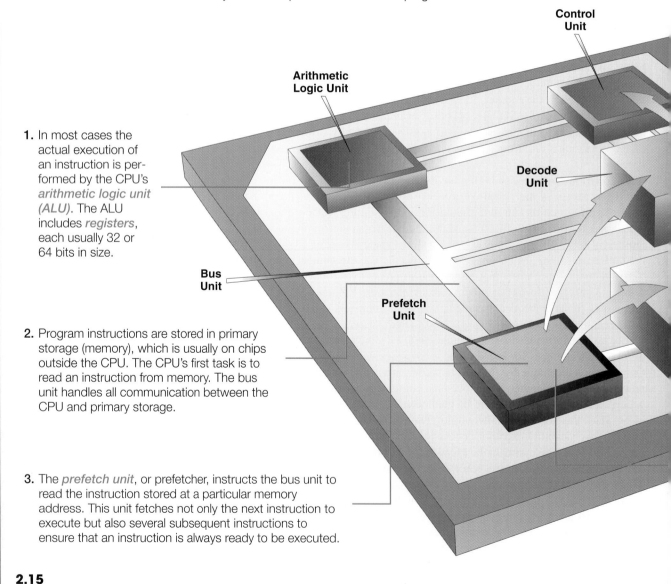

Control Unit

Arithmetic Logic Unit

Decode Unit

Bus Unit

Prefetch Unit

1. In most cases the actual execution of an instruction is performed by the CPU's *arithmetic logic unit (ALU)*. The ALU includes *registers*, each usually 32 or 64 bits in size.

2. Program instructions are stored in primary storage (memory), which is usually on chips outside the CPU. The CPU's first task is to read an instruction from memory. The bus unit handles all communication between the CPU and primary storage.

3. The *prefetch unit*, or prefetcher, instructs the bus unit to read the instruction stored at a particular memory address. This unit fetches not only the next instruction to execute but also several subsequent instructions to ensure that an instruction is always ready to be executed.

2.15

4. The *decode unit* takes the instruction read by the prefetcher and translates it into a form suitable for the CPU's internal processing. It does this by looking up the steps required to complete an instruction in the control unit.

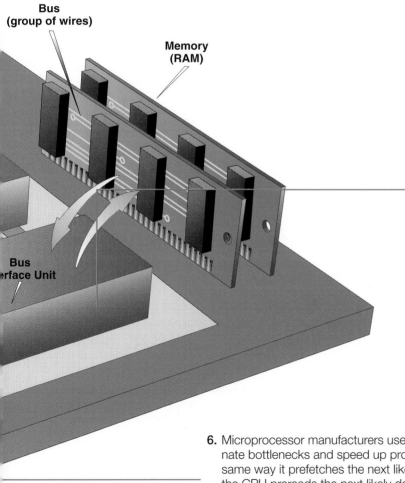

**Bus
(group of wires)**

**Memory
(RAM)**

**Bus
...erface Unit**

5. If an instruction requires that information be sent out from the CPU—for example, written into memory—then the final phase of execution is *writeback*, in which the bus unit writes the results of the instruction back into memory or to some other device.

6. Microprocessor manufacturers use many techniques to eliminate bottlenecks and speed up processing. For example, in the same way it prefetches the next likely instructions to be read, the CPU prereads the next likely data to be used into a cache in memory, called a *Level 2 cache (L2 cache)*, or, for faster access, in the CPU itself (a *Level 1 cache*).

Popular CPU Families and Where to Find Them

	CPU Family	Word Size	Developer/ Manufacturer	Where It Is Used
	Itanium family	64-bit	Intel Corporation	High-end servers and workstations.
	Pentium family (including Celeron and Xeon)	32-bit	Intel Corporation	PCs, notebooks, workstations, and servers. Celeron is designed for low-end systems; Xeon is designed for workstations and servers.
	Opteron family (compatible with Intel Pentium family)	32/64-bit	Advanced Micro Devices (AMD)	High-end PCs, workstations, and servers.
	Athlon family (compatible with Intel Pentium family)	32-bit	AMD	PCs and notebooks.
	Crusoe family (compatible with Intel Pentium family)	32-bit	Transmeta	Ultramobile notebook PCs and embedded devices.
	PowerPC family (including G3, G4, and G5)	64-bit (G5) and 32-bit (G3, G4)	IBM and Motorola	Macintosh computers, notebooks, embedded computers, and servers.
	SPARC	64-bit	Sun Microsystems	High-end UNIX servers, workstations, and embedded computers.
	Xscale	32-bit	Intel Corporation	PDAs and handheld computers.

2.16

The Computer's Memory

The CPU's main job is to follow the instructions encoded in programs. But like Alice in *Through the Looking Glass*, the CPU can handle only one instruction and a few pieces of data at a time. The computer needs a place to store the rest of the program and data until the processor is ready for them. That's what RAM is for.

"**What's one** and **one** and **one** and **one** and **one** and **one** and **one** and **one** and **one** and **one**?" "**I don't know**," said Alice. "I lost count." "**She can't do addition**," said the Red Queen.

—*Lewis Carroll, in* Through the Looking Glass

Random access memory (RAM) is the most common type of primary storage, or computer memory. RAM chips contain circuits that store program instructions and data temporarily. The computer divides each RAM chip into many equal-sized memory locations. Memory locations, like houses, have unique addresses so the computer can tell them apart when it is instructed to save or retrieve information. You can store a piece of information in any RAM location—you can pick one at random—and the computer can, if so instructed, quickly retrieve it. Hence the name random access memory.

The information stored in RAM is nothing more than a pattern of electrical current flowing through microscopic circuits in silicon chips. This means that when the power goes off, the computer instantly forgets everything it was remembering in RAM. RAM is sometimes referred to as volatile memory because information stored there is not held permanently.

This could be a serious problem if the computer didn't have another type of memory to store information that you don't want to lose. This **nonvolatile memory** is called **read-only memory (ROM)** because the computer can only read information from it; it can never write any new information on it. The information in ROM was etched in when the chip was manufactured, so it is available whenever the computer is operating, but it can't be changed except by replacing the ROM chip. All modern computers use ROM to store start-up instructions and other critical information. You can also find ROM inside preprogrammed devices with embedded processors, such as pocket calculators and microwave ovens. Printers use ROM to hold information about character sets.

Other types of memory are available; most are seldom used outside of engineering laboratories. There are two notable exceptions:

- *Complementary metal oxide semiconductor (CMOS)* is a special low-energy kind of RAM that can store small amounts of data for long periods of time on battery power. CMOS RAM stores the date, time, and calendar in a PC. (CMOS RAM is called *parameter RAM* in Macintoshes.)
- *Flash memory* chips, like RAM chips, can be written and erased rapidly and repeatedly. But unlike RAM, flash memory is nonvolatile; it can keep its contents without a flow of electricity. Digital cameras, cell phones, pagers, portable computers, handheld computers, PDAs, and other digital devices use flash memory to store data that needs to be changed from time to time. Data flight recorders also use it. Flash memory is still too expensive to replace RAM and other common storage media, but it may in the future replace disk drives and memory chips.

It takes time for the processor to retrieve data from memory—but not very much time. The *access time* for most memory is measured in *nanoseconds (ns)*—billionths of a second. Compare this with hard disk access time, which is measured in *milliseconds (ms)*—thousandths of a second. Memory speed (access time) is another factor that affects the computer's overall speed.

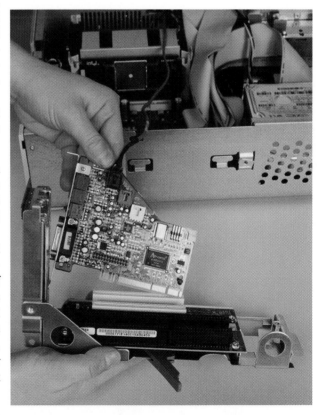

2.17 Slots and ports enable the CPU to communicate with the outside world via peripheral devices. Here an add-on card is being inserted into an internal slot in the PC. (The circuit board containing the slot has been removed for easier viewing.)

How It **Works**

<u>2.4 Memory</u>

Memory is the work area for the CPU. In order for the CPU to execute instructions or manipulate data, these instructions or data must be loaded into memory. Think of memory as millions of tiny storage cells, each of which can contain a single byte of information. Like mailboxes in a row, bytes of memory have unique addresses that identify them and help the CPU keep track of where things are stored. Personal computers contain a large amount of random access memory (RAM) and a small amount of read-only memory (ROM).

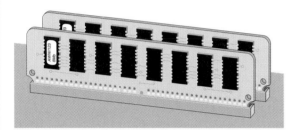

Two SIMMs plugged into a circuit board

A typical personal computer has from 256 megabytes (millions of bytes) to 2 gigabytes (billions of bytes) of RAM. The CPU can store (write) information into RAM and retrieve (read) information from RAM. The information in

RAM may include program instructions, numbers for arithmetic, codes representing text characters, digital codes representing pictures, and other kinds of data. RAM chips are usually grouped on small circuit boards called *single in-line memory modules (SIMMs)* and *dual in-line memory modules (DIMMs)* and are plugged into the motherboard. RAM is volatile memory, meaning that all the information is lost when power to the computer is turned off.

Personal computers also have a small amount of ROM. Information is permanently recorded on the ROM, meaning the CPU can read information from the ROM, but cannot change its contents. On most computer systems, part of the operating system is stored in ROM. Programs stored in ROM are called firmware.

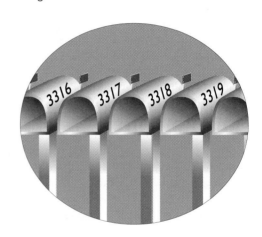

2.18

2.19 A portable computer typically has one or two PC card slots to accommodate credit-card-sized add-on cards such as this one.

Buses, Ports, and Peripherals

In a desktop computer, the CPU, memory chips, and other key components are attached to the motherboard. Information travels between components on the motherboard through groups of wires called **system buses**, or just **buses**. Buses typically have 32 or 64 wires, or data paths; a bus with 32 wires is called a *32-bit bus* because it can transmit 32 bits of information at a time, twice as many as an older 16-bit bus. Just as multilane freeways allow masses of automobiles to move faster than they could on single-lane roads, wider buses can transmit information faster than narrower buses. Newer, more powerful computers have wider buses so they can process information faster.

Buses connect to storage devices in **bays**—open areas in the system box for disk drives and other devices. Buses also connect to **expansion slots** (sometimes just called *slots*) inside the computer's housing. Users can customize their computers by inserting special-purpose circuit boards (called *expansion cards*, or just *cards*) into these slots. Buses also connect to external buses and **ports**—sockets on the outside of the computer chassis. The back of a computer typically has a variety of ports to meet a variety of needs. Some of these ports—where you might plug in the keyboard and mouse, for example—are connected

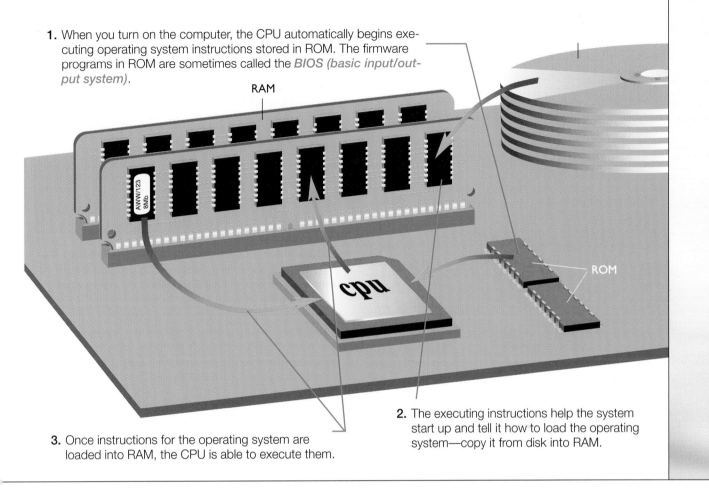

1. When you turn on the computer, the CPU automatically begins executing operating system instructions stored in ROM. The firmware programs in ROM are sometimes called the *BIOS (basic input/output system)*.

RAM

ROM

cpu

2. The executing instructions help the system start up and tell it how to load the operating system—copy it from disk into RAM.

3. Once instructions for the operating system are loaded into RAM, the CPU is able to execute them.

directly to the system board. Others, such as the monitor port, are generally attached to an expansion card. In fact, many expansion cards do little more than provide convenient ports for attaching particular types of peripherals.

In portable computers, where size is critical, most common ports go directly to the system board. Because portable computers don't have room for full-sized cards, many have slots for **PC cards**—credit-card-sized cards that contain memory, miniature peripherals, and additional ports. (When these cards were first released, they were known as PCMCIA cards. One writer humorously suggested that this stood for "People Can't Memorize Computer Industry Acronyms" though the unfortunate acronym actually means "Personal Computer Memory Card International Association." Thankfully, the name was shortened to the simpler PC card.)

Slots and ports make it easy to add external devices, called peripherals, to the computer system so the CPU can communicate with the outside world and store information for later use. Without peripherals, CPU and memory together are like a brain without a body. Some peripherals, such as keyboards and printers, serve as communication links between people and computers. Other peripherals link the computer to other machines. Still others provide long-term storage media. In the next chapter, we explore a variety of input, output, and storage peripherals and then revisit the buses, slots, and ports that connect those peripherals to the CPU and memory.

Inventing the FUTURE

Tomorrow's Processors

The only thing that has consistently **grown faster** than hardware in the last 40 years is **human expectation**.

—*Bjarne Stroustrup, AT&T Bell Labs, designer of the C++ programming language*

Many research labs are experimenting with alternatives to today's silicon chips. For example, IBM researchers have developed plastic chips that are more durable and energy efficient than silicon chips. Intel, Motorola, and AMD are working with the U.S. government to develop new laser etching technology called *extreme ultraviolet lithography* (EUVL) that could reduce chip size and increase performance radically. Motorola researchers have created chips that combine silicon with gallium arsenide, a semiconductor that conducts electricity faster than silicon and emits light that can be used for information applications; the research should soon produce chips that are much faster than any currently available. IBM and Motorola researchers are making progress producing chips based on carbon rather than silicon. Carbon-based nanoscale processors would be much smaller and consume far less electricity than conventional silicon-based microprocessors.

Researchers are pursuing other radical research technologies, too. Superconductors that transmit electricity without heat loss could increase computer speed a hundredfold. Unfortunately, superconductor technology generally requires a supercooled environment, which isn't practical for most applications. A more realistic alternative is the optical computer, which transmits information in light waves rather than in electrical pulses.

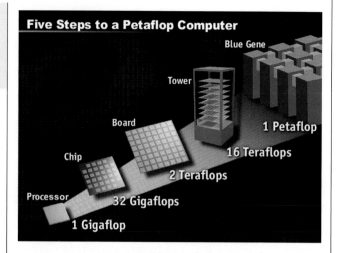

Five Steps to a Petaflop Computer

2.20b This illustration shows how IBM researchers envision the evolution of high-performance computers from simple processors to Blue Gene, IBM's next-generation supercomputer.

Optical computers outside research labs are currently limited to a few narrow applications, such as robot vision. But when the technology is refined, general-purpose optical computers may process information hundreds of times faster than silicon computers do.

Some of the most revolutionary work in computer design involves not what's inside the processors, but how computers are put together. One example is IBM's Blue Gene, a supercomputer being developed to help scientists crack the secrets of proteins in the human body. Blue Gene will have 1 million small, simple processors, each capable of handling eight threads of instructions simultaneously. The processors won't have power-hungry embedded caches, but they will have built-in memory to improve speed. The network of processors will be self-healing; it will detect failed components, seal them off, and direct work elsewhere. If it works as planned, Blue Gene will be the first *petaflop* computer, capable of handling 1 quadrillion (1,000,000,000,000,000) instructions per second—2 million times more than today's PC! (Today's fastest computers have reached *teraflop* speeds—trillions of operations per second.) ∼

2.20a Researchers are exploring ways to apply fiber-optic technology to circuit board and chip design to produce faster processors.

Silicon Hogs *Katharine Mieszkowski*

When we consider how computers are changing the world, we don't often think about its environmental impact. In this article, which first appeared in the online magazine Salon *on Nov. 13, 2002, senior writer Katharine Mieszkowski discusses a hidden cost of our digital devices.*

If we all had to lug around the true environmental weights of the microchips in our iPods, cellphones or laptops, most of those portable gadgets would never make it off their docking stations, much less out the front door.

It takes 3.7 pounds of fossil fuels and other chemicals and 70.5 pounds of water to produce a single two-gram microchip, according to a study in the Dec. 15 [2002] issue of *Environmental Science & Technology,* a publication of the American Chemical Society.

"The technology is not free," says Eric Williams of the United Nations University in Tokyo, one of the co-authors of the study. "The environmental footprint of the device is much more substantial than its small physical size would suggest."

The technology industry has been heralded as a clean alternative to smoke-belching industrial factories of yore, but in recent years, its squeaky-clean image has eroded with news reports about high cancer rates among clean-room workers, and old CPUs and monitors piling up in landfills.

This study suggests that not only is chip manufacturing toxic, it's just plain wasteful. And the waste starts not when last year's cast-off model ends up at the dump, but when a chip is born.

Sixty-nine billion integrated-circuits were produced last year, according to the Semiconductor Industry Association. The production of a silicon wafer—"the purest product manufactured on a commercial scale," according to the study, is a complex, energy intensive procedure. The six-stage process consumes 2130 kilowatt-hours of electricity for every kilogram of silicon. When multiplied against billion of chips, the consequent consumption of fossil fuels necessary just to provide the power is enormous. Then the wafers are repeatedly doped with chemicals, rinsed with ultra-pure water to remove impurities, etched, rinsed again and doped with more chemicals.

Not everyone agrees with the critical analysis: Some scientists point out that the study only looks at one-half of the equation—what goes into the chips, not what they're used for. Chip use could potentially save as much energy and resources as their manufacture consumes. Still, the new data is raising eyebrows.

"We've certainly known about the significant problems that happen at the end of the computer's life cycle as e-waste," says Joel Makower, editor of the Green Business Letter. "But this is as pointed a reference as has been made yet as to the extraordinary amount of waste that is created at the front end."

Hard data about the resources that go into producing chips is scarce. "We have been trying for 10 years to find ways to get the semiconductor industry to report their inputs and outputs on a per unit basis," says Ted Smith, executive director of the Silicon Valley Toxics Coalition. For this study, Williams, Heller and co-author Robert U. Ayres of INSEAD used data provided by an anonymous plant.

Among the study's conclusions: It's 160 times more energy-intensive to create a silicon wafer out of quartz than to produce regular silicon. That's because chips are extremely highly organized forms of matter, or "low-entropy."

The findings fly in the face of the high-tech theory of "dematerialization," which holds that technological progress should lead to the use of increasingly fewer resources. "The smaller you make it, the less forgiving you are of defects," Heller explains. "In this case, dematerialization may lead to increased energy intensity to achieve a high level of purity and low defect levels."

Just how energy-demanding is this process? Consider that it takes 3,300 pounds of fossil fuel and other chemicals to fabricate a whole car, and just 3.7 pounds to create a chip. But if you compare the resources used to create a car to the weight of the vehicle, the ratio is 2-1. For a chip, that same ratio is 630-1.

But not everyone concerned with the impact of chips on the environment is convinced that such a car and chip comparison is meaningful.

"The weight of a product is not a logical basis for normalizing the environmental impact," says Farhang Shadman, director of the NSF/SRC Engineering Research Center for Environmentally Benign Semiconductor Manufacturing at the University of Arizona, which receives some of its funding from the chip industry.

And even the scientists behind the study caution against tarring chips for environmental malfeasance based on what it takes to produce them, since the study considers the chip's creation, but not the impact of its use. "What is the chip replacing?" Heller asks. "Should you compare it to a vacuum tube? Should we be comparing e-mail to surface mail?"

How a chip is used could make up for its consumptive beginnings. "That little tiny chip may actually save vast amounts of electricity," says Jonathan Koomey, a staff scientist and leader of the end-use forecasting group at Lawrence Berkeley National Laboratory. Chips are deployed to make everything from industrial production to household appliances more energy-efficient. For example, the chip-powered sensor in a dishwasher that tells the machine the dishes are clean and to stop sloshing the water around. "So what if the chip uses a lot of power relative to its mass, if it saves vastly more than that in the system?" says Koomey.

But this argument doesn't impress environmental critics. Makower argues that chip manufacturing can be made more resource-efficient. His example: Intel reduced water consumption at a number of plants in water-starved areas such as Albuquerque, N. M., when local communities demanded it. Since 1994, Intel's water usage in Albuquerque has decreased by 47 percent.

"Now that the bubble has burst, it gives us all a chance to look a little less bleary-eyed at these industries that we've spawned, and what their genuine impacts are," says Makower.

Discussion Questions

1. Do you think that silicon chips save more energy and resources than they consume? Explain.

2. Do you favor laws requiring computer manufacturers to minimize their negative environmental impact? Why or why not?

Summary

Whether it's working with words, numbers, pictures, or sounds, a computer is manipulating patterns of bits—binary digits of information that it can store in switching circuitry and that are represented by two symbols. Groups of bits can be treated as numbers for calculations using the binary number system. Bits can be grouped into coded messages that represent alphabetic characters, pictures, colors, sounds, or just about any other kind of information. Even the instructions computers follow—the software programs that tell the computer what to do—must be reduced to strings of bits before the computer accepts them. Byte, kilobyte, megabyte, and other common units for measuring bit quantities are used in descriptions of memory, storage, and file size.

The microprocessor, or central processing unit (CPU), follows software instructions to perform the calculations and logical manipulations that transform input data into output. Not all CPUs are compatible with each other; each is capable of processing a particular set of instructions, so a software program written for one family of processors can't necessarily be understood by a processor from another family. Engineers are constantly improving the clock speed and architecture of CPUs, making computers capable of processing information faster.

The CPU uses RAM (random access memory) as a temporary storage area—a scratch pad—for instructions and data. Another type of memory, ROM (read-only memory), contains unchangeable information that serves as reference material for the CPU as it executes program instructions.

The CPU and main memory are housed in silicon chips on the motherboard and other circuit boards inside the computer. Buses connect to slots and ports that enable the computer to communicate with internal devices and external peripherals.

Key Terms

Interactive Activities

1. The *Computer Confluence* CD-ROM contains self-test quiz questions related to this chapter, including multiple-choice, true or false, and matching questions.

2. The *Computer Confluence* Web site, **http://www.computerconfluence.com**, contains self-test exercises related to this chapter. Follow the instruc-tions for taking a quiz. After you've completed your quiz, you can email the results to your instructor.

3. The Web site also contains open-ended discussion questions called Internet Explorations. Discuss one or more of the Internet Exploration questions for this chapter.

True or False

1. The term "information" is always defined in terms of value.

2. The data processed by digital computers is made up of discrete units, or digits.

3. A simple on/off switch can store exactly one bit of information.

4. There are more than enough characters in standard ASCII codes to represent all of the major world languages.

5. A kilobyte (KB) is twice as big as a kilobit (Kb).

6. If a processor is backward compatible with another, older processor, it can run older programs written for that processor.

7. A CPU with a clock speed of 3.2 gigahertz can perform all tasks at least twice as fast as a processor that runs at 1.5 gigahertz.

8. The information stored in RAM is nothing more than a pattern of electrical current flowing through microscopic circuits in silicon chips.

9. The access time for most memory is slower than the access time for a typical hard disk.

10. Slots and ports make it possible for the CPU to communicate with the outside world through peripherals.

Multiple Choice

1. How many options does a binary choice offer?
   a. None
   b. One
   c. Two
   d. It depends on the amount of memory in the computer.
   e. It depends on the speed of the computer's processor.

2. A collection of bits in the computer's memory might be treated as
   a. Binary numbers that can be added and subtracted
   b. ASCII codes representing letters and other characters
   c. Program instructions that tell the computer what to do
   d. Any of the above
   e. None of the above

3. How many values can be represented by a single byte?
   a. 2
   b. 8
   c. 16
   d. 64
   e. 256

4. One megabyte equals approximately
   a. 1,000 bits
   b. 1,000 bytes
   c. 1 million bytes
   d. 1 million bits
   e. 2,000 megabits

5. A new coding scheme that supports 65,000 unique characters has the name
   a. ASCII
   b. EBCDIC
   c. Esperanto
   d. Unicode
   e. URL

6. Transformation of input into output is performed by
   a. Peripherals
   b. Memory
   c. Storage
   d. The CPU
   e. The ALU

7. Why are program instructions represented in binary notation within the computer?
   a. Binary notation is more compact than other representations.
   b. Computer memory is made out of binary digits (bits).
   c. There are only two different directions for electricity to move along a wire.
   d. Computer programmers prefer to think in binary.
   e. A CPU can execute no more than two instructions at one time.

8. What does the speed of a computer depend on?
   a. The architecture of the processor
   b. The clock speed of the processor
   c. The word size of the processor
   d. The number of processors
   e. All of the above

9. Why will software written for the Pentium III CPU generally run on the Pentium 4 CPU?
   a. Microsoft uses special encoding techniques that only work with Pentium CPUs.
   b. The Pentium 4 has special compatibility registers in RAM.
   c. The Pentium 4 is designed to be backward compatible with earlier Pentium chips.
   d. Every CPU is, by definition, compatible with the Pentium III.
   e. All software written for the Pentium 4 is compiled on Pentium III processors.

10. When you are working on a document on a PC, where is the document temporarily stored?
    a. RAM
    b. ROM
    c. The CPU
    d. Flash memory
    e. The CD-ROM

11. When you first turn on a computer, the CPU is preset to execute instructions stored in
    a. RAM
    b. ROM
    c. Flash memory
    d. The CD-ROM
    e. The ALU

12. Information travels between components on the motherboard through
    a. Flash memory
    b. CMOS
    c. Bays
    d. Buses
    e. Peripherals

13. PC cards (formerly called PCMCIA cards) are
    a. Cards that are designed to be inserted into slots on desktop PCs
    b. High-speed cards that are designed to work with workstations
    c. Compact cards that are designed to work with notebook computers
    d. Cards that attach directly to the PC motherboard
    e. None of the above

14. Nonvolatile memory
    a. Can be thrown in a fire without exploding
    b. Cannot be used to store programs
    c. Can keep its contents without a flow of electricity
    d. Loses its contents without a flow of electricity
    e. Dissolves in water

15. Storage devices can be connected to the CPU and memory via
    a. Expansion slots
    b. Ports
    c. Bays
    d. All of the above
    e. None of the above

Review Questions

1. Provide a working definition of each of the key words listed in the "Key Terms" section. Check your answers in the glossary.

2. Draw a block diagram showing the major components of a computer and their relationships. Briefly describe the function of each component.

3. Think of this as computer input: *123.4*. The computer might read this as a number or as a set of ASCII codes. Explain how these concepts differ.

4. Why is information stored in some kind of binary format in computers?

5. Why can't you normally run Macintosh software on a PC with an Intel Pentium 4 CPU?

6. Clock speed is only one factor in determining a CPU's processing speed. What is another?

7. Why is it important that computers support both internal and external expansion?

8. Explain how symmetrical multiprocessing can increase a computer's performance; use an example or a comparison with the way people work if you like.

9. What is the difference between RAM and ROM? What is the purpose of each?

10. What is the difference between primary and secondary storage?

Discussion Questions

1. Currently ASCII is the most popular code for representing characters. What would be the advantages and disadvantages of a universal conversion to the Unicode scheme?

2. Why are computer manufacturers constantly releasing faster computers? How do computer users benefit from the increased speed?

3. Why do computer manufacturers typically make their new processors backward compatible with earlier processors?

4. How is human memory similar to computer memory? How is it different?

Projects

1. Collect computer advertisements from newspapers, magazines, and other sources. Compare how the ads handle discussions of speed. Evaluate the usefulness of the information in the ads from a consumer's point of view.

2. Examine advertisements in a recent personal computing magazine, or visit a computer store. Collect information about the storage capacities and prices of hard disk drives for either Macintoshes or IBM PC-compatibles, but not both. Draw a graph that plots capacity versus price.

3. Interview a salesperson in a computer store. Find out what kinds of questions people ask when buying a computer. Develop profiles for the most common types of computer buyers. What kinds of computers do these customers buy, and why?

4. Systems supporting the keyboard input of Chinese can be put into three types, depending on whether they rely upon encoding, pronunciation, or the structure of the characters. Research these systems, and report on the relative strengths and weaknesses of each system type.

Sources and Resources

Books

Building IBM: Shaping an Industry and Its Technology, by Emerson W. Pugh (Cambridge, MA: MIT Press, 1995). This book traces IBM's history from Herman Hollerith's invention of the punch card machine more than a century ago. This thoroughly researched and clearly written book is a valuable resource for anyone interested in understanding IBM's history.

Who Says Elephants Can't Dance? Inside IBM's Historic Turnaround, by Louis V. Gerstner, Jr. (New York: Harper Business, 2002). Written by the ex-CEO of IBM, this fascinating book looks at IBM's late-1990s comeback, the IBM culture, and why IBM still matters in a world seemingly dominated by Microsoft. Famous for his quote "the last thing IBM needs right now is a vision," Gerstner is credited with changing IBM into a highly successful and profitable services company.

Information Anxiety 2, by Richard Saul Wurman (Indianapolis: Que, 2001). This is a revised and updated version of Wurman's popular 1989 book, which foresaw the data clutter problem we now face. The style and organization are sometimes quirky, but the content is useful and thought-provoking. Wurman discusses the nature and value of information and offers advice about how to cope with the explosion of non-information—"stuff that doesn't inform."

The Soul of a New Machine, by Tracy Kidder (New York: Back Bay Books, 2000). This Pulitzer Prize–winning book provides a journalist's inside look at the making of a new computer in the late 1970s, including lots of insights into what makes computers (and computer people) tick. It's still a good read—and highly relevant—more than two decades after it was first published.

How Computers Work, Seventh Edition, by Ron White (Indianapolis: Que, 2003). The first edition of *How Computers Work* launched a successful series that inspired many imitators. Like its predecessor, this revised and expanded edition clearly illustrates with beautiful pictures and accessible prose how each component of a modern personal computer system works. If you're interested in looking under the hood, this is a great place to start. The explanations and illustrations are based on IBM-compatible computers, but most of the concepts apply to computers in general. A Windows-only CD-ROM includes a multimedia tour of a computer.

How the Mac Works, by John Rizzo and K. Daniel Clark (Indianapolis: Que, 2000). This book covers the basics of Macintosh anatomy in the same style as *How Computers Work* and includes Mac-related technologies such as Firewire, networks, and printing.

Personal Computers for Technology Students, by Charles Raymond (Upper Saddle River, NJ: Prentice Hall, 2001). This is a technical but readable text on the PC, from CPU to peripherals. It includes a useful glossary of acronyms, in case you ever need to know what SRAM or SVGA stands for.

Peter Norton's New Inside the PC, by Scott Clark, Peter Norton, and Scott H. A. Clark (Indianapolis: Sams, 2002). Norton's name is almost a household word among PC enthusiasts, many of whom consider Norton Utilities to be indispensable software. This book offers clear, detailed explanations of the inner workings of the PC, from CPU to peripherals, from hardware to software. You don't need to be a technical wizard to understand and learn from this book.

The Essential Guide to Computing: The Story of Information Technology, by E. Garrison Walters (Upper Saddle River, NJ: Prentice Hall, 2001). This is a highly readable and surprisingly broad overview of computer technology, with coverage of hardware, software, and networks. The book provides historical and industry perspectives along with solid technical information that goes beyond the usual introductory books.

Web Pages

Most computer hardware manufacturers have Web pages on the Internet. Use a Web browser to visit some of these sites for information about the latest hardware from these companies. It's not hard to guess the Web addresses of computer companies; most follow the pattern suggested by these examples:

http://www.apple.com
http://www.dell.com
http://www.ibm.com

The *Computer Confluence* Web site, http://www.computerconfluence.com, will guide you to these and other hardware pages of interest.

Multimedia

~ Interactive Computer Buyer's Guide

~ An interactive demonstration showing how monitors create color images

~ Additional activities on input devices and the evolution of digital storage devices

~ An interactive on disk storage

~ A video clip on buggy computers

~ Interactive self-study quizzes

~ Instant access to glossary and key word references

~ Interactive demonstrations showing how analog input is digitized

. . . and more.

 computerconfluence.com

Objectives

After you read this chapter you should be able to:

▶ **List several examples of input devices and explain how they can make it easier to get different types of information into the computer**

▶ **List several examples of output devices and explain how they make computers more useful**

▶ **Explain why a typical computer has different types of storage devices**

▶ **Diagram how the components of a computer system fit together**

CHAPTER 3

STEVE WOZNIAK, STEVE JOBS, AND THE GARAGE THAT GREW APPLES

What Steve Wozniak and all those other people failed to foresee was the personal computer revolution—a revolution that he helped start. Wozniak, a brilliant engineer called Woz by his friends, worked days as a calculator technician at Hewlett-Packard; he was refused an engineer's job because he lacked a college degree. At night, he designed and constructed a scaled-down computer system that would fit the home hobbyist's budget. When he completed it in 1975, he offered it to HP, but they turned it down.

Wozniak took his invention to the Homebrew Computer Club in Palo Alto, where it caught the imagination of another college dropout, Steve Jobs. A freethinking visionary, Jobs persuaded Wozniak to quit his job in 1976 to form a company born in Jobs'

It's **not** like we were all **smart enough** to see a **revolution coming** coming. Back then I thought there might be a revolution in **opening** your garage door, **balancing** your checkbook, **keeping** your recipes, that sort of thing. There are a **million people** who study markets and analyze economic trends, people who are **more brilliant than I am**, people who worked for companies like Digital Equipment and IBM and Hewlett-Packard. **None of them foresaw** what was going to happen either.

—*Steve Wozniak*

garage. They marketed the machine as the Apple I.

With the help and financial backing of A. C. Markkula, a businessman, the two Steves turned Apple into a thriving business. Wozniak created the Apple II, a more refined machine, and in the process, he invented the first personal computer disk operating system. Because it put computing power within the reach of individuals, the Apple II became popular in businesses, homes, and especially schools. Apple became the first company in American history to join the Fortune 500 in less than five years. Still in his mid-twenties, Jobs was running a corporate giant. But troubled times were ahead for Apple.

When IBM introduced its PC in 1982, it overshadowed Apple's presence in the business world, where people were accustomed to working with IBM main-

Hardware Basics
Peripherals

3.1 The original Apple I computer in its wooden case.

3.3 Steve Jobs eventually returned to the helm at Apple, where he introduced the best-selling iMac, iPod, iTunes Music Store, and other widely imitated products and services.

frames. Other companies developed PC clones, treating the IBM PC as a standard—a standard that Apple refused to accept. Inspired by a visit to Xerox's Palo Alto Research Center (PARC), Jobs worked with a team of Apple engineers to develop the Macintosh, a futuristic computer Jobs hoped would leapfrog IBM's advantage. When Jobs insisted on focusing most of Apple's resources on the Macintosh, Wozniak resigned to pursue other interests.

Businesses failed to embrace the Mac, and Apple stockholders grew uneasy with Jobs' controversial management style. In 1985, a year and a half after the Macintosh was introduced, Jobs was ousted. He went

on to form NeXT, a company that produced expensive workstations and software. He also bought Pixar, the computer animation company that later captured the public's attention with *Toy Story*, the first computer-generated full-length motion picture.

After Apple's fortunes declined under a string of CEOs, the company bought NeXT in 1997 and invited an older and wiser Jobs to retake the helm. He agreed to share his time between Pixar and Apple. Under his leadership, Apple has regained its innovative edge, releasing a flurry of elegant and trend-setting products. Although its share of the PC market is small, Apple retains a fanatically loyal customer base and now focuses mainly on the consumer, creative, and education markets. While Jobs continues to lead Apple and Pixar, Woz runs a wireless product design company called Wheels of Zeus (WOZ). ∿

3.2 Today, Steve Wozniak runs a wireless product design company called Wheels of Zeus.

The Apple II's phenomenal success wasn't due to a powerful processor or massive memory; the machine had at its core a relatively primitive processor and only 16K of memory. But the Apple II was more than a processor and memory; it included a keyboard, a monitor, and disk and tape drives for storage. While other companies sold computer kits to technical tinkerers, the two Steves delivered complete computer systems to hobbyists, schools, and businesses. They recognized that a computer wasn't complete without peripherals.

In this chapter, we'll complete the tour of hardware we started in the previous chapter. We've seen the CPU and memory at the heart of the system unit; now we'll explore the peripherals that radiate out from those central components. We'll start with input devices, then move on to output devices, and finish with a look at external storage devices. As usual, the main text provides the basic overview; if you want or need to know more about the inner workings, consult the How It Works boxes scattered throughout the chapter.

Input: From Person to Processor

The nuts and bolts of information processing are usually hidden from the user, who sees only the input and output, or as the pros say, *I/O*. This wasn't always the case. Users of the first computers communicated one bit at a time by flipping switches on massive consoles or plugging wires into switchboards; they had to be intimately familiar with the inner workings of the machines before they could successfully communicate with them. In contrast, today's users have a choice of hundreds of input devices that make it easy to enter data and commands into their machines. Of these input devices, the most familiar is the computer keyboard.

> A computer terminal is **not** some **clunky old** television with a typewriter in front of it. It is an **interface** where the **mind** and **body** can **connect** with the **universe** and **move bits** of it about.
>
> —*Douglas Adams, author of* The Hitchhiker's Guide to the Galaxy

The Keyboard

In spite of nearly universal acceptance as an input device, the QWERTY keyboard (named for the top row of letter keys) seems strangely out of place in a modern computer system. The weird arrangement of letters dates back to the earliest manual typewriters. The letter placement was chosen to reduce typing speed, making it less likely that a typist would hit two keys at the same time and cause the machine to jam. Technological traditions die hard, and the QWERTY keyboard became standard equipment on typewriters and later on virtually all PCs.

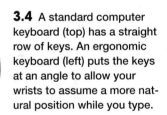

3.4 A standard computer keyboard (top) has a straight row of keys. An ergonomic keyboard (left) puts the keys at an angle to allow your wrists to assume a more natural position while you type.

Some modern computer keyboards stray from the traditional typewriter design, however. Typing on a standard keyboard, with keys lined up in straight rows, forces you to hold your arms and wrists at unnatural angles. Evidence suggests that long hours of typing this way may lead to medical problems, including repetitive-stress injuries, such as tendonitis and Carpal Tunnel Syndrome. Ergonomic keyboards place the keys at angles that are easier on your arms and hands without changing the ordering of the keys.

Whether it's straight or ergonomic, a typical keyboard sends signals to the computer through a cable of some sort. A *wireless keyboard* can send wireless signals (similar to

3.6 Some pocket computers have QWERTY keyboards even though they're too small for touch-typing.

3.5 This portable keyboard, designed for various Palm and Pocket PC handhelds, folds so that it can easily fit in your pocket.

those of a TV remote control, although modern keyboards use newer technology), so it isn't tethered to the rest of the system by a cable.

Other variations on keyboard design include folding keyboards for use with palm-sized computers, miniature keyboards built into pocket-sized devices, one-handed keyboards for people who need to (or prefer to) keep one hand free for other work, and keyboards printed on membranes that can be rolled or folded like paper. Innovative ideas are still emerging from that ancient typewriter technology.

Pointing Devices

Computer users today use their keyboards mostly to enter text and numeric data. For other traditional keyboard functions, such as sending commands and positioning the cursor, they typically use a mouse. The mouse is designed to move a pointer around the screen and point to specific characters or objects. Until recently, the most common type of mouse had a ball on its underside that allowed the user to roll it around on the desktop. But a newer type of mouse uses reflected light to detect movement. Either way, most mice have one or more buttons that the user can press to send signals to the computer, conveying messages such as "Perform this command," "Activate the selected tool," and "Select all the text between these two points." Many mice also include a scroll wheel between the two standard buttons.

It's virtually impossible to find a new computer today that doesn't come with a mouse as standard equipment, but there is one exception: The mouse is impractical as a pointing device on portable computers because these machines are often used where there's no room for a mouse to roam across a desktop. Portable computer manufacturers provide a variety of alternatives to the mouse as a general-purpose pointing device, and some of these devices are becoming popular as desktop solutions as well:

3.7 The most common type of computer mouse has two or more buttons. The Microsoft mouse (right) has multiple buttons and a scroll wheel to streamline the process of scrolling through documents or graphical windows. The Apple mouse has only a single button; in this mouse (left) the entire top surface of the mouse acts as a button.

- The touchpad (sometimes called *trackpad*) is a small flat panel that's sensitive to light pressure. The user moves the pointer by dragging a finger across the pad.
- The pointing stick (often called TrackPoint, IBM's brand name for the device) is a tiny handle that sits in the center of the keyboard, responding to finger pressure by moving the pointer in the direction in which you push it. It's like a miniature embedded joystick.
- The trackball resembles an upside-down mouse. It remains stationary while the user moves the large protruding ball to control the pointer on the screen. Trackballs are also available as an ergonomic mouse alternative for desktop machines.

Other pointing devices offer advantages for specific types of computer work (and play). Here are some examples:

- The joystick is a gearshift-like device that's a favorite controller for arcade-style computer games. Other gaming devices, like a game pad, racing wheel, and multifunction devices with multiple programmable buttons, help gamers become more immersed in different game types.
- The graphics tablet is popular with artists and designers. Most touch tablets are pressure sensitive, so they can send different signals depending on how hard the user presses on the tablet with a stylus. The *stylus* performs the same point-and-click functions as a mouse does. A similar screen used on Tablet PC devices uses a screen with an active digitizer to track a specially made stylus, letting users input data in their own handwriting.
- The touch screen responds when the user points to or touches different screen regions. Computers with touch screens are frequently used in public libraries, airports, and shopping malls, where many users are unfamiliar with computers. Touch screens are also used in many handheld computers, PDAs, and smart displays; a stylus can be used for pointing or writing on these small screens.

3.8 The Apple iBook (above left), like many portable computers, includes a built-in touchpad as a pointing device. The IBM ThinkPad (above center top) has a tiny pointing stick, called a TrackPoint, embedded in the center of its keyboard for moving the cursor on the screen. Some computer users choose to use a trackball (above center bottom) as a pointing device. Joysticks (above right) and game pads are often used by computer gamers. Some portable computers, like the Tablet PC (lower left), use a stylus as the pointing device. Touch-screen monitors are often used in kiosks, ATM machines, self-serve checkout stands in stores, and in home automation stations (lower right).

3.9 Computers use specialized input devices to read information stored as optical marks, bar codes, and specially designed characters.

Reading Tools

In spite of their versatility, pointing devices are woefully inefficient for the input of large quantities of text into computers, which is why the mouse hasn't replaced the keyboard on the standard personal computer. Still, there are alternatives to typing for entering numbers and words into computers. Some types of devices, specifically designed for computer input, allow computers to rapidly read marks that represent codes:

- **Optical mark readers** use reflected light to determine the location of pencil marks on standardized test answer sheets and similar forms.
- **Magnetic ink character readers** read those odd-shaped numbers printed with magnetic ink on checks.
- **Bar code readers** use light to read *universal product codes (UPCs)*, inventory codes, and other codes created from patterns of variable-width bars. In many stores, bar code readers are attached to **point-of-sale (POS) terminals**. These terminals send scanned information to a mainframe computer. The computer determines the item's price, calculates taxes and totals, and records the transaction for future use in inventory, accounting, and other areas.
- **Radio frequency identification (RFID) readers** use radio waves to communicate with **Radio frequency identification (RFID) tags**. When energized by a nearby RFID reader, an RFID tag broadcasts its unique identification number to the reader, which digitizes the information for input into a computer. An RFID tag can be as large as a deck of cards or as small as a grain of rice. Larger tags can be read from a greater distance. The hard plastic antitheft cards attached to clothes at department stores contain RFID tags. RFID tags are also used to identify railroad cars, automobiles at toll booths, library books at checkout counters, and pallets of goods being shipped to stores.

Because test forms, magnetic ink characters, bar codes, and RFID tags were designed to be read by computers, the devices that read them are extremely accurate. Reading text from books, magazines, and other printed documents is more challenging because of the great variety of printed text. **Optical character recognition (OCR)** is the technology of recognizing individual characters on a printed page, so they can be stored and edited as text.

Before a computer can recognize handwriting or printed text, it must first create a digital image of the page that it can

3.10 This self-service POS terminal uses three input devices for gathering information about a purchase: A touch screen for entering commands and answering questions, a bar code reader for scanning product information, and a scale for security and accuracy. Before the transaction is completed, another input device reads information encoded in the magnetic strip on the customer's credit card.

3.11 A pen scanner can capture text from a printed document and transfer it to a PC.

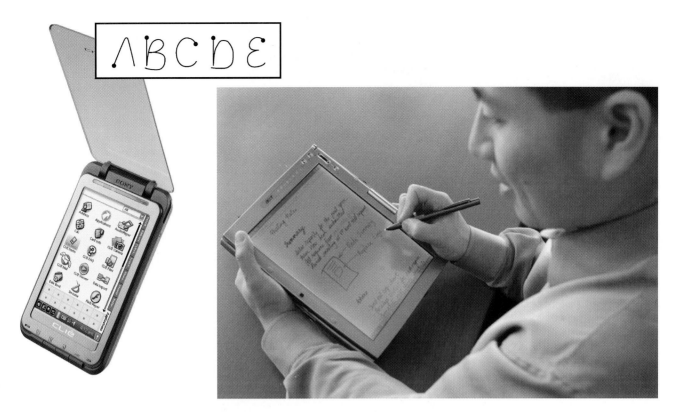

3.12 The Palm OS software uses the Graffiti system (above) to let users input single-stroke characters using a stylus. This type of input is used in devices like the Sony CLIE (left). The larger Tablet PC (right) is a full-fledged Windows XP notebook computer with stylus input capabilities.

store in memory. This is usually done with an input device known as a *scanner*. There are many types of scanners, as you'll see in the next section. A scanner doesn't actually read or recognize letters and numbers on a page—it just makes a digital "picture" of the page available to the computer. The computer can then use OCR software to interpret the black-and-white scanned patterns as letters and numbers.

Actually, a few special-purpose scanners take care of the OCR work themselves. *Pen scanners* look like highlighters, but they're actually wireless scanners that can perform character recognition on the fly. When you drag a pen scanner across a line of printed text, it creates a text file in its built-in memory, where it's stored until you transfer it into your computer's memory through a cable or infrared beam. A wireless pen scanner actually contains a small computer programmed to recognize printed text. This kind of optical character recognition isn't 100 percent accurate, but it's getting better all the time.

Handwriting recognition is far more difficult and error-prone than printed character recognition is. But handwriting recognition has many practical applications today, especially in **pen-based computers**, such as the Tablet PC. A pen-based computer can work without a keyboard and can accept input from a stylus applied directly to a flat-panel screen. The computer electronically simulates the effect of using a pen and pad of paper. **Handwriting recognition software** translates the user's handwritten forms into ASCII characters. In the past, such systems required users to modify their handwriting so that it was consistent and unambiguous enough for the software to decipher reliably, but Tablet PCs have dramatically increased the accuracy and efficiency of this machine type.

Personal digital assistants (PDAs) are handheld pen computers that serve as pocket-sized organizers, notebooks, appointment books, and communication devices. These popular, versatile devices can also be programmed for specialized work, ranging from sports scorekeeping to medical analysis. Newer models feature multimedia functionality, such as music playback and video and photo viewing.

3.13 A smart whiteboard can send its contents to a PC, simplifying and stream-lining the note-taking process for meetings and classes.

The . . . **number-one peripheral device** is not a drive. It's not a printer, scanner, hub, or network. It's you, the user.

—*John K. Rizzo and K. Daniel Clark, in* How the Mac Works

Handwriting recognition software can even be applied to notes scrawled on a whiteboard in a meeting room or class-room. A *smart whiteboard* can serve as an input device for a PC, so each board full of information is stored as a digital image on the computer's disk. If the writing is clear enough, handwriting recognition software can turn the whiteboard notes into a text file that can be emailed to meeting or class participants. (OCR and hand-writing recognition are covered in more detail in later chapters.)

Digitizing Devices

Before a computer can recognize hand-writing or printed text, a scanner or other input device must **digitize** the informa-tion—convert it into a digital form. Because real-world information comes in so many forms, a variety of input devices have been designed for capturing and dig-itizing information. In this section, we'll examine several of these devices, from common scanners to exotic sensors.

A **scanner** is an input device that can create a digital representation of a printed image. The most common models today are *flatbed scanners,* which look and work like photocopy machines, except that they create computer files instead of paper copies. Inexpensive flatbed scanners are designed for home and small business use. More expensive models used by graphics professionals are capable of producing higher-quality reproductions and, with attachments, scanning pho-tographic negatives and slides. Some scanners, called *slide scanners*, can scan only slides

3.14 Flatbed scanners (left) capture and digitize images from external paper sources, while slide and photo scanners (right) can reproduce photographs from slides and nega-tives. A slide scanner can produce high-quality digital reproductions from photographic negatives and slides.

3.15 Consumer cameras, like the one shown in the top-right photo, sell for a few hundred dollars or less; professional models, like the one in the top-left photo, cost much more. Many cell phones, like the one in the center, include picture- and movie-taking capabilities and can send these images to other phone users. Digital video cameras, like the one in the bottom-left photo, can deliver video directly to a PC or Macintosh. A Web cam, like the one shown in the lower-right photo, can continuously feed still pictures or video directly to an attached PC or Mac.

and negatives, but generally produce higher-quality results than flatbed scanners do when scanning transparencies. *Drum scanners* are larger and more expensive than flatbeds are; they're used in publishing applications where image quality is critical. At the other end of the spectrum, *sheetfed scanners* are small, portable, and inexpensive. Regardless of its type or capabilities, however, a scanner converts photographs, drawings, charts, and other printed information into bit patterns that can be stored and manipulated in a computer's memory, usually using graphics software.

In the same way, a **digital camera** can capture snapshots of the real world as digital images. Unlike a scanner, a digital camera isn't limited to capturing flat printed images; it can record anything that a normal camera can. A digital camera often looks like a normal camera. But instead of capturing images on film, a digital camera stores bit patterns on disks or other digital storage media.

A *video digitizer* is a collection of circuits that can capture input from a video camera, videocassette recorder, television, or other video source and convert it to a digital signal that can be stored in memory and displayed on computer screens. A *digital video camera* can send video signals directly into a computer without a video digitizer, because its video images are digitized when they're captured by the camera. Digital video input makes it possible for professionals and hobbyists and even consumers to edit videos with a computer. Digital video is also used for multimedia applications, such as Web page and CD-ROM development. And a growing number of businesses use video cameras and PCs for desktop *videoconferencing*. With videoconferencing software and hardware, people in diverse locations can see and hear each other while they conduct long-distance meetings; their video images are transmitted through networks. These video applications are discussed in more detail in later chapters.

How It **Works**

3.1 **Digitizing the Real World**

We live in an analog world, where we can perceive smooth, continuous changes in color and sound. Modern digital computers store all information as discrete binary numbers. To store analog information in a computer, we must digitize it—convert it from analog to digital form.

Digitizing involves using an input device, such as a digital camera or sound card, to take millions of tiny samples of the original image or sound. A sample of an image might be one pinpoint-sized area of the image;

each sample from an audio source is like a brief recording of the sound at a particular instant.

The value of a sample can be represented numerically and therefore stored on a computer. A representation of the original image or sound can be reconstructed by assembling all the samples in sequence.

In the example below, you can see how a digital camera and a microphone connected to a computer's sound card can capture photographs and sound recordings of a wolf.

Analog Input

A digital camera captures the wolf's image.

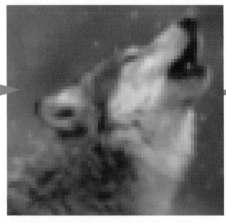

Inside the digital camera, the image is divided into a grid of tiny cells called pixels. Filters separate light into the three primary colors: red, blue, and green. A *charge-coupled device (CCD)* converts light into electrons. An *analog-to-digital converter (ADC)* converts the electrical charges into discrete values. A single byte (eight bits) represents the intensity of each primary color; a three-byte code represents the color of each pixel. After compression, the byte codes are stored as a JPEG file.

A microphone transmits the wolf's howl to a sound card inside the computer.

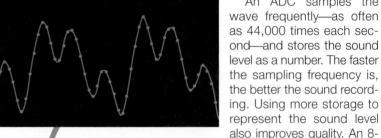

An ADC samples the wave frequently—as often as 44,000 times each second—and stores the sound level as a number. The faster the sampling frequency is, the better the sound recording. Using more storage to represent the sound level also improves quality. An 8-bit sample can represent 256 different levels; a 16-bit sample can represent 65,536 different levels.

A *digital signal processing (DSP)* chip compresses the stream of bits before it is transmitted to the CPU.

3.16

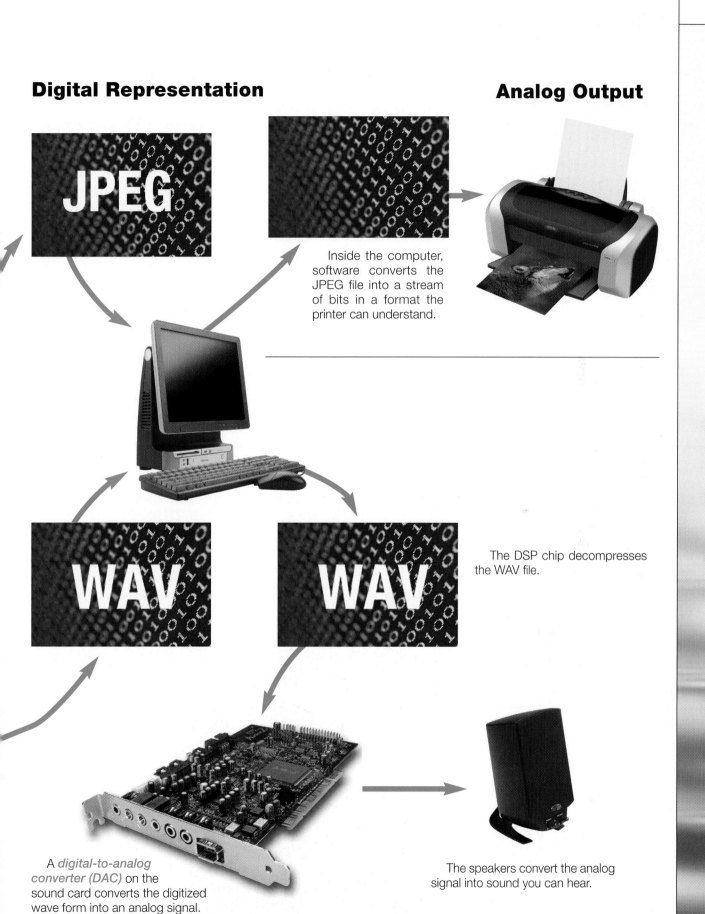

Digital Representation

Analog Output

JPEG

Inside the computer, software converts the JPEG file into a stream of bits in a format the printer can understand.

WAV

WAV

The DSP chip decompresses the WAV file.

A *digital-to-analog converter (DAC)* on the sound card converts the digitized wave form into an analog signal.

The speakers convert the analog signal into sound you can hear.

3.17 Speech recognition software allows this officer to record spoken notes without using a keyboard.

3.18 Sensors in this LifeShirt monitored life signs of this Indy Racing League driver when he crashed in the 2001 Indy 500.

Audio digitizers contain circuitry to digitize sounds from microphones and other audio devices. Digitized sounds can be stored in a computer's or PDA's memory and modified with software. Of course, audio digitizers can capture spoken words as well as music and sound effects. But digitizing spoken input isn't the same thing as converting speech into text. Like scanned text input, digitized *voice input* is just data to the computer. Speech recognition software, a type of artificial intelligence software, can convert voice data into words that can be edited and printed. *Speech recognition* software has been available for years, but until recently it wasn't reliable enough to be of much practical use. The latest products are still too limited to replace keyboards for most people. They generally must be trained to recognize individual voices. They typically require the speaker to articulate each word carefully, and they often work with only a limited vocabulary. Still, they're invaluable for people with disabilities and others who can't use their hands while they work. The promise and problems of automated speech recognition will be explored in later chapters.

Sensors designed to monitor temperature, humidity, pressure, and other physical quantities provide data used in robotics, environmental climate control, weather forecasting, medical monitoring, biofeedback, scientific research, and hundreds of other applications. Even our sense of smell can be simulated with sensors. Such sensors might soon be used to detect spoiled foods, land mines, chemical spills, or halitosis.

Computers can accept input from a variety of other sources, including manufacturing equipment, telephones, communication networks, and other computers. New input devices are being developed all the time as technologies evolve and human needs change. By stretching the computer's capabilities, these devices stretch our imaginations to develop new ways of using computers. We'll consider some of the more interesting and exotic technologies later; for now we turn our attention to the output end of the process.

Output: From Pulses to People

As a rule, men **worry more** about **what they can't see** than about what they can.

—*Julius Caesar*

A computer can do all kinds of things, but none of them is worth anything to us unless we have a way to get the results out of the box. Output devices convert the computer's internal bit patterns into a form that humans can understand. The first computers were limited to flashing lights, teletypewriters, and other primitive communication devices. Most computers today produce output through two main types of devices: display screens for immediate visual output and printers for permanent paper output.

Screen Output

The **display**, also called a **monitor**, serves as a one-way window between the computer user and the machine. Early computer displays were designed to display characters—text, numbers, and tiny graphic symbols. Today's displays are as likely to present graphics, photographic images, animation, and video as they are to display text and numbers. Because of the display's ever-expanding role as a graphical output device, computer users need to know a bit about the factors that control image size and quality.

Display size, like television size, is measured as the length of a diagonal line across the screen; a typical desktop display today measures from 15 to 21 inches diagonally, but the actual viewable area is often smaller. Images on a display are composed of tiny dots, called *pixels* (for picture elements). A square inch of an image on a display is typically a grid of dots about 96 pixels on each side. Such a monitor has a **resolution** of 96 dots per inch (dpi). The higher the resolution is, the closer together the dots and the clearer the image. Another

3.19 These four images show the same photograph displayed in four different bit depths: 1, 4, 8, and 24 bits.

way to describe resolution is to refer to the total number of pixels displayed on the screen. Assuming that two displays are the same size, the one that places the dots closer together displays more pixels and creates a sharper, clearer image. When describing resolution in this way, people usually indicate the number of columns and rows of pixels rather than the total number of pixels. For example, a 1,024 × 768 image is composed of 1,024 columns by 768 rows of pixels, for a total of 786,432 pixels.

Resolution isn't the only factor that determines image quality. Computer displays are limited by *color depth*—the number of different colors they can display at the same time. Color depth is sometimes called *bit depth*, because a wider range of colors per pixel takes up more bits of space in video memory. If each pixel is allotted 8 bits of memory, the resulting image can have up to 256 different colors on screen at a time. (There are 256 unique combinations of 8 bits to use as color codes.) In other words, 8-bit color, common in older PCs, has a color depth of 256. Most graphics professionals use 24-bit color, or *true color*, because it allows more than 16 million color choices per pixel—more than enough for photorealistic images. Older *monochrome monitors* can display only monochrome

3.20 Most desktop computers have historically used CRT monitors because they're inexpensive and they produce high-quality images at a variety of resolutions. However, sales of flat-panel LCD monitors are starting to surpass CRTs as their prices drop and image quality improves (right). LCDs are also used in projectors that allow computer screen images to be projected for large viewing audiences (left).

How It Works

3.2 Color Video

Like television sets, computer displays refresh or update their images many times per second. If a CRT monitor refreshes its image fewer than 70 times per second (70 hertz), the flicker may be enough to cause eyestrain, headaches, and nausea. Many CRT monitors slow down their refresh rates if the resolution is increased, so if you're shopping for a CRT monitor, buy one with a refresh rate of more than 70 hertz at the maximum resolution you expect to be using. Because flat-panel LCD displays don't refresh their images in the same way as CRT monitors, flicker is not an issue with these devices; most LCDs refresh at 60 hertz and have no flickering at all.

Another factor that should figure into your purchasing decision is the monitor's dot pitch—the measurement of how close the holes in the grid are to each other. The smaller the dot pitch, the closer the holes and the sharper the image.

1. The colors in some CRT video images glow because the monitor is a luminous source of light using additive color synthesis—colors are formed by adding different amounts of red, green, and blue light.

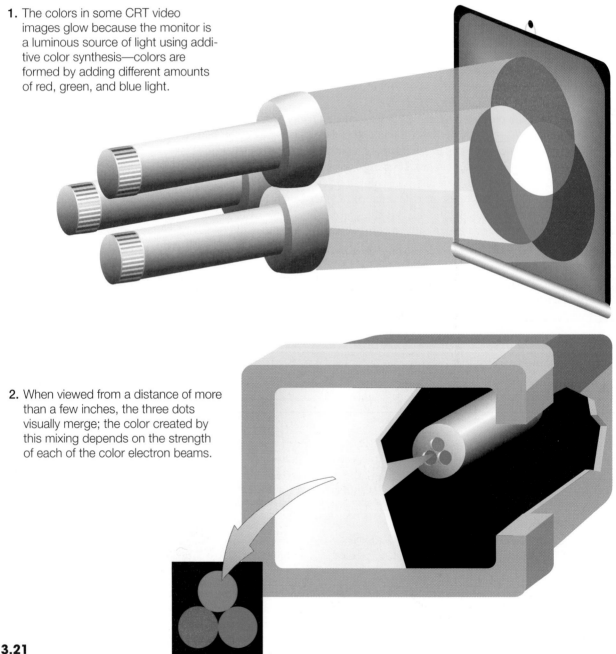

2. When viewed from a distance of more than a few inches, the three dots visually merge; the color created by this mixing depends on the strength of each of the color electron beams.

3.21

images. *Gray-scale monitors*, which can display black, white, and shades of gray but no other colors, and *color monitors*, which can display a range of colors, have greater color depth. A modern PC or Macintosh can portray different combinations of resolution and color depth on the same display.

The monitor is connected to the computer by way of the *video adapter*, which is typically a circuit board installed in a slot inside the main system unit. An image on the monitor exists inside the computer in video memory, or *VRAM*, a special portion of RAM on the video adapter dedicated to holding video images. The amount of VRAM determines the maximum resolution and color depth that a computer system can display. The more video memory a computer has, the more detail it can present in a picture.

Most displays fall into one of two classes: television-style **cathode-ray tube (CRT) monitors** and flat-panel **liquid crystal display (LCD) displays**. Once used primarily in portable computers, LCDs are dropping in price, and they are turning up on more and more desktops. LCD displays are now more popular than the older, bulky, CRT monitors. *Overhead projection panels* and *video projectors* also use LCDs to project computer screen images for meetings and classes.

Paper Output

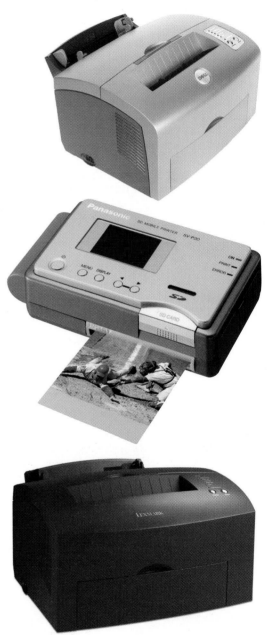

Output displayed on a monitor is immediate but temporary. A **printer** can produce a hard copy on paper of any static information that can be displayed on the computer's screen. Printers come in several varieties, but they all fit into two basic groups: *impact printers* and *nonimpact printers*.

Older **impact printers** include line printers and dot matrix printers. Printers of this type share one common characteristic: They form images by physically striking paper, ribbon, and print hammer together, the way a typewriter does. Mainframes use line printers to produce massive printouts; these speedy, noisy beasts hammer out thousands of lines of text per minute. You might have seen form letters from banks and stores, bills from utility companies, and report cards from schools that were printed with **line printers**. Because they're limited to printing characters, line printers are inadequate for applications such as desktop publishing in which graphics are essential.

Dot matrix printers print text and graphics with equal ease. Instead of printing each character as a solid object, a dot matrix printer uses pinpoint-sized hammers to transfer ink to the page.

Except for those applications, such as billing, where multipart forms need to be printed, **nonimpact printers** have replaced impact printers in most offices, schools, and homes. The two main types of nonimpact printers are laser printers and inkjet printers. **Laser printers** can quickly print numerous pages per minute of high-quality text and graphical output. Because of their speed, durability, and reliability, they're often shared between PCs in office environments. Laser printers use the same technology as photocopy machines: A laser beam creates patterns of electrical charges on a rotating drum; those charged patterns attract black toner and transfer it to paper as the drum rotates. Color laser printers can print multicolor images by mixing different toner shades.

People who work in color tend to use less-expensive **inkjet printers**, which spray ink directly onto paper to produce printed text and graphic images. Inkjets generally print fewer pages per minute than laser printers do. But high-quality color inkjet printers cost far less than color laser printers cost, and many are less expensive than the cheapest black-and-white laser printers are. Inkjet printers are also smaller and lighter than laser printers are. Portable inkjet printers designed to travel with laptops weigh only a couple of pounds each. Newer inkjet printers, often called **photo printers**, are specially optimized to print high-quality photos

3.22 An inkjet printer (top), a portable photo printer (center), and a laser printer (bottom) all provide different types of hard copy output.

How It **Works**

3.3 **Color Printing**

Printed colors can't be as vivid as video colors, because printed images don't produce light the way monitors do; they only reflect light. Most color printers use subtractive synthesis to produce colors: They mix various amounts of cyan (light blue), magenta (reddish purple), yellow, and black pigments to create a color.

Most printers, like monitors, are raster devices; they form images from little dots. The resolution of raster printers is normally measured in dots per inch (dpi). Printers have resolutions of hundreds—or even thousands—of dpi.

Matching on-screen color with printed color is difficult because monitors use additive color synthesis to obtain the color, whereas printers use subtractive synthesis. Monitors are able to display more colors than printers can, although printers can display a few colors that monitors can't. But the range of colors that humans can perceive extends beyond either technology.

You can demonstrate subtractive synthesis by painting overlapping areas of cyan, magenta, and yellow ink. The combination of all three is black; combinations of pairs produce red, green, and blue, which are secondary colors of the subtractive system.

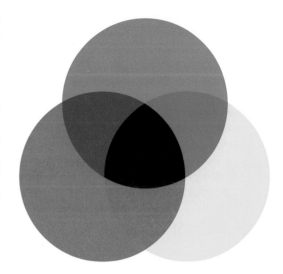

3.23

---

captured with digital cameras and scanners; these printouts are often indistinguishable from the photos you might order from a professional photo-printing service.

Both laser and inkjet printers produce output with much higher resolution—usually 600 or more dots per inch—than is possible with older dot matrix models. At these resolutions, it's hard to tell with the naked eye that characters are, in fact, composed of dots. Because of their ability to print high-resolution text and pictures, nonimpact printers dominate the printer market today.

Multifunction printers (MFP, also called *all-in-one devices*) take advantage of the fact that different tools can use similar technologies. A multifunction printer usually combines a scanner, a laser or inkjet printer, and a fax modem (described in the next section). Such a device can serve as a printer, a scanner, a color photocopy machine, and a fax machine.

For certain scientific and engineering applications, a **plotter** is more appropriate than a printer for producing hard copy. A plotter is an automated drawing tool that can produce large, finely scaled drawings, engineering blueprints, and maps by moving the pen and/or the paper in response to computer commands.

Fax Machines and Fax Modems

A **facsimile (fax) machine** is a fast and convenient tool for transmitting information stored on paper. When you send a fax of a paper document, the sending fax machine scans each page, converting the scanned image into a series of electronic pulses and sending those signals over phone lines to another fax machine. The receiving fax machine uses the signals to construct and print black-and-white facsimiles or copies of the original pages. In a sense, when combined, fax machines and telephone lines serve as a long-distance photocopy machine.

A computer can send on-screen documents through a fax modem to a receiving fax machine. The **fax modem** translates the document into

3.24 A multifunction printer combines a printer with a scanner and a fax modem so that it can print, scan, fax, and photocopy.

signals that can be sent over phone wires and decoded by the receiving fax machine. In effect, the receiving fax machine acts like a remote printer for the document. A computer can also use a fax modem to receive transmissions from fax machines, treating the sending fax machine as a kind of remote scanner. A faxed letter can be displayed on-screen or printed to paper, but it can't immediately be edited with a word processor the way an email message can. Like a scanned document, a digital facsimile is nothing more than a collection of black-and-white dots to the computer. Before a faxed document can be edited, it must be processed by optical character recognition (OCR) software.

Output You Can Hear

Most modern PCs include sound cards. A sound card enables the PC to accept microphone input, play music and other sound through speakers or headphones, and process sound in a variety of ways. (All Macintoshes and some PCs have audio circuitry integrated with the rest of the system, so they don't need separate sound cards.) With a sound card, a PC can play digital recordings of all kinds of sounds, from personal recordings made with the PC and a microphone to music downloaded from the Internet.

Most sound cards also include synthesizers—specialized circuitry designed to generate sounds electronically. These *synthesizers* can be used to produce music, noise, or anything in between. A computer also can be connected to a stand-alone music synthesizer so that the computer has complete control of the instrument. Computers can also generate synthesized speech with the right software. Of course, to produce any kind of sound, the computer needs to include or be attached to speakers or headphones.

3.25 Moby, like many modern musicians, uses computers and electronic synthesizers for composing and performing music.

Controlling Other Machines

In the same way that many input devices convert real-world sights and sounds into digital pulses, many output devices work in the other direction, taking bit patterns and turning them into nondigital movements or measurements. Robot arms, telephone switchboards, transportation devices, automated factory equipment, spacecraft, and a host of other machines and systems accept their orders from computers.

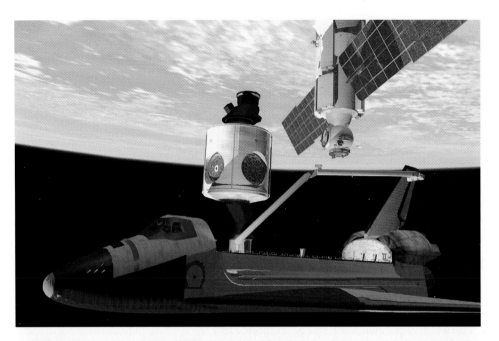

3.26 Using output devices that operate on similar principles, computers control the movements of spacecraft and virtual reality arcade games.

In one example familiar to computer gamers, an enhanced input device delivers output. The *force feedback joystick* can receive signals from a computer and give tactile feedback—jolts, scrapes, and bumps—that matches the visual output of the game or simulation. Many video arcades take the concept further by having the computer shake, rattle, and roll the gamer's chair while displaying on-screen movements that match the action. Output devices that generate synthetic smells are also beginning to appear. If these devices catch on, Web sites might commonly include smells as well as sights and sounds. While you're virtually visiting your favorite beach resort, you might smell synthetic surf, sand, and sunblock.

Of course, computers can send information directly to other computers, bypassing human interaction altogether. The possibilities for computer output are limited only by the technology and the human imagination, both of which are stretching further all the time.

Storage Devices: Input Meets Output

Some computer peripherals are capable of performing both input and output functions. These devices, which include tape and disk drives, are the computer's *storage devices*. They're sometimes referred to as *secondary storage* devices, because the computer's memory is its *primary storage*. Unlike RAM, which forgets everything when the computer is turned off, and ROM, which can't learn anything new, storage devices enable the computer to record information semipermanently so it can be read later by the same computer or by another computer.

> A **retentive memory** may be a good thing, but **the ability to forget** is the true token of greatness.
>
> —*Elbert Hubbard*

Magnetic Tape

Tape drives are common storage devices on most mainframe computers and some PCs. A tape drive can write data onto, and read data off of, a magnetically coated ribbon of tape. The reason for the widespread use of *magnetic tape* as a storage medium is clear: A magnetic tape can store massive amounts of information in a small space at a relatively low cost. The spinning tape reels that symbolized computers in so many old science fiction movies have for the most part been replaced by tape cartridges based on similar technology.

3.27 Tape back-up devices have replaced spinning tape reels as backup storage devices.

Magnetic tape has one clear limitation: Tape is a *sequential-access* medium. Whether a tape holds music or computer data, the computer must zip through information in the order in which it was recorded. Retrieving information from the middle of a tape is far too time-consuming for most modern computer applications, because people expect immediate response to their commands. As a result, magnetic tape is used today primarily for backing up data and a few other operations that aren't time-sensitive.

Magnetic Disks

Like magnetic tape, a *magnetic disk* has a magnetically coated surface that can store encoded information; a *disk drive* writes data onto the disk's surface and reads data from the surface. But unlike a tape drive, a *disk drive* can rapidly retrieve information from any part of a magnetic disk without regard for the order in which the information was recorded, in the same way you can quickly select any track on an audio compact disc. Because of their *random-access* capability, disks are the most popular media for everyday storage needs.

Many computer users are familiar with the 3.5-inch *disk* (also called *floppy disk*)—a small, magnetically sensitive, flexible plastic wafer housed in a

3.28 Internal hard drives and smaller microdrives are based on very similar technologies, despite the differences in size.

Working Wisdom

Ergonomics and Health

Along with the benefits of computer technology comes the potential for unwelcome side effects. For people who work long hours with computers, the side effects include risks to health and safety due to radiation emissions, repetitive-stress injuries, or other computer-related health problems. Inconclusive evidence suggests that low-level radiation emitted by CRT monitors and other equipment might cause health problems, including miscarriages in pregnant women and leukemia. The scientific jury is still out, but the mixed research results so far have led many computer users and manufacturers to err on the side of caution.

More concrete evidence relates keyboarding to occurrences of *repetitive-stress injuries,* such as *Carpal Tunnel Syndrome,* a painful affliction of the wrist and hand that results from repeating the same movements over long periods. Prolonged computer use also increases the likelihood of headaches, eyestrain, fatigue, and other symptoms of "techno-stress."

Ergonomics (sometimes called *human engineering*) is the science of designing work environments that enable people and things to interact efficiently and safely. Ergonomic studies suggest preventative measures you can take to protect your health as you work with computers:

➡ *Choose equipment that's ergonomically designed.* When you're buying computer equipment, look beyond functionality. Use Web site and magazine reviews, manufacturer's information, and personal research to check on health-related factors, such as monitor radiation and glare, disk-drive noise levels, and keyboard layout. Many computer users prefer flat-panel LCD monitors because they reduce eyestrain and radiation risks in addition to saving desk space. A growing number of computer products, such as split, angled ergonomic keyboards, are specifically designed to reduce the risk of equipment-related injuries.

➡ *Create a healthy workspace.* Keep the paper copy of your work at close to the same height as your screen. Position your monitor and lights to minimize glare. Sit at arm's length from your monitor to minimize radiation risks.

➡ *Build flexibility into your work environment.* Whenever possible work with an adjustable chair, an adjustable table, an adjustable monitor, and a removable keyboard. Change your work position frequently.

➡ *Rest your eyes.* Look up from the screen periodically and focus on a faraway object or scene. Blink frequently. Take a 15-minute break from using a CRT monitor every two hours.

➡ *Stretch.* While you're taking your rest break, do some simple stretches to loosen tight muscles. Occasional stretching of the muscles in your arms, hands, wrists,

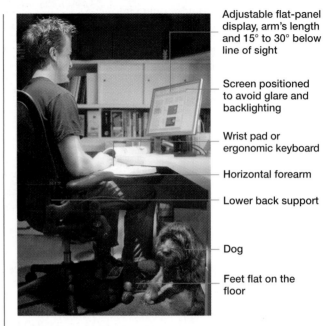

Adjustable flat-panel display, arm's length and 15° to 30° below line of sight

Screen positioned to avoid glare and backlighting

Wrist pad or ergonomic keyboard

Horizontal forearm

Lower back support

Dog

Feet flat on the floor

3.29a A healthy workspace can reduce the chances of developing computer-related injuries.

back, shoulders, and lower body can make hours of computer work more comfortable and less harmful.

➡ *Listen to your body.* If you feel uncomfortable, your body is telling you to change something or take a break. Don't ignore it. Ergonomic keyboards, such as the split, angled keyboard, allow computer users to hold their hands and arms in more natural positions while typing to reduce the risk of repetitive-stress injuries.

➡ *Seek help when you need it.* If your wrists start hurting when you work, you have persistent headaches, or you are feeling some other problem that may be related to excessive computer work, talk to a professional. A medical doctor, chiropractor, physical therapist, or naturopath may be able to help you to head off the problem before it becomes chronic.

3.29b This unusual keyboard is designed to minimize strain on wrists and possibility of injury.

plastic case. The disk was once routinely used for transferring data files between machines, though their limited capacity—typically just 1.44MB—and slow speed make them less useful today. Today, Macintoshes and some PCs no longer include disk drives as standard equipment.

Virtually all PCs include hard disks as their main storage devices. A **hard disk** is a rigid, magnetically sensitive disk that spins rapidly and continuously inside the computer chassis or in a separate box connected to the computer housing. This type of hard disk is usually not removed by the user. Information can be transferred to and from a hard disk much faster than from a floppy disk. A hard disk might hold hundreds of gigabytes (thousands of megabytes) of information—more than enough room for every word and picture in this book, an entire music collection, several movie-length video clips, and years of photographs.

To fill the gap between low-capacity, slow disks and nonremovable, fast hard disks, manufacturers have developed high-capacity transportable storage solutions. There are many choices beyond disks in **removable cartridge media**. The most popular is the *Zip disk*, developed by Iomega. A Zip disk looks like a thicker version of a standard disk. The most common Zip disks can hold up to 100MB of data; a newer variety can hold up to 750MB. Zip drives cannot read or write standard floppy disks, even though they use a similar technology. Zip disks, like floppy disks, are declining in popularity today because of advances in optical disc storage technology.

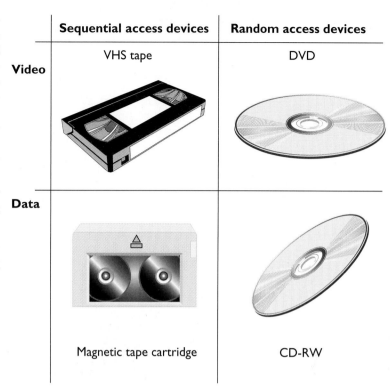

	Sequential access devices	**Random access devices**
Video	VHS tape	DVD
Data	Magnetic tape cartridge	CD-RW

3.30 Home theater systems include sequential-access devices—VHS tape decks—and random-access devices—DVD players. The advantages of random access are the same for stereos as for computers.

Optical Discs

An **optical disc drive** uses laser beams rather than magnets to read and write bits of data on a reflective aluminum layer of the disk. A transparent plastic disc surface protects the aluminum layer from routine physical damage while letting laser light through. Access speeds are slower for optical discs than for magnetic hard disks.

While optical discs are generally reliable for long-term storage, they can deteriorate. A severe scratch in the plastic coating can allow air to reach the aluminum layer, leading to oxidation and a loss of information. Surprisingly, the upper surface of the disc (with the label) is more sensitive to scratching than the lower surface, because the protective plastic layer is thinner on that side.

From CD-ROM to DVD-R/CD-RW, there's an alphabet soup of choices in optical disc drives for PCs today. The names can be especially confusing because they aren't consistent. Does R stand for Read, Recordable, Rewriteable, or Random? It depends on the context. Many of these drive types will undoubtedly fall by the wayside as the cost of the expensive all-purpose drives comes down. But until then, it's helpful to know something about these oddly named devices.

The most common optical drive in computers is the **CD-ROM drive**. A CD-ROM drive can read data from **CD-ROM** (compact disc—read-only memory) discs—data disks that are physically identical to music compact discs. The similarity of audio and data CDs is no accident; it makes it possible for CD-ROM drives to play music CDs under computer control. A CD-ROM can hold up to about 800MB of data—more raw text than you could type in your lifetime. But because CD-ROM drives are read-only devices, they can't be used as

How It Works

3.4 Disk Storage

MAGNETIC DISKS

Both hard disks and floppy disks are coated with a magnetic oxide similar to the material used to coat cassette tapes and videotapes. The read/write head of a disk drive is similar to the record/play head on a tape recorder; it magnetizes parts of the surface to record information. The difference is that a disk is a digital medium—binary numbers are read and written. The typical hard disk consists of several *platters*, each accessed via a read/write head on a movable *armature*. The magnetic signals on the disk are organized into concentric tracks; the tracks in turn are divided into sectors. This is the traditional scheme used to construct addresses for data on the disk.

Hard disks spin much faster than floppy disks do and have a higher storage density (number of bytes per square inch). The *read/write head* of a hard disk glides on a thin cushion of air above the disk and never actually touches the disk.

CD-ROM

A CD-ROM drive contains a small laser that shines on the surface of the disk, "reading" the reflections. Audio CDs and computer CD-ROMs have similar formats; that's why you can play an audio CD with a CD-ROM drive. Information is represented optically—the bottom surface of the CD, under a protective layer of plastic, is coated with a reflective metal film. A laser burns unreflective pits into the film to record data bits. After a pit is burned, it can't be smoothed over and made shiny again; that's why CD-ROMs are read-only.

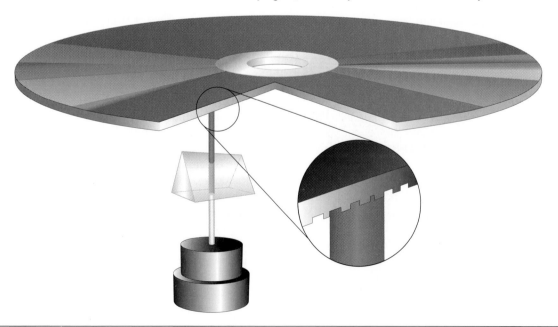

3.31

DVD-ROM

A DVD-ROM drive works on the same principle as a CD-ROM drive does; the main difference is that the pits are packed much closer together on a DVD, so about seven times as many can fit on the disk surface. (To read these tightly packed bits, the DVD-ROM uses a narrower laser beam.) A DVD can hold even more data—up to 8.5GB—if it has a second layer of data. On a layered DVD, the top layer is semireflective, allowing a second readback laser to penetrate to the layer below. The laser can "see through" the top layer, just as you can see through a picket fence when you look at it from exactly the right angle. For truly massive storage jobs, a DVD can have data on both sides—up to 17GB. Two-sided DVDs usually have to be turned over for the reader to read both sides; future drives may use additional readback lasers to read the second side without flipping the disk.

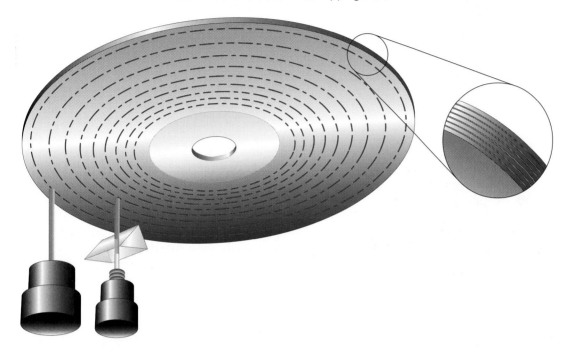

RECORDABLE CD AND DVD DRIVES

Recordable CD and DVD drives use laser beams to write data on recordable disks. But recordable optical media have layers with chemical structures that react to different temperatures created by different types of lasers. To write data, a high-intensity laser beam produces high temperatures that break down the crystalline structure of the original surface. The resulting pits dissipate, rather than reflect, low-level lasers during the process of reading recorded data. To erase data, a laser heats the pits to about 400 degrees, causing them to revert to their original reflective crystalline state.

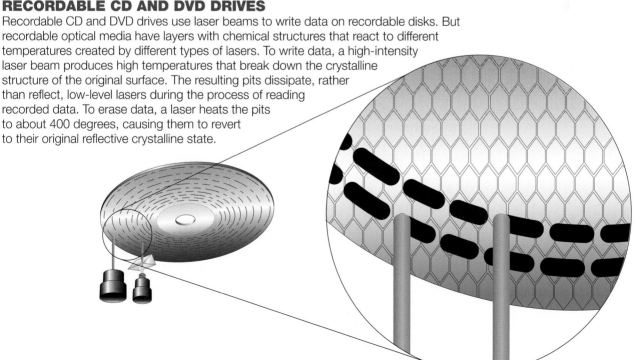

storage devices. Instead, they're mostly used to read commercially pressed CD-ROMs containing everything from business applications to multimedia games and reference libraries.

Many PCs now include **CD-RW drives** (sometimes referred to as *CD-R/RW drives*) instead of CD-ROM drives. Like a CD-ROM drive, a CD-RW drive can read data from CD-ROMs and play music from audio CDs. But a CD-RW drive can also *burn*, or record, data onto CD-R and CD-RW disks.

CD-R (compact disc—recordable) disks are *WORM* (write-once, read-many) media. That is, a drive can write onto a blank (or partially filled) CD-R disk, but it can't erase the data after it's burned in. CD-Rs are commonly used to make archival copies of large data files, back-up copies of software CDs, and personal music CDs. They're also useful for creating master copies of CD-ROMs and audio CDs for professional duplication.

CD-RW (compact disc—rewritable) discs are more expensive than CD-R media, but they have the advantage of being erasable. A drive can write, erase, and rewrite a CD-RW disk repeatedly. Some people use CD-RW disks instead of removable cartridge media for storing, transporting, and backing up large quantities of data.

CD-RW drives are advertised with three different speeds: a speed for *burning* (writing) CD-Rs, a speed for writing CD-RWs, and a much faster speed for reading CD-ROMs. All three *data transfer rates* are expressed as multiples of 150K per second, the speed of the original CD-ROM drives. A typical drive might have maximum speeds specified as 52X/24X/52X. Actual drives speeds don't always measure up to these values, and even the fastest CD-RW drives are pokey compared to a magnetic hard drive.

3.32 A CD-RW drive can read CD-ROMs, play audio CDs, and burn audio and data CDs using recordable and rerecordable discs.

Several types of DVD drives are also used as replacements for CD-ROM drives in PCs. The **DVD** is the same size as a standard CD-ROM, but can hold between 4.7 and 17GB of information, depending on how the information is stored. DVD originally stood for *digital video disc*, because the discs were designed to replace VHS tapes in video stores. Today, many people say DVD stands for *digital versatile discs*, because these high-capacity discs are used to store and distribute all kinds of data.

DVD-ROM drives can play DVD movies, read DVD data discs, read standard CD-ROMs, and play audio CDs. But because they're read-only, they can't record data, music, or movies.

A combination *DVD/CD-RW drive* offers the advantages of a DVD-ROM drive and a CD-RW drive in a single unit that can play DVD movies and audio CDs, record and erase data on CD-RW disks, and burn audio CDs and CD-ROMs. But this type of drive can't record movies or other large files on blank DVDs; it can only record on CD-R and CD-RW media. For that functionality, you need a recordable DVD drive. Unfortunately, manufacturers haven't yet agreed on a single standard for these drives, so choosing a drive can be confusing.

DVD-RAM drives can read, erase, and write data (but not DVD video) on multigigabyte *DVD-R* (but not CD-R or CD-RW) media. A *DVD-RW drive* can read all the standard CD and DVD disc types and record on CD-R, CD-RW, DVD-R (recordable) and *DVD-RW* (rewritable) media. (Apple refers to its DVD-R drive as the SuperDrive.) A competing standard, the *DVD+RW drive*, can read all the standard CD and DVD disc types and record on CD-R, CD-RW, *DVD+R* (recordable) and *DVD+RW* (rewritable) media. And an emerging new standard, *DVD+MRW* (also called *Mt. Rainier*), offers similar functionality. Some companies, including Sony, have released combination drives that support both

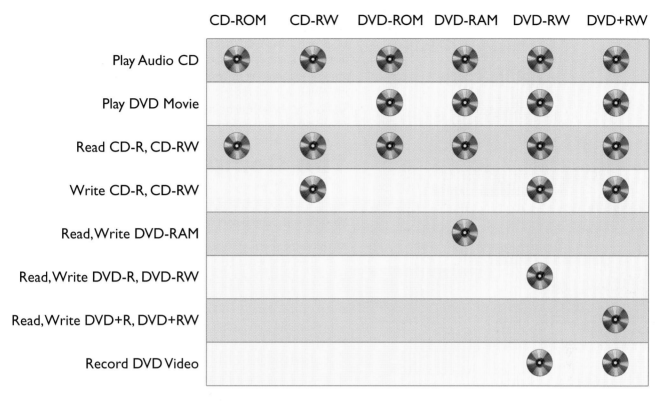

	CD-ROM	CD-RW	DVD-ROM	DVD-RAM	DVD-RW	DVD+RW
Play Audio CD	●	●	●	●	●	●
Play DVD Movie			●	●	●	●
Read CD-R, CD-RW	●	●	●	●	●	●
Write CD-R, CD-RW		●			●	●
Read, Write DVD-RAM				●		
Read, Write DVD-R, DVD-RW					●	
Read, Write DVD+R, DVD+RW						●
Record DVD Video					●	●

3.33 This chart summarizes the common features of several optical disc formats.

DVD-RW and DVD+RW media. With the right software, most of these recordable DVD drives can be used to create DVD videos that you can play on DVD movie players.

Solid-State Storage Devices

Until recently, disk drives were the only realistic random-access storage devices for most computer applications. In spite of their popularity, disk drives present problems for today's computer users. The moving parts in disk drives are more likely to fail than other computer components. For airline travelers and others who must depend on battery power for long periods of time, spinning disk drives consume too much energy. Disk drives can be noisy—a problem for musicians and others who use computers for audio applications. And disk drives are bulky when compared with computer memory; they're often not practical for palm-sized computers and other applications where space is tight and battery life is at a premium.

Flash memory is a type of erasable memory chip that can serve as a reliable, low-energy, quiet, compact alternative to disk storage. Until recently, flash memory was too expensive for most storage applications. But flash memory today has many practical applications. Some flash memory devices are designed for specific applications, such as storing pictures in digital cameras and transferring them to PCs for editing. Sony's Memory Stick is an all-purpose digital storage card about the size of a stick of gum. *USB flash drives* are becoming popular for storing

3.34 USB flash drives can store up to hundreds of megabytes of data; they plug into a computer's USB port. This Swiss Army knife has a built-in USB flash memory device.

3.35 This CompactFlash card represents one of the most popular kinds of solid-state storage used in digital cameras and other digital media devices.

and transporting data files. These tiny devices typically hold less data than CD-ROM discs do and plug directly into the computer's USB port (discussed later in this chapter.) Most experts believe that flash memory or some other type of solid-state storage technology—storage with no moving parts—will eventually replace disk and tape storage in computers and other digital devices. Today, most flash memory devices ship in sizes ranging from 16MB all the way up to 1GB.

The Computer System: The Sum of Its Parts

Most personal computers fall into one of four basic design classes:

- *Tower systems*—tall, narrow boxes that generally have more expansion slots and bays than other designs
- Flat *desktop systems* (sometimes called "pizza box" systems) designed to sit under the monitor like a platform
- *All-in-one systems* (like the iMac) that combine monitor and system unit into a single housing
- *Portable computers*, which include all the essential components, including keyboard and pointing device, in one compact box

Whatever the design, a PC must allow for the attachment of input, output, and storage peripherals. That's where slots, ports, and bays figure in. Now that we've explored the peripherals landscape, we can look again at the ways of hooking those peripherals into the system.

Ports and Slots Revisited

The computer is by all odds the most **extraordinary** of the **technological clothing** ever devised by man, since it is an **extension** of our **central nervous system**. Beside it **the wheel is a mere hula hoop** . . .

—*Marshall McLuhan, in* War and Peace in the Global Village

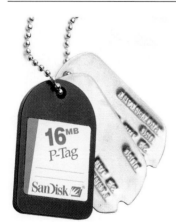

3.36 This flash memory card is small enough to wear on a wristband and contains enough information to save a life in an emergency

The system board, or motherboard, of a computer system generally includes several ports, some of which are now considered *legacy ports*, because the most common ports on system boards have been standard on PCs for years. They include the following:

- A *serial port* for attaching a modem or other device that can send and receive messages one bit at a time
- A *parallel port* for attaching a printer or other device that communicates by sending or receiving bits in groups, rather than sequentially
- *Keyboard/mouse ports* for attaching a keyboard and a mouse

Other ports are typically included on expansion boards rather than on the system board:

- A *video port* for plugging a color monitor into the video board
- *Microphone, speaker, headphone, and musical instrument digital interface (MIDI)* ports for attaching sound equipment to the sound card

All of these ports follow interface standards agreed on by the hardware industry so that devices made by one manufacturer can be attached to systems made by other companies. The downside of industry standards is that they can sometimes hold back progress. For example, today's color printers are often kept waiting by the pokey parallel port.

Computer manufacturers and owners use expansion cards to get around the limitations of these standard ports. For example, many modern computers include an internal *modem* in an expansion slot; this modem card adds a standard phone jack as a communication port. For faster connection to a local-area network (LAN), most modern PCs include a *network card* that adds a LAN port. For faster communication with external drives, scanners, and other peripherals, a PC might include a small computer systems interface (*SCSI*, pronounced "scuzzy") card that adds a SCSI port to the back of the system box. SCSI is becoming less common, however, as standard hard-drive technology improves.

Internal and External Drives

Disk drives generally reside in *bays* inside the system unit. A new PC often includes a floppy disk drive in one bay, a hard drive in another, and some kind of CD or DVD drive in a third bay. Some PCs have extra bays for additional internal hard drives or removable media. Tall tower models generally have more expansion bays than flat desktop systems designed to sit under monitors do. But even if there's no room in the system unit for additional internal drives, external drives can be connected to the system through ports.

Most portable computers are too small to include three drive bays. But some models have bays that enable you to swap drives. For example, you might remove the CD-ROM drive from a laptop and insert a floppy disk drive or extra battery. Some models enable you to **hot swap** devices—remove and replace them without powering down. All portables enable you to attach external peripherals through ports. Some portables can be plugged into docking stations that contain, or are attached to, all the necessary peripherals. When docked, a portable can function like a desktop computer, complete with large-screen monitor, full-sized keyboard, mouse, sound system, and a variety of other peripherals.

3.37 This rear view of a tower system unit shows several ports, including some (below) that are included in add-on-boards in slots. (Courtesy of: © 2004 Gateway, Inc., used with permission.)

Expansion Made Easy

It's clear that the *open architecture* of the PC—the design that enables you to add expansion cards and peripherals—gives it flexibility and longevity that it wouldn't have otherwise. Many hobbyists have been using the same computer system for years; they just swap in new cards, drives, and even CPUs and motherboards to keep their systems up to current standards. But most computer users today prefer to use their computers, not take them apart. Fortunately, new interface standards are emerging that will enable casual computer users to add the latest and greatest devices to their systems without cracking the box.

A **USB**, or *universal serial bus*, can transmit data at approximately 11 megabits per second (Mbps)—roughly 100 times faster than the PC serial port—and a newer, faster version called *USB 2.0* is even faster, offering transfer rates of 480Mbps. Theoretically, up to 126 devices, including keyboards, mice, digital cameras, scanners, and storage devices, can be chained together from a single USB port. USB devices can be hot swapped, so the system instantly recognizes the presence of a new device when it is plugged in. And USB is *platform independent*, so USB devices can often work on both PCs and Macintoshes. In fact, this paragraph is being typed on a keyboard that's shared by a PC and a Mac through a USB hub. All new PCs and Macintoshes include several USB or USB 2.0 ports. In time, computer manufacturers may phase out other ports made unnecessary by USB's presence. Some produce *legacy-free PCs* that cost less because they use USB ports instead of older serial, parallel, keyboard, mouse, and SCSI ports.

Another interface standard that shows promise is **FireWire**, a high-speed connection standard developed by Apple. Some PC makers refer to FireWire by the less friendly designation, *IEEE 1394*, assigned by the Institute of Electrical and Electronics Engineers when they approved it as a standard. (Sony calls its version iLink.) FireWire can move data between devices at 400Mbps—far faster than most peripheral devices

3.38 This tower system has its side panel removed so you can see the storage bays containing disk drives (top left) and the expansion boards inserted into slots (lower right). (Courtesy of: © 2004 Gateway, Inc., used with permission.)

Working Wisdom

Computer Consumer Concepts

> The best computer for your specific needs is the one that will come on the market **immediately after** you actually purchase some other model.
>
> —*Dave Barry, humorist*

This book's appendix, CD-ROM, and Internet Web site contain specific information about the nuts and bolts of buying hardware and software to make your own computer system. Of course, any brand-specific advice on choosing computer equipment is likely to be outdated within a few months of publication. Still, some general principles remain constant while the technology races forward. Here are some consumer criteria worth considering, even if you have no intention of buying your own computer:

➡ **Cost.** Buy what you can afford, but be sure to allow for extra memory, extended warranties, peripherals (printer, extra storage devices, modem, cables, speakers, and so on), and software. If you join a user group or connect to an online shareware site, you'll be able to meet some of your software needs at low (or no) cost. But you'll almost certainly need some commercial software too. Don't be tempted to copy copyrighted software from your friends or public labs; software piracy is theft, prosecutable under federal laws. (Choosing software isn't easy, but many periodicals and Web sites publish regular reviews to help you sort out the best programs.)

➡ **Capability.** Is it the right tool for the job? Buy a computer that's powerful enough to meet your needs. Make sure the processor is fast enough to handle your demands. If you want to take advantage of state-of-the-art multimedia programs, consider only machines that meet the latest standards. If you want to create state-of-the-art multimedia programs, you'll need a powerful computer that can handle audio and video input as well as output—FireWire (IEEE 1394) if you'll be using a digital video camera. Be sure the machine you buy can do the job you need it to do, now and in the foreseeable future.

➡ **Capacity.** If you plan to do graphic design, publishing, or multimedia authoring, make sure your machine has enough memory and disk storage to support the resource-intensive applications you'll need. Consider adding removable media drives for backing up and transporting large files.

➡ **Customizability.** Computers are versatile, but they don't all handle all jobs with equal ease. If you'll be using word processors, spreadsheets, and other mainstream software packages, just about any computer will do. If you have off-the-beaten-path needs (advanced video editing, instrument monitoring, and so on), choose a system with enough slots and ports to enable it to be extended for your work.

➡ **Compatibility.** Will the software you plan to use run on the computer you're considering? Most popular computers have a good selection of compatible software, but if you have specific needs, such as being able to take your software home to run on Mom's computer,

study the compatibility issue carefully. Total compatibility isn't always possible or necessary. A typical Windows-compatible computer, for example, will probably not run every "Windows-compatible" program. Many people don't care if all their programs will run on another kind of computer; they just need data compatibility—the ability to move documents back and forth between systems on disk or through a network connection. It's common, for example, for Windows users and Macintosh users to share documents over a network.

➡ **Connectivity.** In today's networked world, it's short-sighted to see your computer as a self-contained information appliance. Make sure you include a high-speed modem and/or network connection in your system so you can take full advantage of the communication capabilities of your computer.

➡ **Convenience.** Just about any computer can do most common jobs, but which is the most convenient for you? Do you value portability over having all the peripherals permanently connected? Is it important to you to have a machine that's easy to install and maintain so you can take care of it yourself? Or do you want to choose the same kind of machine as the people around you so you can get help easily when you need it? Which user interface makes the kind of work you'll be doing easiest?

➡ **Company.** If you try to save money by buying an off-brand computer, you may find yourself the owner of an orphan computer. High-tech companies can vanish overnight. Make sure you'll be able to get service and parts down the road.

➡ **Curve.** Most personal computer models seem to have a useful life span of just a few years—if they survive the first year or two. If you want to minimize financial risk, avoid buying a computer during the first year of a model's life, when it hasn't been tested on the open market. Also avoid buying a computer that's over the hill; you'll know it because most software developers will have abandoned this model for greener CPUs. In the words of eighteenth-century British poet Alexander Pope, "Be not the first by whom the new are tried, nor yet the last to lay the old aside."

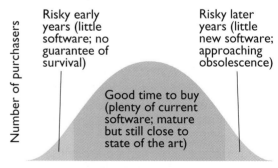

Computer consumer's curve

Number of purchasers

Risky early years (little software; no guarantee of survival)

Risky later years (little new software; approaching obsolescence)

Good time to buy (plenty of current software; mature but still close to state of the art)

0–1 year   Age of computer model   3–6 years

3.39

can handle it. This high speed makes it ideal for working with data-intensive applications such as digital video. Most modern digital video cameras have FireWire ports, so they can be connected directly to 1394-equipped PCs. Like USB, FireWire allows multiple devices to be connected to the same port and to be hot swapped. FireWire can also supply power to peripherals so they don't need an external power supply. Because of its speed and versatility, FireWire is expected to be standard equipment on all new PCs soon. A newer version, *FireWire 800*, was recently introduced on Macintosh systems. This new version of FireWire offers 800Mbps transfer speeds. (Apple now refers to the comparatively pokey FireWire as FireWire 400.)

Putting It All Together

A typical computer system might have several different input, output, and storage peripherals. From the computer's point of view, it doesn't matter which of these devices is used at any given time. Each input device is just another source of electrical signals; each output device is just another place to send signals; each storage device is one or the other, depending on what the program calls for. Read from here, write to there—the CPU doesn't care; it dutifully follows instructions. Like a stereo receiver, the computer is oblivious to which input and output devices are attached and operational, as long as they're compatible.

3.40 A typical desktop computer system includes a computer, a display, and several peripheral devices.

Networks: Systems Without Boundaries

Unlike a stereo system, which has clearly defined boundaries, a computer system can be part of a network that blurs the boundaries between computers. When computers are connected in a network, one computer can, in effect, serve as an input device for another computer, which serves as an output device for the first computer. Networks can include hundreds of different computers, each of which might have access to all peripherals on the system. Many public and private networks span the globe by taking advantage of satellites, fiber-optic cables, and other communication technologies. Using a modem, a computer can connect to a network through an ordinary phone line. The rise in computer networks is making it more difficult to draw lines between individual computer systems. If you're connected to the Internet, your computer is, in effect, just a tiny part of a global system of interconnected networks. We'll take a closer look at networks in Chapter 8.

Software: The Missing Piece

In the span of a few pages, we've surveyed a mind-boggling array of computer hardware, but, in truth, we've barely scratched the surface. Nonetheless, all this hardware is worthless without software to drive it. In the next few chapters, we'll take a look at the software that makes a computer system come to life.

Inventing the FUTURE

Tomorrow's Peripherals

> You can count how many **seeds are in the apple**, but not how many **apples are in the seed**.
>
> —*Ken Kesey, author of*
> *One Flew over the Cuckoo's Nest*

Silicon chips aren't the only parts of computers that are evolving. Here's a sampler of peripheral technologies that are making their way from research labs into products.

TOMORROW'S STORAGE

The trend of smaller disks that hold more will continue, resulting in tiny hard disks that can store astronomical quantities of data. But solid-state storage breakthroughs will threaten the dominance of disks in a few years. For example, Cambridge University researchers funded by Hitachi have developed a single-electron memory chip the size of a thumbnail that can store all the sounds and images of a full-length feature film. This experimental chip consumes very little power and retains memory for up to 10 years when the power is switched off.

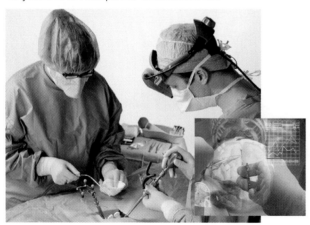

3.41a This surgeon's retinal scanner display makes video images and the patient's vital signs continually visible throughout the surgical procedure.

TOMORROW'S OUTPUT

Flat-panel screens are replacing desktop CRTs at an ever-increasing rate. Soon we'll be using ultra-high-resolution displays that are thin enough to hang on walls like pictures and efficient enough to run on batteries for days. LCD goggle displays—the visual equivalent to headphones—may soon be common for portable PC users who want to shut the rest of the world out. Those who need to see what's going on around them and inside their computer can wear eyeglasses with built-in transparent heads-up displays. Researchers at the University of Washington have developed a *retinal display* that works without a screen; it shines a focused beam of light through the wearer's pupil, moving across the field of vision to draw pixels directly on the retina. Fighter pilots, neurosurgeons,

and people with limited vision are using these displays to see critical computer data without taking their eyes off of their work. We may eventually see these displays attached to PDAs and mobile phones.

3.41b This page of electronic paper is being reloaded with a fresh image.

TOMORROW'S INPUT: SENSORS

Technology forecaster Paul Saffo predicts that the next major breakthroughs will occur as researchers develop—and companies market—inexpensive sensors that enable digital devices to monitor the analog world. Temperature sensors, optical sensors, motion sensors, and other types of sensors already make it possible for computers to track a variety of real-world activities and conditions. But as these technologies mature, more sophisticated devices will serve as eyes, ears, and other types of sense organs for computer networks. Saffo wrote in a special anniversary issue of the *Communications* of the ACM:

Two parallel universes currently exist—an everyday analog universe that we inhabit, and a newer digital universe created by humans, but inhabited by digital machines. We visit this digital world by peering through the portholes of our computer screens, and we manipulate with keyboard and mouse much as a nuclear technician works with radioactive material via glovebox and manipulator arms. . . . Now we are handing sensory organs and manipulators to the machines and inviting them to enter into analog reality. The scale of possible surprise this may generate over the next several decades as sensors, lasers, and microprocessors co-evolve is breathtakingly uncertain. ~

3.41c "Smart dust" computers at the University of California at Berkeley help monitor and control heating and cooling systems using environmental sensors and wireless communication links.

Shifting Into Overdrive *J. Bradford DeLong*

Computer journalists and salespeople tend to focus on the CPU when discussing PC evolution. In this article, first published in the May 2003 issue of Wired, *Bradford DeLong discusses the rapid changes in computer storage capacity and the impact those changes will have on our lives.*

Those of us with one foot far enough in the grave to have been using computers in the mid-1980s remember our extraordinary liberation from the floppy disk. We were freed from the requirement that all our programs and operating systems and files come in 360-kilobyte, 5½-inch chunks. It was a marvelous advance, the revolution in hard disk technology that gave us 10-megabyte mass storage devices for $1,000.

But it is the advances since then—and those we can firmly see our future promising—that are even more marvelous. Right now I am sitting in front of a whirring 60-gigabyte hard disk that cost less than $100. Do the math: If back then 10 megabytes cost $1,000, then 60 gigabytes would have cost x, where x = $6,000,000 and "back then" = 18 years ago. I'm sitting in front of $6,000,000 worth of mass storage, measured at mid-1980s prices. Happy me!

We have Moore's law for microprocessors. But who's coined a law for hard disks? In mass storage we have seen a 60,000-fold fall in price—more than a dozen times the force of Moore's law, with less than one-hundredth the press excitement.

My entire music library—1,803 tracks, 128.8 hours of relatively high-quality MP3 files—now sits in what seems like a small 8-gigabyte corner of my hard disk. *San Jose Mercury News* columnist Dan Gillmor carries the entire *Encyclopaedia Britannica* on his laptop—the thing that fills 6½ linear feet on my family room bookshelf takes up 4 percent of his disk space. Today, a $350 investment in mass storage can buy enough space to hold approximately 250 hours—one and a half 24-hour-a-day weeks—of moderate-quality digital video. And tomorrow? I'm willing to guess that by 2012 the $100 mass storage option for PCs should hold a full terabyte.

Computing power and connectivity hogged the headlines in the past decade, but mass storage will take the lead for three reasons. The first is regulatory: It does not look as though we in the United States will get the capital and regulatory structures of telecommunications right fast enough to see the bandwidth explosion that we know is technically possible during the next several years. The second is that keeping up with Moore's law in silicon is becoming more and more expensive. Intel, IBM, et al. are designing the next generations of microprocessors right now. But the cost of a semiconductor fab is now $3 billion and rising—few companies can afford one. The third is that mass storage is very simple: You write marks, you read marks, whether on modern magneto-optical or Babylonian clay-tablet media. What matters is the size and precision of your chisel, and our engineers' technical creativity makes it a favorable bet that the next five or ten years will see connectivity and Moore's law lagging behind the explosion of mass storage.

So, what will the world look like if mass storage is not a limiting factor?

First, the cheaper the disk space, the more dead the traditional business models of the entertainment industry. Money will come from new content for which a premium price based on must-haveness can still be justified, much like the hardcover-softcover distinction in bookselling. Substantial money will also come from special big-screen, live, and other experiences that cannot be duplicated at home. It's not that information—in the multimedia content sense—wants to be free. Deep in people's minds is a powerful human drive to exchange, to reciprocate, to not just take but also give. But reciprocity works only if the terms of the exchange are seen as fair.

Second, the overwhelming cheapness of storage will lead to the apotheosis of librarianship—or, rather, of search. Overwhelmingly cheap storage means that we will save copies of everything. But saved copies of everything are useful only when you can find what you are looking for. I already find it much, much easier to locate things on the publicly accessible part of my hard disk that is www.j-bradford-delong.net than in my private directories. Why? Google. Other people have omnivorously plowed through the directories opened up to the world, and Google has aggregated the Web traces they have made. Intelligence—artificial or otherwise—at assessing the value of documents and their relevance to you may well become the truly scarce factor. And one of the basic principles of economics is that the truly scarce factor is highly rewarded. Google's children will be a big part of the picture. Tomorrow's movie studio profits may well accrue to the studio that can write the best algorithms to download copies of the 50 films you'd most enjoy to your hard disk overnight.

Finally, and most important, your memory will improve. There will be space to store whatever you wish to recall from your day—pictures of people you saw (grabbed from the Internet), words you heard (recorded via laptop microphone and then translated into text), not to mention whatever thoughts you found time to write down. Your life is your archive, and your archive is your life. Forgetting will be much more difficult—unless, of course, you want to. Then you can always edit it.

Discussion Questions

1. Do you agree that mass storage, not CPUs, will "hog the headlines" in the coming decade? Why or why not?

2. Do you agree that advancements in storage technology will help your memory to improve? Why or why not?

Summary

A computer with just a CPU and internal memory is of limited value; peripherals allow that computer to communicate with the outside world and store information for later use. Some peripherals are strictly input devices. Others are output devices. Some are external storage devices that accept information from and send information to the CPU.

The most common input devices today are the keyboard and the mouse, but a variety of other input devices can be connected to the computer. Trackballs, touch-sensitive pads, touch screens, and joysticks provide alternatives to the mouse as a pointing device. Bar code readers, optical mark readers, and magnetic ink readers are designed to recognize and translate specially printed patterns and characters. Scanners and digital cameras convert photographs, drawings, and other analog images into digital files that the computer can process. Sound digitizers do the same thing to audio information. All input devices are designed to do one thing: convert information signals from an outside source into a pattern of bits that the computer can process.

Output devices perform the opposite function: They accept strings of bits from the computer and transform them into a form that is useful or meaningful outside the computer. Video displays, including CRT monitors and LCDs, are almost universally used to display information continually as the computer functions. A variety of printers are used for producing paper output. Fax machines and fax modems let you share printed information using standard phone lines. Sound output from the computer, including music and synthesized speech, is delivered through audio speakers. Output devices also allow computers to control other machines.

Unlike most input and output peripherals, storage devices such as disk drives and tape drives are capable of two-way communication with the computer. Because of their high-speed random-access capability, magnetic disks—high-capacity hard disks, inexpensive disks, and a variety of removable media—are the most common forms of storage on modern computers. Sequential-access tape devices are generally used to archive only information that doesn't need to be accessed often. Optical discs are used mostly as high-capacity, read-only media, but newer types of optical drives can both read and write data. In the future, solid-state storage technology will probably replace disks and tapes for most applications.

The hardware for a complete computer system generally includes at least one processor, memory, storage devices, and several I/O peripherals for communicating with the outside world. Network connections make it possible for computers to communicate with one another directly. Networks blur the boundaries between individual computer systems. With the hardware components in place, a computer system is ready to receive and follow instructions encoded in software.

Key Terms

bar code reader ....(p. 106)
cathode-ray tube (CRT)
    monitor ....(p. 115)
CD-R ....(p. 124)
CD-ROM ....(p. 121)
CD-ROM drive ....(p. 121)
CD-RW...................................(p. 124)
CD-RW drive.........................(p. 121)
digital camera ....(p. 109)
digitize...................................(p. 108)
disk (floppy disk) ....(p. 119)
disk drive ....(p. 119)
display ....(p. 112)
dot matrix printer..................(p. 115)
DVD ....(p. 124)
DVD-ROM drive ....(p. 124)
ergonomic keyboard..............(p. 103)
ergonomics ....(p. 120)
facsimile (fax) machine.........(p. 116)
fax modem..............................(p. 116)
FireWire (IEEE 1394, FireWire 400,
    FireWire 800) ....(p. 127)
flash memory.........................(p. 125)
graphics tablet ....(p. 104)

handwriting recognition
    software ....(p. 107)
hard disk ....(p. 121)
hot swap.................................(p. 127)
impact printer ....(p. 115)
inkjet printer.........................(p. 115)
interface standards.................(p. 126)
joystick ....(p. 104)
keyboard ....(p. 103)
laser printer...........................(p. 115)
line printer ....(p. 115)
liquid crystal display (LCD)..(p. 115)
magnetic disk.........................(p. 119)
magnetic ink character reader.(p. 106)
magnetic tape.........................(p. 119)
monitor ....(p. 112)
mouse ....(p. 104)
multifunction printer (MFP)..(p. 116)
nonimpact printer ....(p. 115)
optical character recognition
    (OCR) ....(p. 106)
optical disc drive ....(p. 121)
optical mark reader...............(p. 106)
pen-based computer...............(p. 107)

photo printer ....(p. 115)
plotter ....(p. 116)
pointing stick (TrackPoint)....(p. 104)
point-of-sale (POS) terminal .(p. 106)
printer ....(p. 115)
radio frequency identification
    (RFID) reader ....(p. 106)
radio frequency identification
    (RFID) tag ....(p. 106)
random access ....(p. 119)
removable cartridge media ....(p. 121)
repetitive-stress injuries........(p. 103)
resolution...............................(p. 112)
scanner....................................(p. 108)
sensor......................................(p. 112)
sequential access ....(p. 119)
solid-state storage.................(p. 126)
sound card ....(p. 117)
storage device.......................(p. 119)
tape drive ....(p. 119)
touch screen...........................(p. 104)
touchpad (trackpad)..............(p. 104)
trackball..................................(p. 104)
universal serial bus (USB).....(p. 127)

Interactive Activities

1. The Computer Confluence CD-ROM contains self-test quiz questions related to this chapter, including multiple choice, true or false, and matching questions.

2. The Computer Confluence Web site, **http://www.computerconfluence.com**, contains self-test exercises related to this chapter. Follow the instructions for taking a quiz. After you've completed your quiz, you can email the results to your instructor.

True or False

1. The disk drive was invented at about the same time the first computers came into existence.

2. Palm-sized computers can't have keyboards because the stylus is the only input device they can recognize.

3. The touchpad on a notebook computer serves the same function as a QWERTY keyboard on a desktop PC.

4. Because bar codes were designed to be read by computers, the devices that read them are extremely accurate.

5. A scanner creates an analog representation of a printed digital image.

6. The display quality of a monitor is determined in large part by the monitor's resolution and color depth.

7. Most PC printers today are laser printers, because color laser printers are far less expensive to buy than color inkjet printers.

8. A CD-RW drive can be used to store and back up data files.

9. Several years ago the computer industry agreed on a universal standard for rewriteable DVD storage, so today virtually all drives are based on the same standard.

10. Legacy-free computers don't include early PC standards, such as the serial port, that are inefficient when compared with more recent technologies like USB.

Multiple Choice

1. Why was the arrangement of keys on the QWERTY keyboard chosen?
   a. Because it corresponds to alphabetical order in the Esperanto language
   b. Because it corresponds to alphabetical order in the Polish language
   c. To reduce typing speed
   d. To minimize finger motion to reach the most commonly typed characters
   e. To make it easy for the inventor to type his name and address

2. The mouse is standard equipment on virtually all modern PCs except
   a. PCs without USB or FireWire ports
   b. IBM PCs
   c. iMacs
   d. portable PCs
   e. workstation PCs

3. Which of these is both an input and an output device?
   a. A bar-code reader
   b. A flatbed scanner
   c. A touch screen
   d. A sensor
   e. A plotter

4. Optical character recognition can be used to extract text from writing on
   a. Smart whiteboards
   b. Tablet PCs
   c. PDAs
   d. Scanned letters
   e. All of the above

5. LCD technology is used in
   a. Notebook computer displays
   b. Many desktop computer displays
   c. Video projectors
   d. All of the above
   e. None of the above

6. The size of a display is measured
   a. Across the top of the display
   b. Down the left side of the display
   c. Across the middle of the display
   d. Down the center of the display
   e. From the upper-left corner to the lower-right corner of the display

7. What is the bit depth of the video displays used by most graphics professionals?
   a. 8
   b. 16
   c. 24
   d. 32
   e. 64

8. A multifunction printer generally includes several devices, including
   a. A scanner
   b. A CRT monitor
   c. A QWERTY keyboard
   d. A mouse
   e. All of the above

9. Architects needing to produce detailed drawings on paper several feet wide rely upon which of the following?
   a. Line printers
   b. Dot matrix printers
   c. Photo printers
   d. Plotters
   e. Scanners

10. Magnetic tape is not practical for applications where data must be quickly recalled because tape is
    a. A random-access medium
    b. A sequential-access medium
    c. A read-only medium
    d. Fragile and easily damaged
    e. An expensive storage medium

11. The floppy diskette is considered obsolete by many professionals because
    a. It is strictly read-only
    b. It is especially vulnerable to hacker attacks
    c. It doesn't have enough storage capacity for today's large data files
    d. It isn't as reliable as a modern floppy disk
    e. All of the above

12. Hard disk drives have the disadvantage that
    a. They hold less information than diskettes do
    b. They are more likely to fail than other computer components
    c. They cannot be backed up
    d. Their contents are lost when they lose power
    e. All of the above

13. Most digital cameras today store images using
    a. DVD-RAM
    b. CD-ROM
    c. Flash memory
    d. Digital ink
    e. None of the above

14. Which of these technologies is being phased out on modern PCs?
    a. USB 2.0
    b. FireWire 800
    c. The parallel printer port
    d. Expansion slots
    e. Hot-swappable devices

15. Which of these is most like the open architecture of the modern PC?
    a. A modern car with a computer-controlled emissions system that can be adjusted by factory-authorized mechanics
    b. A "smart" microwave with an embedded computer that allows for complex recipes and scheduling
    c. A stereo system that allows speakers, disc players, and other components to be replaced by the owner
    d. A handheld computer with built-in firmware for all of the most common PDA tasks
    e. A music keyboard that includes a built-in synthesizer and an LCD display

Review Questions

1. Provide a working definition for each of the key terms listed in the Key Terms section. Check your answers in the glossary.

2. List five input devices and three output devices that might be attached to a PC. Describe a typical use for each.

3. Name and describe three special-purpose input devices people commonly use in public places, such as stores, banks, and libraries.

4. Many people find that the mouse is impractical for use as a pointing device on a laptop computer. Describe at least three alternatives that are more appropriate.

5. What are the advantages of CRT monitors over LCDs?

6. Name at least two hardware devices that use LCDs because using a CRT would be impractical.

7. What are the advantages of nonimpact printers, such as laser printers, over impact printers? Are there any disadvantages?

8. Some commonly used peripherals can be described as both input and output devices. Explain.

9. What is the difference between sequential-access and random-access storage devices? What are the major uses of each?

Discussion Questions

1. If we think of the human brain as a computer, what are the input devices? What are the output devices? What are the storage devices?

2. What kinds of new input and output devices do you think future computers might have? Why?

3. Many computer users have become addicted to multi-player online role-playing games. Some of them spend 8 hours or more a day playing these games, even though the interactions are through a keyboard, mouse, and video display. Do you think computer addiction will become a bigger problem when more sophisticated peripherals such as LCD goggle displays become commonplace?

Projects

1. The keyboard is the main input device for computers today. If you don't know how to touch-type, you're effectively handicapped in a world of computers. Fortunately, many personal computer software programs are designed to teach keyboarding. If you need to learn to type, try to find one of these programs and use it regularly until you are a fluent typist.

2. Using the inventory of computers you developed in Project 4 in Chapter 1, determine the major components of each (input devices, output devices, storage, and so on).

3. Visit a bank, store, office, or laboratory. List all the computer peripherals you see, categorizing them as input, output, or storage devices.

4. Using computer advertisements in magazines, newspapers, and catalogs, try to break down the cost of a computer to determine, on the average, what percentage of the cost is for the system unit (including CPU, memory, and disk drives), what percentage is for input and output devices, and what percentage is for software. How do the percentages change as the price of the system goes up?

Sources and Resources

Books

Insanely Great: The Life and Times of Macintosh, the Computer That Changed Everything, Reissue Edition, by Steven Levy (New York: Penguin, 2000). Apple fan and *Newsweek* columnist Steven Levy recounts the first 10 years of the Macintosh's history in breathless detail.

The Second Coming of Steve Jobs, by Alan Deutschman (New York: Broadway Books, 2000). This book focuses on Apple's controversial CEO in the years at NeXT and his return to Apple. Jobs is a controversial, complex, and private person who has achieved fame that rivals rock stars. His story makes good reading.

Disclosure, by Michael Crichton (New York: Ballantine Books, 1994). This book-turned-movie provides an inside look at a fictional Seattle corporation that manufactures computer peripherals. Even though the author has clearly tampered with credibility for the sake of a suspenseful plot, the story provides insights into the roles money and power play in today's high-stakes computer industry. It also features some cool and realistic computer technology of the near future.

Real World Scanning and Halftones, Third Edition, by David Blanner, Conrad Chavez, Glenn Fleishman, and Steve Roth (Berkeley, CA: Peachpit Press, 2004). It's easy to use a scanner, but it isn't always easy to get high-quality scans. This illustrated book covers scanner use from the basics to advanced tips and techniques.

Digital Photographer's Handbook, by Tom Ang (London, UK: DK Publishing, 2002). This heavily illustrated book from renowned photographic lecturer Ang covers everything from the basics to the advanced image manipulation and editing.

The Essential Guide to Computer Data Storage: From Floppy to DVD, by Dr. Andrei Khurshudov (Upper Saddle River, NJ: Prentice Hall, 2001). This book provides in-depth explanations of a variety of PC peripherals and interface standards, including magnetic disks, optical discs, and storage for cameras and MP3 music players.

Direct from Dell: Strategies That Revolutionized an Industry, by Michael Dell with Catherine Fredman (New York: HarperBusiness, 2000). The inside story of how a college student from Texas turned his dorm room into the start of America's most successful computer company. Dell brought the "direct model" to the PC industry, forever changing the way PC makers do business, and his company was the first lasting Internet success story, as he successfully transitioned from print ad sales to e-commerce.

Desktop Yoga, by Julie T. Lusk (New York: Perigee, 1998). Like any activity, computer work can be hazardous to your health if you don't exercise care and common sense. This book describes stretching and relaxation exercises for deskbound workers and students. If you spend hours a day in front of a computer screen, these activities can help you to take care of your body and mind.

Periodicals

E-media. This monthly magazine, aimed at multimedia professionals, includes extensive coverage of input, output, and storage technologies.

Computer Shopper. This monthly typically includes a few consumer-oriented articles, but it has evolved over time from an ad-based reference to a print version of CNET's popular shopper.com Web site, with reprints of reviews and editorials by the site's leading writers.

Web Pages

Most computer peripheral manufacturers have Web pages. The Computer Confluence Web site will guide you to many of the most interesting pages.

Multimedia

on the CD-ROM and the Web:

~ Activities on how **operating systems** work and how programs are executed

~ Video explaining what **Linux** is and why you might want to use it

~ **Instant** access to glossary and key word references

~ **Interactive** self-study quizzes

. . . and more.

 computerconfluence.com

Objectives

After you read this chapter you should be able to:

▶ Describe three fundamental categories of software and their relationships

▶ Explain the relationship of algorithms to software

▶ Discuss the factors that make a computer application a useful tool

▶ Describe the role of the operating system in a modern computer system

▶ Describe how file systems are organized

▶ Outline the evolution of user interfaces from early machine-language programming to futuristic virtual reality interfaces

▶ Explain why the unauthorized copying of software is against the law

LINUS TORVALDS AND THE SOFTWARE NOBODY OWNS

When Linus Torvalds bought his first PC in 1991, he never dreamed it would become a critical weapon in a software liberation war. He just wanted to avoid waiting in line to get a terminal to connect to his university's mainframe. Torvalds, a 21-year-old student at the University of Helsinki in Finland, had avoided buying a PC because he didn't like the standard PC's "crummy architecture with this crummy MS-DOS operating system." But Torvalds had been studying operating systems, and he decided to try to build something on his own.

He based his work on Minix, a scaled-down textbook version of the powerful UNIX operating system designed to run on PC hardware. Little by little, he cobbled together pieces of a kernel, the part of the system where the real processing and control work is done.

When he mentioned his project on an Internet discussion group, a member offered him space to post it on a university server. Others copied it, tinkered with it, and sent the changes back to Torvalds. The communal work-in-progress eventually became known as Linux (pronounced "Linn-uks" by its creator). Within a couple of years, it was good enough to release as a product.

Instead of copyrighting and selling Linux, Torvalds made it freely available under the GNU General Public License (GPL) developed by the Free Software Foundation. According to the GPL, anyone can give away, modify, or even sell Linux, as long as the source code—the program instructions—remain freely available for others to improve. Linux is the best-known example of open-source software, and now it spearheads the popular open-source software movement.

Thousands of programmers around the world have worked on Linux, with Torvalds still at the center of the activity. Some do it because they believe there should be alternatives to expensive corporate products; others do it because they can customize the software; still others

> I had **no idea** what I was doing. I knew I was the **best programmer in the world.** Every 21-year-old programmer knows that. "**How hard can it be,** it's just **an operating system?"**
>
> —*Linus Torvalds*

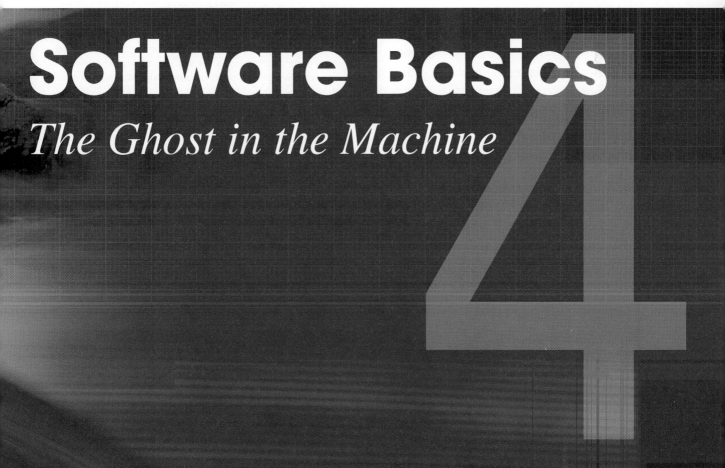

Software Basics
The Ghost in the Machine

4.1 Linus Torvalds talking to Linux fans

with a pseudo–open-source strategy covering its embedded products that compete directly with Linux.

Today, Torvalds is an Internet folk hero. Web pages pay homage to him, his creation, and the stuffed penguin, Tux, that has become the Linux mascot. In 1996, he completed his master's degree in computer science and went to work for Transmeta Corp., a chip design company in Silicon Valley. In November 2003, Torvalds joined Open Source Development Labs, saying, "It feels a bit strange to finally officially work on what I've been doing for the past twelve years." ~

do it just for fun. As a result of all their efforts, Linux has matured into a powerful, versatile product with millions of users.

Today, Linux powers Web servers, film and animation workstations, scientific supercomputers, a handful of handheld computers, some general-use PCs, and even Internet-savvy appliances like refrigerators. Linux is especially popular among people who do computing on a tight budget—particularly in debt-ridden Third World countries.

The success of Linux has inspired Apple, Sun, Hewlett-Packard, and other software companies to release products with open-source code. Even the mighty Microsoft is paying attention as this upstart operating system grows in popularity, and the company has responded

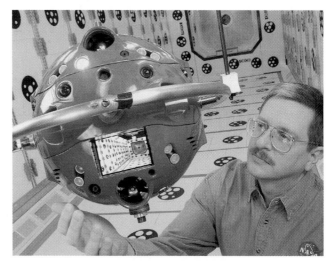

4.2 A novel use of the Linux operating system is in the NASA personal satellite assistant, currently under development. The 6-inch sphere will float around the International Space Station and act as an environmental monitor and communications device. Its design was inspired by the light saber training droid used by Luke Skywalker in the movie *Star Wars*.

Chapters 2 and 3 told only part of the story about how computers do what they do. Here's a synopsis of our story so far:

On one side we have a person—you, me, or somebody else—it hardly matters. We all have problems to solve—problems involving work, communication, transportation, finances, and more. Many of these problems cry out for computer solutions.

On the other side we have a computer—an incredibly sophisticated bundle of hardware capable of performing all kinds of technological wizardry. Unfortunately, the computer *recognizes only zeros and ones*.

A great chasm separates the person who has a collection of vague problems from the stark, rigidly bounded world of the computer. How can humans bridge the gap to communicate with the computer?

That's where software comes in. Software enables people to communicate certain kinds of problems to computers and makes it possible for computers to communicate solutions back to those people.

Modern computer software didn't materialize out of the atmosphere; it evolved from the plug boards and patch cords and other hardware devices that were used to program early computers like the ENIAC. Mathematician John von Neumann, working with ENIAC's creators, J. Presper Eckert and John Mauchly, wrote a 1945 paper suggesting that program

4.3 The communication gap . . .

instructions could be stored with the data in memory. Every computer created since has been based on the *stored-program concept* described in that paper. That idea established the software industry.

Instead of flipping switches and patching wires, today's programmers write *programs*—sets of computer instructions designed to solve problems—and feed them into the computer's memory through keyboards and other input devices. These programs are the computer's software. Because software is stored in memory, a computer can switch from one task to another and then back to the first without a single hardware modification. For instance, the computer that serves as a word processor for writing this book can, at the click of a mouse, turn into an email terminal, a browser into the World Wide Web, a reference library, an accounting spreadsheet, a drawing table, a video-editing workstation, a musical instrument, or a game machine.

What is software, and how can it transform a mass of circuits into an electronic chameleon? This chapter provides some general answers to that question along with details about each of the three major categories of software:

- Compilers and other translator programs, which enable programmers to create other software
- Software applications, which serve as productivity tools to help computer users solve problems
- System software, which coordinates hardware operations and does behind-the-scenes work the computer user seldom sees

Processing with Programs

Software is invisible and complex. To make the basic concepts clear, we start our exploration of software with a down-to-earth analogy.

> **Leonardo da Vinci** called music **"the shaping of the invisible"** and his phrase **is even more apt** as a description of **software**.
>
> —*Alan Kay, conceiver of the notebook computer, and user-interface architect*

Food for Thought

Think of the hardware in a computer system as the kitchen in a short-order restaurant: It's equipped to produce whatever output a customer (user) requests, but it sits idle until an order (command) is placed. Robert, the computerized chef in our imaginary kitchen, serves as the CPU, waiting for requests from the users/customers. When somebody provides an input command—say, an order for a plate of French toast—Robert responds by following the instructions in the appropriate recipe.

As you may have guessed, the recipe is the software. It provides instructions telling the hardware what to do to produce the output the user desires. If the recipe is correct, clear, and precise, the chef turns the input data—eggs, bread, and other ingredients—into the desired output—French toast. If the instructions are unclear, or if the software has **bugs**, or errors, the output may not be what the user wanted.

For example, suppose Robert has this recipe for "Suzanne's French Toast Fantastique."

This seemingly foolproof recipe has several trouble spots. Since step 1 doesn't say otherwise, Robert might include the shells in the "slightly beaten eggs." Step 2 says nothing about separating the six slices of bread before dipping them in the batter; Robert would be within the letter of the instruction if he dipped all six at once. Step 3 has at least two potential bugs. Since it doesn't specify what to fry in butter, Robert might conclude that the mixture, not the bread, should be fried. Even if Robert decides to fry the bread, he may let it overcook waiting for the butter to turn golden brown, or he may wait patiently for the top of the toast to brown while the bottom quietly blackens. Robert, like any good computer, just follows the instructions he's given.

SUZANNE'S FRENCH TOAST FANTASTIQUE

1. Combine 2 slightly beaten eggs with 1 teaspoon vanilla extract, $^1/_2$ teaspoon cinnamon, and $^2/_3$ cup milk.
2. Dip 6 slices of bread in mixture.
3. Fry in small amount of butter until golden brown.
4. Serve bread with maple syrup, sugar, or tart jelly.

4.4 Suzanne's French Toast Fantastique

A Fast, Stupid Machine

The **most useful** word in any computer language is **"oops."**

—*David Lubar, in* It's Not a Bug, It's a Feature

Our imaginary automated chef may not seem very bright, but he's considerably more intelligent than a typical computer's CPU. Computers are commonly called "smart machines" or "intelligent machines." In truth, a typical computer is incredibly limited, capable of performing only the most basic arithmetic operations (such as $7 + 3$ and $15 - 8$) and a few simple logical comparisons ("Is this number less than that number?" "Are these two values identical?").

Computers *seem* smart because they can perform these arithmetic operations and comparisons quickly and accurately. A typical desktop computer can perform thousands of calculations in the time it takes you to pull your pen out of your pocket. A well-crafted program can tell the computer to perform a sequence of simple operations that, when taken as a whole, print a term paper, organize the student records for your school, or simulate a space flight. Amazingly, everything you've ever seen a computer do is the result of a sequence of extremely simple arithmetic and logical operations done very quickly. The challenge for software developers is to devise instructions that put those simple operations together in ways that are useful and appropriate.

SUZANNE'S FRENCH TOAST FANTASTIQUE: THE ALGORITHM

1. Prepare the batter by following these instructions.
   1a. Crack 2 eggs so whites and yolks drop in bowl; discard shells.
   1b. Beat eggs 30 seconds with wire whisk, fork, or mixer.
   1c. Mix in 1 teaspoon vanilla extract, $^1/_2$ teaspoon cinnamon, and $^2/_3$ cup milk.
2. Place 1 tablespoon butter in frying pan and place on 350° heat.
3. For each of six pieces of bread, follow these steps:
   3a. Dip slice of bread in mixture.
   3b. For each of the two sides of the bread do the following steps:
      3b1. Place the slice of bread in the frying pan with this (uncooked) side down.
      3b2. Wait 1 minute and then peek at underside of bread; if lighter than golden brown, repeat this step.
   3c. Remove bread from frying pan and place on plate.
4. Serve bread with maple syrup, sugar, or tart jelly.

4.5 Suzanne's French Toast Fantastique: The algorithm

Suzanne's recipe for French toast isn't a computer program; it's not written in a language that a computer can understand. But it could be considered an algorithm—a set of step-by-step procedures for accomplishing a task. A computer program generally starts as an algorithm written in English or some other human language. Like Suzanne's recipe, the initial algorithm is likely to contain generalities, ambiguities, and errors.

The programmer's job is to turn the algorithm into a program by adding details, hammering out rough spots, testing procedures, and debugging—correcting errors. For example, if we were turning Suzanne's recipe into a program for our electronic-brained short-order cook, we might start by rewriting it like the recipe shown in Figure 4.5.

We've eliminated much of the ambiguity from the original recipe. Ambiguity, while tolerable (and sometimes useful) in conversations between humans, is a source of errors for computers. In its current form, the recipe contains far more detail than any human chef would want but not nearly enough for a computer. If we were programming a computer (assuming we had one with input hardware capable of recognizing golden brown French toast and output devices capable of flipping the bread), we'd need to go into excruciating detail, translating every step of the process into a series of absolutely unambiguous instructions that could be interpreted and executed by a machine with a vocabulary smaller than that of a two-year-old child!

The Language of Computers

Every computer processes instructions in a native machine language. Machine language uses numeric codes to represent the most basic computer operations—adding numbers, subtracting numbers, comparing numbers, moving numbers, repeating instructions, and so on. Early programmers were forced to write every program in a machine language, tediously translating each instruction into binary code. This process was an invitation to insanity; imagine trying to find a single mistyped character in a page full of zeros and ones!

> The programmer, **like the poet**, works only slightly removed from **pure thought-stuff**. He builds **castles in the air**, creating by exertion of the **imagination**. Yet the program construct, unlike the poet's words, is **real** in the sense that **it moves and works**, producing visible outputs **separate from the construct itself.**
>
> —*Frederick P. Brooks, Jr., in* The Mythical Man Month

Today, most programmers use programming languages, such as C++, C#, Java, and Visual Basic.NET, that fall somewhere between natural human languages and precise machine languages. These languages, referred to as high-level languages, make it possible for scientists, engineers, and businesspeople to solve problems using familiar terminology and notation rather than cryptic machine instructions. For a computer to understand a program written in one of these languages, it must use a translator program to convert the English-like instructions to the zeros and ones of machine language.

To clarify the translation process, let's go back to the kitchen. Imagine a recipe translator that enables our computer chef to look up phrases like "fry until golden brown." Like a reference book for beginning cooks, this translator fills in all the details about testing and flipping foods in the frying pan, so Robert understands what to do whenever he encounters "fry until golden brown" in any recipe. As long as our computer cook is equipped with the translator, we don't need to include so many details in each recipe. We can communicate at a higher level. The more sophisticated the translator, the easier the job of the programmer. The most common type of translator program is called a compiler because it compiles a complete translation of the program in a high-level computer language (such as C#) before the program runs for the first time. The compiled program can run again and again; it doesn't need to be recompiled unless instructions need to be changed.

Programming languages have steadily evolved during the last few decades. Each new generation of languages makes the programming process easier by taking on, and hiding from the programmer, more of the detail-oriented work. The computer's unrelenting demands for technical details haven't gone away; they're just handled automatically by

4.1 **Executing a Program**

Most programs are composed of millions of simple machine-language instructions. Here we'll observe the execution of a tiny part of a running program: a series of instructions that computes the 5% sales tax on a $99.00 purchase. The machine instructions are similar to those in actual programs, but the details have been omitted. The computer has already loaded (copied) the program from disk into RAM so that the CPU can see it.

The Program Counter inside the CPU keeps track of the address of the next instruction to be executed. Executing instructions is a three-step process: fetch the instruction, increment the Program Counter, and perform the specified task. In this example, four instructions tell the CPU to read two numbers from memory (locations 2000 and 2004), multiply them, and store the result in memory (location 2008). The CPU goes through 12 steps to execute these four instructions.

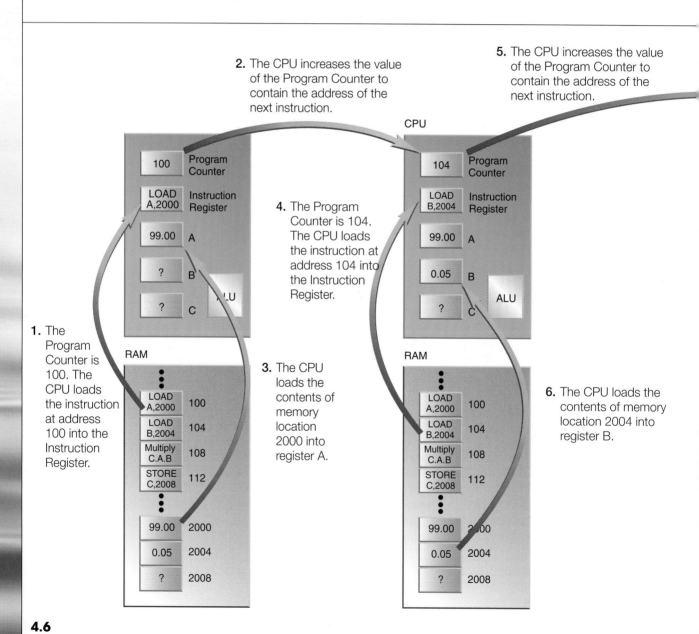

2. The CPU increases the value of the Program Counter to contain the address of the next instruction.

5. The CPU increases the value of the Program Counter to contain the address of the next instruction.

CPU

4. The Program Counter is 104. The CPU loads the instruction at address 104 into the Instruction Register.

1. The Program Counter is 100. The CPU loads the instruction at address 100 into the Instruction Register.

3. The CPU loads the contents of memory location 2000 into register A.

6. The CPU loads the contents of memory location 2004 into register B.

4.6

Translated into English, the instructions at memory addresses 100–112 look like this:

- (100) Copy the number stored in memory location 2000 into register A inside the CPU.
- (104) Copy the number stored in memory location 2004 into register B inside the CPU.
- (108) Multiply the contents of registers A and B, putting the result in register C.
- (112) Copy the contents of register C into memory location 2008.

In this example, memory location 2000 contains the purchase price (99.00), and memory location 2004 contains the sales tax rate (0.05).

The computer actually stores all instructions and data values as binary numbers, but we have represented them as letters or decimal numbers to make the example easier to follow.

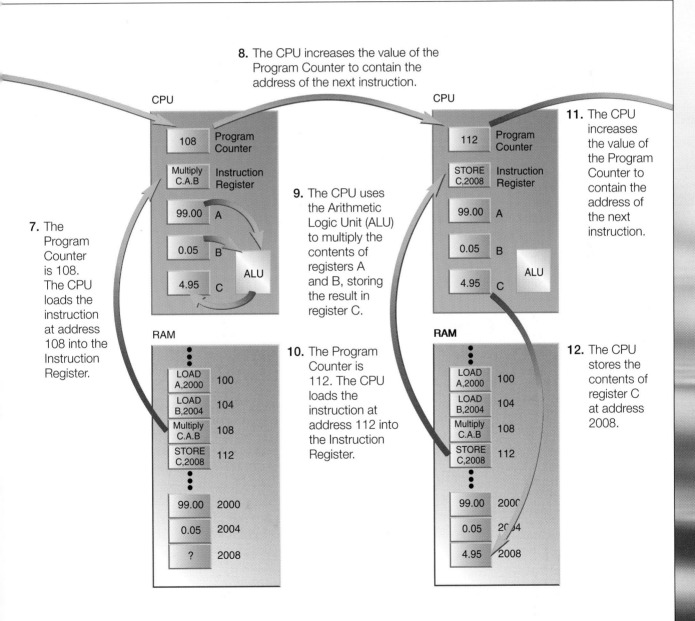

8. The CPU increases the value of the Program Counter to contain the address of the next instruction.

7. The Program Counter is 108. The CPU loads the instruction at address 108 into the Instruction Register.

9. The CPU uses the Arithmetic Logic Unit (ALU) to multiply the contents of registers A and B, storing the result in register C.

10. The Program Counter is 112. The CPU loads the instruction at address 112 into the Instruction Register.

11. The CPU increases the value of the Program Counter to contain the address of the next instruction.

12. The CPU stores the contents of register C at address 2008.

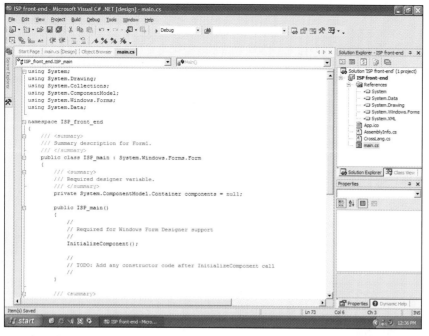

4.7 Compilers enable programmers to write in high-level languages, such as C# (shown), C++, or Java.

translation software. As a result, programming is easier and less error prone. As translators become more sophisticated, programmers can communicate in computer languages that more closely resemble **natural languages**—the languages people speak and write every day.

Even with state-of-the-art computer languages, programming requires a considerable investment of time and brainpower. Fortunately, many tasks that required programming two decades ago can now be accomplished with spreadsheets, graphics programs, and other easy-to-use software applications.

Programming languages are still used to solve problems that can't be handled with off-the-shelf software, but virtually all computer users manage to do their work without programming. Programming today is done mainly by professional software developers, who use programming languages to create and refine the applications and other programs the rest of us use.

Software Applications: Tools for Users

The computer is only a **fast idiot**; it has **no imagination**; it **cannot originate** action. It is, and will remain, **only a tool to man**.

—*American Library Association reaction to the UNIVAC computer exhibit at the 1964 New York World's Fair*

Software applications enable users to control computers without having to think like programmers do. We now turn our attention to applications.

Consumer Applications

Computer and software stores, consumer electronics stores, and mail-order houses sell thousands of software titles: publishing programs, accounting software, personal-information managers, graphics programs, multimedia tools, educational titles, games, and more. The process of buying computer software is similar to the process of buying music software (audio CDs) to play on a stereo system. But there are some important differences; we'll touch on a few here.

Documentation

A computer software package generally includes printed documentation with instructions for installing the software on a computer's hard disk. Some software packages also include tutorial manuals and reference manuals that explain how to use the software. Many software companies have replaced these printed documents with tutorials, reference materials, and *help files* that appear on-screen at the user's request. Most help files are supplemented and updated with *online help* that can be accessed through the local help files or at the company's Web site. Many programs are so easy to use that it's possible to put them to work without reading the documentation. But many programs include advanced features that aren't obvious through trial-and-error experimentation.

Upgrading

Most software companies continually work to improve their products by removing bugs and adding new features. As a result, new versions of many popular programs are released every year or two. To distinguish between versions, program names are generally followed by version numbers, such as the 7.0 in Filemaker Pro 7.0. Most companies use decimals to indicate minor revisions and whole numbers to indicate major revisions. For example, you can assume that Adobe Premiere 5.1, a video-editing program, includes only a few more features than Premiere 5.0 does, while Premiere 6.0 should be significantly different from version 5.1. Not all software follows this logical convention. For example, the last several versions of Microsoft's consumer operating system have been marketed as Microsoft Windows 95, Windows 98, Windows Millennium Edition (Windows Me), and Windows XP Home Edition. When you buy a software program, you generally buy the current version. When a new version is released, you can **upgrade** your program to the new version by paying an upgrade fee to the software manufacturer.

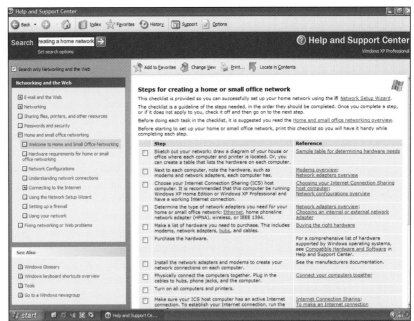

4.8 Most modern computer software provides some kind of online help on demand. Microsoft Windows provides context-sensitive help—help windows with content that depends on what else is currently on the screen. Many software companies, including Microsoft, use Web databases to augment the help included with the system.

Compatibility

A computer software buyer must be concerned with **compatibility**. When you buy an audio CD, you don't need to specify the brand of your CD player, because all manufacturers adhere to common industry standards. But no complete, universal software standards exist in the computer world, so a program written for one type of computer system may not work on another. Software packages contain labels with statements such as "Requires Windows 9x, Me, or XP with 128MB of RAM." (An x in a version specification generally means "substitute any number" so "Windows 9x" means "Windows ninety-*something*.") These demands should not be taken lightly; without compatible hardware and software, most software programs are worthless.

Disclaimers

According to the little-read warranties included with many software packages, some applications might technically be worthless even if you have compatible hardware and software. Here's the first paragraph from a typical software warranty, which is part of a longer **end-user license agreement** (*EULA*, pronounced "yoo-la"):

> *This program is provided "as is" without warranty of any kind. The entire risk as to the result and performance of the program is assumed by you. Should the program prove defective, you—and not the manufacturer or its dealers—assume the entire cost of all necessary servicing, repair, or correction. Further, the manufacturer does not warranty, guarantee, or make any representations regarding the use of, or the result of the use of, the program in terms of correctness, accuracy, reliability, for being current, or otherwise, and you rely on the program and its results solely at your own risk.*

Software companies hide behind disclaimers because nobody's figured out how to write error-free software. Remember our problems providing Robert with a foolproof set of instructions for producing French toast? Programmers who write applications such as word-proccessing programs must try to anticipate and respond to all combinations of commands and actions users might perform under any conditions. Given the difficulty of this task, most programs work amazingly well—but not perfectly.

Licensing

When you buy a typical computer software package, you're not actually buying the software. Instead, you're buying a software license to use the program, typically on a single machine. While end-user licensing agreements vary from company to company, most include limitations on your right to copy disks, install software on hard drives, and transfer information to other users. Many companies offer *volume licenses*—special licenses for entire companies, schools, or government institutions. Some companies even rent software to corporate and government clients.

Virtually all commercially marketed software is copyrighted. Copyrighted software can't be legally duplicated for distribution to others. Some software CDs and DVDs (mostly entertainment products) are physically *copy protected* so they can't be copied *at all*. A milder, more common form of copy protection is to require the user to type his or her name and a product serial number before a newly installed program will work. Between these two extremes, some software doesn't work properly until the owner registers the software purchase via the Internet.

Because programming is so difficult, software development is expensive. Software developers use copyrights and copy protection to ensure that they sell enough copies of their products to recover their investments and stay in business to write programs.

Software piracy is the term frequently used to describe the unauthorized copying and selling of software. By some estimates, global software piracy costs U.S. companies tens of billions of dollars in lost revenues every year. At the end of the chapter, we'll discuss laws protecting the rights of software developers.

Distribution

Software is distributed through direct sales forces to corporations and other institutions. Software is sold to consumers in computer stores, software specialty stores, book and record stores, and other retail outlets. Much software is sold through mail-order catalogs and Web sites. Web distribution makes it possible for some companies to offer software without packaging or disks. For example, you might download (copy) a demo version of a commercial program from a company's Web site or some other source; the demo program is identical to the commercial version, but with some key features disabled or a time limit placed on its usage. After you try the program and decide you want to buy it, you can often contact the company (by phone or through its Web site), pay (by credit card) for the full version of the program, and receive (by email) a code that you can type to unlock the disabled features of the program.

Not all software is copyrighted and sold through commercial channels. Web sites, user groups, and other sources commonly offer public domain software (free for the taking) and shareware (free for the trying, with a send-payment-if-you-keep-it honor system) along with demonstration versions of commercial programs. Unlike copyrighted commercial software, public domain software, shareware, and demo software can be legally copied and shared freely.

Why We Use Applications

It may seem strange that anyone would pay several hundred dollars for a product that comes with no warranty and dozens of legal restrictions about how you can use it. In fact, the rapidly growing software industry has spawned dozens of programs that have sold millions of copies. Why do so many people buy and use these hit programs? Of course, the answer varies from person to person and from product to product. But in general, most successful software products share these two important characteristics:

■ *They are built around visual metaphors of real-world tools.* A drawing program turns the screen into a sheet of drawing paper and a collection of drawing tools. Spreadsheets resemble an accountant's ledger sheets. Video editing software puts familiar VCR controls on the screen. But if these programs merely mimicked their real-world counterparts, people would have no compelling reason to use them.

■ *They extend human capabilities in some way.* Popular programs enable people to do things they can't do easily, or at all, with conventional tools. An artist using a graphics program can easily add an eye-catching distortion effect to a drawing and just as easily remove it if it doesn't look right. Spreadsheet programs enable managers to project future revenues based on best guesses and then instantly recalculate the bottom line with a different set of assumptions. And the possibilities opened up by computer video editing are mind-boggling. All kinds of software applications that extend human capabilities are the driving forces behind the computer revolution.

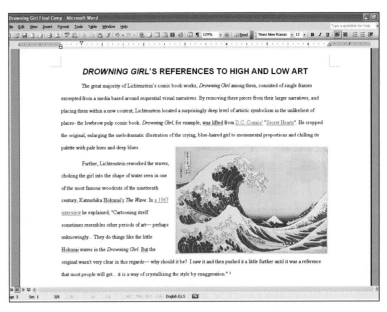

4.9 Word processors are based on the visual metaphor of a typewriter, but a modern word processor makes it easy to add graphics, video, and even Web links to an on-screen document.

Integrated Applications and Suites: Software Bundles

Although most software packages specialize in a particular application, such as word-proccessing or photographic editing, low-priced **integrated software** packages include several applications designed to work well together. Popular integrated packages, such as AppleWorks, Corel Suite, Microsoft Works, and Star Office generally include simple word-processing, database, spreadsheet, graphics, telecommunication, and personal-information management (PIM) modules.

The parts of an integrated package may not have all the features of their separately packaged counterparts, but integrated packages still offer advantages. They apply a similar look and feel to all of their applications so users don't need to memorize different commands and techniques for doing different tasks. The best integrated programs blur the lines between applications so, for example, you can create a table full of calculations right in the middle

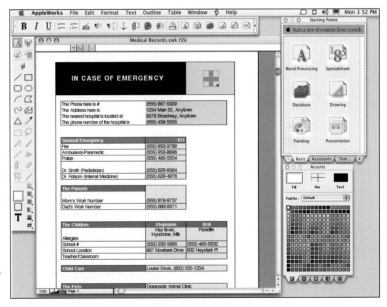

4.10 AppleWorks is an integrated application program that combines several popular applications in an easy-to-use package.

of a typed letter without explicitly switching from a word processor to a spreadsheet. Interapplication communication enables the automatic transfer of data among applications, so, for example, changes in a financial spreadsheet are automatically reflected in a graphic table embedded in a word-processed memo.

These advantages aren't unique to integrated packages. Many software companies offer **application suites**—bundles containing several full application programs that are also sold as separate programs. The best-selling application suite, Microsoft Office System, comes in several versions designed for different types of users. The core programs in Microsoft Office include Microsoft Word (a word processor), Excel (a spreadsheet program), PowerPoint (a presentation graphics program), Access (a database program), and Outlook

4.11 The open-source application suite OpenOffice.org provides compatibility with Microsoft Office documents but runs on a variety of platforms, including Windows, Linux, and the Mac OS.

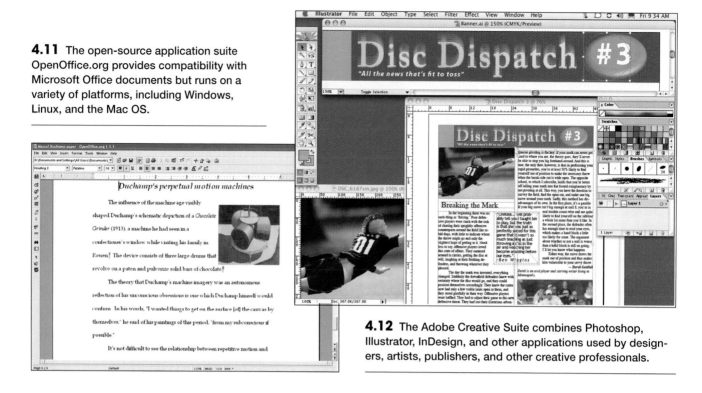

4.12 The Adobe Creative Suite combines Photoshop, Illustrator, InDesign, and other applications used by designers, artists, publishers, and other creative professionals.

(an email/personal-information management program). Microsoft has designed these applications so that they have similar command structures and easy interapplication communication. The price of a suite such as Microsoft Office is generally less than the total price of its applications purchased separately, but more than the cost of an integrated package such as Microsoft Works. Suites have more features than integrated programs do but also make greater demands on system memory, disk storage, and the CPU. Many older computers simply aren't powerful enough to run a modern application suite. Still, Microsoft Office is the most widely used application package on newer PCs and Macintoshes.

Vertical-Market and Custom Software

Because of their flexibility, word processors, spreadsheets, databases, and graphics programs are used in homes, schools, government offices, and all kinds of businesses. But many computer applications are so job specific that they're of little interest or use to anybody outside a given profession. Medical-billing software, library-cataloging software, legal-reference software, restaurant-management software, and other applications designed specifically for a particular business or industry are called **vertical-market applications** or **custom applications**.

Vertical-market applications tend to cost far more than mass-market applications, because companies that develop the software have very few potential customers through which to recover their development costs. In fact, some custom applications are programmed specifically for single clients. For example, the software used to control the space shuttle was developed with a single customer—NASA—in mind.

4.13 Vertical-market software helps this researcher track geographic information.

System Software: The Hardware-Software Connection

When you're typing a paper or writing a program, you don't need to concern yourself with low-level details, like which parts of the computer's memory hold your document, the segments of the word-proccessing software currently in the computer's memory, or the output instructions sent by the computer to the printer. System software, a class of software that includes the *operating system* and *utility programs*, handles these details and hundreds of other tasks behind the scenes.

Originally, **operating systems** were envisioned as a way to handle one of the **most complex** input/output operations: **communicating** with a variety of **disk drives**. But, the operating system quickly **evolved** into **an all-encompassing bridge** between your PC and the software you run on it.

—*Ron White, in* How Computers Work

What the Operating System Does

Virtually every general-purpose computer today, whether it's a timesharing supercomputer or laptop PC, depends on an operating system (OS) to keep hardware running efficiently and to make the process of communication with that hardware easier. Operating-system software runs continuously whenever the computer is on, providing an additional layer of insulation between you and the bits-and-bytes world of computer hardware. Because the operating system stands between the software application and the hardware, application compatibility is usually defined by the operating system as well as by the hardware.

The operating system, as the name implies, is a system of programs that performs a variety of technical operations, from basic communication with peripherals to complex networking and security tasks.

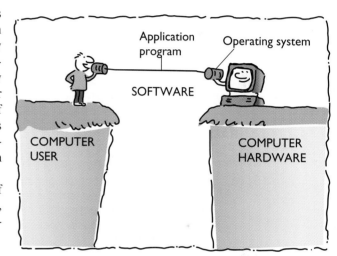

4.14 The user's view: When a person uses an application, whether a game or an accounting program, the person doesn't communicate directly with the computer hardware. Instead, the user interacts with the application, which depends on the operating system to manage and control hardware.

Communicating with Peripherals

Some of the most complex tasks performed by a computer involve communicating with screens, printers, disk drives, and other peripheral devices. A computer's operating system includes programs that transparently communicate with peripherals.

Coordinating the Concurrent Processing of Jobs

Large, multiuser computers often work on several jobs, or tasks, at the same time—a technique known as concurrent processing. State-of-the-art parallel-processing machines use multiple CPUs to process jobs simultaneously. But a typical computer has only one CPU, so it must work on several tasks by rapidly switching back and forth between them. The computer takes advantage of idle time in one process (for example, waiting for input) by working on another program. (Our computerized chef, Robert, might practice concurrent processing by slicing fruit while he waits for the toast to brown.) A timesharing computer practices concurrent processing whenever multiple users are connected to the system. The computer quickly moves from terminal to terminal, checking for input and processing each user's data in turn. If a PC has multitasking capabilities, the user can issue a command that initiates a process (for example, to print this chapter) and continue working with other applications while the computer executes the command.

How It **Works**

4.2 **The Operating System**

Most of what you see on-screen when you use an application program and most of the common tasks you have the program perform, such as saving and opening files, are being performed by the operating system at the application's request.

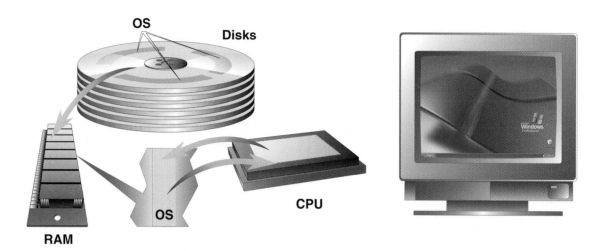

When a computer is turned off, there's nothing in RAM, and the CPU isn't doing anything. The operating system (OS) programs must be in memory and running on the CPU before the system can function. When you turn on the computer, the CPU automatically begins executing instructions stored in ROM. These instructions help the system boot, and the operating system is loaded from disk into part of the system's memory.

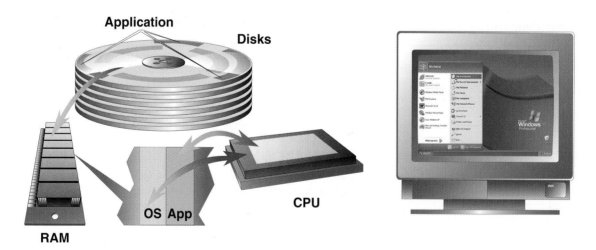

Using the mouse, you "ask" the operating system to load a word-proccessing application program into memory so it can run.

4.15

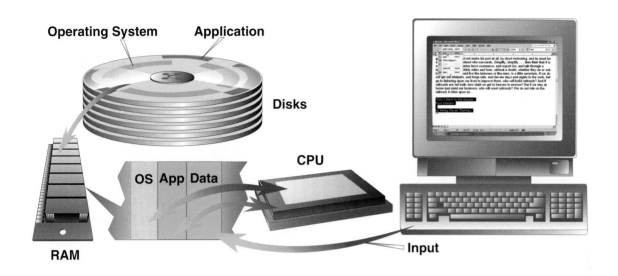

The loaded application occupies a portion of memory, leaving that much less for other programs and data. The OS remains in memory, so it can provide services to the application program, helping it to display on-screen menus, communicate with the printer, and perform other common actions. Because the OS and application are in constant communication, control—the location in memory where the CPU is reading program instructions—jumps around. If the application calls the OS to help display a menu, the application tells the CPU, "Go follow the menu display instructions at address x in the operating system area; when you're done, return here and pick up where you left off."

To avoid losing your data file when the system is turned off, you save it to the disk, meaning you have the OS write it into a file on the disk for later use. The OS handles communication between the CPU and the disk drive, ensuring that your file doesn't overwrite other information. (Later, when you reopen the file, the OS locates it on the disk and copies it into memory so the CPU—and therefore any program—can see it and work with it.)

Memory Management

When several jobs are being processed concurrently, the operating system must keep track of the way the computer's memory is being used and make sure that no job encroaches on another's territory.

Memory management is accomplished in a variety of ways, from simple routines that subdivide the available memory between jobs to elaborate schemes that temporarily swap information between the computer's memory and external storage devices. One common technique for dealing with memory shortages is to set aside part of a hard disk as **virtual memory.** Thanks to the operating system, this chunk of disk space looks just like internal memory to the CPU, even though access time is considerably slower than the access time to the internal memory is.

Resource Monitoring, Accounting, and Security

Many multiuser computer systems are designed to charge users for the resources they consume. These systems keep track of each user's time, storage demands, and pages printed so accounting programs can calculate and print accurate bills. Each user generally has a unique identification name and password, so the system can track and bill for individual resource usage. Even in environments where billing isn't an issue, the operating system should monitor resources to ensure the privacy and security of each user's data.

Program and Data Management

In addition to serving as a traffic cop, a security guard, and an accountant, the operating system acts as a librarian, locating and accessing files and programs requested by the user and by other programs. Later in the chapter we'll look in more detail at how file systems work.

Coordinating Network Communications

Until recently, network communications weren't handled by typical desktop operating systems used by consumers; instead, they were handled by specialized network operating systems. But modern operating systems are designed to serve as gateways to networks, from the inner office to the Internet, so networking is now a central feature of all modern operating systems. These network communication functions are described in detail in later chapters.

Utility Programs and Device Drivers

Even the best operating systems leave some housekeeping tasks to other programs and to the user. **Utility programs** serve as tools for doing system maintenance and repairs that aren't automatically handled by the operating system. Utilities make it easier for users to copy files between storage devices, repair damaged data files, translate files so that different programs can read them, guard against viruses and other potentially harmful programs (as described in the chapter on computer security and risks), compress files so they take up less disk space, and perform other important, if unexciting, tasks.

The operating system can directly invoke many utility programs, so they appear to the user to be part of the operating system. For example, **device drivers** are small programs that enable I/O devices—keyboard, mouse, printer, and others—to communicate with the computer. Once a device driver—say, for a new printer—is installed, the printer driver functions as a behind-the-scenes intermediary whenever the user requests that a document be printed on that printer. Some utility programs are included with the operating system. Others, including many device drivers, are bundled with peripherals. Still others are sold or given away as separate products.

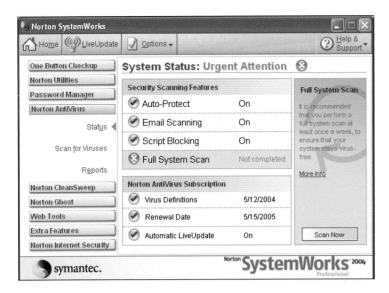

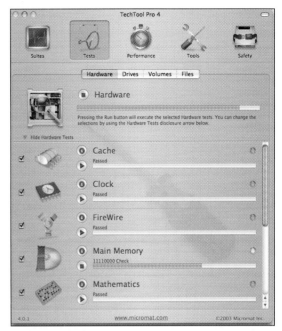

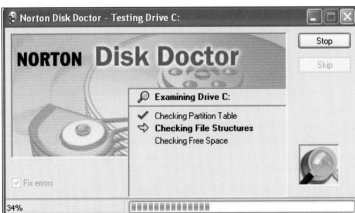

4.16 Norton SystemWorks (left) is a popular Windows utility package that includes software tools such as Norton Disk Doctor for recovering damaged files, repairing damaged disks, and improving performance. Techtool Pro (above) performs similar functions for Mac OS.

Where the Operating System Lives

Some computers—mostly game machines, handheld computers, and special-purpose computers—store their operating systems permanently in ROM (read-only memory) so they can begin working immediately when the user turns them on. But since ROM is unchangeable, operating systems on these machines can't be modified or upgraded without hardware transplants. Some computers, including many handheld devices, store their operating system in flash memory so it can be upgraded. But most computers, including all modern PCs, hold only a small portion of the operating system in ROM. The remainder of the operating system is loaded into memory in a process called **booting**, which occurs when you turn on the computer. (The term *booting* is used because the computer seems to pull itself up by its own bootstraps.)

Most of the time the operating system works behind the scenes, taking care of business without the knowledge or intervention of the user. But occasionally it's necessary for a user to communicate directly with the operating system. For example, when you boot a PC, the operating system takes over the screen, waiting until you tell it—with the mouse, the keyboard, or some other input device—what to do. If you tell it to open a graphics application, the operating system locates the program, copies it from disk into memory, turns the screen over to the application, and then accepts commands from the application while you draw pictures on the screen.

Interacting with the operating system, like interacting with an application, can be intuitive or challenging. It depends on something called the *user interface*. Because of its profound impact on the computing experience, the user interface is a critically important component of almost every piece of software.

The User Interface: The Human–Machine Connection

The anthropologist Claude Levi-Strauss has called human beings **tool makers** and **symbol makers**. The user interface is potentially **the most sophisticated** of these constructions, one in which the **distinction between tool and symbol is blurred.**

—Aaron Marcus and Andries van Dam, user interface experts

Early computer users had to spend tedious hours writing and debugging machine-language instructions. Later users programmed in languages that were easier to understand but still technically challenging. Today, users spend much of their time working with preprogrammed applications, such as word processors, that simulate and amplify the capabilities of real-world tools. As software evolves, so does the user interface—the look and feel of the computing experience from a human point of view.

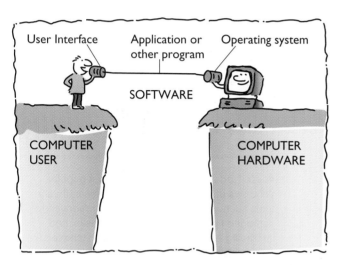

4.17 The user's view revisited: The user interface is the part of the computer system that the user sees. A well-designed user interface hides the bothersome details of computing from the user.

Desktop Operating Systems

The earliest PC operating systems, created for the Apple II, the original IBM PC, and other machines, looked nothing like today's Macintosh and Windows operating systems. When IBM introduced its first personal computer in 1981, a typical computer monitor displayed 24 80-column lines of text, numbers, and/or symbols. The computer sent messages to the monitor telling it which character to display in each location on the screen. To comply with this hardware arrangement, the PC's dominant operating system, MS-DOS, was designed with a character-based interface—a user interface based on characters rather than on graphics.

MS-DOS (Microsoft Disk Operating System, often simply called DOS) became the standard operating system on IBM-compatible computers—computers functionally identical to an IBM personal computer and therefore capable of running IBM-compatible software. Unlike the Windows desktop, MS-DOS used a command-line interface that required the user to type commands to which the computer responded. Some MS-DOS-compatible applications had a command-line interface, but it was more common for applications to have a menu-driven interface that enabled users to choose commands from on-screen lists called menus.

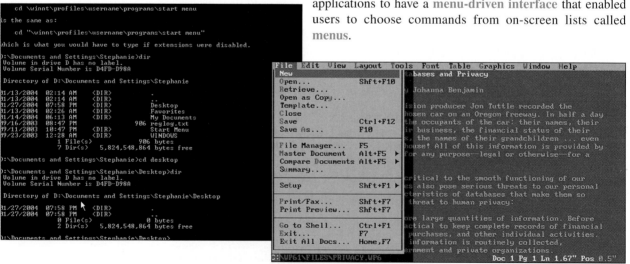

4.18 When typing commands to the OS or selecting options from menus in applications, MS-DOS users work with a character-based interface.

In the years since the introduction of the original IBM PC, graphic displays have become the norm. A computer with a graphic display is not limited to displaying rows and columns of characters; it can individually control every dot on the screen. When the Apple Macintosh was introduced in 1984, it was the first low-cost computer that had an operating system designed with a graphic display in mind. The **Mac OS** sports a **graphical user interface**—abbreviated **GUI**, and pronounced "gooey."

Instead of reading typed commands and filenames from a command line, the Macintosh operating system determines what the user wants by monitoring movements of the mouse. With the mouse, the user points to **icons** (pictures) that represent applications, **documents** (files, such as term papers and charts created with applications), **folders** (collections of files, sometimes called *directories*), and disks. These pictures are arranged on a metaphorical **desktop**—a virtual workspace designed to resemble in some ways the physical desktops we use in day-to-day work. Documents are displayed in **windows**—framed areas that can be opened, closed, and rearranged with the mouse. The user selects commands from **pull-down menus** at the top of the screen. **Dialog boxes** enable users to specify preferences by simply filling in on-screen blanks and clicking check boxes and buttons.

Though it was first to market, the Macintosh was eclipsed in the GUI operating system market by a product from Microsoft, the company that produces MS-DOS. Originally, **Microsoft Windows** (commonly called *Windows*) was a type of program, known as a **shell**, that put a graphical face on MS-DOS. The Windows shell stood between the user and the operating system, translating mouse movements and other user input into commands that could be recognized by MS-DOS. With the introduction of Windows 95 in 1995, Microsoft began transitioning Windows from an operating system shell into a full

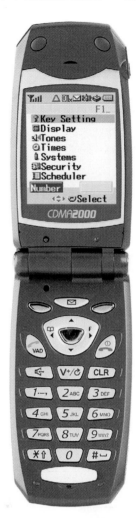

4.19 Many consumer devices today, including VCRs, cell phones, and pagers, have character-based user interfaces.

4.20 Mac OS X refines the traditional graphical user interface with a modern take on windows, icons, and pull-down menus.

4.21 Windows XP has an innovative task-based user interface that adapts to the data the user is viewing.

operating system that seldom showed its MS-DOS roots. Today, the latest Windows version, Windows XP, has no ties at all to the DOS past.

Windows and the Mac OS have evolved over the years, adding new features to their GUIs to make them easier to use. The Windows *task bar* provides one-click access to open applications and other windows, making it easy to switch back and forth among different tasks. **Hierarchical menus** in Windows and Mac OS organize frequently needed commands into compact, efficient submenus, and **pop-up menus** can appear anywhere on the screen. **Context-sensitive menus** offer choices that depend on which on-screen object the user has currently selected.

While there are many differences between Windows and Mac OS, the two now have user interfaces that are more alike than different. Many applications, including Adobe Photoshop and Microsoft Office, are almost identical on Windows and the Mac OS. Many users effortlessly switch between the two operating systems every day. (For a more thorough introduction to Windows and Mac OS, see Chapter 0: "The Basics.")

Multiple-User Operating Systems: UNIX and Linux

Because of its historical ties to academic and government research sites, the Internet is still heavily populated with computers running the **UNIX** operating system. UNIX, developed at Bell Labs over a decade before the first PCs, enables a timesharing computer to communicate with several other computers or terminals at one time. UNIX has long been the operating system of choice for workstations and mainframes in research and academic settings. In recent years it has taken root in many business environments. In spite of competition from Microsoft, UNIX is still the most widely available multiuser operating system today. Some form of UNIX is available for personal computers, workstations, servers, mainframes, and supercomputers.

Because of widespread licensing, commercial brands of UNIX are available from many companies, including Sun (Solaris), Hewlett-Packard (HP-UX), and IBM (AIX). Most Mac users don't know it, but Mac OS X is built around a version of UNIX. Linux, a UNIX clone described at the beginning of this chapter, is widely distributed for free and supported without cost by a devoted, technically savvy group of users.

At its heart, in all its versions, UNIX is a command-line, character-based operating system. The command-line interface is similar to that of MS-DOS, although the commands aren't the same. For most tasks the UNIX command-line interface feels like a single-user system, even when many users are *logged in*— connected to and using the system. But today's UNIX systems don't just work with typed commands. Several companies, including Apple, Sun, and IBM, market UNIX variations and shells with graphical interfaces.

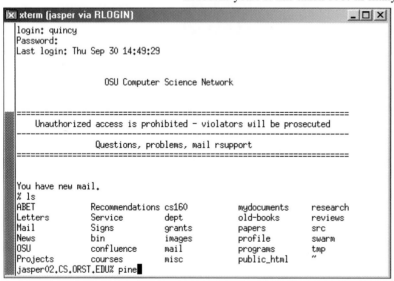

4.22 In its basic form, UNIX is a character-based operating system. This screen shows the beginning of a session on a school's multiuser Unix mainframe. After the user (quincy) types his login name and password, the system responds with some introductory messages and a prompt (in this case, %). Quincy types the "ls" command to view the names of files in his home directory. The system lists the files and then displays a new prompt. Quincy types "pine" to run the pine email program. The session continues this way until quincy responds to a prompt with a command to log off the system. In practice, many UNIX users never see this type of command line interface because of software shells with GUIs similar to Windows or Mac OS.

Screen Test

Using a Linux GUI

GOAL *To open and print a document, this time with Linux. You'll use GNOME, a shell that puts a graphical desktop environment between you and the Linux command-line environment.*

TOOLS *Linux, GNOME, and OpenOffice*

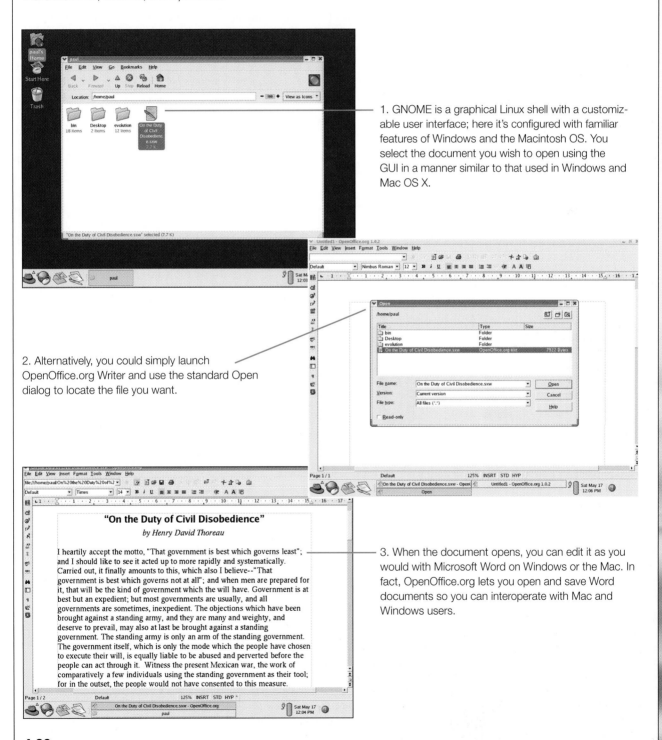

1. GNOME is a graphical Linux shell with a customizable user interface; here it's configured with familiar features of Windows and the Macintosh OS. You select the document you wish to open using the GUI in a manner similar to that used in Windows and Mac OS X.

2. Alternatively, you could simply launch OpenOffice.org Writer and use the standard Open dialog to locate the file you want.

3. When the document opens, you can edit it as you would with Microsoft Word on Windows or the Mac. In fact, OpenOffice.org lets you open and save Word documents so you can interoperate with Mac and Windows users.

4.23

Hardware and Software Platforms

In most electronic devices, the operating system operates invisibly and anonymously. But some operating systems, especially those in PCs, are recognized by name and reputation. The most well-known operating systems include:

- *Microsoft Windows XP.* This is Microsoft's flagship product introduced in 2001. Microsoft sells different versions of Windows XP, including Windows XP Home Edition, for home users; Windows XP Professional, for business users; Windows XP Tablet PC Edition, for Tablet PC-style notebooks; and Windows XP Media Center Edition, for a new generation of multimedia-enabled PCs that are typically used in a family room instead of the home office. All of these products are based on the same core operating system code. Windows XP is a more recent and enhanced version of Windows 2000 Professional, which was aimed solely at business users. Both Windows XP and Windows 2000 are technically successors to Windows NT, not Windows 9x/DOS.

- *Windows Server 2003.* Essentially the server-based counterpart to Windows XP and the successor to the Windows 2000 Server product family, this version of Windows runs on everything from small Web servers to the mightiest hardware on the planet. This product competes directly with many server versions of UNIX and Linux.

- *Microsoft Windows Millennium Edition (Windows Me)/Windows 9x.* This is Microsoft's last "consumer" operating system before XP Home Edition. It represents the end of the DOS-based Windows versions. Previous versions of this OS include Windows 98, Windows 95, and Windows 3.1; Windows 98 is still widely used.

- *Microsoft Windows CE.NET.* This stripped-down Windows variant is designed mostly for embedded, connected devices, and a special version of the OS, targeted at handheld computers like the Pocket PC and smart cell phones, competes directly with Palm's operating system (see following).

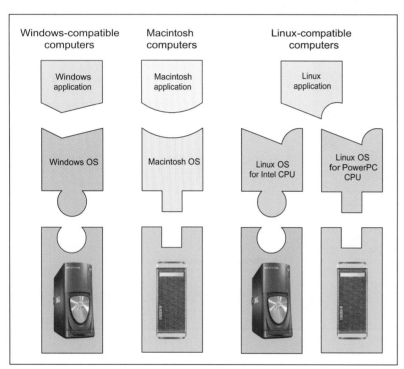

4.24 Compatibility issues: Hardware platforms and software environments.

- *Palm OS.* This OS, originally developed for the Palm Pilot, is now used in handheld devices manufactured by many companies, including Palm, Handspring, and Sony. Its pen-based user interface is simple and convenient to use. The Palm OS has communication capabilities that make it easy to transfer data between a handheld device and another computer. Palm OS is now also available in phones and other communication devices.

- *Mac OS X (10).* Introduced in 2001, OS X is the latest operating system for the Mac. It sports a stylish, animated user interface. Underneath its friendly exterior, OS X is built on UNIX, the powerful OS known for security and stability rather than simplicity. OS X runs only on Macintosh hardware.

- *Mac OS 9.* This is the last in a long line of Macintosh operating systems that started with the original Mac system in 1984. OS 9 and its predecessors run only on Macs.

- *Linux, Sun Solaris, and other UNIX variations.* Some form of UNIX or Linux can be found on PCs, Macs, workstations, supercomputers, mainframes, and a variety of other devices. Linux is especially popular because it is free—and freely supported by its partisans. Since Linux doesn't offer as many application programs as Windows does, some people use *dual-boot PCs* that can switch back and forth between Windows and Linux by simply rebooting.

Operating systems by themselves aren't very helpful to people. They need application software so they can do useful work. But application software can't exist by itself; it needs to be built on some kind of **platform**. People often use the term *platform* to describe the combination of hardware and operating system software on which application software is built. *Cross-platform applications*, such as Microsoft Office and Adobe Photoshop, are programs that are available in similar versions for multiple platforms.

The trends are unmistakable. In the early days of the personal computer revolution, there were dozens of different platforms—machines from Apple, Atari, Coleco, Commodore, Tandy, Texas Instruments, and other companies. All of these products have vanished from the marketplace, sometimes taking their parent companies with them. Today's market for new PC hardware and software is dominated by three general platforms: Windows in all its variations, the Mac OS, and various versions of UNIX/Linux. UNIX isn't often found in desktop PCs; it's mostly used in servers and high-end workstations. While the Mac commands a decent share of specialized markets like graphic design, publishing, music, video, and multimedia, it runs far behind Windows in the massive corporate and home markets.

Most personal computers today are built on what's sometimes called the "Wintel" platform: some form of the Windows OS running on an Intel (or compatible) CPU. The Macintosh platform—Mac OS software running on PowerPC processors—makes up a much smaller segment of the market. The Linux OS can run on many hardware platforms, including Intel and PowerPC processors, but different versions of Linux aren't necessarily compatible.

To interoperate with the Windows-dominated world, Mac users can buy software programs that create a simulated Windows machine in the Mac, translating all Windows-related instructions into signals the Mac's operating system and CPU can understand. Translation takes time, however, so software *emulation* often isn't adequate when speed is critical. But emulation blurs the lines between platforms and enables users to avoid having to choose a single operating system and user interface.

With the growing importance of the Internet and other networks, future applications may be more tied to networks than to desktop computer platforms. Computer users are spending less time dealing with information stored locally on their desktop computers and more time on the Web. Microsoft has responded to that trend with **.NET**, a strategy that blurs the line between the Web and Microsoft's operating systems and applications. As .NET evolves, more and more software components will be delivered by the network rather than residing on the desktop.

Microsoft's .NET strategy is a response to the popularity of **Java**, a platform-neutral computer language developed by Sun Microsystems for use on multiplatform networks. Programs written in Java can run on computers running Windows, Macintosh, UNIX, and other operat-

4.25 Virtual-machine software, such as Virtual PC, available on both Mac and Windows platforms, lets users run Windows and Linux environments inside of a window on the host OS and move data between the virtual machine and the host OS.

ing systems, provided those computers have *Java virtual machine* software installed. However, like emulation software, Java applications run more slowly than applications targeted to a specific OS platform do. Small Java *applets*—miniature application pieces designed to work with other applications or applets—are often included in World Wide Web pages today to add animation and interactivity. As this technology matures, it may make it possible for computer users to do their work without knowing—or caring—where in the world their software is.

File Management: Where's My Stuff?

The first principle of human interface design, whether for a **doorknob** or a **computer**, is to keep in mind the **human being** who wants to use it. **The technology is subservient to that goal.**

—Donald Norman, in The Art of Human–Computer Interface Design

You've seen how the modern operating system provides an interface layer between the computer user and the user's data. In this section we'll look behind the Windows and Mac GUIs to see how information is stored and organized on a computer's hard disk.

Organizing Files and Folders

As we've seen, Windows and the Mac OS employ a user interface that makes an analogy between a computer system and a business office. The monitor becomes a virtual desktop, and the reports, photographs, and other objects manipulated by the computer become files appearing on the desktop. To prevent the desktop from becoming too cluttered, files may be placed inside folders. After a while, the number of folders can become overwhelming, so operating system designers stretch the analogy a little bit and allow users to place a folder inside another folder.

A computer's files and folders are actually stored on a nonvolatile storage device, such as a hard disk, floppy disk, or optical disc. The Windows operating system uses letters to refer to particular storage devices. A Windows PC's floppy disk drive typically is assigned the letter "A", while the computer's primary hard disk is usually given the letter "C". Every file and folder has a unique **pathname**, which describes the nesting of folders containing it. Within the pathname, the backslash character "\" separates the name of the folders.

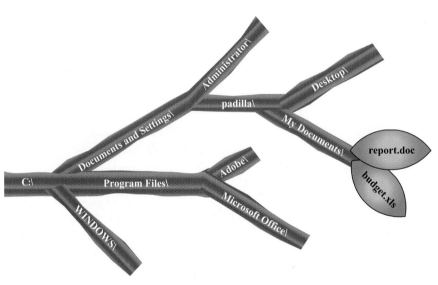

4.26 Because many folders and files may be put into the same folder, you can think of the file directory structure as a kind of tree, where the root directory is the trunk, the folders are the branches, and the files are the leaves. In this particular file directory structure the pathname C:\Documents and Settings\padilla\My Documents\budget.xls refers to an Excel spreadsheet.

For example, on a Windows XP system, the files and folders appearing on the desktop of user "padilla" are most likely kept in the directory

C:\Documents and Settings\padilla\Desktop

Let's interpret this pathname. The main folder on the C drive, called the **root directory**, contains all the other files and folders kept on the disk. The beginning of the pathname,

"C:\", refers to the root directory. The root directory contains a folder named "Documents and Settings". Within folder "Documents and Settings" is another folder named "padilla". Within folder "padilla" is another folder named "Desktop". Within folder "Desktop" is a list of the files and folders appearing on the Windows desktop of user "padilla". (Pathnames on Macintoshes are similar to Windows pathnames, except that there's no requirement that drives be given one-letter names. As a result, most drives have names such as "Padilla HD1" and "Backup drive" rather than C and D.)

File-Management Utilities

A **file-management utility** lets you view, rename, copy, move, and delete files and folders. In the Mac OS, the file-management utility is called the Finder; in Windows it is called Windows Explorer. In both cases, the file-management utility is included with the operating system; few computer users know they're using a separate program when they use these utilities.

You can use a file-management utility to see the location of a file or folder in a storage device's hierarchy and view its pathname. You can also configure the utility to display information about a particular file, such as its size, its type, and the last time it was modified.

File-management utilities simplify copying, moving, and deleting files and folders. Each of these operations, as well as creating new folders, is reduced to a few simple mouse operations. Renaming a file or folder is as simple as clicking the object's icon and typing the new name.

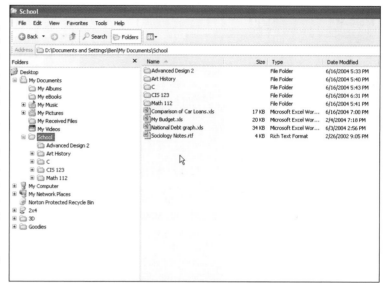

4.27 Windows Explorer allows you to see both the contents of a folder and the location of the folder in the storage device's hierarchy.

Managing Files from Applications

Most applications manipulate objects that can be stored in files. For example, a word processor allows you type a new document or start with a previously saved document. In either case, you have the ability to save a copy of the new or revised document. An email program allows you to save some or all of the emails you have sent or received. An entertainment application may give you the opportunity to save the state of a game and restart the game from that point. Most applications support four basic file-management operations: Open, Save, Save As, and Close.

The *Open* operation allows you to select the file containing the project you would like to work on. After you select the file, the application reads its contents into memory. The state of the application changes to reflect the contents of the file. For example, when you open a file containing a spreadsheet, the contents of the spreadsheet file are displayed for you to view and manipulate.

The *Save* operation writes the current state of the application as a disk file. Suppose you are enhancing a spreadsheet that has been in existence for a while. You used the Open operation to retrieve the previous version of the spreadsheet. After adding some new formulas to the spreadsheet, you replace the previous version with the new, improved version. The Save operation overwrites the prior version of the spreadsheet with the enhanced version.

The *Save As* operation allows you to choose the location and name of the file you want to contain the current state of the application. The Save As operation must be used when a new object has been created. For example, suppose you are running a word processor to create a report from scratch. Since you began with a blank document, there is no filename associated with it. The first time you save the report, the application must be given the

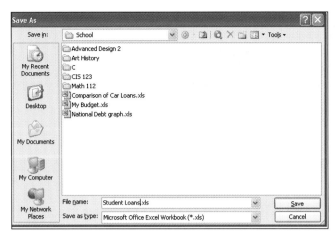

4.28 The "Save As" operation lets you choose the location and the name of the file that will store the current state of the application.

name and location of the file. Another time to use the Save As operation is when you do not want to overwrite the previously saved version. Suppose you open a file containing a digital photograph and use a photo editor to touch it up. You would like to save your work, but you do not want to lose the original in case you've accidentally made a mistake with your retouching. You can keep the original copy and save the new copy by using the Save As operation to give the new copy a different name than the original.

The *Close* operation allows you to stop working on a project but remain in the application program. A Close operation is often followed by an Open operation to read in a new project. When you Close a project, its current state is not saved to a file. Changes you have made to the project since the last Save or Save As operation are lost. If you attempt to close a modified project without saving it, the application probably will display a pop-up window that asks you if you would like to save the project before closing it.

Locating Files

Even if you start with a brand new computer, it doesn't take long to create a huge number of files scattered all over the file system. It's hard to manage data that you can't even find. Of course, it's easier to find files if they're organized logically. To this end, both Windows and the Mac support common system folders with self-explanatory names. For example, your documents might be stored in a folder called *My Documents* (*Documents* in Mac OS X). Likewise, digital photos can be stored in *My Pictures* (*Pictures*) and digital music files can be stored in *My Music* (*Music*). These folders are specific to each user, so multiple users on a single PC will each have unique data in their system folders.

Modern operating systems include search tools that can help you find files wherever they're stored. You can search for filenames, but you can also search for words or phrases inside a file. So if you don't know the name of a file but do know some text that might be contained in that file, you can use the search tool to find your data.

The Search and Find commands are designed to help answer the common computer user's question, "Where's my stuff?" Windows and Mac OS were originally designed when low-capacity floppy disk drives seemed spacious. Today's massive hard drives can hold thousands of files, from email messages to media files. In recent years, Apple and Microsoft have developed new file-management tools to help computer users keep track of their music libraries, photograph collections, email messages, and other files.

Applications such as Apple's iTunes and iPhoto and Microsoft's Windows Media Player go beyond the limitations of the folders-and-windows GUI for cataloging, organizing, and finding media files. For example, Apple's view-based interface enables music collectors to see their collections in a variety of ways. A particular song in an iTunes library might be found by title, artist, recording date, file size, genre, or number of times played. It might also show up in one or many playlists created by the user or by the computer.

4.29 The powerful file management tools in Apple's iTunes allow users to view and organize song collections in a variety of ways. Similar tools for organizing and navigating computer files are at the heart of Mac OS X 10.4 and a future version of the Windows OS.

This type of organizational tool—essentially a database interface—works well for large media collections. But it also works for data files in general. The next major Windows version will include database capabilities in the file system so that you can more easily locate information stored anywhere in your PC. Like the smart playlist feature in Apple iTunes, this feature will help users find their stuff more quickly and easily, while shielding them from the intricacies of the underlying system. And as we move toward distributed computing environments, where data might be stored on different systems on a network or across the Internet, these technologies will become even more valuable.

Defragmentation: The Cure for Fragmented Files

Before the operating system can store files on a hard disk, the disk must be formatted. Formatting a disk means putting electronic marks on the disk, dividing the disk into a series of concentric *tracks* and dividing each track into a collection of *sectors*. (You may never have had to format a hard disk yourself, because computer manufacturers format the hard disks of new computers in order to install the operating system and application programs.) Formatting removes any information that was previously stored on the disk, so you should make sure you never reformat a disk that contains important information.

Sectors are quite small compared to the size of the files most frequently stored on a disk. For this reason disk drives usually bundle sectors into *clusters* or *blocks*. Because many files are larger than a single cluster, the file system must provide a way to link multiple clusters to store larger files. To keep track of the files kept on a disk, the file system maintains a table (also stored on the disk) that indicates which clusters are assigned to each file. The file system also maintains a list of empty clusters. It dips into the pool of empty clusters when you want to create a new file or add to an existing file.

Accessing the information in a file is faster if the file is assigned to contiguous clusters. That way, the disk

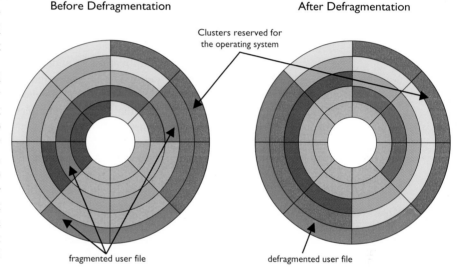

Before Defragmentation

After Defragmentation

Clusters reserved for the operating system

fragmented user file

defragmented user file

4.30 Having a lot of fragmented files can degrade the performance of a hard disk. In this figure, clusters reserved for operating system files are red. Other colors represent application and user files (one file per color). After defragmentation, files are assigned to contiguous clusters whenever possible. For example, before defragmentation, the four sectors holding the user file shown in blue are scattered over three tracks. After defragmentation, all four sectors occupy a single track.

head reading the information does not have to move from track to track as often. Moving the disk head takes several milliseconds, a long time on modern PCs that can perform more than a million instructions every millisecond! Assigning a file to contiguous clusters minimizes the movement of the disk head when the contents of the file are read into memory.

As you work with a file, its contents may become scattered over distant clusters. Suppose you have been editing a Word document, and you ask the file system to save a newer, longer version of the document. If the document no longer fits in the cluster(s) to which it was assigned, the file system looks to see whether the next cluster is empty. If so, it can allocate that cluster to the document, keeping it stored in contiguous clusters. However, if the next cluster is already allocated to another file, the operating system must find another empty cluster. A fragmented file is a file allocated to noncontiguous clusters. As you create, edit, and delete files, more and more of them become fragmented, degrading the performance of the hard disk.

A defragmentation utility eliminates (as much as possible) fragmented files by changing the assignment of clusters to files. Depending upon how fragmented a disk is, the defragmentation process may take hours. For this reason, it's a good idea to let a defragmentation program run overnight. Because defragmentation can significantly improve the performance of a disk drive, some experts recommend that PC users defragment their disks at least once a month. However, if the defragmentation process fails for some reason, a file system can be left in a corrupted state, and the information stored on a disk can be lost. For this reason, it's a good idea to make sure that you've backed up the important files on your hard drive before you defragment the file system, just in case.

Software Piracy and Intellectual Property Laws

Information wants to be free. Information also wants to be expensive. Information wants to **be free** because it has become so cheap to distribute, copy, and recombine—**too cheap to meter. It wants to be expensive** because it can be **immeasurably valuable** to the recipient. **That tension will not go away**.

—*Stewart Brand, in* The Media Lab

Software piracy—the illegal duplication of copyrighted software—is rampant. Millions of computer users have made copies of programs they don't legally own and distributed them to family members, friends, and, sometimes, total strangers. Because so few software companies use physical copy protection methods such as dongles to protect their products, copying software is as easy as duplicating an audio CD or photocopying a chapter of a book. Unfortunately, many people aren't aware that copying software, recorded music, and books can violate federal laws protecting intellectual property. Many others simply look the other way, convinced that software companies, music companies, and publishers already make enough money.

The Piracy Problem

The software industry, with a world market of more than $50 billion a year, loses billions of dollars every year to software pirates. The Business Software Alliance (BSA) estimates that more than one-third of all software in use is illegally copied, costing the software industry tens of thousands of jobs. Piracy can be particularly hard on small software companies. Developing software is just as difficult for them as it is for big companies like Microsoft and Oracle, but they often lack the financial and legal resources to cover their losses they suffer through piracy.

Software industry organizations, including the BSA and SPA Anti-Piracy (a division of the Software & Information Industry Association), work with law enforcement agencies to crack down on piracy. At the same time, they sponsor educational programs to make computer users aware that piracy is theft, because laws can't work without citizen understanding and support.

Software piracy is a worldwide problem, with piracy rates highest in developing nations. In China, approximately 95 percent of all new software installations are pirated; in Vietnam, the piracy rate is 97 percent. A few Third World nations refuse to abide by international copyright laws. They argue that the laws protect rich countries at the expense of underdeveloped nations. In 1998 the Argentine Supreme Court ruled that the country's copyright laws don't apply to computer software.

Intellectual Property and the Law

Legally, the definition of intellectual property includes the results of intellectual activities in the arts, science, and industry. Copyright laws have traditionally protected forms of literary expression, including books, plays, songs, paintings, photographs, and movies. Trademark law has protected symbols, pictures, sounds, colors, and smells used by a business to identify goods. Patent law has protected mechanical inventions, and contract law has covered trade secrets. Software doesn't fit neatly into any of these categories under the law. Copyright laws protect most commercial software programs, but a few companies have successfully used patent laws to protect software products.

The purpose of intellectual property laws is to ensure that mental labor is justly rewarded and to encourage innovation. Programmers, inventors, scientists, writers, editors, filmmakers, and musicians depend on ideas and the expression of those ideas for their incomes. Ideas are information, and information is easy to copy—especially in this electronic age. Intellectual property laws are designed to protect these professionals and encourage them to continue their creative efforts so society can benefit from their future work.

Most of the time, these laws help them to achieve their goals. A novelist can devote two or three years of her life to writing a masterpiece, confident that she won't find bootleg copies for sale on street corners when she finishes it. A movie studio can invest millions of dollars in a film, knowing that the investment will be returned, a little at a time, through ticket sales and video rentals. An inventor can work long hours to create a better mousetrap and know that MegaMousetrap City won't steal her idea.

But sometimes intellectual property laws are applied in such a way that they may stifle the innovation and creativity they're designed to protect. In 1999 Amazon.com was awarded a controversial patent for "one-click shopping," preventing other e-commerce sites from giving their customers a similar, simple shopping experience. Similarly, SightSound patented all paid downloads of "desired digital video or digital audio signals." RealNetworks patented streaming audio and video, and British Telecom claims to hold a 1976 patent that covers every Web hyperlink! Most experts agree that these ideas are too simple and broad to be owned by one company. And in many cases, the patent owner isn't the inventor of the concept; Douglas Engelbart demonstrated hyperlinking as early as 1967 at Stanford Research Institute. Such broad patents generally end up in court, where legal experts and technology experts debate the merits and scope of the ideas and the laws designed to protect them. Meanwhile, legislators attempt to update the laws to address ever-changing technological advances.

Most existing copyright and patent laws, which evolved during the age of print and mechanical inventions, are outdated, contradictory, and inadequate for today's information technology. Many laws, including the Computer Fraud and Abuse Act of 1984, clearly treat software piracy as a crime. The NET (No Electronic Theft) Act of 1997 closed a narrow loophole in the law that allowed people to give away software on the Internet.

The Digital Millennium Copyright Act (DMCA) of 1998 represents the most comprehensive reform of U.S. copyright law in a generation. The DCMA includes several controversial provisions that need to be clarified by the courts. According to the law, it is illegal to write a program that circumvents copy protection schemes, no matter if that program is used to copy DVDs, electronic books, or other protected material illegally. The DMCA also makes it a crime to share information about how to crack copy protection. Critics argue that the law suppresses freedom of speech, academic freedom, and the principle of fair use—the time-honored right to make copies of copyrighted material for personal and academic use and for other noncompetitive purposes.

In 2001 the Recording Industry Association of America (RIAA) used the DMCA to shut down the Napster music-sharing service; by 2003 the RIAA was invoking the DMCA to force Internet service providers to reveal the identities of individual song pirates. While the courts eventually ruled that Internet service providers did not have to give this information to the RIAA, questions about the scope and reach of the DMCA remain. Meanwhile, millions of people continue to exchange music, movies, and other copyrighted works over KaZaA and other file-sharing networks. Some organizations, such as the Electronic Frontier Foundation, are advocating a reform of the copyright system that would legalize file sharing while still providing a way for musicians to receive a fair financial return for their creative efforts.

In matters of software, the legal system is sailing in uncharted waters. Whether dealing with issues of piracy or monopoly, lawmakers and judges must struggle with difficult questions about innovation, property, freedom, and progress. The questions are likely to be with us for quite a while.

4.31 In 1999, Moscow police attempted to make a dent in the illegal software market by destroying mountains of pirated software. Their efforts were largely unsuccessful, however. At this time, Russia has one of the highest software piracy rates in the world, close to that of China's.

Inventing the FUTURE

Tomorrow's User Interfaces

Twenty years ago, the typical computer could be operated only by a highly trained professional, and using a computer was pretty much synonymous with programming a computer. Today, computers are so easy to use that they're sold at shopping malls and operated by preschoolers.

The graphical user interface pioneered by Xerox and popularized by Apple and Microsoft has become an industry standard, making it possible for users to move between computer types almost as easily as drivers can adjust to different brands of cars. But experts expect user interfaces to continue to evolve before they settle down into the kind of long-lasting standard we're used to in automobiles. Today's WIMP (windows, icons, menus, and pointing devices) interface is easier to learn and use than earlier character-based interfaces, but it's not the end of the user interface evolution.

Researcher Raj Reddy uses another acronym to describe emerging user interface technologies: SILK, for speech, image, language, and knowledge capabilities. SILK incorporates many important software technologies:

➡ *Speech and language.* Although we still don't have a language-translating telephone or a foolproof dictation-taking "talkwriter," speech technology is maturing into a practical alternative to keyboard and mouse input. Voice-recognition systems are used for security systems, automated voicemail systems, hands-free Web navigation, and other applications. New applications are being developed and marketed every day. With or without speech, natural-language processing will be part of future user interfaces. It's just a matter of time before we'll be able to communicate with computers in English, Spanish, Japanese, or some other natural language. Today, many computers can reliably read subsets of these languages or can be trained to understand spoken commands and text. Tomorrow's machines should be able to handle much day-to-day work through a natural-language interface, written or spoken. Researchers expect that we'll soon be using programs that read documents as we create them, edit them according to our instructions, and file them based on their content.

➡ *Image.* In the last decade, computer graphics have become an integral part of the computing experience. Tomorrow's graphics won't be still, flat images; they'll include three-dimensional models, animation, and video clips. Today's two-dimensional desktop interfaces will give way to three-dimensional workspace metaphors complete with 3-D animated objects—virtual workspaces unlike anything we use today. Virtual reality (VR) user interfaces will create the illusion that

4.32 Virtual reality user interfaces can enhance research and recreation. In Argonne's CAVE (top), a scientist can interactively study the relationships between the nucleic acids of the molecule. In a similar CAVE (bottom) at the Center for Supercomputer Applications at the University of Illinois, a student plays a CAVE version of Quake II, a 3-D video game.

the user is immersed in a world inside the computer—an environment that contains both scenes and the controls to change those scenes. (Virtual reality is discussed in more detail in the Chapter 6 *Inventing the Future*.)

➡ *Knowledge.* Many experts predict that knowledge will be the most important enhancement to the user interface of the future. Advances in the technology of knowledge will enable engineers to design self-maintaining systems that can diagnose and correct common problems without human intervention. Advances in knowledge will make user interfaces more friendly and forgiving. Intelligent applications will be able to decipher many ambiguous commands and correct common errors as they happen. But more important, knowledge will enable software agents to really be of service to users. Software agents are discussed in next chapter's *Inventing the Future*. ∼

The Bugs in the Machine *by Brendan I. Koerner*

Computer software is plagued by bugs—errors in the instructions that create incorrect results, system failures, or worse. In this article from the August 2002 issue of Wired, *writer Brendan I. Koerner explores the implications of buggy software that's burned into firmware. Are bugs making our tools and toys unsafe?*

Ed Yourdon was on a tarmac in Pittsburgh when he got a glimpse of the coming software hell. His New York shuttle had been cleared for takeoff when the pilot pulled a U-turn and headed back to the gate. The flaps were stuck. "We're going to have to power down and reboot," the pilot announced. It was the aeronautical equivalent of Ctrl+Alt+Delete. "Makes you think," says Yourdon, author of *Byte Wars.* "Maybe they had Windows 95 underneath the hood."

He's not necessarily joking. The so-called embedded systems crammed into jets, cars, and "smart" appliances increasingly rely on the same bug-ridden code that corrupts PowerPoint slides, freezes Ultima games midquest, and costs corporate America $293 billion a year in lost productivity. "They're starting to put Windows CE into automobile dashboards," says Philip Koopman, a computer engineer at Carnegie Mellon University. "What used to be some gears and springs is now a sophisticated computing complex. Think about it."

Or don't, if you scare easily. The software industry's nasty secret is that—surprise!—off-the-shelf code doesn't magically turn trustworthy once it's jammed behind a steering wheel. This sleight of hand wouldn't be so alarming if lives weren't at stake. But imagine the blue screen of death at highway speed.

The problem is built into the software industry. There are 5 to 15 flaws in every 1,000 lines of code, the Software Engineering Institute estimates. Mindful of cost-benefit ratios, vendors have little incentive to boost quality; it's cheaper to write postrelease patches than to spend months triple-checking every string of code. Even if they wanted to churn out more reliable products, most programmers lack the skills. Point-and-click development aids like Visual C++ have turned software creation into a For Dummies exercise.

That reality is now making its way into embedded systems. Code-imbued hardware, once built as a cohesive whole by in-house designers, is more and more likely to incorporate off-the-shelf software. Only 40 percent of embedded operating systems are made from scratch, a figure sure to drop as Microsoft and its Linux rivals push their cheaper options. Why assemble a novel OS when you can shoehorn in Windows 2005 Embedded?

So laptops crash, government servers botch Medicaid requests, and the occasional NASA robot goes haywire on Mars—*c'est la vie digitale*, right? Except that buggy software is creeping into systems where failure can't be dismissed with curses and a sigh. Consider: DARPA is using wearable computers designed to beam tactical information to the "data visors" of combat troops. The devices run Windows 2000, an OS so flawed that its bug-cleansing "service packs" run to 100 Mbytes. A sniper-filled valley near Mazar-i-Sharif would be a particularly lousy spot to encounter a Runtime Error pop-up. Or take mobile phones. They worked fine when telephony was their sole task. Now that they're equipped with Web browsers and GPS chips, software glitches are routine. If you're one of the 200,000 Americans a day who dial 911 on a cell, shabby code could be a real downer. And the problem will only get worse as the tech industry's weakness for bloatware infects all those code-enriched gizmos now on the drawing board—refrigerators that email repairmen, alarms that sniff chemical leaks, cars with drive-by-wire setups.

Yet the shoddiness of these products is hardly inevitable. With a bit more elbow grease, software designers can write increasingly reliable code. One smart move would be to use mutation testing, a quality-control technique that flushes out errors by analyzing the behavior of software that's deliberately infested with bugs. Though effective, it's rarely used by commercial coders because it adds to development costs. But if software jockeys are going to be responsible for lives as well as spreadsheets, their fixation on the bottom line must change.

ONE SOLUTION IS TO UNLEASH THE LAWYERS

If it doesn't, there's always the American way: Unleash the lawyers. At the moment, shrink-wrap licenses and click-through agreements shield software makers from damage claims—even if they broke it, you bought it. Just as the legal fallout from exploding Pintos shamed Detroit, exposing software to class-action lawsuits might induce Silicon Valley to code more cautiously.

Of course, there will be bobsledding in Hades before the software industry willingly accepts such an arrangement. Software is intrinsically complex, lobbyists might aver, and bugs are an ineradicable part of the bargain. Let them think that—at least until the day they find themselves aloft in a plane that needs to reboot.

Discussion Questions

1. Are you troubled by the idea of a car or airplane running on Windows, Linux, or some other commercial operating system? Why or why not?

2. What do you think can be done to make products with embedded code safer?

Summary

Software provides the communication link between humans and their computers. Because software is soft—stored in memory rather than hard-wired into the circuitry—it can easily be modified to meet the needs of the computer user. By changing software, you can change a computer from one kind of tool into another.

Most software falls into one of three broad categories: compilers and other translator programs, software applications, and system software. A compiler is a software tool that enables programs written in English-like languages such as Visual Basic, .NET, and C# to be translated into the zeros and ones of the machine language the computer understands. A compiler frees the programmer from the tedium of machine language programming, making it easier to write quality programs with fewer bugs. But even with the best translators, programming is a little like communicating with an alien species. It's a demanding process that requires more time and mental energy than most people are willing or able to invest.

Fortunately, software applications make it easy for most computer users today to communicate their needs to the computer without learning programming. Applications simulate and extend the properties of familiar real-world tools like typewriters, paintbrushes, and file cabinets, making it possible for people to do things with computers that would be difficult or impossible otherwise. Integrated software packages combine several applications in a single unified package, making it easy to switch between tools. For situations in which a general commercial program won't do the job, programmers for businesses and public institutions develop vertical-market and custom packages.

Whether you're writing programs or simply using them, the computer's operating system is functioning behind the scenes, translating your software's instructions into messages that the hardware can understand. Popular operating systems today include several versions of Microsoft Windows, the Mac OS, and several versions of UNIX. An operating system serves as the computer's business manager, taking care of the hundreds of details that need to be handled to keep the computer functioning. A timesharing operating system has the particularly challenging job of serving multiple users concurrently, monitoring the machine's resources, keeping track of each user's account, and protecting the security of the system and each user's data. One of the most important jobs of the operating system is managing the program and data files stored on nonvolatile memory devices, such as hard disks and optical discs. Utility programs can handle many of those system-related problems that the operating system can't solve directly. Popular operating systems today include several versions of Microsoft Windows, the Mac OS, and several versions of UNIX.

Applications, utilities, programming languages, and operating systems all must, to varying degrees, communicate with the user. A program's user interface is a critical factor in that communication. User interfaces have evolved over the years to the point where sophisticated software packages can be operated by people who know little about the inner workings of the computer. A well-designed user interface shields the user from the bits and bytes, creating an on-screen façade or shell that makes sense to the user. Today, the computer industry has moved away from the tried-and-true command-line interfaces toward a friendlier graphical user interface that uses windows, icons, mice, and pull-down menus in an intuitive, consistent environment. Tomorrow's user interfaces are likely to depend more on voice, three-dimensional graphics, and animation to create an artificial reality.

Commercial software programs enjoy copyright protection. The purpose of granting copyrights to the owners of intellectual property is to stimulate creativity. However, copyright law can stifle creativity if it prevents people from building on the work of others. For this reason, a tension exists between the needs and desires of producers and the needs and desires of consumers. Despite copyright protections for computer programs, software piracy has flourished, particularly in countries like China and Russia.

Key Terms

Interactive Activities

1. The *Computer Confluence* CD-ROM contains self-test multiple-choice quiz questions related to this chapter.

2. The *Computer Confluence* Web site, **http://www.computerconfluence.com**, contains self-test exercises related to this chapter. Follow the instructions for taking a quiz. After you've completed your quiz, you can email the results to your instructor.

3. The Web site also contains open-ended discussion questions called Internet Explorations. Discuss one or more of the Internet Exploration questions at the section for this chapter.

True or False

1. Linux is the original Microsoft operating system with a command-line interface.

2. An algorithm is a computer program written in machine language.

3. When you buy a software program, you're really buying a license to use the program according to rules specified by the software company.

4. Shareware is a type of software application used for sharing files over a network or the Internet.

5. Operating system software runs continuously whenever a PC is on.

6. Your computer can't print documents unless it has a device driver that allows it to communicate with your printer.

7. The first low-cost operating system with a graphical user interface was an early version of Microsoft Windows.

8. It is impossible to run Windows applications on a Macintosh computer.

9. A PC can have only one operating system installed on its hard disk at a time.

10. The PC's user interface isn't likely to change significantly in the next decade.

Multiple Choice

1. Which of the following is the most famous example of open source software?
   a. Microsoft Windows
   b. Mac OS X
   c. UNIX
   d. Linux
   e. Palm OS

2. What is correcting errors in a program called?
   a. Compiling
   b. Debugging
   c. Grinding
   d. Interpreting
   e. Translating

3. A compiler translates a program written in a high-level language into
   a. Machine language
   b. An algorithm
   c. A debugged program
   d. C#
   e. Natural language

4. What does a program's end-user license agreement (EULA) typically include?
   a. Rules specifying how the software may be used
   b. Warranty disclaimers
   c. Rules concerning the copying of the software
   d. All of the above
   e. None of the above

5. When you buy a typical computer software package, you are purchasing
   a. A guarantee that the software has no bugs in it
   b. A share of stock in the company making the software
   c. The software
   d. A license to use the software
   e. Free upgrades to the software

6. Microsoft Office is
   a. Shareware
   b. Public-domain software
   c. Open-source software
   d. A vertical-market application
   e. An application suite

7. What does the computer's operating system do?
   a. Communicates with peripherals
   b. Coordinates concurrent processing of jobs
   c. Monitors resources and handles basic security
   d. All of the above
   e. None of the above

8. Which of the following can handle most system functions that aren't handled directly by the operating system?
   a. Vertical-market applications
   b. Utilities
   c. Algorithms
   d. Integrated software
   e. Compilers

9. The operating system is stored in ROM or flash memory in most
   a. Windows and Macintosh computers
   b. Mainframes and supercomputers
   c. Handheld and special-purpose computers
   d. Open-source and public-domain computers
   e. Workstations and servers

10. What happens when you boot up a PC?
    a. Portions of the operating system are copied from disk into memory.
    b. Portions of the operating system are copied from memory onto disk.
    c. Portions of the operating system are compiled.
    d. Portions of the operating system are emulated.
    e. None of the above

11. Device drivers are
    a. Small, special-purpose programs
    b. Tiny power cords for external storage devices
    c. Experts who know how to maximize the performance of devices
    d. The innermost part of the operating system
    e. Substitutes for operating systems

12. What is the main folder on a storage device called?
    a. Platform
    b. Interface
    c. Root directory
    d. Desktop
    e. Device driver

13. UNIX is
    a. A multiuser operating system designed more than three decades ago
    b. At the heart of Mac OS X
    c. The operating system that is widely used for Internet servers
    d. All of the above
    e. None of the above

14. Future PC user interfaces will almost certainly involve more use of
    a. Machine language
    b. Natural language
    c. High-level language
    d. Assembly language
    e. Algorithmic language

15. Most commercial software programs enjoy a form of intellectual property protection called
    a. Copyright
    b. Open source
    c. Patent
    d. Trademark
    e. Trade secret

Review Questions

1. What is the relationship between a program and an algorithm?

2. Most computer software falls into one of three categories: compilers and other translator programs, software applications, and system software. Describe and give examples of each.

3. Which must be loaded first into the computer's memory, the operating system or software applications? Why?

4. Write an algorithm for changing a flat tire. Check your algorithm carefully for errors and ambiguities. Then have a classmate or your instructor check it. How did your results compare?

5. Describe several functions of a single-user operating system. Describe several additional functions of a multiuser operating system.

6. What does it mean when software is called IBM-compatible or Macintosh-compatible? What does this have to do with the operating system?

7. Why is the user interface such an important part of software?

8. What is a graphical user interface? How does it differ from a character-based interface? What are the advantages of each?

9. What are the three main platforms for desktop computers today? Briefly describe each of them.

Discussion Questions

1. In what way is writing instructions for a computer more difficult than writing instructions for a person? In what way is it easier?

2. How would using a computer be different if it had no operating system? How would programming be different?

3. Speculate about the user interface of a typical computer in the year 2010. How would this user interface differ from those used in today's computers?

4. If you had the resources to design a computer with a brand-new user interface, what would your priorities be? Make a rank-ordered list of the qualities you'd like to have in your user interface.

5. How do you feel about the open software movement? Would you be willing to volunteer your time to write software or help users for free?

6. Suppose you've spent all your spare time for the past eight months programming a new PC game. Your friends have tried it and say it is great. They have started bugging you for copies of the game. Would you give the game away or try to sell it?

Projects

1. Write a report about available computer applications in your field of study or in your chosen profession.

2. Take an inventory of computer applications available in your computer lab. Describe the major uses for each application.

3. Poll 50 college students and find out what kind of computer they own, if any. Compute the percentage of students that own a computer. Of the students who do own a computer, determine the percentage of students owning a system running a version of Windows, the percentage of students owning a system running a version of the Mac OS, and the percentage of students owning a system running Linux.

4. Interview five people who own a PC running a version of the Windows operating system, and interview five people who own a PC running a version of the Mac OS. Ask each person to explain what they like best about their computer's operating system, as well as what they dislike the most about their computer's operating system. After you are done with your interviews, look for similarities and differences between the likes and dislikes of Windows and Mac users.

Sources and Resources

Books

Just for Fun: The Story of an Accidental Revolutionary, by Linus Torvalds and David Diamond (New York: HarperBusiness, 2002). Red Herring Executive Editor convinced Linus Torvalds to tell his story. The result is this book, a quirky collection of tidbits from the life of the creator of Linux.

Rebel Code: Linux and the Open Source Revolution, by Glyn Moody (New York: Perseus, 2002). This book tells the Linux story in a style that's more conventional, and for many readers, more readable, than the Torvalds/Diamond book.

The Cathedral and the Bazaar: Musings on Linux and Open Source by an Accidental Revolutionary, Revised Edition, by Eric S. Raymond (Sebastapol, CA: O'Reilly, 2001). This widely praised book is an expanded version of the original manifesto for the open-source software movement—the movement that threatens to revolutionize the software industry. Tom Peters calls it "wonderful, witty, and, ultimately, wise."

Windows XP for Dummies, by Andy Rothbone (Indianapolis, IN: Hungry Minds, 2001). The Dummies series that started with DOS for Dummies has expanded to cover everything from antiquing to yoga. Unlike Microsoft, this book series isn't a monopoly. There are hundreds of books on Windows for dummies and nondummies alike.

The Robin Williams Mac OS X Book, Panther Edition, by Robin Williams and John Tollette (Berkeley, CA: Peachpit Press, 2004). Robin Williams has written many great books about computers, desktop publishing, graphic design, Web design, and (especially) the Macintosh. She's known for her clear, approachable writing style. In this book, she and John Tollett explain the ins and outs of the Mac's operating system.

UNIX: Visual QuickStart Guide, Second Edition, by Deborah S. Ray and Eric J. Ray (Berkeley, CA: Peachpit Press, 2003). Many UNIX books assume that you speak fluent technojargon and that you want to know all about the operating system and how it works. This book is designed for people who want to (or need to) use UNIX but don't particularly want to read a massive volume of UNIX lore. No book can make mastering UNIX simple, but this one at least makes getting started with UNIX simpler.

Palm Organizers Visual QuickStart Guide, Third Edition, by Jeff Carlson (Berkeley, CA: Peachpit Press, 2004). Palm organizers are essential tools for many busy people. This book can help you tap the power of a Palm.

Piloting Palm: The Inside Story of Palm, Handspring and the Birth of the Billion Dollar Handheld Industry, by Andrea Butter and David Pogue (New York: John Wiley & Sons, 2002). In this fascinating behind-the-scenes look at the making of the original Palm Pilot, we learn how a new industry was created in the aftermath of previous technological failures.

StarOffice Companion and OpenOffice.org 1.0 Resource Kit, by Solveig Haugland, Floyd Jones (Upper Saddle River, NJ: Prentice Hall, 2002–2003). There are dozens of books on Microsoft Office and other commercial PC applications, but very few on freeware applications. These books can serve as an introduction and a valuable reference for anyone wanting to use the powerful, free StarOffice and OpenOffice.org suites on Windows or Linux.

Things That Make Us Smart: Defending Human Attributes in the Age of the Machine, by Donald A. Norman (New York, NY: Perseus, 1994). Norman left his position as the founding Chairman of the Department of Cognitive Science at the University of California, San Diego, to work in the computer industry. His research on the relationship between technology and the human cognitive system is especially relevant in an industry where user interface decisions affect millions of users every day. This book, like Norman's others, is informative, thought provoking, and enjoyable. His argument for a more human-centered technology should be required reading for all software designers.

Ethics for the Information Age, by Michael J. Quinn (Boston, MA: Pearson Addison Wesley, 2005). This book contains in-depth discussions of many ethical issues raised by the introduction of information technology. One of its chapters focuses on intellectual property and debates issues related to the rights of producers and consumers, including whether creators of computer programs and music have a right to own their creations and whether consumers have an obligation to respect copyright laws.

Web Pages

Software companies, like hardware companies, have established their presence on the Net. Most of the companies use addresses that follow the formula <u>http://www.companyname.com</u>. Examples include <u>http://www.microsoft.com, http://www. apple.com,</u> and <u>http://www.adobe.com</u>. Content varies from company to company; you might find technical support, product descriptions, demo software, software updates, and user tips on a typical software home page. For more software information, check the home pages of publishers that specialize in computer books. For example, Peachpit Press (<u>http://www.peachpit.com</u>), McGraw-Hill (<u>http://www.books.mcgraw-hill.com</u>), and other publishers include sample chapters from software books on their Web sites. As usual, <u>http://www.computerconfluence.com</u> provides up-to-date links to a variety of valuable Web resources.

Multimedia

Objectives

After you read this chapter you should be able to:

▶ **Describe how word-processing and desktop-publishing software have revolutionized writing and publishing**

▶ **Discuss the potential impact of desktop publishing and Web publishing on the concept of freedom of the press**

▶ **Speculate about future developments in word processing and digital publishing**

▶ **Describe the basic functions and applications of spreadsheets and other types of statistical and simulation programs**

▶ **Explain how computers can be used to answer what if questions**

▶ **Explain how computers are used as tools for simulating mechanical, biological, and social systems**

DOUG ENGELBART EXPLORES HYPERSPACE

On a December day in 1950, Doug Engelbart looked into the future and saw what no one had seen before. Engelbart had been thinking about the growing complexity and urgency of the world's problems and wondering how he could help solve those problems. In his vision of the future, Engelbart saw computer technology augmenting and magnifying human mental abilities, providing people with new powers to cope with the urgency and complexity of life.

If you **look out in the future**, you can see how best to **make right choices**.

—*Doug Engelbart*

Engelbart decided to dedicate his life to turning his vision into reality. Unfortunately, the rest of the world wasn't ready for Engelbart's vision. His farsighted approach didn't match the prevailing ideas of the time, and most of the research community denounced or ignored Engelbart's work. In 1951, there were only about a dozen computers in the world, and those spent most of their time doing military calculations. It was hard to imagine ordinary people using computers to boost their personal productivity. So Engelbart put together the Augmentation Research Center at the Stanford Research Institute to create working models of his visionary tools.

In 1968, he demonstrated his Augment system to an auditorium full of astonished computer professionals and changed forever the way people think about computers. A large screen showed a cascade of computer graphics, text, and video images, controlled by Engelbart and a coworker several miles away. "It was like magic," recalls Alan Kay, one of the young computer scientists in the audience. Augment introduced the mouse, video-display editing (the forerunner to word processing), mixed text and graphics, windowing, outlining, shared-screen video conferencing, computer conferencing, groupware, and hypermedia. Although Engelbart used a large computer, he was really demonstrating a futuristic "personal" computer—an interactive multimedia workstation for enhancing individual abilities.

Today, many of Engelbart's inventions and ideas are commonplace. He is widely recognized for one small part of his vision: the mouse. But Engelbart hasn't

Basic Productivity Applications 5

stopped looking into the future. He now heads the Bootstrap Institute at Stanford University, a nonprofit think tank dedicated to helping organizations make decisions with the future in mind. In a world where automation can dehumanize and eliminate jobs, Engelbart is still committed to replacing automation with augmentation. But now he focuses more on the human side of the equation, helping people chart a course into the future

5.2 Doug Engelbart's visionary 1968 presentation showed the world how computers could be used as collaborative tools.

5.1 Doug Engelbart

guided by intelligent, positive vision. He talks about turning organizations into "networked improvement communities" and demonstrates ways to "improve the improvement process." If anyone understands how to build the future from a vision, Doug Engelbart does. ～

Doug Engelbart was one of the first people to recognize that computer technology could be used to augment human capabilities. Thanks in large part to his visionary work, people all over the world use computer applications to enhance their abilities to write papers and articles, publish periodicals and books, perform complex calculations, conduct scientific research, and even predict the future.

In this chapter, we survey a variety of applications that people use to manipulate words and numbers. We consider software tools for working with words, from outliners to sophisticated reference tools, and numbers, from spreadsheets to statistical packages and money managers. We look at how desktop publishing technology has transformed the publishing process and provided more people with the power to communicate in print. We examine how scientific visualization software can help us understand relationships that are invisible to the naked eye and how computers simulate reality for work and pleasure.

The Wordsmith's Toolbox

I . . . **cannot imagine** now that I **ever** wrote with a typewriter.

—*Arthur C. Clarke, author and scientist*

The way in which we write has forever been transformed by software. Instead of suffering through the painful process of typing and retyping in pursuit of a "clean" draft, a writer can focus on developing ideas and let the machine take care of laying out the words neatly on the page. Word-processing technology makes it possible for just about any literate person to communicate effectively in writing.

Word Processing Tools and Techniques

Working with a word processor involves several steps:

- Entering text
- Editing text
- Formatting the document
- Proofreading the document
- Saving the document on disk
- Printing the document

Early word-processing systems generally forced users to follow these steps in a strict order. Some systems still in use—mainly on mainframes and other timesharing systems—segregate these processes into steps that can't easily be mixed. Most writers today use word processors that allow them to switch freely between editing and formatting, in some cases doing both at the same time. With virtually all modern word processors, words appear on the screen almost exactly as they will appear on a printed page. This feature is often referred to as **WYSIWYG**, short for "what you see is what you get" and pronounced "wizzy-wig."

Text formatting commands enable you to control the format of the document—the way the words will look on the page. Most modern word processors include commands for controlling the formats of individual characters and paragraphs as well as complete documents.

With character formatting commands, you can select the font and the point size of the document's characters. Other character formatting commands let you do such things as change the color of a character, put it in boldface and/or italics, or underline it.

Other formatting commands apply to paragraphs rather than characters: those commands that control margins, space between lines, indents, tab stops, and justification. **Justification** refers to the alignment of text on a line. Four justification choices are commonly available: left justification (with a smooth left margin and ragged right margin), right justification, full justification (both margins are smooth), and centered justification.

Some formatting commands apply to entire documents. For example, Microsoft Word's Page Setup command enables you to control the margins that apply throughout the document. Other commands enable you to specify the content, size, and style of **headers** and **footers**—blocks that appear at the top and bottom of every page, displaying repetitive information, such as chapter titles, author names, and automatically calculated page numbers.

Most word-processing programs provide even more features. Advanced formatting features enable you to perform the following tasks:

- Define **stylesheets** containing custom styles for each of the common elements in a document. (For example, you can define a style called "subhead" as a paragraph that's left-justified in a boldface, 12-point Helvetica font with standard margins and then apply that style to every subhead in the document without reselecting all three of these commands for each new subhead. If you decide later to change the subheads to 14-point Futura, your changes in the subhead style are automatically reflected throughout the document.)
- Define alternate headers, footers, and margins so that left- and right-facing pages can have different margins, headers, and footers.
- Create documents with multiple variable-width columns.
- Create, edit, and format multicolumn tables.
- Incorporate graphics created with other applications.

5.3 Many word processors are able to convert formatted documents to HTML so they can be published as Web pages.

5.1 Font Technology

When a computer displays a character on a monitor or prints it on a laser, inkjet, or dot matrix printer, the character is nothing more than a collection of dots in an invisible grid. Bitmapped fonts store characters in this way, with each pixel represented as a black or white bit in a matrix. A bitmapped font usually looks fine on screen in the intended point size but doesn't look smooth when printed on a high-resolution printer or enlarged on screen.

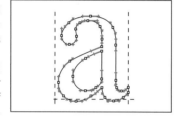

A bitmapped font becomes pixelated when enlarged.

Most computer systems now use scalable outline fonts to represent type in memory until it is displayed or printed. A scalable font represents each character as an outline that can be scaled—increased or decreased in size without distortion. Curves and lines are smooth and don't have stair-stepped, jagged edges when they're resized. The outline is stored inside the computer or printer as a series of mathematical statements about the position of points and the shape of the lines connecting those points.

This outline for a lowercase "a" retains its original shape at any size or resolution.

Downloadable fonts (soft fonts) are stored in the computer system (not the printer) and downloaded to the printer only when needed. These fonts usually have matching screen fonts and are easily moved to different computer systems. Most important, you can use the same downloadable font on many printer models.

Laser printers are really dedicated computer systems that contain their own CPU, RAM, ROM, and specialized operating system. Printer fonts are stored in the printer's ROM and are always available for use with that printer, but you may not be able to achieve WYSIWYG if your computer doesn't have a screen font to match your printer font. And if you move your document to a different computer and printer, the same printer font may not be available on the new system.

Fonts are most commonly available in two scalable outline forms: Adobe PostScript and Apple/Microsoft TrueType. Because Apple and Microsoft supply TrueType downloadable fonts with their operating systems, TrueType fonts are more popular among general computer users. PostScript fonts usually require additional software but are the standard among many graphics professionals. PostScript is actually a complete page description language particularly well suited to the demands of professional publishers.

For the past few years, Adobe and Microsoft have been codeveloping OpenType, a universal font format that combines TrueType and PostScript technology. OpenType enables character shapes to travel with documents in compressed forms so that a document transmitted electronically or displayed on the World Wide Web will look like the original even if the viewer's system doesn't include the original document's fonts.

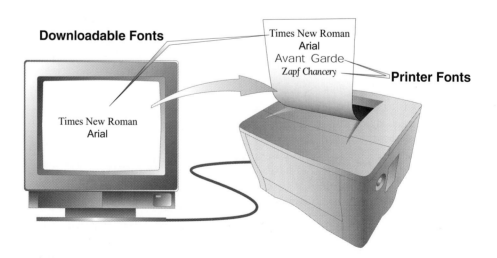

Downloadable Fonts

Times New Roman
Arial

Times New Roman
Arial
Avant Garde
Zapf Chancery

Printer Fonts

5.4

- Use **automatic footnoting** to save you from having to place footnotes and endnotes; the program automatically places them where they belong on the page.
- Use **automatic hyphenation** to divide long words that fall at the ends of lines.
- Use **automatic formatting (autoformat)** to automatically apply formatting to your text; for example, to automatically number lists (like the exercises at the end of this chapter) and apply proper indentation to those lists.
- Use **automatic correction (autocorrect)** to catch and correct common typing errors. For example, if you type *THe* or *Teh*, the software will automatically change it to *The*.
- Generate tables of contents and indexes for books and other long works (with human help for making judgments about which words belong in the index and how they should be arranged).
- Attach hidden comments that can be seen without showing up in the final printed document.
- Use coaching or help features (sometimes called **wizards**) to walk you through complex document formatting procedures.
- Convert formatted documents to **HTML (hypertext markup language)** so they can be easily published on the Web.

In addition to basic editing and formatting functions, a typical word processor might include a built-in outliner, spelling checker, and thesaurus. But even word processors that don't include those features can be enhanced with stand-alone programs specifically designed to accomplish the same things. We examine a few of these tools next.

Outliners and Idea Processors

If any man wishes to **write** in a **clear style**, let him first **be clear** in his **thoughts**.

—Johann W. von Goethe

For many of us, the hardest part of the writing process is collecting and organizing our thoughts. Traditional English-class techniques, including outlines and 3-by-5 note cards, involve additional work. But when computer technology is applied, these time-honored techniques are transformed into high-powered tools for extending our minds and streamlining the process of turning vague thoughts into solid prose.

Outliners, such as the *Outline View* option built into Microsoft Word, are, in effect, idea processors. Outliners are particularly effective at performing three functions:

1. Arranging information into hierarchies or levels so that each heading can be fleshed out with more detailed subheads, which can then be broken into smaller pieces
2. Rearranging ideas and levels so that subideas are automatically moved with their parent ideas
3. Hiding and revealing levels of detail as needed so that you can examine the forest, the trees, or an individual leaf of your project

For a project that requires research, you can use an outliner as a replacement for note cards. Ideas can be collected, composed, refined, rearranged, and reorganized much more efficiently when they're stored in an outline. When the time comes to turn research into a research paper, you don't need to retype the notes; you can polish them with standard text-editing techniques. If the outliner is built into the word processor, the line between notes and finished product blurs to the point where it almost disappears.

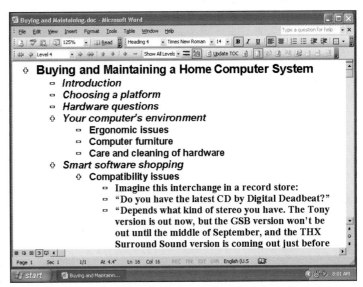

5.5 Microsoft Word's Outline view enables you to examine and restructure the overall organization of a document, while showing each topic in as much detail as you need. When you move headlines, the attached subheads and paragraphs follow automatically.

Digital References

The difference between the **right word** and the **almost-right word** is the difference between the **lightning** and the **lightning bug**.

— *Mark Twain*

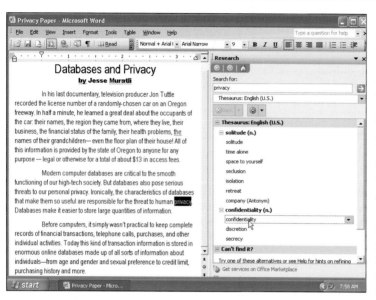

5.6 Microsoft Word's Thesaurus feature puts synonyms at your fingertips. In this case, the computer is providing synonyms for the word *privacy*.

Writers rely on dictionaries, quotation books, encyclopedias, atlases, almanacs, and other references. Just about all of these resources are now available in digital form on CD-ROM, DVD, and the Web.

Searching for subjects or words by computer is usually faster than thumbing through a book. Well-designed electronic references make it easy to jump between related topics in search of elusive facts. In addition, copying quotes electronically takes a fraction of the time it takes to retype information from a book. Of course, this kind of quick copying makes plagiarism—using someone else's words without giving credit—easier than ever and may tempt more writers to violate copyright laws and ethical standards. If you're tempted to plagiarize someone else's writing, remember that electronic references make detecting plagiarism easier than ever, too!

The classic synonym finder, or **thesaurus**, is an invaluable tool for finding the right word, but it's not particularly user-friendly. A computerized thesaurus is another matter altogether. With a good thesaurus, it's a simple matter to select a word and issue a command for a synonym search. The computerized thesaurus provides almost instant gratification, display-

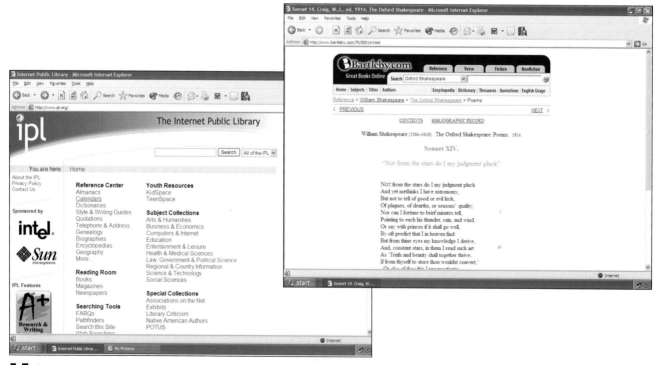

5.7 Students and other researchers can save time when searching for facts, quotes, ideas, or inspiration by using specially designed reference sites on the Web.

ing all kinds of possible replacements for the word in question. If you find a suitable substitute in the list, you can indicate your preference with a click or a keystroke; the software even makes the switch for you.

Because pictures, maps, and drawings take up so much disk space (and Internet transmission time), they're sometimes removed or modified in computerized references. On the other hand, many digital references include sounds, animation, video, and other forms of information that aren't possible to include in books.

Reference materials are everywhere on the Web. Unfortunately, not all of those sources are useful or reliable. Still, the Web offers a combination of currentness and cross-referencing that can't be found in any other reference source. We'll revisit Web references in later chapters.

Spelling Checkers

It's a **darn poor mind** that can only think of **one way** to spell a word.

—Andrew Jackson

Although many of us sympathize with Jackson's point of view, the fact remains that correct spelling is an important part of most written communication. That's why a word processor typically includes a built-in **spelling checker**. A spelling checker compares the words in your document with words in a disk-based dictionary. Every word that's not in the dictionary is flagged as a suspect word—a potential misspelling. In many cases, the spelling checker suggests the corrected spelling and offers to replace the suspect word. Ultimately, though, it's up to you to decide whether the flagged word is, in fact, spelled incorrectly.

Spelling checkers are wonderful aids, but they can't replace careful proofreading by alert human eyes. When you're using a spelling checker, it's important to keep two potential problems in mind:

■ *Dictionary limitations and errors.* No dictionary includes every word, so you have to know what to do with unlisted words—proper names, obscure words, technical terms, foreign terms, colloquialisms, and other oddities. If you add words to your spelling checker's dictionary, you run the risk of adding an incorrectly spelled word, making future occurrences of that misspelling invisible to the spelling checker and to you.

■ *Errors of context.* The fact that a word appears in a dictionary does not guarantee that it is correctly spelled in the context of the sentence. The following passage, for example, contains eight spelling errors, none of which would be detected by a spelling checker:

I wood never have guest that my spelling checker would super seed my editor as my mane source of feed back. I no longer prophet from the presents of an editor while I right.

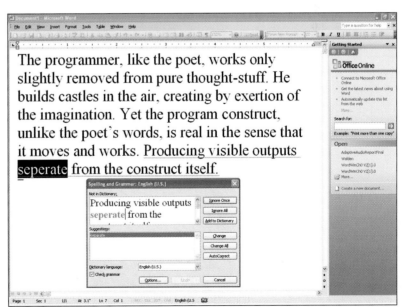

5.8 Most spelling checkers, including the one in Microsoft Word, offer the user several choices for handling words that aren't in the dictionary. (Text in window adapted from *The Mythical Man Month* by Frederick P. Brooks, Jr.)

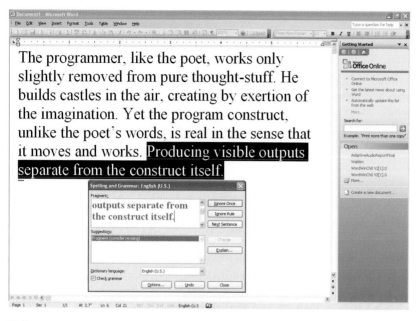

5.9 Grammar-and-style-checking software flags possible errors and makes suggestions about how they might be fixed. Here, Microsoft Word suggests a way to change a particular sentence. (Text in window adapted from *The Mythical Man Month* by Frederick P. Brooks, Jr.)

Grammar and Style Checkers

The errors in the preceding quote would have slipped by a spelling checker; but many of them would have been detected by a **grammar and style checker**. In addition to checking spelling, grammar-and-style-checking software analyzes each word in context, checking for errors of context (I wood never have guest), common grammatical errors (Ben and me went to Boston), and stylistic foibles (Suddenly the door was opened by Bethany). In addition to pointing out possible errors and suggesting improvements, it can analyze prose complexity using measurements such as sentence length and paragraph length. This kind of analysis is useful for determining whether your writing style is appropriate for your target audience.

Grammar-and-style-checking software is, at best, imperfect. A typical program misses many true errors, while flagging correct passages. Still, it can be a valuable writing aid, especially for students who are mastering the complexities of a language for the first time. But software is no substitute for practice, revision, editing, and a good English teacher.

Form-Letter Generators

Congratulations, Mr. \<last name\>. You may already have won!

—Junk mail greeting

Most word processors today have **mail merge** capabilities for producing personalized form letters. When used with a database containing a list of names and addresses, a word processor can quickly generate individually addressed letters and mailing labels. Many programs can incorporate custom paragraphs based on the recipient's personal data, making each letter look as if it were individually written. Direct-mail marketing companies exploited this kind of technology for years before it became available in inexpensive PC software.

Collaborative Writing Tools

Writing only leads to **more writing**.

—Colette

Most large writing projects, including the one that produced this book, involve groups of people working together. Computer networks make it easy for writers and editors to share documents; but it's not always easy for one person to know how a document has been changed by others. **Groupware**—software designed to be used by a workgroup—can keep track of a document's history as it's passed among group members and make sure that all changes are incorporated into a single master document. Using groupware, each writer can monitor and make suggestions concerning the work of any other writer on the team. Editors can "blue pencil" corrections and attach notes directly to the electronic manuscript.

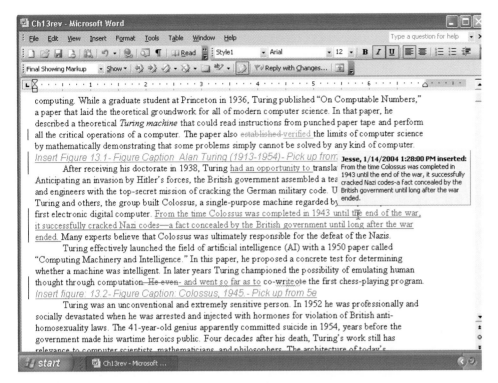

5.10 The Track Changes feature in Microsoft Word enables writers, editors, and other collaborative document creators to contribute to the same document and see each other's changes.

The notes can be read by any or all of the writers—even those who are on the other side of the continent. This kind of collaborative writing and editing doesn't require specialized software anymore; it can be done with many word-processing and publishing programs. For example, Microsoft Word's Track Changes option can record and display contributions from several writers and editors; it can also compare document versions and highlight differences between versions.

Emerging Word Tools

Word-processing software has evolved rapidly in the last few years. The evolution isn't over; current trends suggest big changes are coming in word-processing technology.

> The **real technology**—behind all of our other technologies—is **language**. It actually creates **the world our consciousness lives in**.
>
> —*Norman Fischer, Abbot, Green Gulch Farm Zen Center*

Processing Handwritten Words

For a small but growing population, pen-based systems provide an alternative tool for entering text. Handwriting recognition doesn't come easy to computers; it requires sophisticated software that can interpret pen movements as characters and words. The diversity in handwriting makes it difficult for today's software to translate all of our scribbles into text. Powerful pen-based systems like the Tablet PC work reliably because they use all the processing punch of modern notebook PCs and advanced handwriting-recognition algorithms. Simpler pen-based systems, such as those based on the Palm OS, require users to print characters using a carefully defined system that minimizes errors.

Processing Words with Speech

I think that the **primary means of communication** with computers in the next millennium will be **speech**.

—Nicholas Negroponte, director of MIT's Media Lab

Ultimately, most writers long for a computer that can accept and reliably process *speech* input—a *talkwriter*. With such a system, a user can tell the computer what to type—and how to type it—by simply talking into a microphone. The user's speech enters the computer as a digital audio signal. **Speech-recognition software** looks for patterns in the sound waves and interprets sounds by locating familiar patterns, segmenting input sound patterns into words, separating commands from the text, and passing those commands to the word-processing software.

Speech-recognition software systems have been around for many years, but until recently, most were severely limited. It takes a great deal of knowledge to understand the complexities of human speech. Most current commercial systems need to be trained to recognize a particular person's voice before they can function reliably. Even then, many systems require that the user speak slowly in a quiet environment and use a small, predefined vocabulary. Otherwise the machine might interpret, say, "recognize speech" as "wreck a nice beach." Research in speech recognition today focuses on overcoming these limitations and producing systems that can accomplish the following tasks:

■ Recognize words without being trained to an individual speaker, an ability known as *speaker independence*
■ Handle speech without limiting vocabulary
■ Handle continuous speech—natural speech in which words run together at normal speed

Researchers are making great strides toward these goals. Several companies have developed programs that can achieve two of them. No one has yet developed a system that consistently achieves all three goals, the human body excepted.

Although it's not yet trouble-free or error-free, PC speech-recognition software is growing in popularity, especially for people who can't use keyboards because of physical disabilities or job restrictions. As the technology improves, the microphone may become the preferred input device for PC users. Cell phones and PDAs may soon become digital dictation machines.

5.11 Speech recognition software enables this doctor to dictate notes and other documents into her computer.

Intelligent Word Processors

Speech recognition is just one aspect of artificial intelligence research that's likely to end up in future word processors. Many experts foresee word processors that are able to anticipate the writer's needs, acting as an electronic editor or coauthor. Today's grammar and style checkers are primitive forerunners of the kinds of electronic writing consultants that might appear in a few years.

Here are some possibilities:

■ As you're typing a story, your word processor reminds you (via a pop-up notification message on the screen or an auditory message) that you've used the word *delicious* three times in the last two paragraphs and suggests that you choose an alternative from the list shown on the screen.

■ Your word processor continuously analyzes your style as you type, determines your writing habits and patterns, and learns from its analysis. If your writing tends to be technical and formal, the software modifies its thesaurus, dictionary, and other tools so they're more appropriate for that style.

■ You're writing a manual for a large organization that uses specific style guidelines of documentation. Your word processor modifies your writing as you type so that it conforms to the organizational style.

■ You need some current figures to support your argument on the depletion of the ozone layer. You issue a command, and the computer does a quick search of the literature on the Web and reports to you with several relevant facts.

All these examples are technically possible now. The trend toward intelligent word processors is clear. Nevertheless, you're in for a long wait if you're eager to buy a system with commands such as Clever Quote, Humorous Anecdote, and Term Paper.

The Desktop Publishing Story

Freedom of the press belongs to the person who **owns** one.

—A. J. Liebling, the late media critic for The New Yorker

Just as word processing changed the writer's craft in the 1970s, the world of publishing was radically transformed in the 1980s when Apple introduced its first LaserWriter printer and a new company named Aldus introduced PageMaker, a Macintosh program that could take advantage of that printer's high-resolution output capabilities. Publishing—traditionally an expensive, time-consuming, error-prone process—instantly became an enterprise that just about anyone with a computer and a little cash could undertake.

What Is Desktop Publishing?

The process of producing a book, magazine, or other publication includes several steps:

■ Writing text
■ Editing text
■ Producing drawings, photographs, and other graphics to accompany the text
■ Designing a basic format for the publication
■ Typesetting text
■ Arranging text and graphics on pages
■ Typesetting and printing pages
■ Binding pages into a finished publication

In traditional publishing, many of these steps required expensive equipment, highly trained specialists to operate the equipment, and lots of time. With desktop-publishing (DTP) technology, the bulk of the production process can be accomplished with tools that are small, affordable, and easy to use. A desktop-publishing system generally includes one or more Macs or PCs, a scanner, a high-resolution printer, and software. It's now possible for a single person with a

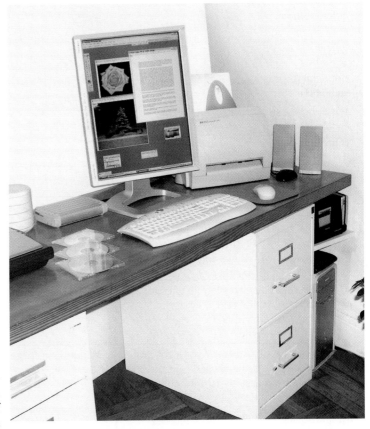

5.12 A typical desktop-publishing system includes a personal computer, a high-resolution printer, a scanner and other imaging hardware, and a variety of graphical software programs.

Working Wisdom

Creating Professional-Looking Documents

Many first-time users of WYSIWYG word processors and desktop-publishing systems become intoxicated with all the power at their fingertips. It's easy to get carried away with all those fonts, styles, and sizes and to create a document that makes supermarket tabloids look tasteful. Although there's no substitute for a good education in the principles of design, it's easy to avoid tacky-looking documents if you follow a few simple guidelines:

➡ ***Plan before you publish.*** Design (or select) a simple, visually pleasing format for your document, and use that format throughout the document.

➡ ***Use appropriate fonts.*** Limit your choices to one or two fonts and sizes per page, and be consistent throughout your document.

➡ ***Don't go style-crazy.*** Avoid overusing italics, bold-face, ALL CAPS, underlines, and other styles for emphasis. When in doubt, leave it out.

BAD

Title is out of proportion to rest of page.

Page uses too many different fonts.

Underlining adds no value here.

Center-justified text is harder to read.

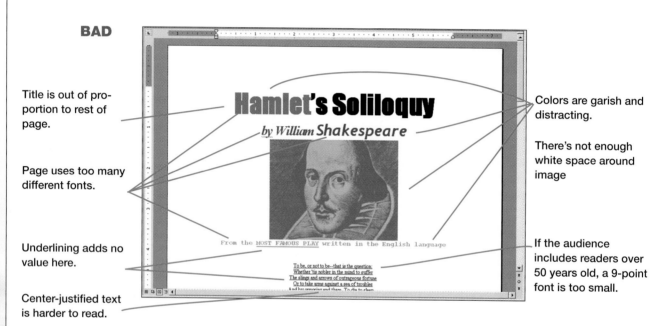

Colors are garish and distracting.

There's not enough white space around image

If the audience includes readers over 50 years old, a 9-point font is too small.

Rules of Thumb for Text Justification		
Justification	When to Use	When to Avoid
This text illustrates full justification. For fully justified text, spaces between words are adjusted to make both margins straight.	Formal documents, such as textbooks and academic reports	Informal documents or documents with narrow columns
This text illustrates left justification. For left-justified text the left margin is straight and the right margin is ragged.	Informal documents, such as letters and newsletters	Formal documents
This text illustrates right justification. For right-justified text the right margin is straight and the left margin is ragged.	Headers and footers	Body of a document (entire paragraphs)
This text illustrates centered justification. For centered text both margins are ragged.	Titles and subtitles	Body of a document (entire paragraphs)

5.13

- ➡️ *Look at your document through your reader's eyes.* Make every picture say something. Don't try to cram too much information on a page. Don't be afraid of white space. Use a format that speaks clearly to your readers. Make sure the main points of your document stand out.
- ➡️ *Learn from the masters.* Study the designs of successful publications. Use design books, articles, and classes to develop your aesthetic skills along with your technical skills. With or without a computer, publishing is an art.
- ➡️ *Know your limitations.* Desktop publishing technology makes it possible for anyone to produce high-quality documents with a minimal investment of time and money. But your equipment and skills may not be up to the job at hand. For many applications, personal desktop publishing is no match for a professional design artist or typesetter. If you need the best, work with a pro.
- ➡️ *Remember the message.* Fancy fonts, tasteful graphics, and meticulous design can't turn shoddy ideas into words of wisdom, or lies into the truth. The purpose of publishing is communication; don't try to use technology to disguise the lack of something to communicate.

GOOD

The Economist magazine inspires this design.

Color enlivens the black-and-white etching without dominating the text.

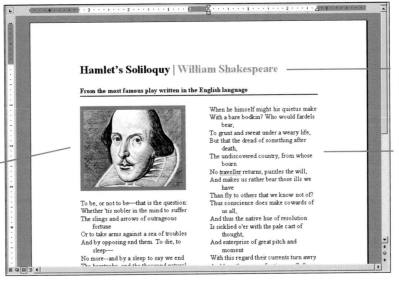

The heading is in proportion to the rest of the page.

A 12-point font and left-justified text make Shakespeare's words easy to read.

Font Category	Examples	Appropriate Use	Inappropriate Use
Serif fonts	Times New Roman Georgia Book Antiqua Palatino	Just about anywhere	
Sans-serif fonts	Arial Helvetica Futura Lucida Sans	Titles, subtitles, captions, and boxed text	Body of a document (pages of text)
Monospaced fonts	Courier Courier New Lucida Console	Representing computer programs or user input to a computer with a character-based interface	Anywhere else
Display fonts	Comic Sans MS Birch Tekton	Posters and flyers	Body of a document (entire paragraphs)
Symbol fonts	Συμβολ (Symbol) ◆✋■㏊✋■㏊◆ (Wingdings)	When special characters are needed or as dingbats at end of stories in newsletter	Anywhere else

modest equipment investment to do all the writing, editing, graphic production, design, page layout, and typesetting for a desktop publication. Of course, few individuals have the skills to handle all of these tasks, so most publications are still the work of teams that include writers, editors, designers, artists, and supervisors. But even if the titles remain the same, each of these jobs is changing because of desktop publishing technology.

The first steps in the publishing process involve producing **source documents**—articles, chapters, drawings, maps, charts, and photographs that are to appear in the publication. Desktop publishers generally use standard word processors and graphics programs to produce most source documents. Scanners with image-editing software are used to transform photographs and hand-drawn images into computer-readable documents. **Page-layout software**, such as QuarkXPress, Adobe PageMaker, or Adobe InDesign, is used to combine the various source documents into a coherent, visually appealing publication. Pages are generally laid out one at a time on-screen, although most programs have options for automating multiple-page document layout.

Page-layout software provides graphic designers with control over virtually every element of the design, right down to the spacing between each pair of letters (*kerning*) and the spacing between lines of text (*leading*). Today's word-processing programs include basic page-layout capabilities, too; they're sufficient for creating many types of publications. But to produce more complex layouts for newspapers, newsletters, magazines, and flyers, publishers need the kind of advanced formatting capabilities found only in dedicated desktop-publishing applications. (Word processors and desktop publishers often work hand-in-hand: For example, writers usually use word processors to create the text that is poured into a desktop publishing layout.)

For users without backgrounds in layout and design, most page-layout and word-processing programs include **templates**—professionally designed "empty" documents that can easily be adapted to specific user needs. Even without templates, it's possible for beginners to create professional-quality publications with a modest investment of money and time.

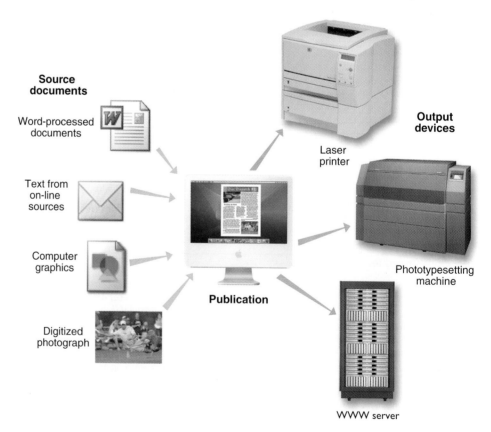

Source documents

Word-processed documents

Text from on-line sources

Computer graphics

Digitized photograph

Publication

Output devices

Laser printer

Phototypesetting machine

WWW server

5.14 Source documents are merged in a publication document, which can be printed on a laser or inkjet printer, printed on high-resolution phototypesetter, or published on the Web.

Screen Test

Desktop Publishing with Adobe InDesign

GOAL *To create a four-page newsletter for ultimate disc players*

TOOLS *Adobe Photoshop, Adobe InDesign*

1. Fill in the newsletter length.

2. Select the page size and orientation.

3. Select number of text columns per page.

4. Adjust the margin size.

5. Click OK to approve your design choices.

6. Import a graphic containing the newsletter's masthead you created with Adobe Photoshop.

7. Import photos you captured with a digital camera and edited with Adobe Photoshop.

8. Create text boxes to hold the cover story.

9. Use the Get Text command to import text from a Word document.

10. Modify the size of the article's title.

11. Add another text box in the middle of the page. The story text automatically rearranges to flow around the box. Type a quote into the new box.

12. Continue the layout process on the remaining pages and print the finished document.

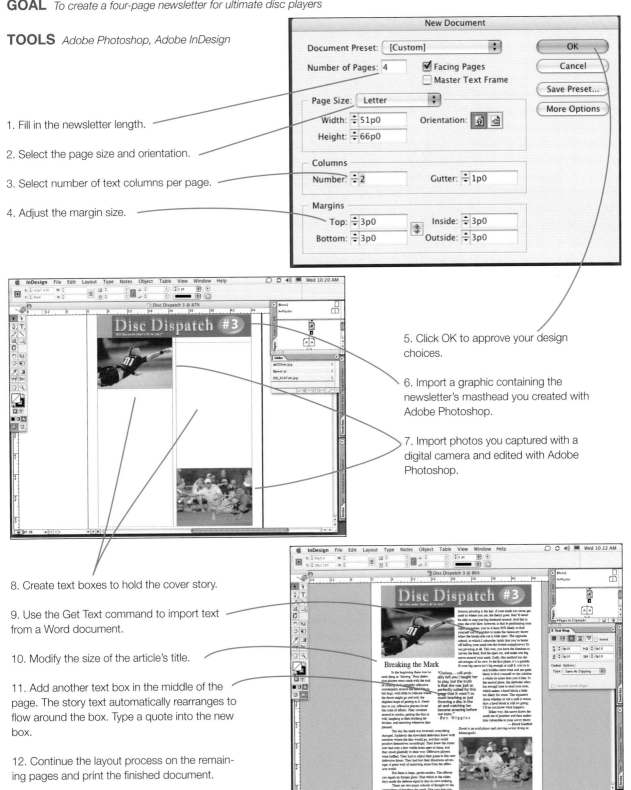

5.15

Desktop publishing becomes more complicated when color is introduced. *Spot color*—the use of a single color (or sometimes two) to add interest—is relatively easy. But *full-color* desktop publishing, including color photos, drawings, and paintings, must deal with the inconsistencies of different color output devices. Because printers and monitors use different types of color-mixing technologies, as described in the How It Works boxes in Chapter 3, what you see on the screen isn't always what you get when you print it. It's even difficult to get two monitors (or two printers) to produce images with exactly the same color balance. Still, color desktop publishing is big business, and advances in color-matching technology are making it easier all the time.

Most desktop publications are printed on inkjet and laser printers capable of producing output with a resolution of at least 600 dots per inch (dpi). The number of dots per inch influences the resolution and clarity of the image. Output of 600 dpi is sufficiently sharp for most applications, but it's less than the 1,200 dpi that is the traditional minimum for professional typesetting. High-priced devices, called phototypesetting machines or image-setters, enable desktop publications to be printed at 1,200 dpi or higher. Many desktop publishers rely on outside service bureaus with phototypesetting machines to print their final camera-ready pages—pages that are ready to be photographed and printed.

Why Desktop Publishing?

Desktop publishing offers several advantages for businesses. Desktop publishing saves money. Publications that used to cost hundreds or thousands of dollars to produce through outside publishing services can now be produced in-house for a fraction of their former cost. Desktop publishing also saves time. The turnaround time for a publication done on the desktop can be a few days instead of the weeks or months it might take to publish the same thing using traditional channels. Finally, desktop publishing can reduce the quantity of publication errors. Quality control is easier to maintain when documents are produced in-house.

The real winners in the desktop publishing revolution might turn out to be not big businesses but everyday people with something to say. With commercial TV networks, newspapers, magazines, and book publishers increasingly controlled by a few giant corporations, many media experts worry that the free press guaranteed by our First Amendment is seriously threatened by de facto media monopolies. Desktop-publishing technology offers new hope for every individual's right to publish. Writers, artists, and editors whose work is shunned or ignored by large publishers and mainstream media now have affordable publishing alternatives. The number of small presses and alternative, low-circulation periodicals is steadily increasing as publishing costs go down. If, as media critic A. J. Liebling suggested, freedom of the press belongs to the person who owns one, that precious freedom is now accessible to more people than ever before.

Beyond the Printed Page

Paper, often underrated as a communication medium, **will not be eliminated** by the growth of electronic media. It remains **inexpensive**, extremely **portable**, and **capable** of carrying very high-resolution images.

—*Mark Duchesne, Vice President, AM Multigraphics*

The first books were so difficult to produce that they were considered priceless. They were kept in cabinets with multiple locks so that they couldn't be removed without the knowledge and permission of at least two monks. Today, we can print professional-quality publications in short order using equipment that costs less than a used car. But the publishing revolution isn't over yet.

Paperless Publishing and the Web

A common prediction is that desktop publishing—and paper publishing in general—will be replaced by paperless electronic media. Paper still offers advantages for countless

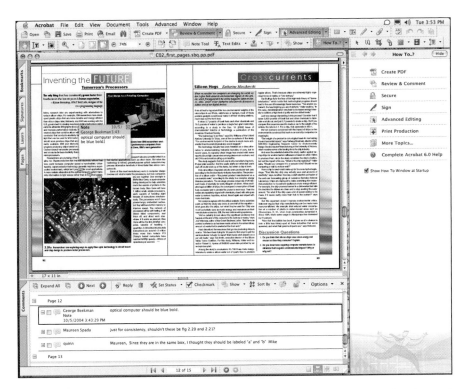

5.16 Adobe Acrobat is a cross-platform software program that enables the electronic sharing of PDF documents, eliminating the need for paper in many publishing projects. People who worked on *Computer Confluence* attached their comments to PDF pages and shared them electronically using Acrobat.

communication tasks. Reading printed words on pages is easier on the eyes than reading from a screen. Paper documents can be read and scribbled on almost anywhere, with or without electricity. And there's no electronic equivalent for the aesthetics of a beautifully designed, finely crafted book. Predictions aside, the printed word isn't likely to go away anytime soon.

Still, digital media forms *are* likely to eclipse paper for many applications. Email messages now outnumber post office letter deliveries. CD-ROM encyclopedias briskly outsell their overweight paper counterparts. Adobe's *PDF (Portable Document Format)* enables documents of all types to be stored, viewed, or modified on any Windows or Macintosh computer, making it possible for organizations to reduce paper flow.

The Web offers unprecedented mass publishing possibilities to millions of Internet users. Programs as diverse as Microsoft Word, AppleWorks, and PageMaker can

5.17 Mountains of waste paper like this one should become less common as paperless publishing grows in popularity. That's the theory, anyway.

5.18 Many popular periodicals, from *Newsweek* to *Rolling Stone*, are published electronically on the Web. *Salon* is an example of a high-quality, popular magazine that is available only on the Web.

save documents in HTML format, so they can be published on the Web. Other programs, specifically designed for Web publishing, offer advanced capabilities for graphics, animation, and multimedia publishing. (We'll explore some of these tools in later chapters when we discuss multimedia and the Web in greater depth.)

Never before has a communication medium made it so easy or inexpensive for an individual to reach such a wide audience. For a few dollars a month, an Internet service provider can provide you with space to publish your essays, stories, reviews, and musings. It doesn't matter whether you're a student, a poet, an artist, a government official, a labor organizer, or a corporate president; on the Web all URLs are created equal.

Of course, the most popular commercial Web sites cost their owners more than a few dollars a month. A typical Web storefront costs a million dollars just to build. And one of the biggest challenges in Web publishing is attracting people to your site once it's online. Copyright protection is another problem for Web publishers; anything that's published on the Web for the world to see is also available for all the world to copy. How can writers and editors be paid fairly for their labors if their works are so easy to duplicate?

Still, the Web is far more accessible to small-budget writers and publishers than any other mass medium. And many experts predict that Web technology will eventually include some kind of mechanism for automatic payment to authors whose works are downloaded. In any case, the free flow of ideas may be more significant than the flow of money. In the words of writer Howard Rheingold, the World Wide Web "might be important in the same way that the printing press was important. By expanding the number of people who have the power to transmit knowledge, the Web might trigger a power shift that changes everything."

Electronic Books and Digital Paper

Science fiction writers have long predicted the **electronic book**, or **ebook**—a handheld device that can contain anything from today's top news stories to an annotated edition of *War and Peace*. Until recently, these types of devices have been commercial failures for two reasons: First, the screens were hard to read and second, content for them was not easily accessible.

LCD technology has made great strides in recent years, and screens are brighter and easier to read than ever before. Recent advances in font technologies from Microsoft and Adobe should help, too. Microsoft's ClearType enhances the clarity of text on flat-panel LCD screens, reducing pixel "blockiness." Adobe has developed a similar technology called Precision Graphics. Easy-on-the-eyes ebooks are likely to take advantage of these technologies soon.

5.19 A Tablet PC like this one can replace a stack of textbooks, novels, and other reading material thanks to its pervasive ebook features.

To make it easier for ebook owners to find content—books, periodicals, and other software to download into their devices—several companies are cooperating to develop an open ebook standard. After industrywide standards are in place, electronic book publishing will be more practical—and popular. Future students may download texts rather than carry them out of bookstores. Everybook CEO Daniel Munyan predicts that college freshmen will load their ebooks with their notes and texts for the next four years and receive future updates via the Internet.

Ebooks today are mostly read on devices with rigid LCD screens—laptop computers, handheld computers, and special-purpose ebook readers that resemble tables. But researchers may soon perfect a form of digital paper that will enable ebooks (as well as emagazines and enewspapers) to look and feel more like their paper counterparts. **Electronic paper**, or **epaper**, is a flexible, portable, paperlike material that can dynamically display black-and-white text and images on its surface. Unlike traditional paper, digital paper can erase itself and display new text and images as the reader "turns" the page. A busy commuter might soon be able to carry a complete morning newspaper and several important business documents in a sheet of digital paper stuffed in his pocket!

5.20 Electronic paper is currently under development by several companies: This demo suggests that practical products aren't too far into the future.

The Spreadsheet: Software for Simulation and Speculation

Compare the **expansion of business** today to the **conquering of the continent** in the nineteenth century. The spreadsheet in that comparison is like **the transcontinental railroad**. It **accelerated the movement**, made it possible, and **changed the course** of the nation.

—Mitch Kapor, creator of the Lotus 1-2-3 spreadsheet software

More than any other type of stand-alone PC software, the spreadsheet has changed the way people do business. In the same way a word processor can give a computer user control over words, spreadsheet software enables the user to take control of numbers, manipulating them in ways that would be difficult or impossible otherwise. A spreadsheet program can make short work of tasks that involve repetitive calculations: budgeting, investment management, business projections, grade books, scientific simulations, checkbooks, and so on. A spreadsheet can also reveal hidden relationships between numbers, taking much of the guesswork out of financial planning and speculation.

The Malleable Matrix

The goal was that it had to be better than the **back of an envelope**.

—Dan Bricklin, inventor of the first spreadsheet program

Almost all spreadsheet programs are based on a simple concept: the malleable matrix. A spreadsheet document, called a worksheet, typically appears on the screen as a grid of numbered rows and lettered columns. The box representing the intersection of a row and a column is called a cell. Every cell in this grid has a unique address made up of a column letter and row number. For example, the cell in the upper-left corner of the grid is called cell A1 (column A, row 1) in most spreadsheet applications. All the cells are empty in a new worksheet; it's up to the user to fill them. Each cell can contain a numeric value, an alphabetic label, or a formula representing a relationship with numbers in other cells.

Values (numbers) are the raw material the spreadsheet software uses to perform calculations. Numbers in worksheet cells can represent wages, test scores, weather data, polling results, or just about anything that can be quantified.

To make it easier for people to understand the numbers, most worksheets include labels at the tops of columns and at the edges of rows, such as "Monthly Wages," "Midterm Exam 1," "Average Wind Speed," or "Final Approval Rating." To the computer, these labels are meaningless strings of characters. The label "Total Points" doesn't tell the computer to calculate the total and display it in an adjacent cell; it's just a road sign for human readers.

To calculate the total points (or the average wind speed or the final approval rating), the worksheet must include a formula—a step-by-step procedure for calculating the desired number. The simplest spreadsheet formulas are arithmetic

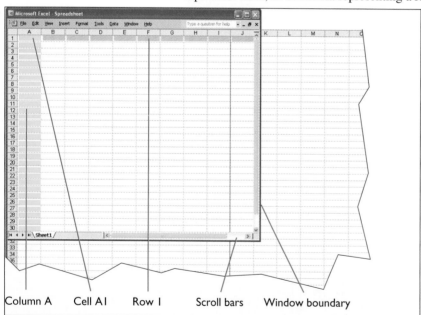

Column A   Cell A1   Row 1   Scroll bars   Window boundary

5.21 The worksheet may be bigger than what appears on your screen. The program enables you to scroll horizontally and vertically to view the larger matrix. (After column Z, columns are labeled with double letters: AA, BB, and so on.)

Screen Test

Creating a Worksheet with Microsoft Excel

GOAL *To create a computerized version of a worksheet showing projected expenses for one college student's fall term.*

TOOLS *Microsoft Excel*

1. Each column represents a month. Type descriptive labels for the month names. The last column will contain total expenses, category by category.

2. Each row represents an expense category. Type labels for these categories. The last row will contain total expenses, month by month.

3. Type numeric values representing the dollars spent in a particular category in a particular month. For example, the September tuition bill is $1,300, so you type 1300.

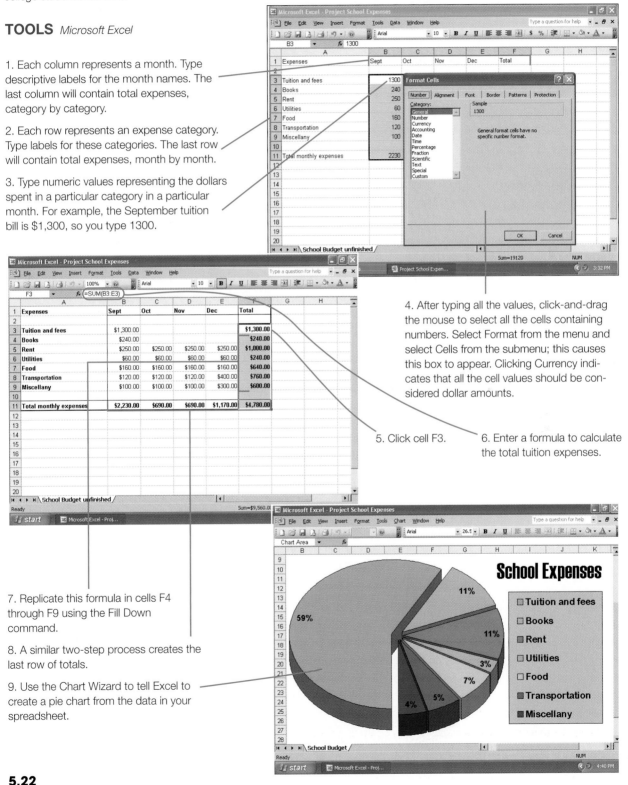

4. After typing all the values, click-and-drag the mouse to select all the cells containing numbers. Select Format from the menu and select Cells from the submenu; this causes this box to appear. Clicking Currency indicates that all the cell values should be considered dollar amounts.

5. Click cell F3.

6. Enter a formula to calculate the total tuition expenses.

7. Replicate this formula in cells F4 through F9 using the Fill Down command.

8. A similar two-step process creates the last row of totals.

9. Use the Chart Wizard to tell Excel to create a pie chart from the data in your spreadsheet.

5.22

expressions using symbols, such as + (addition), – (subtraction), * (multiplication), and / (division). For example, cell B5 might contain the formula =(B2+B3)/2. This formula tells the computer to add the numbers in cells B2 and B3, divide the result by 2, and display the final result in the cell containing the formula, cell B5.

You don't see the formula in cell B5; you just see its effect. It doesn't matter whether the numbers represent test scores, dollars, or nothing at all; the computer obediently calculates their average and displays the results. If the number in cell B2 or B3 changes, the number displayed in B5 automatically changes, too: In many ways, this is the most powerful feature of a spreadsheet.

Different brands of spreadsheets, such as those included in Microsoft Office, StarOffice, OpenOffice.org, and AppleWorks, are distinguished by their features, their user interfaces, and which operating system platforms they support. In spite of their differences, all popular spreadsheet programs work in much the same way and share most of these features:

- *Lists.* Despite the availability of powerful and advanced features in virtually all spreadsheets, most individuals still use these applications for fairly mundane tasks, such as making and managing lists of grocery items, to-do tasks, phone numbers, and other related information. For most of these lists, the spreadsheet's calculation capabilities will go untapped; however, because spreadsheets have sophisticated data-formatting capabilities, they are often used like this.
- *Automatic replication of values, labels, and formulas.* Most worksheets contain repetition: Budgetary amounts remain constant from month to month; exam scores are calculated the same way for every student in the class; a scheduling program refers to the same seven days each week. Many spreadsheet commands streamline the entry of repetitive data, labels, and formulas. Replication commands are, in essence, flexible extensions of the basic copy-and-paste functions found in other software. The most commonly used replication commands are the Fill Down and Fill Right commands. Formulas can be constructed with *relative references* to other cells, as in the example on the previous page, so they refer to different cells when replicated in other locations, or as *absolute references* that don't change when copied elsewhere.
- *Automatic recalculation.* Automatic recalculation is one of the spreadsheet's most important capabilities. It not only makes possible the easy correction of errors but also makes it easy to try different values while searching for solutions. For large, complicated worksheets, recalculation can be painfully slow, so most spreadsheets enable you to turn off the automatic recalculation feature and recalculate the worksheet only when necessary.
- *Predefined functions.* The first calculators made computing a square root a tedious and error-prone series of steps. On today's calculators a single press of the square-root button tells the calculator to do all the necessary calculations to produce the square root. Spreadsheet programs contain built-in functions that work like the calculator's square-root button. A function in a formula instructs the computer to perform some predefined set of calculations. For example, the formula =SQRT(C5) calculates the square root of the number in cell C5. Modern spreadsheet applications have large libraries of predefined functions. Many, such as SUM, AVERAGE (or AVG), MIN, and MAX, represent simple calculations that are performed often in all kinds of worksheets. Others automate complex financial, mathematical, and statistical calculations that would be extremely difficult to calculate manually. The IF function enables the worksheet to decide what to do based on the contents of other cells, giving the worksheet logical decision-making capability. (For example, if the number of hours worked is greater than 40, calculate pay using the overtime schedule.) Like the calculator's square-root button, these functions can save time and reduce the likelihood of errors.
- *Macros.* A spreadsheet's menu of functions, like the menu in a fast-food restaurant, is limited to the most popular selections. For situations in which the built-in functions don't fill the bill, most spreadsheets enable you to capture sequences of steps as reusable macros—custom-designed procedures that you can add to the existing menu

of options. Some programs require you to type macros using a special macro language; others enable you to turn on a macro recorder that captures every move you make with the keyboard and mouse and records those actions in a macro transcript. Later, you can ask the computer to carry out the instructions in that macro. Suppose, for example, you use the same set of calculations every month when preparing a statistical analysis of environmental data. Without macros, you'd have to repeat the same sequence of key-strokes, mouse clicks, and commands each time you created the monthly report. But by creating a macro called, for instance, Monthstats, you can effectively say, "Do it again" by issuing the Monthstats command.

■ *Formatting*. Most modern spreadsheets enable you to control typefaces, text styles, cell dimensions, and cell borders. They also enable you to include pictures and other graphic embellishments in documents.

■ *Templates and wizards*. Even with functions and macros, the process of creating a com-plex worksheet from scratch can be intimidating. Many users take advantage of work-sheet templates that contain labels and formulas but no data values. These reusable tem-plates produce instant answers when you fill in the blanks. Some common templates are packaged with spreadsheet software; others are marketed separately. A similar feature, called a wizard, automates the process of creating complex worksheets that meet partic-ular needs. Well-designed templates and wizards can save considerable time, effort, and anguish.

■ *Validation*. Some spreadsheets incorporate artificial intelligence to guide users through complex procedures. To help users check complex worksheets for consistency of entries and formula logic, spreadsheet programs now include *validators*—the equivalent of spelling and grammar checkers for calculations. For example, suppose you enter six numbers into consecutive cells of a Microsoft Excel spreadsheet; then you create a formula that finds the sum of only the first five of these values. Excel produces a warning message suggesting that you may have left out a value from the sum.

■ *Linking*. Sometimes a change in one worksheet produces changes in another. For example, a master sales summary worksheet for a business should reflect changes in each department's sales summary worksheet. Most spreadsheet pro-grams can create **automatic links** among worksheets so when values change in one, all linked work-sheets update automatically. Some programs can create three-dimen-sional worksheets by stacking and linking several two-dimensional sheets. Some spreadsheet programs can create links to Web pages so data can be downloaded and updated automatically.

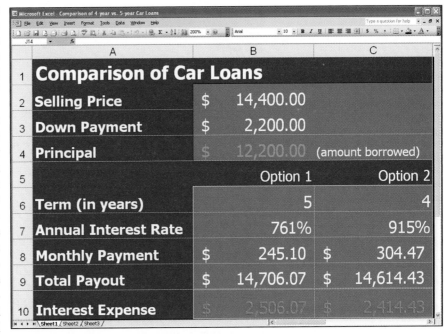

5.23 You can use a spreadsheet to compare car loans.

■ *Database capabilities*. Many spreadsheet programs can perform basic database func-tions: storage and retrieval of information, searching, sorting, generating reports, merg-ing mail, and such. With these features, a spreadsheet can serve users whose database needs are modest. For those who require a full-featured database management system, spreadsheet software might still be helpful; many spreadsheet programs support auto-matic two-way communication with database software.

"What If?" Questions

The purpose of computation is not **numbers** but **insight**.

—*R. W. Hamming*

A spreadsheet program is a versatile tool, but it's especially valuable for answering **"what if?" questions**: "What if I don't complete the third assignment? How will that affect my chances for getting an A?" "What if I put my savings in a high-yield, tax-sheltered IRA account with a withdrawal penalty? Will I be better off than if I leave it in a low-yield pass-book account with no penalty?" "What if I buy a car that gets only 15 miles per gallon instead of a car that gets 40? How much more will I pay altogether for fuel over the next four years?" Because it enables you to change numbers and instantly see the effects of those changes, spreadsheet software streamlines the process of searching for answers to these questions.

Some spreadsheet programs include **equation solvers** that turn "what if?" questions around. Instead of forcing you to manipulate data values until formulas give you the numbers you're looking for, an equation solver enables you to define an equation, enter your target value, and watch while the computer determines the necessary data values. For example, an investor might use an equation solver to answer the question "What is the best mix of these three stocks for minimizing risk while producing a 10 percent return on my investment?"

Spreadsheet Graphics: From Digits to Drawings

Our work . . . is to present things that are **as they are**.

—*Frederick II (1194–1250), King of Sicily*

Most spreadsheet programs include charting and graphing functionality that can turn worksheet numbers into charts and graphs automatically. The process of creating a chart is usually as simple as filling in a few blanks in a dialog box.

The growth in election campaign spending seems more real as a line shooting toward the top of a graph than as a collection of big numbers on a page. The federal budget makes more (or less?) sense as a sliced-up dollar pie than as a list of percentages. The correct chart can make a set of stale figures come to life, awakening our eyes and brains to trends and relationships that we might not have otherwise seen. The charting and graphing functionality in spreadsheet programs offers a variety of basic chart types and options for embellishing charts. The differences among these chart types are more than aesthetic; each chart type is well-suited for communicating particular types of information.

Pie charts show the relative proportions of the parts to a whole. **Line charts** are most often used to show trends or relationships over time or to show relative distribution of one variable through another. (The classic bell-shaped normal curve is a line chart.) **Bar charts** are similar to line charts, but they're more appropriate when data falls into a few categories. Bars can be stacked in a **stack chart** that shows how proportions of a whole change over time; the effect is similar to a series of pie charts. **Scatter charts** are used to discover, rather than display, a relationship between two variables. A well-designed chart can convey a wealth of information, just as a poorly designed chart can confuse or mislead.

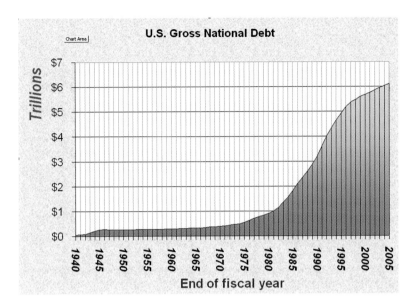

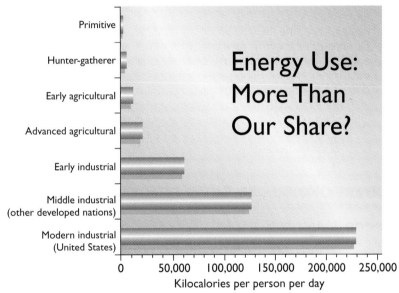

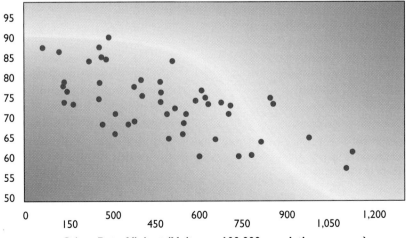

5.24 Line and bar charts show trends over time or distribution over categories. Scatter charts show relationships between variables.

Eradicating Spreadsheet Errors

Spreadsheet errors are easy to make and easy to overlook. When creating a worksheet, you can minimize errors by following a few basic guidelines:

➡ *Plan the worksheet before you start entering values and formulas.* Think about your goals, and design the worksheet to meet those goals.

➡ *Make your assumptions as accurate as possible.* Answers produced by a worksheet are only as good as the assumptions built into the data values and formulas. A worksheet that compares the operating costs of a gas guzzler and a gas miser must make assumptions about future trips, repair costs, and, above all, gasoline prices. The accuracy of the worksheet is tied to all kinds of unknowns, including the future of Middle East politics. The more accurate the assumptions, the more accurate the predictions.

➡ *Double-check every formula and value.* Values and formulas are input for worksheets, and input determines output. Computer professionals often describe the dark side of this important relationship with the letters GIGO—garbage in, garbage out. One highly publicized spreadsheet transcription error for Fidelity Investments resulted in a $2.6 billion miscalculation because of a single missing minus sign!

You may not be working with values this big, but it's still important to proofread your work carefully.

➡ *Make formulas readable.* If your software can attach names to cell ranges, use meaningful names in formulas. It's easier to create and debug formulas when you use readily understandable language, such as payrate*40+1.5*payrate*overtime, instead of a string of characters, like C2*40+1.5*C2*MAX(D2-40,0).

➡ *Check your output against other systems.* Use another program, a calculator, or pencil and paper to verify the accuracy of a sampling of your calculations.

➡ *Build in cross-checks.* Compare the sum of row totals with the sum of column totals. Does everything add up?

➡ *Change the input data values and study the results.* If small input adjustments produce massive output changes, or if major input adjustments result in few or no output changes, something may be wrong.

➡ *Take advantage of preprogrammed functions, templates, and macros.* Why reinvent the wheel when you can buy a professionally designed vehicle?

CHART CHOICE CAN GUIDE READERS TO A PROBLEM RESOLUTION . . .

GOOD

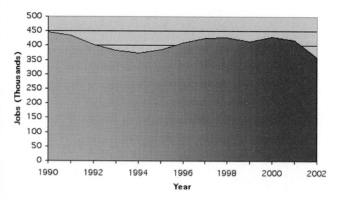

The data values come first, and the employment trend is easy to evaluate. High-tech manufacturing employment in California dropped about 20% between 1990 and 2002.

FAIR: Obscures data values

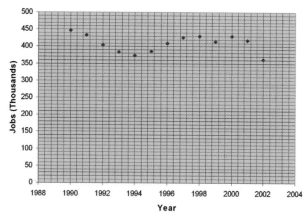

The proliferation of grid lines distracts the reader from the actual data values.

5.25

- *Use a spreadsheet as a decision-making aid, not as a decision maker.* Don't put too much faith in an answer, just because it was produced by a computer. Stay alert and skeptical. Some errors aren't obvious and others don't show up immediately.
- *Take advantage of built-in error-checking tools.* Modern spreadsheet programs have a variety of built-in tools to help you identify errors and track down faulty formulas.
- *Good charts help readers draw the right conclusions from spreadsheet data.* A chart can be a powerful communication tool if it's designed intelligently. If it's not, the message may miss the mark. Here are some guidelines for creating charts that are easy to read and understand.
- *Keep your goal in mind.* The role of a figure may be to describe a trend, facilitate exploration of the data, or tabulate values. A chart is better than a table of numbers for the first two purposes.
- *Choose the right chart for the job.* Think about the message you're trying to convey. Line charts, bar charts, and scatter charts are not interchangeable. Pie charts are rarely appropriate.
- *Put the data first.* Avoid adding elements to your charts that obscure the data values. Too many grid lines make the data values hard to see. If your purpose is tabulating values, perhaps you should be creating a table.
- *Do not distract the reader.* The chart should encourage the reader to think about the meaning of the data values, not which program was used to create the chart, or its interesting color scheme. Avoid filling in blank spaces with clip art or other design elements that have nothing to do with the data.
- *Make it easy to compare data.* If the chart illustrates a single trend, make sure the trend is clear. If the chart shows multiple trends, make sure the reader can distinguish between trends and compare them.
- *Do not distort the data.* By hiding the baseline, you can deceive a reader into thinking that the actual change in a data value is larger or smaller than it really is. Your goal should be to reveal the truth, not hide it.
- *Relate to the rest of the document.* If your chart is part of a written report, make sure that the information you provide in your chart is consistent with the descriptions and analyses in your report.
- *Learn from the experts.* Use high-quality charts in magazines, books, and newspapers as models.

THE WRONG CONCLUSION . . .

DECEIVING: Hides the baseline

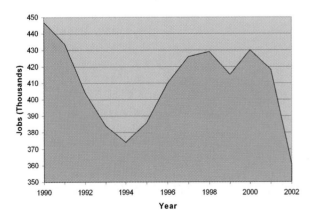

High-Tech Manufacturing Employment in California

The loss of jobs is exaggerated because the bottom of the chart represents 350,000 jobs, not 0 jobs. The chart implies that 90% of the high-tech manufacturing jobs were lost.

OR SIMPLY CONFUSION!

BAFFLING: Hides the trend

High-Tech Manufacturing Employment in California (in Thousands)

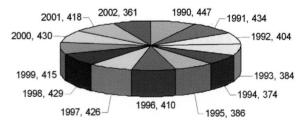

A pie chart is not an appropriate way to show a trend over time. It is almost impossible for the reader to understand how employment has changed by looking at the pie slices. The only use for a pie chart is to show how various parts add up to a whole. Even then, pie charts reveal little information for the amount of space they occupy, and they do not order the data values they contain. For these reasons some experts say pie charts should never be used.

Statistical Software: Beyond Spreadsheets

Science is what we understand well enough to **explain to a computer; art** is **everything else**.

—Donald Knuth, author of The Art of Computer Programming

Spreadsheet software is remarkably versatile, but no program is perfect for every task. Other types of number-manipulation software are available for situations in which spreadsheets don't quite fit the job.

Money Managers

Spreadsheet software has its roots in the accountant's ledger sheets, but spreadsheets are seldom used for business accounting and bookkeeping. Accounting is a complex concoction of rules, formulas, laws, and traditions, and creating a worksheet to handle the details of the process is difficult and time-consuming. Instead of relying on general-purpose spreadsheets for accounting, most businesses (and many households) use professionally designed accounting and financial-management software.

Whether practiced at home or at the office, accounting involves setting up accounts—monetary categories to represent various types of income, expenses, assets, and liabilities—and keeping track of the flow of money among those accounts. An accountant routinely records transactions—checks, cash payments, charges, and other activities—that move money from one account to another. Accounting software, such as Intuit's popular Quicken, automatically adjusts the balance in every account after each transaction. What's more, it records every transaction so that you can retrace the history of each account step by step. This audit trail is a necessary part of business financial records, and it is one reason accountants use special-purpose accounting packages rather than spreadsheet programs.

In addition to keeping records, financial-management software can automate check writing, bill paying, budgeting, and other routine money matters. Periodic reports and charts can provide detailed answers to questions such as "Where does the money go?" and "How are we doing compared to last year?"

Through an Internet connection, a home-accounting program can recommend investments based on up-to-the-hour performance statistics, track investment portfolios, comparison shop for insurance and mortgages, and link to specialized online calculators and advisors. Hundreds of financial institutions offer online banking services, making it possible to pay bills, check account balances, and transfer funds using software.

5.26 Inexpensive personal financial-management programs make the accounting process easier to understand by simulating the look of checks and other familiar documents on the screen. Portable versions of these applications run on devices that use Palm OS and the Pocket PC.

Most accounting and financial-management programs don't calculate income taxes, but they can export records to programs that do. Tax-preparation software works like a prefabricated worksheet. As you enter numbers into the blanks in on-screen forms, the program automatically fills in other blanks. Every time you enter or change a number, the bottom line is recalculated automatically. When the forms are completed, they're ready to print, sign, and mail to the Internal Revenue Service. Many taxpayers now bypass paper forms altogether by sending the completed forms electronically to the IRS.

Automatic Mathematics

Most of us seldom do math more complicated than filling out our tax forms. But higher mathematics is an essential part of the work of many scientists, researchers, engineers, architects, economists, financial analysts, teachers, and other professionals. Mathematics is a universal language for defining and understanding natural phenomena as well as a tool for creating all kinds of products and structures. Whether or not we work with it directly, our lives are constantly being shaped by mathematics.

Many professionals and students whose mathematical needs go beyond the capabilities of spreadsheets depend on symbolic mathematics-processing software to grapple with complex equations and calculations. Mathematics processors make it easier for mathematicians to create, manipulate, and solve equations in much the same way word processors help writers. Features vary from program to program, but a typical mathematics processor can do polynomial factoring, symbolic and numeric calculus, real and complex trigonometry, matrix and linear algebra, and three-dimensional graphics.

Mathematics processors generally include an interactive, wizardlike question-and-answer mode, a programming language, and tools for creating interactive documents that combine text, numerical expressions, and graphics. Although mathematics processors have been available for only a few years, they've already changed the way professionals use mathematics and the way students learn it. By handling the mechanics of mathematics, these programs enable people to concentrate on the content and implications of their work.

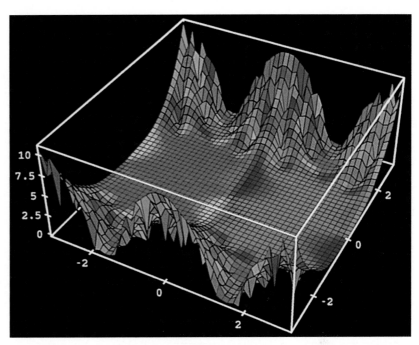

5.27 An abstract mathematical relationship is easier to understand when it is turned into a visible object with software, such as Mathematica.

Statistics and Data Analysis

Yet **to calculate** is not in itself **to analyze**.

—*Edgar Allan Poe, 1841*

One branch of applied mathematics that has become more important in the computer age is statistics—the science of collecting and analyzing data. Modern computer technology provides us with mountains of data—census, political, consumer, economic, sports, weather, scientific, and more. We often refer to the data as statistics. ("The government released unemployment statistics today.") But the numbers by themselves tell only part of the story. The analysis of those numbers—the search for patterns and relationships among them—can provide meaning for the data. ("Analysts note that the rise in unemployment is confined to cities most heavily impacted by the freeze on government contracts.") Statisticians in government, business, and science depend on computers to make sense of raw data.

Do people who live near nuclear power plants run a higher cancer risk? Does the current weather pattern suggest the formation of a tropical storm? Are rural voters more likely to support small-town candidates? These questions can't be answered with absolute certainty; the element of chance is at the heart of statistical analysis. But **statistical-analysis software** can suggest answers to questions such as these by testing the strength of data relationships. Statistical software can also produce graphs showing how two or more variables relate to each other. Statisticians can often uncover trends by browsing through two- and three-dimensional graphs of data, looking for unusual patterns in the dots and lines that appear on the screen. This kind of visual exploration of data is an example of a type of application known as scientific visualization.

Scientific Visualization

The **wind blows** over the lake and **stirs the surface** of the water. Thus, **visible effects** of the **invisible** are manifested.

—The I Ching

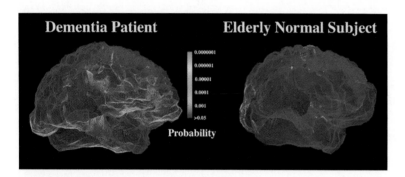

5.28 These two visualizations, created at the Laboratory of Neuro Imaging (LONI), map physical differences between a normal human brain and one with a form of dementia.

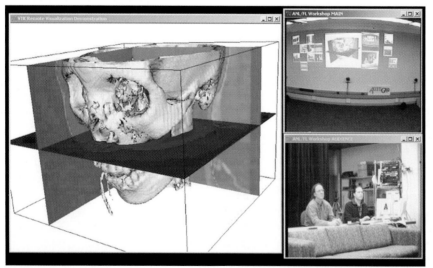

5.29 Using a tool called Access Grid, researchers work with a shared visualization called the Visible Human.

Scientific-visualization software uses shape, location in space, color, brightness, and motion to help us understand relationships that are invisible to us. Like mathematical and statistical software, scientific-visualization software is no longer confined to mainframes and supercomputers; some of the most innovative programs have been developed for use on high-end personal computers and workstations, working alone or in conjunction with more powerful computers.

Scientific visualization takes many forms, all of which involve the graphical representation of numerical data. The numbers can be the result of abstract equations, or they can be data gleaned from the real world. Either way, turning the numbers into pictures enables researchers and students to see the unseeable and sometimes, as a result, to know what was previously unknowable. Here are two examples:

- Margaret Geller of Harvard University created a 3-D map of the cosmos from data on the locations of known galaxies. While using her computer to "fly through" this three-dimensional model, she saw something that no one had seen before: the mysterious clustering of galaxies along the edges of invisible bubbles.

How It **Works**

5.2 **Fractal Geometry and Simulation**

Computers have long been used to analyze and visualize scientific data collected through experiments and observation. A computer can also serve as a virtual laboratory that simulates a physical process without real-world experiments. Of course, an inaccurate simulation can give incorrect results. The problems of creating an accurate simulation helped initiate the study of chaos and fractals. Chaos is now a vast field of study with applications in many disciplines.

The "Chaos Game" illustrates how computers can quickly complete repetitive tasks in experiments that would otherwise be impractical or impossible. You could perform the first few steps of such an experiment with pencil, paper, and ruler, like this:

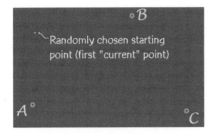

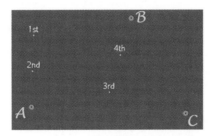

1. Draw three widely separated points on the paper to form a triangle; label the points A, B, and C. Draw a random starting point anywhere on the paper. This will be the first "current" point.

2. Repeat the following process four times: Randomly choose from among points A, B, and C, and draw a new point halfway (on an imaginary straight line) between the current point and the chosen point. The newly drawn point then becomes the new current point.

3. If you use a simple computer program to plot 100,000 repeats of step 2 (excluding the first few points from the drawing), you'll see a pattern emerge rather than a solid mass of dots. This pattern, called a Sierpinski gasket, is a fractal—an object in which pieces are miniatures of the whole figure. You will see a pattern like this.

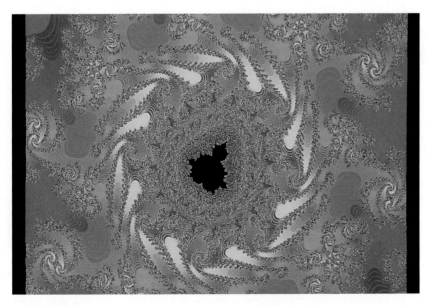

The Mandelbrot set, discovered by the mathematician Benoit Mandelbrot (who coined the term fractal) while he was working at IBM's Thomas J. Watson Research Facility, is one of the most famous fractals to emerge from the theory of chaos.

5.30 Because some fractal formulas mimic the patterns of natural objects, such as coastlines and mountains, chaos has found applications in computer-generated scenery and special effects for movies and television shows.

■ Dr. Mark Ellisman of the University of California, San Diego, School of Medicine used a 30-foot electron microscope to collect data from cells of the brain and enter it into a supercomputer, which rendered a 3-D representation of the brain cell. When Ellisman's team displayed the data on a graphic workstation, they saw several previously undiscovered aberrations in brains of patients who had Alzheimer's disease—aberrations that may turn out to be clues for discovering the cause and cure for this disease.

In these examples and hundreds of others like them, visualization helps researchers see relationships that might have been obscure or even impossible to grasp without computer-aided visualization tools.

Calculated Risks: Computer Modeling and Simulation

We have the ability to **model**—to prototype—**faster, better, and cheaper** than ever before. The old back-of-the-envelope is becoming **supercomputer driven** louver!

—*Michael Schrage, author of* Serious Play

Whether part of a simple worksheet or a complex set of equations, numbers often symbolize real-world phenomena. Computer modeling—the use of computers to create abstract models of objects, organisms, organizations, and processes—can be done with spreadsheets, mathematical applications, or standard programming languages. A business executive who creates a worksheet to project quarterly profits and losses is trying to model the economic world that affects the company. An engineer who uses a mathematics processor to test the stress capacity of a bridge is modeling the bridge mathematically. Even a statistician who starts by examining data collected in the real world creates statistical models to describe the data.

5.31 Consumer-oriented simulations enable people to experience and view artificial life. The Sims is a popular video game title in which users control and observe simulated people, or "Sims," in a virtual world. The Marine Aquarium screen saver offers a stunningly realistic artificial fish tank in which the occupants move and act naturally.

5.32 Flight simulators for home computers and video game consoles are based on the same simulation technology that's used in military flight trainers that pilots use to train for war.

Computer models aren't always serious; most computer games are models. Chessboards, pinball games, battlefields, sports arenas, ant colonies, cities, medieval dungeons, interplanetary cultures, and mythological societies have all been modeled in computer games. Students use computer models to travel the Oregon Trail, explore nuclear power plants, invest in the stock market, and dissect digital frogs.

Whether it's created for work, education, or play, a computer model is an *abstraction*—a set of concepts and ideas designed to mimic some kind of system. But a computer model isn't static; you can put it to work in a computer simulation to see how the model operates under certain conditions. A well-designed model should behave like the system it imitates.

Suppose, for example, an engineer constructs a computer model of a new type of airplane to test how the plane will respond to human commands. In a typical flight simulation, the "pilot" controls the plane's thrust and elevator angle by feeding input data to the model plane. The model responds by adjusting air speed and angle of ascent or descent, just as a real plane would. The pilot responds to the new state of the aircraft by adjusting one or more of the controls, which causes the system to respond by revising the aircraft's state again. This feedback loop, where plane and pilot react to data from each other, continues throughout the simulation.

A flight simulator might have a graphical user interface that makes the computer screen look and act like the instrument panel of a real plane so that human pilots can run it intuitively. Or it might display nothing more than numbers representing input and output values, and the input values might be generated by a simulated pilot—another computer model! Either way, it can deliver a wealth of information about the behavior of the plane, provided the model is accurate.

Computer Simulations: The Rewards

> We are reaching the stage where **problems** that we **must solve** are going to become **insolvable** without computers. **I do not fear computers**; I fear the **lack of them**.
>
> —*Isaac Asimov, scientist and science fiction writer*

Computer simulations are widely used for research in the physical, biological, and social sciences and in engineering. Schools, businesses, and the military also use simulations for training. There are many reasons:

- *Safety.* Although it's safer to learn piloting skills while sitting in front of a computer rather than actually flying in the air, it's still possible to learn to fly without a computer simulation. Some activities, however, are so dangerous that they aren't ethically possible without computer simulations. How, for example, can scientists study the effects of a nuclear power plant meltdown on the surrounding environment? Unless a meltdown occurs, there's only one practical answer: computer simulation.
- *Economy.* It's far less expensive for an automobile manufacturer to produce a digital model of a nonexistent car than to build a prototype out of steel. The company can test the computer model for strength, handling, and efficiency in a series of simulations before it builds and tests a physical prototype. The cost of the computer model is small when compared with the possible expense of producing a defective car.
- *Projection.* Without computers, it could take decades for biologists to determine whether the rising deer population on an island threatens other species, and by the time they discovered the answer, it would be too late to do anything about it. A computer model of the island's ecosystem could speed up natural biological processes so scientists could measure their effects over several generations in a matter of minutes. A computer simulation can, in effect, serve as a time machine for exploring one or more possible futures.
- *Visualization.* Computer models make visualization possible, and visualization enables researchers and students to see and understand relationships that might otherwise go unnoticed. Computer models can speed time up or slow it down; they can make subatomic particles big and the universe small.
- *Replication.* In the real world, it can be difficult or impossible to repeat a research project with slightly different conditions. But this kind of repetition is an important part of serious research. An engineer needs to fine-tune dimensions and angles to achieve peak performance. A scientist studies the results of one experiment and develops a new hypothesis that calls for further testing. An executive needs to test a business plan under a variety of economic scenarios. If the research is conducted on a computer model, replication is just a matter of changing input values and running a new simulation.

Computer Simulations: The Risks

All information is **imperfect**.

—Jacob Bronowski

The downside of computer simulation can be summed up in three words: Simulation isn't reality. The real world is a subtle and complex place, and capturing even a fraction of that subtlety and complexity in a computer simulation is a tremendous challenge.

GIGO Revisited

The accuracy of a simulation depends on how closely its mathematical model corresponds to the system being simulated. Mathematical models are built on assumptions, many of which are difficult or impossible to verify. Some models suffer from faulty assumptions; others contain hidden assumptions that may not even be obvious to their creators; still others go astray simply because of clerical or human errors.

The daily weather report is the result of a complex computer model. Our atmosphere is far too complex to capture exactly in a computer model; that's why the weather forecast is sometimes wrong. Occasionally simulation errors produce disastrous results. Faulty computer models have been responsible for the deadly flooding of the Colorado River, the collapse of the roof of a Salt Lake City shopping mall, and the crash of a test plane on its first flight. These kinds of disasters are rare. It's much more common for computer models to help avert tragedies by pointing out design flaws. In fact, sometimes things go wrong because people *ignore* the results of accurate simulations. Still, *garbage in, garbage out* is a basic rule of simulation.

Making Reality Fit the Machine

Simulations are computation intensive. Some simulations are so complex that researchers need to simplify models and streamline calculations to get them to run on the best hardware available. Even when there's plenty of computing power available, researchers face a constant temptation to reshape reality for the convenience of the simulation. In one classic example, a U.S. Forest Service computer model reduced complex old-growth forests to "accumulated capital." Aesthetics, ecological diversity, and other hard-to-quantify factors didn't exist in this model.

Sometimes this simplification of reality is deliberate; more often it's unconscious. Either way, information can be lost, and the loss may compromise the integrity of the simulation and call the results into question.

The Illusion of Infallibility

Risks can be magnified because people take computers seriously. People tend to emphasize computer-generated reports, often at the expense of other sources of knowledge. Executives use worksheets to make decisions involving thousands of jobs and millions of dollars. Politicians decide the fate of military weapons and endangered species based on summaries of computer simulations. Doctors use computer models to make life-and-death decisions involving new drugs and treatments. All of these people, in some sense, are placing their trust in computer simulations. Many of them trust the data precisely because a computer produced it.

A computer simulation, whether generated by a PC spreadsheet or churned out by a supercomputer, can be an invaluable decision-making aid. The risk is that the people who make decisions with computers will turn over too much of their decision-making power to the computer. The Jedi Master in *Star Wars* understood the danger when he encouraged Luke Skywalker in the heat of battle to turn off his computer simulation rather than let it overpower his judgment. His admonition was simple: "Trust your feelings."

Inventing the FUTURE

Truly Intelligent Agents

I don't want to sit and move stuff around on my screen all day and look at figures and have it recognize my **gestures** and listen to my **voice**. I want to tell it what to do and then go away; I don't want to babysit this computer. I want it to act **for me, not with me**.

—Esther Dyson, computer industry analyst and publisher

At Xerox PARC Alan Kay and his colleagues developed the first user interface based on icons—images that represent tools to be manipulated by users. Their pioneering work helped turn the computer into a productivity tool for millions of people. According to Kay, future user interfaces will be based on agents rather than tools.

Agents are software programs designed to be managed rather than manipulated. An intelligent software agent can ask questions as well as respond to commands, pay attention to its user's work patterns, serve as a guide and a coach, take on its owner's goals, and use reasoning to fabricate goals of its own.

Many PC applications include *wizards* and other agent-like software entities to guide users through complex tasks and answer questions when problems arise. The computer opponents you interact with in games, such as *Civilization* III, are also intelligent agents. The Internet is home to a rapidly growing population of bots—software robots that crawl around the Web collecting information, helping consumers make decisions, answering email, and even playing games. But today's wizards, bots, and agents aren't smart enough to manage the many details that a human assistant might juggle.

Tomorrow's agents will be better able to compete with human assistants, though. A well-trained software agent in the future might accomplish these tasks:

➡ *Remind you that it's time to get the tires rotated on your car, and make an appointment for the rotation*
➡ *Distribute notes to the other members of your study group or work group, and tell you which members opened those notes*
➡ *Keep you posted on new articles on subjects that interest you, and know enough about those subjects to be selective without being rigid*
➡ *Manage your appointments and keep track of your communications*
➡ *Teach you new applications and answer reference questions*
➡ *Defend your system and your home from viruses, intruders, and other security breaches*
➡ *Help protect your privacy on and off the Net*

Agents are often portrayed with human characteristics; *2001*'s Hal and the computers on TV's *Star Trek* are famous examples. Of course, agents don't need to look or sound human—they just need to possess considerable knowledge and intelligence.

Future agents may possess a degree of sensitivity, too. Researchers at MIT and IBM are developing *affective computers* that can detect the emotional states of their users and respond accordingly. Affective computers use sensors to determine a person's emotional state. Sensors range from simple audiovisual devices to mouse-embedded sensors that work like lie detectors, monitoring pulse or skin resistance. Early research has shown limited success at identifying emotions, but the machines still have much to learn. They can't, for example, tell the difference between love and hate, because, from a physiological point of view, they look pretty much the same! ~

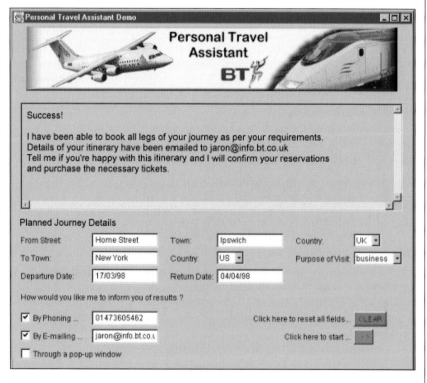

5.33 BT's Personal Travel Assistant is an agent that can assist travelers by booking reservations and purchasing tickets.

Copy Protection Robs the Future *Dan Bricklin*

Dan Bricklin, inventor of the first spreadsheet program, argues here that copy protection may make today's computer documents indecipherable tomorrow. This thought-provoking piece is an edited version of an article on his Web site, www.danbricklin.com.

The other day I wanted to listen to a song from my youth. I took the record out of its sleeve and put it on my aging turntable. I dropped the needle onto the track, and out came the music, but it was way too fast. My turntable now plays everything at 45 rpm instead of 33. Bummer!

This got me to thinking about preserving old works of composers, musicians, authors, and other creative individuals. How does that preserving come about and will today's works produced on digital media last into the future?

As human beings, we benefit greatly from the works of others. Artists, thinkers, scholars, and performers create works that we all enjoy, learn from, and are inspired by. Many works are timeless. We often hear of authors, artists, or composers who have their greatest impact after their death, sometimes many years later.

How are these works passed down through the generations? Other people make it their job to preserve the works and pass them on. These jobs are either formal, like librarians, or informal, like hobbyists.

How are the works preserved? Sometimes just storing the work is sufficient, but in most cases a change in environment is needed. The artist's original location may be sold for another use. The work may be created in a material that is affected by air and water, and must be kept in a temperature- and humidity-controlled room.

For some works, it's enough to just preserve the words themselves. For others, copies are what we preserve, such as recordings of performances, or microfilm copies of newspapers. We produce the copies in more stable media, or ones that are easier from which to reproduce.

With every changing technology, in order to preserve many works we will need to move them ahead, copying them to each new media form before the previous one becomes obsolete. Also, we need to preserve the knowledge of the methods of converting from one media to another, so we can access the old works that have not yet been moved ahead. This is crucial. Without this information, even preserved works could be unreadable.

The most famous example of that type of translation information was an inscribed slab of rock from 196 BC found in 1799. It contained a decree written in Greek that was also written in two forms of Egyptian. It's called the Rosetta Stone. It let scholars finally read ancient works in hieroglyphics that they had physical possession of but whose language had been a mystery for 1,400 years.

There are things happening that make me worry that the future may not be bright for preserving many of the works we create today. For example: Companies are preparing to produce music CDs that cannot be copied into many other formats (something allowed by law as "fair use"). Most ebooks are copy protected. A new law requires all digital devices to enforce copy protection schemes for copyrightable material.

An existing law makes it a crime to tell people how to make copies of protected works.

I believe copy protection will break the chain necessary to preserve creative works. It will make them readable for a limited time and not be able to be moved ahead as media deteriorates or technologies change. Only those works that are thought to be profitable at any given time will be preserved by their "owners" (if they are still in business). We know from history that what's popular at any given time is no certain indication of what will be valuable in the future. Without not-copy protected "originals," archivists, collectors, and preservers will be unable to maintain them the way they would if they weren't protected. We won't even be able to read media in obsolete formats, because the specifications of those formats will not be available. To create a "Rosetta Stone" of today's new formats will be asking to go to jail and having your work banned.

This is different than encryption or patent protection. With encryption, as long as the keys survive, and a description of the method of decryption, you can recreate the unprotected original. It's even better—you can prove authenticity. Patent protection just keeps you from creating and using your unlicensed reader for a limited period of time. For long-term preservation of works patented techniques are good because they discourage secrets and eventually put things in the public domain.

One of the most popular parts of this web site is a copy of the original IBM PC version of VisiCalc. It's not the same exact program you could buy. The original VisiCalc was only shipped on $5\frac{1}{4}$" copy protected diskettes. I received permission from the copyright holder to distribute the copies, but VisiCalc hadn't been produced for years and they lost track of any original masters they had owned. Luckily for me, an employee of Software Arts kept a "test" copy that was created without the copy protection code. Thanks to those not-copy protected copies it is much more likely that future generations will be able to learn about early PC programs by running VisiCalc.

Copy protection, like poor environment and chemical instability before it for books and works of art, looks to be a major impediment to preserving our cultural heritage.

Artists and authors need to create their works and still make a living. Copy protection is arising as a "simple fix" to preserve business models based upon the physical properties of old media and distribution. Our new media and distribution techniques need new business models that don't shortchange the future. Trying to keep those old business models in place is as inappropriate as continuing to produce only 33 rpm vinyl records.

Discussion Questions

1. Do you agree that copy protection will break the chain necessary to preserve creative works? Explain your answer.

2. What kind of "new business model" do you think the author is suggesting in the last paragraph?

Summary

Even though the computer was originally designed to work with numbers, it quickly became an important tool for processing text as well.

Word-processing software enables the writer to use commands to edit text on the screen, eliminating the chore of retyping pages until the message is right. With a word processor, you can control the typefaces, spacing, justification, margins, columns, headers, footers, and other visual components of your documents. Most professional word-processing programs automate footnoting, hyphenation, and other processes that are particularly troublesome to traditional typists.

Outlining software turns the familiar outline into a powerful, dynamic organizational tool. Spelling checkers and grammar and style checkers partially automate the proofreading process, although they leave the more difficult parts of the job to literate humans. Online thesauruses, dictionaries, and other computer-based references automate reference works.

As word processors become more powerful, they take on many of the features previously found only in desktop-publishing software. Still, many publishers use word processors and graphics programs to create source documents that can be used as input for page-layout programs. Desktop publishing has revolutionized the publishing process by enabling publishers and would-be publishers to produce professional-quality text-and-graphics documents at a reasonable cost. Amateur and professional publishers everywhere use desktop-publishing technology to produce everything from comic books to reference books.

The near-overnight success of desktop publishing may foreshadow other changes in the way we communicate with words as new technologies emerge. Computer networks in general and the World Wide Web in particular have made it possible for potential publishers to reach mass audiences without the problems associated with printing and distributing paper documents. Typing may no longer be a necessary part of the writing process as handwriting and speech-recognition technologies improve, and word-processing software that incorporates other artificial intelligence technologies may become as much a coach as a tool for future writers.

Spreadsheet programs, first developed to simulate and automate the accountant's ledger, can be used for tracking financial transactions, calculating grades, forecasting economic conditions, recording scientific data and just about any other task that involves repetitive numeric calculations. Spreadsheet documents, called worksheets, are grids with individual cells containing alphabetic labels, numbers, and formulas. Changes in numeric values can cause the spreadsheet to update any related formulas automatically. The responsiveness and flexibility of spreadsheet software make it particularly well-suited for providing answers to "what if" questions. Most spreadsheet programs include charting commands to turn worksheet numbers into a variety of graphs and charts. The process of creating a chart from a spreadsheet is automated to the point where human drawing isn't necessary; the user simply provides instructions concerning the type of chart and the details to be included in the chart, and the computer does the rest.

Number crunching often goes beyond spreadsheets. Specialized accounting and tax preparation software packages perform specific business functions without the aid of spreadsheets. Symbolic mathematics processors can handle a variety of higher mathematics functions involving numbers, symbols, equations, and graphics. Statistical-analysis software is used for data collection and analysis. Scientific visualization can be done with math processors, statistical packages, graphics programs, or specialized programs designed for visualization.

Modeling and simulation are at the heart of most applications involving numbers. When people create computer models, they use numbers to represent real-world objects and phenomena. Simulations built on these models can provide insights that might be difficult or impossible to obtain otherwise, provided that the models reflect reality accurately. If used wisely, computer simulation can be a powerful tool for helping people understand their world and make better decisions.

Key Terms

Interactive Activities

1. The *Computer Confluence* CD-ROM contains self-test multiple-choice quiz questions related to this chapter.

2. The *Computer Confluence* Web site, **http://www.computerconfluence.com**, contains self-test exercises related to this chapter. Follow the instruc-

tions for taking a quiz. After you've completed your quiz, you can email the results to your instructor.

3. The Web site also contains open-ended discussion questions called Internet Explorations. Discuss one or more of the Internet Exploration questions at the section for this chapter.

True or False

1. WYSIWYG stands for "What you see is what you get."

2. With most word-processing programs, text editing must be completed before text formatting is started.

3. A monospaced font assigns equal horizontal space to all characters of the same point size.

4. Desktop-publishing software does essentially the same thing as word-processing software, but it can process larger documents.

5. One of the biggest problems with desktop-publishing technology is that its high cost makes it impractical for small businesses and individuals.

6. Electronic publishing is replacing some forms of print publishing, but paper documents aren't likely to go away anytime soon.

7. Charting software, such as the chart tools built into spreadsheet software, generally contains safeguards that prevent the misrepresentation of information.

8. Most accounting and financial-management programs don't calculate income taxes, but they can export records to programs that do.

9. Statistical-analysis software can suggest answers to scientific questions by testing the strength of data relationships.

10. People tend to emphasize computer-generated reports, often at the expense of other knowledge sources.

Multiple Choice

1. Which of these is a text-formatting feature of a word-processing program?
   a. Drag and drop
   b. Cut and paste
   b. Word wrap
   c. Stylesheets
   e. None of the above

2. Which of these is a text-editing feature of a word-processing program?
   a. Drag and drop
   b. Font choice
   c. Justification tools
   d. Stylesheets
   e. None of the above

3. To which of the following does justification generally apply?
   a. Individual characters
   b. Words
   c. Paragraphs
   d. Fonts
   e. All of the above

4. Center justification is particularly useful when formatting
   a. Boldface characters
   b. Footnotes
   c. Foreign languages
   d. Titles
   e. All of the above

5. When might full justification be a poor choice?
   a. The column is very narrow.
   b. The column is very wide.
   c. The characters are printed in a serif font.
   d. The characters are printed in italics.
   e. None of the above. Full justification is always a good choice.

6. According to the experts, a serif font is better than a sans serif font when formatting.
   a. Titles and subtitles
   b. The body of a document (pages of text)
   c. Figure captions
   d. Text boxes (side bars)
   e. All of the above

7. To represent full-color images accurately, what must desktop-publishing systems use?
   a. Laser printers
   b. Service bureaus
   c. Color-matching technology
   d. Spot color
   e. Phototypesetting machines

8. A document created with a desktop publishing system can be
   a. Printed on a color printer
   b. Converted into a PDF document for electronic distribution
   c. Displayed on the Web
   d. Printed on a phototypesetting machine at a service bureau
   e. All of the above

9. Which of the following is a fundamentally important principle of spreadsheets?
   a. They eliminate the need for any other kind of programming language.
   b. They never change the values of cells unless explicitly instructed to by the user.
   c. They provide a bar-chart graphical user interface for data input.
   d. Formulas automatically recalculate results when any of their inputs change.
   e. All of the above

10. If you change the value of numbers in a spreadsheet, changes may occur in other cells containing
    a. Values
    b. Macros
    c. Formulas
    d. Labels
    e. Templates

11. Which type of chart is most appropriate for showing the percentages of the U.S. federal budget that go to domestic spending, military spending, other spending, and interest on the national debt?
    a. Bar chart
    b. Line chart
    c. Scatter chart
    d. Pie chart
    e. Bullet chart

12. Which of these types of software is used for creating models?
    a. Spreadsheet software
    b. Accounting software
    c. Mathematics-processing software
    d. All of the above
    e. None of the above

13. Scientific-visualization software
    a. Requires visual input devices to work properly
    b. Is the scientific equivalent of desktop publishing software
    c. Creates pictures from numbers
    d. Requires supercomputer power to run
    e. Doesn't exist yet, but it will be a reality before the end of the decade

14. Simulation software offers many advantages, including all of these *except*:
    a. It can save money.
    b. It can be much safer than "real-world" experience.
    c. It is generally more accurate than standard experimental research.
    d. It can save time.
    e. It makes experimental replication easier.

15. A wizard inside a PC application is a primitive example of
    a. An intelligent agent
    b. A spreadsheet program
    c. A scientific simulation
    d. A computer virus
    e. A fractal

Review Questions

1. How is word processing different from typing?

2. How many different ways can a paragraph or line of text be justified? When might each be appropriate?

3. How is working with an outliner (or idea processor) different from working with a word processor?

4. Describe three different ways a spelling checker might be fooled.

5. How does desktop publishing differ from word processing?

6. Is it possible to have a desktop publishing system that is not WYSIWYG? Explain.

7. An automated speech-recognition system might have trouble telling the difference between a "common denominator" and a "comedy nominator." What must the speaker do to avoid confusion? What other limitations plague automated speech-recognition systems today?

8. In what ways are word processors and spreadsheet programs similar?

9. What are some advantages of using a spreadsheet over using a calculator to maintain a budget? Are there any disadvantages?

10. If you enter "=A1*B1" in cell C1 of a worksheet, the formula is replaced by the number 125 when you press the Enter key. What happened?

11. Explain the difference between a numeric value and a formula.

12. Describe or draw examples of several different types of charts, and explain how they're typically used.

13. Describe several software tools used for numeric applications too complex to be handled by spreadsheets. Give an example of an application of each.

14. List several advantages and disadvantages of using computer simulations for decision making.

Discussion Questions

1. What do you think of the arguments that word processing reduces the quality of writing because it makes it easy to write in a hurried and careless manner and it puts the emphasis on the way a document looks rather than on what it says?

2. Like Gutenberg's development of the movable-type printing press more than 500 years ago, the development of desktop publishing puts powerful communication tools in the hands of more people. What impact will desktop-publishing technology have on the free press and the free exchange of ideas guaranteed in the United States Constitution? What impact will the same technology have on free expression in other countries?

3. Spreadsheets are sometimes credited with legitimizing the personal computer as a business tool. Why do you think they had such an impact?

4. The statement "Computers don't make mistakes, people do" is often used to support the reliability of computer output. Is the statement true? Is it relevant?

5. Before spreadsheets, people who wanted to use computers for financial modeling had to write programs in complex computer languages to do the job. Today, spreadsheets have replaced those programs for many financial applications. Do you think spreadsheets will be replaced by some easier-to-use software tool in the future? If so, try to imagine what it will be like.

Projects

1. Use a word-processing or a desktop-publishing system to produce a newsletter, brochure, or flyer in support of an organization or cause that is important to you. Base your design on an attractive, mass-marketed publication.

2. Buy four magazines from your local newsstand. Create a table that documents the text fonts and styles each magazine uses for titles, subtitles, figure captions, text boxes, and the body of each article. For each magazine, create a collage that shows the color scheme used inside the magazine (excluding advertisements). Evaluate the similarities and differences among the magazines.

3. Use a spreadsheet or a financial-management program to develop a personal budget. Try to keep track of your income and expenses for the next month or two, and record the transactions with your program. At the end of that time, evaluate the accuracy of your budget, and discuss your reactions to the process.

4. Use a spreadsheet to search for answers to a "what if?" question that's important to you. Possible questions: If I lease a car instead of buying it, am I better off? If I borrow money for school, how much does it cost me in the long run?

5. Use a spreadsheet to track your grades in this (or another) class. Apply weightings from the course syllabus to your individual scores, calculating a point total based on those weightings.

6. Scan the graphics appearing in some newspapers or magazines. Find a graphic that distorts the data values by hiding the baseline. Find a graphic containing superfluous elements that distract from the data values. Find a graphic in which it is difficult to compare data values (for example, a pie chart used inappropriately).

Sources and Resources

Books

Bootstrapping: Douglas Engelbart, Coevolution, and the Origins of Personal Computing, by Thierry Bardini (Stanford, CA: Stanford University Press, 2000). This long-overdue book shines a spotlight on the visionary, revolutionary work of Douglas Engelbart at SRI.

The Handbook of Digital Publishing, Volumes I & II, by Michael L. Kleper (Upper Saddle River, NJ: Prentice Hall, 2001). These two books, which are available in a boxed set, cover every aspect of digital publishing, including typography, design, imaging, page layout, color management, workflow, multimedia, Web publishing, and careers.

The Non-Designer's Design Book, Second Edition, by Robin Williams (Berkeley, CA: Peachpit Press, 2003). In this popular book, Robin Williams provides a friendly introduction to the basics of design and page layout in her popular, down-to-earth style. The first half of the book illustrates the four basic design principles (proximity, alignment, repetition, and contrast). The second half focuses on using type as a design element. This book is highly recommended for anyone new to graphic design.

Looking Good in Print, Fifth Edition, by Roger C. Parker (Scottsdale, AZ: Paraglyph Publishing, 2003). This book covers the nontechnical side of desktop publishing. Now that you know the mechanics, how can you make your work look good? Parker and Berry clearly describe the basic design tools and techniques and then apply them in sample documents ranging from brochures to books.

Designing for Print: An In-depth Guide to Planning, Creating, and Producing Successful Design Projects, by Charles Conover (New York: Wiley, 2003). This book clearly explains and shows how to design successful publications using type, photos, illustrations, and other elements in creative ways.

Bugs in Writing: A Guide to Debugging Your Prose, Second Edition, by Lyn Dupre (Reading, MA: Addison-Wesley, 1998). This entertaining little book is designed to help computer science and computer information systems students, who presumably already know how to debug their programs, debug their prose. It's a friendly, readable tutorial that can help almost anybody to be a better writer.

The Elements of Style, Fourth Edition, by William Strunk, Jr., and E. B. White (Needham Heights, MA: Allyn & Bacon, 2000). If you want to improve your writing, this book is a classic.

The Microsoft Manual of Style for Technical Publications, Third Edition (Redmond, WA: Microsoft Press, 2003). This style guide is a useful alphabetical reference when you need to write about computer hardware and software. Especially useful is its appendix that lists industry acronyms and abbreviations.

Adobe Acrobat Professional Classroom in a Book (San Jose, CA: Adobe Press, 2004). Adobe's PDF is the industry standard for paperless publishing, and Acrobat is the standard tool for creating and editing PDF documents. This tutorial, like others in Adobe's excellent Classroom in a Book series, explains the ins and outs of the software in an easy-to-follow format.

Creating a Newsletter in InDesign: Visual QuickProject, by Katrin Straub and Torsten Buck (Berkeley, CA: Peachpit Press, 2005). Peachpit's Visual Quickproject series reduces projects to most basic instructions. This approach works well if you just want to get something done without mastering the software.

Scrolling Forward: Making Sense of Documents in the Digital Age, by David M. Levy (Arcade Publishing, 2001). How are computers, the Internet, and digital technology changing the notion of documents? The future of books, paper, copyrights, and libraries are discussed in this thought-provoking book.

The Visual Display of Quantitative Information, Second Edition, by Edward R. Tufte (Cheshire, CT: Graphics Press, 2001). Tufte is widely recognized as the master of statistical graphics. In this book he presents his rules for good design and illustrates them with dozens of wonderful (and terrible) graphics that have actually appeared in print.

How to Lie with Statistics, by Darrell Huff (New York: W. W. Norton, 1993). This classic book, first published in 1954, has more relevance in today's computer age than it did when it was written.

The Sum of Our Discontent: Why Numbers Make Us Irrational, by David Boyle (Texere, 2001). Computers, television, and other media bombard us with more numbers than most of us can digest. Boyle argues that all those numbers make it harder, not easier, to understand what's going on around us.

Designing Infographics, by Eric K. Meyer (Indianapolis, IN: Hayden Books, 1997). This book provides an excellent overview of the theory and the practice of designing the modern graphs, charts, and other informative illustrations found in such publications as *USA Today*. It covers tools, techniques, forms, and applications of quantitative and informative graphics; there's even a section on statistical ethics.

Serious Play: How the World's Best Companies Simulate to Innovate, by Michael Schrage (Cambridge, MA: Harvard Business School Press, 1999). "When talented innovators innovate, you don't listen to the specs they quote. You look at the models they've created," says Michael Schrage, MIT Media Lab fellow and Fortune magazine columnist. In this book, Schrage looks at the kind of "serious play" being done at innovative companies, such as Disney, 3M, Sony, and Hewlett Packard.

Web Pages

Created as a tool for scientific researchers and engineers, the Web is full of fascinating sites about mathematics, statistics, scientific visualization, and simulation and is an endless resource for publishers, writers, and page designers. Some, like **http://www.adobe.com**, are obvious; others are harder to find but no less useful. Check the *Computer Confluence* Web site at **http://www.computerconfluence.com** for links to the best pages.

Multimedia

~ Interactive **tutorial** on making presentations

~ Additional content on digital music

~ An example of how **data compression** works

~ Interactive **self-study** quizzes

. . . and more.

www computerconfluence.com

Objectives

After you read this chapter you should be able to:

▶ **Explain the difference between painting software, image-processing software, drawing software, and 3-D modeling software**

▶ **Explain effective techniques for improving the quality of slides prepared with presentation-graphics software**

▶ **Explain the difference between analog video and digital video**

▶ **Describe how data compression works**

▶ **Describe several present and future applications for multimedia technology**

CHAPTER 6

The Internet has long been a powerful communication medium and a storehouse of valuable information. But until recently, few people mastered the cryptic codes and challenging languages that were required to unlock the Internet's treasures. The Net was effectively off-limits to most of the world's people. Tim Berners-Lee changed all that when he single-handedly invented the World Wide Web and gave it to all of us.

Tim Berners-Lee was born in London in 1955. His parents met while programming the Ferranti Mark I, the first commercial computer. They encouraged their son to think unconventionally. He developed a love for electronics and even built a computer out of spare parts and a TV set when he was a physics student at Oxford.

Berners-Lee took a software engineering job at CERN, the European Particle Physics Laboratory in Geneva, Switzerland. While he was there, he developed a program to help him track all his random notes. He

TIM BERNERS-LEE WEAVES THE WEB FOR EVERYBODY

> The whole idea you can have some idea and **make it happen** means that **dreamers** all over the world should **take heart** and **not stop**.
>
> —*Tim Berners-Lee, creator of the World Wide Web*

tried to make the program, called Enquire, deal with information in a "brainlike way." Enquire was a primitive hypertext system that allowed related documents on his computer to be linked with numbers rather than mouse clicks. (Back in 1980, PCs didn't have mice.)

Berners-Lee wanted to expand the concept of Enquire so he could link documents on other computers to his own. His idea was to create an open-ended, distributed hypertext system without boundaries, so scientists everywhere could link their work.

Over the next few years, he single-handedly built a complete system to realize his dream. He designed the URL scheme for giving every Internet document a unique address. He developed HTML, the language for encoding and displaying hypertext documents on the Web. He created HTTP, the set of rules that allows hypertext documents to be linked across the Internet. And he built the first software browser for viewing those documents from remote locations.

Graphics, Digital Media, and Multimedia

When he submitted the first paper describing the Web to a conference in 1991, the conference organizers rejected it because the Web seemed too simple to them. They thought that Berners-Lee's ideas would be a step backward when compared to hypertext systems that had been developed by Ted Nelson, Doug Engelbart, and others over the previous 25 years. It's easy to see now that the simplicity of the Web was a strength, not a weakness.

Rather than try to own his suite of inventions, Berners-Lee made them freely available to the public. Suddenly, vast tracts of the Internet were open to just about anyone who could point and click a mouse. Other programmers added multimedia capabilities to the Web, and its popularity spread like a virus. In a few short years, the Internet was transformed from a forbidding fortress of cryptic commands and codes into an inviting multimedia milieu for the masses.

When he created the Web, Tim Berners-Lee created a new medium of

communication. Few people in history have had so great an impact on the way we communicate. In the words of writer Joshua Quittner, Tim Berners-Lee's accomplishments are "almost Gutenbergian."

Tim Berners-Lee now works in an unassuming office at MIT, where he heads the World Wide Web Consortium (W3C). The W3C is a standards-setting organization dedicated to helping the Web evolve in positive directions rather than disintegrating into incompatible factions. The work of Tim Berners-Lee and the W3C will help ensure that the World Wide Web continues to belong to everyone. ～

6.1 Tim Berners-Lee, the inventor of the World Wide Web.

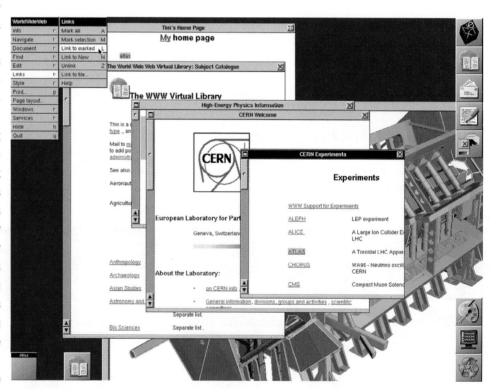

6.2 Berners-Lee implemented the first Web browser on a NeXT workstation in 1990.

The work of Tim Berners-Lee brought multimedia to millions of people around the world. Today, the Web is a source of images, sounds, animations, video clips, and rich interactive documents that merge multiple media types. Even without the Web, though, today's PC can serve as a digital hub for a network of creative media tools, from digital cameras and graphics tablets to musical instruments and video systems. In this chapter we look into these cutting-edge technologies and see how they're changing the ways we create and communicate.

Focus on Computer Graphics

The previous chapter explored a variety of computer applications, from basic word-processing programs to powerful mathematical software packages that can analyze data and generate quantitative charts and graphs from numbers. But computer graphics today go far beyond page layouts and pie charts. In this section, we explore a variety of graphical applications, from simple drawing and painting tools to complex programs used by professional artists and designers.

Mastering technology is only part of what it means **to be an artist** in the twenty-first century. The other hurdle is **mastering creative expression**, so that art has **something substantial** to say. **Expression** has been **the one constant** among artists **from the Stone Age** until now. The only thing that has changed is the **technology**.

—*Steven Holtzman, author of* Digital Mantras

Painting: Bitmapped Graphics

Everything you **imagine** is real.

—*Pablo Picasso*

An image on a computer screen is made up of a matrix of pixels—tiny dots of white, black, or color arranged in rows. The words, numbers, and pictures we see on the computer display are nothing more than patterns of pixels created by software. Most of the time, the user doesn't directly control those pixel patterns; software creates the patterns automatically in response to commands. For example, when you press the *e* key while word processing, the software constructs a pattern that appears on the screen as an *e*. Similarly, when you issue a command to create a bar chart from a spreadsheet, software automatically constructs a pixel pattern that looks like a bar chart. Automatic graphics are convenient, but they can also be restrictive. When you need more control over the details of the screen display, another type of graphics software might be more appropriate.

Painting software enables you to "paint" pixels on the screen with a pointing device. A typical painting program accepts input from a mouse, joystick, trackball, touch pad, or stylus, translating the pointer movements into lines and patterns on-screen. A professional artist might prefer to work with a stylus on a pressure-sensitive tablet because it can, with the right software, simulate a traditional pen or paintbrush more accurately than other pointing devices can. A painting program typically offers a palette of tools on-screen. Some tools mimic real-world painting tools, while others can do things that are difficult, even impossible, on paper or canvas.

6.3 When it's used with compatible software, a stylus on a pressure-sensitive tablet can simulate the feel of a paintbrush on paper. As the artist presses harder on the stylus, the line becomes thicker and denser on the screen.

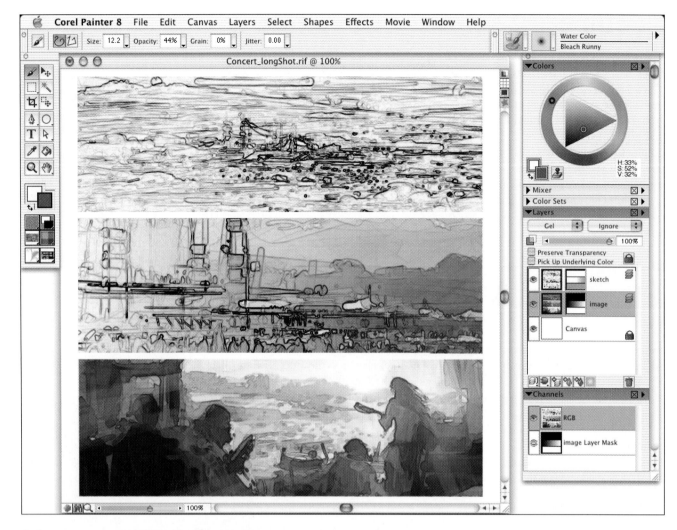

6.4 Natural painting programs, such as Corel Painter, allow artists and nonartists to create digital paintings that simulate real-world tools like watercolors, oil paints, and charcoal.

Painting programs create **bitmapped graphics**, or, as they're sometimes called, **raster graphics**. To the computer, these pictures are simple maps showing how the pixels on the screen should be represented. For the simplest bitmapped graphics, a single bit of computer memory represents each pixel. Because a bit can contain one of two possible values, 0 or 1, each pixel can display one of two possible colors, usually black or white. Allocating more memory per pixel, so each pixel can display more possible colors or shades, produces even higher-quality graphics. **Gray-scale graphics** allow each pixel to appear as black, white, or one of several shades of gray. A program that assigns 8 bits per pixel allows up to 256 different shades of gray to appear on the screen—more than the human eye can distinguish.

Realistic color graphics require more memory. Many older computers have hardware to support 8-bit color, allowing 256 possible colors to be displayed on the screen at a time—enough to display rich images, but not enough to reproduce photographs exactly. Photorealistic color requires hardware that can display millions of colors at a time—24 or 32 bits of memory for each pixel on the screen. Modern personal computers are equal to this task.

The number of bits devoted to each pixel—called **color depth** or **bit depth**—is one of two technological factors limiting an artist's ability to create realistic on-screen images with a bitmapped graphics program. The other factor is **resolution**—the density of the

6.5 This painting served as the cover art for a Herbie Hancock CD called *Dis is de Drum*. Photographer Sanjay Kothari created the image through the process of digital photographic manipulation. Several of the photos used in the final collage are shown along the side of the main image. At the bottom of the collage, three small images show how the photos were merged to create the final image.

pixels, usually described in *dots per inch*, or *dpi*. Not surprisingly, these are also the two main factors controlling image quality in monitors, as described in Chapter 3, "Hardware Basics: Peripherals." But some graphics images are destined for the printer after being displayed on-screen, so the printer's resolution comes into play, too. When displayed on a 96-dpi computer screen—on a Web page, for example—a 96-dpi picture looks fine. But when printed on paper, that same image lacks the fine-grained clarity of a photograph. Diagonal lines, curves, and text characters have tiny "jaggies"—jagged, stair-step-like bumps that advertise the image's identity as a collection of pixels.

Screen Test

Creating a CD Cover

GOAL *To create a CD cover by modifying a digital photograph of the artist.*

TOOL *Adobe Photoshop CS, part of the Adobe Creative Suite.*

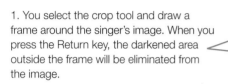

1. You select the crop tool and draw a frame around the singer's image. When you press the Return key, the darkened area outside the frame will be eliminated from the image.

2. There are still a few distracting details in the corners of the cropped photo that need to be removed. Using the marquee tool, you select an oval area to hide the distractions.

3. You click the mask tool to hide everything outside the selected area.

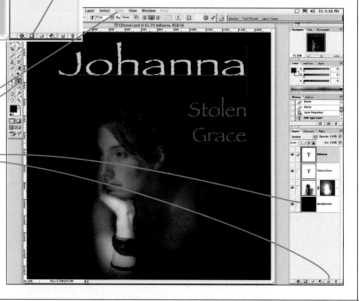

4. You click the Quick Masking icon and refine the shape of the mask by painting with the mouse.

5. You apply a filter to soften the image and give it a painterly effect.

6. You create a new black background layer and place it behind the photo layer.

7. Using the text tool, you add titles.

6.6

Painting programs get around the jaggies by allowing you to store an image at 300 dots per inch or higher, even though the computer screen can't display every pixel at that resolution and normal magnification. Of course, these high-resolution pictures demand more memory and disk space. But for printed images, the results are worth the added cost. The higher the resolution, the harder it is for the human eye to detect individual pixels on the printed page.

Practically speaking, resolution and bit-depth limitations are easy to overcome with today's hardware and software. Artists can use paint programs to produce works that convincingly simulate watercolors, oils, and other natural media, and transcend the limits of those media. Similarly, bitmapped image-editing software can be used to edit photographic images.

Image Processing: Photographic Editing by Computer

Like a picture created with a high-resolution paint program, a digitized photograph or a photograph captured with a digital camera—often simply referred to as a *digital photo*—is a bitmapped image. **Image-processing software** enables the photographer to manipulate digital photos and other high-resolution images with tools similar to those found in paint programs. Image-processing software, such as Adobe Photoshop, is in many ways similar to paint software; both are tools for editing high-resolution bitmapped images.

6.7 Apple's iPhoto, like many PC photo applications, makes it easy to import, edit, and organize photos. iPhoto also automates the creation of custom photo albums that can be turned into professionally bound books via an online store.

The aim of every artist is to **arrest motion**, which is **life**, by artificial means and **hold it fixed** so that **a hundred years later**, when a stranger looks at it, **it moves again** since it is life.

—*William Faulkner*

Digital image-processing software makes it easier for photographers to remove unwanted reflections, eliminate "red eye," and brush away facial blemishes. These kinds of editing tasks were routinely done with magnifying glasses and tiny brushes before photographs were digitized. But digital photographic editing is far more powerful than traditional photo-retouching techniques. With image-processing software, it's possible to distort photos, apply special effects, and fabricate images that range from artistic to other-worldly. It's also possible to combine photographs into composite scenes that show no obvious evidence of tampering. Supermarket gossip tabloids routinely use these tools to create sensationalistic cover photos. Many experts question whether photographs should be allowed as evidence in the courtroom now that they can be doctored so convincingly.

A digital camera typically stores images in a small amount of onboard RAM or on a flash memory card; images are typically downloaded from camera to computer via a USB connection. Digital *photo-management software* programs such as Apple iPhoto and Microsoft PictureIt! simplify and automate common tasks associated with capturing, organizing, editing, and sharing digital images. Most consumer-oriented digital photo managers make it easy to import photos from digital cameras, remove red eye, adjust color and contrast, fix small errors, print photos on a color printer, upload images to a Web site, email copies to friends and family, store photo libraries on CD or DVD, and order paper prints or hardbound photo albums online.

Creating Smart Art

Modern graphics software isn't just for professional artists. Almost anybody can create pictures and presentations. Here are some guidelines to help you make the most of the computer as a graphic tool:

➡ **_Reprogram yourself . . . relax._** For many of us the hardest part is getting started. We are all programmed by messages we received in our childhood, which for many of us included "You aren't creative" and "You can't draw." Fortunately, a computer can help us overcome this early programming and find the artist locked within us. Most drawing and painting programs are flexible, forgiving, and fun. Allow yourself to experiment; you'll be surprised at what you can create if you're patient and playful.

➡ **_Choose the right tool for the job._** Will your artwork be displayed on the computer screen or printed? Does your output device support color? Would color enhance the finished work? Your answers to these questions will help you determine which software and hardware tools are most appropriate. As you're thinking about options, don't rule out low-tech tools. The best approach may not involve a computer, or it may involve some combination of computer and nonelectronic tools.

➡ **_Borrow from the best._** Art supply stores sell _clip art_—predrawn images that artists can legally cut out and paste into their own pictures or posters. Computer artists can choose from hundreds of digital clip art collections. Computer clip art images can be cut, pasted, and edited electronically. Some computer clip art collections are in the public domain (that is, they are free); others can be licensed for a small fee. Computer clip art comes in a variety of formats, and it ranges from simple line drawings to scanned color photographs. If you have access to a scanner, you can create your own digitized clip art from traditional photos and drawings.

➡ **_Don't borrow without permission._** Computers, scanners, and digital cameras make it all too easy to create unauthorized copies of copyrighted photographs, drawings, and other images. There's a clear legal and ethical line between using public domain or licensed clip art and pirating copyrighted material. If you use somebody else's creative work, make sure you have written permission from the owner.

➡ **_Understand your rights._** Copyright laws aren't just to protect other people's work. Your creative work is copyrighted, too. The papers you write, the photographs you take, the doodles you put down on napkins—as soon as your creative work takes on a fixed form, it is your property and enjoys copyright protection. (If an employer is paying you to create the work, the employer is considered to be the author for copyright purposes.) If one of your creations is particularly valuable, you may want to register it with the U.S. Copyright Office. For more information, go to the U.S. Copyright Office Web site: **http://lcweb. loc.gov/copyright/**

➡ **_Consider letting others build on your work._** Under current copyright law, you can't use someone else's work without asking their permission. That means others can't use your work either without asking your permission. The current environment is great for lawyers, but tough on those who want to use the Internet to stimulate the creative reuse of intellectual property. If you want to allow certain uses of your creative work, or if you want it to become public domain (freely usable by anyone), you can give your permission up front by associating a Creative Commons license with your work. See the Creative Commons Web site for more details (**www.creative commons.org**).

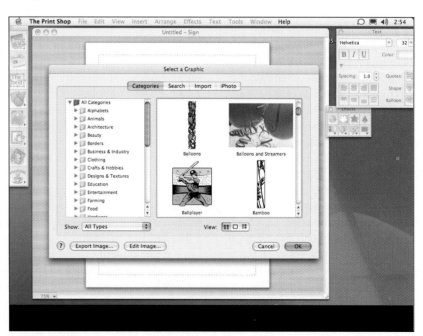

Many graphics applications, including The Print Shop, include extensive clip art collections.

6.8

Drawing: Object-Oriented Graphics

Because high-resolution paint images and photographs are stored as bitmaps, they can make heavy storage and memory demands. Another type of graphics program can economically store pictures with virtually *infinite* resolution, limited only by the capabilities of the output device. Drawing software stores a picture not as a collection of dots, but as a collection of lines and shapes. When you draw a line with a drawing program, the software doesn't record changes in the underlying pixels. Instead, it calculates and remembers a mathematical formula for the line. A drawing program stores shapes as shape formulas and text as text. Because pictures are collections of lines, shapes, and other objects, this approach is often called object-oriented graphics or vector graphics. In effect, the computer is remembering "a blue line segment goes here and a red circle goes here and a chunk of text goes here" instead of "this pixel is blue and this one is red and this one is white."

Many drawing tools—line, shape, and text tools—are similar to painting tools in bitmapped programs. But the user can manipulate objects and edit text without affecting neighboring objects, even if the neighboring objects overlap. On the screen, an object-oriented drawing looks similar to a bitmapped painting. But when it's printed, a drawing appears as smooth as the printer's resolution allows. (Of course, not all drawings are designed to be printed. You may, for example, use a drawing program to create images for publication on a Web page. Because many Web browsers recognize only bitmapped images, you'll probably convert the drawings to bitmaps before displaying them.)

Many professional drawing programs, including Adobe Illustrator and Macromedia Freehand, store images using PostScript—a standard page-description language for describing text fonts, illustrations, and other elements of the printed page. PostScript is built into ROM in many laser printers and other high-end output devices, so those devices can understand and follow PostScript instructions. PostScript-based drawing software constructs a PostScript program as the user draws. This program provides a complete set of instructions for reconstructing the picture at the printer. When the user issues a Print command, the computer sends PostScript instructions to the printer, which uses those instructions to construct the grid of microscopic pixels that will be printed on each page. Most desktop-publishing software uses PostScript in the same way. Mac OS X uses PostScript to display on-screen graphics.

Object-oriented drawing and bitmapped painting each offer advantages for certain applications. Bitmapped image-editing programs give artists and photo editors unsurpassed control over textures, shading, and fine detail; they're widely used for creating screen displays (for example, in

> Actually, a root word of technology, **techne**, originally meant "**art**." The ancient Greeks never separated **art** from **manufacture** in their minds, and so never developed **separate words** for them.
>
> —*Robert Pirsig, in* Zen and the Art of Motorcycle Maintenance

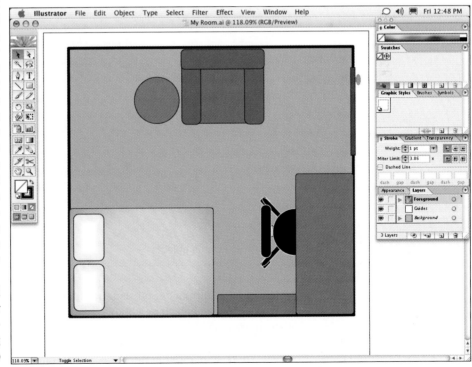

6.9 This room floor plan was created in minutes with Macromedia Freehand, a professional drawing and illustration program. Each piece of furniture can be moved as an independent object in the drawing.

Pixels versus Objects

How do you edit a picture? It depends on what you're doing and how the picture is stored.

The task . . .	Using bit-mapped graphics	Using object-oriented graphics
Moving and removing parts of pictures	Easier to work with regions rather than objects (note), especially if those objects overlap	Easier to work with individual objects or groups of objects, even if they overlap
Working with shapes	Shapes stored as pixel patterns can be edited with eraser and drawing tools	Shapes stored as math formulas can be transformed mathematically
Magnification	Magnifies pixels for fine detail editing	Magnifies objects, not pixels
Text handling	Text "dries" and can't be edited, but can be moved as a block of pixels When paint text "dries" it can't be edited like other text	Text can always be edited Draw text always can be changed
Printing	Resolution of printout can't exceed the pixel resolution of the stored picture	Resolution is limited only by the output device
Working within the limits of the hardware	Photographic quality is possible but requires considerable memory and disk storage	Complex drawings require considerable computational power for reasonable speed

6.10 Pixels versus objects

video games, multimedia presentations, and Web pages), for simulating natural paint media, and for embellishing photographic images. Object-oriented drawing and illustration programs are better choices for creating printed graphs, charts, and illustrations with clean lines and smooth shapes. Some integrated programs, including Corel Draw and AppleWorks, contain both drawing and painting modules, allowing you to choose the right tool for each job. Some programs merge features of both in a single application, blurring the distinction and offering new possibilities for amateur and professional illustrators.

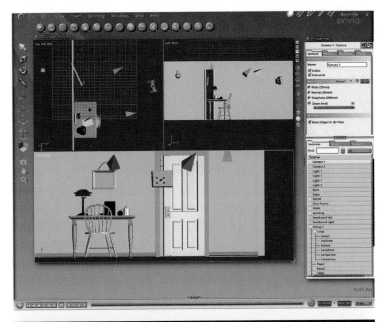

6.11 This scene was created using Amapi 7 Designer 3-D modeling software. The upper screen shows three different views of the scene being modeled. The lower screen shows the completed scene, including lighting and surface textures.

3-D Modeling Software

Working with a pencil, an artist can draw a representation of a three-dimensional scene on a two-dimensional page. Similarly, an artist can use a drawing or painting program to create a scene that appears to have depth on a two-dimensional computer screen. But in either case, the drawing lacks true depth; it's just a flat representation of a scene. With **3-D modeling software** graphic designers can create 3-D objects with tools similar to those found in conventional drawing software. You can't touch a 3-D computer model; it's no more real than a square, a circle, or a letter created with a drawing program. But a 3-D computer model can be rotated, stretched, and combined with other model objects to create complex 3-D scenes.

Illustrators who use 3-D software appreciate its flexibility. A designer can create a 3-D model of an object, rotate it, view it from a variety of angles, and take two-dimensional "snapshots" of the best views for inclusion in final printouts. Similarly, it's possible to "walk through" a 3-D environment that exists only in the computer's memory, printing snapshots that show the simulated space from many points of view. For many applications, the goal is not a printout but an animated presentation on a computer screen or videotape. Animation software, **presentation-graphics software**, and multimedia-authoring

6.12 Animated 3-D figures using technology from LifeFX can simulate human expressions for use in Internet-based video communications.

software (all described later in this chapter) can display sequences of screens showing 3-D objects being rotated, explored, and transformed. Many modern television and movie special effects involve combinations of live action and simulated 3-D animation. Techniques pioneered in *The Matrix*, *Jurassic Park*, *Finding Nemo*, and other films continually push computer graphics to new levels of realism.

CAD/CAM: Turning Pictures into Products

Three-dimensional graphics also play an important role in the branch of engineering known as **computer-aided design (CAD)**—the use of computers to design products. CAD software allows engineers, designers, and architects to create designs on-screen for products ranging from computer chips to public buildings. Today's software goes far beyond basic drafting and object-oriented graphics. It allows users to create three-dimensional "solid" models with physical characteristics such as weight, volume, and center of gravity. These models can be visually rotated and viewed from any angle. The computer can evaluate the structural performance of any part of the model by applying imaginary force to the object. Using CAD, an engineer can crash-test a new model of an automobile before it ever leaves the computer screen. CAD tends to be cheaper, faster, and more accurate than traditional design-by-hand techniques. What's more, the forgiving nature of the computer makes it easy to alter a design to meet project goals.

Computer-aided design is often linked to **computer-aided manufacturing (CAM)**. When the design of a product is completed, the numbers are fed to a program that controls the manufacturing of parts. For electronic parts, the design translates directly into a template for etching circuits onto chips. The emergence of CAD/CAM has streamlined many design and manufacturing processes. The combination of CAD and CAM is often called **computer-integrated manufacturing (CIM)**; it's a major step toward a fully automated factory.

6.13 Engineers use CAD software running on powerful workstations to design everything from microscopic electronic circuits to massive structures.

Presentation Graphics: Bringing Lectures to Life

One common application for computer graphics today is the creation of visual aids—slides, transparencies, graphics displays, and handouts—to enhance presentations. Although drawing and painting programs can create these aids, they aren't as useful as programs designed with presentations in mind.

Presentation-graphics software helps automate the creation of visual aids for lectures, training sessions, sales demonstrations, and other presentations. Presentation-graphics programs are most commonly used for creating and displaying a series of on-screen "slides" to serve as visual aids for presentations. Slides might include photographs, drawings, spreadsheet-style charts, or tables. These different graphical elements are usually integrated into a series of **bullet charts** that list the main points of a presentation. Slides can be output as 35-mm color slides, overhead transparencies, or handouts. Presentation-graphics programs can also display "slide shows" directly on computer monitors or LCD projectors, including animation and video clips along with still images. Some can convert presentations into Web pages automatically.

Because they can be used to create and display on-screen presentations with animated visual effects and video clips, presentation-graphics programs, such as Microsoft's PowerPoint, are sometimes called multimedia-presentation tools. These programs make it easy for nonartists to combine text, graphics, and other media in simple multimedia presentations. But more dramatic effects are possible. A free add-on for PowerPoint, called Producer, makes it possible for users to publish video presentations to the Web or CD/DVD. Producer presentations can include a video of the presenter speaking, a revolving slide show, and a navigable chapter listing.

We now turn our attention to several types of media that go beyond the limitations of the printed page or the static screen; then we look at how multimedia-authoring software can combine these diverse media types to produce dynamic, interactive documents.

Making Powerful Presentations

You've probably had to suffer through at least one terrible computer-assisted presentation—a speech or lecture that used ugly, hard-to-understand computer-generated slides to distract from, rather than drive home, the basic messages of the talk. Presentation-graphics software makes it easy to create presentations, but it doesn't guarantee that those presentations will be good. These guidelines will help you produce first-rate presentations.

Before you create any slides . . .

➡ **Remember your goal.** Know what you're trying to communicate. Keep your goal in mind throughout the process of creating the presentation.

➡ **Remember your audience.** How much do they know about your topic? How much do they need to know? Do key terms need to be defined?

➡ **Plan a story.** Determine the best way to take your listeners from where they are to where you want them to be. A powerful presentation smoothly guides the audience from one point to the next, as if it were telling a story.

➡ **Determine your slide count.** Depending on your topic and speaking style, you'll probably spend between 30 seconds and 2 minutes per slide. Figure out how many slides you need to create to match the total presentation time. Then estimate how many slides to devote to each point you want to make.

➡ **Tell them what you're going to tell them, then tell them, then tell them what you told them.** It's the speechmaker's fundamental rule, and it applies to presentations, too.

As you create the slides . . .

➡ **Outline your ideas.** If you can't express your plan in a clear, concise outline, you probably won't be able to create a clear, concise presentation. After your outline is done, you can import it into your presentation-graphics software and massage it into a presentation.

➡ **Don't expect too much from one slide.** A single page of this book has more pixels than 200 computer screens. A visual presentation is not a replacement for a detailed written report with data-rich diagrams.

➡ **Keep each slide focused.** Each screen should convey one idea clearly, possibly with a few concrete supporting points.

➡ **Be stingy with words.** Limit yourself to seven lines per list and a short phrase per line. Whenever possible, eliminate low-information-content words such as "a," "an," "and," and "the."

➡ **Use signposts.** Help listeners keep track of where you are in the presentation through the use of signpost slides. A signpost slide lists the major topics and indicates which one is going to be covered next.

➡ **Use a consistent design.** Make sure all your slides look like they belong together. Use the same fonts, backgrounds, and colors throughout your presentation. Consider using predesigned templates.

➡ **Cool colors make better backgrounds.** Blues and greens are better than yellows, oranges, and reds. It's hard to go wrong with a dark blue background.

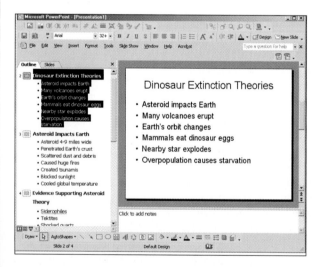

The presentation software converts an outline into slides.

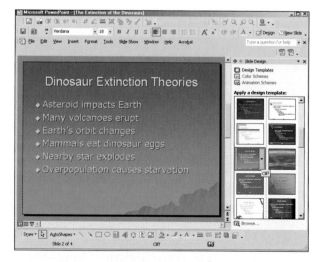

You can choose a professionally designed template from a collection provided with the software.

6.14

- *Use large letters.* The smallest letters on the slide should be at least 24 point to ensure readability for audience members in the back of the room.
- *Avoid use of all capital letters.* Text printed in ALL CAPITAL LETTERS is harder to read.
- *Be smart with art.* Don't clutter your presentation with random clip art. Make sure each illustration contributes to your message. Use simple graphs that support your main points. When you do use illustrations, make sure you coordinate them with the colors and design of the rest of the presentation.
- *Keep it simple.* Avoid useless decorations and distractions. Avoid fancy borders and backgrounds. Don't use a different transition on each slide.

When you make your presentation . . .

- *Stand to the left of the screen.* The eyes of the audience members won't have to cross the screen when they shift their gaze from you to a new slide or list item.
- *Do not read your slides.* Talk in complete sentences but only put short phrases on the slide.
- *Reveal no line before its time.* If you unveil the entire contents of a slide all at once, expect audience members to read the slide rather than listen to you.
- *Use wipe right to reveal lines.* The wipe right animation allows audience members to begin reading the text before it is completely written.
- *Pause when you reveal a new slide or bullet.* Give your listeners a chance to read the slide title or list item before you elaborate on it.
- *Vary pace or volume to make a point.* To emphasize a particular point, you can repeat yourself, pause for a moment after saying it, or noticeably change the volume of your voice.

BAD

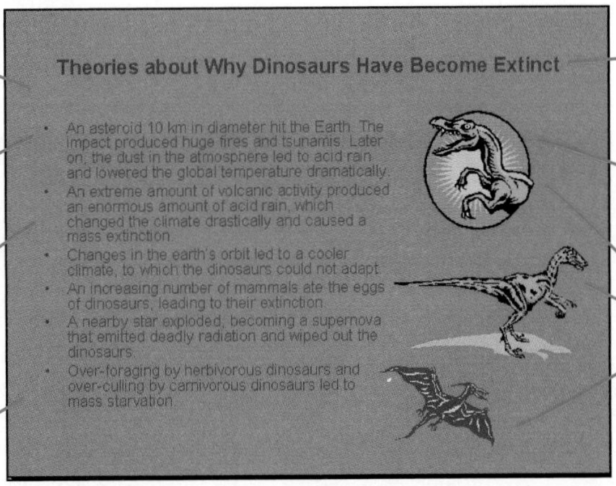

Blue on red and red on blue are the worst possible color choices.

Each bullet contains a complete sentence. The audience will be tempted to read the sentences, not listen to you speak.

The excessive number of words causes text to be too small.

Background is a hot color.

Title is too long, forcing letter size to be too small.

Graphic images do not add information. Images distract from text.

Images are taken from different libraries and do not match each other.

GOOD

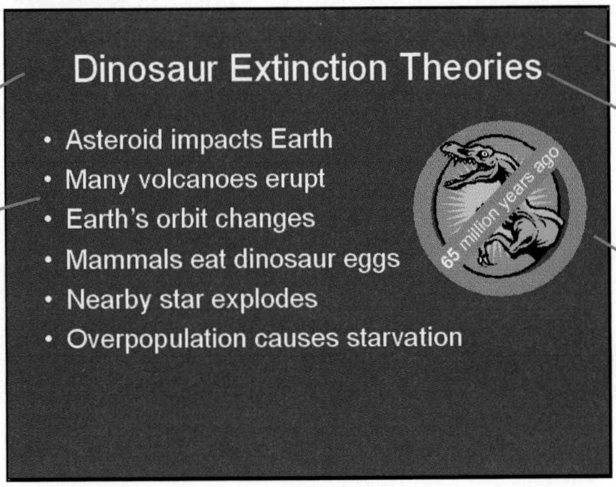

High contrast between letters and background improves readability.

Because there are only six lines and only three or four words per line, text is large and easy to read.

Background is a cool color.

Short title allows large text size.

The graphic contributes information. An animation in which the "No" symbol stamps out the dinosaur would be a nice touch.

Dynamic Media:
Beyond the Printed Page

The world is **complex, dynamic, multidimensional;** the paper is **static, flat**. How are we to represent the **rich visual world** of experience and measurement on mere **flatland**?

—*Edward R. Tufte, in* Envisioning Information

Most PC applications—painting and drawing programs, word processors, desktop publishers, and so on—are designed to produce paper documents. But many types of modern media can't be reduced to pixels on printouts because they contain dynamic information—information that changes over time or in response to user input. Today's multimedia computers enable us to create and edit animated sequences, video clips, sound, and music along with text and graphics. Just as words and pictures serve as the raw materials for desktop publishing, dynamic media such as animation, video, audio, and hypertext are important components of interactive multimedia projects.

Animation: Graphics in Time

We're on the threshold of a moment in cinematic history that is unparalleled. **Anything** you can **imagine** can be done. If you can **draw it**, if you can **describe it**, we can **do it**. It's just a matter of cost.

—*James Cameron, filmmaker*

Creating motion from still pictures—this illusion is at the heart of all **animation**. Before computers, artists drew animated films by hand, one still picture, or **frame**, at a time. Modern computer-graphics technology has transformed amateur and professional animation by automating many of the most tedious aspects of the animation process.

In its simplest form, the techniques used in creating computer-based animation are similar to traditional frame-by-frame animation techniques; each frame is a computer-drawn

6.15 The animated films *Shrek* and *Shrek 2* feature computer-generated characters with amazingly emotive faces.

Screen Test

Creating a Flash Animation

GOAL *To create an animated space ship for a science fiction fan Web site.*

TOOLS *Flash MX 2004, part of Macromedia Studio MX 2004.*

1. You draw the ship and thrusters using the line, shape, and paint tools in the tools palette.

2. You draw the flame using the same tools. The space ship, thrusters, and the flame are stored as separate objects—graphic symbols that can be manipulated over time in the animation.

3. Each object has its own timeline. You move the playback head through the flame's timeline, slightly changing the flame's shape at a few key frames.

4. To smooth the flame's motion, you use the Shape Tweening command between each pair of key frames.

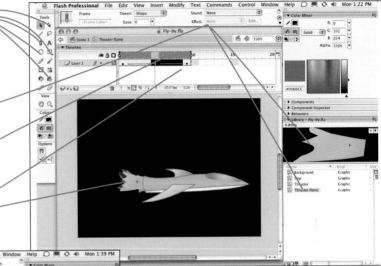

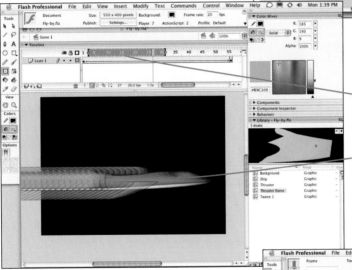

5. Returning to the stage (main) timeline, you create keyframes for the beginning and end points of the space ship's journey across the screen. You apply motion tweening to create a smooth movement between these two points. You preview the animation in Onion Skin mode to see multiple points in time on a single screen.

6. Using a masking effect, you cause text to appear in the wake of the moving ship. Your animation is now ready to publish on a Web page.

Sci-Fanatic.com

6.16

picture, and the computer displays those frames in rapid succession. With an animation program, an animator can create key frames and objects and use software to help fill in the movement of the objects in the in-between frames—a process known as *tweening*. The most powerful animation programs include tools for working with animated objects in three dimensions, adding depth to the scene on the screen.

Animation on the Web ranges from simple GIF animations to complex cartoon animations created with programs like Macromedia's Shockwave Flash MX and Director MX. An animated GIF is simply a bundle of bitmapped GIF images that appear in a sequence similar to the pages of a children's flip book. A more sophisticated way to represent an animation is through the use of vector graphics. A vector-graphics animation describes a collection of objects and how they change over time. The two most popular vector graphics formats are *Shockwave Flash Format (SWF)*, associated with the Macromedia Flash player, and *Scalable Vector Graphics (SVG)*, an open standard promoted by the W3C.

As a way of representing Web animations, vector graphics animations have several advantages over animated GIFs. Vector-graphics animations occupy less space, which means they can be downloaded faster. Because vector-graphics animations describe images in terms of objects and locations, rather than colored pixels, it is possible to write software that makes the images look good on a wide variety of displays, such as those found on personal computers, pocket PCs, and cell phones. Finally, SVG files represent the words inside images as plain text characters. Future versions of Web search engines may include the contents of animations in their indices, making it easier for them to return animations in response to queries.

Computer animation has become commonplace in everything from television commercials to feature films. Sometimes computer animation is combined with live-action film; Harry Potter, Spider-Man, the Terminator, and a host of other characters depend on computer animation to make their larger-than-life actions seem real. Other films, including *Toy Story, Shrek, Finding Nemo*, and *The Incredibles*, use computer animation to create every character, scene, and event, leaving only the soundtrack for live actors and musicians to create.

Digital editing software

Firewire cable

Video camera

6.17 Video can be easily transferred from a variety of video sources to a computer's hard drive. Separate interfaces are required for digital and analog video sources: Typically, digital video is transferred via FireWire, while analog video can be transferred via USB or proprietary AV converter hardware.

Desktop Video: Computers, Film, and TV

Digital technology is the **same revolution** as adding **sound** to pictures and the same **revolution** as adding **color** to pictures. **Nothing more** and **nothing less**.

—*George Lucas, filmmaker*

There's more to the digital video revolution than computer animation. Computers can be used to edit video, splice scenes, add transitions, create titles, and do other tasks in a fraction of the time—and at a fraction of the cost—of precomputer techniques. The only requirement is that the video be in a digital form so the computer can treat it as data.

Analog and Digital Video

Conventional television and video images are stored and broadcast as analog (smooth) electronic waves. A video digitizer can convert analog video signals from a television broadcast or videotape into digital data. Most video digitizers must be installed as add-on cards or external devices that plug into serial or USB ports. Broadcast-quality digitizers are relatively expensive; low-cost models are available for consumers who can settle for less-than-perfect images.

Many video digitizers can import signals from televisions, videotapes, video cameras, and other sources and display them on the computer's screen in *real time*—at the same time they're created or imported. The computer screen can serve as a television screen or, with a network connection, a viewing screen for a live video teleconference. For many applications, it's not important to display digitized images in real time; the goal is to capture entire video sequences and convert them into digital "movies" that can be stored, edited, and played on computer screens without external video equipment.

Video professionals and hobbyists who use *digital video cameras* don't need to digitize their video footage before working with it in a computer, because it's already in digital form. Digital video cameras capture and store all video footage as digital data. Most digital video cameras have FireWire (IEEE 1394) ports (see Chapter 3) that can be used to copy raw video footage from tape to a computer and later copy the edited video back from computer to tape. Because digital video can be reduced to a series of numbers, it can be copied, edited, stored, and played back without any loss of quality. Digital video will soon replace analog video for most applications.

Video Production Goes Digital

A typical video project starts with an outline and a simple *storyboard* describing the action, dialogue, and music in each scene. The storyboard serves as a guide for shooting and editing scenes.

Today, most video editing is done using *nonlinear editing* technology. For nonlinear editing, video and audio clips are stored in digital form on a computer's hard disk. Using

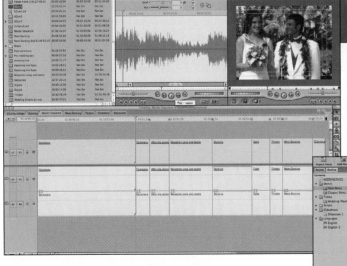

6.18 Software can turn a desktop or notebook computer into a video-editing and production station. Programs like Apple's iMovie and iDVD (above) make it easy for nonprofessionals to capture and edit video footage, add special effects and audio, and publish the finished movie on a DVD, tape, CD-ROM, or Web site. Professional programs, such as Apple's Final Cut Pro and DVD Studio Pro (below), perform the same functions to the exacting standards of industry professionals.

on-screen tools and commands, you can organize, rearrange, enhance, and combine these digital clips. Nonlinear editing is faster and easier than older editing techniques are, and it allows filmmakers to do things that aren't possible without computers. Video editing makes massive storage and memory demands on a computer. Until recently, nonlinear editing technology was available only to professionals. But falling hardware prices and technological advances make it possible for hobbyists to edit video with inexpensive desktop machines.

Video-editing software, such as Adobe Premiere, Apple iMovie, and Microsoft Windows Movie Maker 2, makes it easy to eliminate extraneous footage, combine clips from multiple takes into coherent scenes, splice together scenes, insert visual transitions, superimpose titles, synchronize a soundtrack, and create special effects. High-end editing software can combine live action with computer animation. Software can also create *morphs*—video clips in which one image metamorphoses into another. Photoshop-style tools allow artists to, for example, paint one or two frames with a green polka-dotted sky and then automatically apply those painting effects to the other frames.

After it's edited, you can output the video clip to a videotape. The process is simplest and most effective in an all-digital system using FireWire and a digital camcorder. With a DVD-R drive and software, such as Apple's iDVD or Sonic MyDVD, you can press video footage onto a DVD, complete with menus and navigational features not available on tape.

Edited video doesn't need to be exported to tape or DVD. Many digital clips end up in multimedia presentations. On-screen digital movies can add realism and excitement to educational, training, presentation, and entertainment software. Video clips are also common on the Web. Media players, such as Apple's cross-platform QuickTime, Microsoft Windows Player, and RealNetworks RealONE, make it possible for any multimedia-capable computer to display digital video clips without additional hardware.

Data Compression

Digital movies can make heavy hardware demands; even a short full-screen video clip can quickly fill a large hard disk or CD-ROM. To save storage space and allow the processor to keep up with the quickly changing frames, digital movies designed for the Web or CD-ROM are often displayed in small windows with fewer frames per second than the

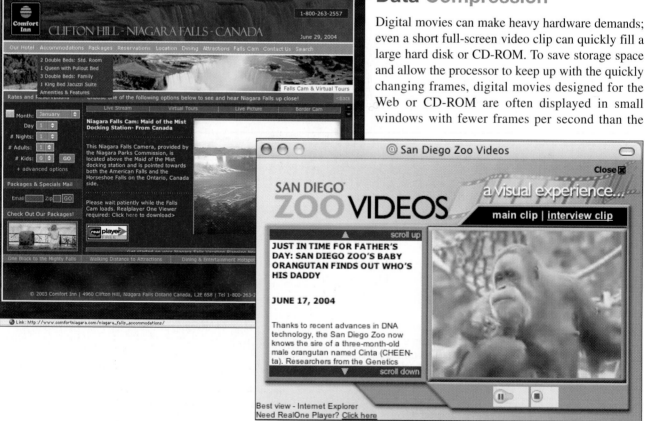

6.19 Many Web sites deliver streaming video content to viewers with fast broadband Internet connections.

standard 30. In addition, data compression software and hardware squeeze data out of movies so they can be stored in smaller spaces, often with a slight loss of image quality, though newer formats like MPEG-4 and Windows Media Video 9 lessen this problem. General data compression software can be used to reduce the size of almost any kind of data file; specialized *image-compression software* is generally used to compress graphics and video files. Modern media players, such as QuickTime and Windows Media Player, include several common software compression schemes. Some compression schemes involve specialized hardware as well as software.

Even highly compressed video clips gobble up storage space quickly. As compression and storage technologies continue to improve, digital movies will become larger, longer, smoother, and more common in everyday computing applications.

Professionals in the motion picture, television, and video industries create their products using graphics workstations that cost hundreds of thousands of dollars. Today, it's possible to put together a Windows- or Macintosh-based system that can perform most of the same graphics functions for a fraction of the cost. Low-cost desktop video systems are transforming the film and video industry in the same way that desktop publishing has revolutionized the world of the printed word. They're also making it possible for individuals, schools, and small businesses to create near-professional quality videos.

The Synthetic Musician: Computers and Audio

Sound and music can turn a visual presentation into an activity that involves the ears, the eyes, and the whole brain. For many applications, sound puts the *multi* in *multimedia*. Computer sounds can be sampled—digitally recorded—or synthesized—synthetically generated. Windows PCs (using sound cards; see Chapter 3) and Macintoshes (which have sound hardware already built in) can produce sounds that go far beyond the basic beeps of early computers; most of them can also digitize sounds.

> It's **easy to play** any musical instrument: all you have to do is **touch the right key** at the right time and **the instrument will play itself**.
>
> —*J. S. Bach*

Digital Audio Basics

An audio digitizer can record just about any sound as a sample—a digital sound file. Digitized sound data, like other computer data, can be loaded into the computer's memory and manipulated by software. Sound-editing software can change a sound's volume and pitch, add special effects such as echoes, remove extraneous noises, and even rearrange musical passages. Sound data is sometimes called *waveform audio* because this kind of editing often involves manipulating a visual image of the sound's waveform. To play a digitized sound, the computer must load the data file into memory, convert it to an analog sound, and play it through a speaker.

Recorded sound can consume massive amounts of space on disk and in memory. As you might expect, higher-quality sound reproduction generally requires more memory. The difference is due in part to differences in *sampling rate*—the number of sound "snapshots" the recording equipment takes each second. A higher sampling rate produces more realistic digital sounds in the same way that higher resolution produces more realistic digital photographs; it allows for more accurate modeling of the analog source. The number of bits per sample, usually 8 or 16, also affects the quality of the sound; this is similar to a digital photograph's bit depth.

Music is digitized on audio CDs at a high sampling rate and bit depth—high enough that it's hard to tell the difference between the original analog sound and the final digital recording. But CD audio is memory intensive; a three-minute song takes about 30 megabytes of space on a compact disc. Files that large are expensive to store and slow to transmit through networks. That's why most computer sound files are recorded at a lower sampling rate and bit depth and therefore don't have the sound quality of an audio CD recording. Sound data compression, like image compression, can make a file even smaller. Since computers can

How It **Works**

6.1 **Data Compression**

A full-screen 256-color photograph or painting takes about a megabyte of storage—the same as the complete text from a typical paperback book! Graphic images, digital video, and sound files can consume massive amounts of storage space on disk and in memory; they can also be slow to transmit over computer networks. Data-compression technology allows large files to be temporarily squeezed to reduce the amount of storage space and network transmission time they require. Before you can use them, you must decompress compressed files. (In the physical world, many companies "compress" goods to save storage and transportation costs: When you "just add water" to a can of concentrated orange juice, you're "decompressing" the juice.)

All forms of compression involve removing bits; the trick is to remove bits that can be replaced when the file can be restored. Different compression techniques work best for different types of data.

Suppose you want to store or transmit a large text file. Your text compression software might follow steps similar to those shown here:

1. Each character in the uncompressed ASCII file occupies eight bits; a seven-character word—*invoice*, for example—requires 56 bits of storage.

i   n   v   o   i   c   e

(space)   p   a   y   a   b   l   e

Portion of a dictionary		
A	○○○○○○○○	○○○○○○○●
a	○○○○○○○○	○○○○○○●○
aback	○○○○○○○○	○○○○○○●●
abacus	○○○○○○○○	○○○○○●○○
. . .		
invoice	○○●○○●○●	○○●●●○○●
invoiced	○○●○○●○●	○○●●●○●○
invoke	○○●○○●○●	○○●●●○●●
. . .		
pay	○●○○●○●●	●○●○○○●○
payable	○●○●○●●●	●○●○○●●●
. . .		
zygote	●●●●●●●●	●●●●●●●●

%   9   V   ú

2. A two-byte binary number can contain code values ranging from 0 to 65,535—enough codes to stand for every commonly used word in English. This partial code dictionary shows the code values for a few words, including *invoice* and *payable*.

3. To compress a file using a code dictionary, the computer looks up every word in the original file; in this example, *invoice* and *payable*. It replaces each word with its two-byte code value. In this example, they are % 9 and V ú. The seven-character word now takes up only 16 bits—less than one-third of its original size.

4. In a compressed file, these two-byte code values would be used to store or transmit the information for *invoice* and *payable*, using fewer bits of information either to increase storage capacity or to decrease transmission time.

5. To reverse the process of compression, the same dictionary (or an identical one on another computer) is used to decompress the file, creating an exact copy of the original. A computer program quickly performs all the tedious dictionary lookup.

Compression programs usually work on patterns of bits rather than on English words. One type of digital video compression stores values for pixels that change from one frame to the next; there's no need to store values repeatedly for pixels that are the same in every frame. For example, the only pixels that change in these two pictures are the ones that represent the unicycle and the shadows.

In general, compression works because most raw data files contain redundancy that can be "squeezed out." *Lossless compression* systems allow a file to be compressed and later decompressed without any loss of data; the decompressed file will be an identical copy of the original file. Popular lossless compression systems include ZIP/PKZIP (DOS/Windows), StuffIt (Macintosh), tar (UNIX), and GIF (general graphics). A *lossy compression* system can usually achieve better compression than a lossless one but it may lose some information in the process; the decompressed file isn't always identical to the original. This is tolerable in many types of sound, graphics, and video files but not for most program and data files. JPEG is a popular lossy compression system for graphics files.

MPEG is a popular compression system for digital video. An MPEG file takes just a fraction of the space of an uncompressed video file. Because decompression programs demand time and processing power, the playback of compressed video files can sometimes be jerky or slow. Some computers get around the problem with MPEG hardware boards that specialize in compression and decompression, leaving the CPU free for other tasks. *Hardware compression* is likely to be built into most computers as multimedia becomes more commonplace.

The original photographic image (above) has an uncompressed size of 725 KB. With aggressive JPEG compression, the image on the right occupies only 1/38th as much disk space (19 KB), but looks almost as good.

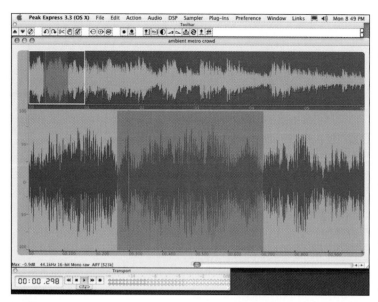

6.21 You can edit waveform audio files in a variety of ways using software tools like Peak, from Bias, Inc.

read standard audio CDs, it's easy to *rip*, or copy, songs from a CD to the computer's hard drive, and *burn*, or copy, audio CDs that contain ripped songs. Until recently, high-quality sounds required large files, and compact files compromised quality. But relatively new methods of compression, including **MP3** (for MPEG Audio Layer 3), Advanced Audio Codec (*AAC*), and Windows Media Audio (*WMA*) can squeeze music files to a fraction of their original CD-file sizes, often with an imperceptible loss of quality. MP3, AAC, and WMA make it practical to transmit songs and other recordings through the Internet, store them on hard disks, and play them on pocket-sized devices without disk or tape. Audio files are available for free on hundreds of Web sites. Many are contributed by undiscovered musicians who want exposure; others are ripped from copyrighted CDs and distributed illegally (giving a new meaning to the old phrase "ripped off").

A few years ago, *online peer-to-peer (P2P) file sharing* services such as Napster popularized the illegal sharing of stolen music. Napster is no longer the center of illegal file trading, but music piracy thrives in other Internet venues. Still, there are many online sources for legally downloading music files using AAC and WMA formats. One of the first commercial online music services, Apple's iTunes Music Store, pioneered the concept of selling individual songs rather than entire albums. The iTunes Music Store and others that followed offer convenience for customers without robbing musicians and others who work in the music industry. Customers can play their purchases on their computers, burn them to CDs, or download them into iPods and other portable music players.

Ethical and legal issues raised by digital audio files will be discussed in more detail in Chapter 9, *Inside the Internet and the World Wide Web*, and Chapter 10, *Computer Security and Risks*.

Samplers, Synthesizers, and Sequencers: Digital Audio and MIDI

Multimedia computers can control a variety of electronic musical instruments and sound sources using Musical Instrument Digital Interface (**MIDI**)—a standard interface used to send commands between computers and musical instruments. MIDI commands can be interpreted by a variety of music *synthesizers* (electronic instruments that synthesize sounds using mathematical formulas), *samplers* (instruments that can digitize, or sample, audio sounds, turn them into notes, and play them back at any pitch), and hybrid instruments that play sounds that are part sampled and part synthesized. But most PCs can also interpret and execute MIDI commands using sampled sounds built into their sound cards or stored in software form. Whether the sounds are played back on external instruments or internal devices, the computer doesn't need to store the entire recording in memory or on disk; it just has to store commands to play the notes in the proper sequence. A MIDI file containing the MIDI messages for a song or soundtrack requires only a few kilobytes of memory.

Anyone with even marginal piano-playing skills can create MIDI music files. A piano-style keyboard sends MIDI signals to the computer, which interprets the sequence of MIDI commands using **sequencing software**. (While the keyboard is the most common MIDI controller for sequencing, MIDI communication capabilities are built into other types of instruments, including drums, guitars, and horns.) Sequencing software turns a computer into a musical composing, recording, and editing machine. The computer records MIDI signals as

Digital Audio Do's and Don'ts

Whether you are digitizing your audio CD collection or are subscribed to an online music service, your digital audio experiences will go more smoothly if you understand a few simple rules.

➡ ***Don't steal.*** It's okay to copy audio CDs to your PC, use those songs on portable audio devices, and mix CDs you create, but only if you own the originals. Don't "borrow" music from a friend or steal music online.

➡ ***Understand streaming and downloading.*** Internet radio stations typically *stream* music to your system in real time, so the songs are never actually downloaded and stored locally on your computer. When you download a song from a service like the iTunes Music Store, you are receiving a physical file that you can back up and copy to other systems, depending on the rights granted to you via the service's DRM scheme (See below). Streaming audio is fleeting—the stream dries up the second your Internet connection goes down or you disconnect from the service. Downloadable music is persistent, because it stays on your system.

➡ ***Know your file formats.*** Uncompressed audio CD files can gobble up hard disk space at an alarming rate. The MP3 compression format is popular because it produces files that sound almost identical to uncompressed audio files. But MP3 isn't the only popular audio compression format. Many audio files are stored in the relatively new AAC format, which includes *digital rights management (DRM)* technology designed to protect the artists' intellectual property. Many

The iTunes Music Store enables Mac and Windows users to purchase music by their favorite artists in a protected digital format.

Windows users prefer Microsoft's WMA format, which can offer quality comparable to MP3 at smaller file sizes; WMA also offers DRM capabilities.

➡ ***Don't overcompress.*** Audio compression is lossy, so there's always a loss of quality when you compress a sound file. There's no way to put back the bits that you squeeze out in the compression process. Most people can't distinguish between a 160 Kbps MP3 file or a 128 Mbps AAC or WMA file and an original audio CD recording. But if you choose too low a bit rate when compressing a file, you may squeeze the life out of the music.

Popular Digital Audio Formats.			
Format	Downloadable	Streamable	Typically used for . . .
MP3	Yes	Yes	Ripping (copying) CDs to the computer and to portable audio players
WMA	Yes	Yes	Ripping CDs to the computer and for purchased music from online music stores
AAC	Yes	Yes	Purchased music from online music stores
RealAudio	Yes	Yes	Audio streams from commercial Web sites like CNN
MIDI	Yes	Yes	Contains no audio—just sequences of commands to control musical instruments and music samples on a PC

6.22   Popular Digital Audio Formats

6.23 In the modern music studio, computer keyboards and music keyboards often sit side by side.

a musician plays each part on a keyboard. The musician can use the computer to layer instrumental tracks, substitute instrument sounds, edit notes, cut and paste passages, transpose keys, and change tempos, listening to each change as it's made. The finished composition can be played by the sequencing software or exported to any other MIDI-compatible software, including a variety of multimedia applications.

Music recording and composition software isn't limited to sequencing MIDI commands; most programs can record digital audio tracks as well as MIDI tracks, making it possible to include voices and nonelectronic instruments in the mix. The audio and MIDI data is recorded directly onto the computer's hard disk, making tape unnecessary.

A typical electronic music studio includes a variety of synthesizers, samplers, and other instruments. But the trend today is to replace many bulky, expensive hardware devices with *virtual instruments*—instruments that exist only in software. With today's powerful CPUs and massive storage devices, it's possible to have a professional-level multitrack recording and editing studio that fits in a suitcase.

You can use digital audio technology to imitate (with varying degrees of success) anything from a Bach fugue to a rock jam.

Professional musicians use computers for composing, recording, performing, and publishing music, and for educating would-be musicians. Digital audio technology cuts across genres; it's used for everything from Bach to rock. The technology has spawned whole new branches of music that fit loosely into a category called *electronica*—music designed from the ground up with digital technology. Just as computer graphics technology has changed the way many artists work, electronic music technology has transformed the world of the musician. What's more, computer music technology has the power to unleash the musician in the rest of us.

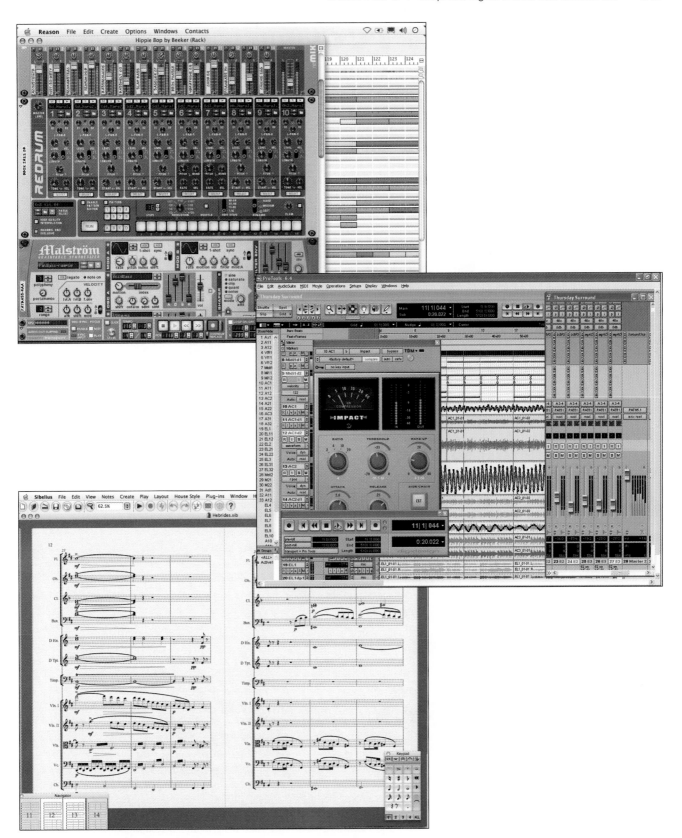

6.24 Music software allows musicians to put Macintoshes and Windows PCs to work in a variety of ways. Reason (top) is a complete software studio, including a variety of virtual instruments and tools. Pro Tools (middle) is widely used for recording, sequencing, and editing music. Sibelius (bottom) is a music publishing program that can create sheet music from MIDI files and other sources.

How It Works

6.2 Computer-Based Music Production

Music-processing software comes in a variety of forms, but most programs are built on the same fundamental concepts. A musical composition is typically made up of several tracks that represent individual instrumental and vocal parts. For example, a song might have a lead vocal track, a guitar track, a bass track, a drum track, and three backup vocal tracks. You can record and edit each of these tracks separately; you can play them back in any combination.

A software mixer can adjust the relative volumes to achieve the desired balance before you mix the piece down to a final digital stereo recording. The same principles apply for acoustic, electric, or electronic music; the differences between these types of music are reflected mainly in the way the individual tracks are created and stored. Most software can work with two kinds of tracks: digital audio samples, represented as waveforms, and MIDI sequences, depicted as a series of bars representing notes.

1. Real-world instruments and sounds can be sampled by plugging an instrument or microphone into the sound in port on the computer.

2. Any sample, such as this recording of a percussionist playing a drum kit, can be looped, which simply repeats the sample until the desired length is reached.

3. Because waveforms are stored as a series of numbers, many music production tools use math to manipulate those numbers and alter qualities, such as the tempo, pitch, and volume of the recording.

4. Software-based filters can be used to manipulate the sonic qualities of your samples and loops; this particular effect lends an acoustic, echo-filled, ethereal quality to the guitar part.

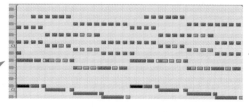

5. MIDI instruments send performance information, such as when and where each note is played in a sequence, and how hard each note is struck. Because MIDI stores your performance as a series of notes rather than an audio sample, you are able to later correct notes, transpose to a different key, alter the tempo, and even change the instrument used to play back your performance. You can easily correct for human error using a feature known as quantizing, which cleans up the timing of a passage by "rounding off" performance data to the nearest points on the rhythmic grid.

6.25

6. Software allows you to control characteristics of sound over time. For example, the master volume controller fades the song out as it nears the song's end.

7. A finished composition can be output in a variety of forms.

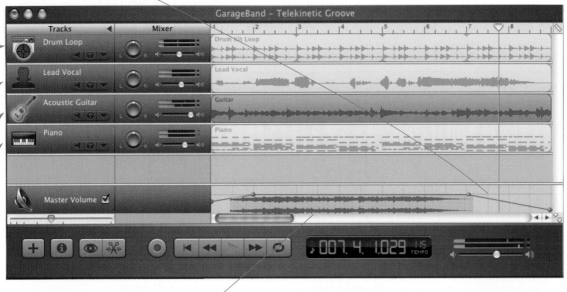

8. The final mix can be exported as a stereo waveform.

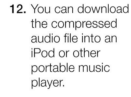

11. Compression software can produce a much smaller sound file.

12. You can download the compressed audio file into an iPod or other portable music player.

9. Speakers or headphones attached to the computer provide the most direct output, giving the composer and performers immediate sonic feedback.

13. You can upload a compressed audio file to the Web and share it with the online community.

10. You can burn the stereo file onto an audio CD.

14. You can import the audio file into a video-editing program for use in a movie soundtrack.

Hypertext and Hypermedia

Human Beings are naturally predisposed **to hear, to remember, and to tell stories**. The **problem**—for teachers, parents, government leaders, friends, and **computers**—is to have **more interesting stories** to tell.

—Roger Schank et al., in Tell Me a Story: Narrative and Intelligence

Word processors, drawing programs, and most other applications today are WYSIWYG—what you see (on the screen) is what you get (on the printed page). But WYSIWYG isn't always necessary or desirable. If a document doesn't need to be printed, it doesn't need to be structured like a paper document. If we want to focus on the relationship between ideas rather than the layout of the page, we may be better off with another kind of document—a dynamic, cross-referenced super document that takes full advantage of the computer's interactive capabilities.

Since 1945 when President Roosevelt's science advisor, Vannevar Bush, first wrote about such an interactive cross-referenced system, computer pioneers like Doug Engelbart and Ted Nelson, who coined the term hypertext, pushed the technology toward that vision. Early efforts were called hypertext because they allowed textual information to be linked in *nonsequential* ways. Conventional text media, such as books, are linear, or *sequential*: They are designed to be read from beginning to end. A hypertext document contains links that can lead readers quickly to other parts of the document or to other related documents. Hypertext invites readers to cut their own personal trails through information.

Hypertext first gained widespread public attention in 1987 when Apple introduced HyperCard, a hypermedia system that could combine text, numbers, graphics, animation, sound effects, music, and other media in hyperlinked documents. (Depending on how it's used, the term hypermedia might be synonymous with interactive multimedia.) Today, millions of Windows and Macintosh users routinely use hypertext whenever they consult online Help files, and handheld computer and Tablet PC users navigate hypermedia-enabled ebooks. But the biggest hotbed of hypertext/hypermedia activity is the World Wide Web, where hypertext links connect documents all over the Internet.

But in spite of its popularity, hypertext isn't likely to replace paper books any time soon. Web users and others who use hypertext have several legitimate complaints:

■ Hypermedia documents can be disorienting and leave readers wondering what they've missed. When you're reading a book, you always know where you are and where you've been in the text. That's not necessarily true in hypermedia.

■ Hypermedia documents don't always have the links readers want. Hypermedia authors can't build every possible connection into their documents, so some readers are frustrated because they can't easily get "there" from "here."

■ Hypermedia documents sometimes contain "lost" links, especially on the Web, where even a popular page can disappear without a trace.

■ Hypermedia documents don't encourage scribbled margin notes, highlighting, or turned page corners for marking key passages. Some hypermedia documents provide controls for making "bookmarks" and text fields for adding personal notes, but they aren't as friendly and flexible as traditional paper mark-up tools.

■ Hypermedia hardware can be hard on humans. Most people find that reading a computer screen is more tiring than reading printed pages, although modern screen like Microsoft ClearType seeks to reduce this problem. Many people complain that extended periods of screen-gazing cause eyestrain, headache, backache, and other ailments. It's not always easy to stretch out under a tree or curl up in an easy chair with a Web-linked computer, though notebooks and Tablet PCs are making anywhere–everywhere computing more viable.

The art of hypermedia is still in its infancy. Every new art form takes time to develop. How can writers develop effective plot lines if they don't know what path their readers will choose through their stories? This is just one of the hundreds of questions with which hypermedia authors are struggling. Still, hypermedia is not all hype. As the art matures, advances in software and hardware design will take care of many of these problems. Even today hypermedia documents provide extensive cross-referencing, flexibility, and instant keyword searches that simply aren't possible with paper media.

Interactive Multimedia: Eye, Ear, Hand, and Mind

We live in a world rich in sensory experience. Information comes to us in a variety of forms: pictures, text, moving images, music, voice, and more. As information processing machines, computers are capable of delivering information to our senses in many forms. Until recently, computer users could work with only one or two forms of information at a time. Today's multimedia computers allow users to work with information-rich documents that intermix a variety of audiovisual media.

> The hybrid or the meeting of two media is a **moment of truth and revelation** from which a **new form** is born.
>
> —*Marshall McLuhan, in* Understanding Media; The Extensions of Man

Interactive Multimedia: What Is It?

The term multimedia generally means using some combination of text, graphics, animation, video, music, voice, and sound effects to communicate. By this definition an episode of *Sesame Street* or the evening news might be considered multimedia. In fact, computer-based multimedia tools are used heavily in the production of *Sesame Street*, the evening news, and hundreds of other television programs. Entertainment-industry professionals use computers to create animated sequences, display titles, construct special video effects, synthesize music, edit soundtracks, coordinate communication, and perform dozens of other tasks crucial to the production of modern television programs and motion pictures.

So when you watch a typical TV program, you're experiencing a multimedia product. With each second that passes, you are bombarded with millions of bits of information. But television and video are passive media; they pour information into our eyes and ears while we sit and take it all in. We have no control over the information flow. Modern computer technology allows information to move in both directions, turning multimedia into interactive multimedia. Unlike TV, radio, and video, interactive multimedia allow the viewer/listener to take an active part in the experience. The best interactive multimedia software puts the user in charge, allowing that person to control the information flow.

Interactive multimedia software is delivered to consumers on a variety of platforms. Today, multimedia computers equipped with fast processors, large memories, CD-ROM or DVD-ROM drives, speakers, and sound cards are everywhere. Thousands of education and entertainment multimedia programs are available on CD-ROM and DVD-ROM for these machines. Many more multimedia software titles are designed to be used

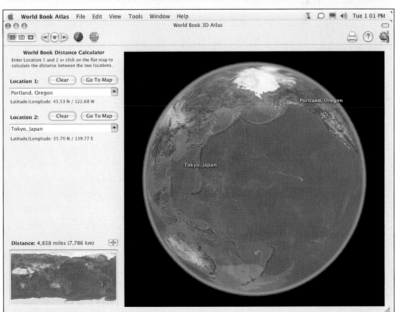

6.26 Interactive multimedia CD-ROMs and DVDs often combine education with entertainment. Sierra's Starry Night Sky turns your computer into a virtual planetarium. The World Book combines an encyclopedia with other reference tools in an easy-to-use interactive package.

with television sets and controlled by game machines and other *set-top boxes* from Sony, Microsoft, Nintendo, and other companies. Many multimedia documents are created for use in kiosks in stores, museums, and other public places. A typical multimedia kiosk is a PC-in-a-box with a touch screen instead of a keyboard and mouse for collecting input.

Interactive multimedia materials are all over the Web, too. But multimedia on the Web today is full of compromises, because many of today's Web pipelines can't deliver large media files quickly enough. Still, Web technology is improving rapidly, and more people are connecting to the Net with faster broadband technology, making many experts wonder whether disk-based multimedia will eventually be unnecessary. In the meantime, cable, telephone, and other companies are rushing to provide multimedia services, including video on demand.

Multimedia Authoring: Making Mixed Media

Style used to be an interaction between the **human soul** and **tools** that were **limiting**. In the digital era, it will have to come from **the soul alone**.

—Jaron Lanier, virtual reality pioneer

Multimedia-authoring software is used to create and edit multimedia documents. Similar to desktop publishing, interactive multimedia authoring involves combining source documents—including graphics, text files, video clips, and sounds—in an aesthetically pleasing format that communicates with the user. Multimedia-authoring software, like page-layout software, serves as glue that binds documents created and captured with other applications. But since a multimedia document can change in response to user input, authoring involves specifying not just *what* and *where* but also *when* and *why*. Some authoring programs are designed for professionals. Others are designed for children. Many are used by both.

Some authoring programs, including HyperStudio and MetaCard, use the card-and-stack user interface originally introduced with Apple's HyperCard. According to this metaphor, a multimedia document is a stack of cards. Each screen, called a card, can contain graphics, text, and **buttons**—hot spots that respond to mouse clicks. Buttons can be programmed to transport the user to another card, play music, open dialog boxes, launch other applications, rearrange information, perform menu operations, send messages to hardware devices, or do other things. Some authoring programs, including ToolBook, use a similar user interface with a book-and-page metaphor: A book replaces the stack and a page replaces the card. The World Wide Web uses metaphorical pages to represent screens of information; many authoring tools are designed specifically to create Web pages. The most widely used professional multimedia-authoring tool, Macromedia's Director, has a different kind of user interface. A Director document is a movie rather than a stack of cards or a book of pages. A button can transport a user to another frame of a movie rather than to another card or page. Macromedia Flash, a popular tool for adding multimedia to the Web, is based on an interface similar to Director's. Some authoring tools, such as Authorware, use flowcharts as tools for constructing documents.

6.27 Multimedia authoring involves programming objects on the screen to react, or behave, in particular ways under particular circumstances. Macromedia Director MX, one of the most popular of such packages, includes prewritten behaviors that can be attached to on-screen buttons, images, and other objects.

Creating an Effective Interactive Experience

Whether you're creating a simple presentation or a full-blown multimedia extravaganza, your finished product will communicate more effectively if you follow a few simple guidelines:

➡ **Be consistent.** Group similar controls together, and maintain a consistent visual appearance throughout the presentation.

➡ **Make it intuitive.** Use graphical metaphors to guide viewers, and make your controls do what they look like they should do.

➡ **Strive for simplicity.** A clean, uncluttered screen is more inviting than a crowded one—and easier to understand, too.

➡ **Keep it lively.** If your presentation doesn't include motion, sound, or user interaction, it probably should be printed and distributed as a paper document.

➡ **The message is more important than the media.** Your goal is to communicate information, not saturate the senses. Don't let the bells and whistles get in the way of your message.

➡ **Put the user in the driver's seat.** Include controls for turning down sound, bypassing repetitive animation, and turning off annoying features. Provide navigation aids, search tools, bookmarks, online help, and "Where am I?" feedback. Never tell the user, "You can't get there from here."

➡ **Let real people test your designs.** The best way to find out whether your multimedia works is to test it on people who aren't familiar with the subject. If they get lost or bored, find out why, fix the problem, and test it again.

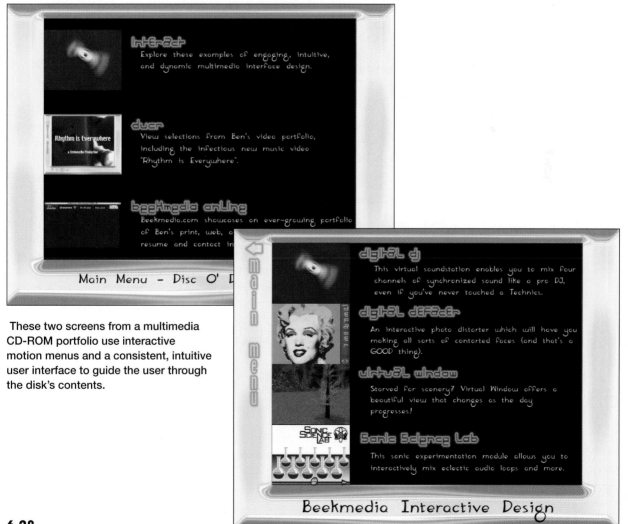

These two screens from a multimedia CD-ROM portfolio use interactive motion menus and a consistent, intuitive user interface to guide the user through the disk's contents.

6.28

The authoring tool's interface metaphor is important to the person creating the multimedia document, but not to the person viewing the finished document, who sees only the user interface that was built into the document by the author. When you're using a well-designed multimedia document, you can't tell whether it was created by Director, Authorware, or another authoring tool.

With the growing interest in the Internet, many people expect the Web to replace CD-ROMs for most multimedia delivery. Most multimedia-authoring tools can create Web-ready multimedia documents. For example, by using Macromedia's Shockwave technology, you can convert documents created by Authorware and Director into Web documents. Shockwave software compresses multimedia documents so they can appear and respond more quickly on the Web. But even with compression, the Internet isn't fast enough to deliver the high-quality audio and video that's possible with CD-ROM and DVD-ROM. On the other hand, the contents of a disk are static; they can't be continually updated like a Web site. And CD-ROMs don't offer opportunities for communication with other people the way a Web site can. Many multimedia manufacturers today produce hybrid disks—media-rich CD-ROMs and DVD-ROMs that automatically draw content and communication from the Web. Hybrid discs hint at the types of multimedia experiences that will be possible without discs through tomorrow's faster Internet.

Multimedia-authoring software today puts a great deal of power into the hands of computer users, but it doesn't solve all the technical problems in this new art form. Many of the problems with hypertext and hypermedia outlined earlier are even more serious when multiple media are involved. Still, the best multimedia productions transcend these problems and show the promise of this emerging technology.

Interactive Media: Visions of the Future

For most of recorded history, the **interactions of humans with their media** have been **primarily passive** in the sense that marks on paper, paint on walls, even motion pictures and television, **do not change** in response to the viewer's wishes. (But computers can) **respond to queries and experiments**—so that the message may involve the learner in a **two-way conversation**.

—Alan Kay

For hundreds of thousands of years, two-way interactive communication was the norm: One person talked, another responded. Today television, radio, newspapers, magazines, and books pour information into billions of passive people every day. For many people, one-way passive communication has become more common than interactive discourse.

According to many experts, interactive multimedia technology offers new hope for turning communication back into a participatory sport. With interactive multimedia software the audience is a part of the show. Interactive multimedia tools can give people control over the media—control traditionally reserved for professional artists, filmmakers, and musicians. The possibilities are far-reaching, especially when telecommunication enters the picture. Consider these snapshots from a not-too-distant future:

- Instead of watching your history professor flip through overhead transparencies, you control a self-paced interactive presentation complete with video footage illustrating key concepts.
- Using an electronic whiteboard, a professor's writings are automatically transmitted to your wireless notebook or Tablet PC, allowing you to take notes on what he says, and not what he writes. Students can present questions in real time, using an electronic ballot.
- In your electronic mailbox you find a "letter" from your sister. The letter shows her performing all of the instrumental parts for a song she composed, followed by a request for you to add a vocal line.

- Your favorite TV show is an interactive thriller that allows you to control the plot twists and work with the main characters to solve mysteries.
- While working on a biology project in the field, you come across an unusual bird with a song you don't recognize. Using a pocket-sized digital device, you record some audio/video footage of the bird as it sings. Using the same device, you dial your project partner's phone number and send the footage directly to her computer for editing and analysis.
- You share your concerns about a proposed factory in your hometown at the televised electronic town meeting. Thousands of others respond to questions from the mayor by pressing buttons on their remote control panels. The overwhelming citizen response forces the city council to reconsider the proposal.

Of course, the future of interactive multimedia may not be all sunshine and roses. Many experts fear that these exciting new media possibilities will further remove us from books, other people, and the natural world around us. If television today can mesmerize so many people, will tomorrow's interactive multimedia TVs cause even more serious addiction problems? Or will interactive communication breathe new life into the media and the people who use them? Will interactive electronic media make it easier for abusers of power to influence and control unwary citizens, or will the power of the push button create a new kind of digital democracy? Will interactive digital technology just turn "sound bites" into "sound bytes," or will it unleash the creative potential in the people who use it? For answers, stay tuned.

6.29 Animators at Pixar Studios work on film projects, including *Finding Nemo* and *The Incredibles*. Many of these projects spawn games, educational software programs, and other interactive multimedia products.

Inventing the FUTURE

Shared Virtual Spaces

> What I'm hoping is that **inside virtual worlds**, eventually, people can both have the **power and excitement of imagination** while also **being connected** with other people because the virtual world is really **shared with the real world**, even though you make it up.
>
> —*Jaron Lanier, virtual reality pioneer*

Tomorrow's multimedia is likely to extend beyond the flat screen, creating immersive experiences that challenge our notion of reality.

VIRTUAL REALITY

Since the 1960s researchers have experimented with *virtual worlds*—computer-generated worlds that created the illusion of immersion. Virtual worlds typically involve special hardware; for input, a glove or body suit equipped with motion sensors, and for output, a head-mounted display—a helmet with eye-sized screens with views that change as the helmet moves. This equipment, when coupled with appropriate software, enables the user to explore an artificial world of data as if it were three-dimensional physical space. *Virtual reality* combines virtual worlds with networking, placing multiple participants in a virtual space. People see representations of each other, sometimes called *avatars*. Most avatars today are cartoonish, but they convey a sense of presence and emotion.

TELE-IMMERSION

Jaron Lanier, who coined the term *virtual reality*, is now the lead scientist in the National Tele-Immersion Initiative. *Tele-immersion* uses multiple cameras and high-speed networks to create an environment in which multiple remote users can interact with each other and with computer-generated objects. (Lanier was a consultant for Spielberg's *Minority Report*, a movie that shows a similar technology.) Tele-immersion combines virtual reality techniques with new vision technologies that allow participants to move around in shared virtual spaces, while maintaining their unique points of view. Today's systems require participants to wear special glasses; future versions may not.

Tele-immersion systems, when coupled with tomorrow's high-speed Internet2 (see Chapter 9), will allow engineers, archaeologists, and artists, among others,

6.30a Virtual reality (VR) pioneer Jaron Lanier.

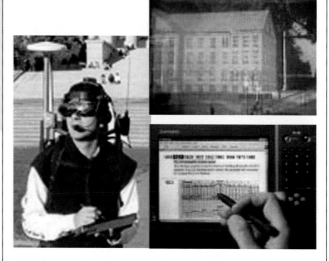

6.30b Using an experimental system at Columbia University, this student explores the campus with a unique historical perspective. He can see and walk around a 3-D image of the Bloomingdale Asylum—the previous occupant of the campus space—in its original location; additional historical information is displayed on his handheld tablet.

to collaborate long-distance in shared virtual workspaces. It may allow musicians and actors to give personal interactive performances. Tele-immersion may significantly reduce the need for business travel within a decade.

AUGMENTED REALITY

Another promising offshoot of VR research is *augmented reality (AR)*—the use of computer displays that add virtual information to a person's sensory perceptions. Unlike VR, AR supplements rather than replaces the world the user sees.

The first-down line that's superimposed on TV football fields is a simple example of AR, but the future offers many more practical applications. With AR, a repair person might see instructions superimposed on a machine part; a surgeon might see inside a patient with live ultrasound scans of internal organs overlaid on the patient's body; a firefighter might see the layout of a burning building.

AR researcher Steven K. Feiner predicts "the overlaid information of AR systems will become part of what we expect to see at work and at play: labels and directions when we don't want to get lost, reminders when we don't want to forget and, perhaps, a favorite cartoon character popping out from the bushes to tell a joke when we want to be amused. When computer user interfaces are potentially everywhere we look, this pervasive mixture of reality and virtuality may become the primary medium for a new generation of artists, designers, and storytellers who will craft the future." ～

Memory Overload *Jim Lewis*

Multimedia technology is unleashing the creative potential in budding photographers and video artists. But what will become of all of the digital works created by these amateur archivists? In this essay, first published in the February 2003 issue of Wired, *writer Jim Lewis suggests that we're storing way too much on our hard drives.*

There's a famous allegory about a map of the world that grows in detail until every point in reality has its counterpoint on paper; the twist being that such a map is at once ideally accurate and entirely useless, since it's the same size as the thing it's meant to represent.

Something very similar is happening in the world around us, though the phenomenon captured is time, not space, and the medium is digital memory rather than paper and ink. Consider, for example, a paradox well known to new parents: Mom and Dad buy a video camera expecting to document Junior's first years, only to find that, while they do indeed shoot anything and everything, they never get around to watching all they recorded. There aren't enough hours in the day for such marathons of consumption.

There was an era when a mechanically captured memory was a rare and precious thing: a formal photo, a faint recording of someone's voice. Nowadays it's all you can do to avoid leaving a recording behind as you go about your day—especially as hard drives get bigger and devices more ubiquitous. The average American is caught at least a dozen times a day on surveillance cameras: at bank machines, above intersections, outside tourist spots, on the dashboards of police cruisers. Businesses log every keystroke made by their employees; help centers store audio of telephone calls, as does 911. DigiMine CEO Usama Fayyad, a computer scientist turned data mining entrepreneur, calculates that the data storage curve is now rocketing upward at a rate of 800 percent per year. "It makes Moore's law look like a flat line," he says. "Companies are collecting so much data they're overwhelmed."

You may know the feeling. Since Kodachrome made way for JPEG, pictures accumulate on hard drives like wet leaves in a gutter. If you wanted to, you could make a fair-quality audio recording of everything that reaches your ears for a month and store it on an iPod that fits in your pocket. Though, of course, you'd need another month to listen to it. Whence the rub: If life gets recorded in real time, it hardly counts as a record at all. It certainly has less impact, and in extreme examples it's self-defeating.

Mechanical memory—to its unexpected advantage—degrades. Colors fade, negatives crack, manuscripts grow brittle, grooves get scratched. What emerges from these depredations is a crucial sense of both the pastness of the past, and its presence. Time takes just enough out of acetate and celluloid to remind us of the distance between now and then, while leaving just enough to remind us of the nearness of our own history.

But digital memory—ubiquitous, fathomless, and literally gratuitous—serves neither idea: The past is always here and always perfect; everything can be represented, no moment need be lost. Moreover, all of it is as good as new, and every copy identical to the original. What's missing is a cadence, a play of values, or a respect for the way loss informs our experience of time. Like the map that's as big as the world itself, it's useless precisely because it's too good.

In a way, we've engineered ourselves back in time. When it was rare and expensive, mechanical memory swamped the real thing; what you most vividly recalled from your vacation wasn't necessarily the most striking part, but what you had the best picture of. Recollecting my own early childhood, I can't tell the experiences from the photographs of them that I've seen since. As recently as 160 years ago, such a phenomenon would have been inconceivable—there simply was no such thing as a photo, film, an audiotape. Now there's a surfeit, to the same effect. Moments are no longer fixed as monuments around which memories accrue—the picture in your wallet, your favorite uncle's Super 8 movies, a single song on a 45. There's just a constant downpour of experience, some of it real and some of it representation, a fluid and uninflected cataract.

Whether this is a boon or a disaster I can't say. Such subtle patterns in the history of human experience tend to escape that kind of judgment. But the result is a telling contradiction: Our culture has become engulfed in its past and can make no use of it at all.

Discussion Questions

1. When you think about your early childhood, do you have trouble, as the author does, distinguishing memories from photographs? Do you think digital technology will make this phenomenon more or less common? Explain.

2. Do you think the proliferation of recorded experience is a boon or a disaster? Explain your answer.

Summary

Computer graphics today encompass more than quantitative charts and graphs generated by spreadsheets. Bitmapped painting programs enable users to "paint" the screen with a mouse, pen, or other pointing device. The software stores the results in a pixel map, with each pixel having an assigned color. The more possible colors there are and the higher the resolution (pixel density) is, the more the images can approach photorealism. Object-oriented drawing programs also allow users to draw on the screen with a pointing device, with the results stored as collections of geometric objects rather than as maps of computer bits.

Bitmapped graphics and object-oriented graphics each offer advantages in particular situations; trade-offs involve editing and ease of use. Both types of graphics have applications outside the art world. Bitmapped graphics are used in high-resolution image-processing software for on-screen photo editing. Object-oriented graphics are at the heart of 3-D modeling software and computer-aided design (CAD) software used by architects, designers, and engineers. Presentation-graphics software, which may include either one or both graphics types, automates the process of creating slides, transparencies, handouts, and computer-based presentations, making it easy for nonartists to create visually attractive presentations.

With today's computers, you aren't limited to working with static images; they're widely used to create and edit documents in media that change over time or in response to user interaction. For animation and digital video work, PCs mimic many of the features of expensive professional workstations at a fraction of the cost. Similarly, today's personal computers can perform a variety of sound- and music-editing tasks that used to require expensive equipment and numerous musicians.

The interactive nature of the personal computer makes it possible to create nonlinear documents that enable users to take individual paths through information. Early nonlinear documents were called hypertext because they could contain only text. Today, we can create or explore hypermedia documents—interactive documents that mix text, graphics, sounds, and moving images with on-screen navigation buttons—on disc and on the World Wide Web.

Multimedia computer systems make a new kind of software possible—software that uses text, graphics, animation, video, music, voice, and sound effects to communicate. Interactive multimedia documents are available for desktop computers, video game machines, set-top boxes connected to televisions, and networks. Regardless of the hardware, interactive multimedia software enables the user to control the presentation rather than watch or listen passively. Only time will tell whether these new media will live up to their potential for enhancing education, training, entertainment, and cultural enrichment.

Key Terms

3-D modeling software..........(p. 231)
animation..............................(p. 237)
audio digitizer.......................(p. 241)
augmented reality (AR).........(p. 256)
bit depth................................(p. 224)
bitmapped graphics ....(p. 224)
bullet charts ....(p. 233)
button...................................(p. 252)
color depth............................(p. 224)
compression..........................(p. 241)
computer-aided design
    (CAD)..............................(p. 232)
computer-aided manufacturing
    (CAM) ....(p. 233)
computer-integrated manufacturing
    (CIM)...............................(p. 233)
digital video..........................(p. 238)

drawing software ....(p. 229)
frame.....................................(p. 237)
gray-scale graphics................(p. 224)
hypermedia...........................(p. 250)
hypertext...............................(p. 250)
image-processing
    software ....(p. 227)
interactive multimedia...........(p. 251)
MIDI.....................................(p. 244)
morph ....(p. 240)
MP3 ....(p. 244)
multimedia............................(p. 251)
multimedia-authoring
    software ....(p. 252)
object-oriented graphics ....(p. 229)
page-description language.....(p. 229)
painting software ....(p. 223)

palette ....(p. 223)
pixel......................................(p. 223)
PostScript ....(p. 229)
presentation-graphics
    software ....(p. 233)
public domain.......................(p. 228)
raster graphics ....(p. 224)
resolution..............................(p. 224)
sample...................................(p. 241)
sequencing software ....(p. 244)
synthesized ....(p. 241)
tele-immersion......................(p. 256)
vector graphics ....(p. 229)
video digitizer.......................(p. 238)
video-editing
    software ....(p. 240)
virtual reality ....(p. 256)

Interactive Activities

1. The *Computer Confluence* CD-ROM contains self-test multiple-choice quiz questions related to this chapter.

2. The *Computer Confluence* Web site, http://www.computerconfluence.com, also contains self-test exercises related to this chapter. Follow the instructions for taking a quiz. After you've completed your quiz, you can email the results to your instructor.

True or False

1. Through the use of mathematical formulas, bitmapped graphics represent lines, shapes, and characters as objects.

2. Photographic image-editing software can produce images so realistic that some now question the validity of photographic evidence in the courtroom.

3. 3-D graphics play an important role in the branch of engineering known as computer-aided design (CAD).

4. Presentation-graphics programs, such as PowerPoint, can automatically generate pie charts and bar charts but not bullet charts.

5. Based on trends in animation technology today, it's likely that the first fully computer-animated feature-length film will happen in the second decade of the twenty-first century.

6. Sequencing software allows musicians to record audio and MIDI tracks, edit them, and play them back.

7. Because uncompressed video requires massive amounts of storage, virtually all digital video files are compressed.

8. Hypermedia isn't possible without a PC.

9. Today multimedia-authoring software is used almost exclusively for creating animated Web pages.

10. Interactive multimedia on the Web are limited in quality by the bandwidth restrictions of many Internet connections.

Multiple Choice

1. Which kind of technology are photographic image-editing programs largely based on?
   a. Object-oriented graphics
   b. Presentation graphics
   c. Bitmapped graphics
   d. Quantitative graphics
   e. CAD/CAM graphics

2. If a photographic image looks fine when displayed on a computer screen but appears jagged and rough when printed, the problem has to do with the image's
   a. Bit depth
   b. Dimensions
   c. Vector
   d. Raster
   e. Resolution

3. Which of the following might professional artists, seeking an input device that can more accurately simulate a pen or paintbrush, choose to draw with?
   a. A mouse
   b. A joystick
   c. A trackball
   d. A stylus on a pressure-sensitive pad
   e. An infrared system that tracks their eye movements

4. Which technology is 3-D graphics software based largely on?
   a. Object-oriented graphics
   b. Presentation graphics
   c. Bitmapped graphics
   d. Photographic image-editing software
   e. Hypermedia

5. Presentation-graphics software is typically used to prepare a
   a. Series of on-screen "slides"
   b. Web animation
   c. Movie for recording on 35 mm film
   d. Music video
   e. Realistic, computer-generated scene

6. The process of tweening in animation is similar to which of these video concepts?
   a. Averaging
   b. Morphing
   c. Sequencing
   d. Synthesizing
   e. Easterizing

7. Which of these movies relies upon computer animation for all of its images?
   a. *Finding Nemo*
   b. *The Incredibles*
   c. *Shrek*
   d. *Toy Story*
   e. All of the above

8. What must you do to use a computer to edit footage captured with a digital video camera?
   a. Install a video digitizer in the PC
   b. Import the video footage using a FireWire cable or the equivalent
   c. Digitize the video footage
   d. Store the video clips on a DVD
   e. All of the above

9. For nonlinear video editing, what are video and audio clips stored on?
   a. Tape
   b. DVD
   c. CD
   d. Floppy disks
   e. Hard disk(s)

10. Even short digital movies can require a lot of storage space. What is the least expensive way to solve this problem?
    a. Use cheap hard disk drives made in China
    b. Use nonlinear editing
    c. Use PostScript
    d. Use data compression
    e. Use miniature holographic storage cubes

11. Which of the following is a method that many legal online music stores use to attempt to prevent piracy?
    a. Sell music files with built-in digital rights-management technology
    b. Require customers to sign antipiracy pledges
    c. Perform background checks on potential customers
    d. Sell only MP3 files, because MP3 is widely known to be secure
    e. Compress files with lossless compression technology

12. Why is MP3 is a popular format for music file sharing?
    a. MP3 files typically contain video as well as audio data.
    b. MP3 files work equally well for text, graphics, and music.
    c. MP3 compression reduces file sizes considerably with minimal loss of music quality.
    d. MP3 compression is lossless.
    e. MP3 files contain DRM technology.

13. Why is a MIDI file of a Beethoven piano concerto much smaller than a CD audio file of the same piece?
    a. MIDI uses efficient MP3 technology.
    b. MIDI uses MPEG-4 compression.
    c. MIDI uses software rather than hardware for compression.
    d. The MIDI file contains only instructions for playing notes; the note sounds are stored in the computer or musical instrument.
    e. Actually, MIDI files are larger than MP3 files.

14. What does hypermedia software give computer users?
    a. Nonsequential access to text, numbers, graphics, music, and other media
    b. Incredibly fast access to documents stored anywhere on the Web
    c. Instantaneous downloading of full-length feature movies
    d. Immersive virtual-reality interaction with other computer users
    e. All of the above

15. What is the most important difference between an interactive multimedia version of *Sesame Street* and a *Sesame Street* television program?
    a. The interactive multimedia version allows the viewer to have more control over the experience.
    b. The interactive multimedia version offers a richer mix of media types.
    c. The interactive multimedia version requires a joystick or game controller.
    d. The interactive multimedia version can't be displayed on a standard TV screen.
    e. The interactive multimedia version exists only in theory; it's not technically possible yet.

Review Questions

1. Define or describe each of the key terms listed in the "Key Terms" section. Check your answers using the glossary.

2. What is the difference between bitmapped graphics and object-oriented graphics? What are the advantages and disadvantages of each?

3. Which two technological factors limit the realism of a bitmapped image? How are these related to the storage of that image in the computer?

4. How is the digital image processing of photographs related to bitmapped painting?

5. Describe several practical applications for 3-D modeling and CAD software.

6. Why is image compression an important part of digital video technology?

7. Describe three different technologies for adding music or other sounds to a multimedia presentation. Describe a practical application of each sound source.

8. How do hypertext and other hypermedia differ from linear media?

9. Describe several practical applications for hypermedia.

10. What are the main disadvantages of hypermedia when compared with conventional media such as books and videos?

11. Is it possible to have hypermedia without multimedia? Is it possible to have multimedia without hypermedia? Explain your answers.

12. How does presentation-graphics software differ from multimedia-authoring software? Give an example of a practical application of each.

Discussion Questions

1. How does modern digital image-processing technology affect the reliability of photographic evidence? How does digital audio technology affect the reliability of sound recordings as evidence? How should our legal system respond to this technology?

2. Scanners, video digitizers, and audio digitizers make it easier than ever for people to violate copyright laws. What, if anything, should be done to protect the intellectual property rights of the people who create pictures, videos, and music? Under what circumstances do you think it's acceptable to copy sounds or images for use in your own work?

3. Do you think hypermedia documents will eclipse certain kinds of books and other media? If so, which ones and why?

4. Thanks to modern electronic music technology, one or two people can make a record that would have required dozens of musicians 20 years ago. What impact will electronic music technology ultimately have on the music profession?

5. Try to answer each of the questions posed at the end of the section called "Interactive Media: Visions of the Future."

Projects

1. Draw a familiar object or scene using a bitmapped painting program. Draw the same object or scene with an object-oriented drawing program. Describe how the process changed using different software.

2. Modify a photograph using an image-processing software package, such as Adobe Photoshop. If the photograph is not already in digital form, use a scanner to create a digitized image. With the image-processing software, add some special effects that demonstrate the power of a computer to create images that cannot be seen in the "real world." Which image-processing tools were easiest to use? Which tools were hardest to use?

3. Create visual aids for a speech or lecture using presentation-graphics software. In what ways did the software make the job easier? What limitations did you find?

4. Produce a ten-minute video on a subject related to one of your classes. Begin by creating a storyboard outlining the action, dialogue, and music in each scene. Use a digital video camera to record the scenes. Download the video and music files into a computer. Edit the movie using a video-editing software package such as Adobe Premier, Apple iMovie, or Microsoft Windows Movie Maker 2. Save the finished movie onto videotape or DVD. Reflect on the movie production process. Describe possible improvements to the software that would have made your job easier.

5. Compose some original music using a synthesizer, a computer, and a sequencer. Reflect on the process of producing the piece of music. Describe possible improvements to the software that would have made your job easier.

6. Review several interactive multimedia titles. Discuss their strengths and weaknesses as communication tools. In what ways did their interactivity enhance their usefulness? (Extra challenge: Make your review interactive.)

Sources and Resources

Books

Most of the best graphics, video, music, and multimedia applications books are software specific. When you decide on a software application, choose books based on your chosen software and on the type of information you need. If you want quick answers with a minimum of verbiage, you'll probably be delighted with a book from Peachpit's *Visual Quickstart* series. Most of the titles in the following list aren't keyed to specific applications.

Weaving the Web, by Tim Berners-Lee. (San Francisco, CA: Harper San Francisco, 1999). This is the story of the creation of the Web straight from the word processor of the man who did it. Few people in history have had more impact on the way we communicate than this unassuming man.

How the Web Was Born: The Story of the World Wide Web, by Robert Cailliau, James Gillies, and R. Cailliau. (London: Oxford University Press: 2000). This book provides another account of the events leading up to and following the creation of the Web. The authors provide a context that helps explain how Tim Berners-Lee made critical decisions in shaping the Web.

Computer Graphics Companion, edited by Jeffrey J. McConnell, Anthony Ralston, Edwin D. Reilly, and David Hemmendinger (New York, NY: John Wiley & Sons, 2002). This is a collection of articles from the *Computer Science Dictionary* plus some additional material written specifically for this volume. Some of the articles are technical, but there's plenty of useful information here.

Graphic Communications Dictionary, by Daniel J. Lyons (Upper Saddle River, NJ: Prentice Hall, 2000). This is an excellent alphabetic reference for anyone wrestling with the terminology of graphic design.

The New Drawing on the Right Side of the Brain: A Course in Enhancing Creativity and Artistic Confidence, by Betty Edwards and Jeremy P. Tarcher (Los Angeles, CA: J. P. Tarcher, 1999). If you're convinced you have no artistic ability, give this book a try; you might surprise yourself.

The Arts and Crafts Computer: Using Your Computer as an Artist's Tool, by Janet Ashford (Berkeley, CA: Peachpit Press, 2001). This lavishly illustrated book covers basic principles of drawing, painting, photography, typography, and design with computers. But unlike other books on computer art, this one goes beyond the computer screen and the printed page as output possibilities. If you want to create original fabric art, greeting cards, labels, decals, bumper stickers, or toys, you'll find a wealth of ideas here.

Digital Photography Top 100 Simplified Tips & Tricks, by Gregory Georges (Hoboken, NJ: Wiley, 2003). If you want to take pictures that are more than snapshots, this highly graphical book can help. It's packed with useful tips accompanied by clear illustrations.

Photoshop CS for Windows and Macintosh: Visual Quickstart Guide, by Elaine Weinmann and Peter Lourekas (Berkeley, CA: Peachpit Press, 2004). Peachpit's *Visual Quickstart Guides* are popular because they provide maximum instruction for a minimal investment of time. This Photoshop guide is one of the best. Using lots of pictures and few words, it unlocks the secrets of the program that is the industry standard for professional photo- and bitmap-editing software.

Photoshop CS Artistry, by Barry Haynes and Wendy Crumpler (Berkeley, CA: Peachpit Press, 2004). If the stripped-down *Visual Quickstart* approach is too sparse for you, this book is an excellent alternative. Combining clear explanations, numerous color screen shots, hands-on tutorials, and a handy CD-ROM, the authors deliver a complete course in Photoshop.

Adobe Creative Suite Idea Kit, by Katrin Straub (Berkeley, CA: Adobe Press, 2004). The Adobe Creative Suite includes Photoshop, InDesign, Acrobat, Illustrator, and other industrial-strength digital media applications. This friendly book can show you how to create a variety of projects, from newsletters to animated Web sites, using these powerful application.

Looking Good in Presentations, Third Edition, by Molly W. Joss (Scottsdale, AZ: Coriolis Group, 1999). Programs like PowerPoint can help nondesigners create stylish presentations, but they're not foolproof. This is a great book for anyone creating presentations, from simple slide shows to full-featured multimedia extravaganzas. Starting with "How to Not Be Boring" in Chapter 1, you'll find plenty of tips to make your presentations shine.

The Art of 3-D Computer Animation and Effects, Third Edition, by Isaac V. Kerlow (New York: Wiley, 2004). Films like *Shrek* and *Finding Nemo* have turned 3-D graphics into a big business and a popular art form. This book clearly explains the technology that makes it all possible.

Macromedia Studio MX 2004: Training from the Source, by Shaowen Bardzell and Jeffrey Bardzell (Berkeley, CA: Macromedia Press, 2004). Macromedia's Training from the Source books provide clear, easy-to-follow tutorials for using their most popular products. This one provides an overview of Studio MX 2004, the popular multimedia suite that includes Flash, Freehand, Dreamweaver, and Fireworks. Other books in the series cover Macromedia applications in more detail.

Real World Digital Video, Second Edition, by Pete Shaner and Gerald Everett Jones (Berkeley, CA: Peachpit Press, 2004). This book covers the entire video production process, from buying equipment to producing a final video product. You can avoid many of the pitfalls of video production by reading this book before you start.

Developing Digital Short Films, by Sherri Sheridan (Indianapolis: New Riders, 2004). This illustrated guide is a great companion for budding digital filmmakers. The focus is on the art of storytelling through video, rather than technical trivia. An accompanying CD-ROM includes a music video project, tools, and demo software.

Essentials of Music Technology, by Mark Ballora (Upper Saddle River, NJ: Prentice Hall, 2003). This book provides a systematic introduction to music technology, from basic acoustics to digital instruments.

The Streaming Media Handbook, by Eyal Menin (Upper Saddle River, NJ: Prentice Hall, 2003). This book, by one of the pros in the field, provides solid information for anyone interested in streaming audio or video on the Web.

Streaming Audio: The FezGuy's Guide, by Jon R. Luini and Allen E. Whitman (Indianapolis, IN: New Riders, 2002). This book gives step-by-step instructions for setting up streaming audio on the Web using all the popular formats and platforms.

MTIV: Process, Inspiration and Practice for the New Media Designer, by Hillman Curtis (Indianapolis, IN: New Riders, 2002). This bold, colorful book presents a successful new media designer's perspective on creating media that work well. The title stands for "Making the Invisible Visible." If you're interested in graphic design for the Internet age, this book is worth seeking.

Pause and Effect: The Art of Interactive Narrative, by Mark Stephen Meadows (Indianapolis, IN: New Riders, 2003). One of the biggest challenges in new media is the difficulty of putting the narrative form to nonlinear packages. This beautiful book examines the brave new world at the intersection of storytelling, visual art, and interactivity.

Theoretical Foundations of Multimedia, by Robert S. Tannenbaum (New York: W.H. Freeman, 1998). Multimedia is an ideal profession for a modern Renaissance person. To be truly multimedia literate, a person needs to understand concepts from fields as diverse as computer science, physics, design, law, psychology, and communication. This introductory text/CD-ROM surveys each of these fields from the multimedia perspective, providing valuable conceptual background with practical value.

Understanding Media: The Extensions of Man, by Marshall McLuhan (Cambridge, MA: MIT Press, 1994). This classic, originally published in 1964, explores the relationship of mass media to the masses. The new introduction in this thirtieth anniversary reissue reevaluates McLuhan's visionary work 30 years later.

net_condition: art and global media (Electronic Culture: History, Theory, and Practice), edited by Peter Weibel and Timothy Druckery (Cambridge, MA: MIT Press, 2001). This book surveys the global landscape of digital art and its impact on our culture.

Multimedia: From Wagner to Virtual Reality, Expanded Edition, edited by Randall Packer and Ken Jordan (New York: Norton, 2002). This collection of essays by William Burroughs, John Cage, Tim Berners-Lee, and others offers a broad overview of the historical roots of multimedia.

Periodicals

Artbyte. This stylish magazine explores the world and culture of digital art and design.

Digital Camera. This magazine covers the rapidly changing world of digital photography.

DV. This monthly magazine is aimed at digital video professionals and serious amateurs.

EMedia. This monthly covers the new media landscape, with an emphasis on CDs, DVDs, and other disc based media.

Keyboard and *Electronic Musician.* These two magazines are among the best sources for up-to-date information on computers and music synthesis.

Web Pages

The Web is known as the multimedia part of the Internet, and there are plenty of Web sites for learning about—and experiencing first-hand—a variety of mixed media types.

Multimedia

on the CD-ROM and the Web:

~ Bill Gates talks about what's wrong with PCs

~ An interactive activity for understanding database queries

~ Instant access to glossary and key word references

~ Interactive self-study quizzes

. . . and more.

 computerconfluence.com

Objectives

After you read this chapter you should be able to:

▶ **Explain what a database is and describe its basic structure**

▶ **Identify the kinds of problems that can best be solved with database software**

▶ **Describe different kinds of database software, from simple file managers to complex relational databases**

▶ **Describe database operations for storing, sorting, updating, querying, and summarizing information**

▶ **Give examples of ways in which large, easily accessible databases make our lives safer or more convenient**

▶ **Explain how databases threaten our privacy**

In the early days of the personal computer revolution, Bill Gates and Paul Allen formed a company called Microsoft to produce and market a version of the Basic programming language for microcomputers. Microsoft Basic quickly became the standard language installed in virtually every microcomputer.

When IBM went shopping for an operating system for its PC, Microsoft moved aggressively to get IBM's business. Microsoft purchased an operating system from a small company, reworked it to meet IBM's specifications, renamed it MS-DOS (for Microsoft Disk Operating System), and charged IBM only $80,000 for a *nonexclusive*, royalty-free license to use MS-DOS forever. Gates's goal was to make money by licensing MS-DOS to *other* manufacturers making PC-compatible computers. His gamble paid off. MS-DOS became the dominant operating system for the IBM PC, and Microsoft made billions of dollars when Compaq and other PC-compatible makers captured most of the market.

BILL GATES RIDES THE DIGITAL WAVE

The goal is **information at your fingertips**.

—Bill Gates

Today, Bill Gates and Microsoft dominate the PC software industry, selling operating systems, applications programs, server software, and software development tools. Software has made Gates the richest man on earth.

Microsoft's desktop dominance was threatened in the mid-1990s by the Internet explosion. For many people, computers became little more than portals into the Internet. Gates responded by making the Internet a critical part of Microsoft's software strategy. Today, Microsoft's Internet Explorer Web browser is a central component of the Windows OS; Microsoft desktop applications have links to the Internet, and Microsoft has partnerships with dozens of Web-related businesses worldwide.

According to writer Steven Levy, Gates "has the obsessive drive of a hacker working on a tough technical dilemma, yet has an uncanny grasp of the marketplace, as well as a firm conviction of what the future will be like and what he should do about it." The future, says Gates, will be digital. To prepare for this all-digital future,

Database Applications and Privacy Implications

7

7.1 Bill Gates.

Microsoft is extending its reach beyond software into all kinds of information-related business ventures, from online banking and shopping to the MSNBC cable TV network.

Many competitors and customers insist that Microsoft uses unethical business practices to ruthlessly—and sometimes illegally—stomp out competition and choice. In 1998, 20 states joined the U.S. government in a widely publicized lawsuit against Microsoft's anticompetitive practices. That same year, the European Union filed two antitrust lawsuits against the company. Microsoft responded with arrogant denials and a massive P.R. campaign; one state official received pro-Microsoft form letters from hundreds of people, including some who had died years before.

In 2000, a federal judge ruled that Microsoft illegally maintained its desktop operating system monopoly and that Microsoft's crimes had hurt consumers as well as other businesses. The ruling was confirmed by an appeals court in 2001, but the government settled out of court in exchange for minor concessions from the company. Today, Microsoft still faces numerous antitrust-related lawsuits around the world, but the company appears to have escaped from its most dangerous legal challenge.

In recent years, Bill Gates and Microsoft have given billions of dollars to public schools, AIDS research, and other charities. Cynics argue that these gifts are calculated to improve the company's public image in the face of legal troubles. Whatever the motivation, the donations are helping people all over the world.

In early 2000, Gates stepped aside as CEO of Microsoft to become the company's chairman and chief software architect. Today, he spearheads the development of future versions of Windows, moving the OS closer to his "information at your fingertips" vision by making it easier for computer users to find files on their computers and networks. In the future we will have all kinds of information at our fingertips; Bill Gates hopes that Microsoft will provide the tools for delivering that information. ∼

7.2 Bill Gates and Paul Allen as students.

We live in an information age. We're bombarded with information by television, radio, newspapers, magazines, books, and computers. It's easy to be overwhelmed by the sheer quantity of information we're expected to deal with each day. Computer applications, such as word processors and spreadsheets, can aggravate the problem by making it easier for people to generate more documents full of information.

A *database program* is a data manager that can help alleviate information overload. Databases make it possible for people to store, organize, retrieve, communicate, and manage information in ways that wouldn't be possible without computers. To control the flood of information, people use databases of all sizes and shapes—from massive mainframe database managers that keep airliners filled with passengers, to computerized appointment calendars on palmtop computers, to public database kiosks in shopping malls.

First the good news: Information at your fingertips can make your life richer and more efficient in a multitude of ways. Ready cash from street-corner ATMs, instant airline reservations from the Web at any time of the day, catalog shopping with overnight mail-order delivery, exhaustive online searches in seconds; none of these conveniences would be possible without databases.

Now the bad news: Some of the information stored in databases is about you and your activities, and you have little or no control over who has it and how it is used. Ironically, the database technology that liberates us in our day-to-day lives is, at the same time, chipping away at our privacy. We explore both sides of this important technology in this chapter.

The Electronic File Cabinet: Database Basics

The next best thing to **knowing**, is knowing **where to find It**.

—Samuel Johnson

We start by looking at the basics of databases. Like word processors, spreadsheets, and graphics programs, database programs are applications—programs for turning computers into productive tools. If a word processor is a computerized typewriter and a spreadsheet is a computerized ledger, you can think of a database program as a computerized file cabinet.

While word processors and spreadsheets generally are used to create printed documents, database programs are designed to maintain *databases*—collections of information stored on computer disks. A database can be as simple as a list of names and addresses, or as complex as an airline reservation system. An electronic version of a phone book, a recipe file, a library's card catalog, an inventory file stored in an office file cabinet, a school's student grade records, a card index containing the names and addresses of business contacts, or a catalog of your compact disc collection—just about any collection of information can be turned into a database.

What Good Is a Database?

Why do people use computers for information-handling tasks that can be done with index cards, three-ring binders, or file folders? Computerized databases offer several advantages over their paper-and-pencil counterparts:

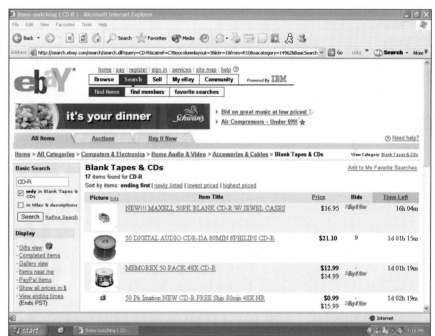

7.3 Internet auction Web sites, such as eBay, wouldn't be possible without database technology.

- *Databases make it easier to store large quantities of information.* If you have only 20 or 30 compact discs, it may make sense to catalog them in a notebook. But if you have 2,000 or 3,000 CDs, your notebook may become as unwieldy as your CD collection. The larger the mass of information, the bigger the benefit of using a database.
- *Databases make it easier to retrieve information quickly and flexibly.* It might take a minute or more to look up a phone number in a card file or telephone directory, but the same job can be done in seconds with a database. If you look up 200 numbers every

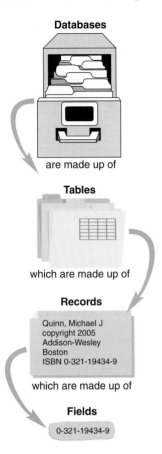

Databases

are made up of

Tables

which are made up of

Records

Quinn, Michael J
copyright 2005
Addison-Wesley
Boston
ISBN 0-321-19434-9

which are made up of

Fields

0-321-19434-9

7.4

week, the advantage of a database is obvious. That advantage is even greater when your search doesn't match your file's organization. For example, suppose you have a phone number on a scrap of paper and you want to find the name and address of the person with that number. That kind of search may take hours if your information is stored in a large address book or file alphabetized by name, but the same search is almost instantaneous with a computerized database.

▪ *Databases make it easy to organize and reorganize information.* Paper filing systems force you to arrange information in one particular way. Should your book catalog be organized by author, by title, by publication date, or by subject? There's a lot riding on your decision, because if you decide to rearrange everything later, you will waste a lot of time. With a database, you can instantly switch between these organizational schemes as often as you like; there's no penalty for flexibility.

▪ *Databases make it easy to print and distribute information in a variety of ways.* Suppose you want to send letters to hundreds of friends inviting them to your post graduation party. You'll need to include directions to your place for out-of-towners but not for home-towners. A database, when used with a word processor, can print personalized form letters, including extra directions for those who need them, and print preaddressed envelopes or mailing labels in a fraction of the time it would take you to do it by hand and with less likelihood of error. You can even print a report listing invitees sorted by ZIP code so you can suggest possible car pools. (And if you want to bill those who attend the party, your database can help with that, too.)

Database Anatomy

As you might expect, a specialized vocabulary is associated with databases. Unfortunately, some terms take on different meanings depending on their context, and different people use these words in different ways. We'll begin by charting a course through marketing hype and technical terminology to find our way to the definitions most people use today.

For our purposes, a **database** is a collection of information stored in an organized form in a computer, and a **database program** is a software tool for organizing storage and retrieval of that information. A variety of programs fit this broad definition, ranging from simple address book programs and other list managers to massive inventory-tracking systems. We explore the differences between types of database programs later in the chapter, but for now we treat them as if they are more or less alike.

Early PC databases were simple file managers; they made it easy for users to store, organize, and retrieve information—names, numbers, prices, whatever—from structured data files. This type of data management is really list management, since these files are just structured lists. Today's spreadsheet software can easily handle this kind of simple list management. Today's database software isn't limited to this kind of simple file management; it can handle complex tasks involving multiple data files.

A database is typically composed of one or more tables. A **table** is a collection of related information; it keeps that information together the way a folder in a file cabinet does. If a database is used to record sales information for a company, separate tables might contain the relevant sales data for each year. For an address database, separate tables might hold personal and business contacts. It's up to the designer of the database to determine whether information in different categories is stored in separate tables, which are, in turn, stored in files on the computer's disk.

A database table is a collection of records. A **record** is the information related to one person, product, or event. In the library's card catalog database, a record is equivalent to one card with information about a book. In an address book database, a record contains information about one person. A compact disc catalog database would have one record per CD.

Each discrete chunk of information in a record is called a **field**. A record in the library's card catalog database would contain fields for author, title, publisher, address, date, and title code number. Your CD database could break records into fields by title, artist, and so on.

The type of information a field can hold is determined by its *field type* or *data type*. For example, the author field in the library database would be defined as a text field, so it could contain text. A field specifying the number of copies of a book would be defined as a *numeric field*, so it could contain only numbers—numbers that can be used to calculate totals and other arithmetic formulas, if necessary. A date-of-purchase field might be a *date field* that could contain only date values. In addition to these standard field types, many database programs allow fields to contain graphics, digitized photographs, sounds, or video clips. **Computed fields** contain formulas similar to spreadsheet formulas; they display values calculated from values in other numeric fields. For example, a computed field called GPA might contain a formula for calculating a student's grade point average using the grades stored in other fields.

Most database programs provide you with more than one way to view the data, including *form views*, which show one record at a time, and *list views*, which display several records in lists similar to a spreadsheet. In any view, you can rearrange fields without changing the underlying data.

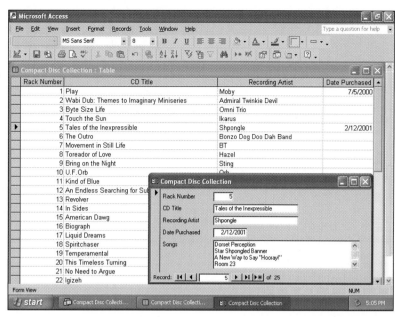

7.5 These two windows show the list and form views of a database.

Database Operations

Information has **value**, but it is as **perishable** as fresh fruit.

—Nicholas Negroponte, founder and director of the MIT Media Lab

After the structure of a database is defined, it's easy to enter information; it's just a matter of typing. Typing may not even be necessary if the data already exists in some computer-readable form. Most database programs can easily **import data** or receive data in the form of text files created with word processors, spreadsheets, or other databases. When information changes or errors are detected, records can be modified, added, or deleted.

Browsing

The challenging part of using a database is retrieving information in a timely and appropriate manner. Information is of little value if it's not accessible. One way to find information is to **browse** through the records of the database just as you would if they were paper forms in a notebook. Most database programs provide keyboard commands, on-screen buttons, and other tools for navigating quickly through records. But this kind of electronic page turning offers no particular advantage over paper, and it's painfully inefficient for large databases. Fortunately, most database programs include a variety of commands and capabilities that make it easy to get the information you need when you need it.

Database Queries

The alternative to browsing is to ask the database for specific information. In database terminology, an information request is called a **query**. A query may be a simple **search** for a specific record (say, one containing information on Abraham Lincoln) or a request to **select** *all* records that match a set of criteria (for example, records for all U.S. presidents who served more than one term). After you've selected a group of records, you can browse

Creating an Address Book with FileMaker Pro

GOAL *To create a database file containing names, addresses, and phone numbers, replacing the bundle of business cards in your desk drawer and the scribbled list of numbers posted by your phone.*

TOOL *FileMaker Pro*

1. You decide which fields should be in each record of the database and define those fields. (This dialog box shows several fields you've already defined.)

2. You type the name of the next field.

3. You select the type of the field.

4. Once all of the fields are defined, you enter data into each field for all of your contacts.

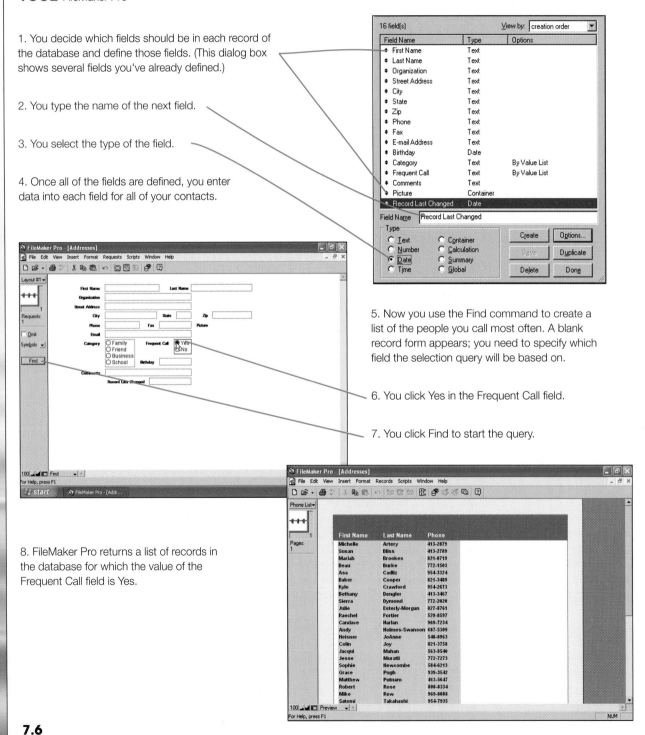

5. Now you use the Find command to create a list of the people you call most often. A blank record form appears; you need to specify which field the selection query will be based on.

6. You click Yes in the Frequent Call field.

7. You click Find to start the query.

8. FileMaker Pro returns a list of records in the database for which the value of the Frequent Call field is Yes.

7.6

through it, produce a printout, or do just about anything else you might do with the complete table. Many databases allow you to record, or store, commonly used queries so you can access them quickly in the future. The ability to generate a *stored query* is a powerful feature that helps databases blur the line between application programs and development tools.

Sorting Data

Sometimes it's necessary to rearrange records to make the most efficient use of data. For example, a mail-order company's customer file might be arranged alphabetically by name for easy reference, but it must be rearranged in order by ZIP code to qualify for postal discounts on bulk catalog mailings. A **sort** command allows you to arrange records in alphabetic or numeric order based on values in one or more fields.

Printing Reports, Labels, and Form Letters

In addition to displaying information on the screen, database programs can produce a variety of printouts. The most common type of database printout is a **report**—an ordered list of selected records and fields in an easy-to-read format. Most business reports arrange data in tables with rows for individual records and columns for selected fields; they often include summary lines containing calculated totals and averages for groups of records.

You can also use database programs to produce mailing labels and customized form letters. Many database programs don't actually print letters; they simply **export data**, or transmit the necessary records and fields, to word processors with mail merge capabilities, which then take on the task of printing the letters.

Complex Queries

Queries may be simple or complex, but either way they must be precise and unambiguous. With appropriate databases, queries could be constructed to find the following:

- In a hospital's patient database, the names and locations of all of the patients on the hospital's fifth and sixth floors
- In a database of airline flight schedules, the least expensive way to fly from Boston to San Francisco on Tuesday afternoon
- In a politician's database, all voters who contributed more than $1,000 to last year's legislative campaign and who wrote to express concern over gun control laws since the election

These may be legitimate targets for queries, but they aren't expressed in a form that most database programs can understand. The exact method for performing a query depends on the user interface of the database software. Most programs enable the user to specify the rules of the search by filling in a dialog box or a blank on-screen form. Some require the user to type the request using a special **query language** that's more precise than English is. For example, to view the records for males between 18 and 35, you might type

Select * From Population Where
Sex = M and Age >= 18 and Age <= 35

Many database programs include programming languages, so queries can be included in programs and performed automatically when the programs are executed. Although the details of the process vary, the underlying logic is consistent from program to program.

Most modern database-management programs support a standard language called **SQL** (from *Structured Query Language*; often pronounced "sequel") for programming complex queries. Because SQL is available for many different database-management systems, programmers and sophisticated users don't need to learn new languages when they work with different hardware and software systems. Users are usually insulated from the complexities of the query language by graphical user interfaces that allow point-and-click queries.

Querying a Web Search Database

GOAL *To research the use of solar energy to provide electricity for remote indigenous communities.*

TOOL *Internet Explorer*

1. You go to google.com and type "solar OR energy OR indigenous" to find Web sites that contain those three words.

2. The search reveals that more than twelve million pages contain at least one of the three target words. Your search strategy was flawed. Most of the articles listed for "solar" probably have nothing to do with indigenous peoples, so you've selected a large collection of mostly irrelevant titles.

3. You replace the ORs and ANDs in the search field and try again.

4. Google reminds you that AND is unnecessary in the search string; Google assumes you mean AND unless you type OR between two target words in a search string.

5. The search reveals 135,000 pages that contain all three words, including some at the top of the list that look relevant.

6. Switching OR to AND in this example reminds you of the importance of choosing every word carefully when defining a database query. If you don't find what you're looking for in this list, you might need to try different search strategies or search engines.

7.7

Special-Purpose Database Programs

Specialized database software is preprogrammed for specific data storage and retrieval purposes. Users of special-purpose databases don't generally need to define file structures or design forms, because these details have been taken care of by the software's designers. In fact, some special-purpose database programs are not even sold as databases; they have names that more accurately reflect their purposes.

Directories and Geographic Information Systems

For example, an electronic phone directory can pack millions of names and phone numbers onto a single CD-ROM or Web site. Using an *electronic phone directory* for the United States, you can track down phone numbers of people and businesses all over the country—even if you don't know where they are. You can look up a person's name if you have the phone number or street address. You can generate a list of every dentist in town—any town. Then using another type of specialized database, an *electronic street atlas*, you can pinpoint each of your finds on a freshly printed map. Many street atlases are designed to work with global positioning system (GPS) receivers on laptop, handheld, or automobile-based computers. GPS satellites feed location information to GPS receivers; mapping software uses that information to provide location feedback for travelers and mobile workers.

Geographical information systems (GISs) go beyond simple mapping and tracking programs. A GIS allows a business to combine tables of data, such as customer sales lists with demographic information from the U.S. Census Bureau and other sources. The right combination can reveal valuable strategic information. For example, a stock brokerage firm can pinpoint the best locations for branch offices based on average incomes and other neighborhood data; a cable TV company can locate potential customers who live close to existing lines. Because GISs can display geographic and demographic data on maps, they enable users to see data relationships that might be invisible in table form.

Personal Information Managers

One type of specialized database program is often called a **personal information manager (PIM)**. This type of program can automate some or all of the following functions:

- *Address/phone book*. Software address books provide options for quickly displaying specific records and printing mailing labels, address books, and reports. Some include automatic phone-dialing options and fields for recording phone notes.
- *Appointment calendar*. A typical PIM calendar enables you to enter appointments and events and display or print them in a variety of formats, ranging from one day at a time to a monthly overview. Many include built-in alarms for last-minute reminders and ways to share your calendar electronically with other users.
- *To-do list*. Most PIMs enable users to enter and organize ongoing lists of things to do and archive lists of completed tasks.
- *Miscellaneous notes*. Some PIMs accept diary entries, personal notes, and other hard-to-categorize tidbits of information.

PIMs have long been popular among people with busy schedules and countless contacts. They're easier to understand and use than general-purpose database programs, and they're faster and more flexible than their leather-bound paper counterparts. For people on the go, PIMs work especially well with notebook computers or handheld computers. For example, software that's built into the Palm OS accepts a pocket-sized device to *hot-sync* with PIM software on a desktop PC or Mac. This instant data linking makes it easy to keep up-to-date personal information in and out of the office.

In many organizations, enterprise information systems, such as Microsoft Outlook, part of Microsoft Office, have replaced PIMs. These systems enable networked coworkers to share calendars and contacts easily and often include email and other communication tools along with basic PIM features. The Web offers another alternative: Several Web sites provide free PIM software that you can access from any Web-accessible computer; many of these applications also permit workgroups to share calendars and other information.

How It **Works**

Years ago, the number of incompatible database languages made it difficult for people using different applications to access the same database. In the mid-1970s, IBM's E. F. Codd proposed a standardized Structured English Query Language, which evolved into SQL. With SQL, users and programmers can employ the same language to access databases from a wide variety of vendors.

SQL combines the familiar database concepts of tables, rows (records), and columns (fields) and the mathematical idea of a set. Here we illustrate a simple SQL command using the Rental Vehicles database from Clem's Transportation Rental ("If it moves, we rent it."). Here's a complete listing of the database records:

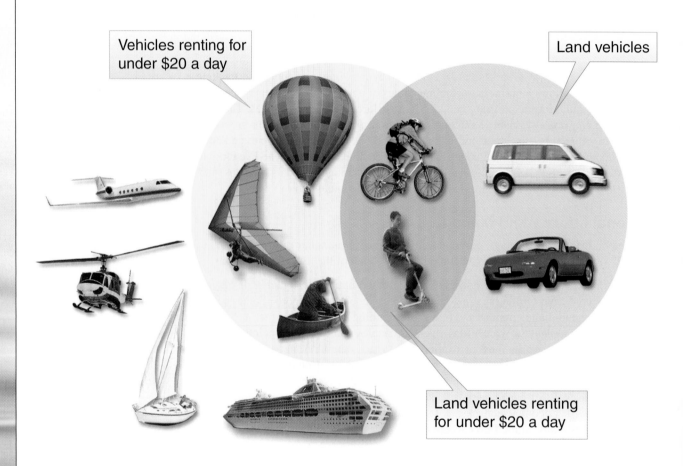

Vehicles renting for under $20 a day

Land vehicles

Land vehicles renting for under $20 a day

7.8

Vehicle_ID	Vehicle_Type	Transport_Mode	Num_Passengers	Cargo_Capacity	Rental_Price
1062	Helicopter	Air	6	500	$1,250.00
1955	Canoe	Water	2	30	$5.00
2784	Automobile	Land	4	250	$45.00
0213	Scooter	Land	1	0	$10.00
0019	Minibus	Land	8	375	$130.00
3747	Balloon	Air	3	120	$340.00
7288	HangGlider	Air	1	5	$17.00
9430	Sailboat	Water	8	200	$275.00
8714	Powerboat	Water	4	175	$210.00
0441	Bicycle	Land	1	10	$12.00
4759	Jet	Air	9	2300	$2,900.00

A typical SQL statement filters the records of a database, capturing only those that meet the specific criteria. For example, suppose you wanted to list the ID numbers and types of the vehicles that travel on land and cost less than $20.00 per day. The SQL statement to perform this task would look like this:

```
SELECT Vehicle_ID, Vehicle_Type FROM Rental_Vehicles WHERE
Transport_Mode = 'Land' AND Rental_Price < 20.00
```

In English, this SQL statement says, "Show me (from the Rental Vehicles database) the vehicle IDs and vehicle types for those vehicles that travel by land and cost less than $20.00 per day to rent."

Two rows in the database meet these criteria, the scooter and bicycle:

```
0213 Scooter
0441 Bicycle
```

The selection rules for SQL are consistent and understandable whether queries are simple or complex. This simple example is designed to give you an idea of how they work.

Screen Test

Synchronizing Data Between Outlook and Portable Devices

GOAL *To ensure the calendar and contacts list on your PC and all of your portable devices are up to date.*

HARDWARE TOOLS *PC computer, Apple iPod, Nokia 6800 phone, Palm Tungsten T3 personal digital assistant (PDA), connector cables*

SOFTWARE TOOLS *Microsoft Outlook, iPodSync, Nokia PC Sync, Palm Outlook Conduits*

1. Microsoft Outlook contains your contact list of names and phone numbers.

2. Outlook also maintains your calendar containing appointments and important dates.

3. You need third-party synchronization software to exchange data between Outlook and your portable devices. You can acquire synchronization utilities from portable device manufacturers or independent software companies.

4. Each portable device has a cable connecting it to a USB port on the PC.

5. A third-party program, such as iPodSync, can connect your iPod to Outlook and download the calendar and contact list.

6. Nokia's PC Sync program synchronizes the Nokia 6800's contacts list and calendar with the information on your PC.

7. Palm Outlook Conduit synchronizes the Tungsten T3 with the information on the PC.

7.9

Beyond the Basics: Database Management Systems

So far we've used simple examples to illustrate concepts common to most database programs. This oversimplification is useful for understanding the basics, but it's not the whole story. In truth, database programs range from simple mailing label programs to massive financial information systems, and it's important to know a little about what makes them different as well as what makes them alike.

> When we try to pick out **anything**, we find it hitched to **everything else in the universe**.
>
> *—John Muir, first director of the National Park Service*

From File Managers to Database Management Systems

Technically speaking, many consumer databases and PIM programs aren't really database managers at all; they're file managers. A **file manager** is a program that enables users to work with one file at a time. A true **database-management system (DBMS)** is a program or system of programs that can manipulate data in a large collection of files—the data-

Transcript file	Financial info file	Class list file
Student ID	Student ID	Course Number
Name	Name	Department
Local Street Address	Local Street Address	Section Number
Apartment No.	Apartment No.	Instructor
City	City	Time
State	State	Location
Zip	Zip	Number of Students
Permanent Street Address	Permanent Street Address	
Apartment No.	Apartment No.	(Student 1 Information)
City	City	Student ID
State	State	Name
Zip	Zip	Class Standing
Sex	Sex	Major
Citizenship	Citizenship	
Year Admitted	Year Admitted	(Student 2 Information)
Class Standing	Class Standing	Student ID
Major	Major	Name
GPA	GPA	Class Standing
		Major
(Course 1 information)		
Department	Tuition	
Number	Deposits	
Credits	Registration Fees	
Grade	Parking Fees	
Date	Housing Fees	
	Lab Fees	
(Course 2 information)		
Department		

7.10 Student information is duplicated in several different files of this poorly designed, error-prone database.

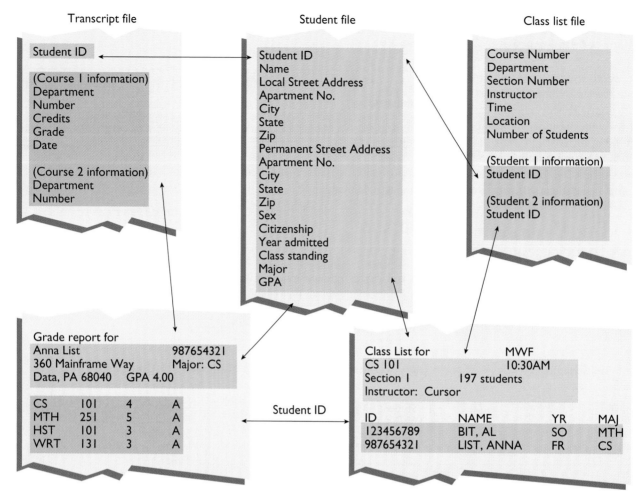

Transcript file Student file Class list file

7.11 The Student table serves as a reference when grade reports and class lists are created. The Student ID fields in the Transcript table and the Class List table are used as a key for locating the necessary student information in the Student table.

base—cross-referencing between files as needed. You can use a DBMS interactively, or control it directly through other programs. A file manager is sufficient for mailing lists and other common data management applications. But for many large, complex jobs there's no substitute for a true database-management system.

Consider, for example, the problem of managing student information at a college. It's easy to see how databases might be used to store this information: a table containing one record for each student, with fields for name, student ID number, address, phone, and so on. But a typical student generates far too much information to store practically in a single table.

Most schools choose to keep several tables containing student information: one for financial records, one for course enrollment and grade transcripts, and so on. Each of these tables has a single record for each student. In addition, a school must maintain class enrollment tables with one record for each class and fields for information on each student enrolled in the class. Three of these tables might be organized as shown in the accompanying figure.

In this database, each of the three separate tables contains basic information about every student. This redundant data not only occupies expensive storage space but also makes it difficult to ensure that student information is accurate and up to date. If a student moves to a different address, several files must be updated to reflect this change. The more changes, the greater the likelihood of a data-entry error.

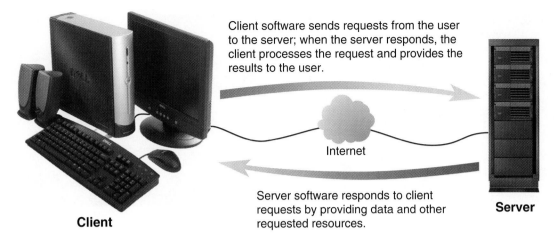

Client software sends requests from the user to the server; when the server responds, the client processes the request and provides the results to the user.

Internet

Server software responds to client requests by providing data and other requested resources.

Client

Server

7.12 Client/server computing involves two-way communications between applications running on the "client" PC and the "server" PC.

With a DBMS there's no need to store all this information in every table. The database can include a basic student table containing demographic information—information that's unique for each student. Because the demographic information is stored in a separate table, it doesn't need to be included in the financial information table, the transcript table, the class list table, or any other table. The student ID number, included in each table, serves as a *key field*; it unlocks the relevant student information in the student table when it's needed elsewhere. The student ID field is, in effect, shared by all tables that use data from this table. If the student moves, the change of address need only be recorded in one place. Databases organized in this way are called *relational databases*.

What Makes a Database Relational?

To most users, a **relational database** program is one that allows tables to be related to each other so that changes in one table are reflected in other tables automatically. To computer scientists, the term *relational database* has a technical definition related to the underlying structure of the data and the rules specifying how that data can be manipulated.

The structure of a relational database is based on the relational model—a mathematical model that combines data in tables. Other kinds of database-management systems are based on different theoretical models, with different technical advantages and disadvantages. But the majority of DBMSs in use today, including virtually all PC-based database-management systems, use the relational model. So from the average computer user's point of view, the distinction between the popular and technical definitions of *relational* is academic.

In the late 1970s Oracle Corporation produced the first commercial relational-database system. Large companies with massive amounts of information to store and retrieve discovered that the relational database model was much more versatile than previous systems were. Oracle Corporation quickly became an industry powerhouse. Today more than half of the FORTUNE 100 companies use Oracle software to manage their databases.

The Many Faces of Databases

Large databases often contain hundreds of interrelated tables. This maze of information could be overwhelming to users if they were forced to deal with it directly. Fortunately, a database-management system can shield users from the complex inner workings of the system, providing them with only the information and commands they need to get their jobs done. In fact, a well-designed database puts on different faces for different classes of users.

Clerk's view

Video rental view used by clerks to access renter information, scan bar codes on videos, and print rental invoices

Video store database

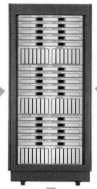

Manager's view

- Inventory-tracking view used by managers to check on rental history and inventory for individual movies
- Policy view used by managers to change pricing, membership, and other policies

Technician/programmer's view

Technical view used by programmer to create other user interfaces and custom queries

7.13 Clerks, managers, programmers, and customers see different views of a movie rental store's database. Customers can browse through listings and reviews of available movies using a touch-screen kiosk. The clerk's view allows for only simple data-entry and checkout procedures. The manager, working with the same database, has control over pricing, policies, and inventory but can't change the structure or user interface of the database. The programmer can work under the hood to fine-tune and customize the database so it can better meet the needs of other employees and customers.

Retail clerks don't need to be able to access every piece of information in the store's database; they just need to enter sales transactions on point-of-sale terminals. Databases designed for retail outlets generally include simple, straightforward terminal interfaces that give the clerks only the information, and the power, they need to process transactions. Managers, accountants, data processing specialists, and customers see the database from different points of view because they need to work with the data in different ways.

Database Trends

It is better to ask **some of the questions** than to know **all of the answers**.

—James Thurber, in Fables for Our Time

Database technology isn't static. Advances in the last two decades have changed the way most organizations deal with data, and current trends suggest even bigger changes in the near future.

Real-Time Computing

The earliest file-management programs could do only **batch processing**, which required computer operators to accumulate transactions and feed them into computers in large batches. These batch systems weren't able to provide the kind of immediate feedback we expect today. Questions like "What's the balance in my checking account?" or "Are there any open flights to Denver next Tuesday?" were likely to be answered "Those records will be updated tonight, so we'll let you know tomorrow."

Today, disk drives, inexpensive memory, and sophisticated software have allowed **interactive processing** to replace batch processing for most applications. Users can now interact with data through terminals, viewing and changing values online in **real time**. Batch processing is still used for printing periodic paychecks, bills, invoices, and reports and for making backup copies of data files—jobs for which it makes sense to do a lot of transactions at once. But for applications that demand immediacy, such as airline reservations, banking transactions, and the like, interactive, multiuser database systems have taken over. These systems are typically run on powerful servers and accessed by users remotely. Oracle, IBM, Microsoft and other companies create the *database servers* used by businesses of all sizes around the world.

This trend toward real-time computing is accelerated by the Internet, which makes it possible to have almost instant access to information stored in databases from anywhere on Earth, inside or outside the boundaries of the enterprise.

Downsizing and Decentralizing

In the pre-PC days, most databases were housed in mainframe computers accessible only to information-processing personnel. But the traditional hard-to-access **centralized database** on a mainframe system is no longer the norm.

Today, many businesses use a **client/server** approach employing database servers: *Client* programs in desktop computers, notebooks, PDAs, or other devices send information requests through a network or the Internet to database servers or mainframe databases; these *servers* process queries and send the requested data back to the client. A client/server system enables users to take advantage of the PC's simple user interface and convenience, while still having access to data stored on large server systems.

Some corporations keep copies of all corporate data in integrated **data warehouses**. In some respects, data warehouses are similar to old-style systems: They're large, relatively expensive, and centralized. But unlike older centralized systems, data warehouses give users more direct access to enterprise data. Data warehouses are most commonly found in large corporations and government departments.

Some companies use **distributed databases**, which spread data across networks on several different computers rather than store it in one central site. Many organizations have data warehouses and distributed databases. From the user's point of view, the differences between these approaches may not be apparent. Connectivity software, sometimes called *middleware*, links the client and server machines, hiding the complexity of the interaction between those machines and creating a *three-tier* design that separates the actual data from the programming logic used to access it. No matter how the data is stored, accessed, and retrieved, the goal is to provide quick and easy access to important information.

Data Mining

Today's technology makes it easy for a business to accumulate masses of information in a database. Many organizations are content to retrieve information using the queries, searches, and reports. But others are finding that there's gold hidden in their large databases—gold that can be extracted only by using a new technology called *data mining*. Data mining is the discovery and extraction of hidden predictive information from large databases. It uses statistical methods and artificial intelligence technology to locate trends and patterns in data that would have been overlooked by normal database queries. For example, a grocery chain used data mining to discover differences between male and female shopping patterns so they could create gender-specific marketing campaigns. (In an industry ad, they announced that some men habitually buy beer and diapers every Friday!) In effect, data-mining technology enables users to "drill down" through masses of data to find valuable veins of information.

Databases and the Web

Many businesses are retooling to take advantage of Internet technology on their internal networks. These *intranets* enable employees to access corporate databases using the same Web browsers and search engines they use to access information outside the company networks. As Internet tools rapidly evolve, database access should become easier and more transparent.

HTML, the language used to construct most Web pages, wasn't designed to build database queries. But a newer, more powerful data description language called XML is designed with industrial-strength database access in mind. Database manufacturers are currently retooling their products so they can process data requests in XML. Because XML can serve as a query language and as a Web page construction tool, it's likely to open up all kinds of databases to the Web, making it easy for you to request and receive information online.

For many organizations, Web database strategies revolve around *directories*. Directories were originally little more than repositories for user phone numbers, addresses, and passwords, and they were commonly buried inside network operating systems. But the explosive growth of the Internet and of e-commerce has expanded the roles of directories for many organizations. Directories can be used to store basic employee and customer information, along with access policies, identity proof, payment information, and security information. Directories are at the heart of many *customer relationship management (CRM)* systems—software systems for organizing and tracking information on customers.

The Web makes it possible for employees and customers alike to have instant access to databases, opening up all kinds of rapid-response e-commerce possibilities. But this kind of broad real-time database access also increases the probability of data errors and the importance of eliminating those errors as quickly as possible.

Data records containing errors are called dirty data. Examples of dirty data are records with spelling or punctuation mistakes, incorrect values, or obsolete values. If you receive a mail order catalog addressed to the prior resident at your address, that's an example of dirty data in the mail order company's database.

High data quality is a critical factor in successful e-commerce. Dirty data can lead to inefficiency, incomplete or incorrect record matching, and bad business decisions. Most large databases use data-checking routines whenever data is entered. But many organizations also depend on software to correct errors that make it though the entry checks. Data scrubbing (also called data cleansing) is the process of going through a database and eliminating dirty data. For errors that aren't corrected by automated cleansing tools, the last wall of defense is typically a human customer service representative who can provide rapid response to customer complaints.

Dealing with Databases

Whether you're creating an address file with a simple file manager or retrieving data from a full-blown relational database management system, you can save yourself a great deal of time and grief if you follow a few common-sense rules:

➡ **Choose the right tool for the job.** Don't invest time and money in a programmable relational database to computerize your address book, and don't try to run the affairs of your multinational corporation with a spreadsheet list manager.

➡ **Think about how you'll get the information out before you put it in.** What kinds of tables, records, and fields will you need to create to make it easy to find things quickly and print things the way you'll want them? For example, use separate fields for first and last name if you want to sort names alphabetically by last name and print first names first.

➡ **Start with a plan, and be prepared to change your plan.** It's a good idea to do a trial run with a small amount of data to make sure everything works the way you think it should.

➡ **Make your data consistent.** Inconsistencies can mess up sorting and make searching difficult. For example, if a database includes residents of Minnesota, Minn., and MN, it's hard to group people by state.

➡ **Databases are only as good as their data is.** When entering data, take advantage of the data-checking capability of your database software. Does the first name field contain nonalphabetic characters? Is the birth date within a reasonable range? Automatic data checking is important, but it's no substitute for human proofreading or for a bit of skepticism when using the database.

➡ **Query with care.** In the words of Aldous Huxley, "People always get what they ask for; the only trouble is that they never know, until they get it, what it actually is that they have asked for." Here's a real example: A student searching a database of classic rock albums requested all records containing the string "Dylan," and the database program obediently displayed the names of several Bob Dylan albums . . . plus one by Jimi Hendrix called Electric Ladyland. Why? Because "dylan" is in Ladyland! Unwanted records can go unnoticed in large database selections, so it's important to define selection rules very carefully.

➡ **If at first you don't succeed, try another approach.** If your search doesn't turn up the answers you were looking for, it doesn't mean the answers aren't there; they may just be wearing a disguise. If you search a standard library database, such as Questia, for "Vietnam War" references, you might miss hundreds of them. Why? Because the government officially classifies the Vietnam War as a conflict, so many references are stored under the subject "Vietnam Conflict." Technology meets bureaucracy!

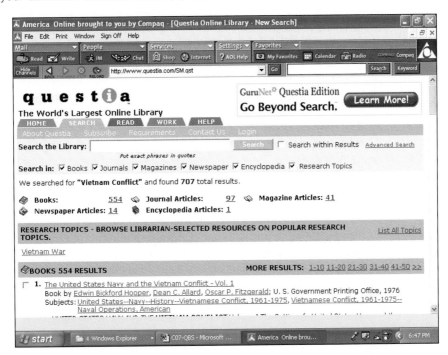

7.14 Library database Questia returns hundreds of hits for the search "Vietnam conflict."

Object-Oriented Databases

Some of the biggest changes in database technology in the next few years may take place under the surface, where they may not be apparent to most users. For example, many computer scientists believe that the relational data model will be supplanted in the next decade by an object-oriented data model and that most future databases will be **object-oriented databases** rather than relational databases. Instead of storing records in tables and hierarchies, object-oriented databases store *objects*. Every object is an instance of a *class*. The class specifies the data contained in the object as well as the kinds of operations that may be performed on the data.

For example, imagine an object-oriented database containing various kinds of images. Within the database is a class for photographs. There is one instance of this class—one object—for every photograph in the database. The data associated with this object are the name of the photographer, a description of the photograph, its copyright status, and the image itself. One of the operations associated with this class is producing a thumbnail-sized miniature of the photo. The association of actions along with the data distinguishes object-oriented databases from relational databases, which do not have this capability.

Compared to relational databases, object-oriented databases make it easier to manipulate many different types of data. They can store and retrieve unstructured data, such as audio and video clips, more efficiently. Programmers developing a new database can save time by reusing objects. For these reasons, designers of multimedia information-management systems are taking a hard look at object-oriented databases. Many companies are experimenting with databases that combine relational and object concepts into hybrid systems. Users will find databases more flexible and responsive as object technology becomes more widespread, even if they aren't aware of the underlying technological reasons for these improvements.

Multimedia Databases

Today's databases can efficiently store all kinds of text and numeric data. But today's computers are multimedia machines that routinely deal with pictures, sounds, animation, and video clips. Multimedia databases can handle graphical and dynamic data along with text and numbers. Multimedia professionals use databases to catalog art, photographs, maps, video clips, sound files, and other types of media files. Media files aren't generally stored in databases because they're too large. Instead, a multimedia database serves as an *index* to all of the separately stored files.

Multimedia databases have applications in law enforcement, medicine, entertainment, and other professions where information needs go beyond words and numbers. In one high-profile example, IBM and Sony are transferring 115,000 hours worth of CNN videotape into a digital database. This database enables CNN producers to work more efficiently with archived clips, but it also opens up the possibility of pay-per-view Web access by consumers through the Internet and wireless devices.

Natural Language Databases

Ultimately, database technology will all but disappear from the user's view as interfaces become simpler, more powerful, and more intelligent. Future databases will undoubtedly incorporate more artificial intelligence technology. We're already seeing databases and data-mining software that can respond to simple *natural language* queries—queries in English or some other human language. Many help sites and search engines on the Web can accept queries in English, German, French, Japanese, and several other languages. Today's natural language technology is far from perfect, but it's getting better quickly. It won't be long before you'll be able to use the same language you use when addressing a human being to ask for data from a computer system.

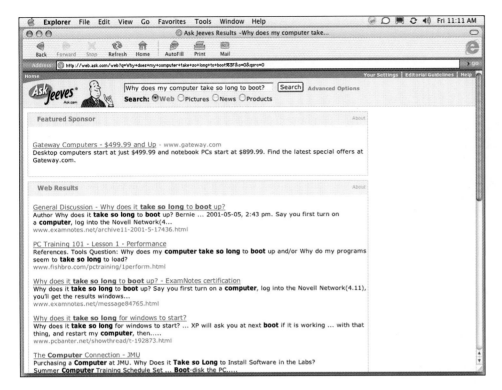

7.15 www.askJeeves.com enables users to ask questions about computers by stating their queries in plain English and other natural languages.

No Secrets:
Computers and Privacy

Instant airline reservations, all-night automated banking, overnight mail, instant library searches, Web shopping—databases provide us with conveniences that were unthinkable a generation ago. But convenience isn't free. In the case of databases, we pay with our privacy.

Advanced technology has created **new opportunities** for America as a nation, but it has also created the possibility for **new abuses** of the individual American citizen. Adequate safeguards must always **stand watch** so that man remains **master** and never the **victim of the computer**.

—Richard Nixon, 37th president of the United States, Feb. 23, 1974

What, exactly, is **privacy**? While experts may disagree on the definition, a common theme in privacy discussions is the notion of access, where *access* means physical proximity to a person or knowledge about that person. People need a certain amount of privacy to maintain their dignity and freedom. (How much freedom and dignity would you have if everyone could read your mind?) On the other hand, information about people can have great value to a society. Direct mail companies can save a great deal of money, and reduce waste, by sending catalogs only to those people who may make a purchase. Many parents want to know the identities of convicted sex offenders living in their neighborhoods. These conflicting desires lead to some interesting dilemmas, especially when computers make gathering, storing, and retrieving information easier than ever.

Personal Data: All About You

You have **zero privacy** anyway. **Get over it**.

— Scott McNealy, founder and CEO of Sun Microsystems

7.16 Subscribers to *Reason* magazine received a personalized issue in June 2004 that had a satellite photo of their home or workplace on the cover.

We live in an information age, and data is one of the currencies of our time. Businesses and government agencies spend billions of dollars every year to collect and exchange information about you and me. More than 15,000 specialized marketing databases contain two billion consumer names, along with a surprising amount of personal information. The typical American consumer is on at least 25 marketing lists. Many of these lists are organized by characteristics, such as age, income, religion, political affiliation, and even sexual preference, and they're bought and sold every day.

Marketing databases are only the tip of the iceberg. Credit and banking information, tax records, health data, insurance records, political contributions, voter registration, credit card purchases, warranty registrations, magazine and newsletter subscriptions, phone calls, passport registration, airline reservations, automobile registrations, arrests, and Internet explorations are all recorded in computers, and we have little or no control over what happens to most of those records after they're collected.

For most of us, this data is out of sight and out of mind. But lives are changed because of these databases. Here are some representative stories:

■ When members of Congress investigated ties between President Jimmy Carter's brother Billy and the government of Libya, they produced a report that detailed, among other things, the exact time and location of phone calls placed by Billy Carter in three different states. The phone records, which revealed a great deal about Billy Carter's activities, were obtained from AT&T's massive network of data-collecting computers. Similar information is available on every phone company customer.

7.17 The Internal Revenue Service workers shown here enter taxpayers' financial information into massive computer databases. When you shop by phone, respond to a survey, or fill out a warranty card, it's likely that a clerk somewhere will enter that data into a computer.

- When a credit bureau mistakenly placed a bankruptcy filing in the file of a St. Louis couple, banks responded by shutting off loans for their struggling construction business, forcing them into real bankruptcy. They sued but lost because credit bureaus are protected by law from financial responsibility for "honest" mistakes!

- A Los Angeles thief stole a wallet and used its contents to establish an artificial identity. When the thief was arrested for a robbery involving murder, the crime was recorded under the wallet owner's name in police databases. The legitimate owner of the wallet was arrested five times in the following 14 months and spent several days in jail before a protracted court battle resulted in the deletion of the record.

- In a more recent, more typical example of identity theft, an imposter had the mail of an innocent individual temporarily forwarded to a post office box so he could easily collect credit card numbers and other personal data. By the time the victim discovered an overdue Visa bill, the thief had racked up $42,000 in bogus charges. The victim wasn't liable for the charges, but it took the better part of a year to correct all of the credit bureau errors.

As these examples indicate, there are many ways that abuse and misuse of databases can take away personal privacy. Sometimes privacy violations are due to government surveillance activities. Sometimes they're the result of the work of private corporations. Privacy breaches may be innocent mistakes, strategic actions, or malicious mischief. The explosive growth of identity theft, which claims millions of victims each year, makes it clear that database technology can be a powerful criminal tool.

Privacy violations aren't new, and they don't always involve computers. The German Nazis, the Chinese Communists, and even Richard Nixon's 1972 campaign committee practiced surveillance without computers. But the privacy problem takes on a whole new dimension in the age of high-speed computers and databases. The same characteristics that make databases more efficient than other information storage methods—storage capacity, retrieval speed, organizational flexibility, and ease of distribution of information—also make them a threat to our privacy.

7.18 This poster was part of a 2004 campaign to educate the public about identity theft.

The Privacy Problem

In George Orwell's *1984*, information about every citizen was stored in a massive database controlled by the ever-vigilant Big Brother. Today's data warehouses in many ways resemble Big Brother's database. Data-mining techniques can be used to extract information about individuals and groups without their knowledge or consent. And database information can be easily sold or used for purposes other than those for which it was collected. Most of the time this kind of activity goes unnoticed by the public. Here are some examples where public knowledge changed privacy policy:

> What has taken me **a lifetime to build**—my trust, my integrity and my identity—has been **tainted**. I don't know if I'm dealing with a **14-year-old messing around with a computer** or if I'm dealing with **organized crime**.
>
> —*Identity theft victim*

Working Wisdom

Your Private Rights

Sometimes computer-aided privacy violations are nuisances; sometimes they're threats to life, liberty, and the pursuit of happiness. Here are a few tips for protecting your right to privacy.

➡ ***Your Social Security number is yours; don't give it away.*** Since your SSN is a unique identifier, it can be used to gather information about you without your permission or knowledge. For example, you could be denied a job or insurance because of something you once put on a medical form. Never write it (or your driver's license number or phone number, for that matter) on a check or credit card receipt. Don't give your SSN to anyone unless they have a legitimate reason to ask for it.

➡ ***Don't give away information about yourself.*** Don't answer questions about yourself just because a questionnaire or company representative asks you to. When you fill out any form—coupon, warranty registration card, survey, sweepstakes entry, or whatever—think about whether you want the information stored in somebody else's computer.

➡ ***Say no to direct mail, phone, and email solicitations.*** Businesses and political organizations pay for your data so they can target you for mail, phone, and email campaigns. You can remove yourself from many lists using forms from the Direct Mail Marketing Association (**www.the-dma.org**). You can block most telemarketers by enrolling in the U.S. Federal Trade Commission's Opt Out program (**www.donotcall. gov**). If these steps don't stop the flow, you might want to try a more direct approach. Send back unwanted letters along with "Take me off your list" requests in the postage-paid envelopes that come with them. When you receive an unsolicited phone marketing call, tell the caller, "I never purchase or donate anything as a result of phone solicitations," and ask to be removed from the list. If they call within 12 months of being specifically told not to, you can sue and recover up to $500 per call according to the Telephone Consumer Protection Act of 1991. Unfortunately, the federal anti-spam law (the CAN SPAM Act) has proven to be ineffective, so you should be especially careful about giving out your email address if you don't like receiving unsolicited email.

➡ ***Say no to sharing your personal information.*** If you open a private Internet account, tell your Internet service provider that your personal data is not for sale. If you don't want your state's Department of Motor Vehicles selling information about you, notify them. A relatively new federal law gives you more control over DMV use of personal data. If you don't want credit agencies sharing personal information, let them know. The Federal Trade Commission's Privacy Web site (**www.ftc.gov/privacy**) includes clear guidelines and forms for contacting your DMV and credit agencies. The Financial Modernization Act of 1999 allows you to tell your banks and other financial institutions not to share your personal information with other institutions; check with those institutions for details.

➡ ***Say no to pollsters.*** Our political system has been radically transformed by polling; most of our "leaders" check the polls before they offer opinions on controversial issues. If you and I don't tell the pollsters what we're thinking, politicians may be more likely to tell us what they're thinking.

➡ ***If you think there's incorrect or damaging information about you in a file, find out.*** The Freedom of Information Act of 1966 requires that most U.S. government agencies records be made available to the

■ In 1999, Amazon.com introduced "Purchase Circles," a feature that allowed customers to see which books, CDs, tapes, and videos are most popular within particular companies, schools, government organizations, and cities. Amazon didn't make individual purchase information available to the public, but it used that information to create customer profiles for groups. Using these Purchase Circle profiles, Amazon's Web site might tell you the most popular books and videos among Microsoft employees, Stephens College students, or residents of Dedham, Massachusetts, for example. In response to protests, Amazon decided to give customers the option of being excluded from Purchase Circles.

■ In 1999, DoubleClick, an online advertising agency, acquired a direct marketing firm along with its database of 90 million households. The company intended to combine supposedly anonymous data on Web user activity with personal information from the massive consumer database, creating data files rich with personal data about consumers. In March 2000, responding to outcries from consumers and privacy watchdog groups, DoubleClick backed away from the data-matching plan, calling it a "big mistake" to try to match information in that way before government or industry standards could be put into place.

public on demand. The Privacy Act of 1974 requires federal agencies to provide you with information in your files related to you and to amend incorrect records. The Fair Credit Reporting Act of 1970 allows you to see your credit ratings—for free if you have been denied credit—and correct any errors. The three big credit bureaus are Equifax (**www.equifax.com**), Trans Union (**www.transunion.com**), and Experian (**www.experian.com**).

➡ *To maximize your privacy, minimize your profile.* If you don't want a financial transaction recorded, use cash. If you don't want your phone number to be public information, use an unlisted number. If you don't want your mailing address known, use a post office box.

➡ *Know your electronic rights.* Privacy protection laws in the United States lag far behind those of other high-tech nations, but they are beginning to appear. For example, the 1986 Electronic Communications Privacy Act provides the same protection that covers mail and telephone communication to some—but not all—electronic communications. The 1988 Computer Matching and Privacy Protection Act regulates the use of government data in determining eligibility for federal benefits.

➡ *Support organizations that fight for privacy rights.* If you value pri-

vacy rights, let your representatives know how you feel, and support the American Civil Liberties Union, Computer Professionals for Social Responsibility, the Electronic Frontier Foundation, the Electronic Privacy Information Center, the Center for Democracy and Technology, Private Citizen, and other organizations that fight for those rights.

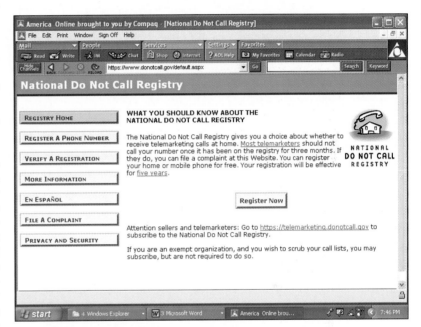

7.19 Tens of millions of households receive fewer telemarketing calls because they put their phone numbers in the free National Do Not Call Registry.

- Prior to February 2001, N2H2, an Internet filtering software company, sold to other companies "class clicks," which were made up of marketing research based on Web usage patterns of children. The company insists that its data didn't threaten any individual's privacy. Still, in response to protests, it stopped selling its data.

- After the terrorist attacks of September 11, 2001, the U.S. Department of Defense established the Information Awareness Office. The goal of the office was to identify potential terrorists by gathering information about people's activities in a central database and looking for patterns of suspicious activity. Privacy advocates were outraged to think that the credit card receipts, utility bills, travel reservations, and tax records of ordinary Americans would be collected and inspected by a government agency. Responding to the public outcry, Congress cut off funding to the Information Awareness Office in February 2003.

Centralized data warehouses aren't necessary for producing computerized dossiers of private citizens. With networked computers, it's easy to compile profiles by combining information from different databases. As long as the tables in the databases share a single unique

7.20 The National Crime Information Center database helped the FBI apprehend Timothy McVeigh, later convicted for his role in the bombing of the federal building in Oklahoma City.

7.21 With credit, we can travel long distances without carrying a large amount of cash. Credit bureau databases verify the reputable state of our finances.

field, such as a Social Security number field, **record matching** is trivial and quick. And when database information is combined, the whole is often far greater than the sum of its parts.

Sometimes the results of record matching are beneficial. The National Crime Information Center, managed by the FBI, contains more than 39 million records related to stolen automobiles, stolen or missing guns, missing persons, wanted persons, convicted persons, suspected terrorists, and more. The NCIC provided the FBI with the information it needed to identify James Earl Ray as the assassin of Dr. Martin Luther King, Jr. It helped the FBI track down Timothy McVeigh, the person convicted of bombing the Alfred P. Murrah Federal Building in Oklahoma City. Because the NCIC is accessible by state and local law enforcement agencies, it facilitates more than 100,000 arrests and the recovery of more than 100,000 stolen cars every year.

Another benefit of record matching is its use in establishing reputations. Because credit bureaus collect data about us, our financial trustworthiness becomes established in cyberspace. Businesses around the globe have access to this information, meaning we can use credit cards almost anywhere in the world. If we want to borrow money to purchase a house, banks around the nation will compete for our business. More competition means lower interest rates and lower monthly payments.

But these benefits come with at least three problems:

◼ *Data errors are common.* A study of 1,500 reports from the three big credit bureaus found errors in 43 percent of the files.

◼ *Data can become nearly immortal.* Because files are commonly sold and copied, it's impossible to delete or correct erroneous records with absolute certainty.

◼ *Data isn't secure.* A *Business Week* reporter demonstrated this in 1989 by using his computer to obtain then Vice President Dan Quayle's credit report. Had he been a skilled criminal, he might have been able to change that report.

The word *privacy* does not appear in the U.S. Constitution. While U.S. Supreme Court decisions have recognized that a **right to privacy** is implied by other constitutional guarantees, legal scholars continue to debate the extent of privacy rights.

The creation of computerized databases led to a general concern about an erosion of individuals' privacy rights. In the early 1970s, a panel of experts produced a report to Congress, which included a *Code of Fair Information Practices*. The Code suggested that there be no secret government databases, that individuals be able to access and correct information about themselves kept in government databases, and that agencies ensure the reliability and security of information kept in the databases.

7.22 Critics of the USA PATRIOT Act say it contradicts constitutionally guaranteed rights against unreasonable searches and seizures.

Surprisingly, the report had a much greater impact in Europe than in the United States. Nearly every European nation passed laws based on the Code of Fair Information Practices. State legislatures have been reluctant to pass laws based on the Code because of intense lobbying by business interests. Legislation passed by the U.S. Congress, called the Privacy Act of 1974, fell far short of the ambitions of privacy advocates. For example, it applies only to databases managed by the federal government; no one in the federal government is responsible for enforcing its provisions, and agencies can "opt out" of its requirements.

However, several key pieces of U.S. legislation have provided individuals with a cluster of privacy rights. The Fair Credit Reporting Act promotes the accuracy and privacy of information used by credit bureaus to create consumer credit reports. It puts limits on how long negative information can be kept on a person's credit report. The Family Education Rights and Privacy Act lets students (or the parents of minor students) access their educational records and request changes to erroneous records. The Video Privacy Protection Act prohibits videotape service providers from disclosing rental records without the consumer's written consent. The Children's Online Privacy Protection Act prohibits Internet-based businesses from collecting information from children 12 years old and younger without their parents' consent. The Health Insurance Portability and Accountability Act limits how doctors, hospitals, pharmacies, and insurance companies can use the medical information they collect from patients.

On the other hand, the USA PATRIOT Act, passed by the U.S. Congress in response to the September 11, 2001, attacks on the World Trade Center and the Pentagon, has made it easier for the FBI to collect certain kinds of information about individuals. The FBI can get a search warrant for educational, medical, business, library, and church/mosque/synagogue records simply by stating that they are related to an ongoing investigation. In other words, the FBI does not need to show probable cause. It is illegal for someone who has supplied such records to reveal the existence of the warrant. Critics of the USA PATRIOT Act, including the governments of more than 100 cities and several states, argue that the legislation weakens constitutional guarantees against unreasonable searches and seizures.

Big Brother and Big Business

If **all records** told the same tale, then **the lie** passed into history and **became truth**.

—George Orwell, in 1984

Database technology clearly poses a threat to personal privacy, but other information technologies amplify that threat:

- Networks make it possible for personal data to be transmitted almost anywhere instantly. The Internet is particularly fertile ground for collecting personal information about you. And the Web makes it alarmingly easy for anyone with a connected computer to examine your personal information.
- Microsoft's Passport, part of its .NET technologies, can optionally collect passwords, credit card numbers, and other consumer information in a central database controlled by Microsoft. The company's stated goal is to make it easier for its customers to take advantage of the Web's many services, but the potential for abuse of this technology may outweigh any possible gains in convenience. As a result, few consumers have taken advantage of these Passport features.
- Workplace monitoring technology enables managers to learn more than ever before about the work habits and patterns of workers. Supervisors can (and do) count keystrokes, monitor Web activity, screen email, and remotely view what's on the screens of employees.

7.23 Surveillance cameras can be used with facial recognition software to locate criminals, but they may also threaten the privacy of law-abiding citizens.

- Surveillance cameras, increasingly used for nabbing routine traffic violators and detecting security violators, can be combined with picture databases to locate criminals and others. Florida law enforcement officials came under fire from privacy groups because they used cameras, face-recognition software, and criminal databases to find and arrest several attendees of the 2001 Super Bowl. After the terrorist attacks of September 11, 2001, surveillance cameras were installed in hundreds of businesses and government agencies to guard against future attacks.
- Surveillance satellites can provide permanent peepholes into our lives for anyone willing to pay the price.
- Cell phones are now required by law to include technology to determine and transmit their locations to emergency personnel responding to 911 calls. Privacy advocates point out that the same technology can easily be used for less noble purposes.

In George Orwell's *1984*, personal privacy was the victim of a centralized Communist police state controlled by Big Brother. Today, our privacy is threatened by many Big Brothers—with new threats emerging almost every day. As Simson Garfinkel says in *Database Nation*, "Over the next 50 years, we will see new kinds of threats to privacy that don't find their roots in totalitarianism, but in capitalism, the free market, advanced technology, and the unbridled exchange of electronic information."

Democracy depends on the free flow of information, but it also depends on the protection of individual rights. Maintaining a balance is not easy, especially when new information technologies are being developed at such a rapid pace. With information at our fingertips, it's tempting to think that more information is the answer. But in the timeless words of populist philosopher Will Rogers, "It's not the things we don't know that get us into trouble, it's the things we do know that ain't so."

Inventing the FUTURE

Embedded Intelligence and Ubiquitous Computing

Computers are disappearing into more of our tools all the time. Information appliances, including cell phones, fax machines, and GPS devices, perform their specialized functions while hiding the technological details from their users. Dozens of household appliances and tools have invisible computers. Even our cars process megabytes of information as we drive down the road.

Some car computers are invisible; others are more obvious. Several companies have introduced dashboard computers that can play CDs and DVDs, recognize spoken commands, alert the driver to incoming email messages, read those messages aloud, store and retrieve contacts and appointments, dial phone numbers, recite directions using GPS-based navigation systems, report mechanical problems, and even track stolen vehicles. IBM researchers are developing an in-dash "artificial passenger" to make commuting safer for drivers. This intelligent agent carries on conversations, watching for signs of fatigue in the driver. If it finds them, it might change the radio station, open a window, or even spray the driver with cold water. In 2001, Volkswagen AG became the first automobile company to mass-produce a car with an Internet connection. (Appropriately, the VW eGeneration was initially sold only on the Net.)

Computers may soon be part of our clothing, too. Most of today's *wearable computers* are strap-on units for active information gatherers. But researchers at MIT and elsewhere are stitching CPUs, keyboards, and touchpads right into the clothes, turning their wearers into wireless Internet nodes. These digital outfits aren't just high-tech fashion statements—when worn with eyeglass monitors (described in Chapter 3's Inventing the Future Box [p. 130]), they might be invaluable for any number of jobs that require both activity and connectivity.

In Japan, computer technology has even found its way into the bathroom. A number of Japanese fixture manufacturers sell computer-controlled smart toilets. Some models automatically collect and store information on blood pressure, pulse, temperature, urine, and weight. The information can be displayed on a LCD display, accumulated for months, and even transmitted by modem to a medical service. Users of these smart toilets get a minicheckup whenever they visit the bathroom. Body-monitoring features give the toilet an entirely new function—a function are that will undoubtedly save lives.

When computers show up in our toilets, we're clearly entering an era of ubiquitous computers—computers everywhere. For several years, researchers at Xerox PARC, Cambridge University, Olivetti, and elsewhere have been experimenting with technology that will make computers even more ubiquitous. PARC's Mark Weiser describes an experimental office equipped with intelligent devices, including smart badges described in Chapter 10: "Doors open only to the right badge wearer, rooms greet people by name, telephone calls can be automatically forwarded to wherever the recipient may be, receptionists actually know where people are, computer terminals retrieve the preferences of whoever is sitting at them, and appointment diaries write themselves." ～

7.24 A dashboard GPS-based navigator is an example of a visible embedded computer system, unlike the computers controlling the engine and the airbags, which are invisible to the driver.

Privacy and Security: Finding a Balance *Michael J. Miller*

After the terrorist attacks of September 11, 2001, security jumped to the forefront of the political landscape. Many laws quickly passed to strengthen U.S. security reduced the privacy of U.S. citizens and others. This article, first published in the April 29, 2003, issue of PC Magazine, *clearly describes the delicate balance between security and privacy.*

Over the past year and a half, the tug of war between privacy and security has reached a new level, and I'm not convinced that people are willing to give up their privacy in pursuit of security. Of course, I'm willing to put up with inconveniences at airports and office buildings; I'm now accustomed to removing my shoes before going through airport metal detectors, and I've had my photo taken many times before getting into elevators in office buildings. But I do have a problem with indiscriminate data gathering that invades people's privacy without really improving security.

The mass collection of personal information and subsequent mining of that data will not solve the security problem. Instead, the government ends up with far more information than any person or any computer can analyze. The problem behind the 9/11 attacks was not that the government had too little information. Rather, it had so much information that it couldn't tell what was important.

Data mining is problematic because it results in extensive watch lists of people who share "suspicious" traits, such as an Arabic surname or a fondness for movies about airplanes. But so many people end up on these lists that the lists become an inefficient way of finding the bad guys. Data mining is better for building a case after the fact than for preventing an attack. The massive data collection measures are more effective at trampling our privacy.

Several technology developments for gathering, sorting, mining, and distributing all kinds of information about people pose potential threats to privacy. Here are just a few of them.

All sorts of records are now digitized. Everything from tax returns and legal settlements to sales receipts is now in digital format, which can be easily copied.

Databases have proliferated. Since everyone from your bank to your local dry cleaner is storing customer information in a database, large data repositories are inviting targets for hackers. Databases also make it easier for people to look up information they have no business accessing.

Databases are increasingly linked. New application integration technologies, such as Web services, are designed to tie databases together easily, allowing business intelligence software to pinpoint specific information in multiple databases.

The Internet makes collecting, sharing, and sending information easy.

Inexpensive digital cameras, particularly Webcams, let people capture images wherever they go.

These technologies are here to stay, and their potential for both good and evil is real. Recently, the NYPD made the right decision to destroy a database it had created of antiwar protesters' prior political activities. But other uses of data-gathering technologies have me concerned.

Under the USA PATRIOT Act, libraries and bookstores can be required to turn over their patron records. This information used to be considered private. The American Library Association has opposed this legislation, and some libraries have been very public about shredding their records.

Meanwhile, the U.S. Department of Defense's Total Information Awareness research project is looking into surveillance through mass data mining of all sorts of public databases. And the Domestic Security Enhancement Act of 2003, now under discussion, would expand the government's power even more, letting it use a database to collect, analyze, and maintain DNA samples and other identification information from suspected terrorists. It would also enable the government to obtain information from private businesses without a subpoena.

In one camp are those who see these steps as necessary measures in the fight against terrorism. I fall in the opposition camp of those who believe that the security gains aren't worth the intrusion of privacy, which I consider a fundamental freedom. Even more disturbing, most of these new restrictions are being implemented after very little public debate.

So we're left with some difficult problems, and I don't have the answers. But I can suggest some safeguards, such as legislated encryption of identifying data to eliminate or minimize abuse of such data, legislated access to one's own records to correct errors, creation of an oversight panel to put a stop to spurious data collection, and a continuing requirement for judicial oversight and subpoenas for the collection of private information.

Most Americans think they have a right to privacy. But check the Constitution: It's not stated there explicitly. If you want to protect your privacy, you need to get involved in the debate now. Some legislators are pressing for changes to these new laws—some arguing for tighter limitations on the government and some for less, while others are trying to make the USA PATRIOT Act permanent. (It's currently set to expire at the end of 2005.)

Discussion Questions

1. Do you think libraries and bookstores should be required to turn over information about their patrons to the government? Why or why not?

2. Do you think increased use of database technology for security purposes is worth the threat to personal privacy? Justify your answer and give specific examples.

Summary

Database programs enable users to store, organize, retrieve, communicate, and manage large amounts of information quickly and efficiently. Each database is made up of tables, which are, in turn, collections of records, and each record is made up of fields containing text strings, numbers, and other chunks of information. Database programs enable users to view data in a variety of ways, sort records in any order, and print reports, mailing labels, and other custom printouts. A user can search for an individual record or select a group of records with a query.

While most database programs are general-purpose tools that can be used to create custom databases for any purpose, some are special-purpose tools programmed to perform a particular set of tasks. Geographical information systems, for example, combine maps and demographic information with data tables to provide new ways to look at data. Personal information managers provide automated address books, appointment calendars, to-do lists, and notebooks for busy individuals.

Many database programs are, technically speaking, file managers because they work with only one file at a time. Database-management systems (DBMSs) can work with several data sources at a time, cross-referencing information among files when appropriate. A DBMS can provide an efficient way to store and manage large quantities of information by eliminating the need for redundant information in different files. A well-designed database provides different views of the data to different classes of users so each user sees and manipulates only the information necessary for the job at hand.

The trend today is clearly away from large, centralized databases accessible only to data processing staff. Instead, most organizations are moving toward a client/server approach that enables users to access data stored in servers throughout the organization's network. While relational databases have been the norm for the past twenty years, a new focus on multimedia records and other complex data sets has sparked the development of object-oriented database systems.

The accumulation of data by government agencies and businesses is a growing threat to our right to privacy. Massive amounts of information about private citizens are collected and exchanged for a variety of purposes. Today's technology makes it easy to combine information from different databases, producing detailed profiles of individual citizens. Although there are many legitimate uses for these procedures, there's also a great potential for abuse. It's encouraging to reflect on the number of times that groups of citizens or their elected representatives have halted the deployment of systems that went too far.

Key Terms

Interactive Activities

1. The *Computer Confluence* CD-ROM contains self-test quiz questions related to this chapter, including multiple-choice, true or false, and matching questions.

2. The *Computer Confluence* Web site, http://www. computerconfluence.com, contains self-test exercises related to this chapter. Follow the instructions for tak-

ing a quiz. After you've completed your quiz, you can email the results to your instructor.

3. The Web site also contains open-ended discussion questions called Internet Explorations. Discuss one or more of the Internet Exploration questions at the section for this chapter.

True or False

1. In a typical database, a record contains the information related to one person, product, or event.

2. In a database, a numeric field can contain only computed formulas similar to formulas in spreadsheets.

3. Typical database software allows you to view one record at a time in form view or several records at a time in list view.

4. The most common type of database printout is called an export.

5. To query a database, you must learn at least some SQL, the universal query language of databases.

6. A database-management system (DBMS) can manipulate data in a large collection of files, cross-referencing them as needed.

7. XML is a middleware product designed to link Windows XP databases to HTML Web pages.

8. The right to privacy is explicitly guaranteed by the U.S. Constitution.

9. Democracy depends on the free flow of information and on the protection of individual rights; database technology threatens to upset the balance between these two principles.

10. Middleware is a special class of software designed to link databases in PDAs to databases in PCs.

Multiple Choice

1. Why do people use databases rather than paper-based filing systems for information-handling tasks?
   a. Databases make it easier to store large quantities of information.
   b. Databases make it easier to retrieve information quickly and flexibly.
   c. Databases make it easy to organize and reorganize information.
   d. Databases make it easy to print and distribute information in a variety of ways.
   e. All of the above

2. Early PC databases were simple file managers; today most of the jobs done with these programs can be performed easily and efficiently with
   a. Equation-solving software
   b. Financial-management software
   c. Spreadsheet software
   d. Word-processing software
   e. Authoring software

3. Which of these is the correct hierarchy for a standard database?
   a. Database, field, record, table
   b. Database, record, field, table
   c. Database, record, table, field
   d. Database, table, field, record
   e. Database, table, record, field

4. Which of these is not a specialized database program?
   a. A geographic information system
   b. A personal information manager (PIM)
   c. A program for organizing and managing photos
   d. The software that manages MP3 files in music players like the iPod
   e. All of these are specialized database programs.

5. Which of the following defines a relational database?
   a. A database that contains several related records
   b. A database that contains several related fields
   c. A database that has a relationship with other databases
   d. A database whose structure combines data in tables based on the relational model
   e. A database with more than 1,000 records

6. What is the purpose of a database query?
   a. To update information kept within a record
   b. To retrieve information from all appropriate records
   c. To count the number of records in the database
   d. To convert a relational database into an object-oriented database
   e. To delete the appropriate records

7. Because of advances in hardware and software, which of the following procedures can today's databases perform in real time?
   a. Batch processing
   b. Interactive processing
   c. Structured processing
   d. Unstructured processing
   e. File-management processing

8. A college's database administrator writes a program to examine the records of all its students over the past decade, looking for patterns that might explain why some students drop out. What is the administrator's program an example of?
   a. Browsing
   b. Interactive processing
   c. Data exporting
   d. Data importing
   e. Data mining

9. Data warehouses are similar in some ways to old-style centralized databases; but unlike those older systems, data warehouses
   a. Depend on middleware to produce reports
   b. Give users more direct access to enterprise data
   c. Are built on distributed database systems
   d. Are powered by simple file-management software
   e. All of the above

10. Which of these Web applications depends on database technology?
    a. Online auctions, such as eBay
    b. Search engines, such as Google
    c. Online stores, such as Amazon.com.
    d. Customer relationship management (CRM) systems
    e. All of the above

11. Object-oriented databases
    a. Are likely to replace relational databases for many applications in the coming decade
    b. Are likely to be replaced by relational databases for many applications in the coming decade
    c. Are likely to replace most distributed databases for many applications in the coming decade
    d. Are likely to be replaced by file managers for many applications in the coming decade
    e. Are not likely to become practical for the coming decade

12. Even without centralized data warehouses, how can government agencies quickly produce detailed dossiers on millions of private citizens?
    a. Through the World Wide Web
    b. By using XML technology
    c. Through record matching
    d. Through identity theft
    e. With middleware

13. What is the act of removing erroneous data from a database called?
    a. Data scrubbing
    b. Data deletion
    c. Data synchronization
    d. Data doodling
    e. Record matching

14. The Code of Fair Information Practices had the greatest impact in the legislation of
    a. The U.S. Congress
    b. State legislatures
    c. European governments
    d. The former Soviet Union
    e. The People's Republic of China

15. The USA PATRIOT Act has generated controversy because some say it weakens Constitutional guarantees against
    a. The separation of church and state
    b. Freedom of the press
    c. Self-incrimination
    d. Unreasonable searches and seizures
    e. All of the above

Review Questions

1. Define or describe each of the key terms listed in the Key Terms section. Check your answers in the glossary.

2. What is the difference between a file manager and a database-management system? How are they similar?

3. Describe the structure of a simple database. Use the terms *file*, *record*, and *field* in your description.

4. What is a query? Give examples of the kinds of questions that might be answered with a query.

5. What steps are involved in producing a standard multi-column business report from a database?

6. What are the advantages of personal information management software over paper notebook organizers? What are the disadvantages?

7. What does it mean to sort a data file?

8. How can a database be designed to reduce the likelihood of data-entry errors?

9. Describe how record matching is used to obtain information about you. Give an example.

10. Do we have a legal right to privacy? On what grounds?

11. Why are computers important in discussions of invasion of privacy?

Discussion Questions

1. Grade books, checkbooks, and other information collections can be managed with either a database program or a spreadsheet program. How would you decide which type of application is most appropriate for a given job?

2. What have you done this week that directly or indirectly involved a database? How would your week have been different in a world without databases?

3. How important is it to you to have instant access to your credit card and checking account balances? How often do you inquire about your balances?

4. "The computer is a great humanizing factor because it makes the individual more important. The more information we have on each individual, the more each individual counts." Do you agree with this statement by science fiction writer Isaac Asimov? Why or why not?

5. Suppose you have been incorrectly billed for $100 by a mail-order house. Your protestations are ignored by the company, which is now threatening to report you to a collection agency. What do you do?

6. The National Crime Information Center (NCIC) allows local, state, and federal law enforcement personnel to share information with each other. What advantages and disadvantages does a computerized law enforcement system have for law-abiding citizens?

7. Would you be upset or worried if the FBI obtained copies of your educational, medical, and library records?

8. In what ways were George Orwell's "predictions" in the novel *1984* accurate? In what ways were they wrong?

Projects

1. Design a database for your own use. (If you're having a hard time thinking of a theme for the database, think about a database related to one of your hobbies. For example, if you like to bowl, you could create a database in which each record contains the date, the location where you bowled, the lane number(s), and your score(s).) Create several records, sort the data, and print a report.

2. Find out as much as you can about someone (for example, yourself or a public figure) from public records like tax records, court records, voter registration lists, and motor vehicle files. How much of this information were you able to get directly from the Web? How much was available for free?

3. Find out as much as you can about your own credit rating. The three major credit bureaus are Equifax (**www.equifax.com**), Experian (**www.experian.com**), and Trans Union (**www.transunion.com**).

4. The next time you order something by mail or phone, try encoding your name with a unique middle initial so you can recognize when the company sells your name and address to other companies. Use several different spellings for different orders if you want to do some comparative research.

5. Determine what information about you is stored in your school computers. What information are you allowed to see? What information are others allowed to see? Exactly who may access your files? Can you find out who sees your files? How long is the information retained after you leave school?

6. Keep track of your purchases for a few weeks. If other people had access to this information, what conclusions might they be able to draw about you? For example, could they estimate your income? Could they determine your hobbies? Would they be able to make an educated guess about your favorite kinds of food?

Sources and Resources

Books

Like word processors, spreadsheet software, and multimedia programs, databases have inspired hundreds of how-to tutorials, user's guides, and reference books. If you're working with a popular program, you should have no trouble finding a book to help you develop your skills.

Database Design for Mere Mortals: A Hands-On Guide to Relational Database Design, Second Edition, by Michael J. Hernandez (Reading, MA: Addison-Wesley Professional, 2003). This book can save time, money, and headaches for anyone who's involved in designing and building a relational database. After defining all the critical concepts, the author clearly outlines the design process using case studies to illustrate important points.

A Manager's Guide to Database Technology: Building and Purchasing Better Applications, by Michael R. Blaha (Upper Saddle River, NJ: Prentice Hall, 2001). This little book presents clear explanations of database technology and applications from a management perspective. The author does a good job of focusing on strategy rather than getting bogged down in technical details.

The Practical SQL Handbook: Using Structured Query Language, Third Edition, by Judith S. Bowman, Sandra L. Emerson, and Marcy Darnovsky (Reading, MA: Addison-Wesley, 1996). If you want to learn to communicate with relational databases using the standard database query language, this book can help you learn the language.

SQL Fundamentals, Second Edition, by John J. Patrick (Upper Saddle River, NJ: Prentice Hall, 2002). This introduction applies the principles of SQL to Microsoft Access and Oracle, two of the most widely used database products.

PHP and MySQL for Dynamic Web Sites: Visual QuickPro Guide, by Larry Ullman (Berkeley, CA: Peachpit Press, 2003). MySQL is the world's most popular open source database. A combination of PHP and MySQL can turn a static Web site into a dynamic, database-driven site. This book provides an introduction to this dynamic duo.

Data Smog: Surviving the Information Glut, Revised and Updated Edition, by David Shenk (New York: HarperEdge, 1998). It's possible to have too much information at your fingertips. David Shenk's book clearly describes the hazards to individuals and society of all this information.

Surveillance Society: Monitoring Everyday Life (Issues in Society), by David Lyon (Berkshire, UK: Open University Press, 2001). This book intelligently analyzes the deterioration of personal privacy in our information society without getting bogged down in jargon.

Database Nation: The Death of Privacy in the 21st Century, by Simson Garfinkel (Cambridge, MA: O'Reilly, 2001). This is a frightening, sobering account of the erosion of our personal privacy as a result of misuse of technology—databases, on-the-job monitoring, data networks, biometric devices, video surveillance, and more. Simson Garfinkel skillfully mixes chilling true stories and futuristic scenarios with practical advice for reclaiming our individual and collective rights to privacy. Highly recommended.

The Unwanted Gaze: The Destruction of Privacy in America, by Brian Doherty (New York: Knopf, 2001). This book ties together the impeachment of President Clinton with the threat computers present to our control over personal information. The unifying thread is the deterioration of the private space earlier generations of Americans enjoyed.

The Transparent Society: Will Technology Force Us to Choose Between Freedom and Privacy?, by David Brin (Cambridge, MA: Perseus Publishing, 1999). Brin, a mathematician and award-winning science fiction writer, presents a compelling case that personal privacy is doomed by technology. He argues that our best hope is to provide equal access to all information, rather than let the biggest brothers have the only windows into our lives. Compelling reading.

Videos

Many popular films and television shows, from *Clear and Present Danger* to *The X-Files*, deal directly or indirectly with issues related to privacy and technology. One recent action film, *Enemy of the State*, used those issues as central themes. There's plenty of fantasy in this nonstop thriller about a man on the run and a government that can watch his every move. But there's a good deal of truth here, too.

Periodicals

The Privacy Journal (http://www.privacyjournal.net). This widely quoted monthly newsletter covers all issues related to personal privacy.

Organizations

Privacy Foundation (http://www.privacyfoundation.org). The Privacy Foundation isn't an advocacy group; its mission is to report on technology-based privacy threats and circulate alerts.

Computer Professionals for Social Responsibility (http://www.cpsr.org). CPSR provides the public and policymakers with realistic assessments of the power, promise, and problems of information technology. Much of their work deals with privacy-related issues. Their newsletter is a good source of information.

The Electronic Frontier Foundation (http://www.eff.org). EFF strives to protect civil rights, including the right to privacy, on emerging communication networks.

Electronic Privacy Information Center (http://www.epic.org). EPIC serves as a watchdog over government efforts to build surveillance capabilities into the emerging information infrastructure.

American Civil Liberties Union (http://www.aclu.org). The ACLU tirelessly defends constitutional rights, including privacy rights.

Private Citizen (http://www.private-citizen.com). This organization can help keep you off junk phone lists—for a price.

Web Pages

Check the *Computer Confluence* Web site for links to many of the organizations listed in the previous section, along with links to other database and privacy-related sites.

Multimedia

on the CD-ROM and the Web:

~ Additional content on modem and network technology

~ An activity on home computer networking

~ An interactive on netiquette and text messaging

~ Instant access to glossary and key word references

~ Interactive self-study quizzes

. . . and more.

 computerconfluence.com

Objectives

After you read this chapter you should be able to:

▶ **Describe the basic types of technology that make telecommunication possible**

▶ **Describe the nature and function of local area networks and wide area networks**

▶ **Discuss the uses and implications of email, instant messaging, teleconferencing, and other forms of online communication**

▶ **Explain how wireless network technology is transforming the ways people work and communicate**

▶ **Describe current and future trends in telecommunications and networking.**

CHAPTER 8

ARTHUR C. CLARKE'S MAGICAL PROPHECY

Besides coining Clarke's laws, British writer Arthur C. Clarke has written more than 100 works of science fiction and nonfiction. His most famous work was the monumental 1968 film *2001: A Space Odyssey*, in which he collaborated with movie director Stanley Kubrick. The film's villain, a faceless English-speaking computer with a lust for power, sparked many public debates about the nature and risks of artificial intelligence. These debates continue today.

But Clarke's most visionary work may be a paper published in 1945 in which he predicted the use of *geostationary communications satellites*—satellites that match the Earth's rotation so they can hang in a stationary position relative to the spinning planet below and relay wireless transmissions between locations. Clarke's paper pinpointed the exact height of the orbit required to match the movement of the satellite with the planetary rotation. He also suggested that these satellites could replace many telephone cables and radio towers, allowing electronic signals to be beamed across oceans, deserts, and mountain ranges, linking the people of the world with a single communications network.

If an elderly but distinguished scientist says that something is possible he is almost **certainly right**, but if he says that it is impossible he is **very probably wrong**. The only way to find the **limits of the possible** is to go beyond them into the impossible. Any sufficiently advanced technology is **indistinguishable from magic**.

—*Clarke's Three Laws*

8.1 Arthur C. Clarke

Networking and Telecommunication

A decade after Clarke's paper appeared, powerful rockets and sensitive radio receiving equipment made communications satellites realistic. In 1964 the first synchronous TV satellite was launched, marking the beginning of a billion-dollar industry that has changed the way people communicate.

Today Clarke is often referred to as the father of satellite communications. In his 80s and largely confined to a wheelchair, Clarke lives in Sri Lanka, where he continues his work as a writer, though he now uses a personal computer and beams his words around the globe to editors using the satellites he envisioned half a century ago. ~

8.2 Geostationary communications satellite.

The Battle of New Orleans, the bloodiest battle of the War of 1812, was fought two weeks after the war officially ended; it took that long for the cease-fire message to travel from Washington, D.C. to the front line. In 1991, 179 years later, six hard-line Soviet communists staged a coup to turn back the tide of democratic and economic reforms that were sweeping the U.S.S.R. Within hours, messages zipped between the Soviet Union and Western nations on telephone and computer networks. Cable television and computer conferences provided up-to-the-minute analyses of events—analyses that were beamed to computer bulletin boards inside the Soviet Union. Networks carried messages among the resistors, allowing them to stay steps ahead of the coup leaders and the Soviet military machine. People toppled the coup and ultimately the Soviet Union—not with guns, but with courage, will, and timely information.

8.3 Students use PCs to connect with online information sources and perform research for a class.

Telecommunication technology—the technology of long-distance communication—has come a long way since the War of 1812, and the world has changed dramatically as a result. After Samuel Morse invented the telegraph in 1844, people could, for the first time, send long-distance messages instantaneously. Alexander Bell's invention of the telephone in 1876 extended this capability to the spoken word. Today, systems of linked computers enable us to send data and software across the room or around the world. The technological transformation has changed the popular definition of the word *telecommunication*, which today means long-distance electronic communication in a variety of forms.

In this chapter, we look at the computer as part of a network rather than as a self-contained appliance. We examine the hardware and software technologies that make computer networks possible, and we discuss ways in which such linked computers are used for communication and information gathering. We also consider how networks are changing the way we live and work, as well as security and privacy issues raised by new network technologies.

In the next chapter, we'll delve deeper into the Internet—the global computer network at the heart of the latest telecommunication revolution. We'll explore how the Internet is set up, the various ways to access the Internet, and the software foundations of the World Wide Web. We will discuss using the Web for publishing information, finding information, and supporting electronic commerce.

But first things first. Let's start by considering the various kinds of computer networks and how they are constructed.

Basic Network Anatomy

A computer network is any system of two or more computers that are linked together. Why is networking important? The answers to this question revolve around the three essential components of every computer system:

> After more than a century of electric technology, we have **extended our central nervous system** itself in a global embrace, **abolishing both space and time** as far as our planet is concerned.
>
> —*Marshall McLuhan, in* Understanding Media

- *Hardware.* Networks enable people to share computer hardware resources, reducing costs and making it possible for more people to take better advantage of powerful computer equipment.
- *Software.* Networks enable people to share data and software programs, increasing efficiency and productivity.
- *People.* Networks enable people to work together, or collaborate, in ways that are otherwise difficult or impossible.

Important information is hidden in these three statements. But before we examine them in more detail, we need to look at the hardware and software that make computer networks possible.

Networks Near and Far

Computer networks come in all shapes and sizes, but most can be categorized as either local area networks or wide area networks.

A **local area network (LAN)** is a network in which the computers are physically close to each other, usually in the same building. A typical LAN includes a collection of computers and peripherals; each computer and networked peripheral is an individual *node* on the network. Nodes are connected to *hubs* or *switches*, which allow any node on the network to communicate with any other node. A hub allows only a single message at a time to move across the LAN, while a switch can carry multiple messages simultaneously. For this reason, a switch provides a significant advantage over a hub on a busy LAN.

> Pretty soon you'll have no more idea of **what computer you're using** than you have an idea of **where your electricity comes from**.
>
> —*Danny Hillis, computer designer*

One way to connect a node to a hub or a switch is by using a physical cable. The most common type of LAN cable, known as *twisted pair*, contains copper wires that resemble those in standard telephone cables. Some networks, mostly in homes, use existing household electrical or telephone wiring to transmit data. But the biggest trend in LAN technology today is the explosive growth in wireless networks.

In a **wireless network**, each node has a tiny radio (or, less commonly, infrared) transmitter connected to its network port so it can send and receive data through the air rather than through cables. Wireless network connections are especially convenient for workers who are constantly on the move. They're also used for creating small networks in homes and small businesses because they can be installed without digging or drilling. However, wireless networks are generally slower than wired LANs are.

All computers on a LAN do not have to use the same operating system. For example, a single network might include Macintoshes, Windows PCs, and Linux workstations. The computers can be connected in many different ways, and many rules and industry-defined standards dictate what will and won't work. Most organizations depend on *network administrators* to take care of the behind-the-scenes details so others can focus on using the network. For *enterprise network systems*—large, complex networks with hundreds of computers—network administrators depend on *network management system software* to help them track and maintain healthy networks.

A *metropolitan area network (MAN)* is a service that links two or more LANs within a city. MAN service is typically provided by a telephone or telecommunications company. With a MAN, a company can keep employees linked even if they're blocks away from each other.

A **wide area network (WAN)**, as the name implies, is a network that extends over a long distance. In a WAN, each network site is a node on the network. Data is transmitted long-distance between networks on a collection of common pathways known as the *backbone*. Large WANs are possible because of the web of telephone lines, microwave relay towers, and satellites that span the globe. Most WANs are private operations designed to link geographically dispersed corporate or government offices.

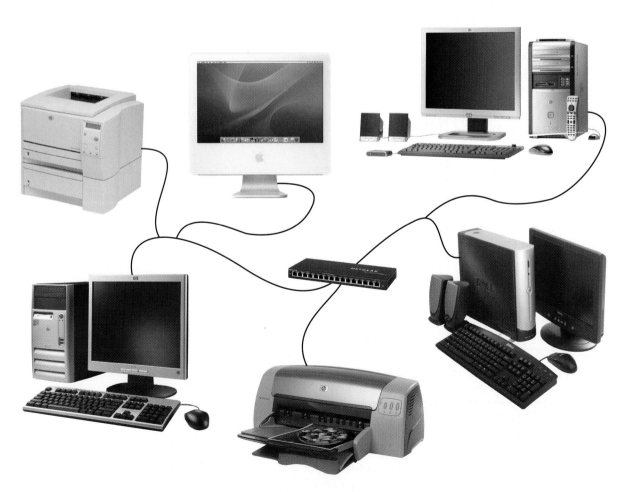

8.4 A LAN can contain a variety of interconnected computers and peripherals.

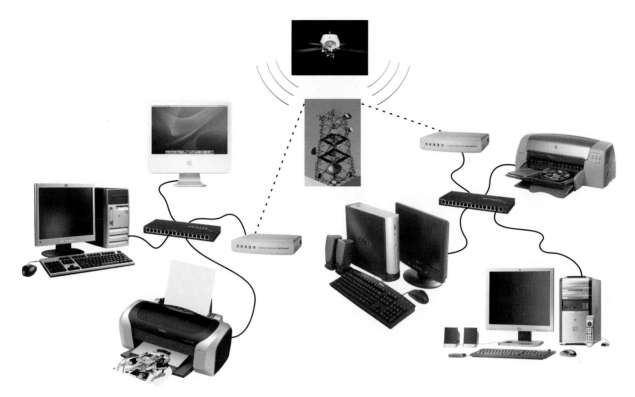

8.5 WANs are often made up of LANs linked by phone lines, microwave towers, and communications satellites.

In today's internetworked world, communication frequently happens between LANs and WANs. **Bridges** and **gateways** are hardware devices that can pass messages between networks and, in some cases, translate messages so they can be understood by networks that obey different software protocols. (Software protocols are discussed later in the chapter.) **Routers** are hardware devices or software programs that route messages as they travel between networks via bridges and gateways. Bridges, gateways, and routers make it possible to connect to the Internet just about anywhere and communicate with computers connected to the Internet through other networks around the planet.

Specialized Networks: From GPS to Financial Systems

It would be a mistake to think of all computer networks as collections of PCs linked to the Internet. Some specialized networks are designed to perform specific functions; these networks may not be directly connected to the Internet.

One such specialized network is the U.S. Department of Defense **Global Positioning System (GPS)**. The GPS includes 24 satellites that circle the Earth. They are carefully spaced so that from any point on the planet, at any time, four satellites will be above the horizon. Each satellite contains a computer, an atomic clock, and a radio. On the ground, a *GPS receiver* can use signals broadcast by three or four visible satellites to determine its position. Handheld GPS receivers can display locations, maps, and directions on small screens; GPS receivers can also be embedded in automobile navigation systems or connected to laptop computers. Members of the U.S. military use GPS receivers to keep track of where they are, but so do scientists, engineers, motorists, hikers, boaters, and others. Mobile phones now include GPS receivers so they can be located quickly when used for emergency calls.

8.6 A global positioning system helps this blind person navigate.

Probably the most widely used specialized computer networks are the networks that keep our global financial systems running. When you strip away the emotional trappings, money is another form of information. Dollars, yen, pounds, and rubles are all symbols that make it easy for people to exchange goods and services. Money can be just about anything, provided people agree to its value. During the last few centuries, paper replaced metal as the major form of money. Today, paper is being replaced by digital patterns stored in computer media. Money, like other digital information, can be transmitted through computer networks. That's why it's possible to withdraw cash from your checking account using an *automated teller machine (ATM)* at an airport or shopping mall thousands of miles from your home bank. An ATM (not to be confused with the communication protocol with the same initials) is a specialized terminal linked to a bank's main computer through a commercial banking network. Financial networks also make possible credit card purchases, automatic bill paying, electronic funds transfer, and all kinds of electronic commerce (e-commerce). E-commerce will be discussed in more detail in later chapters.

The Network Interface

Imagine how useful an office would be **without a door**.

—*Doug Engelbart, Internet pioneer, on the importance of network connections*

In Chapter 2 and Chapter 3, you saw how information travels among the CPU, memory, and other components within a computer as electrical impulses that move along collections of parallel wires called buses. A network extends the range of these information pulses, allowing them to travel to other computers. The Internet is a vast network of interconnected networks that effectively extends the roaming range of those pulses to the entire planet. By connecting to a network that's part of the Internet, a computer can connect to millions of other computers that are connected to the Internet.

A computer may have a **direct connection** to a network; for example, it might be one of many machines linked in an office, or it might be part of a university network. On the other hand, a computer might have **remote access** to a network through a phone line, a television cable system, or a satellite link.

No matter how it is connected, the computer communicates with the network through a **port**—a socket that enables information to pass in and out of the system. As described in Chapter 2, "Hardware Basics: Inside the Box," *parallel ports* enable bits to pass through in groups of 8, 16, or 32. They are commonly used to connect older printers to computers. *Serial ports*, on the other hand, require bits to pass through one at a time. The standard serial port is designed to attach peripherals, such as modems, not to connect directly to networks. Older PCs (and many newer ones) have at least one serial port and one parallel port. (Older Macintoshes have one or more multipurpose serial ports but no parallel ports.) Standard PC serial and parallel ports—sometimes called *legacy ports*—are being quickly replaced by newer technology. Modern Macs and PCs have multiple *USB* and *FireWire (IEEE 1394)* ports that are much faster and more flexible than traditional serial and parallel ports.

A **network interface card** (**NIC**, pronounced "nick") adds a special serial port to the computer—one that's designed for a direct network connection. The network interface card controls the flow of data between the computer's RAM and the network cable. At the same time, it converts the computer's internal low-power signals into more powerful signals that can be transmitted through the network. The type of card a computer has depends on the type of network connection needed. The most common types of networks today require some kind of Ethernet card or port in each computer. **Ethernet** is a popular networking architecture developed in the 1970s at Xerox PARC. Most newer PCs include an *Ethernet port* on the main circuit board, so they don't require NICs to connect to Ethernet networks. Details vary, and there are many details, but the same general principles apply to all common network connections.

8.7 Every day, stock traders move billions of dollars in funds electronically through world markets.

In the simplest networks, two or more computers are linked by cables. But direct connection is impractical for computers that are miles or oceans apart. For computers to communicate over long distances, they need to transmit information through other paths. To connect directly, the computer needs a *network interface port*, typically an *Ethernet port*. For a remote connection, it generally needs a *modem* or some type of *broadband* connection device.

Communication á la Modem

An intricate network of cables, radio transmitters, and satellites enables people to talk by telephone between just about any two places on the planet. The telephone network is capable of connecting remote computers, although it was designed to carry sound waves, not streams of bits. Before a **digital signal**—a stream of bits—can be transmitted over a standard phone line, it must be converted to an **analog signal**— a continuous wave. At the receiving end, the analog signal first must be converted back into the bits, representing the original digital message. Each of these tasks is performed by a **modem** (short for modulator/demodulator)—a hardware device that connects a computer to a telephone line.

An *internal modem* is installed on a circuit board inside the computer's chassis. An *external modem* sits in a box linked to a serial port or USB port. Both types use phone cables to connect to the telephone network through standard modular phone jacks.

A *fax modem* can communicate with *facsimile (fax) machines* as well as computers. With a fax modem, a PC can "print" any document on a remote fax machine by dialing the number of that machine and sending a series of electrical pulses that represent the marks on the pages of the document. When it receives a fax, the PC constructs an on-screen document based on the pulses it receives from the transmitting machine.

Modems differ in their transmission speeds, measured in **bits per second (bps)**. Many people use the term *baud rate* instead of bps, but

8.8 A network interface card, or NIC, allows a PC to connect to a network.

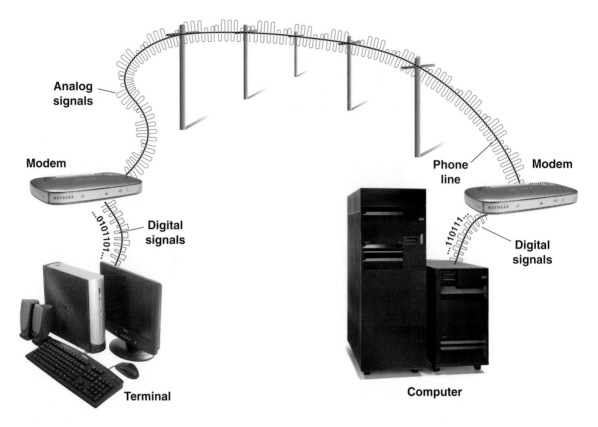

8.9 A modem converts digital signals from a computer into analog signals that can be transmitted through telephone wires to another modem, which then converts them back into digital signals another computer can understand.

bps is technically more accurate for high-speed modems. Modems today commonly transmit at 28,800 bps to 56.6K (56,600) bps over standard phone lines. Communication by modem is slower than communication between computers that are directly connected on a network. High-speed transmission isn't usually critical for text messages, but it can make a huge difference when the data being transmitted includes graphics, sound, video, and other multimedia elements—the kinds of data commonly found on the Web.

Broadband Connections

Most people who have explored multimedia on the Web have experienced small, jerky videos, sputtering audio, and (especially) long waits. The cause of most of these problems on the Internet (and other networks) is a lack of *bandwidth* at some point in the path between the sending computer and the receiving computer. The word has a technical definition, but in the world of computer networks bandwidth generally refers to the quantity of information that can be transmitted through a communication medium in a given amount of time. In general, increased bandwidth means faster transmission speeds. Bandwidth is typically measured in kilobits (thousands of bits) or megabits (millions of bits) per second. (Since a byte is 8 bits, a megabit is 1/8 of a megabyte. The text of this chapter is about 200 kilobytes, or 1600 kilobits, of information. A physical medium capable of transmitting 100 megabits per second could theoretically transmit this chapter's text more than 50 times in 1 second.) Bandwidth can be affected by many factors, including the physical media that make up the network, the amount of network traffic, the software protocols of the network, and the type of network connection.

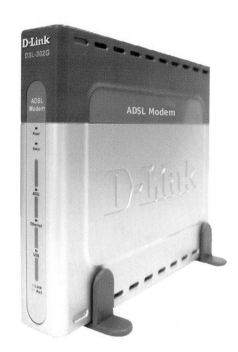

Some people find it easier to visualize bandwidth by thinking of a network cable as a highway. One way to increase bandwidth in a cable is to increase the number of parallel wires in that cable—the equivalent of adding more lanes to a freeway. Another way is to increase the speed with which information passes through the cable; this is the same as increasing the speed of the vehicles on the freeway. Of course, it's easier and safer to increase highway speed limits if you have a traffic flow system that minimizes the chance of collisions and accidents; in the same way, more efficient, reliable software can increase network bandwidth. But increasing a highway's throughput doesn't help much if cars pile up at the entry and exit ramps; in the same way, a high-bandwidth network seems like a low-bandwidth network if you're connected through a slow modem.

8.10 Broadband connections require cable modems or DSL modems. These aren't really modems but are so named because they are functionally similar to modems.

For faster remote connections, many businesses and homes bypass standard modems and use some kind of *broadband connection*—a connection with much greater bandwidth than modems have. Several competing broadband technologies are available to computer users in many areas: DSL, cable, satellite, and wireless broadband connections.

- DSL uses standard phone lines and is provided by phone companies in many areas.
- Cable modems provide fast network connections through cable television networks in many areas.
- High-speed wireless connections can connect computers to networks using radio waves rather than wires.
- Satellite dishes can deliver fast computer network connections as well as television programs.

These broadband technologies are discussed in more detail later in this chapter.

Fiber-Optic Connections

These are the days of **lasers in the jungle**.
Lasers in the jungle somewhere . . .

—*Paul Simon, in* "The Boy in the Bubble"

Broadband network connections through cable modems and DSL are faster than standard modems are because they have greater bandwidth. But DSL and cable modems have nowhere near the bandwidth of fiber-optic cables that are replacing copper wires in the

Networks Are Built on Physical Media

Type		Uses	Maximum Operating Distance (without amplification)	Cost
Twisted pair		Small LANS	300 feet	Low
Coaxial cable		Large LANs	6,002,500 feet	Medium
Fiber-optic		network backbones; WANs	125 miles	High
Wireless/infrared		LANs	3–1,000 feet (line of sight)	Medium
Wireless/radio		Connecting things that move	100 to 300 feet	Medium

8.11 Different types of networks are built with different physical media, which can play a huge role in the overall performance of the network.

worldwide telephone network. Fiber-optic cables use light waves to carry information at blinding speeds. A single fiber-optic cable can transmit half a gigabit (500 *million* bits) per second, replacing 10,000 copper telephone cables.

A fiber-optic network can rapidly and reliably transmit masses of multimedia data at the same time it's handling voice messages. Digital fiber-optic networks now connect major communication hubs around the world. Many large businesses and government institutions are connected to the global fiber-optic network. But most small businesses and homes still depend on copper wires for the "last mile," as it's often referred to in the industry—the link to the closest on-ramp to the fiber-optic freeway. Fiber-optic communication lines will eventually find their way into most homes, radically changing our lives in the process. These cables will provide two-way links to the outside world for our phones, televisions, radios, computers, and a variety of other devices.

Wireless Network Technology

A lightning-fast network connection to your desktop is of little use if you're away from your desk most of the time. When bandwidth is less important than mobility and portability, wireless technology can provide practical solutions.

Infrared wireless technology has been around for many years. Many laptops and handheld computers have infrared ports that can send and receive digital information short distances. Infrared technology isn't widely used in networks because of distance and line-of-sight limitations. Still, infrared technology has practical applications—especially for mobile users. For example, Palm users routinely share programs and data by beaming them through infrared links.

The fastest-growing wireless LAN technology is known as Wi-Fi, or *802.11*. There are three different flavors of Wi-Fi, known as 802.11a, 802.11b, and 802.11g. All of these wireless networking technologies allow multiple computers to connect to a LAN through a base station (also called a wireless access point) up to 150 feet away. The first Wi-Fi networks (including Apple's Airport) met the 802.11b standard. The next type of Wi-Fi network to hit the market was 802.11a. It is more expensive than 802.11b is, but it provides higher bandwidth. The newest Wi-Fi networks, called 802.11g, combine the advantages of the previous standards; they are low cost and high bandwidth. (Apple labels its 802.11g network devices Airport Extreme.)

Wi-Fi isn't as fast as a hard-wired Ethernet connection, but it's fast enough for most applications, including multimedia Web downloads. A home Wi-Fi network allows computers to connect from any room without cables. Wi-Fi base stations are showing up in airports, coffee shops, phone booths, and other public places. On many campuses, Wi-Fi networks allow students to connect their laptops to the Internet effortlessly from dorm rooms, classrooms, or tree-lined gardens. Free Wi-Fi access points are sprouting everywhere, part of a grassroots movement to provide universal wireless access to the Net.

Another type of wireless technology is Bluetooth, named for a Danish king who overcame his country's religious differences. Bluetooth technology overcomes differences between mobile phones, handheld computers, and PCs, making it possible for all of these devices to communicate with each other regardless of their operating system. Bluetooth uses radio technology similar to that of Wi-Fi, but its transmissions are limited to about 30 feet. Bluetooth isn't designed to compete with Wi-Fi. It is intended to replace the wires that are often required to connect devices like cell phones, PDAs, and printers. With Bluetooth it's possible to create a *personal*

> Wireless technology is a **liberating force**. It will make possible **human-centered computers**. This wasn't possible before because we were **anchored to a PC**, and we had to go to it like going to a temple to **pay our respects**.
>
> —*Michael Dertouzos, Director, MIT Laboratory for Computer Science*

8.12 This University of Tennessee student can connect to the Internet using the campus wireless network.

Wireless Network Standards

Technical Name	Popular Name	Range	Technology	Speed	Typical Use
IrDA-Data	IrDA	1 meter	Infrared	9600 bps	Exchange data between PDAs
802.15	Bluetooth	10 meters	Radio	1 Mbps	Room-sized "personal area network"
802.11a	Wi-Fi	30 meters	Radio	54 Mbps	Local area network
802.11b	Wi-Fi	30 meters	Radio	11 Mbps	Local area network
802.11g	Wi-Fi	30 meters	Radio	54 Mbps	Local area network

8.13 Wireless technologies compared

area network (PAN)—a network that links a variety of personal electronic devices so they can communicate with each other. Bluetooth technology is currently limited to simple device connectivity, but in the future it will open up all kinds of possibilities:

- A pacemaker senses a heart attack and notifies the victim's mobile phone to dial 911.
- A car radio communicates with parking-lot video cameras to find out where spaces are available.
- A pen scans business cards and sends the information to a PDA inside a briefcase.
- A medical wristband transmits an accident victim's vital information to a doctor's hand-held computer.
- A cell phone tells you about specials on clothes (available in your size) as you walk past stores in a mall. (Many fear that this technology will usher in a new era of junk phone calls.)

Wi-Fi and Bluetooth aren't part of mass culture yet, but wireless communication through mobile phones certainly is. In two decades, mobile phones have gone from simple analog systems to powerful digital devices that can handle Internet data, text messages, photos, and other data along with voice traffic.

8.14 Many students living in Japan use their mobile phones regularly for instant messaging and multiplayer games.

Mobile phone Internet connections are more common in Europe and Asia than they are in the United States. While many Americans enjoy sharing photos with their cell phones, phone users in Europe and Asia are more likely to use their phones as multifunction devices. In Japan, people routinely use their phones to send and receive email, exchange instant messages, check news headlines, shop, play games, share photos, and even do karaoke. The next generation of mobile wireless technology, often called *3G*, promises high-bandwidth connections that will support true multimedia, including real-time video. Some experts believe that Wi-Fi's rapidly growing popularity will force cell phone companies to embrace it rather than 3G. Either way, the boundaries that separate phone networks and computer networks will continue to blur.

The convenience of wireless technology carries a price in security. Wireless networks are far more vulnerable to eavesdropping, data snooping, and hacking than wired networks are. Many techniques and tools can help preserve privacy and security, but the most effective ones are expensive and available to large companies only. As a result, most wireless home networks today are extremely insecure. These problems are discussed in more detail later in this chapter and in Chapter 10, "Computer Security and Risks."

8.15 Emerging wireless standards, such as Bluetooth, allow cell phones, PDAs, and computer peripherals, such as this mouse, to announce themselves and describe their capabilities to other devices and PCs in personal area networks.

Communication Software

Whether connected by cables, radio waves, or a combination of modems and telephone lines, to interact computers need some kind of communication software. To communicate with each other, two machines must follow the same protocols—rules for the exchange of data between a terminal and a computer or between two computers. One such protocol is transmission speed: If one machine is "talking" at 56,600 bps and the other is "listening" at 28,800 bps, the message doesn't get through. (Most modems can avoid this particular problem by adjusting their speeds to match each other.) Protocols include prearranged codes for messages such as "Are you ready?" "I am about to start sending a data file," and "Did you receive that file?" For two computers to understand each other, the software on both machines must be set to follow the same protocols. Communication software establishes a protocol that is followed by the computer's hardware.

All the **most promising technologies** making their debut now are chiefly due to communication between computers—that is, to **connections** rather than to **computations**. And since **communication is the basis of culture**, fiddling at this level is indeed **momentous**.

—*Kevin Kelly, former* Wired *Executive Editor*

The most famous protocol for computer networking is TCP/IP. Strictly speaking, the Internet is the network of computers that uses TCP/IP to control the exchange of data. We'll discuss the Internet in more detail in Chapter 9, "Inside the Internet and the World Wide Web."

Communication software can take a variety of forms. For users who work exclusively on a local area network, many communication tasks are taken care of by a network operating system (NOS), such as Novell's Netware or Microsoft's Windows Server. Just as a personal computer's operating system shields the user from most of the nuts and bolts of the computer's operation, a NOS shields the user from the hardware and software details of routine communication between machines. But unlike a PC operating system, the NOS must respond to requests from many computers and must coordinate communication throughout the network. Today, many organizations are replacing the specialized PC-based NOS with an intranet system—systems built around the open standards and protocols of the Internet, as described in more detail in the next chapter.

The function and location of the network operating system depend in part on the LAN model. Some LANs are set up according to the client/server model, a hierarchical model

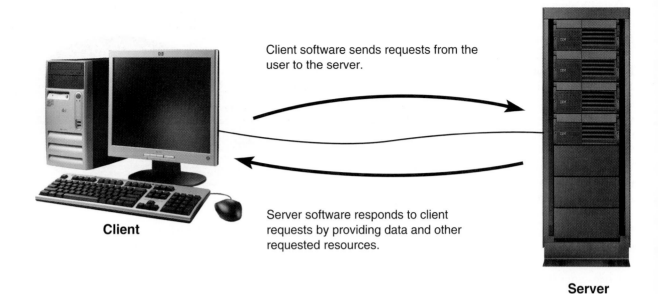

Client software sends requests from the user to the server.

Client

Server software responds to client requests by providing data and other requested resources.

Server

8.16 Client/server computing involves two-way communication between so-called client and server programs, each of which runs on a separate PC.

in which one or more computers act as dedicated servers and all the remaining computers act as clients. Each server is a high-speed, high-capacity computer containing data and other resources to be shared with client computers. Using NOS server software, the server fulfills requests from clients for data and other resources. In a client/server network the bulk of the NOS resides on the server, but each client has NOS client software for sending requests to servers.

Many small networks are designed using the **peer-to-peer model** (sometimes called *p-to-p* or *P2P*), which enables every computer on the network to be both client and server. In this kind of network, every user can make files publicly available to other users on the network. Some desktop operating systems, including many versions of Windows and the Mac OS, include all the software necessary to operate a peer-to-peer network. In practice, many networks are hybrids, combining features of the client/server and peer-to-peer models.

Outside of a LAN, the most basic type of communication software is primitive **terminal emulation software**, which enables a computer to function as a character-based "dumb" terminal—a simple input/output device for sending messages to and receiving messages from the host

8.17 Servers like these powerful IBM devices can provide software and data for hundreds or thousands of networked computers.

computer. A terminal program handles phone dialing, protocol management, and the miscellaneous details necessary for making a PC and a modem work together. With terminal software and a modem, a personal computer can communicate through phone lines with another PC, a network of computers, or, more commonly, a large multiuser computer. The Windows and Macintosh operating system packages include terminal emulation programs.

Basic terminal emulators are fine for bare-bones computer-to-computer connections, but their character-based user interfaces can be confusing to people who are used to point-and-click GUIs. What's more, they can't be used to explore media-rich destinations on and off the World Wide Web. That's why most online explorers today use Web browsers and other specialized graphical client software instead of generic terminal programs. At the other end of the line, communications software is usually built into the multiuser operating system of the *host system*—the computer that provides service to multiple users. This software enables a timesharing computer to communicate with several other computers or terminals at once. The most widely used host operating system today is UNIX, the 30-year old OS that has many variants, including the open source Linux OS discussed in Chapter 4, "The Ghost in the Machine."

The Network Advantage

A network becomes more valuable as **it reaches more users**.

—Metcalfe's Law, by Bob Metcalfe, inventor of Ethernet

With this background in mind, let's reconsider the three reasons people use networks:

■ *Networks enable people to share computer hardware resources, reducing costs and making it possible for more people to take better advantage of powerful computer equipment.* When computers and peripherals are connected in a LAN, computer users can share expensive peripherals. Before LANs, the typical office had a printer connected to each computer. Today, it's more common to find a large group of computers and users sharing a small number of high-quality networked printers. In a client/server network, each printer may be connected to a *print server*—a server that accepts, prioritizes, and processes print jobs. Although it may not make much sense for users to try to share a printer on a wide area network, WAN users often share other hardware resources. Many WANs include powerful mainframes and supercomputers that can be accessed by authorized users at remote sites.

■ *Networks enable people to share data and software programs, increasing efficiency and productivity.* In offices without networks, people often transmit data and software by sneakernet—that is, by carrying disks between computers. In a LAN, one or more computers can be used as *file servers*—storehouses for software and data that are shared by several users. With client software a user can, without taking a step, *download* software and data—copy it from a server. Of course, somebody needs to *upload* the software—copy it to the server—first. A large file server is typically a dedicated computer that does nothing but serve files.

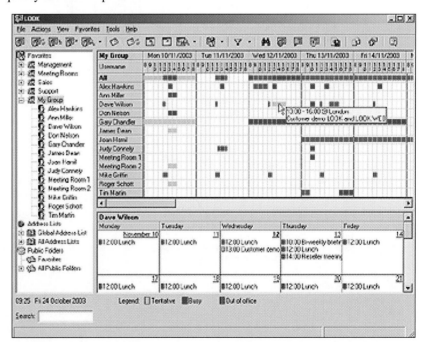

8.18 Microsoft Exchange, the most widely used groupware product, combines email, scheduling, contacts, tasks, and other personal information management features to facilitate information sharing and workgroup collaboration.

How It **Works**

Internet

1. A cable or DSL line provides high-bandwidth access to the Internet.

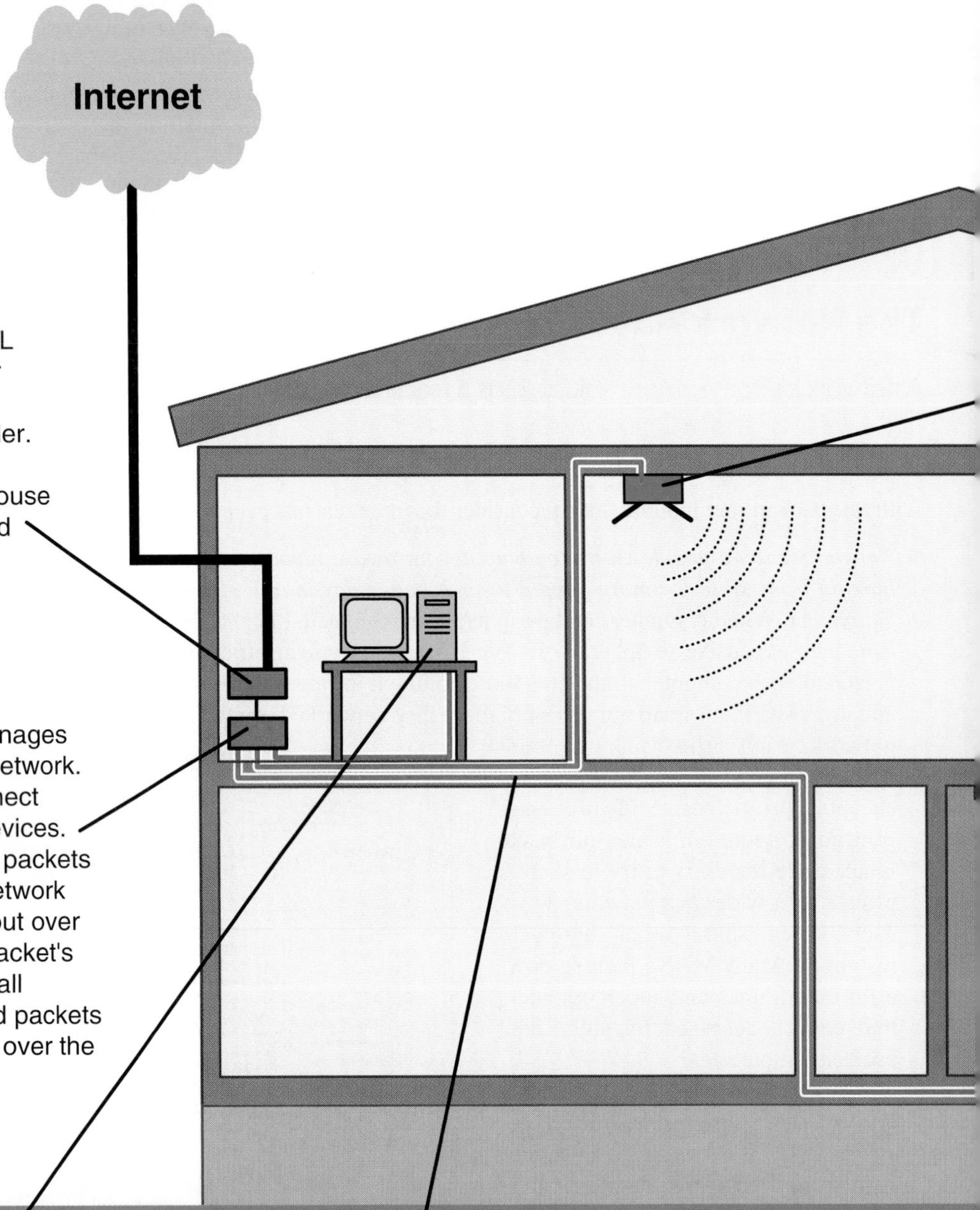

2. A cable modem or DSL modem connects your home network to an Internet service provider. It converts the analog signal entering your house into a digital signal and vice versa.

3. A combination router/firewall/hub manages traffic on your home network. The hub lets you connect multiple networked devices. The router takes data packets coming in over one network link and sends them out over a link leading to the packet's destination. The firewall prevents unauthorized packets from being forwarded over the network.

4. A PC contains a network card rated at 100 Mbps —100 million bits per second. (Older, slower cards support only 10 Mbps).

5. Cat 5 cables connect Ethernet-equipped devices. The cables look like telephone cables, but the connectors are slightly different. Cat 5 cables are easier to work with than older coaxial cables.

8.19

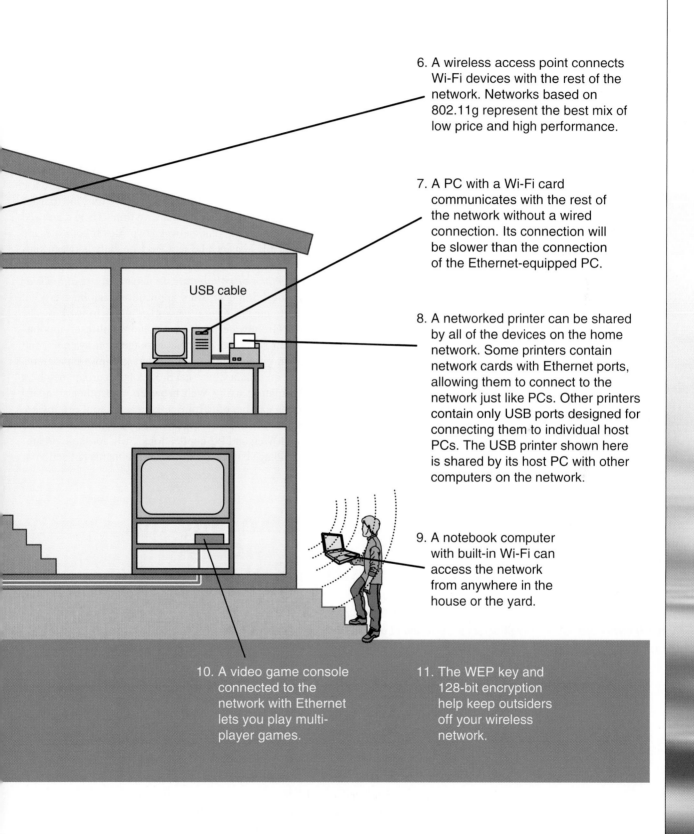

6. A wireless access point connects Wi-Fi devices with the rest of the network. Networks based on 802.11g represent the best mix of low price and high performance.

7. A PC with a Wi-Fi card communicates with the rest of the network without a wired connection. Its connection will be slower than the connection of the Ethernet-equipped PC.

USB cable

8. A networked printer can be shared by all of the devices on the home network. Some printers contain network cards with Ethernet ports, allowing them to connect to the network just like PCs. Other printers contain only USB ports designed for connecting them to individual host PCs. The USB printer shown here is shared by its host PC with other computers on the network.

9. A notebook computer with built-in Wi-Fi can access the network from anywhere in the house or the yard.

10. A video game console connected to the network with Ethernet lets you play multi-player games.

11. The WEP key and 128-bit encryption help keep outsiders off your wireless network.

But a peer-to-peer approach, allowing any computer to be both client and server, can be an efficient, inexpensive way to share files on small networks. Of course, sharing computer software on a network can violate software licenses (see Chapter 4) if not done with care. Many, but not all, licenses allow the software to be installed on a file server as long as the number of simultaneous users never exceeds the number of licensed copies. Some companies offer site licenses or network licenses, which reduce costs for multiple copies or remove restrictions on software copying and use at a network site. (Software copying is discussed in more detail in the next two chapters.) Networks don't eliminate compatibility differences between different computer operating systems, but they can simplify data communication between machines. Users of Windows-compatible computers, for example, can't run Macintosh applications just because they're available on a file server. But they can, in many cases, use data files and documents created on a Macintosh and stored on the server. For example, a poster created with Adobe Illustrator on a Macintosh could be stored on a file server so it can be opened, edited, and printed by Illustrator users on Windows PCs. File sharing isn't always that easy. If users of different systems use programs with incompatible file formats, they need to use *data translation software* to read and modify each other's files. On WANs, the transfer of data and software can save more than shoe leather; it can save time. There's no need to send printed documents or discs by overnight mail between two sites if both sites are connected to the same network. Typically, data can be sent electronically between sites in a matter of seconds.

■ *Networks enable people to work together, or collaborate, in ways that are difficult or impossible without network technology.* Some software applications can be classified as groupware—programs designed to enable several networked users to work on the same documents at the same time. Groupware programs include multiuser appointment calendars, project-management software, database-management systems, and software for group editing of text-and-graphics documents. Many groupware programs today, such as Lotus Notes, are built on standard Internet protocols, so group members can communicate and share information using Web browsers and other standard Internet software tools. Workgroups can benefit from networks without groupware packages. Most groupware features—email, message posting, calendars, and the rest—are generally available through Web and PC applications. Still, for large organizations a full-featured groupware package can be easier to manage than a collection of separate programs.

Email, Instant Messaging, and Teleconferencing: Interpersonal Computing

New technology gives us two kinds of **newfound freedom**: The ability to **reach each other** 24/7—and the chance to **avoid one another** as never before.

—*Lori Gottlieb, Author of* Stick Figure

For many LAN and WAN users, network communication is limited to sending and receiving messages. A recent study found that the typical Internet user spends about 70 percent of connected time communicating with others. Electronic messaging can profoundly change the way people and organizations work. In the next section, we take a close look at the advantages and implications of interpersonal communication with computers.

The Many Faces of Email

Whether you're connected to a LAN, a WAN, a timesharing mainframe, and/or the Internet, you probably have access to an email system that enables you to send and receive messages to others on the network. (Chapter 0, "Basics," covered the basics of email.) There's no single way to send and receive email. What you see on the screen depends on

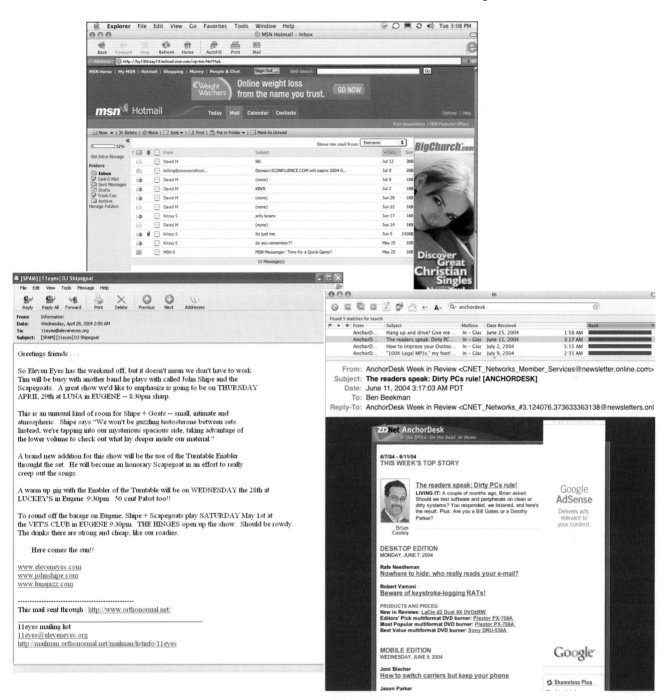

8.20 Email programs sport a variety of user interfaces. Web-based email clients such as Hotmail (top) provide email access to people familiar with Web browsers. Microsoft Outlook Express (left) is a widely-used email client that connects to a variety of email server types. Apple's Mail program (right), part of Mac OS X, is popular because of its ease of use and its intelligent spam (junk mail) filters.

the type of connection you have and the mail client program you use. If you have a standard modem connection to a UNIX-based Internet host, you might send and receive mail using PINE, the UNIX mail program developed at the University of Washington. Because it's character based, PINE works with almost any kind of Internet connection, but it's less friendly than today's graphical mail applications. Modern GUI mail programs, such as Microsoft Outlook Express, Apple OS X Mail, and Qualcomm Eudora Pro, are easier to learn and offer more flexibility than most character-based programs do. Many email services, including several free ones, are designed to be accessed through Web browsers rather than through separate email client programs.

Web-based email systems and many older UNIX-based programs require that read and unread messages be stored in post office boxes or folders on the remote mail servers. Most newer non-Web email clients enable PCs and Macs to download and handle mail locally rather than depending on a remote host as a post office.

Many email messages are plain ASCII text. Plain text messages can be viewed with any mail client program, including those in email-capable PDAs and phones. Many email programs can (optionally) send, receive, edit, and display email messages formatted in HTML, the formatting language used in most Web pages. HTML messages can include text formatting, pictures, and links to Web pages. The email client software hides the HTML source code from the sender and the recipient, displaying only the formatted messages. If the recipient views an HTML-encoded message with a mail program that doesn't recognize HTML, the formatting doesn't appear.

Even if their software can display HTML mail, not all email users *want* it. HTML encoding can slow down an email program. An HTML email message can also carry a *Web bug*—an invisible piece of code that silently notifies the sender about when the message was opened and may report other information about their machine or email software at the same time. Web bugs, which operate through specially encoded one-pixel graphics files, are increasingly common in commercial Web pages as well as HTML email messages. Fortunately, newer email applications can turn off Web bugs, preventing junk mailers and others from getting information about you when you read their messages.

Most email programs can send and receive formatted word processor documents, pictures, and other multimedia files as **attachments** to messages. Attachments need to be temporarily converted to ASCII text using some kind of encoding scheme before they can be sent through Internet mail. Most modern email programs take care of the encoding and decoding automatically. Of course, attachments aren't practical with many PDAs, cell phones, and other text-only email devices. And attachments can contain viruses and other unwelcome surprises, as described in Chapter 10, "Computer Security and Risks."

Mailing Lists

Email is a valuable tool for communicating one-to-one with individuals around the globe, but it's also useful for communicating one-to-many. **Mailing lists** enable you to participate in email discussion groups on special-interest topics. Lists can be small and local, or large and global. They can be administered by a human being or automatically administered by programs with names like Listserv and Majordomo. Each group has a mailing address that looks like any Internet address.

You might belong to one student group that's set up by your instructor to carry on discussions outside of class, another group that includes people all over the world who use Macromedia Flash to animate Web pages, a third that's dedicated to saving endangered species in your state, and a fourth for customers of an online bookstore. When you send a message to a mailing list address, every subscriber receives a copy. And, of course, you receive a copy of every mail message sent by everyone else to those lists.

Subscribing to a busy list might mean receiving hundreds of messages each day. To avoid being overwhelmed by incoming mail, many list members sign up to receive them in daily digest form; instead of receiving many individual messages each day, they receive one message that includes all postings. But digest messages can still contain lots of repetitive, silly, and annoying messages. Some lists are moderated to ensure that the quality of the discussion remains high. In a *moderated group*, a designated moderator acts as an editor, filtering out irrelevant and inappropriate messages and posting the rest.

8.21 Wirelessly connected handheld devices let users access their email and the Web without a PC.

Network News

You can participate in special-interest discussions without overloading your mailbox by taking advantage of **newsgroups**. A newsgroup is a public discussion on a particular subject consisting of notes written to a central Internet site and redistributed through a worldwide newsgroup network called USENET. You can check into and out of a newsgroup discussion whenever you want; all messages are posted on virtual bulletin boards for anyone to read anytime. There are groups for every interest and taste . . . and a few for the tasteless. Newsgroups are organized hierarchically, with dot names like rec.music.makers.percussion and soc.culture.french. You can explore network newsgroups through several Web sites, including Google, or with a newsreader client program.

Many newsgroups contain the same kind of free-flowing discussions you'll find in Internet mailing lists, but there are two important differences:

- Listserv mail messages are delivered automatically to your mailbox, but you have to seek out information in newsgroups.
- Mailing list messages are sent to a specific group of people, whereas newsgroup messages are available for anyone to see . . . for years to come.

Newsgroup discussions can get bogged down by repetitive questions from newcomers, childish rants, off-topic trivia, and other counterproductive messages. *Moderated newsgroups* contain only messages that have been filtered by designated moderators. The moderator discards inappropriate messages, making it easier for others to find the information they're looking for. Yahoo, MSN, AOL, and other portals and information services have discussion groups that are similar to USENET newsgroups; the main difference is that they aren't distributed as widely.

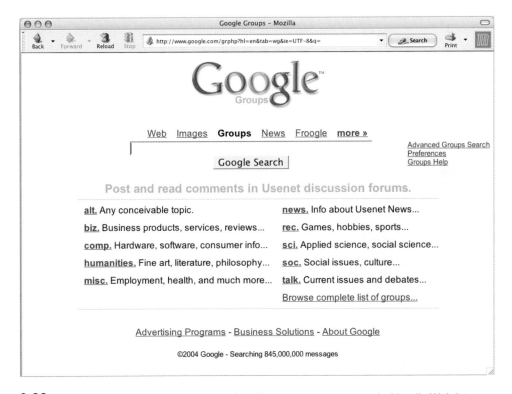

8.22 Google Groups lets users access USENET newsgroup content via friendly Web interface.

Online Survival Tips

When you're online, you're using a relatively new communication medium with new rules. Here are some suggestions for successful online communication:

➡ *Let your system do as much of the work as possible.* If your email program can sort mail, filter mail, or automatically append a signature file to your mail, take advantage of those features. If you find yourself sending messages to the same group of people repeatedly, create an *alias* that includes all of those people—a distribution list that can save you the trouble of typing or selecting all those names each time

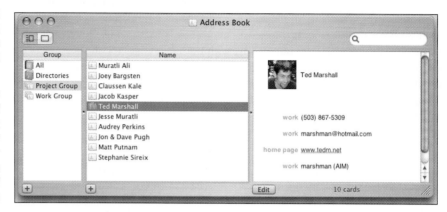

Store your email addresses in a software address book to save time and minimize errors.

➡ *Store names and addresses in a computer-accessible address book.* Email addresses aren't always easy to remember and type correctly. If you mistype even a single character, your message will probably either go to the wrong person or bounce—come back to you with some kind of undeliverable mail message. An online address book enables you

You can't always trust online sources, so cross-check your facts.

to select addresses without typing them each time you use them. Use your email program's back-up or export capability to back up your address book.

➡ *Don't share your email address.* It's easy to think of an email address like a physical address, sharing it with roommates, partners, and others who use the same computer. But email works best if each person has a unique address. A personal email address is more secure and private, but it's also more practical; when someone sends a message to you, the sender knows that you are the person who will receive the message.

➡ *Protect your privacy.* Miss Manners said it well in a *Wired* interview: "For email, the old postcard rule applies. Nobody else is supposed to read your postcards, but you'd be a fool if you wrote anything private on one."

➡ **Cross-check online information sources.** Don't assume that every information nugget you see online is valid, accurate, and timely. If you read something online, treat it with the same degree of skepticism that you would if you heard it in a cafeteria or coffee shop.

➡ *Be aware and awake.* It's easy to lose track of yourself and your time online. In his book *Virtual Community*, Howard Rheingold advises, "Rule Number One is to pay attention. Rule Number Two might be: Attention is a limited resource, so pay attention to where you pay attention.

➡ *Avoid information overload.* When it comes to information, more is not necessarily better. Search selectively. Don't waste time and energy trying to process mountains of online information. Information is not knowledge, and knowledge is not wisdom.

8.23

Instant Messaging and Teleconferencing: Real-Time Communication

Mailing lists and newsgroups are delayed or use **asynchronous communication** because the sender and the recipients don't have to be logged in at the same time. Computer networks offer many possibilities for **real-time communication**, too. **Instant messaging (IM)** has been possible since the days of text-only Internet access. Internet relay chat (IRC) and Talk enable UNIX users to exchange instant messages with their online friends and coworkers. But newer, easier-to-use messaging systems from AOL, Microsoft, Yahoo, Apple, and others have turned instant messaging into one of the most popular Internet activities. Instant messaging programs enable users to create buddy lists, check for "buddies" who are logged in, and exchange typed messages and files with those who are. Most of these programs are available for free. Many businesses now use instant messaging to keep employees connected. IM technology is even built into many mobile phones. Online services also offer **chat rooms**—public or private virtual conference rooms where people with similar interests or motivations can type messages to each other and receive near-instant responses.

Some IM programs, chat rooms, and multiplayer games on the Web use graphics to simulate real-world environments. Participants can represent themselves with *avatars*—graphical "bodies" that might look like simple cartoon sketches, elaborate 3-D figures, or exotic abstract icons.

Several IM programs make it possible to carry on two-way **video teleconferences**. A video teleconference enables two or

> **No other medium** gives every participant the capability to communicate **instantly** with thousands and thousands of people.
>
> —*Tracy LaQuey, in* The Internet Companion

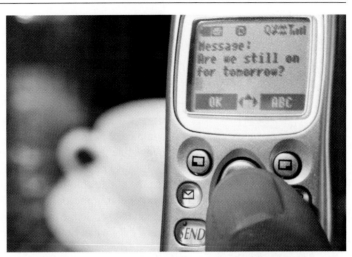

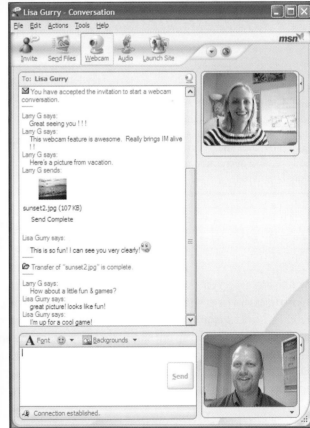

8.24 Real-time text-, audio-, and video-based conversations are supported by instant messaging software running on cell phones and PCs.

more people to communicate face-to-face over long distances by combining video and computer technology. Until a few years ago, most video teleconferences were conducted in special rooms equipped with video cameras, microphones, television monitors, and other specialized equipment. Today, it's possible to participate in multiperson video teleconferences using a video camera attached to a PC with a high-speed Internet connection. Internet video images don't measure up to the images beamed to professional conference rooms, but they're more than adequate for most applications. With some IM systems, participants caother ways.

Computer Telephony

A **voicemail** system is a voice messaging system with many of the features of an email system, including the ability to store, organize, and forward messages. Voicemail is a familiar example of a growing trend toward *computer telephony integration (CTI)*—the linking of computers and telephones to gain productivity. Many PCs have **telephony** software and hardware that allow them to serve as speakerphones, answering machines, and complete voicemail systems. A typical computer telephony system connects to a standard phone line through a modem capable of handling voice conversations.

It's also possible to send voice signals through a LAN, a WAN, or the Internet, bypassing the phone companies (and their charges) altogether. Many programs enable you to use a computer's microphone and speaker to turn the Internet into a toll-free long-distance telephone service. Most **Internet telephony (IP telephony** or **voice-over IP)** programs work only when both parties are running the same program at the same time, and they're not nearly as trouble-free as traditional long-distance service. Still, many experts predict that this kind of technology will soon pose a serious competitive threat to the current telephone infrastructure.

On the mobile front, the line between computers and telephones is especially fuzzy. Many mobile phones can connect to the Internet, do instant messaging, upload and download short email messages, and display miniature Web pages. Handheld PDAs from Palm, Dell, Hewlett Packard, and other companies can do the same things, but with larger screens and friendlier input devices. These handheld computers use software to integrate the functions of a PDA, a phone, and an Internet terminal. Hybrid PDAs and phones involve trade-offs; do you want to use a boxy PDA as a phone or type email on a tiny phone keypad? But most analysts expect rapid advances in these converging technologies over the next few years—advances such as reliable speech recognition that will make these devices much more useful for people on the go.

8.25 Modern cell phones are basically miniature portable computers including electronic address books, calendars, image and video viewers, and even onboard digital cameras.

Online Issues: Reliability, Security, Privacy, and Humanity

Well there's egg and bacon; egg, sausage and bacon; egg and spam; bacon and **spam**; egg, bacon, sausage and **spam; spam**, bacon, sausage and **spam; spam**, egg, **spam, spam**, bacon and **spam; spam, spam, spam**, egg and **spam; spam, spam, spam, spam, spam, spam**, baked beans, **spam, spam, spam** and **spam**; or lobster thermidor aux crevettes with a mornay sauce garnished with truffle paté, brandy, and a fried egg on top of **spam**.

—Waitress in Monty Python's Flying Circus

Everyone knows email is a powerful technology. It combines the advantages of the telephone and the letter. Like a telephone call, an email message is a way of instantaneously communicating with someone else, even if that person is on the other side of the globe. Like a letter, an email is nonintrusive. An email doesn't interrupt you the same way a telephone call does. An email conversation can take place over a period of hours, days, or even weeks.

Most of us use email because it is a practical and powerful tool. However, any new technology introduces new problems, and online communication is no exception. Here are some of the most important:

■ *Email and teleconferencing are vulnerable to machine failures, network glitches, human errors, and security breaches.* A system failure can cripple an organization that depends on email for critical communications. Internet users have experienced email blackouts caused by power outages, satellite failures, system overloads, and other technological breakdowns. Email attachment viruses have caused billions of dollars worth of damage worldwide. (See Chapter 10 for more on viruses.)

■ *Email can be overwhelming.* Many people receive hundreds of messages every day. Sifting through all those messages can consume hours that could have been used in other ways. Email overload has become such a serious problem that some businesses have implemented email-free Fridays to give their employees time to catch up on other work.

■ *Email can be unsolicited.* Because it's easy, fast, and free, email is often used to send blanket messages to masses of people without permission. Some of this unsolicited mail is innocent (and not-so-innocent) humor. Some is designed to spread the word for a good cause. (Some "good cause" campaigns are, in fact, fraudulent or misinformed; even so, they continue to circulate.) Most unsolicited email is designed to sell something—weight-loss plans, insurance, vacation homes, cigarettes, pornography, cheap loans, political campaigns, or just about anything that people can pay for with a credit card. Junk email is known as spam because it can be just as annoying and repetitive as the menu in the Monty Python skit quoted previously. But spam can also be a security risk, as you'll see in the next two chapters. Many email clients and Internet service providers offer antispam technology, including filters that recognize and delete obvious spam and challenge-response systems that require unrecognized email senders to reply to questions that can't easily be answered by automated systems. But none of these systems is foolproof, so antispam legislation is probably necessary to curb the problem. The CAN-SPAM Act of 2003 made some types of spam illegal in the United States, but it also overturned much stricter antispam laws in several states. Most experts expect that this law isn't strong enough to stem the tide of spam. In fact, the amount of spam clogging our electronic mailboxes continues to rise; spam now constitutes over 50 percent of all email messages sent worldwide.

■ *Email can pose a threat to privacy.* The U.S. Postal Service has a centuries-old tradition of safeguarding the privacy of first-class mail. Electronic communication is not grounded in that tradition. Although most email messages are secure and private, there's always a potential for eavesdropping by an organization's system administrators and crafty system snoopers. Many businesses routinely monitor email sent by employees. In 1999 an online bookseller was found guilty of intercepting a competitor's email to gain a market advantage. That same year, users of Microsoft's popular Hotmail service learned that their private email messages and address books

8.26 Many email client programs, including Eudora, include intelligent filters that automatically route spam into junk mailboxes. But it's not always easy to tell whether a message is spam or legitimate email. Many spammers disguise their lowly intentions with subject lines that look like legitimate mail. Other spammers use odd spellings of "hot" words so their messages won't automatically be filtered into the recipient's junk bin.

Working Wisdom

Netiquette and Text Messaging Etiquette

The Internet is a new type of community that uses new forms of communication. Like any society, the Net has acceptable behavior rules and guidelines. If you follow these rules of netiquette, you'll be doing your part to make life on the Net easier for everybody—especially yourself.

➡ *Say what you mean, and say it with care.* After you send something electronically, there's no way to call it back. Compose each message carefully, and make sure it means what you intend it to mean. If you're replying to a message, double-check the heading to make sure your reply is going only to those people you intend to send it to. Even if you took only a few seconds to write your message, it may be broadcast far and wide and be preserved forever in online archives.

➡ *Keep it short.* Include a descriptive subject line, and limit the body to a screen or two. If you're replying to a long message, include a copy of the relevant part of the message, but not the whole message. Remember that many people receive hundreds of email messages each day, and they're more likely to read and respond to short ones.

➡ *Proofread your messages.* A famous *New Yorker* cartoon by Peter Steiner shows one dog telling another, "On the Internet no one knows you're a dog." You may not be judged by the color of your hair or the clothes you wear when you're posting messages, but that doesn't mean appearances aren't important. Other people will judge your intelligence and education by the spelling, grammar, punctuation, and clarity of your messages. If you want your messages to be taken seriously, present your best face.

➡ *Don't assume you're anonymous.* Your messages can say a lot about you. Those messages might be seen by more than your intended audience, and they won't necessarily go away when you want them to. Researcher Jonathan G. S. Koppell suggests a more contemporary caption for the *New Yorker* cartoon mentioned above: "On the Internet, everyone knows you're an aging, overweight, malamute-retriever mix living in the southwest, and with a preference for rawhide."

➡ *Learn the "nonverbal" language of the Net.* A simple phrase like "Nice job!" can have very different meanings depending on the tone of voice and body language behind it. Since body language and tone of voice can't easily be stuffed into a modem, online communities have developed text-based or graphical substitutes, sometimes called *emoticons*. The table below shows a few of the most common emoticons.

➡ *Know your abbreviations.* Text messaging is slow and tedious on cell phones and PDAs. To speed things up, a shorthand has developed for many common phrases. Knowing the meaning of abbreviations will save you time and help you understand the text messages you receive. See the table on the facing page for a list of some of the most common abbreviations.

➡ *Keep your cool.* Many otherwise timid people turn into raging bulls when they're online. The facelessness of Internet communication makes it all too easy to shoot from the hip, overstate arguments, and get caught up in a digital lynch-mob mentality. There's nothing wrong with expressing your emotions, but broadside attacks and half-truths can do serious damage to your online relationships. Online or off, freedom of speech is a right that carries responsibility.

➡ *Don't be a source of spam.* It's so easy to send multiple copies of email messages that it's tempting to broadcast too widely. Target your messages carefully; if you're trying to sell tickets to a local concert or advertise your garage sale, don't tell the whole world. If you do send a mass mailing, hide the recipient list to protect the privacy of your recipients. One way is to send the message to yourself and put everyone else in the bcc (blind carbon copy) field. And if you send repeated mass mailings, make sure you always include a message telling people how they can get off your list.

Common Emoticons

Emoticon	Vertical variant	Graphic	Meaning
:-)	(^^)		Humor or sarcasm
:-(	(;_;)		Sadness or anger
;-)	(^_-)		Sarcasm
:-/			Wry humor
:-P			I'm grossed out!

A few of the most common emoticons

8.27

- **Say no to spam.** People send spam because it gets results—mouse clicks to Web links, email replies, purchases, and more. If you want to do your part to wipe out spam, *never* reward spammers with your time or money.
- **Send no-frills mail.** Even if your email program makes it easy to use fancy formatting, embed HTML, and include attachments, it's usually better to err on the side of simplicity. Graphics and fancy formatting make message files bigger and slower to download. Many people turn off the HTML capabilities of their email programs to protect themselves from Web bugs (HTML code that sends messages back to the sender). And many email veterans fear attachments because of the risk of email viruses. If you don't need the extra baggage, why not leave it out?
- **Lurk before you leap.** People who silently monitor mailing lists and newsgroups without posting messages are called *lurkers*. There's no shame in lurking, especially if you're new to a group; it can help you to figure out what's appropriate. After you've learned the culture and conventions of a group, you'll be better able to contribute constructively and wisely.
- **Check your FAQs.** Many newsgroups and mailing lists have FAQs (pronounced "facks")—posted lists of frequently asked questions. These lists keep groups from being cluttered with the same old questions and answers, but only if members take advantage of them.
- **Give something back.** The Internet includes an online community of volunteers who answer beginner questions, archive files, moderate newsgroups, maintain public servers, and provide other helpful services. If you appreciate their work, tell them in words and show them in actions; do your part to help others in the Internet community.

Common Text Message Abbreviations

Message	Meaning
101	Beginner
2moro	Tomorrow
404	Clueless
4YI	For your information
AAMOF	As a matter of fact
AFAICT	As far as I can tell
AFK	Away from keyboard
aQr8	Accurate
AYT	Are you there?
B4N	Bye for now
BRB	Be right back
BTW	By the way
CID	Consider it done
dlAd	Delayed
doh	How stupid of me
FWIW	For what it's worth
HHOK	Ha ha only kidding
HRU	How are you?
IMHO	In my humble opinion
LOL	Laughing out loud
ROFL	Rolling on the floor laughing
RUF2C	Are you free to chat?
RUF2T	Are you free to talk?
RUOK	Are you OK?
TMB	Text me back
TNK	Thanks
WDYT	What do you think?

Text messaging abbreviations and their meanings

could be easily accessed by anyone with a basic knowledge of how Web addresses work. Microsoft corrected the problem, but questions about email security remain.

- *Email can be faked.* Email forgery can be a serious threat on a surprising number of email systems. The protocols at the heart of today's email system weren't designed with today's Internet in mind; they don't have mechanisms for ensuring that the sender of a message is who that person claims to be. Some systems have safeguards against sending mail using someone else's ID, but none completely eliminates the threat. In time, it's likely that a digital signature will be encoded into every email message (using cryptography technology described in Chapter 10). Until then, forgery is a problem.

- *Email works only if everybody plays.* Just as the postal system depends on each of us checking our mailboxes daily, an email system can work only if all subscribers regularly log in and check their mail. Most people develop the habit quickly if they know important information is only available online.

- *Email and instant messaging filter out many "human" components of communication.* When Bell invented the telephone, the public reaction was cool and critical. Business people were reluctant to communicate through a device that didn't allow them to look each other in the eye and shake hands. Although this reaction might seem strange today, it's worth a second look given the even more impersonal nature of email and IM. When people communicate, part of the message is hidden in body language, eye contact, voice inflections, and other nonverbal signals. The telephone strips visual cues out of a message, and this can lead to misunderstandings. Most online communication systems peel away the sounds as well as the sights, leaving only plain words on a screen—words that might be misread if they aren't chosen carefully. What's more, email and teleconferences seldom replace casual water cooler conversations—those chance meetings that result in important communications and connections.

Problems notwithstanding, email and instant messaging have become fixtures in businesses, schools, and government offices everywhere.

Wireless Issues: Access, Security, and Privacy

A **magical thing** happens when you get your first **e-mail** from someone who says, **"Me, too."**

Meg Hourihan, blogger

Publicly accessible wireless access points (called *hot spots*) are popping up all over the place. Most hot spots charge users for access, but free access is available in certain locations. Many colleges and universities now support free campus-wide hot spots to their students. Hermosa Beach, California, is installing access points, giving every resident in the town free wireless access to the Internet. The City of Spokane, Washington, has established a free wireless network covering 100 city blocks of its downtown core.

The growing popularity of Internet-accessible mobile devices creates a need for people to find hot spots. *Warchalking* is an unofficial, grassroots movement to mark hot spots. Warchalkers identify a wireless access point by writing a symbol on a nearby sidewalk or wall. The symbol identifies whether the node is open, closed, or protected by WEP. The Wi-Fi Alliance is more organized, "establishment" effort to identity hot spots. The organization has created the Wi-Fi ZONE program, with its own logo, that commercial enterprises can display to indicate they are operating a hot spot.

Offering free wireless access is a way for an organization to market itself, but there are downsides to providing this service. Suppose a small coffee shop decides to become a cybercafe by setting up a hot spot for its customers. The hot spot may prove to be a draw for new customers, but will these customers expect technical support, too? Are baristas capable of helping people who are having trouble connecting their notebook computers to the network? Customers who are reading email or surfing the Web stay longer than those who are simply drinking a cup of coffee. It may hurt a coffee shop's profits if some customers occupy a table for an hour or more during lunch. Some cybercafes have solved this problem by turning off the network during peak business hours, but that decision has its risks, too.

ssid

bandwidth

Open Node

ssid

bandwidth

Closed Node

ssid

access
contact

bandwidth

WEP Node

8.28 Hot spots are unofficially identified through warchalking (first three symbols) and the Wi-Fi ZONE program (rightmost symbol). The ssid is the password you type to connect your device to the network.

Wireless networks introduce new security concerns. A wireless access point broadcasts packets in all directions. The network forms a sphere with a diameter of up to 300 feet (the length of a football field). If the network is not secured, anyone with a laptop inside this virtual sphere can "sniff" network traffic and read what you're writing, and collect email addresses, phone numbers, and other personal information. The *WEP* (Wired Equivalent Privacy) encryption scheme improves the security of wireless networks. WEP makes your data as secure as it would be on an unencrypted, wired Ethernet. However, it does not make data completely secure. Businesses that need extra security for their networks can take two additional steps. They can treat their wireless network as an insecure network and put a *firewall* between their wireless network and their wired network. (A firewall blocks unauthorized data transfers. We'll discuss how firewalls work in Chapter 10.) They can also make a wireless network more secure through the use of *VPN* (Virtual Private Network), which provides another layer of encryption to the messages.

If you are using a public hot spot, be aware that the data you send and receive may not be secure. It is a bad idea to transmit valuable information, such as your phone number, Social Security number, credit card numbers, or even your email address when you're using a public hot spot. You never know who may be eavesdropping.

Digital Communication in Perspective

The lines that separate the telephone industry, the computer industry, and the home entertainment industry are blurring as voices, video, music, and messages flow through a complex web of wires, fiber-optic cables, and wireless connections. Many services we take for granted today—video rentals, cable TV, newspapers, and magazines, for example—will be transformed or replaced by digital, high-bandwidth, interactive delivery systems of the future. At the same time, entirely new forms of communication are likely to emerge. Telecommunications technology is rapidly changing our lives, and the changes will accelerate as the technology improves. We'll explore these changes in the next chapter as we focus on the Internet—the network of networks at the center of the communication revolution.

Before we do, let's step back and put electronic communication in a larger perspective. As futurist Stewart Brand reminded us in his groundbreaking book, *The Media Lab*:

> *We can be grateful for the vast dispersed populations of peasant and tribal cultures in the world who have never used a telephone or a TV, who walk where they're going, who live by local subsistence skills honed over millennia. You need to go on foot in Africa, Asia, South America to realize how many of these people there are and how sound they are. If the world city goes smash, they'll pick up the pieces, as they've done before. Whatever happens, they are a reminder that electronic communication may be essential to one kind of living, but it is superfluous to another.*

Inventing the FUTURE

A World Without Wires

We stand at the brink of a transformation. It is a moment that echoes the birth of the Internet in the mid-'70s. . . . This time it is not wires but the air between them that is being transformed.

—Chris Anderson, Editor in Chief, Wired

Most people who access the Internet still make their connections through wires—telephone lines, TV cables, or specialized data-only conduits. But there's a wireless revolution afoot, and it is beginning to change the game for millions of Internet users. Wi-Fi represents the first major victory in the revolution. Wireless LANs based on the Wi-Fi standard are turning up in home networks, public buildings, and neighborhood freenets. Wi-Fi has captured the attention of populists who see Wi-Fi as a way to provide free Internet access to everyone. Whether these dreams are realized, Wi-Fi has definitely made it easier for people on the move to maintain Internet access.

But current Wi-Fi technology isn't the end of the wireless road. Several other promising technologies are being tested and refined in research labs. Here's a sampler:

➡ *802.11n* is a wireless LAN standard with approximately three times the bandwidth of 802.11g. When 802.11n products appear, moving data to and from mobile devices will be faster than ever, accelerating the migration to wireless networks.

➡ *802.11e* is yet another Wi-Fi-related standard that focuses on quality of service, particularly the timely delivery of data packets. That's important for data streaming applications, such as video conferencing and voice-over IP.

➡ *802.11i* adds another level of security to Wi-Fi, which will enable businesses to use wireless networks for more sensitive transactions.

➡ *WiMax* will give consumers a wireless alternative to cable or DSL service. A WiMax station will provide high-speed Internet access to customers up to 30 miles away. To use WiMax, customers will need to mount a dish antenna outside their building. An extension to WiMax, called *802.16e*, will let mobile computer users access the WiMax network.

➡ *Ultrawideband* is a short-range wireless technology that transmits ultra-high-speed signals over a wide spectrum of frequencies. **8.29**

This low-power technology could transform entertainment and communication systems if it can be refined so it doesn't interfere with more critical communication systems.

➡ *Mesh networks* are an alternative to today's networks that rely on centralized routers. In a mesh network, a message hops from wireless device to wireless device until it finds its destination; there's no need to go through a central hub on the way. Mesh networks might offer faster and cheaper connections than today's networks, but they also raise new security issues.

➡ *Adaptive radio* is a technology that enables wireless devices to transmit messages selectively based on other wireless network traffic. By monitoring messages sent by other devices and sending its own messages in unused gaps in the spectrum, an adaptive device will be able to avoid the interference that plagues many other wireless technologies.

➡ *Software-defined radio* is a technology that allows a single wireless hardware device to be reprogrammed on the fly to serve a variety of functions. Just as software can transform a PC from a communication tool to a music workstation to an accountant's ledger, it can be used to change a single wireless tool into a cell phone, a garage door opener, a game machine, a baby monitor, a messaging machine, a Web browser, or a TV remote. Researchers are working on the chip technology to make such a universal communicator a reality, hopefully eliminating much of the techno-clutter that litters our lives.

It's not clear how all of these emerging technologies will converge. What is clear is that the wireless revolution is far from over. ～

Time to Do Everything Except Think *David Brooks*

Is there a downside to the digital communication explosion? In this lighthearted article, first published in the April 30, 2001, issue of Newsweek, *David Brooks raises some serious questions about being overconnected. Brooks is the author of* Bobos in Paradise.

Somewhere up in the canopy of society, way above where normal folks live, there will soon be people who live in a state of perfect wirelessness. They'll have mobile phones that download the Internet, check scores and trade stocks. They'll have Palm handhelds that play music, transfer photos and get Global Positioning System read-outs. They'll have laptops on which they watch movies, listen to baseball games and check inventory back at the plant. In other words, every gadget they own will perform all the functions of all the other gadgets they own, and they will be able to do it all anywhere, any time.

Wireless Woman will do a full day's work on the beach in her bikini: her personal digital assistant comes with a thong clip so she can wear it on her way to the pina colada stand. Her phones beep, her pagers flash red lights; when they go off, she looks like a video arcade. Wireless Man will be able to put on his performance underwear, hop in his SUV and power himself up to the top of a Colorado mountain peak. He'll be up there with his MP3 device and his carabiners enjoying the view while conference-calling the sales force, and playing Mega-Death with gamers in Tokyo and Sydney. He'll be smart enough to have enough teeny-tiny lithium batteries on hand to last weeks, and if he swallows them they'd cure depression for life. He's waiting for them to develop a lap-top filled with helium that would actually weigh less than nothing, and if it could blow up into an inflatable sex doll he'd never have to come down.

So there he sits in total freedom on that Rocky Mountain peak. The sky is blue. The air is crisp. Then the phone rings. His assistant wants to know if he wants to switch the company's overnight carrier. He turns off his phone so he can enjoy a little spiritual bliss. But first, there's his laptop. Maybe somebody sent him an impor-tant email. He wrestles with his conscience. His con-science loses. It's so easy to check, after all . . .

Never being out of touch means never being able to get away. But Wireless Man's problem will be worse than that. His brain will have adapted to the tempo of wireless life. Every 15 seconds there is some new thing to respond to. Soon he has this little rhythm machine in his brain. He does everything fast. He answers emails fast and sloppily. He's bought the fastest machines, and now the idea of waiting for something to download is a personal insult. His brain is operating at peak RPMs.

He sits amid nature's grandeur and says, "It's beautiful. But it's not moving. I wonder if I got any new voice mails." He's addicted to the perpetual flux of the information net-works. He craves his next data fix. He's a speed freak, an info junkie. He wants to slow down, but can't.

Today's business people live in an overcommunicated world. There are too many Web sites, too many reports, too many bits of information bidding for their attention. The successful ones are forced to become deft machete wielders in this jungle of communication. They ruthlessly cut away at all the extraneous data that are encroaching upon them. They speed through their tasks so they can cover as much ground as possible, answering dozens of emails at a sitting and scrolling past dozens more. After all, the main scarcity in their life is not money; it's time. They guard every precious second, the way a desert wan-derer guards his water.

The problem with all this speed, and the frantic energy that is spent using time efficiently, is that it undermines creativity. After all, creativity is usually something that hap-pens while you're doing something else: when you're in the shower your brain has time to noodle about and cre-ate the odd connections that lead to new ideas. But if your brain is always multitasking, or responding to techno-prompts, there is no time or energy for undirected mental play. Furthermore, if you are consumed by the same information loop circulating around everyone else, you don't have anything to stimulate you into thinking dif-ferently. You don't have time to read the history book or the science book that may actually prompt you to see your own business in a new light. You don't have access to unexpected knowledge. You're just swept along in the same narrow current as everyone else, which is swift but not deep.

So here's how I'm going to get rich. I'm going to design a placebo machine. It'll be a little gadget with voice recog-nition and everything. Wireless People will be able to log on and it will tell them they have no messages. After a while, they'll get used to having no messages. They'll be able to experience life instead of information. They'll be able to reflect instead of react. My machine won't even require batteries.

Discussion Questions

1. Do you think Wireless Woman and Wireless Man are realistic? Explain.

2. Do you agree that speed and efficiency undermine creativity? Explain.

Summary

Networking is one of the most important trends in computing today. Computer networks are growing in popularity because they allow computers to share hardware, and to send software and data back and forth. They enable people to work together in ways that would be difficult or impossible without networks.

LANs are made up of computers that are close enough to be directly connected with cables or wireless radio transmitters/receivers. Most LANs include shared printers and file servers. WANs are made up of computers separated by a considerable distance. The computers are connected to each other through the telephone network, which includes cables, microwave transmission towers, and communication satellites. Many computer networks are connected together through the Internet so messages and data can pass back and forth among them. Some specialized networks serve unique functions, including global positioning systems and financial systems.

Most computer networks today use the Ethernet architecture; an Ethernet port is a standard feature on most modern PCs. Computers can be directly connected to networks through Ethernet ports. When high-speed direct connections aren't possible, a PC can transmit and receive signals over standard phone lines with a modem. The modem converts the PC's digital signals to analog so they can travel through standard phone lines. Broadband connections offer much more bandwidth than standard modem connections do, so they can transmit large amounts of information more quickly. These include DSL, which uses standard phone lines; cable modems, which use cable TV lines; satellite,

which uses TV satellite dishes; and Wi-Fi, which uses short-range wireless 802.11 transmitters. Wi-Fi is a type of wireless network technology that's exploding in popularity because of its potential for providing universal Internet access. All of these technologies offer connections to Internet backbones, many of which transmit astronomical amounts of data quickly through fiber-optic cables.

Communication software takes care of the details of communication between machines—details like protocols that determine how signals will be sent and received. Network operating systems typically handle the mechanics of LAN communication. Many popular PC operating systems include peer-to-peer networking software, so any PC or Mac on a network can serve as a server as well as a client. Terminal programs enable personal computers to function as character-based terminals when connected to other PCs or to timesharing computers. Other types of specialized client programs have graphical user interfaces and additional functionality. Timesharing operating systems enable multiuser computers to communicate with several terminals at a time.

Email, instant messaging, and teleconferencing are the most common forms of communication between people on computer networks. They offer many advantages over traditional mail and telephone communication and can shorten or eliminate many meetings. But because of several important limitations, email and teleconferencing cannot completely replace older communication media. People who communicate with these new media should follow simple rules of netiquette and exercise a degree of caution to avoid many of the most common problems.

Key Terms

Interactive Activities

1. The *Computer Confluence* CD-ROM contains self-test quiz questions related to this chapter, including multiple-choice, true or false, and matching questions.

2. The *Computer Confluence* Web site, http://computerconfluence.com, contains self-test exercises related to this chapter. Follow the instructions for taking a quiz. After you've completed your quiz, you can email the results to your instructor.

3. The Web site also contains open-ended discussion questions called Internet Explorations. Discuss one or more of the Internet Exploration questions at the section for this chapter.

True or False

1. Today virtually all computer networks are general-purpose networks connected to the Internet.

2. The standard PC serial port is being phased out and replaced by a standard parallel port.

3. The most common types of networks today use a standard networking architecture known as Ethernet.

4. A single fiber-optic cable has the bandwidth of thousands of copper telephone cables.

5. Because peer-to-peer networking software is built into the Windows and Macintosh operating systems, a modern desktop computer can act as both client and server on a network.

6. If you want your Windows PC to read a file created on a Macintosh, you must use data-translation software.

7. Depending on your email client program and your preferences, your mail might be stored on a remote host or downloaded and stored on your local machine.

8. The line that separates computer communication and telephone communication is being blurred by devices and technologies that operate in both realms.

9. Simple technological solutions can eliminate the spam problem for email users.

10. Email and instant messaging can filter out many human components of communication, increasing the chance of misinterpreted messages.

Multiple Choice

1. Computer networks
   a. Allow people to share hardware resources
   b. Make it easier for people to share data
   c. Support collaboration through tools, such as email and instant messaging
   d. All of the above
   e. None of the above

2. What is a service that connects computers and peripherals in the same building called?
   a. Connection area network (CAN)
   b. Local area network (LAN)
   c. Metropolitan area network (MAN)
   d. Remote area network (RAN)
   e. Wide area network (WAN)

3. What is a service that connects two or more networks within a city called?
   a. Connection area network (CAN)
   b. Local area network (LAN)
   c. Metropolitan area network (MAN)
   d. Remote area network (RAN)
   e. Wide area network (WAN)

4. A modem
   a. Allows a computer to communicate with its peripherals, such as printers and scanners
   b. Increases the speed with which a computer can communicate over a telephone line
   c. Converts a digital signal into an analog signal and vice versa
   d. Allows a Windows PC to run Macintosh applications
   e. Performs the same functions as an Ethernet port, except faster

5. Which of the following does not affect bandwidth?
   a. The amount of network traffic
   b. The software protocols of the network
   c. The type of network connection
   d. The type of information being transmitted
   e. The physical media that make up the network

6. What is the most common reason for installing a Wi-Fi hub in a home?
   a. To enable a PC to connect to a cell phone
   b. To make client/server computing possible
   c. To make it possible to connect Bluetooth-enabled devices to a network
   d. To allow PCs to connect to a network without wires
   e. To create a wireless alternative to hi-fi home entertainment systems

7. If you want to share a document with other people whose computers are connected to your LAN, you should upload the document to a
   a. File server
   b. Client server
   c. Print server
   d. Document server
   e. Upload server

8. What is an important difference between Internet newsgroups and mailing lists?
   a. A mailing list message goes to only a specific group of people, whereas a newsgroup message is available for anyone to see.
   b. A mailing list message is posted via email, whereas a newsgroup message requires special posting software.
   c. A mailing list message is posted to a special Web mailbox, whereas a newsgroup message is delivered directly to group member mailboxes.
   d. All of the above are true.
   e. There are no significant differences between the two.

9. What is the main difference between instant messaging (IM) and email?
   a. The use of moderated groups for IM
   b. The ability of email to handle real-time communication
   c. The GUI of the IM client software
   d. The asynchronous nature of email communication
   e. There are no significant differences between the two.

10. The number of email messages delivered each day far exceeds the number of letters delivered by the U.S. postal service. Why?
    a. Email is faster than snail mail is.
    b. Email is asynchronous communication.
    c. Email facilitates group communication.
    d. Email can save money.
    e. All of the above

11. Today's email system is built on protocols that
    a. Don't ensure that each sender has a verifiable identity
    b. Automatically filter spam based on objectionable content
    c. Can be modified by anyone with systems administration clearance
    d. Apply directly to instant messaging systems
    e. All of the above

12. What percentage of email messages is junk email (spam)?
    a. Less than 10 percent
    b. About 20 percent
    c. About 30 percent
    d. About 40 percent
    e. More than 50 percent

13. Which of these is okay according to the generally accepted rules of netiquette?
    a. Sending a message to ten thousand members of a worldwide society of birdwatchers inviting them to your local club's weekly outing
    b. Lurking in a hang-glider enthusiasts newsgroup without posting any messages
    c. Quickly posting on a DJ newsgroup 15 "help me" beginner questions about the second-hand turntables you just bought without manuals
    d. Responding to an antiwar group email with a heated message that attacks the personal integrity of the sender
    e. Sending 36 unsolicited high-resolution family photos to everyone on your list of email friends

14. Many experts say we're at the beginning of a revolution that is creating a vast grassroots network of public and private wireless hubs based on
    a. 3G technology
    b. Mesh network technology
    c. Wi-Fi technology
    d. Bluetooth technology
    e. Adaptive radio technology

15. What should people who use a public hot spot be aware of?
    a. There is no such thing as free access to the Internet.
    b. Wireless connections cannot be used to surf the Web.
    c. A notebook computer must be plugged into a power source in order to connect to the network.
    d. Exposure to radio waves is harmful to pregnant women.
    e. Data transmitted over networks without WEP key encryption can be viewed by malicious eavesdroppers.

Review Questions

1. Define or describe each of the key terms listed in the Key Terms section. Check your answers using the glossary.

2. Give three general reasons for the importance of computer networking. (*Hint*: Each reason is related to one of the three essential components of every computer system.)

3. How do the three general reasons listed in Question 2 relate specifically to LANs?

4. How do the three general reasons listed in Question 2 relate specifically to WANs?

5. Under what circumstances is a modem necessary for connecting computers in networks? What does the modem do?

6. Describe at least two different kinds of communication software.

7. How could a file server be used in a student computer lab? What software licensing issues would be raised by using a file server in a student lab?

8. What are the differences between email and instant messaging systems?

9. Describe some things you can do with email that you can't do with regular mail.

10. Describe several potential problems associated with email and teleconferencing.

11. "Money is just another form of information." Explain this statement, and describe how it relates to communication technology.

12. Wi-Fi and Bluetooth wireless technologies are designed to serve different purposes than mobile phone technology does. Explain this statement.

13. Why is netiquette important? Give some examples of netiquette.

Discussion Questions

1. Suppose you have an important message to send to a friend in another city, and you can use the telephone, email, real-time teleconference, fax, or overnight mail service. Discuss the advantages and disadvantages of each. See if you can think of a situation for each of the five options in which that particular option is the most appropriate choice.

2. Some people choose to spend several hours every day online. Do you see potential hazards in this kind of heavy modem use? Explain your answer.

3. Should spam be illegal? Explain your answer.

4. In the quote at the end of the chapter, Stewart Brand points out that electronic communication is essential for some of the world's people and irrelevant to others. What distinguishes these two groups? What advantages and disadvantages does each have?

5. Do you think Wi-Fi and other wireless technology put us on the brink of a communication revolution? Why or why not?

Projects

1. Find out about your school's computer networks. Are there many LANs? How are they connected? Who has access to them? What are they used for?

2. Spend a few hours exploring an online service like AOL. Describe the problems you encounter in the process. Which parts of the service are the most useful and interesting?

3. Imagine you are living in a house with three other students, and everyone has a PC. Determine what you would need to purchase to create a home network that would enable all four of you to access the Internet with only a single subscription to a high-speed Internet provider (either cable or DSL). Compare the cost of a wired network based on 100 Mbps Ethernet versus a wireless network based on 802.11g.

4. Identify a wireless hot spot in your city or town. Interview a staff person at the establishment. Does the hot spot provide free access or does it require payment? If it requires payment, how does it charge for access? What security measures does it have in place? What have been the consequences (both good and bad) of creating a wireless hot spot?

Sources and Resources

Books

The Communications Miracle: The Telecommunication Pioneers from Morse to the Information Superhighway, by John Bray (New York: Plenum, 1995). This book gives the communication revolution a historical perspective by mixing technical explanations with human stories.

How Networks Work, Sixth Edition, by Frank J. Derfler, Jr., and Les Freed (Indianapolis, IN: Que, 2003). This book follows the model popularized with the *How Computers Work* series. It uses a mix of text and graphics to illuminate the nuts and bolts of PC networks.

The Essential Guide to Networking, by James Edward Keogh (Upper Saddle River, NJ: Prentice Hall, 2000). This book is part of a series of technical *Essential* books for nontechnical professionals. This one provides a broad overview of network technology, from LANs and WANs to the Internet and wireless networks.

The Essential Guide to Telecommunications, Third Edition, by Annabel Z. Dodd (Upper Saddle River, NJ: Prentice Hall, 2002). This popular book presents a clear, comprehensive guide to the telecommunications industry and technology, including telephone systems, cable systems, wireless systems, and the Internet. If you want to understand how the pieces of our communication networks fit together, this book is a great place to start.

The Wireless Network Start Kit: The Practical Guide to Wi-Fi Networks for Windows and Macintosh, Second Edition, by Adam Engst and Glenn Fleishman (Berkeley, CA: Peachpit Press, 2004). This book is an excellent introduction to the wonderful world of Wi-Fi. It answers most any what, why, and how question you're likely to have if you're setting up a wireless network.

The Essential Guide to Wireless Communications Applications: From Cellular Systems to Wi-Fi, Second Edition, by Andy Dornan (Upper Saddle River, NJ: Prentice Hall, 2002). Yet another *Essential Guide,* this one focuses on networks without wires. The book includes clear explanations of technical nuts and bolts, plus a chapter on health risks of wireless technology.

Computer Networks and Internets, Fourth Edition, by Douglas E. Comer, CD-ROM by Ralph Droms (Upper Saddle River, NJ: Prentice Hall, 2003). This text answers the question, "How do computer networks and internets operate?" Coverage includes LANs, WANs, Internet packets, digital telephony, protocols, client/server interaction, network security, and the underpinnings of the World Wide Web. A CD-ROM and a companion Web site supplement the text.

Wireless Nation: The Frenzied Launch of the Cellular Revolution, by James B. Murray (Perseus Books, 2001). The mobile phone and the PC both burst into our culture in the last decades of the twentieth century, and they came together through the Internet. This book chronicles the rise of mobile communication technology.

Tyranny of the Moment: Fast and Slow Time in the Information Age, by Thomas Hylland (London: Pluto Press, 2001). In an age when instantaneous communication has never been easier, time is one of our scarcest commodities. Hylland explores this paradox and discusses the social and political implications of the evaporation of "slow time."

F2f, by Phillip Finch (New York: Bantam, 1997). As communities form on computer networks, they bring with them many of the problems found in other communities. This suspense thriller captures some of the potential risks of online communities in an exciting, tightly written story.

Periodicals

Network Magazine focuses on networks with a business perspective.

Computer Telephony and *Communications Solutions* are two magazines that cover the rapidly changing territory where computers and telephones meet. Both periodicals are aimed at professionals and include a fair amount of technical material.

Web Pages

Computer networking technology is changing faster than publishers can print books and periodicals about it. The *Computer Confluence* Web site can connect you to up-to-date networking information all over the Internet.

Multimedia

on the CD-ROM and the Web:

~ **Animated illustrations** of basic World Wide Web technologies

~ Additional content on how **peer-to-peer file sharing** and TCP/IP work

~ A video of virtual community pioneer Howard Rheingolds

~ Additional content on instant messaging and streaming media

~ Interactive **self-study quizzes**

~ **Instant access** to glossary and key terms references

. . . and more.

www computerconfluence.com

Objectives

After you read this chapter you should be able to:

▶ **Explain how and why the Internet was created**

▶ **Describe the technology that's at the heart of the Internet**

▶ **Describe the technology that makes the Web work as a multimedia mass medium**

▶ **Discuss the tools people use to build Web sites**

▶ **Discuss the trends that are changing the Internet and the way people use it**

▶ **Discuss some of the most important social and political issues raised by the growth of the Internet**

▶ **Describe various ways that governments restrict access to the Internet**

CHAPTER 9

ARPANET PIONEERS BUILD AN UNRELIABLE NETWORK . . . ON PURPOSE

In the 1960s, the world of computers was a technological Tower of Babel; most computers couldn't communicate with each other. When people needed to move data from one computer to another, they carried or mailed a magnetic tape or a deck of punch cards. While most of the world viewed computers only as giant number crunchers, J. C. R. Licklider, Robert Taylor, and a small group of visionary computer scientists saw the computer's potential as a communication device. They envisioned a network that would enable researchers to share computing resources and ideas.

U.S. military strategists during those Cold War years had a vision, too: They foresaw an enemy attack crippling the U.S. government's ability to communicate. The Department of Defense wanted a network that could function even if some connections were destroyed. They provided one million dollars to Taylor and other scientists and engineers to build a small experimental network.

It's a bit like **climbing a mountain**. You don't know how far you've come until you **stop and look back**.

—*Vint Cerf, ARPANET pioneer and first president of the Internet Society*

The groundbreaking result, launched in 1969, was called ARPANET, for Advanced Research Projects Agency NETwork. When a half-dozen researchers sent the first historic message from UCLA to Doug Engelbart's lab at the Stanford Research Institute, no one even thought to take a picture.

ARPANET was built on two unorthodox assumptions: The network itself was unreliable, so it had to be able to overcome its own unreliability, and all computers on the network would be equal in their ability to communicate with other network computers. In ARPANET there was no central authority because that would make the entire network vulnerable to attack. Messages were contained in software "packets" that could travel independently by any number of different paths, through all kinds of computers, toward their destinations.

ARPANET grew quickly into an international network with hundreds of military and university sites. In addition

Inside the Internet and the World Wide Web

9.1 The team that built the predecessor to the Internet included, from front to back: Bob Taylor, Vint Cerf, Frank Heart, Larry Roberts, Len Kleinrock, Bob Kahn, Wes Clark, Doug Engelbart, Barry Wessler, Dave Walden, Severo Ornstein, Truett Thach, Roger Scantlebury, Charlie Herzfeld, Ben Barker, Jon Postel, Steve Crocker, Bill Naylor, and Roland Bryan.

to carrying research data, ARPANET channeled debates over the Vietnam War and intense discussions about Space War, an early computer game. ARPANET's peer-to-peer networking philosophy and protocols were copied in other networks in the 1980s. Vint Cerf and Bob Kahn, two of the original researchers, developed the protocols that became the standard computer communication language, allowing different computer networks to be linked.

In 1990 ARPANET was disbanded, having fulfilled its research mission, but its technology spawned the Internet. In a recent interview, Cerf said about the network he helped create, "It was supposed to be a highly robust technology for supporting military command and control. It did that in the Persian Gulf War. But, along the way, it became a major research support infrastructure and now has become the best example of global information infrastructure that we have."

The ARPANET pioneers have gone on to work on dozens of other significant projects and products. In the words of Bob Kahn, "Those were very exciting days, but there are new frontiers in every direction I can look these days." ∼

The team that designed ARPANET suspected they were building something important. They couldn't have guessed, though, that they were laying the groundwork for a system that would become a universal research tool, a hotbed of business activity, a virtual shopping mall, a popular social hangout, a publisher's clearinghouse of up-to-the-minute information, and one of the most talked about institutions of our time.

The Internet is a technology, a tool, and a culture. Computer scientists originally designed it for computer scientists, and other scientists and engineers are continually adding new features. Consequently, the vocabulary of the Internet often seems like a flurry of technobabble to the rest of us. You don't need to analyze every acronym to make sense of the Internet, but your Net experiences can be far more rewarding if you understand the concepts at the heart of basic netspeak terminology. In this chapter we delve into the Internet to make those concepts clear.

Inside the Internet

It shouldn't be too much of a surprise that the Internet has evolved into a force **strong enough** to reflect the **greatest hopes and fears** of those who use it. After all, it was designed to **withstand nuclear war**, not just the **puny huffs and puffs** of politicians and religious fanatics.

—*Denise Caruso, digital commerce columnist,* New York Times

The Internet includes dozens of national, statewide, and regional networks, hundreds of networks within colleges and research labs, and thousands of commercial sites. Most sites are in the United States, but the Internet has connections in almost every country in the world. More importantly, the

Internet is not controlled by any one government, corporation, individual, or legal system. Several international advisory organizations develop standards and protocols for the evolving Internet, but no one has the power to control the Net's operation or evolution. The Internet is, in a sense, a massive anarchy unlike any other organization the world has ever seen.

Counting Connections

No **LAN** is an **island**.

—*Karyl Scott*, InfoWorld *writer*

In its early days, the Internet connected only a few dozen computers at U.S. universities and government research centers, and the government paid most of the cost of building and operating it. Today, it connects millions of computers in almost every country in the world, and costs are shared by thousands of connected organizations. It's impossible to pin down the exact size of the Internet for several reasons:

- The Internet is growing too fast to track. Millions of new users connect to the Internet every year in the United States alone, and the rest of the world is adding new connections by the minute.
- The Internet is decentralized. There's no "Internet Central" that keeps track of user activity or network connections. To make matters worse for Internet counters, some parts of the Internet can't be accessed by the general public; they're sealed off to protect private information.
- The Internet doesn't have hard boundaries. There are several ways to connect to the Internet (described later in this chapter); these different types of connections offer different classes of services and different degrees of interactivity. As choices proliferate, it's becoming harder to know exactly what it means to "belong to the Internet."

This last point is worth a closer look. It's easier to understand the different types of Internet access if you know a little bit about the protocols that make the Internet work.

9.2 Cyber cafes around the world, like this one in China, enable travelers to stay connected to their homes and the rest of the world. Customers often pay by the minute to log into their home servers to keep up on email, favorite Web sites, and IM contacts.

Internet Protocols

The protocol at the heart of the Internet is called **TCP/IP (Transmission Control Protocol/ Internet Protocol)**. It was developed as an experiment in **internetworking**—connecting different types of networks and computer systems. The TCP/IP specifications were published as **open standards**, not owned by any company. As a result, TCP/IP became the "language" of the Internet, allowing cross-network communication for almost every type of computer and network. These protocols are generally invisible to users; they're hidden deep in software that takes care of communication details behind the scenes. They define how information can be transferred between machines and how machines on the network can be identified with unique addresses.

The **most important quality** of the Internet is that it lends itself to **radical reinvention**. . . . In another 10 years, the **only part** of the Internet as we know it now that will have survived will be **bits and pieces** of the underlying Internet protocol. . . .

—*Paul Saffo, director of the Institute for the Future*

The TCP protocols define a system similar in many ways to the postal system. When a message is sent on the Internet, it is broken into *packets*, in the same way you might pack your belongings in several individually addressed boxes before you ship them to a new

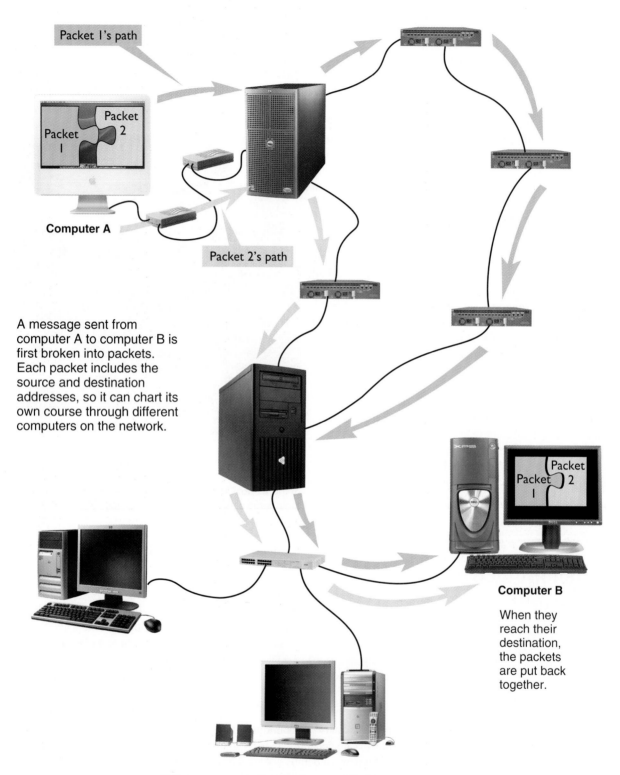

Packet 1's path

Packet 2's path

Computer A

A message sent from computer A to computer B is first broken into packets. Each packet includes the source and destination addresses, so it can chart its own course through different computers on the network.

Computer B

When they reach their destination, the packets are put back together.

9.3 Packet switching gets the message through.

location. Each packet has all the information it needs to travel independently from network to network toward its destination. Different packets might take different routes, just as different parcels might be routed through different cities by the postal system. The host systems that use software to decide how to route Internet transmissions are called *routers*, although sometimes less flexible hardware, *switches*, can do the same routing work faster. Regardless of the route they follow, the packets eventually reach their destination, where they are reassembled into the original message. This **packet-switching** model is flexible and robust, allowing messages to get through even when part of the network is down.

The other part of TCP/IP—the IP part—defines the addressing system of the Internet. Every host computer on the Internet has a unique *IP address*, a string of four numbers separated by periods, or, as they say in Net speak, dots. A typical IP address might look like this: 123.23.168.22 ("123 dot 23 dot 168 dot 22"). Every packet includes the IP address of the sending computer and the receiving computer.

Internet Addresses

In practice, people seldom see or use numerical IP addresses, because the Internet's *domain name system (DNS)* translates the IP address into something that's easier for humans to read and remember. The DNS uses a string of names separated by dots to specify the exact Internet location of the host computer.

Internet addresses are classified by *domains*. In the United States the most widely used top-level domains are general categories that describe types of organizations:

- (.edu) Educational sites
- (.com) Commercial sites
- (.gov) Government sites
- (.mil) Military sites
- (.net) Network administration sites
- (.org) Nonprofit organizations

The Internet Ad Hoc Committee recently created seven additional top-level domain names:

- (.aero) Air transport organizations
- (.biz) Businesses
- (.coop) Cooperative businesses such as credit unions
- (.info) Information services
- (.museum) Museums
- (.name) Personal registration by name
- (.pro) Licensed professionals, including lawyers, doctors, and accountants

Some of these domains, including .com, .net, .org, and .info, are open to anyone without restriction. For example, you could have a Web site or an email address in the .net domain whether or not you're part of a nonprofit organization. Other domains, including .edu and .mil, are restricted so only people in the designated organizations can use them. Outside (and occasionally inside) the United States, top-level domains are two-letter country codes, such as .jp for Japan, .th for Thailand, .au for Australia, .uk for United Kingdom, and .us for United States.

Some domain names are quite valuable. The tiny Pacific nation of Tuvalu has sold its domain name to a U.S. Internet company. The firm markets the .tv domain name to television-related companies. The 10,000 residents of Tuvalu are using the income—$4 million a year—to build new schools, roads, and electrical systems.

The top-level domain name is the last part of the address. The other parts of the address, when read in reverse, provide information that narrows down the exact location on the network. The words in the domain name, like the lines in a post office address, are arranged hierarchically from little to big. They might include the name of the host computer, the name of the department or network within the organization, and the name of the organization.

The domain naming system is used in virtually all email addresses and Web URLs. A Web URL specifies the IP address of the Web server that houses the page. In an email

kelly@cs.allaire.edu

kelly is the login name of the user.

cs is the name of kelly's host network in the Computer Science Department.

allaire is the domain name for Allaire State University's LAN, which includes the cs LAN.

edu is the name of the top-level domain containing Internet educational sites.

9.4 Anatomy of an email address.

---

address, the domain name system is used to pinpoint the Internet location of the host computer that contains the user's mail server. The email address includes the user name and the host address, as illustrated above:

Here are some other examples of email addresses using the domain name system:

- president@whitehouse.gov
- crabbyabby@AOL.com
- hazel_filbertnut@admin.gmcc.ab.ca

User *president* whose mail is stored on the host *whitehouse* in the government domain

User called *crabbyabby* whose mail is handled by AOL, a commercial service provider

User *hazel_filbertnut* at the *admin* server for Grant MacEwan Community College in Alberta, Canada

Internet Access Options

Computers connect to the Internet through three basic types of connections: direct connections, dial-up connections through modems, and broadband connections through high-speed alternatives to modems.

The **grand design** keeps getting grander. A **global computer** is taking shape, and we're **all connected** to it.

—*Stewart Brand, in* The Media Lab

Direct Connections

In many schools and businesses, computers have a direct (dedicated) connection to the Internet through a LAN and have their own IP addresses. A direct connection offers several advantages: You can take full advantage of Internet services without dialing in; your files are stored on your computer, not on a remote host; and response time is much faster, making it possible to transfer large files (like multimedia documents) quickly. Direct-connect digital lines come in many varieties, including *T1* connections, which can transmit voice, data, and video at roughly 1.5Mbps, and *T3*, which is even faster. (On some continents, a technology called E1 is used instead of T1.)

Dial-up Connections

If your computer isn't directly connected to the Internet, you can temporarily connect to an Internet host through a dial-up connection—a connection using a modem and standard telephone lines.

Software that uses point-to-point protocol (*PPP*) allows a computer connected via a modem and phone line to have full Internet access temporarily and a temporary IP address. *Full-access dial-up connections* offer most of the advantages of a direct connection, including Web access, but response time is limited by the modem's speed. A typical connection through a modem and plain old telephone service (*POTS*) is much slower, and often less reliable, than a direct Internet connection. Although modern modems are theoretically capable of delivering data at 56Kb or faster, they're often much slower when connected to typical noisy phone lines. Modem connections are sometimes called narrowband connections because they don't offer much bandwidth when compared to other types of connections.

Broadband Connections

Until a few years ago, a slow dial-up connection was the only alternative to direct Internet for homes and small businesses. Today, millions of Internet users connect via DSL, cable modems, and satellites. These modem alternatives are often called broadband connections because they have much higher bandwidth than standard modem connections do. In some cases, broadband connections offer data transmission speeds comparable to direct connection speeds. Many broadband services offer another big advantage: They're always on. Users of these services don't need to dial in; the Internet is instantly available anytime, like television or radio. The most common broadband alternatives are based on the following technologies:

- *DSL.* Many phone companies offer digital subscriber line (DSL), a technology for bringing high-bandwidth always-on connections to homes and small businesses by sharing the copper telephone lines that carry voice calls. DSL is faster and cheaper than *ISDN*, a digital service offered by phone companies in the 1900s. Most experts believe ISDN will soon be obsolete. DSL customers must be geographically close to phone company service hubs. DSL transmission speeds vary considerably. *Downstream traffic*—information from the Internet to the subscriber—sometimes approaches T1 speeds. A graphics-heavy Web page that takes minutes to download through a conventional modem will load in seconds through a DSL connection.

Internet Connection Speeds

Connection type		Downstream		Upstream
		Potential	Typical	Typical
Dial-up modems: connection modem (56K)		56Kbps	42 to 53Kbps	33.6Kbps
T1		1.544Mbps	1.544Mbps	1.544Mbps
T3		44.736Mbps	44.736Mbps	44.736Mbps
ISDN		128Kbps	64 to 128Kbps	64 to 128Kbps
DSL/xDSL		6.1Mbps	512 Kbps to 1.544Mbps	128Kbps
Cable modem		27Mbps	1.5 to 3Mbps	500Kbps to 2.5Mbps
Satellite connection		1.2Mbps	150 to 1,000 Kbps	50 to 150Kbps
Wireless broadband (802.11g)		54Mbps	15 to 20Mbps	15 to 20Mbps

9.5 Speeds vary widely for different types of Internet connections.

Upstream traffic—data traveling from the home computer to the Internet—typically travels more slowly, but still much faster than over standard modem transmission. A DSL signal can share a standard telephone line with voice traffic, so it can remain on without interfering with telephone calls. DSL connections are available only in limited areas.

■ *Cable modem connections.* Some cable TV companies offer ultra-high-speed Internet connections through cable modems. Cable modems allow Internet connections through the same network of coaxial cables that delivers television signals to millions of homes. Like DSL, cable modem service isn't available everywhere. Cable modem speeds often exceed DSL speeds both downstream and upstream. But because a single cable is shared by an entire neighborhood, transmission speeds can go down when the number of users goes up.

■ *Satellite connections.* Satellite Internet connections are available through many of the same satellite dishes that provide television channels to viewers. Downstream satellite transmission is much faster than conventional modem traffic is, although not as fast as

9.6 Many airports and other public areas now have Wi-Fi wireless networks that enable travelers to connect to the Internet.

DSL or cable modem service. For some satellite services, upstream traffic goes through phone lines at standard modem rates. Some newer services use satellites for upstream and downstream traffic. For many homes and businesses outside of urban centers, satellites provide the only high-speed Internet access options available.

■ *Wireless broadband connections.* People packing portable computers can, in some places, temporarily connect to the Internet through wireless broadband connections. Using Wi-Fi technology, described in detail in Chapter 8, "Networking and Telecommunication," students can connect to the Internet while they move around a wireless-equipped campus, travelers can make Web connections while waiting in some airports, and coffee shops can become Internet cafes for people with wireless receivers in their laptops.

Each of these broadband technologies is widely deployed in the United States and each is rapidly expanding its area of coverage. In the future, many homes and small businesses will have a direct connection to the Internet via fiber-optic cables. But for now, most Internet users can choose between narrowband modems and various broadband services available in their areas.

Internet Service Providers

Internet service providers (ISPs) generally offer several connection options at different prices. Local ISPs are local businesses with permanent connections to the Internet. They provide connections to their customers, usually through local telephone lines, along with other services. For example, an ISP might provide an email address, a server for customers to post Web pages, and technical help as part of a service package. National ISPs, such as EarthLink, offer similar services on a nationwide scale. National ISPs have local telephone numbers in most major cities so travelers can dial into the Net on the road without paying long-distance charges. In some cities, inexpensive or free access to the Internet is available through a freenet—a local ISP designed to provide community access to online forums, announcements, and services.

Many private networks and commercial *online services*, such as AOL, provide Internet access through gateways. A *gateway* is a computer connected to two networks—in this context the Internet and an outside network—that translates communication protocols and transfers information between the two. Some online services, such as MSN, have been rebuilt so they use the same protocols and framework as the Internet does; subscribers use standard

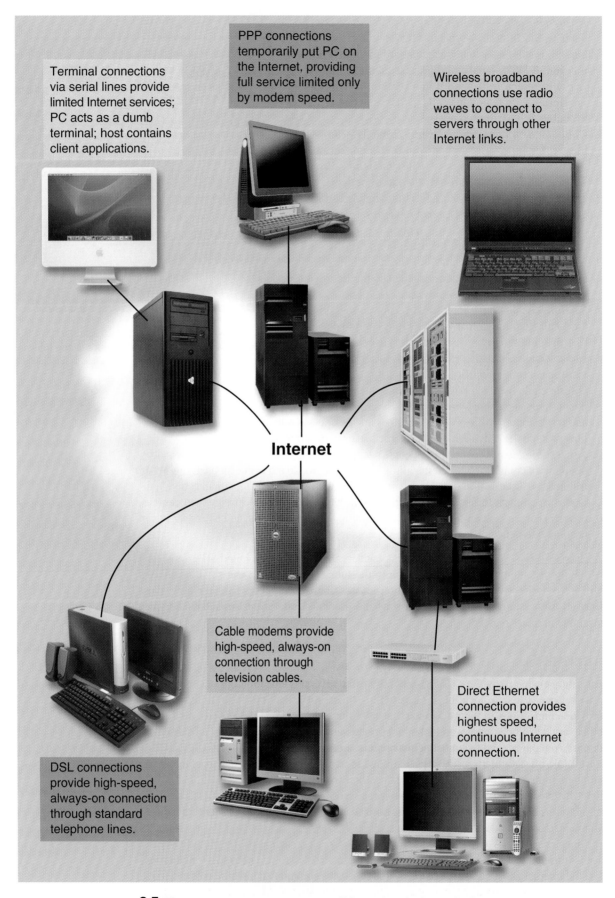

Terminal connections via serial lines provide limited Internet services; PC acts as a dumb terminal; host contains client applications.

PPP connections temporarily put PC on the Internet, providing full service limited only by modem speed.

Wireless broadband connections use radio waves to connect to servers through other Internet links.

Internet

Cable modems provide high-speed, always-on connection through television cables.

Direct Ethernet connection provides highest speed, continuous Internet connection.

DSL connections provide high-speed, always-on connection through standard telephone lines.

9.7 There are many ways to connect a PC or other device to the Internet.

Web browsers and email programs to access services. Others, such as AOL and CompuServe, use proprietary client software to give subscribers access to their services and to the Internet. These services also enable members to use standard Internet software tools to connect to the Web and check email. Whatever their underlying architecture, online services are essentially ISPs that offer extra services to subscribers, including news, research tools, shopping, banking, games, chat rooms, bulletin boards, email, instant messaging, and software libraries.

Internet Servers

Internet applications, like PC applications, are software tools for users. But working with Internet applications is different from working with word processors or spreadsheets because of the distributed nature of the Internet and the client/server model used by most Internet applications. In the client/server model, a client program asks for information, and a server program fields the request and provides the requested information from databases and documents. The client program hides the details of the network and the server from the user.

> The most desirable interaction with a network is one in which **the network itself is invisible and unnoticeable**. Planners often forget that people **do not want to use systems** at all—easy or not. What people want is to **delegate** a task and **not to worry about how** it is done.
>
> —*Nicholas Negroponte, director of MIT's Media Lab*

Different people might access the same server using different client applications with different user interfaces. For example, a user with a direct connection might be using a Web browser with a point-and-click interface to explore a particular server, while another user with a dial-up terminal connection might be typing UNIX commands and seeing only text on-screen. A third user might be viewing the same data, a few words at a time, on the tiny screen of a handheld PDA or mobile phone.

Many Internet applications use specialized servers. Some of the most common server types include the following:

- *Email servers.* An email server acts like a local post office for a particular Internet host—a business, an organization, or an ISP. For example, a college might have an email server to handle the mail of all students, faculty, and staff; their email addresses point to that server. The email server receives incoming mail, stores it, and provides it to the email client programs of the addressees when they request it. Similarly, the email server collects mail from its subscribers and sends those messages toward their Internet destinations. Basically, the email server handles local client requests of two types: "Give me my mail," and "Pick up my mail and send it."

- *File servers.* File servers are common within LANs, but they're also used to share programs, media files, and other computer data across the Internet. The Internet's file transfer protocol (FTP) enables users to download files from remote servers (sometimes called FTP servers) to their com-

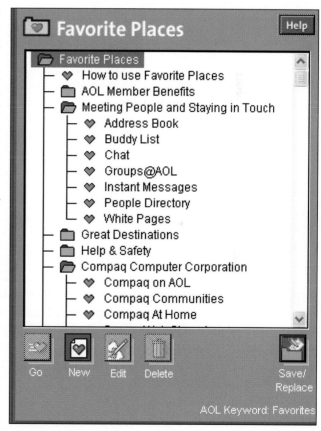

9.8 Online services, such as America Online (AOL), offer a variety of services in a privately controlled environment.

puters—and to upload files they want to share from their computers to these archives. When you click a Web link that downloads a file, the Web browser's request is probably handled using FTP. A newer technology called WebDAV performs the functions of FTP using software with a graphical interface that makes remote servers appear like simple file folders. Wherever they are stored, most files in Net archives are compressed—made smaller using special encoding schemes. File compression saves storage space on disk and saves transmission time when files are transferred through networks. (See Chapter 6, "Graphics, Digital Media, and Multimedia," for more on compression.) After you download files to a PC, they have to be decompressed before you can use them. You don't need to know how compression works to take advantage of it; software makes the process automatic and transparent.

- ■ *Application servers.* An **application server** stores applications—PC office applications, databases, or other applications—and makes them available to client programs that request them. An application server might be used within a large company to keep PCs updated with the latest software. Each PC might have a client program that regularly sends requests for updates to the server. The application server might also be housed at an **application service provider (ASP)**—a company that manages and delivers application services on a contract basis. Users of ASPs don't buy applications; they rent them, along with service contracts. Some application servers supply platform-neutral, Web-centered applications rather than OS-specific PC applications. Many industry watchers believe ASPs will eventually provide most of the software we use. For some companies, ASPs are part of larger Web-services strategies, discussed later.
- ■ *Web servers.* A **Web server** stores Web pages and sends them to client programs—Web browsers—that request them. It may also store and send Web media, including graphics, audio, video, and animation. In the next section we'll turn our attention to the technology behind the Web.

Inside the Web

> The **dream behind the Web** is of a common information space in which we **communicate by sharing information**.
>
> —*Tim Berners-Lee, creator of the World Wide Web*

The **World Wide Web (WWW)** is a distributed browsing and searching system originally developed at CERN (European Laboratory for Particle Physics) by Tim Berners-Lee, a visionary scientist profiled in Chapter 6. He designed a system for giving Internet documents unique addresses, wrote the HTML language for encoding and displaying documents, and built a software browser for viewing those documents from remote locations. Since it was introduced in 1991, the Web has become phenomenally popular as a system for exploring, viewing, and publishing all kinds of information on the Net.

Web Protocols: HTTP and HTML

> The Web was built by **millions of people** simply **because they wanted it**, without need, greed, fear, hierarchy, authority figures, ethnic identification, advertising, or any form of manipulation. **Nothing like this ever happened before in history**. We can be blasé about it now, but it is **what we will be remembered for**. We have been made aware of a **new dimension of human potential**.
>
> —*Jaron Lanier, virtual reality pioneer*

The Web is built around a naming scheme that allows every information resource on the Internet to be referred to using a **uniform resource locator** or, as it's more commonly known, **URL**. Here's a typical URL:

http://weatherunderground.com/ satellite/vis/1k/US.html/

The first part of this URL refers to the protocol that must be used to access information; it might be FTP, news, or something else. It's most commonly *http*, for *hypertext transfer protocol*, the protocol used to transfer Web pages. The second part (the part following the //) is the address of the host containing the resource; it uses the same domain-naming scheme used for email addresses. The third part, following the dot address, describes the *path* to the particular resource on the host—the hierarchical nesting of directories (folders) that contain the resource.

Most Web pages are created using a language called **HyperText Markup Language (HTML)**. An HTML *source document* is a text file that includes codes that describe the format, layout, and logical structure of a hypermedia document. HTML is definitely not

http://www.vote-smart.org/help/database.html

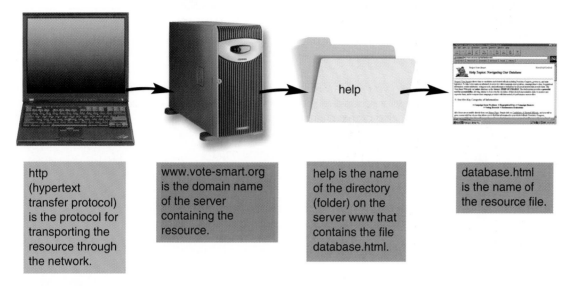

| http (hypertext transfer protocol) is the protocol for transporting the resource through the network. | www.vote-smart.org is the domain name of the server containing the resource. | help is the name of the directory (folder) on the server www that contains the file database.html. | database.html is the name of the resource file. |

9.9 Anatomy of a URL.

WYSIWYG (what you see is what you get); the HTML codes embedded in the document make it look cryptic and nothing like the final page displayed on the screen. But those codes enable a Web browser to translate an HTML source document into that finished page. Because it's a text file, an HTML document can be easily transmitted from a Web server to a client machine anywhere on the Internet.

9.10 HTML source code tells the Web browser how to format the text when it's displayed on the screen.

9.1 **The World Wide Web**

1. When you type a URL into the address box of your Web browser, the browser sends a message through the Internet to the server with the specified domain name **www.appleeater.com**.

Request for ww.appleater.com home page

2. The server responds by sending the specified file to the client browser. The file contains the contents of the requested Web page in HTML format. The HTML commands provide formatting instructions and other information. Because HTML files are all text, they're small and easy to transmit through the Internet.

...<H1>Eat Apples!</H1>For a special treat

3. The browser reads the HTML file and interprets the HTML commands, called tags, embedded in angle brackets <like this>. It uses the formatting tags to determine the look and layout of the text on the page. For example, <H1> indicates a level 1 heading to be displayed in large text, <I> indicates italics, and so on.

4. The HTML file doesn't contain pictures; it's a text file. But it does contain a tag specifying where a picture file is stored and where in the page it is to be displayed. The server responds to this tag by sending the requested graphics file.

Request for www.fugieater.com home page

5. The HTML file also contains a tag indicating a hyperlink to another document with a URL on another server. When the user clicks that link, a message is sent to the new server, and the process of building a Web page in the browser window starts anew.

9.11

Publishing on the Web

You can create a Web page with any word processor or text editor; you just type the HTML commands along with the rest of the text. But you don't need to write HTML code to create a Web page. Many programs, including Microsoft Word, PowerPoint, and FileMaker Pro, can automatically convert basic formatting features (including character styles, indentation, and justification) into HTML codes. Some Web authoring software, including Macromedia Dreamweaver, Adobe GoLive, and Microsoft FrontPage, work like page layout programs that desktop publishers use. You can lay out text and graphics the way you want them to look, and the authoring program creates an HTML document that looks similar to your original layout when viewed through a Web browser. The best of these Web authoring programs enable you to manage entire Web sites using tools that can automate repetitive edits, apply formatting styles across pages, and check for bad links. Some have tools for connecting large sites to databases containing critical, rapidly changing content.

> By expanding the number of people who have **the power to transmit knowledge**, the Web might trigger a **power shift that changes everything**.
>
> —*Howard Rheingold, author of* Virtual Communities

After an HTML document is completed, you need to upload it onto a Web server before it's visible on the Web. Many ISPs provide Web server space as part of their subscription service; other companies rent Web server space to individuals and organizations. By default, most Web pages have URLs that include the ISP or Web server domain names—names like **http://hometown.aol.com/shjoobedebop/index.htm**. Many businesses, organizations, and individuals pay an annual fee to a *domain name registry* company for names that match their organization name and are easy to remember and use. Many customized domain names resemble company or product names—for example, **http://www.prenhall.com** or **http://www.computerconfluence.com**.

Many individuals post daily diaries, ongoing political commentaries, regularly updated business information, photo journals, and similar documents without using HTML or standard Web authoring software. Instead, they use software that's designed specifically to create Weblog, or blog, documents. Blogs are published to Web servers using simple Web interfaces that shield the user from technical details like FTP server addresses and URLs. They even provide custom design templates so that users can modify the look of their sites without knowing any HTML. Blog software provides a way to post diary-like entries to a blog on an ongoing basis. Some suppliers of blog software, like Google's Blogger.com, will even host your blog for free as long as you don't mind advertising their wares. Today, blogs are revolutionizing Web publishing by bringing the power of personal publishing to individuals who would otherwise be uninterested in learning the technical details of HTML and Web authoring. Using a simple and free Web-based tool, anyone can publish views on any topic, at any time, and reach a worldwide audience instantly. Influential blogs have had an impact on public policy by drawing attention to facts and ideas overlooked by commercial news organizations.

From Hypertext to Multimedia

Way back in the early 1990s(!) the first Web pages were straight hypertext. Within a couple of years graphics were common, and a few cutting-edge Web sites enabled browsers to download scratchy video and audio clips to their hard disks. Today, color graphics and

> We are still a **multimedia organism**. If we want to push the envelope of complexity further, we have to use **all of our devices** for accessing information—not all of which are **rational**.
>
> —*Psychologist Mihaly Csikszentmihalyi*

Screen Test

Building a Web Site

GOAL *To create a site representing a small service business.*

TOOLS *Macromedia Dreamweaver and Microsoft Internet Explorer.*

1. The first step in publishing, whether on paper or on the Web, is to plan the layout for the publication. Since a Web site is a hypertext document, a flowchart can make it easier to plan the links between pages.

2. When the plan is complete, you collect and edit the source documents—the images, articles, and other elements that will make up the finished publication.

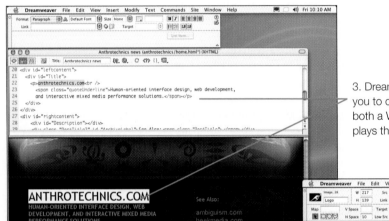

3. Dreamweaver Web authoring software enables you to create, view, and edit your pages using both a WYSIWG editor and a text editor that displays the actual HTML code.

4. You insert graphical elements, Flash animations, and other multimedia objects into each page.

5. You test each page with various Web browsers to make sure they display everything properly.

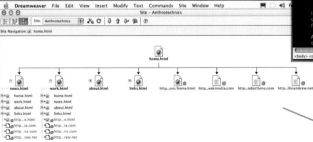

6. After testing the partially completed site with various Web browsers, you compare this site map, created by Dreamweaver, with the original design.

7. When the rest of the pages are completed and tested, you can load the site onto the Web so the world can view it.

9.12

animation are everywhere, and a typical Web site can contain any or all of these:

- *Tables* are spreadsheet-like grids with rows and columns contain neatly laid out text and graphical elements. Tables with invisible cell borders are often used as alignment tools to create simple layouts.
- *Frames* are subdivisions of a Web browser's viewing area that enable visitors to scroll and view different parts of a page, or even multiple pages, simultaneously. Many users find frames confusing, and as the Web evolves frames are becoming less common.
- *Forms* are pages that visitors can fill in to order goods and services, respond to questionnaires, enter contests, express opinions, or add comments to ongoing discussions.
- *Animations* are moving pictures based on a variety of technologies, from simple repetitive GIF animations to complex interactive animations created with authoring tools, such as Macromedia Flash.
- *Search engine* are tools for locating what you're looking for on a site. Most of these site-specific search engines are based on the same technology as Web-wide search engines. Many site builders license search engines from search engine companies.
- *Downloadable audio* clips are compressed sound files that you must download onto your computer's hard disk before the browser or some other application can play them. Some types of audio compression cause significant sound quality degradation. The MP3 compression format is popular because the compressed music files sound almost the same as the uncompressed originals.

9.13 Streaming and downloadable media are available from a variety of Web sites. MSN Radio, shown at top, offers music streams on request. Apple's iTunes Music Store, below, offers hundreds of thousands of downloadable songs.

- *Downloadable video* clips are compressed video files that you can download and view on a computer. Many are small, short, and jerky, but quality is rapidly improving as new video compression technologies mature.
- **Streaming audio** files are sounds that play without being completely downloaded to the local hard disk. Some streaming files play automatically while you view a page, providing background music and sound effects. Others, such as sound samples at music stores, play on request. Unlike downloaded media files, you can view or hear streaming media files within seconds, because they play while you're downloading them. For the same reason, streaming media files don't need to be limited to short clips. Concert-length streaming programs are common. High-quality streaming music requires a fast connection and can be interrupted by Internet traffic jams.

■ **Streaming video** files are video clips that play while you're downloading them. Streaming video is even more dependent on high-bandwidth connection than streaming audio is.

■ *Real-time streaming audio* broadcasts, or *Webcasts* are streaming transmissions of radio broadcasts, concerts, news feeds, speeches, and other sound events as they happen. Many Internet radio stations stream around the clock.

■ *Real-time streaming video* Webcasts are similar to streaming audio Webcasts, but with video.

■ *3-D environments* are drawn or photographed virtual spaces you can explore with mouse clicks.

■ *Personalization* is customization of content made possible because sites can remember information about guests from visit to visit. Some sites use login names and passwords to remember visitors. Others track and remember using **cookies**—small files deposited on the visitor's hard disk. Cookies can make online shopping and other activities more efficient and rewarding, but they can also pose a threat to personal privacy.

Today new Web ideas appear at an astounding rate—so fast that browser makers have trouble keeping up. Fortunately, the most popular browsers can be enhanced with **plug-ins**—software extensions that add new features. When a company introduces a Web innovation, such as a new type of animation, it typically makes a free browser plug-in available to users. Once you download the plug-in and install it in your browser, you can take advantage of any Web pages that include the innovation. Popular plug-ins become standard features in future browser versions, so you don't need to download and install them. Even if a browser can't play or display a particular type of graphics, animation, audio, or video by itself, it might be able to offload the task to a *helper application*—a separate program designed to present that particular media type.

The most popular free cross-platform plug-ins and helper applications include the following:

■ *RealOne* (Real) is one of the most popular programs for playing streaming audio and video, including live Webcasts. RealOne movies and sound files are encoded in proprietary formats so they can't be played with other media players.

■ *Windows Media Player* (Microsoft) is a direct competitor to RealOne, delivering streaming media in proprietary formats that are compatible with other players because Microsoft licenses the technology to other companies.

■ *QuickTime* (Apple) also delivers cross-platform streaming media in proprietary formats. QuickTime movies are generally very high quality, at the expense of being larger than the lower-quality media typically associated with RealOne and Windows Media Player.

■ *Shockwave/Flash* (Macromedia) plug-ins enable Web browsers to present compressed interactive multimedia documents and animations created with Flash MX, Director MX, and other authoring tools.

9.14 This 3-D pool game is just one of many interactive games available from the Web. Like many online games, this one uses a Shockwave/ Flash plug-in to display animation and interactive elements.

■ *Adobe Reader* and *Acrobat* (Adobe) display documents in *Portable Document Format (PDF)* so they look the same on the screen as on paper, even if the documents are viewed on computers that don't have the same fonts installed. Adobe Reader is a free application that can only display PDF documents; the Acrobat products allow you to edit and create PDF documents.

HTML was originally designed to share scientific research documents, not to deliver media-rich documents in which design is as important as content. By popular demand, the HTML standard has been revised several times to incorporate new features. Newer versions of HTML, sometimes called *dynamic HTML*, allow HTML code to modify itself automatically under certain circumstances. Dynamic HTML supports *cascading stylesheets* that can define formatting and layout features that aren't recognized in older versions of HTML.

Dynamic HTML also recognizes *scripts*—short programs—that can add interactivity, animation, and other dynamic features to Web pages. One common use of scripts is to add *rollovers* to onscreen buttons, so they visibly change when the user rolls the pointer over them. Scripts are typically written in a scripting language called *JavaScript*. Web pages that take advantage of the latest dynamic HTML features can be more interesting and interactive, but only if you view them with newer full-featured browsers. Unscrupulous Web programmers can use scripts to embed viruses and other unwanted elements into your computer. We'll explore these risks in the next chapter.

Dynamic Web Sites: Beyond HTML

HTML is flexible, but it's designed for page layout, not programming. By itself, it can't support online shopping, financial transaction processing, library catalogs, daily newspapers, search engines, and other applications with masses of rapidly changing data. This kind of dynamic Web site requires two things that HTML can't

> If you thought a Web site consisted of **HTML** pages organized as a directory, **go back to the 20th century**. A successful Web site today consists primarily of **XML** code and a **database**.
>
> —*Dana Blankenhorn, coauthor of* Web Commerce: Building a Digital Business

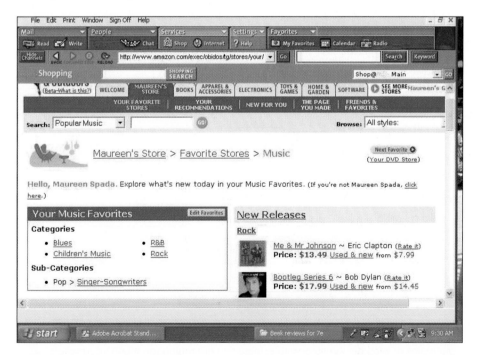

9.15 Amazon.com is the world's largest online retailer, and the site uses massive databases to store items, inventory information, customer data, and transaction information. The dynamic Web site displays data that is personalized for each customer.

Working Wisdom

Weaving Winning Web Sites

It's easy to create a Web site; just about anybody with an Internet connection can do it. It's not so easy to create an effective Web site—one that communicates clearly, attracts visitors, and achieves its goals. Here are a few pointers for making your Web publications work.

➡ **Start with a plan.** The Web is littered with Web sites that seem pointless. Many of those sites were probably constructed without a clear plan or purpose. Start with clear goals and design your entire site with those goals in mind.

➡ **Write for the Web.** Most people won't read long, scrolling documents on computer screens. Limit each page to a couple of screens worth of text. Provide clearly marked links to pages with more details for people who need them. And don't forget to check your spelling and grammar.

➡ **Keep it simple.** Web pages that are cluttered with blinking text, busy backgrounds, repetitive animations, and garish graphics tend to lose their visitors quickly. Stick with clean lines and clear design if you want people to stick around.

➡ **Keep it consistent.** Every page in your site should look like it's related to the other pages in your site. Fonts, graphical elements, colors, buttons, and menus should be consistent from page to page.

➡ **Make it obvious.** Your visitors should be able to tell within a few seconds how your site works. Unless you're building a puzzle palace, make sure the buttons and structure of your site are intuitive.

➡ **Keep it small.** Large photographs, complex animations, video clips, and sounds can make your Web site big and slow to load. People with standard modem connections won't want to wait two minutes for your graphically heavy Web page to load. If you need lots of pictures, use an image-editing program to optimize them for the Web.

➡ **Keep it honest.** Anybody can publish a Web site without the benefit of an editor. Check your facts before you share your pages with the world.

➡ **Offer contact information.** Web communication shouldn't be one-way. Provide a way for your visitors to contact you. But if you include your email address, expect to receive lots of spam—software Web crawlers are always searching for new addresses on the Web. To minimize spam, you might want to refer to your email address indirectly: "My email name is Fuji and my domain name is appleeater.com."

➡ **Think like a publisher and a multimedia designer.** The rules of publishing and design, discussed in earlier chapters, apply to Web publishing, too.

➡ **Test before you publish.** Show your work to others, preferably people in your target audience, and watch their reactions carefully. If they get lost, confused, bored, or upset, you probably have more work to do before launching the final site.

➡ **Think before you publish.** It's easy to publish Web pages for the world—at least that part of the world that uses the Web. Don't put anything on your Web pages that you don't want the world to see; you may, for example, be asking for trouble if you publish your home address, your work schedule, and a photo of the expensive computer system in your study.

➡ **Keep it current.** It's easy to build a Web site, and it's even easier to forget to keep it up to date. If your Web site is worth visiting, it's worth revising. If the contents of your site are constantly in need of revision, consider using a database to house the data so you can automatically update the site when the data changes.

9.16 This screen from www.re-vision.com was created to violate as many principles of Web design as possible, including cramming too much information onto a page, noisy banner ads, overuse of frames, and navigation elements scattered across the page.

easily deliver: a database to store the constantly changing content of the site, and custom programming to make the appropriate data available to Web site visitors.

A data-driven Web site can display dynamic, changeable content without having constantly redesigned pages, thanks to a constantly evolving database that separates the content of the site from its design. For example, an online store's Web site doesn't have a separate HTML page for each catalog item. Instead, it has pages that are coded to display product information drawn from a database that can be continually updated. The Web site is a front end for the database; it serves as the visitor's window into the database. Likewise, the database is a data back end for the Web site.

Programmers use a variety of programming languages for creating dynamic Web sites. The *Perl* scripting language is particularly popular for programming Web servers. Microsoft's Active Server Pages (ASP) and ASP .NET technologies allow programmers to work in their choice of programming languages.

Java, an object-oriented programming language developed by Sun Microsystems, is probably the best-known language for Web programming. (Java and JavaScript have little in common except their names. JavaScript is a simple scripting language for enhancing HTML Web pages; Java is a full-featured cross-platform programming language.) Small Java programs are called *applets* because they're like tiny applications. Java applets can be automatically downloaded onto your client computer through almost any modern Web browser. A Java applet is platform independent; it runs on a Windows PC, a Mac, a UNIX workstation, or anything else as long as the client machine has Java Virtual Machine (JVM) software installed. This JVM software is built into most modern browsers and is available for free download.

Microsoft offers several alternatives to Java. The oldest is *ActiveX*, a collection of programming technologies and tools for creating controls or components—programs that are similar in many ways to Java applets. ActiveX components require a compatible browser, such as Internet Explorer, to run properly.

Experts expect XML (eXtensible Markup language), which includes all of HTML's features plus many additional programming extensions, to replace HTML. XML enables Web developers to control and display data the way they now control text and graphics. Forms, database queries, and other data-intensive operations that can't be completely constructed with standard HTML are much easier to create with XML. In effect, XML combines a programming language with a page layout language. XML is at the heart of Microsoft's .NET and other competing strategies for developing Web services.

XML isn't the only markup language that's emerging to go beyond the capabilities of HTML. XHTML, a sort of cross between HTML and XML, is backward compatible with HTML, making it easier to upgrade older sites. A subset of XHTML called XHTML basic is especially designed to work with phones, PDAs, and other small-screen wireless devices. XHTML and XHTML basic are designed to work together, so that sites designed with XHTML automatically work on handheld devices. XHTML isn't yet widely used, but it has strong support from the wireless industry and from the World Wide Web Consortium (W3C), an organization that sets standards for the Web. W3C is also developing a standard for Synchronized Multimedia Integration Language (SMIL), an HTML-like language designed to make it possible to link time-based streaming media so, for example, sounds, video, and animation can be tightly integrated with each other.

Screen Test

Using Different Search Strategies

GOAL *To find Web pages on the subject of intellectual property piracy using two different types of search tools.*

TOOLS *Microsoft Internet Explorer, the Google search engine, and the Google subject tree.*

1. Using the Google Directory, you click on the subject area that looks most appropriate: Society Issues.

2. This was the right choice; one of the categories is called Intellectual Property. You click on that category.

3. Under Intellectual Property there are 11 categories. One of them is just what you wanted: Piracy. You click on it.

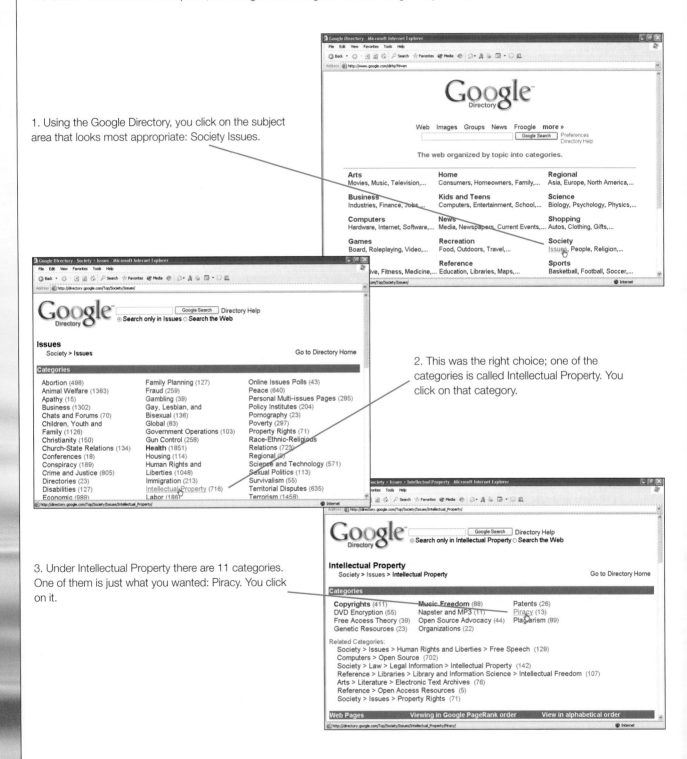

9.17

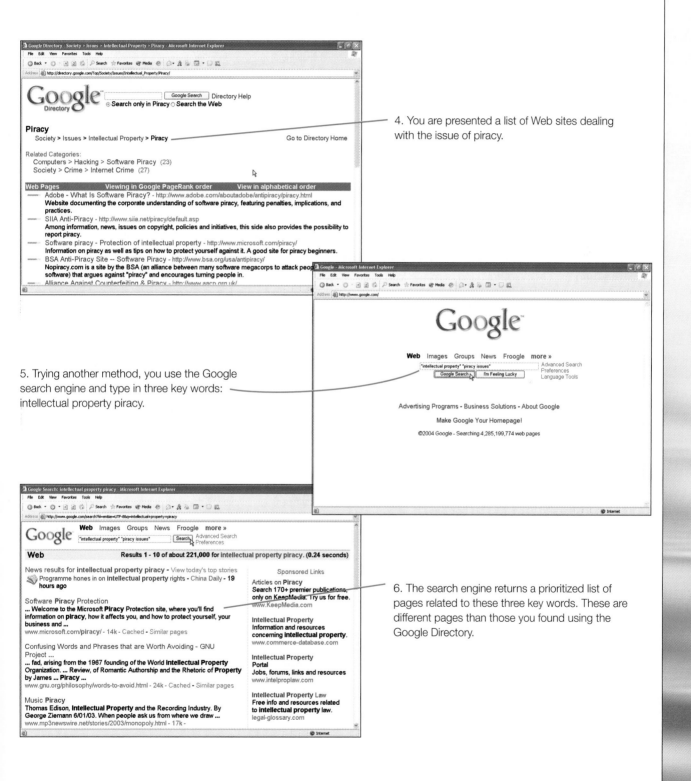

4. You are presented a list of Web sites dealing with the issue of piracy.

5. Trying another method, you use the Google search engine and type in three key words: intellectual property piracy.

6. The search engine returns a prioritized list of pages related to these three key words. These are different pages than those you found using the Google Directory.

Working the Web

The Web is so easy to navigate that it's tempting just to dive in. But like a large library, the Web has more to offer if you learn a few tricks and techniques. Your goals should dictate your Web strategy.

➡ **Get to know your search engines.** Try several, choose your favorites, and learn the more advanced search features so you can minimize the time it takes to find what you're looking for. Search Engine Watch (www.searchenginewatch.com) is a good source of information about search engines.

➡ **Be specific when you search.** A search engine is more likely to give you the answer you're looking for if you search for "Epson USB scanner" than if you just type "scanner". An even better search would specify the scanner's model number.

➡ **Know your plusses and minuses.** In most search engines you can use a plus sign to signify that you want pages that contain all words. For example, "+Alaska +oil +wildlife" searches pages that contain all three words. On the other hand, a minus sign usually means "not." For example, "cancer –astrology" locates pages that contain "cancer" but not "astrology." When you use these symbols, you're using basic Boolean algebra—the logical basis of database queries.

➡ **Be selective.** As Robert P. Lipshutz wrote in *Mobile Computing*, "A few tidbits of accurate, timely and useful information are worth much more than a ream of random data, and bad information is worse than no information at all." When you're assessing a Web page's credibility, consider the author, the writing, the references, and the page sponsor's objectivity and reliability. Be aware that many of the most popular search engines charge companies to be listed prominently in their directories and that some give top billing to their own services and partners.

➡ **Triangulate.** A traditional navigation technique for sailors, triangulation involves using two points, other than yourself, to establish location. Xerox Chief Scientist John Seely Brown suggests that the same concept should be applied to the turbulent waters of the Web. Don't assume something is true because one Web source tells you so, unless you're sure the source is rock solid.

➡ **Organize your favorites.** When you find a page worth revisiting, record it on your list of favorites or bookmarks. Browsers enable you to organize your lists by category—a strategy that's far more effective than just throwing them all in a digital shoebox.

➡ **Protect your privacy.** Many Web servers keep track of all kinds of data about you: which site you visited before you came, where you clicked, and more. When you fill out forms to enter contests, order goods, or leave messages, you're providing more data for your hosts. Don't divulge any private information about yourself. And make sure you don't leave tracks that you're ashamed of as you hip-hop around the Web.

➡ **Be conscious of cookies and bugs.** Many Web servers send cookies to your browser when you visit them or perform other actions. Cookies are tidbits of information about your session that can be read later; they enable Web sites to remember what they know about you between sessions. Cookies make personalized portals and customized shopping experiences possible. Unfortunately, cookies can also provide all kinds of possibilities for snoopers who want to know how you spend your time online. By default, most browsers don't tell you when they leave a cookie. It's easy to change browser settings so your browser will refuse all cookies; accept cookies from the current site but not so-called third-party sites, such as those sent by advertisements that appear on many Web pages. You can accept cookies only from selected sites; or set the browser to ask you, on a cookie-by-cookie basis, whether to accept or refuse cookies. Unfortunately, you can't easily turn off Web bugs— one-pixel graphic images that are programmed to send information about your Web use back to their creators.

➡ **Online shopping isn't always better.** In increasing numbers shoppers are abandoning brick-and-mortar stores for click-and-mortar Web stores. Online shops and auctions can save you money, especially if you comparison shop. But when a product doesn't work as advertised, or when you have after-sale questions, a Web merchant might not be as helpful as a local shopkeeper. Some don't even accept phone queries. If your purchase will require person-to-person communication before or after the sale, you're probably better off patronizing a local merchant. But if you must shop online, be sure to frequent reputable sites.

➡ **Shop with bots.** Bots are software robots, or agents, that can explore the Web and report back their findings. Several bots, such as mySimon at **www. mySimon.com**, are designed to help you find low prices by searching the databases of hundreds of merchants.

> ➡ **Shop with care.** The Web, like the nondigital world, has its share of less-than-honest merchants. Use services such as bizrate (www.bizrate .com) to check out questionable merchants before you lay your digital money down. If you're dealing with a private party or an unknown merchant, consider using a transaction service, such as PayPal (www.paypal.com), to serve as a safe temporary depository for funds until the purchased product reaches you.

> ➡ **Remember why you're there.** The Web's extensive hyperlinks make it all too easy to wander off course when you're searching for important information. If you're using the Web to save time, stay focused or you may find that the Web costs more time than it saves.

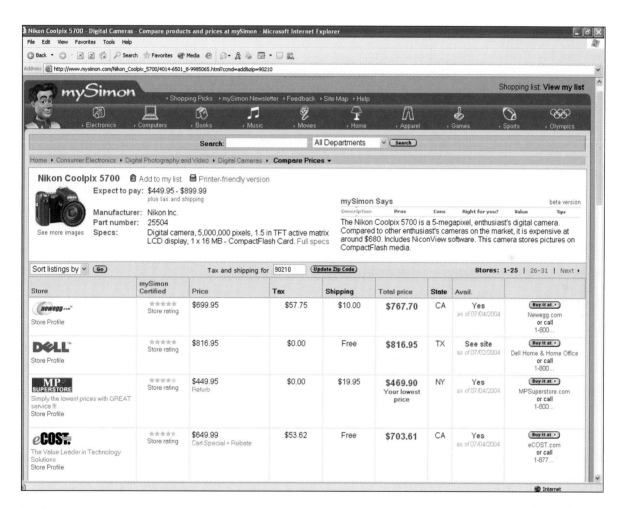

9.18 Bots like mySimon can help you find low prices.

Inside Web Applications

For **time** is the **longest distance** between two points.

—*Tennessee Williams*

The Web today is far more than a simple hypertext publishing medium. We'll now survey a variety of Web applications, from search engines and portals to peer-to-peer technologies and e-commerce applications.

Search Engines

With its vast storehouses of information, the Web is like a huge library. Unfortunately, the Web is a poorly organized library; you might find information on a particular topic almost anywhere. (What can you expect from a library where nobody's in charge?) That's why search engines are among the Web's most popular tools.

All search engines are designed to make it easier to find information on the Web, but they don't all function the same way. A typical search engine uses *web crawlers* or *spiders*— software robots that systematically explore the Web, retrieve information about pages, and index the retrieved information in a database. Different search engines use different search and indexing strategies. For example, one search engine might record detailed information about key words in documents, while another might pay more attention to links to and from other documents. For some search engines, researchers organize and evaluate Web sites in databases; other search engines are almost completely automated.

Most search engines enable you to type queries using key words, just as you might locate information in other types of databases. You can construct complex queries using *Boolean logic* (for example, American AND Indian BUT NOT Cleveland), quotations, and other tools for refining queries. Some search engines enable you to narrow your search repeatedly by choosing subcategories from a hierarchical *directory* or *subject tree*. No matter which search technique you use, you're eventually presented with a rank-ordered list of Web pages. A page might go undetected by one search engine and appear at the top of a list on another. That's why some researchers still use *meta-search engines*, such as MetaCrawler, OneSeek, and Apple's Sherlock. These software tools conduct parallel searches using several different search engines and directories. Of course, getting more hits isn't necessarily better. The best search engines provide you with relatively few high-quality results rather than overwhelming you with marginally relevant links.

Some popular search engines are designed to search for specific types of information. Specialized search engines can help you locate email addresses and phone numbers; others can help you find the lowest prices on the Web. These specialized search engines generally use technology similar to general search engine technology.

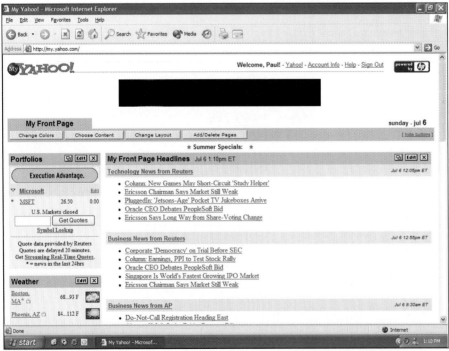

9.19 Like other Web portals, the popular Yahoo! site can be personalized to highlight news, weather, sports, and other information the user specifies.

Most search engines have access to less than 1 percent of the pages on the Web. The rest are out of reach of the public or stored in databases that can't be searched by conventional search engines. Some search engines, including invisibleweb.com, can provide access to information in those databases. Web search technology continues to evolve with the Web.

Portals

Many Web sites that started out as search engines have evolved into portals—Web entry stations that offer quick and easy access to a variety of services. Popular general-interest portals include Yahoo!, MSN, and Netscape Netcenter. *Consumer portals* feature search engines, email services, chat rooms, references, news and sports headlines, shopping malls, other services, and advertisements—many of the same things found in online services, such as AOL. You can personalize many of the portals so they automatically display local weather and sports scores, personalized TV and movie listings, news headlines related to particular subjects, horoscopes, and ads to meet your interests. Most browsers enable users to choose a home page that opens by default when the browser is launched; portals are designed with this feature in mind.

In addition to these general-interest portals, the Web has a growing number of specialized portals. *Corporate portals* on intranets serve the employees of particular corporations. *Vertical portals*, or *vortals*, like vertical market software (see Chapter 4, "Software Basics,") target members of a particular industry or economic sector. For example, webmd.com is a portal for medically minded consumers and health-care professionals. A growing number of specialized portals are competing to be your browser's home page.

Push Technology: Notifications and Alerts

The Web was built with pull technology: Browsers on client computers pull information from server machines. With pull technology the browser needs to initiate a request before any information is delivered. But for some applications, it makes more sense to have information delivered automatically to the client computer. That's the way push technology works.

> **We think we "surf"** the Web now, but what we really do is hopscotch across fragile stepping-stones of texts, or worse, spelunk in a vast unmapped cave of documents. Only when **waves of media** begin to cascade behind our screens—huge swells of unbrowsable stuff—will we truly surf.
>
> —*Kevin Kelly and Gary Wolf, former* Wired *editors*

With push technology, you subscribe to a service or specify the kinds of information you want to receive and the server delivers that information periodically and unobtrusively. Maybe you want up-to-the-minute weather maps displayed in a small window in the corner of your screen. You might prefer to see news headlines (on subjects of your choice) scroll across the top of your screen. You may want to receive new product descriptions automatically from selected companies. Or you might like to have the software on your hard disk automatically upgraded when upgrades are posted on the Web. All of this is possible with push technology.

Technically speaking, today's push technology is really pull technology in disguise. Your computer quietly and automatically pulls information from selected Web servers based on your earlier requests or subscriptions. As convenient as they are, push programs have the same basic problem as Web search engines: They give you what they think you want, but they may not be very smart. Their ability to deliver what you really need, without bombarding you with unwanted data, will get better as artificial intelligence technology improves.

In the meantime, push technology is used mostly for in-house delivery of information on intranets. Outside of the corporate enterprise, most push technology takes the form of *notifications* and *alerts*, services to which you've subscribed. Some notifications and alerts are free. For example, free MSN Alerts services include stock price changes, breaking news from MSNBC, and online auction statuses from eBay.com. Other alerts require fees. For example, MSN subscribers can get scheduling and to-do alerts. Email continues to be the single form of push technology that has been embraced by almost all Internet users.

Peer-to-Peer and Grid Computing

The **genie** does not **go back** in the bottle—**period**.

—*Tom Peters, business guru and best-selling author*

Of all the companies that came out of nowhere during the dot-com boom of the late '90s, Napster generated the most conversation—and controversy. When 19-year-old college student Shawn Fanning put a friendly user interface and a fresh spin on decades-old file-sharing technology, he created a virtual swap meet for students and others who wanted to share MP3 music files. Almost overnight Napster became one of the hottest Internet destinations, with millions of users downloading and sharing MP3s daily using Napster's software. In May of 2000, a tech company hired by the rock band Metallica revealed that 322,000 Napster users were illegally distributing their music. The Recording Industry Association of America sued the company because its software enabled users to download copyrighted recordings without paying the record companies or artists.

The Napster servers didn't contain those illegal recordings; it just displayed links to recordings scattered all over the Net. People who used Napster practiced **peer-to-peer (P2P) computing**, or, more specifically, *peer-to-peer file sharing*, by making music files on their hard drives available to others rather than posting them on central servers. In April of 2001, a U.S. District Court judge ruled that Napster was violating federal copyright law and forced the company to change its software so that users no longer had free access to copyrighted recordings. Napster changed its software and its business model, but the peer-to-peer music exchange lived on through other programs and Web sites. The Gnutella file-sharing system, used by several different file-sharing programs, avoids Napster's legal problems by allowing users to share music, movies, and other files without going through a central directory. According to some experts, Gnutella's rapid growth suggests that it may become a Web standard.

9.20 The SETI@Home project synchronizes the processing power of various connected computers from around the world. Anyone can donate their unused PC time to SETI@Home; the freely downloadable application starts up whenever your PC is not being used.

Technologies like Gnutella make it difficult, or impossible, for laws to contain the peer-to-peer file-sharing phenomenon. Recording artists are divided on the issue; some encourage fans to share their music; others fear that sharing will make it difficult for musicians to support themselves. A growing collection of legitimate music downloading services, such as the Apple iTunes Music Store, which lets consumers inexpensively purchase songs and albums digitally online, provide consumers with a legal way to download music. (Copyright and intellectual property issues were discussed in Chapter 4, "Software Basics.")

Music sharing is just one application of peer-to-peer computing. The technology is being applied to a growing number of diverse applications. Books, movies, and computer software are shared using peer-to-peer technology and with the same legal and ethical concerns. Businesses use P2P for group collaboration, for Web searches, and for sharing updates to virus-control software, among other things.

A related technology—grid computing—is, like P2P, a form of *distributed computing*. But grid computing isn't about sharing files; it's about sharing processing power. The best-known example is SETI@Home (**setiathome.ssl.berkeley.edu/**), a program that puts PCs all over the Internet together into a sort of virtual supercomputer that analyzes space telescope data in the search for extraterrestrial life. The SETI@Home program, when installed on a PC, uses the computer's idle time to do calculations and send the results back to SETI headquarters. Millions of PCs around the world can do the work of a million-dollar supercomputer in much less time. A similar program called FightAIDS@home (**fightaidsathome.com**) enables PCs to contribute spare processing cycles to the fight against AIDS.

Grid computing may soon extend far beyond these processor-sharing programs to a new Internet model that resembles a utility grid. IBM and other companies are supporting initiatives to build a grid-computing environment where anyone can plug in from anywhere and rent processing power and software from anywhere on the Net. Grid-computing applications are currently being used by the U.S. Department of Defense, the U.S. Department of Energy, NASA, the U.K National Grid, and a variety of academic and scientific communities.

Intranets, Extranets, and Electronic Commerce

For many businesses, Internet protocols and software are almost as important as the Net itself. Members of these organizations communicate through intranets— self-contained intraorganizational networks that are designed using the same technology the Internet uses. A typical intranet offers email, newsgroups, file transfer, Web publishing, and other Internet-like services, but not all of these services are available to people outside the organization. For example, an intranet Web document might be accessible only to company employees—not to the entire Internet community. If an intranet has a gateway connection to the Internet, the gateway probably has some kind of *firewall* to prevent unauthorized communication and to secure sensitive internal data.

> Our customers are **moving at Internet speed**. They need us to **respond** at Internet speed.
>
> —*Laurie Tucker, Federal Express vice president*

Some private TCP/IP networks are designed for outside use by customers, clients, and business partners of the organization. These networks, often called extranets, are typically for electronic commerce (e-commerce)—business transactions through electronic networks. Most use *electronic data interchange (EDI)*—a decade-old set of specifications for ordering, billing, and paying for parts and services over private networks.

Some extranets are virtual private networks that use encryption software (described in the next chapter) to create secure "tunnels" through the public Internet. Others use their own lines or lease lines that aren't subject to the traffic and security problems of the public Internet. Extranets are especially useful for business-to-business (B2B) e-commerce— transactions that involve businesses providing goods or services to other businesses.

Business-to-consumer (B2C) e-commerce generally involves transactions that take place on the Internet, rather than on an extranet, because consumers don't have access to private extranets. The Internet has spawned a wide variety of B2C businesses, including the following:

- *Online catalog sales.* Online catalogs save paper, and they offer other advantages for consumers, including search engines, immediate availability reports, custom orders, and instant updates. But some types of merchandise don't lend themselves to online sales, and online customers can be frustrated by confusing user interfaces and minimal customer support.

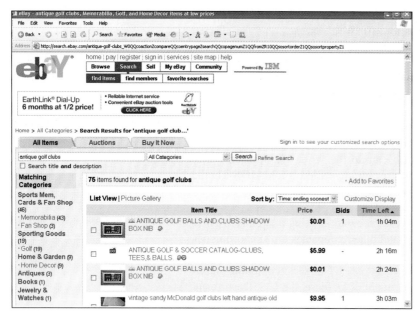

9.21 eBay is a popular online auction site.

■ *Auctions.* The Internet makes long-distance auctions practical, allowing people to bid on all kinds of items. Some retail outlets use auctions to move clearance merchandise; some sites sell everything through auctions.

■ *Reverse auctions.* Some sites allow customers to request goods or services and have merchants bid on prices. Everything from airline tickets to legal services is offered through reverse auctions.

■ *Comparison shopping.* Specialized search engines search the Web for the lowest prices.

■ *Financial services.* Checks, credit cards, and stocks are all available online.

B2C sites can offer a high degree of personalization—for example, suggesting products similar to the ones already ordered by a customer, or remembering a customer's personal preferences and sizes between visits. But personalization raises privacy and security concerns in many customers. (Security issues are discussed in detail in the next chapter.)

E-commerce is changing the way many companies do business. But e-commerce isn't cheap or easy. Profits have proven to be elusive for many online companies. Like the brick-and-mortar world, the Internet presents challenges along with opportunities for enterprising business people.

Web Services

Software costs can be daunting for companies that have to build e-commerce sites from the ground up. Several of the computer industry's biggest companies, including EDS, IBM, Hewlett-Packard, Microsoft, Oracle, and Sun, are developing software tools to make e-commerce solutions easier to build and maintain. These systems have different names and features, but they all fall into a software category called **Web services**. Web services involve new kinds of Web-based applications that can be assembled quickly using existing *software components*. Component technology can, for example, make it easy to plug a shopping-cart component into an existing Web site or to design applications that can be accessed through a variety of Web-enabled devices. XML plays an important role in most Web services systems currently under development.

Unfortunately, the industry hasn't agreed on the details of this emerging technology. Sun, Hewlett-Packard, and IBM are using Java to build their cross-platform service tools. Sun's Web services platform is called J2EE. Microsoft's Web services platform, .NET, uses a wider variety of languages, including C#. Today, C# runs only on Windows platforms, but it is being ported to other platforms, including Linux. The open-source community is working to port even more of .NET to Linux, hoping to keep .NET from being a proprietary system, and they're getting help from Microsoft. Meanwhile, the W3C is attempting to create Web services standards that the entire industry can embrace.

Pervasive Web services systems are still many years away. But they offer great hope for companies struggling with the challenges of creating successful e-commerce sites. Hints of the future are all over the Web. The popular online store Amazon.com pioneered Web services by letting developers freely access their back-end databases using .NET technology. And *Passport*, a .NET-based user authentication service, is used by hundreds of millions of Hotmail and MSN users to provide secure logons to the system from any PC on the planet. In the future, Web services will be as prevalent on the Web as actual Web sites. We just won't realize they're working silently in the background, like the electricity we take for granted today.

The Evolving Internet

The Internet started as a small community of scientists, engineers, and other researchers who staunchly defended the noncommercial, cooperative charter of the network. Today, the Net has swollen into a community of millions, including everybody from children to corporate executives. The rate of growth is so great that it raises questions about the Internet's ability to keep up; the amount of information transmitted may eventually be more than the Net can handle.

> In the short term, the **impact** of new technologies like the Internet will be **less than the hype** would suggest. But in the long term, it will be vastly **larger than we can imagine** today.
>
> —*Paul Saffo, director of the Institute for the Future*

The U.S. government no longer assumes primary responsibility for Internet expansion. Many funding and administrative duties have been passed to private companies, allowing businesses to commercialize the Net. In 1995, for the first time, the number of commercial host sites on the Net exceeded the number of noncommercial sites. In the three-year period that followed, the Net experienced a hundredfold increase in monthly traffic.

Internet2 and the Next Generation Internet

As the Internet evolves into the network of the masses, congestion becomes more problematic for the scientists and researchers who made up the original Internet community. The U.S. government, working in conjunction with several large corporations, launched Internet2 in 1998 to provide faster network communications for universities and research institutions. A related effort from DARPA, the *Next Generation Internet (NGI)*, will consist of a nationwide web of optical fiber integrated with intelligent management software to maintain high-speed connections.

Internet2 will eventually be capable of transmitting data at 9.6 billion bits per second— enough to send all 30 volumes of the Encyclopedia Britannica in 1 second. Internet2 isn't available for commercial or recreational use; it is reserved for research and academic work. Participating universities are building virtual laboratories, digital libraries, telemedicine research facilities, and distance learning applications that take advantage of its tremendous bandwidth. The rest of us will undoubtedly inherit the technologies developed for Internet2.

Internet Issues: Ethical and Political Dilemmas

The commercialization of the Internet has opened a floodgate of new services to users. People are logging into the Internet to view weather patterns, book flights, buy stocks, sell cars, track deliveries, listen to radio broadcasts from around the world, conduct videoconferences, coordinate disaster recovery programs, and perform countless other private and public transactions. The Internet saves time, money, and lives, but it brings problems, too.

> **The Internet** still hasn't figured out how to **conduct itself in public.**. . . Everybody is trying to **develop the rules** by which they can conduct themselves in order to keep a **civil operation** going and not **self-destruct**.
>
> —*George Lucas, filmmaker*

Computer Addiction

One growing problem is *computer addiction*. For a few hard-core networkers, the world on the other side of the modem is more real and more interesting than the everyday physical world. One Alaskan reader wrote to advice columnist Ann Landers: "Computer chat lines can become every bit as addictive as cocaine. I have been hooked on both, and it was easier to get off coke." While this may seem strange, it's not unique. Many people feel the same way about television, spectator sports, or romance novels. Internet addiction, like any addiction, can be a serious problem—for individuals and for society. The problem is growing as more people go online, and no quick fixes are in sight.

Freedom's Abuses

Other problems relate more to greed than need. Commercialization has brought capitalism's dark side to the Internet. Spam scams, get-rich-quick hoaxes, online credit card thefts, email forgery, child pornography hustling, illegal gambling, Web site sabotage, online stalking, and other sleazy activities abound. The Internet has clearly lost its innocence.

Some of these problems have at least partial technological solutions. Concerned parents and teachers can now install **filtering software** that, for the most part, keeps children out of Web sites that contain inappropriate content. Commercial Web sites routinely use encryption so customers can purchase goods and services without fear of having credit card numbers stolen by electronic eavesdroppers. Several software companies and banks are developing systems for circulating **digital cash** on the Internet to make online transactions easier and safer. To protect against email forgery, many software companies are working together to hammer out standards for *digital signatures* using encryption techniques described in the next chapter.

Access and Censorship

Many problems associated with the rapid growth and commercialization of the Internet are social problems that raise important political questions. Online hucksterism and pornography have prompted government controls on Internet content, including the 1996 Communications Decency Act. Opponents to this law and other proposed controls argue that it's important to preserve the free flow of information; they stress the need to protect our rights to free speech and privacy on the Net. In 1996 the U.S. Supreme Court declared the Communications Decency Act unconstitutional, arguing that "the interest in encouraging freedom of expression in a democratic society outweighs any theoretical but unproven benefit of censorship."

However, the public outcry against the corrupting influence of pornography on children continued, and in December of 2000, Congress passed the Children's Internet Protection Act. The act requires public libraries and schools that receive certain types of federal funding to install content filters on computers with Internet access. In June 2003 the U.S. Supreme Court upheld the constitutionality of the Children's Internet Protection Act.

Questions about human rights online probably won't be resolved by legislators and judges, though. The Internet's global reach makes it nearly impossible for a single government to regulate it. Internet pioneer John Gilmore said, "The Net interprets censorship as damage and routes around it." Still, most governments are uncomfortable simply allowing an uninhibited flow of information through the Internet. As we have seen, even democratic nations have taken steps to regulate Internet content. In the United States, the federal government attempts to prevent children from gaining access to pornography, and most states make it illegal to run online casinos. In Germany, neo-Nazi Web sites are banned.

Some nations with more authoritarian governments have been much more aggressive in their attempts to reduce or eliminate the free flow of information over the Internet. For example, the

9.22 As part of the nonprofit Tech Corps program, these computer professionals volunteer their time and skills to help students and teachers put technology to good use.

governments of North Korea and Burma have prohibited ordinary residents from accessing the Internet.

Saudi Arabians had no Internet access until 1999. Today, virtually all Internet traffic to and from Saudi households is routed through a centralized control center. Technicians in the control center attempt to block all Web sites offensive to Islam or the government of Saudi Arabia, including those related to pornography, Middle Eastern politics, non-Islamic religious organizations, women's health and sexuality issues, and gay rights. When a Saudi attempts to access a blocked page, the server returns a message that it cannot display that page.

The People's Republic of China allows Internet service providers to make their own connections, but it requires them to sign a "self-discipline" agreement that forbids them from forwarding politically or morally objectionable Web pages. Objectionable pages include those containing pornography, references to Taiwan or Tibet, or news about Chinese dissidents. Sophisticated software responds to the actions of each user. For example, if a Chinese Web surfer goes to the Google Web site and types in "Falun Gong," not only will the query be ignored, but the user may find Google itself inaccessible for the next hour. To do business in China, Google has modified its software so that Web searches can be censored by the government.

The Digital Divide

During the 1990s the U.S. government pushed for the development of a National Information Infrastructure (NII)—an affordable, secure, high-speed network to provide "universal service" for all Americans. The motivation for the creation of an NII was the realization that a digital divide separates computer haves from have-nots.

Today more than half of the U.S. population has easy access to the Internet—a subset of America that excludes many poor people and minorities. Government programs to wire schools, libraries, and other public facilities have increased access for disadvantaged populations. But many Internet services that used to be free for all are now available only to paying customers. Families can't buy computers or Internet service if they're having trouble paying the rent. The problem of equal access isn't likely to go away without combined efforts of governments, businesses, and individuals.

9.23 The Children's Internet Protection Act requires many public schools and libraries in the United States to install Web filtering software.

Even if the United States achieves a universal-access NII, access issues still confront the rest of the world. The Internet is a global infrastructure, but huge populations all over the world are locked out. For example, less than one percent of Africans have Internet access. Many experts argue that access to the Internet is one of many ingredients necessary for economic development in the twenty-first century. They fear that we'll leave billions of people behind as we move further into the information age. If poverty leads to political instability, wars, and terrorism, then the digital divide could be harmful to all of us unless we find ways to unlock the Internet for everybody who wants it.

Critics of the digital divide mentality ask whether a lack of Internet access leads to a disadvantaged socio-economic position, or if it is the other way around. After all, most new technologies, from color TVs to VCRs to DVD players, were first adopted by the wealthy before gradually being assimilated into the general population. Furthermore, providing Internet access to everyone in the world is not a cure-all. People in many countries are lacking adequate transportation systems, electrical systems, communication systems, water systems, educational systems, and health care systems. Giving these people Internet access would be pointless unless their other needs were met as well.

Cyberspace: The Electronic Frontier

Cyberspace. **A consensual hallucination** experienced daily by billions of legitimate operators, **in every nation**, by children being taught mathematical concepts. . . . A graphic representation of data abstracted from the banks of **every computer in the human system. Unthinkable complexity**. Lines of light ranged in the nonspace of the mind, clusters and constellations of data. Like city lights, receding. . . .

—*William Gibson, in* Neuromancer

Science fiction writers suggest that tomorrow's networks will take us beyond the Internet into an artificial reality that has come to be known as cyberspace, a term coined by William Gibson in his visionary novel *Neuromancer*.

In *Neuromancer*, as in earlier works by Vernor Vinge and others, travelers experience the universal computer network as if it were a physical place, a shared virtual reality, complete with sights, sounds, and other sensations. Gibson's cyberspace is an abstract, cold landscape in a dark and dangerous future world. Vinge's novella *True Names* takes place in a network hideaway where adventurous computer wizards never reveal their true names or identities to each other. Instead, they take on mythical identities with supernatural abilities.

Today's computer networks are still light-years from the futuristic visions of Vinge and Gibson. But the Net today *is* a primitive cyberspace—a world where messages, mathematics, and money can cross continents in seconds. People from all over the planet meet, develop friendships, and share their innermost thoughts and feelings in cyberspace.

John Perry Barlow, cofounder of the Electronic Frontier Foundation, has called the online world an "electronic frontier," suggesting parallels to America's Old West. Until recently, the electronic frontier was populated mostly by free-spirited souls willing to forgo creature comforts. These digital pioneers built the roads and towns that are used today by less adventurous settlers and business interests.

In spite of its rapid commercialization, the electronic frontier is far from tame. Network nomads pick digital locks and ignore electronic fences. Some explore nooks and crannies out of a spirit of adventure. Others steal and tamper with private information for profit or revenge. Charlatans and hustlers operate outside the law. Law enforcement agencies and lawmakers occasionally overreact.

There's a strong sentiment on the Net toward keeping controls to a minimum. Netizens commonly argue that the Web will always be free of control because of the way it's constructed. It's true that governments have so far had trouble regulating many Internet activities. But there's no guarantee that the free-spirited Internet will always remain that way.

In *The Code and Other Laws of Cyberspace*, Lawrence Lessig claims that, because of commerce and other forces, an architecture of control is being built into the Net—control by government and by businesses intent on maximizing Net profits. Lessig argues that the code—the way the Net is programmed—will determine how much freedom we have in the

9.24 After meeting on the Internet, twin sisters Joelle and Florence married twin brothers Gilles and Guy.

future Internet. "We can build, or architect, or code cyberspace to protect values we believe are fundamental, or we can build, or architect, or code cyberspace to allow those values to disappear. There is no middle ground. There is no choice that does not include some kind of *building*."

There are parallels in the nondigital world. Many city planning experts argue that industrialized nations have systematically (if not consciously) rebuilt their cities so that, in many places, it's just about impossible to live without a car. These car-centered cities have generated revenue for businesses and governments, and they've brought a new sense of freedom to many citizens. But for the poor, the disabled, the young, the old, and others who can't drive, these cities are anything but free. At the same time, other cities have thriving masses of car-free people. Design choices (and nonchoices) made decades ago determine the livability of our cities today.

In the same way, the design decisions being made today by software architects, corporate managers, government officials, and concerned citizens will determine the nature of our Internet experiences in the future. Will portals guide us to corporate-approved information sources? Will Netizens feel free to express controversial opinions and criticize powerful institutions without fear of lawsuits and prosecution? Will paths through cyberspace be accessible to everyone? As Mark Stefik says in *Internet Dreams: Archetypes, Myths, and Metaphors,* "Different versions of [cyberspace] support different kinds of dreams. We choose, wisely or not."

Inventing the FUTURE

The Invisible Information Infrastructure

In the future, **everything with a digital heartbeat** will be connected to the Internet.

—Scott McNealy, CEO of Sun Microsystems

Where is the Internet heading? Vint Cerf, one of the Internet's founders, thinks it's headed for space. He's putting much of his time and energy into a project called InterPlaNet, which he hopes will extend the Internet to the other planets in our solar system. According to the plan, electronic "post offices" will orbit other planets, routing messages between space explorers, both human and robot. The obstacles are significant—a message from Mars can take 20 minutes or more to reach Earth, an intolerably long time for Internet servers that "time out" if they don't receive messages quickly. According to Cerf, "the interplanetary network is an example of a much more general concept we call delay-tolerant networks." Even if you aren't expecting email from the red planet, the research being done on InterPlaNet may result in more reliable Internet for you here on Earth.

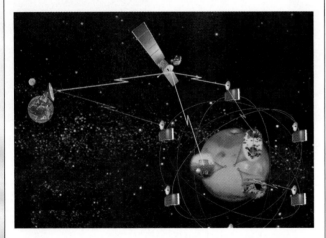

9.25a A visualization of the Marsnet proposed by Vint Cerf.

Whatever happens with InterPlaNet, tomorrow's Net surfers will find it easier to locate what they're looking for on the Web. Tim Berners-Lee, the inventor of the Web, is planning a *Semantic Web*—a Web full of data that's meaningful to computers as well as humans. With a Semantic Web, search engines will be able to deliver exactly what you're looking for instead of bombarding you with hundreds of possibility pages. Here's how Berners-Lee described it to the *Boston Globe*: "You'll tell a search engine, 'find me someplace where the weather is currently rainy and it's within a hundred miles of such and such a city.'. . . A search engine . . . will come back and say, 'Look, I found this place and I can prove to you why I know that it's raining and why I know it's within a hundred miles of this place.' So you'll be dealing with much firmer information."

Technology forecaster Paul Saffo suggests a blurring of the boundaries between the Web and interpersonal communication applications. When we visit a Web site that's being explored by hundreds of other people, we'll actually be able to experience their presence and interact with them in ways that go beyond today's simple chat rooms. In Saffo's words, "We're going to shift away from a model of people accessing information to a model of people accessing other people in an information-rich environment. The information will become the wallpaper surrounding conversational space."

We may be sharing Web space with more people in the future, but we'll also be sharing it with all kinds of gadgets. Today we think of the Web as a network of computers, but the Web isn't just for PCs, mainframes, and servers anymore. A variety of Internet appliances, network computers, set-top boxes, PDAs, mobile phones, and other devices are being connected to the Internet in offices and homes. Everything from coffee makers to traffic lights may be routinely connected to the Web soon. Consider the possibilities:

You tell your alarm clock to wake you in time to catch the 8:00 A.M. flight to Washington. At 5:00 A.M. the clock checks the airline's Web site and determines that the flight has been delayed an hour. It also checks online traffic reports and finds that traffic is light. The clock resets your wakeup time accordingly, giving you an extra hour of sleep. As usual, it turns on the heat and the coffee maker 10 minutes before it wakes you. On the way to the airport, your car routes you around a congested construction spot. When you arrive at the airport, it tells you where to find a vacant parking spot close to the terminal.

9.25b A smart refrigerator with Internet connectivity.

Whether you consider this future fantasy appealing or appalling, the technology is on the horizon. One thing is clear: The Web is changing so fast it's impossible for anybody to predict exactly what it will look like even a few months from today. ～

Info With a Ball and Chain *Steven Levy*

Steven Levy has eloquently written for years about the human issues raised by the Internet. In this article, first published in the June 23, 2003, issue of Newsweek, *Levy looks at the hard questions raised by online music distribution.*

When Steve Jobs introduced the iTunes music store a few weeks ago, the acclaim was nearly universal. Nonetheless, a small but vocal minority viewed the online emporium as a menace—because the iTunes program somewhat limits a consumer's ability to copy and share songs.

Even though Apple had broken ground by getting the record labels to accept fairly liberal terms of use—Apple-oids could listen to purchased songs on three computers and burn CDs—this bunch objected to any restrictions at all. They saw the iTunes store as a sugar-coated inducement for consumers to accept a new reality: some stuff on your computer isn't really under your control. And as far as that goes, the critics are right. Say goodbye to the "Information Wants to Be Free" era. We're entering the age of digital ankle bracelets.

The key to this shift is the technology that protects information from unauthorized or illegal use. It's called digital-rights-management software, or DRM. Like it or not, rights management is increasingly going to be a fact of your life. Not only will music, books and movies be steeped in it, but soon such mundane artifacts as documents, spreadsheet files and e-mail will be joining the domain of restricted information. In fact, the next version of Microsoft Office will enable creators of certain documents to issue restrictions that dictate who, if anyone, can read them, copy them or forward them. In addition, you can specify that the files and mail you send may "sunset" after a specified period of time, evaporating like the little tapes dead-dropped to Peter Graves in "Mission: Impossible."

On the one hand, it seems that digital-rights management is a no-brainer. What's wrong with media companies' building in antitheft devices to protect their property? And shouldn't the creator of a document or e-mail be able to determine who can read or copy it? Surely, piracy is to be condemned and privacy to be cherished: DRM can go a long way toward implementing both those sentiments.

But certain critics consider the very concept anathema. "I don't think that DRM is in and of itself evil," says David Weinberger, who recently published an essay in *Wired* titled "Copy Protection Is a Crime Against Humanity." "But in the real world, it is evil. There's no user demand for it. It's being forced upon us by people with vested interests."

Edward Felton, a Princeton computer scientist, believes that DRM perverts the basic deal of the Internet: the free flow of information benefits all. "The basic problem is that DRM is trying to turn information into something other than information so you can't pass it on," he says. "People want to control their technology, and the more the technology is eroded, the harder it is to use."

DRM's defenders say that the technology actually empowers users. Without protections, entertainment companies would never release their products in the digital marketplace. Microsoft's Erin Cullen says that DRM software is flexible enough to limit illegal uses (like sharing a song with millions of "friends" on the Net) while allowing consumers to enjoy music and films in ways they always have.

In practice, though, DRM can stifle legal activity, too. For instance, copy protection on DVDs blocks not only illegal copying, but the "fair use" ability to copy a frame or short scene into a home movie or school project. (To do this, you have to break the copy-protection scheme—an act that is specifically outlawed by the anticonsumer Digital Millennium Copyright Act.)

Critics like Weinberger also complain that computers enforcing DRM systems lack "the essential leeway by which ideas circulate." Sure, Microsoft rights management will allow creators to set the rules. But will corporations dictate that every e-mail message and document be fitted with a virtual ball and chain: *no copying . . . no forwarding . . . no amending . . . no archiving*? Whistle-blowers won't be able to do what they do," says Joe Kraus of DigitalConsumer.org.

Even Congress, which has so far ignored consumers and coddled rights holders on copy protection, is waking up. Sen. Sam Brownback, a Kansas Republican, is about to introduce a bill "to ensure that our nation's media producers and distributors do not clamp down on the ways in which [consumers] traditionally and legally use media products."

We do need legislative help in keeping DRM under control. But ultimately, its fate will be determined by our own actions. As we have with the iTunes store, we'll vote with our dollars when we're satisfied that restrictions on our music and movies allow us the access we need. And corporations may well come to understand that it's bad policy to strictly hobble the flow of information. Will we suffer the worst-case DRM scenario: a world so constricted that we can't cut or paste a line from a poem, or forward the latest sick Internet joke to our buddies? I doubt it. But I do think that the files that arrive in our in boxes and jukeboxes will be on tighter leashes. And while I understand the reasoning for this, the prospect doesn't gladden my heart.

Discussion Questions

1. Do you agree with David Weinberger's statement that, in the real world, DRM is evil? Why or why not?

2. Do you agree with the provision in the Digital Millennium Copyright Act that makes it illegal to copy a frame or short scene into a home movie or school project? Explain your answer.

Summary

The Internet is a network of networks that connects all kinds of computers around the globe. It grew out of a military research network designed to provide reliable communication even if part of the network failed. The Internet uses standard protocols to allow Internet communication to occur. No single organization owns or controls the Internet.

You can connect to the Internet in any of several ways; these ways provide different degrees of access to Internet services. A direct connection provides the most complete and fastest service, but users can also access most Internet information through modem connections. Broadband connections approach direct connection speeds, but they aren't universally available. Several online services have gateways to the Internet; these gateways enable users to access Internet information resources and send and receive Internet mail.

Most Internet applications are based on the client/server model. The user interface for these applications varies depending on the type of connection and the type of client software the user has. A user might type UNIX commands to a host computer or use point-and-click tools on a personal computer. Different types of servers provide different kinds of Internet services, ranging from mail to the Web.

The earliest Web pages were simple hypertext pages; today the World Wide Web contains thousands of complex, media-rich structures that offer visitors a wealth of choices. The Web uses a set of protocols to make a variety of Internet services and multimedia documents available to users through a simple point-and-click interface. Web pages are generally constructed using a language called HTML. Many Web authoring tools automate the coding of HTML pages, making it easy for nonprogrammers to write and publish their own pages. Other languages and techniques are being developed to extend the power of the Web in ways that go beyond the capabilities of HTML. Today, most large interactive Web sites are database-driven, so content can be updated automatically.

In addition to Web sites, a variety of applications are built on the protocols of the Internet and the Web. For example, people who use the Web depend on search engines to find the information they need. Search engines use a combination of automated searches and indexed databases to catalog Web resources.

Peer-to-peer computing was popularized by music sharing services, but its applications go beyond music sharing. Many businesses are exploring ways to apply P2P technology. Grid computing goes beyond P2P computing by enabling people to share processor power with others. Some organizations are working to build a grid-computing model that would make the Internet work like a shared utility.

E-commerce is built on Internet technology. Businesses use the Internet and the Web for business-to-business and business-to-customer communication. Many businesses have private networks, called intranets, based on Internet technology. Extranets are also private networks based on the same technology; extranets enable businesses to connect with their partners and customers without going through public Internet channels.

As the Internet grows and changes, issues of privacy, security, censorship, criminal activity, universal access, and appropriate Net behavior are surfacing. Even more questions will arise when all kinds of electronic devices are attached to the Web, communicating with each other from our homes, our offices, and our vehicles. We have many questions to answer as the Internet evolves from an electronic frontier into a futuristic cyberspace.

Key Terms

application server ....(p. 352)
application service provider
    (ASP)................................(p. 352)
blog...(p. 355)
broadband connections..........(p. 347)
business-to-business (B2B) ...(p. 369)
business-to-consumer (B2C) .(p. 369)
cable modems.........................(p. 349)
cookie ....(p. 358)
cyberspace ....(p. 374)
data-driven Web site ....(p. 361)
dial-up connection..................(p. 347)
digital cash.............................(p. 371)

digital divide..........................(p. 373)
digital subscriber line
    (DSL)................................(p. 347)
direct (dedicated) connection (p. 347)
electronic commerce
    (e-commerce)....................(p. 369)
email server ....(p. 351)
eXtensible Markup Language
    (XML) ....(p. 361)
extranets ....(p. 369)
file transfer protocol
    (FTP) ....(p. 351)
filtering software ....(p. 372)

grid computing ....(p. 368)
HyperText Markup Language
    (HTML) ....(p. 352)
Internet2 ....(p. 371)
Internet service providers
    (ISP)................................(p. 349)
internetworking ....(p. 343)
intranets ....(p. 369)
Java..(p. 361)
JavaScript ....(p. 359)
narrowband connections........(p. 347)
open standards ....(p. 343)
packet-switching....................(p. 345)

Interactive Activities

1. The *Computer Confluence* CD-ROM contains self-test quiz questions related to this chapter, including multiple-choice, true or false, and matching questions.

2. The *Computer Confluence* Web site, **http://www. computerconfluence.com**, contains self-test exercises related to this chapter. Follow the instructions for tak-

ing a quiz. After you've completed your quiz, you can email the results to your instructor.

3. The Web site also contains open-ended discussion questions called Internet Explorations. Discuss one or more of the Internet Exploration questions at the section for this chapter.

True or False

1. The Internet was originally built on the assumption that all computers on the network would be equal in their ability to communicate with each other.

2. Because of its strongly centralized design, the Internet can withstand most attacks.

3. When a digital video file is sent on the Internet, it is broken into packets that travel independently to the designated destination.

4. The TCP/IP protocols at the heart of the Internet were published as open standards, not owned by any company.

5. The words in a domain name, like the lines in a post office address, are arranged hierarchically from little to big.

6. Technically, every Web URL begins with http://, although most browsers don't require you to type it.

7. Streaming video is distinguished from downloadable video by the fact that it is always real time—that is, it presents events as they happen.

8. Many Internet shopping sites use cookies to keep track of customer orders and preferences.

9. Peer-to-peer file sharing is almost always illegal, but many people do it anyway.

10. Internet2 is designed to replace the current Internet for most commercial applications within the decade.

Multiple Choice

1. The Internet was originally a
   a. LAN at MIT
   b. Code-cracking network during World War II by the U.S. Defense Department
   c. A network cooperatively created by several large hardware and software companies
   d. A small experimental research network called ARPANET
   e. A Microsoft product that quickly became too big for the company to control

2. Where is the Internet's central hub and control center located?
   a. Near Washington D.C..
   b. Near the Microsoft campus in Redmond, Washington.
   c. In a top-secret location.
   d. In Silicon Valley.
   e. Nowhere; the Internet has no central hub.

3. Which of these domains is restricted to qualified organizations?
   a. .com.
   b. .org.
   c. .net.
   d. .edu.
   e. None are restricted; anyone can have a URL in any of these domains.

4. Which of these types of Internet connections is typically the slowest?
   a. Direct connection through T1 lines
   b. Dial-up modem connections through phone lines
   c. DSL connections through phone lines
   d. Cable modem connections through cable TV lines
   e. Satellite connections through satellite dishes

5. Which of these services would you probably not be able to get from a typical Internet service provider (ISP)?
   a. An email address
   b. Access to a Web server
   c. A connection to the Internet
   d. Technical help
   e. Free Windows upgrades

6. Specialized servers are used on the Internet to
   a. Function like email post offices
   b. Accept FTP requests to upload and download files
   c. Store applications that are rented or leased by large corporations
   d. Store and send Web pages
   e. All of the above

7. The first Web pages were
   a. Strictly hypertext with no multimedia content
   b. Designed to simulate printed pages using HTML's table tools
   c. The first true multimedia documents to be published on the Internet
   d. Viewable only with proprietary Microsoft software
   e. Sent via email from Doug Engelbart's office on the Stanford campus

8. Quicktime, RealOne, and Shockwave are among the most popular Web browser
   a. Plug-ins
   b. Cookies
   c. Cascading stylesheets
   d. Search engines
   e. Security tools

9. An online shopping catalog for a large outdoor outfitter is almost certainly
   a. A data-driven Web site that separates site content from design
   b. Carefully hand-coded in pure HTML to minimize errors
   c. Designed to work without cookies
   d. Limited to work with a single type of Web browser for consistency
   e. All of the above

10. The Internet will change drastically in the next decade, but what is the one thing that is likely to remain relatively unchanged?
    a. The dominance of HTML as a Web page creation language
    b. The metaphor of the page as the container of Internet information
    c. The TCP/IP protocol that's used to send and receive Internet messages
    d. The ownership of the Internet by Microsoft
    e. The percentage of non-U.S. Internet users

11. Which of the following is the form of push technology that has been embraced by most Internet users?
    a. Peer-to-peer sharing
    b. Web searching
    c. FTP
    d. email
    e. grid computing

12. What kind of people are drawn to grid computing?
    a. People who need a massive amount of electricity
    b. People who need a massive amount of raw computing power
    c. People who need super-reliable access to the Web
    d. People who receive an extremely large amount of email
    e. All of the above

13. What do you call specialized software tools designed to make e-commerce solutions easier to implement and maintain?
    a. Firewalls
    b. Peer-to-peer networks
    c. Grid tools
    d. Object-oriented programming languages
    e. Web services

14. What do you call software that prevents certain Web pages from being displayed?
    a. Child-safe software
    b. Dutch dike software
    c. Filtering software
    d. Spam blockers
    e. Underage software

15. Which country attempts to limit its residents' access to controversial Web content by routing all incoming Internet traffic through a single control center?
    a. Germany
    b. North Korea
    c. People's Republic of China
    d. Saudi Arabia
    e. United States

Review Questions

1. Define or describe each of the key terms listed in the Key Terms section. Check your answers using the glossary.

2. Why is it hard to determine how big the Internet is today? Give several reasons.

3. Why are TCP/IP protocols so important to the functioning of the Internet? What do they do?

4. How does the type of Internet connection influence the things you can do on the Internet?

5. Explain the relationship between the client/server model and the fact that different users might experience different interfaces while accessing the same data.

6. What do email addresses and URLs have in common?

7. Briefly describe several software tools that can be used to develop Web pages.

8. How might you use remote login while visiting another school? What about file transfer? How might the Web make remote login unnecessary?

9. Why is file compression important on the Internet?

10. Briefly describe several software tools that can be used to develop Web pages.

11. How does push technology differ from standard Web page delivery techniques? How is it used?

12. What new services are available as a result of the commercialization of the Internet? What new problems are arising as a result of that commercialization?

Discussion Questions

1. How did the Internet's Cold War origin influence its basic decentralized, packet-switching design? How does that design affect the way we use the Net today? What are the political implications of that design today?

2. Why is the World Wide Web important as a publishing medium? In what ways is the Web different from any publishing medium that's ever existed before?

3. As scientists, engineers, and government officials develop plans for the future of the Internet, they wrestle with questions about who should have access and what kinds of services to plan for. Do you have any ideas about the kinds of things they might want to consider?

4. Do you know anyone who has experienced Internet addiction? If so, can you describe the experience?

5. How do you think online user interfaces will evolve as bandwidth and processing power increase? Describe what cyberspace will feel like in the year 2010, in the year 2050, and beyond.

6. Residents of the People's Republic of China can have their Internet access blocked for a period of time if they attempt to access banned sites. Do you feel this is an effective way for the Chinese government to control people's behavior on the Internet?

Projects

1. Search the Web for articles related to the history and evolution of the Internet. Create a summary report on paper or on the Web.

2. Create a Web site on a subject of interest to you and link it to other Web sites. (When you're trying to decide what information to include in your home page, remember that it will be accessible to millions of people all over the world.)

3. Research peer-to-peer and grid-computing applications to determine how they're used. Write a report summarizing your findings.

4. Research how access to the Internet in general and Web sites in particular is controlled by the governments of these countries: Brazil, Cuba, France, Germany, India, Israel, Japan, the People's Republic of China, Saudi Arabia, and the United States. Create a chart ranking these countries from "Most free access" to "Least free access." The chart should detail the various restrictions applied by these governments.

5. Research the extent of the digital divide in the United States by collecting information about Internet access by people of different ages and ethnic groups. Which is better predictor of Internet access: age or ethnic group?

6. Read several books and articles about cyberspace and write a paper comparing them. Better yet, write a hypertext document and publish it on the Web.

Sources and Resources

Books

There are thousands of books on the Internet. Many of them promise to simplify and demystify the Net, but they don't all deliver. The Internet is complex and ever-changing. The following list contains a few particularly good titles, but you should also look for more current books released since this book went to press.

When Wizards Stay Up Late: The Origins of the Internet, by Katie Hafner and Matthew Lyon (New York: Simon and Schuster, 1998). If you want to learn more about the birth of the Internet, this book is a great place to start. The authors describe the people, challenges, and technical issues in clear, entertaining prose.

How the Internet Works, Seventh Edition, by Preston Gralla (Indianapolis: Que, 2003). If you like the style of *How Computers Work,* you'll appreciate *How the Internet Works.* You won't learn how to use the Net, but you'll get a colorful tour of what goes on behind the scenes when you connect. There's a surprising amount of technical information in this graphically rich, approachable book.

The Unusually Useful Web Book, by June Cohen (Indianapolis: New Riders, 2003). Some Web books are written for programmers; some are written for designers; some are written for business people. This book, by a former VP of HotWired (the Web site that spun off *Wired* magazine) has something for all three audiences—and more. If you want to build a Web site that people will actually use, this book is a good investment.

HTML for the World Wide Web with XHTML and CSS Visual QuickStart Guide, Fifth Edition, by Elizabeth Castro (Berkeley, CA: Peachpit Press, 2003). There are dozens of books on HTML, but few offer the clear, concise, comprehensive coverage of this bestseller. The latest edition emphasizes the Web's gradual transition to XHTML, which makes the first couple of chapters a little more daunting for beginners. Still, if you want to build your own Web pages, this is a great place to start. Even if you know the basics of HTML, you'll appreciate the coverage of "advanced" topics like DHTML and CGI. After you've read it, you'll almost certainly want to keep it as a reference.

Perl and CGI for the World Wide Web: Visual QuickStart Guide, Second Edition, by Elizabeth Castro (Berkeley, CA: Peachpit Press, 2001). When you fill out a form on a Web page, it's likely that your input is processed by a script that's written in Perl following the CGI protocol. Castro's book takes up where her popular HTML book leaves off, introducing the basics of Perl and CGI for first-time scripters.

JavaScript for the World Wide Web: Visual QuickStart Guide, Fifth Edition, by Tom Negrino and Dori Smith (Berkeley, CA: Peachpit Press, 2003). JavaScript is the most popular cross-platform scripting language for Web pages. A little bit of JavaScript can turn a static Web page into a dynamic interactive page. This book provides a quick introduction to the language, including applications involving forms, frames, files, graphics, and cookies. If you're ready to move beyond basic HTML, this book can help.

Web Style Guide: Basic Design Principles for Creating Web Sites, Second Edition, by Patrick J. Lynch and Sarah Horton (New Haven, CT: Yale University Press, 2002). Yale University was one of the first institutions to publish a Web style guide on the Web. This book, like that site, offers a clear, thoughtful discussion of techniques for designing effective Web sites.

The Non-Designer's Web Book, Second Edition, by Robin Williams and John Tollett (Berkeley, CA: Peachpit Press, 2000). Web publishing, like desktop publishing, can be hazardous if you don't have a background in design. Robin Williams and John Tollett provide a crash course in design for first-time Web authors. They assume you're using an authoring tool that hides the nuts and bolts of HTML; if you're not, you'll need to learn HTML elsewhere.

Return on Design: Smarter Web Design That Works, by Ani Phyo (Indianapolis, IN: New Riders, 2003). Web pro Ani Phyo clearly outlines seven necessary steps for creating usable Web sites. Her user-centered methodology satisfies a wide variety of clients, and this book explains how.

Train of Thought: Designing the Effective Web Experience, by John C. Lenker, Jr. (Indianapolis, IN: New Riders, 2002). This book focuses on the psychology of Web design, emphasizing the creation of Web *experiences*. It's packed with ideas, interviews, and images that just might inspire you to create great Web experiences for others.

From Anarchy to Power: The Net Comes of Age, by Wendy M. Grossman (New York: New York University Press, 2001). The Internet has gone through a radical transition in just a few years. This book chronicles the changes and comments on the profound social and political impact of those changes.

Peer-to-Peer: Harnessing the Power of Disruptive Technologies, edited by Andy Oram (Sebastopol, CA: O'Reilly and Associates, 2001). This collection of essays discusses the philosophy, applications, and implications of peer-to-peer technology, from music sharing to CPU sharing and beyond.

The Code and Other Laws of Cyberspace, by Lawrence Lessig (New York: Basic Books, 2000). This important book presents a strong argument that we might lose our liberty on the Internet unless we consciously work to preserve it. The way we build the Net today will determine what's possible in cyberspace tomorrow. Lessig, a lawyer, is an excellent writer with something important to say.

We the Media: Grassroots Journalism by the People, for the People, by Dan Gillmor (Sebastopol, CA: O'Reilly, 2004). In an age of increasing concentration of media ownership, we get most of our broadcast and print news and information sources owned by a handful of multinational corporations. Web sites, email networks, and blogs are providing concerned citizens with alternatives to the major news and opinion factories. This book offers an in-depth look at the ways the Internet is revolutionizing the world of journalism.

The Future of Ideas: the Fate of the Commons in a Connected World, by Lawrence Lessig (New York: Random House, 2001). In this follow-up book, Lessig puts forward his plan for using the Internet to stimulate an unprecedented era of innovation. He suggests radical changes to intellectual property laws that would accelerate the movement of creative works into the public domain.

Republic.com, by Cass Sunstein (Princeton, NJ: Princeton University Press, 2001). Sunstein looks with alarm at the personalization of entertainment and news. She argues that a free market media system that allows people to control the opinions and topics to which they are exposed could have serious and harmful consequences on a democratic society.

Crypto Anarchy, Cyberstates, and Pirate Utopias, edited by Peter Ludlow (Cambridge, MA: MIT Press, 2001). This lively, thought-provoking collection of essays presents a cyberspace made up of virtual communities that are outside of the circles of corporate and political power.

True Names: And the Opening of the Cyberspace Frontier, by Vernor Vinge and James Frenkel (New York: Tor Books, 2001). In 1981 (three years before the original publication of *Neuromancer*) Vernor Vinge's critically acclaimed novella *True Names* described a virtual world inside a computer network. Vinge didn't use the term *cyberspace*, but his visionary story effectively invented the concept. This book includes the wonderful original *True Names* novella and a collection of articles by cyberspace pioneers about the past, present, and future of cyberspace.

Neuromancer, Reissue Edition, by William Gibson (New York: Ace Books, 2003). Gibson's 1984 cyberpunk classic spawned several sequels, dozens of imitations, and a new vocabulary for describing a high-tech future. Gibson's future is gloomy and foreboding, and his futuristic slang isn't always easy to follow. Still, there's plenty to think about here.

Snow Crash, by Neal Stephenson (New York: Bantam, 2000). This early 1990s science fiction novel lightens the dark, violent cyberpunk future vision a little with Douglas Adams–style humor. Characters regularly jack into the Metaverse, a shared virtual reality network that is in many ways more real than the physical world in which they live. The descriptions of this alternate reality heavily influenced the design of many VR-like Web sites today.

Web Pages

The World Wide Web is especially good at providing information about itself. Whether you want to learn HTML, see the latest Web traffic reports, or explore the technological underpinnings of the Net, you'll find Web links at the *Computer Confluence* Web site (**http://www.computerconfluence.com**) that can help.

Multimedia

on the CD-ROM and the Web:

~ Inside the **hacker's world**

~ An activity on protecting yourself from identity theft

~ Additional content on spyware

~ **Animated illustrations** of how computer viruses and cryptography work

~ **Instant access** to glossary and key word references

~ Interactive **self-study quizzes**

. . . and more.

 computerconfluence.com

Objectives

After you read this chapter you should be able to:

▶ Describe several types of computer crime and discuss possible crime-prevention techniques

▶ Describe the major security issues facing computer users, computer system administrators, and law enforcement officials

▶ Describe how computer security relates to personal privacy issues

▶ Explain how security and computer reliability are related

In 1760 Wolfgang Kempelen, a 49-year-old Hungarian inventor, engineer, and advisor to the court of Austrian Empress Maria Theresa, built a mechanical chess player. This amazing contraption defeated internationally renowned players and earned its inventor almost legendary fame.

A Turkish-looking automaton sat behind a big box that supported a chessboard and chess pieces. The operator of the machine could open the box to "prove" there was nothing inside but a network of cogwheels, gears, and revolving cylinders. After every 12 moves, Kempelen wound the machine up with a huge key. Of course, the chess-playing machine was actually a clever hoax. The real chess player was a dwarf-sized person, who controlled the mechanism from inside and was concealed by mirrors when the box was opened. The tiny player couldn't see the board, but he could tell what pieces were moved by watching magnets below the chessboard.

Kempelen had no intention of keeping the deception going for long; he thought of it as a joke and dismantled

KEMPELEN'S AMAZING CHESS-PLAYING MACHINE

Check.

—The only word ever spoken by Kempelen's chess-playing machine

it after its first tour. But he became a slave to his own fraud, as the public and the scientific community showered him with praise for creating the first "machine-man." In 1780 the Emperor Joseph II ordered another court demonstration of the mechanical chess player, and Kempelen had to rebuild it. The chess player toured the courts of Europe, and the public became more curious and fascinated than ever.

After Kempelen died in 1804, the machine was purchased by the impresario Maelzel, who showed it far and wide. In 1809 it challenged Napoleon Bonaparte to play. When Napoleon repeatedly made illegal moves, the machine-man brushed the pieces from the table. Napoleon was delighted to have unnerved the machine. When he played the next game fairly, Napoleon was badly beaten.

The chess-playing machine came to America in 1826, where it attracted large, paying crowds. In 1834 two different articles—one by Edgar Allan Poe—revealed the secrets of the automated chess player.

Computer Security and Risks

Poe's investigative article was insightful but not completely accurate; one of his 17 arguments was that a true automatic player would invariably win.

After Maelzel's death in 1837, the machine passed from hand to hand until it was destroyed by fire in Philadelphia in 1854. During the 70 years that the automaton was publicly exhibited, its "brain" was supplied by 15 different chess players, who won 294 of 300 games. ∼

10.1 Kempelen's chess-playing machine.

With his elaborate and elegant deception, Kempelen might be considered the forerunner of the modern computer criminal. Kempelen was trapped in his fraud because the public wanted to believe that the automated chess player was real. Desire overtook judgment in thousands of people, who were captivated by the idea of an intelligent machine.

More than two centuries later, we're still fascinated by intelligent machines. In 1997 people all over the world watched (many via the Web) as IBM's Deep Blue computer trounced Garry Kasparov, the reigning international chess champion. But modern computers don't just play games; they manage our money, our medicine, and our missiles. We're expected to trust information technology with our wealth, our health, and even our lives. The many benefits of our partnership with machines are clear. But blind faith in modern technology can be foolish and, in many cases, dangerous. In this chapter we examine some of the dark corners of our computerized society: legal dilemmas, ethical issues, and reliability risks. These issues are tied to a larger question: How can we make computers more secure so that we can feel more secure in our daily dealings with them? We'll look for answers to this question and then ask several more difficult questions about our relationship to computer technology and our future.

Online Outlaws: Computer Crime

Computers are **power**, and **direct contact** with power can bring out the **best** or **worst** in a person.

—Former computer criminal turned corporate computer programmer

Like other professions, law enforcement is being transformed by information technology. The FBI's National Crime Information Center provides police with almost instant information on crimes and criminals nationwide. Investigators use PC databases to store and cross-reference clues in complex cases. Using pattern recognition technology, automated fingerprint identification systems locate matches in minutes rather than months. Computers routinely scan the New York and London stock exchanges for connections that might indicate insider trading or fraud. Texas police use an intranet to cross-reference databases of photographs, fingerprints, and other crime-fighting information. *Computer forensics* experts use special software to scan criminal suspects' hard disks for digital "fingerprints"—traces of deleted files containing evidence of illegal activities. All of these tools help law enforcement officials ferret out criminals and stop criminal activities.

As with guns, people use computers to break laws as well as uphold them. Computers are powerful tools in the hands of criminals, and computer crime is a rapidly growing problem.

The Computer Crime Dossier

Some will rob you with a **six gun**, and some with a **fountain pen**.

—*Woody Guthrie, in "Pretty Boy Floyd"*

Today the computer has replaced both the gun and the pen as the weapon of choice for many criminals. Computer crime is often defined as any crime accomplished through knowledge or use of computer technology.

Nobody knows the true extent of computer crime. Many computer crimes go undetected. Those that are detected often go unreported because businesses fear that they can lose more from negative publicity than from the actual crimes.

According to a 2001 survey of more than 500 companies and government agencies by the FBI and the Computer Security Institute, 85 percent detected computer security breaches in the preceding 12 months. These breaches included system penetration by outsiders, theft of information, the changing of data, financial fraud, vandalism, theft of passwords, and the prevention of legitimate users from gaining access to systems. According to the survey, financial losses due to security breaches topped $377 million. By conservative estimates, businesses and government institutions lose billions of dollars every year to computer criminals.

The majority of computer crimes are committed by company insiders who aren't reported to authorities even when they are caught in the act. To avoid embarrassment, many companies cover up computer crimes committed by their own employees. These crimes are typically committed by clerks, cashiers, programmers, computer operators, and managers who have no extraordinary technical ingenuity. The typical computer criminal is a trusted employee with no criminal record who is tempted by an opportunity, such as the discovery of a loophole in system security. Greed, financial worries, and personal problems motivate this person to give in to temptation.

10.2 A police officer uses his mobile computer to check records in a central law enforcement database.

Of course, not all computer criminals fit this profile. Some are former employees seeking revenge on their former bosses. Some are high-tech pranksters looking for a challenge. A few are corporate or international spies seeking classified information. Organized crime syndicates are turning to computer technology to practice their trades. Sometimes entire companies are found guilty of computer fraud.

The 2001 survey suggests that the explosive growth of Internet commerce is changing the demographics of computer crime: 70 percent reported that Internet connections were frequent points of attack; only 31 percent said that internal systems were frequent points of attack.

Comparing this survey with previous annual surveys shows unmistakable trends: Internet security breaches are on the rise, internal security breaches are on the rise, and computer crime in general is on the rise. All of these increases are happening in spite of increased security and law enforcement efforts.

Theft by Computer

Every system has **vulnerabilities**. Every system **can be compromised**.

—Peter G. Neumann, in Computer Related Risks

Theft is the most common form of computer crime. Computers are used to steal money, goods, information, and computer resources. Here are a few examples:

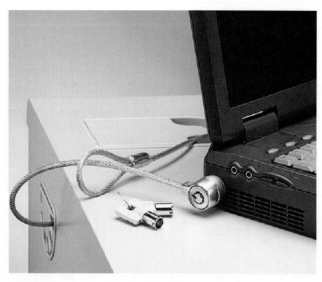

10.3 A portable computer is easy prey for thieves unless it is locked to something stationary and solid.

- In 2000 intruders broke into Creditcards.com, stole 55,000 credit card numbers, and held them for ransom. When their extortion attempt failed, they posted the numbers on the Web. The company has since created a more secure Web site.
- In 2001 two young Russian men were arrested for breaking into several U.S. company networks, stealing sensitive information, and demanding ransom for it. The FBI captured the pair by using a fake computer security company as bait. When they demanded payment from the bogus company, FBI agents agreed. The two men were arrested when they landed in the United States to collect their bounty.
- In May of 2001, Operation Cyber Loss, the FBI's crackdown on Internet fraud, netted 88 people in 10 days. According to the FBI, 56,000 people were defrauded of more than $117 million during the scams.
- In 2004 authorities arrested an America Online software engineer and charged him with using another AOL employee's access code to steal a list of 92 million customer screen names that was later sold to spammers.

One common type of computer theft today is the actual theft of computers. Notebook and handheld computers make particularly easy prey for crooks—especially in airports and other high-traffic, high-stress locations. Notebooks and PDAs are expensive items, but the information stored on a computer can be far more valuable than the computer itself.

Some types of computer crime are so common that they've been given names. A common student scam uses a process called spoofing to steal passwords. The typical spoofer launches a program that mimics the mainframe computer's login screen on an unattended terminal in a public lab. When an unsuspecting student types an ID and password, the program responds with an error message and remembers the secret codes.

Identity Theft

Sometimes thieves use computers and other tools to steal whole *identities*. By collecting personal information—credit card numbers, driver's license numbers, Social Security numbers, and a few other tidbits of data—a thief can effectively pose as someone else, even committing crimes in that person's name. Identity theft doesn't require a computer; many identity thieves get sensitive information by dumpster diving—rummaging through company and personal trash. But computers generally play a role in the process.

Identity theft often involves social engineering—slang for the use of deception to get individuals to reveal sensitive information. According to the FBI, two-thirds of identity thefts begin with an email solicitation. A spammer sends out an email that appears to be from PayPal, Citibank, AOL, or another company with which the recipient may have an account. One such message from "PayPal" reads, "Your credit card will expire soon. To avoid any interruption to your service, please update your credit card expiration date by following the steps below." By filling out and returning the form, unsuspecting consumers give thieves the information they need to steal an identity. Other identity thieves trick people into revealing their credit card numbers by setting up pornographic Web sites. These sites ask viewers to prove they are adults by providing credit card information.

Working Wisdom

Protecting Yourself from Identity Theft

The number of cases of identity theft is on the rise. About 100,000 people in the United States have their identities stolen each year. With a few simple precautions, you can reduce your chances of falling victim to this crime.

➡ *Make all your online purchases using a credit card.* Visa USA, MasterCard International, and American Express all have zero liability programs that waive your liability in case someone uses your credit card number for online fraud. Most debit cards, checking accounts, and money orders don't offer this kind of protection.

➡ *Get a separate credit card with a low credit limit for your online transactions.* If the card number is stolen, the thieves will not be able to run up as large a balance.

➡ *Make sure a secure Web site is managing your online transaction.* Look at the address of the Web site you are visiting. The URL should begin with https, not http. The https designator means the site is using encryption to improve the security of the transaction.

➡ *Don't disclose personal information over the phone.* Remember that a credit card company would never call you and ask you for your credit card number, expiration date, or other personal information; they already know it.

➡ *Handle email with care.* Cunning thieves send email that looks like it comes from a legitimate company like PayPal or Amazon.com, asking you to update your personal information, including your credit card number and expiration date. But when you click the link in the email, the Web site that loads isn't really from the legitimate company, opening unsuspecting users up to credit card theft. Regard all such emails with suspicion and be careful any time you enter a credit card number or other personal information online.

➡ *Don't put your Social Security number or your driver's license number on your checks.* These are key pieces of information sought by identity thieves.

➡ *Shred sensitive mail before you recycle it.* Bills, junk mail credit card offers, and other mail can contain personal information. Looking through people's garbage is a tried-and-true tactic of identity thieves.

➡ *Keep your wallet thin.* Don't carry your Social Security card or extra ID around with you. Cut and toss unused credit cards.

➡ *Copy your cards.* Make photocopies of both sides of your driver's license and credit cards and keep the copies in a safe place If your wallet or purse is stolen, you'll have the information you need to get replacement cards and cancel the stolen ones.

➡ *Scan your bills and statements promptly.* For companies that allow online access to accounts, you may not even need to wait for paper statements to arrive. If you find any unexpected transaction or other unpleasant surprises, report them right away.

➡ *Report identity theft promptly.* Call your credit card companies and the Federal Trade Commission (877-438-4338) right away.

10.4 A fraudulent email message.

The steady increase in electronic commerce has been accompanied by an increase in online fraud. Online auctions seem to be particularly fertile grounds for criminals. "The ePrivacy and Security Report" from market research company eMarketer.com estimated that 87 percent of online fraud cases in 2000 were related to online auctions, with the average cost per victim being around $600. The average age of an identity theft victim is 40. Many victims are used to providing credit card information online and simply get careless.

Software Sabotage: Viruses and Other Malware

The American government can stop me from going to the U.S., **but they can't stop my virus**.

—Virus creator

Another type of computer crime is sabotage of hardware or software. The word sabotage comes from the early days of the Industrial Revolution, when rebellious workers shut down new machines by placing wooden shoes, called sabots, into the gears. Modern computer saboteurs commonly use malware—malicious software—rather than footwear to do destructive deeds. The names given to the saboteurs' destructive programs—viruses, worms, and Trojan horses—sound more like biology than technology, and many of the programs even mimic the behavior of living organisms.

Viruses

A biological virus is unable to reproduce by itself, but it can invade the cells of another organism and use the reproductive machinery of each host cell to make copies of itself; the new copies leave the host and seek new hosts to repeat the process. A software virus works in the same way. Virus software is a piece of code usually hidden in the operating system of a computer or in an application program. When a user executes a program containing a virus, the virus quickly copies itself to an uninfected program; it then allows the user's application to execute. Usually this happens so quickly that the user is unaware the application program contains a virus. A virus can jump from one computer to another when someone uses a disk or a computer network to copy an infected program. Some viruses do nothing but reproduce; others display messages on the computer's screen; still others destroy data or erase disks.

Like most software code, a virus is usually operating-system specific. Windows viruses invade only Windows disks, Macintosh viruses invade only Macintosh disks, and so on. There are exceptions: *Macro viruses* attach themselves to documents that contain *macros*—embedded programs to automate tasks. Macro viruses can be spread across computer platforms if the documents are created and spread using cross-platform applications—most commonly the applications in Microsoft Office. Macro viruses can be spread through innocent-looking email attachments. Viruses spread through email are sometimes called *email viruses*.

One of the most widely publicized email viruses was 1999's Melissa virus. Melissa's method of operation is typical of email viruses: An unsuspecting computer user received an "Important message" from a friend: "Here is that document you asked for . . . don't show it

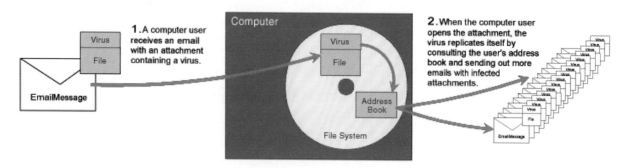

10.5 How a virus spreads via email.

to anyone else ;-)." The attached Microsoft Word document contained a list of passwords for Internet pornography sites. It contained something else: a macro virus written in Microsoft Office's built-in Visual Basic scripting language. When the user opened the document, the macro virus went to work, sending a copy of the email message and infected document to the first 50 names on the user's Outlook address book. Within minutes, 50 more potential Melissa victims received messages apparently from someone they knew—the user of the newly infected computer. Melissa spread like wildfire among Windows systems, infecting 100,000 systems in just a few days. Melissa wasn't designed to do damage to systems, but the sudden flurry of messages brought down some email servers. A nationwide search located the probable author of the Melissa virus, a 30-year-old New Jersey resident with a fondness for a topless dancer named Melissa. A federal judge fined him $5,000 and sentenced him to 20 months in federal prison plus 100 hours of community service.

Shortly after Melissa faded from the headlines, a similar, but more destructive virus, named Chernobyl, infected more than 600,000 computers worldwide. South Korea alone suffered 300,000 attacks; about 15 percent of its PCs were damaged by the virus, at a cost of $250 million. In May of 2000, a Melissa-like virus called Love Bug spread from a PC in the Philippines around the world through innocent-looking "I Love You" email message attachments. In a matter of hours, the Love Bug caused billions of dollars in lost productivity and damage to computer systems.

In the summer of 2003, a rash of viruses plagued PC users, culminating in a massive epidemic caused by a virus called Sobig. Sobig was the fastest-spreading network virus ever. One message-filtering service intercepted more than a million copies of the virus in a single day. The Windows virus deposited a Trojan horse that could scan an infected PC's hard disk for email addresses in documents and address books and send copies of itself to those addresses. Sobig didn't destroy files or damage PCs, but it clogged networks and mailboxes worldwide.

Worms

Like viruses, worms (named for tapeworms) use computer hosts to reproduce themselves. But unlike viruses, worms are complete programs capable of traveling independently over computer networks, seeking out uninfected workstations in which to reproduce. A worm can reproduce until the computer freezes from lack of free memory or disk space. A typical worm segment resides in memory rather than on disk, so the worm can be eliminated by shutting down all of the workstations on the network.

The first headline-making worm was created as an experiment by a Cornell graduate student in 1988. The worm was accidentally released onto the Internet, clogging 6,000 computers all over the United States, almost bringing them to a standstill and forcing operators to shut them all down so every worm segment could be purged from memory. The total cost, in terms of work time lost at research institutions, was staggering. The student was suspended from school and was the first person convicted of violating the Computer Fraud and Abuse Act.

In the summer of 2001, a worm called Code Red made worldwide headlines. Code Red didn't attack PCs; its target was Internet servers running Microsoft server software. The U.S. government and Microsoft issued warnings about the worm and made free software patches available to protect servers. Even so, many servers were crippled by the repeated attacks from the worm, including servers owned and operated by Microsoft.

Trojan Horses

A Trojan horse is a program that performs a useful task while at the same time carrying out some secret destructive act. As in the ancient story of the wooden horse that carried Greek soldiers through the gates of Troy, Trojan horse software hides an enemy in an attractive package. Trojan horse programs are often posted on shareware Web sites with names that make them sound like games or utilities. When an unsuspecting bargain hunter downloads and runs such a program, it might erase files, change data, or cause some other kind of damage. Some network saboteurs use Trojan horses to pass secret data to other unauthorized users.

One type of Trojan horse, a **logic bomb**, is programmed to attack in response to a particular event or sequence of events. For example, a programmer might plant a logic bomb that is designed to destroy data files if the programmer is ever listed as terminated in the company's personnel file. A logic bomb might be triggered when a certain user logs in, enters a special code in a database field, or a performs a particular sequence of actions. If the logic bomb is triggered by a time-related event, it is called a *time bomb*. A widely publicized virus included a logic bomb that was programmed to destroy PC data files on Michelangelo's birthday.

Trojan horses can cause serious problems in computer systems of all sizes. To make matters worse, many Trojan horses carry software viruses.

Spyware

Spyware refers to a technology that collects information from computer users without their knowledge or consent. A spyware application program, sometimes called *tracking software* or a *spybot*, gathers user information and communicates this information to an outsider via the Internet. Spybots can monitor your keystrokes, record which Web sites you visit, and even take snapshots of what's displayed on your monitor. Other spybots cause pop-up advertising to appear on your screen.

A recent survey of PC users with broadband Internet connections found that 91 percent of them had spyware on their computers. That's not surprising, considering the number of ways spyware can get into a PC. Some computer viruses spread spyware. Some freeware or shareware programs include hidden spyware. In *drive-by downloads*, simply visiting certain Web sites causes spyware to be downloaded to your computer.

Virus Wars

The popular press usually doesn't distinguish among Trojan horses, viruses, and worms; they're all called computer viruses. Whatever they're called, these rogue programs make life more complicated and expensive for people who depend on computers. Researchers have identified more than 18,000 virus strains, with 200 new ones appearing each month. At any given time, about 250 virus strains exist in the wild—in circulation.

Modern viruses can spread faster and do more damage than viruses of a few years ago for several reasons. The Internet, which speeds communication all over the planet, also speeds virus transmission. Web pages, macros, and other technologies give virus writers new places to hide their creations. And increased standardization on Microsoft applications and operating systems has made it easier for viruses to spread. Just as natural mixed forests are more resistant to disease than are single-species tree farms, mixed computing environments are less susceptible to crippling attacks than is an organization in which everyone uses the same hardware and software.

When computers are used in life-or-death situations, as they are in many medical and military applications, invading programs can even threaten human lives. The U.S. government and several states now have laws against introducing these programs into computer systems.

Antivirus programs (sometimes simply referred to as AV software) are designed to search for viruses, notify users when they're found, and remove them from infected disks or files. Most antivirus programs continually monitor system activity, watching for and reporting suspicious viruslike actions. But no antivirus program can detect every virus, and these programs need to be frequently revised to combat new viruses as they appear. Most antivirus programs can automatically download new virus-fighting code from the Web as new virus strains appear. But it can take several days for companies to develop and distribute patches for new viruses, and destructive viruses can do a lot of damage in that time.

The virus wars continue to escalate as virus writers develop new ways to spread their works. After a rash of 1999 email viruses, most users learned not to open unidentified email attachments, and software vendors started modifying their email applications to prevent this sort of attack. But before the year was over, a worm called BubbleBoy (named for an episode of TV's Seinfeld) demonstrated that a system could be infected by email even if the mail wasn't opened. Some viruses have even been developed to infect HTML code in Web pages or HTML email messages. HTML viruses can't (so far) infect your computer if you're viewing an infected Web page on another computer; the infected HTML code must be downloaded onto your machine.

Software companies continually test their products for security holes and try to make them more resistant to viruses, worms, and other security breaches. Because Microsoft Windows is the target of the great majority of malware, the company periodically releases security patches—software programs that plug potential security breaches in the operating system. These patches are provided as free downloads or automatic updates to all owners of the OS. But preventive security measures like these can sometimes backfire. In the summer of 2003, a worm called MS Slammer made worldwide headlines, shutting down hundreds of thousands of PCs as it moved from computer to computer looking for vulnerable targets. The worm was deployed more than a month after Microsoft had issued a security patch to fix the very problem that MS Slammer exploited. By publicizing the vulnerability, Microsoft inadvertently inspired malicious programmers to create the worm. These system saboteurs took advantage of the fact that many computer users fail to install security patches, leaving their systems ripe for attack. In response to MS Slammer, a well-intentioned programmer released a helper worm designed to search the Internet for machines that had been infected by MS Slammer and apply the Microsoft security patch to those machines. But this worm caused its own problems, slowing many systems to a crawl by repeatedly checking them for security problems.

Stories like this one happen more often than the information technology industry would like to admit. These stories serve as reminders that the virus wars are far from over. There will always be new ways to compromise connected systems.

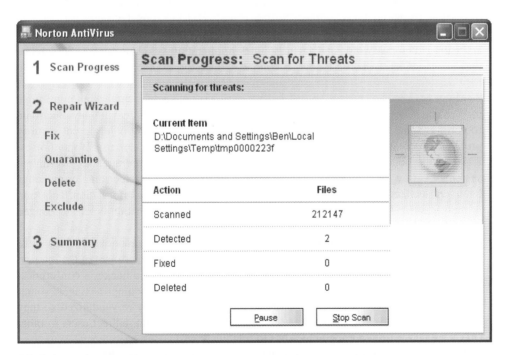

10.6 Antivirus software scans files for viruses, worms, and other software invaders. New versions of the software definition files should be downloaded regularly to ensure the software is up to date.

Hacking and Electronic Trespassing

The Hacker Ethic: Access to computers—and anything which might teach you something about the way the world works—should be **unlimited** and **total**. Always yield to the **Hands-on Imperative**.

All information should be **free**.

Mistrust Authority—Promote Decentralization.

Hackers should be judged by their **hacking**, not bogus criteria such as degrees, age, race, or position.

You can create **art and beauty** on a computer.

Computers can **change your life** for the better.

—*Steven Levy, in* Hackers: Heroes of the Computer Revolution

---

I don't drink, smoke, or take drugs. I don't steal, assault people, or vandalize property. The **only way** in which I am **really different** from most people is in **my fascination** with the ways and means of learning about **computers that don't belong to me**.

—*Bill "The Cracker" Landreth, in* Out of the Inner Circle

In the late 1970s, timesharing computers at Stanford and MIT attracted informal communities of computer fanatics who called themselves *hackers*. In those days, a hacker was a person who enjoyed learning the details of computer systems and writing clever programs, referred to as hacks. Hackers were, for the most part, curious, enthusiastic, intelligent, idealistic, eccentric, and harmless. Many of those early hackers were, in fact, architects of the microcomputer revolution.

Over the years, the idealism of the early hacker communities was at least partly overshadowed by cynicism, as big-money interests took over the young personal computer industry. At the same time, the term hacking took on a new, more ominous connotation in the media. Although many people still use the term to describe software wizardry, it more commonly refers to unauthorized access to computer systems. Old-time hackers insist that this electronic trespassing is really *cracking*, or criminal hacking, but the general public and popular media don't recognize the distinction between hackers and crackers. Today's stereotypical hacker, like his early counterparts, is a young, bright, technically savvy, white, middle-class male who, in addition to programming his own computer, may break into others.

Of course, not all young computer wizards break into systems, and not all electronic trespassers fit the media stereotype. Still, hackers aren't just a media myth; they're real, and there are lots of them. Electronic trespassers enter corporate and government computers using stolen passwords and security holes in operating system software. Sometimes they use modems to dial up the target computers directly; in other cases they "travel" to their destinations through the Internet and other networks.

Many hackers are merely motivated by curiosity and intellectual challenge; once they've cracked a system, they look around and move on without leaving any electronic footprints. Some hackers claim to be acting in the public good by pointing out security problems in commercial software products. Some malicious hackers use Trojan horses, logic bombs, and other tricks of the trade to wreak havoc on corporate and government systems. A growing number of computer trespassers are part of electronic crime rings intent on stealing credit card numbers and other sensitive, valuable information. This kind of theft is difficult to detect and track because the original information is left unchanged when the copy is stolen.

According to the FBI, an Internet hack happens every 30 seconds. Hackers have defaced the Web sites of the White House, the U.S. Senate, the Department of the Interior, presidential candidates, countless online businesses, and even a hacker's conference. Sometimes Web sites are simply defaced with obscene or threatening messages; sometimes they're replaced with satirical substitutes; sometimes they're vandalized so they don't work properly. *Webjackers* hijack legitimate Web pages and redirect users to other sites—anywhere from pornographic sites to fraudulent businesses.

Denial of service (DoS) attacks bombard servers and Web sites with so much bogus traffic that they're effectively shut down, denying service to legitimate customers and clients. In a *distributed denial of service (DDoS) attack* the flood of messages comes from many compromised systems distributed across the Net. In a single week in February 2000, the Yahoo!, E*TRADE, eBay, and Amazon Web sites were crippled by denial of service attacks, costing their owners millions of dollars in business. Two months later, a 15-year-old

Canadian youth, nicknamed "Mafia Boy," was arrested after he bragged online about causing the breakdowns. His expensive pranks didn't require any special expertise; he reportedly downloaded all of the software he used from the Internet. In August 2003, computers affected by the Blaster worm launched a DDoS attack on Microsoft's Windows Update Web site; this time bomb attack ironically prevented users from downloading the software patch that would have rendered Blaster impotent.

One famous case of electronic trespassing was documented in Cliff Stoll's best-selling book, *The Cuckoo's Egg*. While working as a system administrator for a university computer lab in 1986, Stoll noticed a 75-cent accounting error. Rather than letting it go, Stoll investigated the error. He uncovered a system intruder who was searching government, corporate, and university computers across the Internet for sensitive military information. It took a year and some help from the FBI, but Stoll eventually located the hacker—a German computer science student and part of a ring of hackers working for the KGB. Ironically, Stoll captured the thief by using standard hacker tricks, including a Trojan horse program that contained information on a fake Strategic Defense Initiative Network (SDI Net).

This kind of online espionage is becoming commonplace as the Internet becomes a mainstream communication medium. A more recent front-page-story-turned-book involved the 1995 capture of Kevin Mitnick, the hacker who had stolen millions of dollars worth of software and credit card information on the Net. By repeatedly manufacturing new identities and cleverly concealing his location, Mitnick successfully evaded the FBI for years. But when he broke into the computer of computational physicist Tsutomu Shimomura, he inadvertently started an electronic cat-and-mouse game that ended with his capture and conviction. Shimomura was able to defeat Mitnick because of his expertise in computer security—the protection of computer systems and, indirectly, the people who depend on them.

10.7 Kevin Mitnick was the most notorious hacker ever caught, according to federal authorities. Mitnick was a "pure" hacker who illegally accessed remote computers out of curiosity. He spent five years in jail for his hacking activities. Today, Mitnick runs a computer security company whose Web site, ironically, was hacked in early 2003.

Computer Security: Reducing Risks

With computer crime on the rise, computer security has become an important concern for system administrators and computer users alike. Computer security refers to protecting computer systems and the information they contain against unwanted access, damage, modification, or destruction. According to a 1991 report of the Congressional Research Service, computers have two inherent characteristics that leave them open to attack or operating error:

> In the **old world**, if I wanted to attack something physical, there was **one way to get there**. You could put guards and guns around it, **you could protect it**. But a database—or a control system—usually has multiple pathways, **unpredictable routes to it**, and seems intrinsically **impossible to protect**. That's why most efforts at computer security **have been defeated**.
>
> —*Andrew Marshall, military analyst*

1. A computer does exactly what it is programmed to do, including reveal sensitive information. Any system that can be programmed can be reprogrammed by anyone with sufficient knowledge.

2. Any computer can do only what it is programmed to do. "[I]t cannot protect itself from either malfunctions or deliberate attacks unless such events have been specifically anticipated, thought through, and countered with appropriate programming."

Computer owners and administrators use a variety of security techniques to protect their systems, ranging from everyday low-tech locks to high-tech software scrambling.

10.8 Biometric devices provide high levels of computer and network security because they monitor human body characteristics that can't be stolen. IriScan's PC Iris (above) can compare the patterns in the iris of the user against a database of employees and other legitimate users. The U-Match Bio-Link Mouse (right) checks the thumbprint of the user against a database of prints approved for access.

Physical Access Restrictions

One way to reduce the risk of security breaches is to identify people attempting to access computer equipment. Organizations use a number of tools and techniques to identify personnel. Computers can perform some security checks; human security guards perform others. Depending on the security system, you might be granted access to a computer based on the following criteria:

- *Something you have*, such as a key, an ID card with a photo, or a *smart card* containing digitally encoded identification in a built-in memory chip
- *Something you know*, such as a password, an ID number, a lock combination, or a piece of personal history, such as your mother's maiden name
- *Something you do*, such as your signature or your typing speed and error patterns
- *Something about you*, such as a voice print, fingerprint, retinal scan, facial feature scan, or other measurement of individual body characteristics; these measurements are collectively called biometrics.

Because most of these security controls can be compromised—keys can be stolen, signatures can be forged, and so on—many systems use a combination of controls. For example, an employee might be required to show a badge, unlock a door with a key, and type a password to use a secured computer.

In the days when corporate computers were isolated in basements, physical restrictions were sufficient for keeping out intruders. But in the modern office, computers and data are almost everywhere, and networks connect computers to the outside world. In a distributed, networked environment, security is much more problematic. It's not enough to restrict physical access to mainframes when personal computers and network connections aren't restricted. Additional security techniques—most notably passwords—are needed to restrict access to remote computers.

Passwords

Passwords are the most common tools used to restrict access to computer systems. Passwords are effective, however, only if they're chosen carefully. Most computer users choose passwords that are easy to guess: names of partners, children, or pets; words related to jobs or hobbies; and consecutive characters on keyboards. One survey found that the two favorite passwords in Britain were "Fred" and "God"; in America they were "love" and "sex." Hackers know and exploit these clichés; cautious users avoid them. Many security systems refuse to enable users to choose any real words or names as passwords so hackers can't use dictionary software to guess them systematically. Even the best passwords should be changed frequently.

Access-control software doesn't need to treat all users identically. Many systems use passwords to restrict users so they can open only files related to their work. In many cases, users are given read-only access to files that they can see but not change.

To prevent unauthorized use of stolen passwords by outsiders, many companies use call-back systems. When a user logs in and types a password, the system hangs up, looks up the user's phone number, and calls back before providing access.

Firewalls, Encryption, and Audits

Many data thieves do their work without breaking into computer systems; instead, they intercept messages as they travel between computers on networks. Passwords are of little use for hiding email messages when they're traveling through phone lines or Internet gateways. Still, Internet communication is far too important to sacrifice in the name of security. Many organizations use firewalls to keep their internal networks secure while enabling communication with the rest of the Internet. The technical details of firewalls vary considerably, but they're all designed to serve the same function: to guard against unauthorized access to an internal network. In effect, a firewall is a gate with a lock; the locked gate opens only for information packets that pass one or more security inspections. Firewalls aren't just for large corporations anymore. Without firewall hardware or software installed, a home computer with an always-on DSL or cable modem connection can be easy prey for Internet snoopers. Windows XP and Mac OS X include basic software firewalls, but these firewalls must be activated before they can provide protection.

Of course, the firewall's digital drawbridge has to let some messages pass through; otherwise there could be no communication with the rest of the Internet. How can those messages be secured in transit? To protect transmitted information, many organizations and individuals use encryption software to scramble their transmissions. When a user encrypts a message by applying a secret numerical code, called an *encryption key*, the message can be transmitted or stored as an indecipherable garble of characters. The message can be read only after it's been reconstructed with a matching key.

For the most sensitive information, passwords, firewalls, and encryption aren't enough. A diligent spy can "listen to" the electromagnetic signals that emanate from the computer hardware and, in some cases, read sensitive information. To prevent spies from using these spurious broadcasts, the Pentagon has spent hundreds of millions of dollars on a program called Tempest to develop specially shielded machines.

10.9 Hardware firewall products come in all shapes and sizes.

How It Works

10.1 Firewalls

A firewall is a program, often run on a dedicated computer, that filters information between a private network and the rest of the Internet. A set of security rules, created by a network administrator, determines which packets can enter and leave the local network.

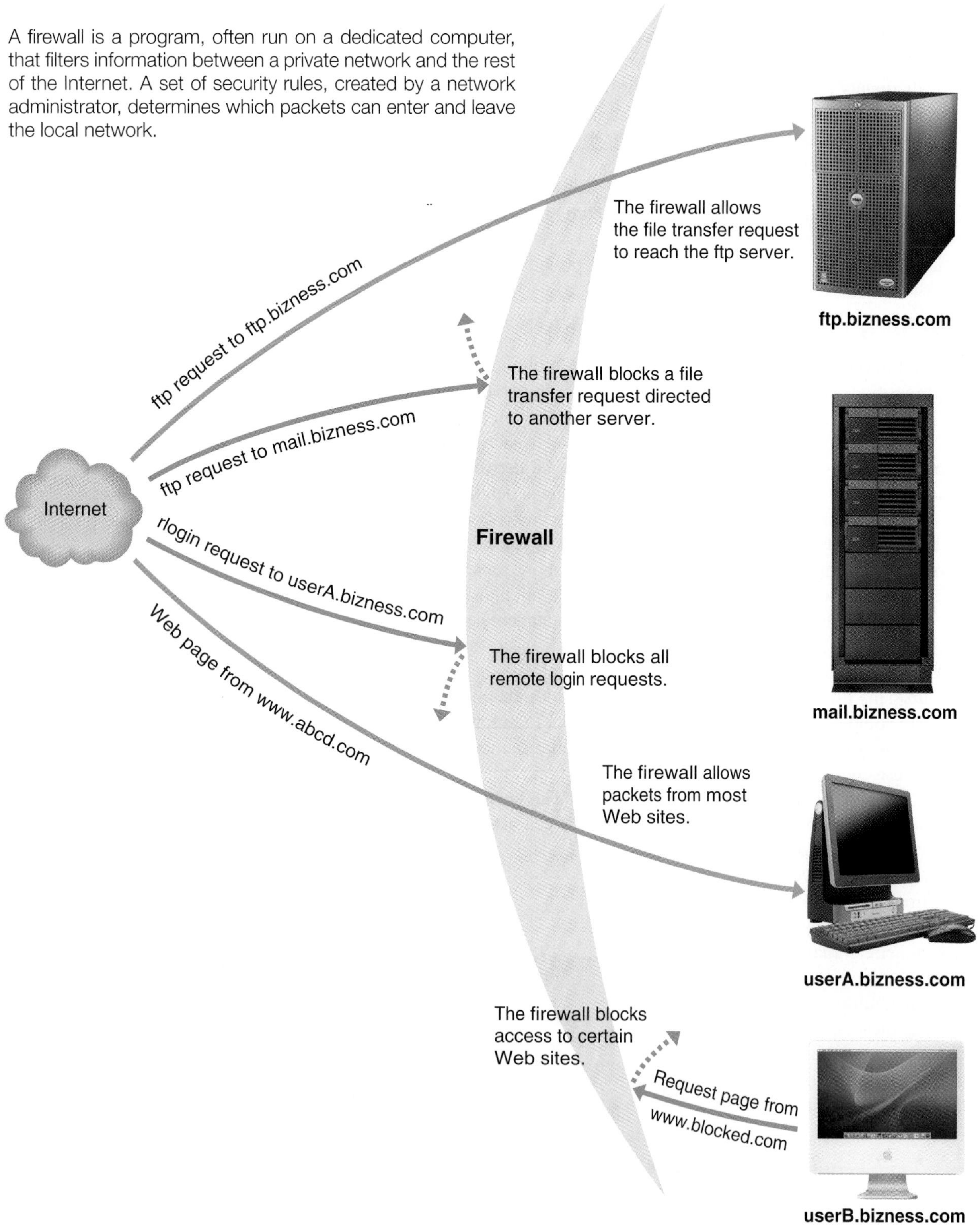

The firewall allows the file transfer request to reach the ftp server.

ftp.bizness.com

ftp request to ftp.bizness.com

ftp request to mail.bizness.com

rlogin request to userA.bizness.com

Web page from www.abcd.com

Internet

The firewall blocks a file transfer request directed to another server.

Firewall

The firewall blocks all remote login requests.

mail.bizness.com

The firewall allows packets from most Web sites.

userA.bizness.com

The firewall blocks access to certain Web sites.

Request page from www.blocked.com

userB.bizness.com

10.10

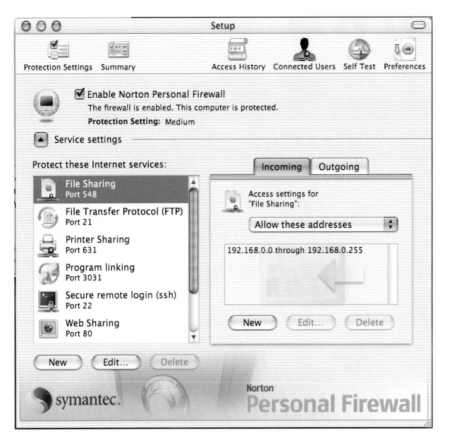

10.11 Software firewalls, such as the one included with Norton Systemworks, help protect home networks from hackers.

Audit-control software is used to monitor and record computer transactions as they happen so auditors can trace and identify suspicious computer activity after the fact. Effective audit-control software forces every user, legitimate or otherwise, to leave a trail of electronic footprints. Of course, this kind of software is of little value unless someone in the organization monitors and interprets the output.

The encrypted message is transmitted through the network.

x48dqq82ked8i3kdi 3i3kd0o290ekwcmg qaoi34ieqhj3o3k,wi woakaqjkurtj2iewow qlekejroqei45783.p

The sender creates, encrypts, and sends the message.

The message is received and decrypted.

10.12 The encryption process.

10.2 **Cryptography**

If you want to be sure that an email message can be read by only the intended recipient, you must either use a secure communication channel or secure the message.

Mail within many organizations is sent over secure communication channels—channels that can't be accessed by outsiders. But you can't secure the channels used by the Internet and other worldwide mail networks; there's no way to shield messages sent through public telephone lines and airwaves. In the words of Mark Rotenberg, director of the Electronic Privacy Information Center, "Email is more like a postcard than a sealed letter."

If you can't secure the communication channel, the alternative is to secure the message. You secure a message by using a cryptosystem to encrypt it—scramble it so it can be decrypted (unscrambled) only by the intended recipient.

Almost all cryptosystems depend on a key—a password-like number or phrase that can be used to encrypt or decrypt a message. Eavesdroppers who don't know the key have to try to decrypt it by brute force by trying all possible keys until they guess the right one.

Some cryptosystems afford only modest security: A message can be broken after only a day or week of brute force cryptanalysis on a supercomputer. More effective systems would take a supercomputer billions of years to break the message.

The traditional kind of cryptosystem used on computer networks is called a symmetric secret key system. With this approach the sender and recipient use the same key, and they have to keep the shared key secret from everyone else.

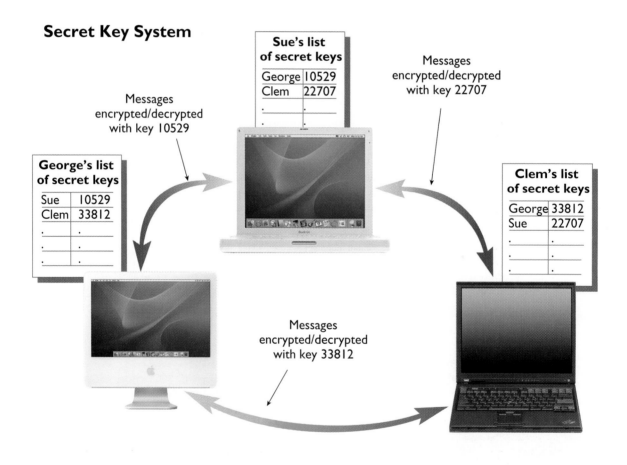

Secret Key System

Sue's list of secret keys

George	10529
Clem	22707
.	.

Messages encrypted/decrypted with key 10529

Messages encrypted/decrypted with key 22707

George's list of secret keys

Sue	10529
Clem	33812
.	.
.	.
.	.

Clem's list of secret keys

George	33812
Sue	22707
.	.
.	.
.	.

Messages encrypted/decrypted with key 33812

10.13

The biggest problem with symmetric secret key systems is key management. If you want to communicate with several people and ensure that each person can't read messages intended for the others, then you'll need a different secret key for each person. When you want to communicate with new people, you have the problem of letting them know what the key is. If you send it over the ordinary communication channel, it can be intercepted.

In the 1970s, cryptographers developed public key cryptography to get around the key management problems. The most popular kind of public key cryptosystem, RSA, is being incorporated into most new network-enabled software. Phillip Zimmerman's popular shareware utility called PGP (for Pretty Good Privacy) uses RSA technology.

Public Key System

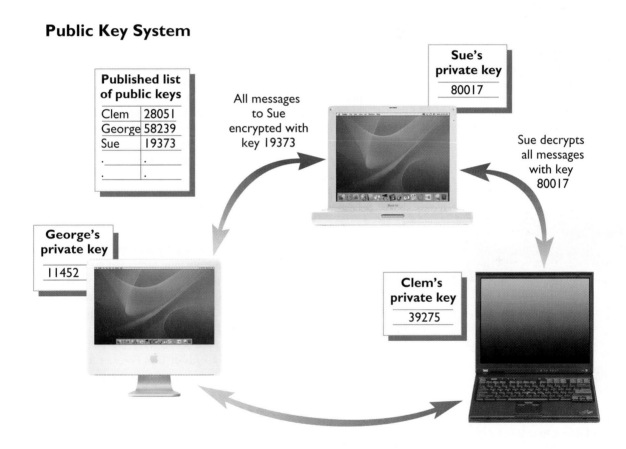

Each person using a public key cryptosystem has two keys: a private key known only to the user and a public key that is freely available to anyone who wants it. Thus a public key system is asymmetric: A different key is used to encrypt than to decrypt. Public keys can be published in phone directories, Web pages, and advertisements; some users include them in their email signatures.

If you want to send a secure message over the Internet to your friend Sue in St. Louis, you use her public key to encrypt the message. Sue's public key can't decrypt the message; only her private key can do that. The private key is specifically designed to decrypt messages that were encrypted with the corresponding public key. Since public/private key pairs can be generated by individual users, the key distribution problem is solved. The only keys being sent over an insecure network are publicly available keys.

You can use the same technology in reverse (encrypt with the private key, decrypt with the public key) for message authentication: When you decrypt a message, you can be sure that it was sent from a particular person on the network. In the future, legal and commercial documents will routinely have digital signatures that will be as valid as handwritten ones.

Backups and Other Precautions

Even the tightest security system can't guarantee absolute protection of data. A power surge or a power failure can wipe out even the most carefully guarded data in an instant. An **uninterruptible power supply (UPS)** can protect computers from data loss during power failures; inexpensive ones can protect home computers from short power dropouts. *Surge protectors* don't help during power failures, but they can shield electronic equipment from dangerous power spikes, preventing expensive hardware failures.

Of course, disasters come in many forms. Sabotage, human errors, machine failures, fire, flood, lightning, and earthquakes can damage or destroy computer data along with hardware. Any complete security system should include a plan for recovering from disasters. For mainframes and PCs alike, the best and most widely used data recovery insurance is a system of making regular **backups**. For many systems, data and software are backed up automatically onto disks or tapes, usually at the end of each workday. Most data processing shops keep several *generations* of backups so they can, if necessary, go back several days, weeks, or years to reconstruct data files. For maximum security, many computer users keep copies of sensitive data in several different locations. Storage technology called *redundant array of independent disk (RAID)* enables multiple hard disks to operate as a single logical unit. RAID systems can, among other things, automatically *mirror* data on multiple disks, effectively creating instant redundancy.

10.14 An uninterruptible power supply (UPS) protects a computer against power surges and momentary power loss.

Human Security Controls: Law, Management, and Ethics

In 2003, the supplier of the world's most used software products launched a "Trustworthy Computing" initiative. Microsoft's long-term goal was to make the software it develops as secure as possible when released, lessening the need for expensive and time-consuming security patches. Security experts throughout the computer industry are constantly developing new technologies and techniques for protecting computer systems from computer criminals. But at the same time, criminals continue to refine their craft. In the ongoing competition between the law and the lawless, computer security generally lags behind. In the words of Tom Forester and Perry Morrison in *Computer Ethics,* "Computer security experts are forever trying to shut the stable door after the horse has bolted."

Ultimately, computer security is a human problem that can't be solved by technology alone. Security is a management issue, and a manager's actions and policies are critical to the success of a security program. An alarming number of companies are lax about computer security. Many managers don't understand the problems and don't think they are at risk. It's important for managers to understand the practical, ethical, and legal issues surrounding security. Managers must make their employees aware of security issues and security risks. If managers don't defend against security threats, information can't be secure.

10.15 A RAID storage device combines hard drives to create a redundant data store that can withstand hardware failures.

The Role of System Administrators

System administrators play a key role in determining the security of a computer network. To begin with, they implement mechanisms to ensure only legitimate users have access to the system, and the privileges of these users are set appropriately. **Authentication mechanisms** ensure only legitimate users have access to the system by asking potential users to identify themselves. Previously in this chapter, you saw examples of knowledge-based, token-based, action-based, and biometric authentication schemes.

Most computer systems rely upon passwords as the sole authentication mechanism. System administrators should put policies in place to ensure that users do not choose passwords that are easy for a hacker to guess. Administrators can run a program that attempts to guess users' passwords by trying dictionary words and other short combinations of letters and numbers. If the program successfully guesses the password, the password is too obvious, and the system administrator can require the user to pick a new password.

Even if a person has the right to use a computer, not every user has the same privileges. **Authorization mechanisms** guarantee that users have permission to perform particular actions. For example, a typical user of a mainframe computer is not authorized to shut down the system. Only a system administrator has the authority to perform that action. Most operating systems assign each user a unique *user identifier*. Information about the user's privileges is associated with every user. The system administrator should ensure that each user's privileges are set correctly.

System administrators can reduce the threat of malware by keeping the operating system up to date with the latest patches provided by the software vendor. Announcements of security patches provide hackers with information they can use to create new worms. Up-to-date systems are immune from these worms.

System administrators are also responsible for performing backups on a regular basis. Data files can be quite valuable, and if files are accidentally or maliciously destroyed, back-up copies are indispensable. Whenever possible, back-up tapes or disks should be kept in a separate building from the computers themselves to provide added protection in case of fire or earthquake.

Security, Privacy, Freedom, and Ethics: The Delicate Balance

It's hard to overstate the importance of computer security in our networked world. Destructive viruses, illegal interlopers, crooked coworkers, software pirates, and cyber-vandals can erode trust, threaten jobs, and make life difficult for

> In this age of advanced technology, **thick walls** and **locked doors** cannot guard our **privacy** or safeguard our **personal freedom**.
>
> —*Lyndon B. Johnson, 36th president of the United States, February 23, 1974*

everyone. But sometimes computer security measures can create problems of their own. Complex access procedures, virus-protection programs, intellectual property laws, and other security measures can, if carried too far, interfere with people getting their work done. In the extreme, security can threaten individual human rights.

When Security Threatens Privacy

As you've seen in other chapters, computers threaten our personal privacy on several fronts. Corporate and government databases accumulate and share massive amounts of information about us against our will and without our knowledge. Internet-monitoring programs and software snoopers track our Web explorations and read our electronic mail. Corporate managers use monitoring software to measure worker productivity and observe their on-screen activities. Government security agencies secretly monitor telephone calls and data transmissions.

When security measures are used to prevent computer crime, they usually help protect privacy rights at the same time. When a hacker invades a computer system, the intruder might monitor the system's legitimate users' private communications. When an outsider breaks into the database of a bank, the privacy of every bank customer is at risk. The same applies to government computers, credit bureau computers, and any other computer containing data on private citizens. The security of these systems is important for protecting people's privacy.

Safe Computing

Even if you're not building a software system for the DOJ or the FBI, computer security is important. Viruses, disk crashes, system bombs, and miscellaneous disasters can destroy your work, your peace of mind, and possibly your system. Fortunately, you can protect your computer, your software, and your data from most hazards.

➡ **Share with care.** A computer virus is a contagious disease that spreads when it comes in contact with a compatible file or disk. Viruses spread rapidly in environments where disks and files are passed around freely, as they are in many student computer labs. To protect your data, keep your disks to yourself, and don't borrow disks from others.

➡ **Beware of email bearing gifts.** Many viruses hide in attachments to email messages that say something like "Here's the document you asked for. Please don't show anyone else." Don't open unsolicited email attachments, especially from senders you don't recognize; just throw them away.

➡ **Handle shareware and freeware with care.** Some viruses enter systems in Trojan horse shareware and freeware programs. Treat public domain programs and shareware with care; test them with a disinfectant program before you install them on your hard disk. Viruses can be embedded in an email message or attachment, so scan attached files before opening them and use AV software regularly.

➡ **Don't pirate software.** Even commercial programs can be infected with viruses. Shrink-wrapped, virgin software is much less likely to be infected than pirated copies. Besides, software piracy is theft, and the legal penalties can be severe.

➡ **Disinfect regularly.** Virus protection programs are available for all kinds of systems, often for free. Use up-to-date virus protection software regularly.

➡ **Treat your removable disks as if they contained something important.** Keep them away from liquids, dust, pets, and (especially) magnets. Don't put your disks close to phones, speakers, and other electronic devices that contain hidden magnets. (Magnets won't harm CD-ROMs or DVD-ROMs, but scratches can make them unusable.)

➡ **Take your passwords seriously.** Choose a password that's not easily guessable, not in any dictionary, and not easy for others to remember. Don't post it by your computer, and don't type it when you're being watched. Change your password occasionally—immediately if you have reason to suspect it has been discovered.

➡ **If it's sensitive, lock it up.** If your computer is accessible to others, protect your private files with passwords and/or encryption. Many operating systems and utilities include options for adding password protection and encrypting files. If others need to see the files, lock them so they can be read but not changed or deleted. If secrecy is critical, don't store the data on your hard disk at all. Store it on removable disks and lock it away in a safe place.

➡ **If it's important, back it up.** Regularly make backup copies of every important file on different disks than the original. Keep copies of critical disks in different locations so that you have backups in case disaster strikes.

➡ **If you're sending sensitive information through the Internet, consider encryption.** Use a utility or a program like freeware PGP (Pretty Good Privacy) to turn your message into code that's almost impossible to crack.

➡ **Don't open your system to interlopers.** If you've got an always-on Internet connection—T1, DSL, or cable modem—consider using firewall hardware or software to detect and lock out snoopers. Set your file-sharing controls so access is limited to authorized visitors.

➡ **Prepare for the worst.** Even if you take every precaution, things can still go wrong. Make sure you aren't completely dependent on the computer for really important things.

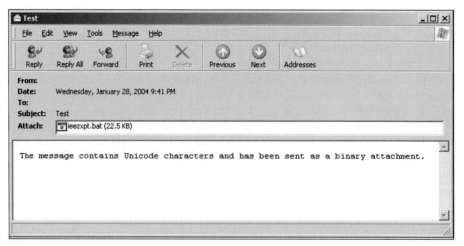

10.16 Don't open attachments to unsolicited emails. They may contain viruses.

But in some cases security and law enforcement can pose threats to personal privacy. Here are some examples:

■ In 1990 Alana Shoar, email coordinator for Epson America, Inc., found stacks of print-outs of employee email messages in her boss's office—messages that employees believed were private. Shortly after confronting her boss, she was fired for "gross misconduct and insubordination." She filed a class-action suit, claiming that Epson routinely monitored all email messages. Company officials denied the charges but took a firm stand on their right to any information stored on, sent to, or taken from their business computers. The courts ruled in Epson's favor. Since then, many other U.S. court decisions have reinforced a company's right to read employee email stored on company computers.

■ A 2004 decision by a federal appeals court went even further, ruling that an Internet service provider has the right to read the email messages of its subscribers. While the Wiretap Act prohibits eavesdropping on telephone calls and other messages sent in real time, the majority opinion stated that a stored message, such as a piece of email, does not have the same protection. The Electronic Frontier Foundation protested the decision, arguing that the ruling "dealt a grave blow to the privacy of Internet communications."

■ In 1995 the U.S. government passed legislation requiring new digital phone systems to include additional switches that allow for electronic surveillance. This legislation protects the FBI's ability to wiretap at the expense of individual privacy. Detractors have pointed out that this digital "back door" could be abused by government agencies and could also be used by savvy criminals to perform illegal wiretaps. Government officials argue that wiretapping is a critical tool in the fight against organized crime.

■ The digital manhunt that led to the arrest of the programmer charged with authoring the Melissa virus was made as a direct result of information provided by America Online Inc. A controversial Microsoft document identification technology—the Global Unique Identifier, or GUID—may also have played a role. While virtually everyone was happy when the virus's perpetrator was apprehended, many legal experts feared that the same techniques will be used for less lofty purposes.

■ In 2000 the U.S. government found Microsoft guilty of gross abuses of its monopolistic position in the software industry. The government's case included hundreds of private email messages between Microsoft employees—messages that often contradicted Microsoft's public testimony.

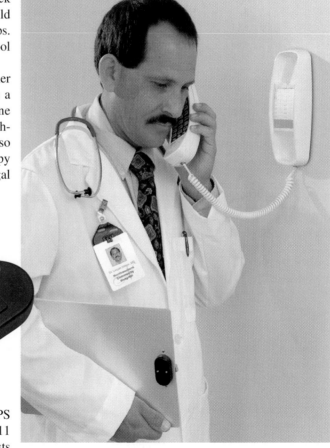

■ A 2001 U.S. law required that mobile phones include GPS technology for transmitting the phone's location to a 911 operator in the case of an emergency call. Privacy activists fear that government agents and criminals will use this E911 technology to track the movements of phone owners.

■ In response to the terrorist attacks of September 11, 2001, the U.S. Congress quickly drafted and passed the USA PATRIOT Act, a sweeping set of law changes that redefined terrorism and the government's authority to combat it. The act defined "cyberterrorism" to include computer crimes

10.17 Active badges allow employees to be tracked as they move. Instead of paging the entire hospital, an operator could use information from a physician's active badge to route the call to the phone nearest his location. This active badge from Versus Technology also includes a button that can be programmed to send a message to a pager, open a locked door, or perform another task.

that cause at least $5,000 in damage or destroy medical equipment. It increased the FBI's latitude to use wiretap technology to monitor suspects' Web browsing and email without a judge's order. Critics argued that this controversial law could easily be used to restrict the freedom and threaten the privacy of law-abiding citizens.

One of the best examples of a technology that can simultaneously improve security and threaten privacy is the active badge (sometimes called the *smart badge*). These microprocessor-controlled badges broadcast infrared identification codes every 15 seconds. Each badge's code is picked up by a nearby network receiver and transmitted to a badge-location database that is constantly being updated. Active badges are used for identifying, finding, and remembering:

- *Identifying*. When an authorized employee approaches a door, the door recognizes the person's badge code and opens. Whenever anyone logs into a computer system, the badge code identifies the person as an authorized or unauthorized user.
- *Finding*. An employee can check a computer screen to locate another employee and find out with whom that person is talking. With active badges there's no need for a paging system, and "while you were away" notes are less common.
- *Remembering*. At the end of the day, an active-badge wearer can get a minute-by-minute printout listing exactly where and with whom he's been.

Some large conferences are using active badges to help the attendees meet each other. Delegates receive personalized active badges containing their contact information, employment history, areas of interest, and hobbies. As the attendees move about, the active badges communicate with each other. If the badge identifies a nearby delegate with similar interests, it alerts the badge wearer.

Is the active badge a primitive version of the communicator on TV's *Star Trek* or a surveillance tool for Big Brother? The technology has the potential to be either or both; it all depends on how people use it. Active badges, like other security devices and techniques, raise important legal and ethical questions about privacy—questions that we, as a society, must resolve sooner or later.

Justice on the Electronic Frontier

Through our scientific genius, we have **made this world a neighborhood**; now through our moral and spiritual development, we must **make of it a brotherhood**.

—*The Rev. Martin Luther King, Jr.*

Federal and state governments have responded to the growing computer crime problem by creating new laws against electronic trespassing and by escalating enforcement efforts. Hackers have become targets for nationwide anticrime operations. Dozens of hackers have been arrested for unauthorized entry into computer systems and for the release of destructive viruses and worms. Many have been convicted under federal or state laws. Others have had their computers confiscated with no formal charges filed.

Some of the victims of these sting operations claim that they broke no laws. In one case, a student was arrested because he published an electronic magazine that carried a description of an emergency 911 system allegedly stolen by hackers. Charges were eventually dropped when it was revealed that the "stolen" document was, in fact, available to the public.

Cases like this raise questions about how civil rights apply in the "electronic frontier." How does the Bill of Rights apply to computer communications? Does freedom of the press apply to online magazines in the same way it applies to paper periodicals? Can an electronic bulletin board operator or Internet service provider be held responsible for information others post on a server? Can online pornography be served from a house located in a neighborhood with antiporn laws? Are Internet service providers responsible when their users illegally trade music online?

Working Wisdom

Computer Ethics

Ethics is moral philosophy—philosophical thinking about right and wrong. Many people base their ethical beliefs on religious rules, such as the Ten Commandments or the Buddhist Eightfold Path. Others use professional codes, such as the doctor's Hippocratic oath, which includes the often quoted "First do no harm." Still others use personal philosophies with principles, such as "It's okay if a jury of observers would approve." But in today's changing world, deciding how to apply the rules isn't always easy. Sometimes the rules don't seem to apply directly, and sometimes they contradict each other. (How should you "Honor thy father" if you learn that he's using the home computer to embezzle money from his employer? Is it okay to allow a friend who's broke to borrow your Microsoft Office CD for a required class project?) These kinds of *moral dilemmas* are central questions in discussions of ethics. Information technology poses moral dilemmas related to everything from copying software to reporting a coworker's sexually explicit screen saver or racist email.

Computer ethics can't be reduced to a handful of rules; the gray areas are always going to require thought and judgment. But principles and guidelines can help to focus thinking and refine judgments when dealing with technology-related moral dilemmas. The Association for Computing Machinery (ACM) Code of Ethics, reprinted in the appendix of this book, is the most widely known code of conduct specifically for computer professionals. The ACM Code is worth understanding and applying even if you don't plan to be a "computer professional." Who shouldn't "Contribute to Society and Human Well-Being" or "Honor Confidentiality?" But these principles take on new meaning in an age of email and databases.

Here are some other guidelines that might help you to decide how to "do the right thing" when faced with ethical dilemmas at school, at work, or at home:

➡ ***Know the rules and the law.*** Many laws, and many organizational rules, are reflections of moral principles. For example, almost everyone agrees that plagiarism—presenting somebody else's work as your own—is wrong. It's also a serious violation of rules in most schools. And if the work is copied without permission, plagiarism can become copyright infringement, a serious legal offense even if the work is not explicitly copyrighted.

➡ ***Don't assume that it's okay if it's legal.*** Our legal system doesn't define what's right and wrong. How can it, when we don't all agree on morality? The law is especially lax in areas related to information technology, because the technology changes too fast for lawmakers to keep up. It's ultimately up to each individual to act with conscience.

➡ ***Think scenarios.*** If you're choosing between different actions, think about what might happen as a result of your actions. If you suspect your employer is falsifying spreadsheets to get around environmental regulations, what's likely to happen if you snoop around on his computer and blow the whistle on him? What's likely to happen if you don't? What are your other alternatives?

➡ ***When in doubt, talk it out.*** Discuss your concerns with people you trust, ideally, people with wisdom and experience dealing with similar situations. For example, if you're unsure about the line between getting computer help from a friend and cheating on homework, ask an instructor.

➡ ***Make yourself proud.*** How would you feel if you saw your actions on the front page of *The New York Times*, your company newsletter, or your family's hometown newspaper? If you'd be embarrassed or ashamed, you probably should choose another course of action.

➡ ***Remember the golden rule: Do unto others as you would have them do unto you.*** This universal principle is central to every major spiritual tradition, and it is amazingly versatile. One example: Before you download that bootleg MP3 file of that up-and-coming singer, think about how you'd feel about bootleggers if you were the singer.

➡ ***Take the long view.*** It's all too easy to be blinded by the rapid-fire rewards of the Internet and computer technology. Consider this guiding principle from a Native American tradition: In every deliberation, consider the impact of your decision on the next seven generations.

10.18 Discussing moral dilemmas with your peers is a good way to be exposed to alternative viewpoints. Ethics is based on the notion that when people stick to the facts and discuss issues logically, better decisions result.

Laws like the Telecommunications Act of 1996 attempt to deal with these questions by outlining exactly what kinds of communications are legal online. Unfortunately, these laws generally raise as many questions as they answer. Shortly after its passage, a major section of the Telecommunications Act, called the Communications Decency Act, was declared unconstitutional by the Supreme Court. The debates continue inside and outside of the courts.

The Digital Millennium Copyright Act of 1998 (discussed in Chapter 4, "Software Basics,") hasn't (so far) been found unconstitutional, but it has resulted in several lawsuits that raise serious human rights questions. In the summer of 2001, a Russian programmer and graduate student named Dmitry Sklyarov was arrested by the FBI after he spoke at a computer security conference in Las Vegas. His alleged crime was writing—not using—a program that cracks Adobe's copy protection scheme for e-books. After a Webwide demonstration against the arrest, Adobe publicly came out in favor of freeing Sklyarov.

The same law was used to silence Professor Edward Felton in 2001. The Princeton University computer scientist was threatened with a lawsuit from the Recording Industry Association of America if he presented a paper analyzing the system that encodes digital music; he withdrew the paper. Several months later, Felton published the paper and the RIAA recanted its threat, but not its right to threaten similar suits in the future.

The DMCA was even used to file a suit against *2600* magazine because of a single Web site link. A Norwegian 15-year-old had written code allowing DVD movies to be played on Linux computers—code that broke the DVD encryption scheme. *2600*'s Web site included a link to another site containing the program. (The *New York Times* Web site contained a link to the same site, but was not sued by the recording industry.)

When Congress passed the Telecommunications Act of 1996 and the Digital Millennium Copyright Act of 1998, it was attempting to make U.S. law more responsive to the issues of the digital age. But each of these laws introduced new problems by threatening rights of citizens—problems that have to be solved by courts and by future lawmakers. These laws illustrate the difficulty lawmakers face when protecting rights in a world of rapid technological change.

Security and Reliability

If the automobile had followed the same development cycle as the computer, a **Rolls Royce would today cost $100**, get a million miles per gallon, and **explode once a year**, killing everyone inside.

—*Robert X. Cringely, PBS computer curmudgeon*

So far our discussion of security has focused mainly on protecting computer systems from trespassing, sabotage, and other crimes. But security involves more than criminal activity. Some of the most important security issues have to do with creating systems that can withstand software errors and hardware glitches.

Bugs and Breakdowns

Computer systems, like all machines, are vulnerable to fires, floods, and other natural disasters, as well as breakdowns caused by the failure of hardware components. But in modern computers, hardware problems are relatively rare when compared with software failures. By any measure, bugs do more damage than viruses and computer burglars put together do. Here are a few horror stories:

■ A new laboratory computer system became backlogged the day after it was installed at the Los Angeles County-USC Medical Center in April 2003. Emergency room doctors, who could not get the test results they needed, instructed the County of Los Angeles to stop sending ambulances. One doctor said, "It's almost like practicing Third World medicine. We rely so much on our computers and our fast-world technology that we were almost blinded."

■ In September 1999, the Mars Climate Orbiter burned up as it approached Mars because controllers had mixed up English and metric units. Three months later, the Mars Polar Lander went silent 12 minutes before touchdown. Investigators suspect software errors are at least partly responsible for this spectacular mission failure.

■ On January 15, 1990, AT&T's 30-year-old signaling system software failed, bringing the long-distance carrier's network to its knees. Twenty million calls failed to go through during the next 18 hours before technicians found the problem: a single incorrect instruction hiding among a million lines of code.

■ On February 25, 1991, 28 American soldiers were killed and 98 others wounded when an Iraqi Scud missile hit a barracks near Dhahran, Saudi Arabia. A tiny bug in a Patriot missile's software threw off its timing just enough to prevent it from intercepting the Scud. Programmers had already fixed the bug, and a new version of the software was being shipped to Dhahran when the attack occurred.

■ In 2001 a bug in a new billing system led Qwest to charge some of its cell phone customers as much as $600 per minute. About 14,000 customers received incorrect bills, including one customer whose monthly statement asked her to pay $57,346.20.

■ On March 1, 2003, Japan's air traffic control system and back-up system failed simultaneously, forcing airports to communicate with each other via telephone. Fortunately, no persons were harmed, but dozens of flights were delayed or cancelled because of the outage.

Every year brings new stories of breakdowns and bugs with catastrophic consequences. But it wasn't until 1999 that a computer bug—the Y2K (year 2000) bug, or millennium bug—became an international sensation. For decades, programmers commonly built two-digit date fields into programs to save storage space, thinking they had no reason to allow space for the first two digits because they never changed. But when 1999 ended, those digits did change, making many of those ancient programs unstable or unusable. Programmers knowledgeable in COBOL, FORTRAN, and other ancient computer languages repaired many of the programs. But others couldn't be repaired and had to be completely rewritten.

Businesses and governments spent more than 100 billion dollars trying to head off Y2K disasters. Many individuals bought generators and guns, stockpiled food and water, and prepared for a collapse of the computer-controlled utility grids that keep our economy running. When the fateful day arrived, the Y2K bug caused scattered problems, ranging from credit card refusals to malfunctioning spy satellites. But for most people, January 1, 2000, was business as usual. It's debatable whether disasters were averted by billions of dollars worth of preventive maintenance, or whether the Y2K scare stories were overblown. The truth is undoubtedly somewhere between these two extremes. In any event, Y2K raised the public's consciousness about its dependence on fickle, fragile technology.

10.19 These South Koreans, like many people around the globe, stocked up on food and cooking gas cans to prepare for possible emergency shortages as a result of Y2K computer failures. Those failures, of course, never happened.

Given the state of the art of programming today, three facts are clear:

1. It's impossible to eliminate all bugs. Today's programs are constructed of thousands of tiny pieces, any one of which can cause a failure if it's incorrectly coded.
2. Even programs that appear to work can contain dangerous bugs. Some bugs are easy to detect and correct because they're obvious. The most dangerous bugs are difficult to detect and may go unnoticed by users for months or years.
3. The bigger the system, the bigger the problem. Large programs are far more complex and difficult to debug than small programs are, and the trend today is clearly toward large programs. For example, Microsoft Windows 95 has 11 million lines of code and was considered huge at the time; Windows XP has over 30 million!

As we entrust complex computerized systems to do everything from financial transaction processing to air traffic control, the potential cost of computer failure goes up. In the last decade, researchers have identified hundreds of cases in which disruptions to computer system operations posed some risk to the public, and the number of incidents has doubled every two years.

Computers at War

Massive networking makes the U.S. the **world's most vulnerable target**.

—John McConnell, former NSA director

Nowhere are the issues surrounding security and reliability more critical than in military applications. To carry out its mission effectively, the military must be sure its systems are secure against enemy surveillance and attack. At the same time, many modern military applications push the limits of information technology farther than they've ever been before.

Smart Weapons

The United States has invested billions of dollars in the development of smart weapons—missiles that use computerized guidance systems to locate their targets. A command-guidance system enables a human operator to control the missile's path while watching a

10.20 In modern weapons systems, like those used by the North America Aerospace Defense Control (NORAD) in its Cheyenne Mountain Complex in Colorado Springs, Colorado, computers are critical components in the command and control process.

missile's-eye view of the target on a television screen. Using infrared heat-seeking devices or visual pattern recognition technology, a missile with a homing guidance system can track a moving target without human help. Weapons that use "smart" guidance systems can be extremely accurate in pinpointing enemy targets under most circumstances. In theory, smart weapons can greatly reduce the amount of civilian destruction in war if everything is working properly.

One problem with high-tech weapons is that they reduce the amount of time people have to make life-and-death decisions. As decision-making time goes down, the chances of making errors goes up. In one tragic example, an American guided missile cruiser on a peacetime mission in the Persian Gulf used a computerized Aegis fleet defense system to shoot down an Iranian Airbus containing 290 civilians. The decision to fire was made by well-intentioned humans, but those humans had little time—and used ambiguous data—to make the decision.

Autonomous Systems

Even more controversial is the possibility of people being left out of the decision-making loop altogether. Yet the trend in military research is clearly toward weapons that demand almost instantaneous responses—the kind that only computers can make. An **autonomous system** is a complex system that can assume almost complete responsibility for a task without human input, verification, or decision making.

The most famous and controversial autonomous system is the Strategic Defense Initiative (SDI)—former President Ronald Reagan's proposed "Star Wars" system for shielding the United States from nuclear attack. Recently resuscitated by President George W. Bush, the SDI system, as planned, will use a network of laser-equipped satellites and ground-based stations to detect and destroy attacking missiles shortly after launch, before they have time to reach their targets. SDI weapons will have to be able to react almost instantaneously, without human intervention. If they sense an attack, these system computers will have no time to wait for the president to declare war, and no time for human experts to analyze the perceived attack.

The automated missile defense system generates intense public debates about false alarms, hardware feasibility, constitutional issues, and the ethics of autonomous weapons. But for many who understand the limitations of computers, the biggest issue is software reliability. The system will require tens of millions of lines of code. The system can't be completely tested in advance because there's no way to simulate accurately the unpredictable conditions of a global war. Yet to work effectively, the system will have to be absolutely reliable. In a tightly coupled worldwide network, a single bug could multiply and expand like a speed-of-light cancer. A small error could result in a major disaster. Many software engineers have pointed out that absolute reliability simply isn't possible now or in the foreseeable future.

In spite of years of political haggling, system failures, and cost overruns, the missile defense system is still in the works, and systems reliability issues remain. Supporters of automated missile defense systems argue that the technical difficulties can be overcome in time, and the U.S. government continues to invest billions in research toward that end. Whether a "smart shield" is ever completed, it has focused public attention on critical issues related to security and reliability.

Warfare in the Digital Domain

Even as the U.S. government spends billions of dollars on smart missiles and missile defense systems, many military experts suggest that future wars may not be fought in the air, on land, or at sea. The front lines of the future may, instead, be in cyberspace. By attacking through vast interconnected computer networks, an enemy could conceivably cripple telecommunications systems, power grids, banking and financial systems, hospitals and medical systems, water and gas supplies, oil pipelines, and emergency government services without firing a shot.

Several recent examples highlight our vulnerability:

■ In 1994 Swedish hackers broke into telecommunications systems in central Florida and blocked several 911 systems by automatically dialing their numbers repeatedly. Anyone who called 911 with a legitimate emergency during the cyberattack was greeted with a busy signal.

■ In 1996 a juvenile hacker disabled a key phone computer servicing a Massachusetts airport, paralyzing the airport control tower for six hours.

■ In 1998 Israeli police working with the FBI, the U.S. Air Force, and NASA arrested three Israeli teens who successfully hacked into Department of Defense computers in both countries.

■ During the 2000 U.S. election, dozens of politically motivated Web attacks occurred for various causes, parties, and countries. The attacks included Web site vandalism, denial of service attacks, and system snooping.

Thankfully, none of these crimes resulted in serious damage or injury. But terrorists, spies, or criminals might use the same techniques to trigger major disasters.

Recognizing the growing threat of system sabotage, then-Attorney General Janet Reno created the *National Infrastructure Protection Center* in early 1998. The NIPC's state-of-the-art command center is housed at FBI headquarters. The center includes representatives of various intelligence agencies (the departments of defense, transportation, energy, and treasury) and representatives of several major corporations.

Corporate participation is critical because private companies own many of the infrastructure systems that are most vulnerable to attack. Unfortunately, many businesses are slow to recognize the potential threat to their systems. They embrace the efficiency that networks bring, but they don't adequately prepare for attack through those networks.

In the wake of the terrorist attacks of September 2001, George W. Bush formed The President's Critical Infrastructure Board, consisting of cabinet members and top presidential aides; this board was later transformed into the U.S. Department of Homeland Security. The cyberterrorism panel was designed to protect utilities and critical public services that depend on information networks.

Network attacks are all but inevitable, and such attacks can have disastrous consequences for all of us. In a world where computers control everything from money to missiles, computer security and reliability are too important to ignore.

Is Security Possible?

Computer thieves. Hackers. Software pirates. Computer snoopers. Viruses. Worms. Trojan horses. Spybots. Wiretaps. Hardware failures. Software bugs. When we live and work with computers, we're exposed to all kinds of risks that didn't exist in the precomputer era. These risks make computer security especially important and challenging.

Because computers do so many amazing things so well, it's easy to overlook the problems they bring with them and to believe that they're invincible. But like Kempelen's chess-playing machine, today's computers hide the potential for errors and deception under an impressive user interface. This doesn't mean we should avoid using computers, only that we should remain skeptical, cautious, and realistic as we use them. Security procedures can reduce but not eliminate risks. In today's fast-moving world absolute security simply isn't possible.

Human Questions for a Computer Age

In earlier chapters we examined many social and ethical issues related to computer technology, including privacy, security, reliability, and intellectual property. These aren't the only critical issues before us. Before closing we'll briefly raise some other important, and as yet unanswered, questions of the information age.

> The **important thing** to forecast is not the automobile but the **parking problem**; not the television but the **soap opera**.
>
> —*Isaac Asimov*

> It's the **end of the world** as we know it and I feel fine.
>
> —*R.E.M.*

Will Computers Be Democratic?

In 1990 a spontaneous protest exploded across computer networks in reaction to the threat to privacy posed by Marketplace, a new CD-ROM product containing consumer information on millions of Americans. The firestorm of protest forced Lotus Development Corporation to cancel distribution of the product. In Santa Monica, California, homeless people used public-access terminals in the library to lobby successfully for more access to public showers. In France, student organizations used computer networks to mobilize opposition to tuition increases. In 1999 environmentalists, labor organizations, human rights groups, and a handful of anarchists used the Internet to mobilize massive protests at the World Trade Organization's Seattle meeting. The protests brought many issues surrounding the secretive WTO into the global spotlight for the first time.

> The higher the technology, the **higher the freedom**. Technology enforces certain solutions: satellite dishes, computers, videos, international telephone lines force pluralism and freedom onto a society.
>
> —*Lech Walesa*

> When machines and computers, profit motives, and property rights are considered **more important than people**, the giant triplets of **racism**, **materialism**, and **militarism** are incapable of being conquered.
>
> —*The Rev. Martin Luther King, Jr.*

Computers are often used to promote the democratic ideals and causes of common people. Many analysts argue that modern computer technology is, by its very nature, a force for equality and democracy. On the other hand, many powerful people and organizations use information technology to increase their wealth and influence.

Will personal computers and the Internet empower ordinary citizens to make better lives for themselves? Or will computer technology produce a society of technocrats and technopeasants? Will computerized polls help elected officials better serve the needs of their constituents? Or will they just give the powerful another tool for staying in power? Will networks revitalize participatory democracy through electronic town meetings? Or will they give tyrants the tools to monitor and control citizens?

Will the Global Village Be a Community?

Progress in commercial information technologies will improve productivity, bring the world closer together, and **enhance the quality of life**.

—*Stan Davis and Bill Davidson, in* 2020 Vision

The **real question** before us lies here: do these instruments further **life and its values** or not?

—*Lewis Mumford in 1934*

A typical computer today contains components from dozens of countries. The modern corporation uses computer networks for instant communication among offices scattered around the world. Information doesn't stop at international borders as it flows through networks that span the globe. Information technology enables organizations to overcome the age-old barriers of space and time, but questions remain.

In the post–Cold War era, will information technology be used to further peace, harmony, and understanding? Or will the intense competition of the global marketplace simply create new kinds of wars—information wars? Will electronic interconnections provide new opportunities for economically depressed countries? Or will they simply make it easier for information-rich countries to exploit developing nations from a distance? Will information technology be used to promote and preserve diverse communities, cultures, and ecosystems? Or will it undercut traditions, cultures, and roots?

Will We Become Information Slaves?

Our inventions are wont to be **pretty toys** which distract our attention from serious things. They are but improved means to an **unimproved end**.

—*Henry David Thoreau*

Computers are useless. They can only give you answers.

—*Pablo Picasso*

The information age has redefined our environment; it's almost as if the human species has been transplanted into a different world. Even though the change has happened almost overnight, most of us can't imagine going back to a world without computers. Still, the rapid changes raise questions.

Can human bodies and minds adapt to the higher stimulation, faster pace, and constant change of the information age? Will our information-heavy environment cause us to lose touch with the more fundamental human needs? Will we become so dependent on our "pretty toys" that we can't get by without them? Will we lose our sense of purpose and identity as our machines become more intelligent? Or will we learn to balance the demands of the technology with our biological and spiritual needs?

Standing on the Shoulders of Giants

If I have seen farther than other men, it is because **I stood on the shoulders of giants**.

—*Isaac Newton*

When we use computers, we're standing on the shoulders of Charles Babbage, Ada King, George Boole, Alan Turing, Grace Hopper, Doug Engelbart, Alan Kay, and hundreds of others who invented the future for us. Because of their foresight and effort we can see farther than those who came before us.

10.21 Prometheus brings fire from the heavens to humanity.

In Greek mythology Prometheus (whose name means "forethought") stole fire from Zeus and gave it to humanity, along with all arts and civilization. Zeus was furious when he discovered what Prometheus had done. He feared that fire would make mortals think they were as great as the gods and that they would abuse its power. Like fire, the computer is a powerful and malleable tool. It can be used to empower or imprison, to explore or exploit, to create or destroy. We can choose. We've been given the tools. It's up to all of us to invent the future.

Inventing the FUTURE

The Future of Internet Security

It is **conceivable**, in theory, for a **hacker** sitting in his easy chair to get **inside a tank**.

—*Colonel Thaddeus Dmuchowski, U.S. Army*

Faster Internet connectivity has opened up new vistas for international communication and collaboration, but it has also allowed malware to spread faster than ever. The Sapphire worm, also called Slammer, infected 90 percent of the vulnerable hosts worldwide in less than 10 minutes. Future worms may spread globally in less than a minute. That's not nearly enough time for humans to get involved in stopping them. Instead, network developers are devising automated systems to thwart attacks.

LAYERED DEFENSES

Organizations with large computer networks will need to resort to a layered defensive approach. They will put ever-more-sophisticated hardware and software systems on the perimeter of their networks. Firewalls, augmented with network intrusion detection software, will try to prevent dangerous packets from entering the organization's networks. Sophisticated pattern-recognition software will help these systems distinguish between legitimate and illegitimate network access attempts.

However, it is unrealistic to expect that the outer defenses will be 100 percent effective. That's why organizations will implement automated systems for coping with worms and viruses that penetrate their networks. Researchers are developing reconfigurable hardware that can quarantine infected subnets. Hardware-imposed quarantines will prevent a worm that gets into a handful of machines on a LAN from spreading throughout the entire organization.

Special-purpose hardware called *security processors* will allow every message to be encrypted, even huge video streams. Security processors will give organizations the confidence that all their messages, even those sent over wireless networks, are secure from eavesdroppers. Programmers are getting into the act, too. Better programming languages, combined with a greater attention to security-related issues by software developers, should result in future operating systems and applications that contain fewer security holes.

THE PEOPLE PROBLEM

Unfortunately, no amount of technological fixing can completely eliminate security problems. The human element is the weak link in many security systems. Despite warnings about malware, some people continue to spread viruses by opening attachments to email from unknown sources. An experiment in London showed that many computer users would reveal their computer password in return for a pen. Employees bring infected notebooks or PDAs to work. Once attached to the employer's network, these devices spread viruses or worms.

10.22 Employees have spread viruses and worms onto corporate networks by bringing infected notebook computers from home.

Ultimately, organizations and individuals must balance security, convenience, and features. Consumers are unlikely to purchase a piece of software that is 100 percent secure but lacks essential features. So software developers must balance the time they spend on security against the time they spend adding features. Organizations must weigh security against convenience. A network may be very secure, but so difficult to use that it hurts the productivity of the computer users. That can hurt an organization's bottom line.

HOW OPEN?

A rising onslaught of malware and spam could tip the scales toward security and put the openness of the Internet in peril. Computer and network system administrators cannot afford to spend all of their time eradicating malicious software, and users do not want to spend large amounts of their time deleting spam messages. While disconnecting from the Internet is not a reasonable option in this age of global enterprises, system administrators and computer users can erect communication barriers. Even now, some corporate networks reject connection attempts from employees' PDAs and notebook computers that don't have up-to-date security patches. Many email users, disgusted by the volume of spam they have received, have created white lists containing the email addresses of people they are willing to receive messages from. Messages from everyone else are rejected. The entire Internet community—users, programmers, hardware designers, system administrators, and managers—will help determine whether the Internet will remain a place of relatively free and open information exchange. ~

Idiocy Imperils the Web *Jim Rapoza*

We normally think of computer virus writers as villains and the people whose machines are infected as victims. Jim Rapoza suggests another way to assign blame for the virus problem in this column from the June 13, 2003, issue of Eweek. Rapoza uses humor to make his point on a very serious matter.

You people are such idiots!

Not *you*, of course. I mean those *other* people, the ones who make it so easy for every simple, standard virus to propagate across the Web. Twice in the last few weeks, I've had the same experience. I receive a security notice on a new virus, first Fizzer and then Palyh. I then find out that they infect Windows-based systems when a user opens an attachment from an unsolicited e-mail message. I then think to myself, "This won't be big; everyone knows you don't open attachments in unexpected e-mails." Then the virus spreads across tens of thousands of systems.

What's up with these people? Over the last few years, there have been hundreds of new viruses that spread in this manner. Most people figure out that if they keep grabbing the electric fence, they'll get a shock every time. So why do they continue to stupidly open attachments they aren't expecting?

To some degree, the fault for this lies with the technology press. We tend to take each new virus too seriously while not taking the time to shame the morons who are making it possible for the viruses to succeed.

Imagine if there were a rash of car thefts where thieves stole a bunch of cars that were left running with the doors open. Reporters wouldn't focus on the cleverness of the car thieves; they would point out the stupidity of the car owners. Or imagine thousands of cases of food poisoning from people eating completely raw chicken. I'm sure we would be reading plenty about the cluelessness of the "victims."

It's time for us to stop admiring virus writers and start dishing out heaping spoonfuls of shame to stupid users.

Instead of a headline like "Dangerous Fizzer Worm Attacks the Internet," how about "Thousands of Morons Open Obviously Virus-Laden E-mail Attachments"? I kind of like it. It has a light, comedic feel similar to headlines found at The Onion. But as Homer Simpson would say, it's funny because it's true. Stories like that should embolden smart users so that, instead of accepting their co-workers' incompetence, they will feel free to mock and ridicule these Typhoid Marys of the computer world.

The shaming wouldn't have to stop there. IT staff could put up posters identifying the stupidest virus-spreaders in the company. Rank-and-file employees could videotape their co-workers opening attachments with obvious virus subjects such as "Cool screensaver." We could have a new TV show, "America's Most Idiotic E-mail Users!" Webcams could be set up peering over the shoulders of those most likely to open an attachment. Watching a virus spread in real time could become a spectator sport.

But seriously, folks. It's very easy to teach even a kid how to avoid infecting most systems with viruses in e-mail attachments. So why isn't this message getting out? Because getting hit with a virus is considered acceptable. Too many people have taken the attitude that viruses are going to happen, and there's nothing you can do to stop them. This isn't true, but many people use it as a convenient excuse for their mistakes.

Obviously, we need to do a better job educating users, but we also need to remove the mystique that surrounds viruses. Virus victims need to realize that many viruses wouldn't exist without them and their careless use of their e-mail accounts.

It doesn't take a whole lot of effort to change. First, users need to be suspicious of the e-mail they receive. If you don't know who it's from and the subject is generic, delete it. If there are multiple versions of the same e-mail, it's most likely a virus or spam. And never, ever, open attachments that you weren't expecting. If you think it's something important, double-check with the sender.

When coupled with a good virus scanner, these simple efforts can keep most users from becoming victims of viruses that are doing little more than taking advantage of their stupidity. I follow these basic procedures, and I haven't had an e-mail-born virus infect one of my systems in more than five years.

So let's change our attitudes and our tactics. Let's get out the word that most of the time, when people get viruses, it's their own fault. Stupidity is nothing to be proud of.

Discussion Questions

1. The author seems to be arguing that being the victim of a computer virus is something to be ashamed of. Do you agree? Explain your answer.

2. The author compares virus victims to careless car owners when he says, "Imagine if there were a rash of car thefts where thieves stole a bunch of cars that were left running with the doors open." A reader responded by asking what the reaction would be if the car companies gave us cars that could easily be stolen by 10-year-old thieves. Do you think this analogy makes sense? What does it suggest concerning solutions to the virus problem?

Summary

Computers play an ever-increasing role in fighting crime. At the same time, law enforcement organizations are facing an increase in computer crime—crimes accomplished through special knowledge of computer technology. Most computer crimes go undetected, and those that are detected often go unreported. But by any estimate, computer crime costs billions of dollars every year.

Some computer criminals use computers, modems, and other equipment to steal goods, money, information, software, and services. Others use Trojan horses, viruses, worms, logic bombs, and other software tricks to sabotage systems. According to the media, computer crimes are committed by young, bright computer wizards called hackers. Research suggests, however, that hackers are responsible for only a small fraction of computer crimes. The typical computer criminal is a trusted employee with personal or financial problems and knowledge of the computer system. The most common computer crime, software piracy, is committed by millions of people, often unknowingly. Piracy is a violation of intellectual property laws, which, in many cases, lag far behind the technology.

Because of rising computer crime and other risks, organizations have developed a number of computer security techniques to protect their systems and data. Some security devices, such as keys and badges, are designed to restrict physical access to computers. But these tools are becoming less effective in an age of personal computers and networks. Passwords, encryption, shielding, and audit-control software are all used to protect sensitive data in various organizations. When all else fails, backups of important data are used to reconstruct systems after damage occurs. The most effective security solutions depend on people at least as much as on technology.

Normally, security measures serve to protect our privacy and other individual rights. But occasionally, security procedures threaten those rights. The trade-offs between computer security and freedom raise important legal and ethical questions.

Computer systems aren't just threatened by people; they're also threatened by software bugs and hardware glitches. An important part of security is protecting systems and the people affected by those systems from the consequences of those bugs and glitches. Since our society uses computers for many applications that put lives at stake, reliability issues are especially important. In modern military applications, security and reliability are critical. As the speed, power, and complexity of weapons systems increase, many fear that humans are being squeezed out of the decision-making loop. The debate over high-tech weaponry is bringing many important security issues to the public's attention for the first time.

Key Terms

access-control software ....(p. 397)
active badge ....(p. 406)
antivirus ....(p. 392)
authentication mechanisms ...(p. 402)
authorization mechanisms .....(p. 403)
autonomous systems..............(p. 411)
backup ....(p. 402)
biometrics ....(p. 396)
Code of Ethics ....(p. 407)
computer crime......................(p. 387)
computer security ....(p. 395)

denial of service (DoS)
    attack ....(p. 394)
encryption.............................(p. 397)
ethics.....................................(p. 407)
firewall..................................(p. 397)
hacking ....(p. 394)
identity theft ....(p. 388)
logic bomb............................(p. 392)
malware ....(p. 390)
passwords ....(p. 397)
plagiarism.............................(p. 407)

sabotage ....(p. 390)
security patch........................(p. 393)
smart weapons ....(p. 410)
social engineering.................(p. 388)
spoofing ....(p. 388)
spyware..................................(p. 392)
Trojan horse...........................(p. 391)
uninterruptible power supply
    (UPS) ....(p. 402)
virus......................................(p. 390)
worms ....(p. 391)

Interactive Activities

1. The *Computer Confluence* CD-ROM contains self-test quiz questions related to this chapter, including multiple-choice, true or false, and matching questions.

2. The *Computer Confluence* Web site, www.computerconfluence.com, contains self-test exercises related to this chapter. Follow the instructions for taking a quiz. After you've completed your quiz, you can email the results to your instructor.

3. The Web site also contains open-ended discussion questions called Internet Explorations. Discuss one or more of the Internet Exploration questions at the section for this chapter.

True or False

1. Computer crimes often go unreported because businesses fear that they can lose more from negative publicity than from the actual crimes.

2. The majority of computer crimes are committed by hackers and vandals with no ties to the victim companies.

3. The software industry loses billions of dollars each year to piracy.

4. In general, computer viruses don't discriminate among operating systems; a typical virus can infect any system, regardless of platform.

5. Access-control software treats all users the same, in the same way a lock provides equal access to everyone with a key that fits the lock.

6. Computer security is ultimately a technological problem with technological solutions.

7. U.S. courts have ruled that your email is not private if you send and receive it on a computer at your workplace.

8. Computer ethics is defined as a collection of clear, unambiguous rules for dealing with computers.

9. While many questions remain about the viability of an automated missile defense system, computer scientists are confident that the software for the system will be reliable.

Multiple Choice

1. According to a recent survey cited in the chapter,
   a. Internet security breaches are on the rise.
   b. Internal security breaches are on the rise.
   c. Computer crime in general is on the rise.
   d. All of the above are true.
   e. None of the above are true.

2. Which of these words means "tricking" or "fooling?"
   a. Bombing
   b. Cracking
   c. Hacking
   d. Hijacking
   e. Spoofing

3. What do you call a piece of code that attaches to an application program and secretly spreads when the application program is executed?
   a. Virus
   b. Worm
   c. Trojan horse
   d. Spybot
   e. Antivirus

4. What do you call a program that has the ability to execute independently and spread over a computer network?
   a. Virus
   b. Worm
   c. Trojan horse
   d. Antivirus
   e. All of the above

5. What do you call a program that secretly records information about a computer user's activities and sends it out over the Internet?
   a. Virus
   b. Worm
   c. Spybot
   d. Antivirus
   e. None of the above

6. What do you call a program that performs a useful task while at the same time carrying out some secret destructive act?
   a. Virus
   b. Worm
   c. Trojan horse
   d. Macro virus
   e. None of the above

7. What do you call a person who accesses a computer system without authorization?
   a. Hacker
   b. Cuckoo
   c. User
   d. Slammer
   e. System administrator

8. What are biometrics often used for?
   a. To measure virus strength
   b. To measure the speed of a spreading worm
   c. To assess the power of a Trojan horse to bring down a computer system
   d. To identify personnel before allowing them to have access to computer systems
   e. None of the above

9. What do you call the process of establishing the identity of a potential computer user?
   a. Authentication
   b. Authorization
   c. Identification
   d. Potentiation
   e. Rationalization

10. What can a firewall do?
    a. Prevent packets from entering a LAN from the Internet
    b. Prevent packets from entering the Internet from a LAN
    c. Prevent requests for service from reaching a particular computer on the LAN from the Internet
    d. Prevent requests for service from reaching the Internet from a particular computer on the LAN
    e. All of the above

11. What can a surge protector protect a system from?
    a. Firewalls
    b. Denial of service (DoS) attacks
    c. Power spikes
    d. Trojan horses and worms
    e. All of the above

12. Which of these statements is true about bugs in computer software today?
    a. It's impossible to eliminate all bugs in a large program.
    b. Even a program that appears to work can contain dangerous bugs.
    c. The bigger the system, the higher the number of bugs.
    d. All of the above are true.
    e. None of the above are true.

13. In our culture, people commonly base their ethical beliefs on all of these except
    a. Religious rules
    b. Professional codes
    c. Personal philosophies
    d. Autonomous systems
    e. Personal principles

14. When or where can computer viruses spread rapidly?
    a. In environments where disks and files are passed around freely
    b. In documents as email attachments
    c. When infected shareware and freeware programs are downloaded onto PCs
    d. All of the above
    e. None of the above

15. According to the FBI, how do most cases of identity theft begin?
    a. With a pop-up Web advertisement
    b. With a stolen credit card
    c. With a stolen Social Security number
    d. During a phone solicitation
    e. During an email solicitation

Review Questions

1. Define or describe each of the key terms listed in the Key Terms section. Check your answers using the glossary.

2. Why is it hard to estimate the extent of computer crime?

3. Describe the typical computer criminal. How does he or she differ from the media stereotype?

4. What is the most common computer crime? Who commits it? What is being done to stop it?

5. What are intellectual property laws, and how do they apply to software?

6. Describe several different types of programs that can be used for software sabotage.

7. What are the two inherent characteristics of computers that make security so difficult?

8. Describe several different computer security techniques, and explain the purpose of each.

9. Every afternoon at closing time, the First Taxpayer's Bank copies all the day's accumulated transaction information from disk to tape. Why?

10. In what ways can computer security protect the privacy of individuals? In what ways can computer security threaten the privacy of individuals?

11. What are smart weapons? How do they differ from conventional weapons? What are the advantages and risks of smart weapons?

Discussion Questions

1. Are computers morally neutral? Explain your answer.

2. Suppose Whizzo Software Company produces a program that looks, from the user's point of view, exactly like the immensely popular BozoWorks from Bozo, Inc. Whizzo insists that it didn't copy any of the code in BozoWorks; it just tried to design a program that would appeal to BozoWorks users. Bozo cries foul and sues Whizzo for violation of intellectual property laws. Do you think the laws should favor Bozo's arguments or Whizzo's? Why?

3. What do you suppose motivates people to create computer viruses and other destructive software? What do you think motivates hackers to break into computer systems? Are the two types of behavior related?

4. Some people think all mail messages on the Internet should be encrypted. They argue that if everything is encrypted, the encrypted message won't stand out, so everybody's right to privacy will be better protected. Others suggest that this would just improve the cover of criminals with something to hide from the government. What do you think, and why?

5. Would you like to work in a business where all employees were required to wear active badges? Explain your answer.

6. How do the issues raised in the debate over the missile defense system apply to other large software systems? How do you feel about the different issues raised in the debate?

Projects

1. Talk to employees at your campus computer labs and computer centers about security issues and techniques. What are the major security threats according to these employees? What security techniques are used to protect the equipment and data in each facility? Are these techniques adequate? Report on your findings.

2. Perform the same kind of interviews at local businesses. Do businesses view security differently than your campus personnel does?

3. If you have a login name and password on a college network, try changing your password. Will the system let you change your password to a common word such as "love" or "fish?" Does the system set a minimum number of characters for passwords? Are you allowed to have a letters-only password, or are you required to include nonalphabetic characters?

4. Is your college or university ID number the same as your Social Security number? If so, find out what steps you need to take to get an alternative ID number from your school.

Sources and Resources

Books

Ethics for the Information Age, by Michael J. Quinn (Boston, MA: Addison Wesley, 2005). This book, written by the *Computer Confluence* co-author, presents a framework for ethical decision-making and uses that framework to evaluate a wide variety of information- and technology-related issues. Major topics covered include networks and censorship, intellectual property, privacy, computer and network security, computer reliability, automation, and globalization.

A Gift of Fire: Social, Legal, and Ethical Issues in Computing, Second Edition, by Sara Baase (Upper Saddle River, NJ: Prentice-Hall, 2003). This book offers a thorough, easy-to-read overview of the human questions facing us as a result of the computer revolution: privacy, security, reliability, accountability, and the rest.

Cyberethics: Morality and Law in Cyberspace, Second Edition, by Richard Spinello (Sudbury, MA: Jones and Bartlett, 2003). This book surveys most of the big issues of computer ethics: intellectual property, privacy, security, free speech, and others. Case studies help make theoretical concepts concrete.

Readings in CyberEthics, Second Edition, edited by Richard A. Spinello and Herman T. Tavani (Sudbury, MA: Jones and Bartlett, 2004). This collection of papers and articles includes sections on freedom of expression, property, privacy, and other critical subjects related to information technology.

Computer Network Security and Cyber Ethics, by Joseph Migga Kizza (Jefferson, NC: McFarland & Co., 2001). This book clearly analyzes the causes, costs, and consequences of computer crime and cracking.

Secrets and Lies: Digital Security in a Networked World, by Bruce Schneier (New York: Wiley, 2000, 2004). Mathematician and computer security expert Schneier tells you in clear, lively prose how to think like a computer thief so you can protect yourself and your organization from that thief.

Tech TV's Security Alert: Stories of Real People Protecting Themselves from Identity Theft, Scams, and Viruses, by Becky Worley (Indianapolis: New Riders, 2004). If you're worried about identity theft, Internet scams, and other hazards of the digital world, this book will help you protect yourself. If you're not worried, this book may change that.

The Hundredth Window: Protecting Your Privacy and Security in the Age of the Internet, by Charles Jennings and Lori Fena (New York: Free Press, 2000). The Internet is only as secure as its weakest link. This practical book can help you to understand where the weakest links are and how to protect your privacy online.

Identity Theft, by John R. Vacca (Upper Saddle River, NJ: Prentice Hall, 2003). This thorough book is written for professionals, but it's accessible enough that any technologically aware person should be able to learn how to safeguard personal information.

Cyberwars: Espionage on the Internet, by Jean Guisnel (New York: Plenum, 1997). If you need proof that the Internet has graduated from its role as a research assistant, read *Cyberwars*. Guisnel, a respected French journalist, exposes the emerging online battle zones where spies, saboteurs, government agents, drug traffickers, and others wage virtual wars. Even though we can't see them happening, we're all victims of the fallout from these dangerous battles.

Hackers: Heroes of the Computer Revolution, by Steven Levy (New York: Delta, 1994, 2001). This book helped bring the word *hackers* into the public's vocabulary. Levy's entertaining account of the golden age of hacking gives a historical perspective to today's antihacker mania.

The Cuckoo's Egg, by Cliff Stoll (New York: Pocket Books, 1989, 1995). This best-selling book documents the stalking of an interloper on the Internet. International espionage mixes with computer technology in this entertaining, engaging, and eye-opening book.

Takedown: The Pursuit and Capture of Kevin Mitnick, America's Most Wanted Computer Outlaw—by the Man Who Did It, by Tsutomu Shimomura with John Markoff (New York: Hyperion Books, 1996) and *The Fugitive Game,* by Jonathon Littman (New York: Little, Brown and Co., 1997). These two books chronicle the events leading up to and including the capture of Kevin Mitnick, America's number-one criminal hacker. *Takedown* presents the story from the point of view of the security expert who captured Mitnick. *The Fugitive Game* is written from a more objective, journalistic point of view.

Cyberpunk—Outlaws and Hackers on the Computer Frontier, Updated Edition, by Katie Hafner and John Markoff (New York: Simon & Schuster, 1995). This book profiles three hackers whose exploits caught the public's attention: Kevin Mitnick, a California cracker who vandalized corporate systems; Pengo, who penetrated U.S. systems for East German espionage purposes; and Robert Morris, Jr., whose Internet worm brought down 6,000 computers in a matter of hours.

The Hacker Crackdown: Law and Disorder on the Electronic Frontier, by Bruce Sterling (New York: Bantam Books, 1992). Famed cyberpunk author Sterling turns to nonfiction to tell both sides of the story of the war between hackers and federal law enforcement agencies. The complete text is available online along with rest-of-the-story updates.

Ender's Game, by Orson Scott Card (New York: Tor Books, 1999). This award-winning, entertaining science fiction opus has become a favorite of the cryptography crowd because of its emphasis on encryption to protect privacy.

The Blue Nowhere, by Jeffery Deaver (New York: Simon & Schuster, 2001). This suspenseful thriller involves a sadistic hacker who invades his victims' computers, meddles with their lives, and lures them to their deaths. Though fictional, the novel presents a terrifyingly accurate analysis of the lack of privacy and security on the Internet.

The Postman, by David Brin (New York: Bantam, 1990). This entertaining science fiction novel weaves a tale of the future that raises many of the same issues raised by Kempelen's chess-playing machine. The disappointing 1997 movie bears little resemblance to the novel.

Periodicals

Many popular magazines, from *Newsweek* to *Wired*, provide regular coverage of issues related to privacy and security of digital systems. Most of the periodicals listed here are newsletters of professional organizations that focus on these issues.

Information Security (**www.infosecuritymag.com**). This magazine focuses on security problems and solutions. Some of the articles are technical, but most are accessible to anyone with an interest in security issues.

The CPSR Newsletter, published by Computer Professionals for Social Responsibility (P.O. Box 717, Palo Alto, CA 94302, 415/322-3778, fax: 415/322-3798, email: **cpsr@csli.stanford.edu**). An alliance of computer scientists and others interested in the impact of computer technology on society, CPSR works to influence public policies to ensure that computers are used wisely in the public interest. Their newsletter has intelligent articles and discussions of risk, reliability, privacy, security, human rights, work, war, education, the environment, democracy, and other subjects that bring together computers and people.

EFFector, published by the Electronic Frontier Foundation (155 Second St., Cambridge, MA 02141, 617/864-0665, fax: 617/864-0866, email: effnews-request@eff.org). This electronic newsletter is distributed by EFF, an organization "established to help civilize the electronic frontier." EFF was founded by Mitch Kapor (see Chapter 6) and John Perry Barlow to protect civil rights and encourage responsible citizenship on the electronic frontier of computer networks.

Ethix: The Bulletin of the Institute for Business, Technology, and Ethics (**www.ethix.org**, email: contact@ethix.org). The IBTE is a relatively new nonprofit corporation working to transform business through appropriate technology and ethical values.

Web Pages

As you might suspect, the Net is the best source of up-to-the-minute information on computer security and related issues. Public and commercial organizations maintain Web pages devoted to these issues, and dozens of newsgroups contain lively ongoing discussions on controversial topics. Check the *Computer Confluence* Web site for the latest links.

ACM Appendix

ACM Code of Ethics and Professional Conduct (Adopted by ACM Council October 16, 1992)

Commitment to ethical professional conduct is expected of every member (voting members, associate members, and student members) of the Association for Computing Machinery (ACM).

This Code, consisting of 24 imperatives formulated as statements of personal responsibility, identifies the elements of such a commitment. It contains many, but not all, issues professionals are likely to face. Section 1 outlines fundamental ethical considerations, while Section 2 addresses additional, more specific considerations of professional conduct. Statements in Section 3 pertain more specifically to individuals who have a leadership role, whether in the workplace or in a volunteer capacity such as with organizations like ACM. Principles involving compliance with this Code are given in Section 4.

The Code shall be supplemented by a set of Guidelines, which provide explanation to assist members in dealing with the various issues contained in the Code. It is expected that the Guidelines will be changed more frequently than the Code.

The Code and its supplemented Guidelines are intended to serve as a basis for ethical decision making in the conduct of professional work. Secondarily, they may serve as a basis for judging the merit of a formal complaint pertaining to violation of professional ethical standards.

It should be noted that although computing is not mentioned in the imperatives of Section 1, the Code is concerned with how these fundamental imperatives apply to one's conduct as a computing professional. These imperatives are expressed in a general form to emphasize that ethical principles which apply to computer ethics are derived from more general ethical principles.

It is understood that some words and phrases in a code of ethics are subject to varying interpretations, and that any ethical principle may conflict with other ethical principles in specific situations. Questions related to ethical conflicts can best be answered by thoughtful consideration of fundamental principles, rather than reliance on detailed regulations.

1. General moral imperatives
2. More specific professional responsibilities
3. Organizational leadership imperatives
4. Compliance with the code

1. General Moral Imperatives

As an ACM member I will ...

1.1 Contribute to Society and Human Well-Being

This principle concerning the quality of life of all people affirms an obligation to protect fundamental human rights and to respect the diversity of all cultures. An essential aim of computing professionals is to minimize negative consequences of computing systems, including threats to health and safety. When designing or implementing systems, computing professionals must attempt to ensure that the products of their efforts will be used in socially responsible ways, will meet social needs, and will avoid harmful effects to health and welfare.

In addition to a safe social environment, human well-being includes a safe natural environment. Therefore, computing professionals who design and develop systems must be alert to, and make others aware of, any potential damage to the local or global environment.

1.2 Avoid Harm to Others

"Harm" means injury or negative consequences, such as undesirable loss of information, loss of property, property damage, or unwanted environmental impacts. This principle prohibits use of computing technology in ways that result in harm to any of the following: users, the general public, employees, and employers. Harmful actions include intentional destruction or modification of files and programs leading to serious loss of resources or unnecessary expenditure of human resources such as the time and effort required to purge systems of "computer viruses."

Well-intended actions, including those that accomplish assigned duties, may lead to harm unexpectedly. In such an event the responsible person or persons are obligated to undo or mitigate the negative consequences as much as possible. One way to avoid unintentional harm is to carefully consider potential impacts on all those affected by decisions made during design and implementation.

To minimize the possibility of indirectly harming others, computing professionals must minimize malfunctions by following generally accepted standards for system design and testing. Furthermore, it is often necessary to assess the social consequences of systems to project the likelihood of any serious harm to others. If system features are misrepresented to users, coworkers, or supervisors, the individual computing professional is responsible for any resulting injury.

In the work environment the computing professional has the additional obligation to report any signs of system dangers that might result in serious personal or social damage. If one's superiors do not act to curtail or mitigate such dangers, it may be necessary to "blow the whistle" to help correct the problem or reduce the risk. However, capricious or misguided reporting of violations can, itself, be harmful. Before reporting violations, all relevant aspects of the incident must be thoroughly assessed. In particular, the assessment of risk and responsibility must be credible. It is suggested that advice be sought from other computing professionals. See principle 2.5 regarding thorough evaluations.

1.3 Be Honest and Trustworthy

Honesty is an essential component of trust. Without trust an organization cannot function effectively. The honest computing professional will not make deliberately false or deceptive claims about a system or system design, but will instead provide full disclosure of all pertinent system limitations and problems.

A computer professional has a duty to be honest about his or her own qualifications, and about any circumstances that might lead to conflicts of interest.

Membership in volunteer organizations such as ACM may at times place individuals in situations where their statements or actions could be interpreted as carrying the "weight" of a larger group of professionals. An ACM member will exercise care to not misrepresent ACM or positions and policies of ACM or any ACM units.

1.4 Be Fair and Take Action Not to Discriminate

The values of equality, tolerance, respect for others, and the principles of equal justice govern this imperative. Discrimination on the basis of race, sex, religion, age, disability, national origin, or other such factors is an explicit violation of ACM policy and will not be tolerated.

Inequities between different groups of people may result from the use or misuse of information and technology. In a fair society, all individuals would have equal opportunity to participate in, or benefit from, the use of computer resources regardless of race, sex, religion, age, disability, national origin or other such similar factors. However, these ideals do not justify unauthorized use of computer resources nor do they provide an adequate basis for violation of any other ethical imperatives of this code.

1.5 Honor Property Rights Including Copyrights and Patents

Violation of copyrights, patents, trade secrets and the terms of license agreements is prohibited by law in most circumstances. Even when software is not so protected, such violations are contrary to professional behavior. Copies of software should be made only with proper authorization. Unauthorized duplication of materials must not be condoned.

1.6 Give Proper Credit for Intellectual Property

Computing professionals are obligated to protect the integrity of intellectual property. Specifically, one must not take credit for other's ideas or work, even in cases where the work has not been explicitly protected by copyright, patent, etc.

1.7 Respect the Privacy of Others

Computing and communication technology enables the collection and exchange of personal information on a scale unprecedented in the history of civilization. Thus there is increased potential for violating the privacy of individuals and groups. It is the responsibility of professionals to maintain the privacy and integrity of data describing individuals. This includes taking precautions to ensure the accuracy of data, as well as protecting it from unauthorized access or accidental disclosure to inappropriate individuals. Furthermore, procedures must be established to allow individuals to review their records and correct inaccuracies.

This imperative implies that only the necessary amount of personal information be collected in a system, that retention and disposal periods for that information be clearly defined and enforced, and that personal information gathered for a specific purpose not be used for other purposes without consent of the individual(s). These principles apply to electronic communications, including electronic mail, and prohibit procedures that capture or monitor electronic user data, including messages, without the permission of users or bona fide authorization related to system operation and maintenance. User data observed during the normal duties of system operation and maintenance must be treated with strictest confidentiality, except in cases where it is evidence for the violation of law, organizational regulations, or this Code. In these cases, the nature or contents of that information must be disclosed only to proper authorities.

1.8 Honor Confidentiality

The principle of honesty extends to issues of confidentiality of information whenever one has made an explicit promise to honor confidentiality or, implicitly, when private information not directly related to the performance of one's duties becomes available. The ethical concern is to respect all obligations of confidentiality to employers, clients, and users unless discharged from such obligations by requirements of the law or other principles of this Code.

2. More Specific Professional Responsibilities

As an ACM computing professional I will ...

2.1 Strive to Achieve the Highest Quality, Effectiveness and Dignity in Both the Process and Products of Professional Work

Excellence is perhaps the most important obligation of a professional. The computing professional must strive to achieve quality and to be cognizant of the serious negative consequences that may result from poor quality in a system.

2.2 Acquire and Maintain Professional Competence

Excellence depends on individuals who take responsibility for acquiring and maintaining professional competence. A professional must participate in setting standards for appropriate levels of competence, and strive to achieve those standards. Upgrading technical knowledge and competence can be achieved in several ways: doing independent study; attending seminars, conferences, or courses; and being involved in professional organizations.

2.3 **Know** and Respect Existing Laws Pertaining to Professional Work

ACM members must obey existing local, state, province, national, and international laws unless there is a compelling ethical basis not to do so. Policies and procedures of the organizations in which one participates must also be obeyed. But compliance must be balanced with the recognition that sometimes existing laws and rules may be immoral or inappropriate and, therefore, must be challenged. Violation of a law or regulation may be ethical when that law or rule has inadequate moral basis or when it conflicts with another law judged to be more important. If one decides to violate a law or rule because it is viewed as unethical, or for any other reason, one must fully accept responsibility for one's actions and for the consequences.

2.4 **Accept** and Provide Appropriate Professional Review

Quality professional work, especially in the computing profession, depends on professional reviewing and critiquing. Whenever appropriate, individual members should seek and utilize peer review as well as provide critical review of the work of others.

2.5 **Give** Comprehensive and Thorough Evaluations of Computer Systems and Their Impacts, Including Analysis of Possible Risks

Computer professionals must strive to be perceptive, thorough, and objective when evaluating, recommending, and presenting system descriptions and alternatives. Computer professionals are in a position of special trust, and therefore have a special responsibility to provide objective, credible evaluations to employers, clients, users, and the public. When providing evaluations the professional must also identify any relevant conflicts of interest, as stated in imperative 1.3.

As noted in the discussion of principle 1.2 on avoiding harm, any signs of danger from systems must be reported to those who have opportunity and/or responsibility to resolve them. See the guidelines for imperative 1.2 for more details concerning harm, including the reporting of professional violations.

2.6 **Honor** Contracts, Agreements, and Assigned Responsibilities

Honoring one's commitments is a matter of integrity and honesty. For the computer professional this includes ensuring that system elements perform as intended. Also, when one contracts for work with another party, one has an obligation to keep that party properly informed about progress toward completing that work.

A computing professional has a responsibility to request a change in any assignment that he or she feels cannot be completed as defined. Only after serious consideration and with full disclosure of risks and concerns to the employer or client, should one accept the assignment. The major underlying principle here is the obligation to accept personal accountability for professional work. On some occasions other ethical principles may take greater priority.

A judgment that a specific assignment should not be performed may not be accepted. Having clearly identified one's concerns and reasons for that judgment, but failing to procure a change in that assignment, one may yet be obligated, by contract or by law, to proceed as directed. The computing professional's ethical judgment should be the final guide in deciding whether or not to proceed. Regardless of the decision, one must accept the responsibility for the consequences.

However, performing assignments "against one's own judgment" does not relieve the professional of responsibility for any negative consequences.

2.7 **Improve** Public Understanding of Computing and Its Consequences

Computing professionals have a responsibility to share technical knowledge with the public by encouraging understanding of computing, including the impacts of computer systems and their limitations. This imperative implies an obligation to counter any false views related to computing.

2.8 Access Computing and Communication Resources Only When Authorized To Do So

Theft or destruction of tangible and electronic property is prohibited by imperative 1.2—"Avoid harm to others." Trespassing and unauthorized use of a computer or communication system is addressed by this imperative. Trespassing includes accessing communication networks and computer systems, or accounts and/or files associated with those systems, without explicit authorization to do so. Individuals and organizations have the right to restrict access to their systems so long as they do not violate the discrimination principle (see 1.4). No one should enter or use another's computer system, software, or data files without permission. One must always have appropriate approval before using system resources, including communication ports, file space, other system peripherals, and computer time.

3. Organizational Leadership Imperatives

Background Note: This section draws extensively from the draft IFIP Code of Ethics, especially its sections on organizational ethics and international concerns. The ethical obligations of organizations tend to be neglected in most codes of professional conduct, perhaps because these codes are written from the perspective of the individual member. This dilemma is addressed by stating these imperatives from the perspective of the organizational leader. In this context "leader" is viewed as any organizational member who has leadership or educational responsibilities. These imperatives generally may apply to organizations as well as their leaders. In this context "organizations" are corporations, government agencies, and other "employers" as well as volunteer professional organizations.

As an ACM member and an organizational leader, I will ...

3.1 Articulate Social Responsibilities of Members of an Organizational Unit and Encourage Full Acceptance of those Responsibilities

Because organizations of all kinds have impacts on the public, they must accept responsibilities to society. Organizational procedures and attitudes oriented toward quality and the welfare of society will reduce harm to members of the public, thereby serving public interest and fulfilling social responsibility. Therefore, organizational leaders must encourage full participation in meeting social responsibilities as well as quality performance.

3.2 Manage Personnel and Resources to Design and Build Information Systems that Enhance the Quality of Working Life

Organizational leaders are responsible for ensuring that computer systems enhance, not degrade, the quality of working life. When implementing a computer system, organizations must consider the personal and professional development, physical safety, and human dignity of all workers. Appropriate human-computer ergonomic standards should be considered in system design and in the workplace.

3.3 Acknowledge and Support Proper and Authorized Uses of an Organization's Computing and Communication Resources

Because computer systems can become tools to harm as well as to benefit an organization, the leadership has the responsibility to clearly define appropriate and inappropriate uses of organizational computing resources. While the number and scope of such rules should be minimal, they should be fully enforced when established.

3.4 Ensure that Users and those Who Will Be Affected by a System Have Their Needs Clearly Articulated During the Assessment and Design of Requirements; Later the System Must Be Validated to Meet Requirements

Current system users, potential users and other persons whose lives may be affected by a system must have their needs assessed and incorporated in the statement of requirements. System validation should ensure compliance with those requirements.

3.5 Articulate and Support Policies that Protect the Dignity of Users and Others Affected by a Computing System

Designing or implementing systems that deliberately or inadvertently demean individuals or groups is ethically unacceptable. Computer professionals who are in decision making positions should verify that systems are designed and implemented to protect personal privacy and enhance personal dignity.

3.6 Create Opportunities for Members of the Organization to Learn the Principles and Limitations of Computer Systems

This complements the imperative on public understanding (2.7). Educational opportunities are essential to facilitate optimal participation of all organizational members. Opportunities must be available to all members to help them improve their knowledge and skills in computing, including courses that familiarize them with the consequences and limitations of particular types of systems. In particular, professionals must be made aware of the dangers of building systems around oversimplified models, the improbability of anticipating and designing for every possible operating condition, and other issues related to the complexity of this profession.

4. Compliance with the Code

As an ACM member I will ...

4.1 Uphold and Promote the Principles of this Code

The future of the computing profession depends on both technical and ethical excellence. Not only is it important for ACM computing professionals to adhere to the principles expressed in this Code, each member should encourage and support adherence by other members.

4.2 Treat Violations of this Code as Inconsistent with Membership in the ACM

Adherence of professionals to a code of ethics is largely a voluntary matter. However, if a member does not follow this code by engaging in gross misconduct, membership in ACM may be terminated.

This Code and the supplemental Guidelines were developed by the Task Force for the Revision of the ACM Code of Ethics and Professional Conduct: Ronald E. Anderson, Chair, Gerald Engel, Donald Gotterbarn, Grace C. Hertlein, Alex Hoffman, Bruce Jawer, Deborah G. Johnson, Doris K. Lidtke, Joyce Currie Little, Dianne Martin, Donn B. Parker, Judith A. Perrolle, and Richard S. Rosenberg. The Task Force was organized by ACM/SIG-CAS and funding was provided by the ACM SIG Discretionary Fund. This Code and the supplemental Guidelines were adopted by the ACM Council on October 16, 1992.

3-D environments p. 357 Drawn or photographed virtual spaces you can explore with mouse clicks.

3-D modeling software p. 231 Software that enables the user to create 3-D objects. The objects can be rotated, stretched, and combined with other model objects to create complex 3-D scenes.

3G p. 315 The next generation of mobile wireless technology, which promises high-bandwidth connections that will support true multimedia, including real-time video.

802.11 p. 313 See Wi-Fi.

802.11e p. 332 A Wi-Fi-related standard that focuses on quality of service, particularly the timely delivery of data packets.

802.11i p. 332 A Wi-Fi-related security technology that will enable businesses to use wireless networks for more sensitive transactions.

802.11n p. 332 A wireless LAN standard with approximately three times the bandwidth of 802.11g.

802.16e p. 332 An extension to WiMax that will let mobile computer users access the WiMax network.

A

AAC p. 244 Advanced Audio Codec, one of a number of relatively new methods of audio compression than can squeeze music files to a fraction of their original CD-file sizes, often without perceptible loss of quality.

access p. 285 Physical proximity to a person, or knowledge about that person, a common theme in privacy discussions.

access time p. 89 The amount of time, measured in nanoseconds, it takes for a CPU to retrieve a unit of data from memory. Also the amount of time, measured in milliseconds, it takes for a CPU to retrieve a unit of data from a disk drive.

access-control software p. 397 Software that only allows user access according to the user's needs. Some users can open only files that are related to their work. Some users are allowed read-only access to files they can see but not change.

accounting and financial management software p. 204 Software especially designed to set up accounts, keep track of money flow between accounts, record transactions, adjust balances in accounts, provide an audit trail, automate routine tasks such as check writing, and produce reports.

active badge p. 406 A microprocessor-controlled ID badge that broadcasts infrared identification codes to a network receiver that updates a badge-location database.

ActiveX p. 361 A collection of programming technologies and tools that can be used to create programs that are similar in many ways to Java applets.

adaptive radio p. 332 A technology that enables wireless devices to selectively transmit messages based on other wireless network traffic, thus avoiding the interference that plagues many other wireless technologies.

address p. 196 In a spreadsheet, the location of a cell, determined by row number and column number.

agents p. 168 Software programs that can ask questions, respond to commands, pay attention to users' work patterns, serve as a guide and a coach, take on owners' goals, and use reasoning to fabricate their own goals.

agricultural age p. 51 The era covering most of the past ten thousand years, during which humanity lived mainly by domesticating animals and growing food using plows and other agricultural tools.

alerts p. 367 Along with notifications a popular noncorporate type of push technology on the Web, mostly offered through services that alert subscribers to stock price changes, breaking news, and the like.

algorithm p. 143 A set of step-by-step instructions that, when completed, solves a problem.

alias p. 23 See user name.

all-in-one devices p. 116 See multifunction printer.

analog signal p. 309 A continuous wave.

analog-to-digital converter (ADC) p 110 A device that converts electrical charges into discrete values, allowing continuous signals to be stored in computers.

animation p. 236 The process of simulating motion with a series of still pictures.

antivirus p. 392 A program designed to search for viruses, notify users when they're found, and remove them from infected files.

applet p. 162 A small compiled program designed to run inside another application—typically a Web browser.

application program (application) p. 52 Software tool that allows a computer to be used for specific purposes.

application server p. 352 A common type of Internet server that stores PC office applications, databases, or other applications and makes them available to client programs that request them.

application service provider (ASP) p. 352 A company that manages and delivers application services on a contract basis.

application suite (office suite) p. 149 A collection of several related application programs that are also sold as separate programs.

architecture p. 85 Design that determines how individual components of the CPU are put together on the chip. More generally used to describe the way individual components are put together to create a complete computer system.

arithmetic logic unit (ALU) p. 86 The part of the CPU that performs data calculations and comparisons.

armature p. 122 The part of a disk drive that moves the read/write head across the disk surface.

ASCII p. 78 American Standard Code for Information Interchange, a code that represents characters as 8-bit codes. Allows the binary computer to work with letters, digits, and special characters.

asynchronous communication p. 325 Delayed communication, such as that used for newsgroups and mailing lists, where the sender and the recipients don't have to be logged in at the same time.

attachments p. 23 A way to send formatted word processor documents, pictures, and other multimedia files via email.

audio digitizers p. 112 Hardware devices or software programs that capture a sound and store it as a data file on a disk.

audit-control software p. 399 Applications that monitor and record computer transactions as they happen so auditors can trace and identify suspicious computer activity after the fact.

augmented reality (AR) p. 256 The use of computer displays that add virtual information to a person's sensory perceptions, supplementing rather than replacing (as in virtual reality) the world the user sees.

authentication mechanisms p. 402 Computer network security measures that ensure that only legitimate users have access to the system by asking potential users to identify themselves.

authorization mechanisms p. 403 Computer network security measures that guarantee that users have permission to perform particular actions.

automated teller machine (ATM) p. 308 A device that enables users to remotely access and deposit money from their bank accounts through the use of a network.

automatic correction (autocorrect) p. 181 A word processing feature that catches and corrects common typing errors.

automatic footnoting p. 181 A word processing feature that places footnotes where they belong on the page.

automatic formatting p. 181 A word processing feature that applies formatting to the text.

automatic hyphenation p. 181 A word processing feature that divides long words that fall at the ends of lines.

automatic link p. 199 A link between worksheets in a spreadsheet that ensures that a change in one worksheet is reflected in the other.

automatic recalculation p. 198 A spreadsheet capability that allows for easy correction of errors and makes it easy to try out different values while searching for solutions.

autonomous systems p. 411 Complex systems that can assume almost complete responsibility for a task without human input, verification, or decision making.

avatars p. 325 Graphical bodies used to represent a person in a virtual meeting place; can range from a simple cartoon sketch to an elaborate 3-D figure or an exotic abstract icon.

B

Back and Forward buttons p. 21 Browser buttons that allow you to retrace your steps while navigating the Web and return to previously visited sites.

backbone p. 306 A collection of common pathways used to transmit large quantities of data between networks in a wide-area network (WAN).

back-up copy p. 16 A copy of a file created as insurance against the loss of the original.

back-up media p. 16 Disks, CD-Rs, and other technologies to hold back-up files and to save computer storage space.

backup p. 402 The process of saving data—especially for data recovery. Many systems automatically back up data and software onto disks or tapes.

backward compatible p. 82 Able to run software written for older CPUs. Also, when referring to a software program, able to read and write files compatible with older versions of the program.

baud rate p. 309 A speed of data transmission; not necessarily equivalent to bits per second (bps), the preferred measurement for high-speed modems.

bandwidth p. 310 The quantity of information that can be transmitted through a communication medium in a given amount of time.

bar chart p. 200 A chart that shows relative values with bars, appropriate when data fall into a few categories.

bar code reader p. 106 A reading tool that uses light to read universal product codes, inventory codes, and other codes created out of patterns of variable-width bars.

batch processing p. 281 Accumulating transactions and feeding them into a computer in large batches.

bay p. 90 An open area in the system box for disk drives and other peripheral devices.

binary p. 75 A choice of two values, such as yes and no or zero and one.

binary number system p. 78 A system that denotes all numbers with combinations of two digits.

biometrics p. 396 Measurements of individual body characteristics, such as a voice print or fingerprint; sometimes used in computer security.

BIOS (basic input/output system) p. 91 The firmware programs in read-only memory.

bit p. 75 Binary digit, the smallest unit of information. A bit can have two values: 0 or 1.

bit depth p. 113 Color depth, the number of bits devoted to each pixel in a color display.

bitmapped graphics p. 224 Graphics in which images are stored and manipulated as organized collections of pixels rather than as shapes and lines. Contrast with object-oriented graphics.

bits per second (bps) p. 309 The standard unit of measure for modem speed.

blocks p. 165 Units of data or memory, made up of bundles of sectors, on a hard disk.

blog p. 355 Short for Web log, a personal Web page that often carries diary-like entries or political commentaries. Blogs are fast proliferating as new software allows users to create Web pages without having to learn the technical details of HTML and Web authoring.

Bluetooth p. 313 A type of wireless technology that enables mobile phones, handheld computers, and PCs to communicate with each other regardless of operating system.

bookmarks p. 21 Personal lists kept on a browser of favorite or memorable Web sites that are often revisited. Also called favorites.

Boolean logic p. 366 A complex query structure supported by most search engines; one example is "American AND Indian BUT NOT Cleveland."

booting p. 155 Loading the non-ROM part of the operating system into memory.

bot p. 212 Software robots that crawl around the Web collecting information, helping consumers make decisions, answering email, and even playing games.

bounce p. 324 The automatic return of an undeliverable email message to its sender.

bridges p. 307 Hardware devices that can pass messages between networks.

broadband connection p. 311 An Internet connection such as DSL or cable modem that offers higher bandwidth, and therefore faster transmission speed, than standard modem connections.

browse p. 269 The process of finding information in a database or other data source, such as the World Wide Web.

bug p. 142 An error in programming.

bullet charts p. 233 Graphical elements, such as drawings and tables, integrated into a series of charts that list the main points of a presentation.

burn p. 124 To record data onto CD-R and CD-RW disks.

bus p. 90 Group of wires on a circuit board. Information travels between components through a bus.

business-to-business (B2B) p. 369 E-commerce transactions that involve businesses providing goods or services to other businesses.

business-to-consumer (B2C) p. 369 E-commerce transactions that involve businesses providing goods or services to consumers.

button p. 8 A hot spot on a screen that responds to mouse clicks. A button can be programmed to perform one of many tasks, such as opening a dialog box or launching an application.

byte pp. 78 Grouping of 8 bits.

C

cable modems p. 349 A type of broadband Internet connection that uses the same network of coaxial cables that delivers TV signals.

camera-ready p. 192 Typeset-quality pages, ready to be photographed and printed.

cards p. 91 See expansion card.

carpal tunnel syndrome p. 120 An affliction of the wrist and hand that results from repeating the same movements over long periods.

cascading style sheets p. 358 A feature of dynamic HTML that gives users more control over how a Web page is displayed. Cascading style sheets can define formatting and layout elements that aren't recognized in older versions of HTML.

CD-R p. 124 Compact disk–recordable, an optical disk you can write information on, but you cannot remove the information.

CD-ROM p. 121 Compact disc—read-only memory, a type of optical disk that contains data that cannot be changed; CD-ROMs are commonly used to distribute commercial software programs.

CD-ROM drive p. 6 A common optical drive in computers that can read data from CD-ROM disks.

CD-RW p. 124 Compact disk–rewritable, an optical disk that allows writing, erasing, and rewriting.

CD-RW drive p. 121 A disk drive that can read and write on rewritable optical disks.

cell p. 196 The intersection of a row and a column on the grid of a spreadsheet.

central processing unit (CPU) p. 6 Part of the computer that processes information, performs arithmetic calculations, and makes basic decisions based on information values.

centralized database p. 281 A database housed in a mainframe computer, accessible only to information-processing personnel.

character-based interface p. 156 A user interface based on text characters rather than graphics.

charge-coupled device (CCD) p. 110 A device, as in a digital camera, that converts light into electrons.

chat room p. 325 Public real-time teleconference.

class p. 284 In an object-oriented database, the data contained in the object as well as the kinds of operations that may be performed on the data.

click p. 8 The action of pressing a button on a mouse.

client/server p. 281 Client programs in desktop computers send information requests through a network to server databases on mainframes, minicomputers, or desktop computers; the servers process queries and send the requested data back to the client.

client/server model p. 315 For a local-area network, a hierarchical model in which one or more computers act as dedicated servers and all the remaining computers act as clients. The server fills requests from clients for data and other resources.

clip art p. 228 A collection of redrawn images that you can cut out and paste into your own documents.

clipboard p. 9 A word processing program text editing tool for temporarily storing chunks of text and other data.

clock p. 84 The timing device producing electrical pulses for synchronizing the computer's operations.

close p. 164 An operation that allows you to stop working on a project but remain in the application program.

cluster p. 85 A grouping of multiple processors or servers to, for example, improve graphic rendering speeds or increase reliability.

CMOS p. 89 Complementary metal oxide semiconductor, a special low-energy kind of RAM that can store small amounts of data for long periods of time on battery power. CMOS RAM is used to store the date, time, and calendar in a PC. CMOS RAM is called parameter RAM in Macintoshes.

code of ethics p. 407 Policies and procedures, such as those developed by companies and by organizations such as the ACM (Association for Computing Machinery), to guide the behavior of information workers.

Code of Fair Information Practices p. 291 A set of guidelines produced for Congress by a panel of experts in the early 1970s that called for a ban on secret government databases, citizen access to personal information kept in government databases, and agency responsibility for database reliability and security.

color depth p. 113 Bit depth, the number of bits devoted to each pixel.

color monitor p. 115 A monitor capable of displaying a wide range of colors, with greater depth than a gray-scale monitor.

columns p. 196 Along with rows, comprise the grid of a spreadsheet.

command-line interface p. 156 User interface that requires the user to type text commands on a command-line to communicate with the operating system.

communication software p. 315 Software that enables computers to interact with each other over a phone line or other network.

compatible (compatibility) p. 82 The ability of a software program to run on a specific computer system. Also, the ability of a hardware device to function with a particular type of computer.

compiler p. 143 A translator program that translates an entire program from a high-level computer language before the program is run for the first time.

compression p. 241 Making files smaller using special encoding schemes. File compression saves storage space on disks and saves transmission time when files are transferred through networks.

computed field p. 269 In a database, a field containing formulas similar to spreadsheet formulas; they display values calculated from values in other numeric fields.

computer addiction p. 371 The condition in which networking and surfing the Net become more real and interesting than the everyday physical world.

computer crime p. 387 Any crime accomplished through knowledge or use of computer technology.

computer forensics p. 386 The use of computer technology and applications as tools to help law enforcement officials stop criminal activities.

computer security p. 395 Protecting computer systems and the information they contain against unwanted access, damage, modification, or destruction.

computer telephony integration (CTI) p. 326 The linking of computers and telephones to gain productivity, such as by allowing PCs to serve as speakerphones, answering machines, and complete voicemail systems.

computer-aided design (CAD) p. 232 The use of computers to draw products or process designs on the screen.

computer-aided manufacturing (CAM) p. 233 When the design of a product is completed, the numbers are fed to a program that controls the manufacturing of parts. For electronic parts the design translates directly into a template for etching circuits onto chips. Also called computer integrated manufacturing (CIM).

computer-integrated manufacturing (CIM) p. 233 The combination of CAD and CAM.

concurrent processing p. 151 A large computer working on several jobs at the same time. The computer uses multiple CPUs to process jobs simultaneously.

consumer portals p. 367 Portals that include search engines, email services, chat rooms, references, news and sports headlines, shopping malls, other services, and advertisements—many of the same things found in online services such as AOL.

context-sensitive menus p. 158 Menus offering choices that depend on the context.

contract p. 166 A type of law that covers trade secrets.

cookie p. 358 Small files deposited on a user's hard disk by Web sites, enabling sites to remember what they know about their visitors between sessions.

copy p. 9 A word processing program text editing tool that allows you to make a copy of a set of words or data and place the copy elsewhere in the same or a different document.

copy protected p. 148 Produced in a way that prevents any physical copying, such as is the case with software CDs and DVDs, especially some entertainment products.

copyright p. 166 A type of law that traditionally protects forms of literary expression.

copyrighted software p. 148 Software that prevents a disk from being copied.

corporate portals p. 367 Specialized portals on an intranet that serve the employees of a particular corporation.

CPU p. 6 See central processing unit.

cracking p. 394 Unauthorized access and/or vandalism of computer systems; short for criminal hacking.

cross-platform applications p. 161 Programs, such as Adobe Photoshop, that are available in similar versions for multiple platforms.

CRT (cathode-ray tube) monitors p. 115 Television-style monitors used as the output device for many desktop computers.

cursor (arrow) key p. 7 A keyboard key that moves the cursor up or down, right or left, on the screen.

cursor p. 7 A line or rectangle, sometimes flashing, that indicates your location on the screen or in a document.

custom application p. 150 An application programmed for a specific purpose, typically for a specific client.

customer relationship management (CRM) p. 282 Software systems for organizing and tracking information on customers.

cut p. 9 A word processing program text editing tool that allows you to delete a set of words or data; often used with the copy function to move text around.

cyberspace p. 374 A term used to describe the Internet and other online networks, especially the artificial realities and virtual communities that form on them. First coined by William Gibson in his novel, *Neuromancer*.

D

data p. 38 Information in a form that can be read, used, and manipulated by a computer.

data files p. 9 Documents that contain passive data rather than instructions.

data mining p. 282 The discovery and extraction of hidden predictive information from large databases.

data scrubbing (data cleansing) p. 282 The process of going through a database and eliminating records that contain errors.

data transfer rates p. 124 The speed at which a drive, for example, can read or write data.

data translation software p. 320 Software that enables users of different systems with incompatible file formats to read and modify each other's files.

data type p. 269 See field type.

data warehouse p. 281 An integrated collection of corporate data stored in one location.

database p. 268 A collection of information stored in an organized form in a computer.

database management system (DBMS) p. 277 A program or system of programs that can manipulate data in a large collection of files (the database), cross-referencing between files as needed.

database program p. 268 A software tool for organizing the storage and retrieval of the information in a database.

database server p. 281 A powerful computer for holding and managing an interactive, multiuser database.

data-driven Web site p. 361 A Web site that can display dynamic, changeable content without having constantly redesigned pages, due to an evolving database that separates the site's content from its design.

date field p. 269 A field containing only dates.

debugging p. 143 Finding and correcting errors—bugs—in computer software.

decode unit p. 87 Takes the instruction read by the prefetcher and translates it into a form suitable for the CPU's internal processing.

defragmentation utility p. 165 A program that eliminates fragmented files by changing the assignment of clusters to files.

Delete key p. 7 A keyboard key that acts as an eraser by, for example, removing highlighted text in a word document.

denial of service (DoS) attack p. 394 A type of computer vandalism that bombards servers and Web sites with so much bogus traffic that they're effectively shut down, denying service to legitimate customers and clients.

desktop p. 157 The virtual workspace on a graphical user interface that resembles the physical desktops found in brick-and-mortar offices.

desktop publishing (DTP) p. 187 Software used mainly to produce print publications. Also, the process of using desktop publishing software to produce publications.

desktop replacements p. 45 Heavy but powerful laptops that perform as well as desktop PCs.

device drivers p. 154 Small programs that allow input/output devices to communicate with the computer.

dialog box p. 157 In a graphical user interface, a box that enables the user to communicate with the computer.

digit p. 75 A discrete, countable unit.

digital p. 75 Information made up of discrete units that can be counted.

digital camera p. 109 A camera that captures images and stores them as bit patterns on disks or other digital storage media instead of using film.

digital cash p. 371 A system for purchasing goods and services on the Internet without using credit cards.

digital divide p. 373 A term that describes the divide between the people who do and do not have access to the Internet.

digital photo p. 227 A photograph captured with a digital camera.

digital rights management (DRM) p. 245 Technology now being used in many audio files to protect musicians' and other artists' intellectual property.

digital signal p. 309 A stream of bits.

digital signatures p. 372 A developing identity verification standard that uses encryption techniques to protect against email forgery.

digital versatile discs (DVD) p.124 Digital video disk or digital versatile disk, a popular type of high-capacity optical disk used in both consumer video playback machines and computers.

digital video camera p. 108 A video camera that captures footage in digital form so that clips can be transferred to and from a computer for editing with no loss of quality.

digital video p. 238 Video reduced to a series of numbers, which can be edited, stored, and played back without loss of quality.

digitize p. 108 Converting information into a digital form that can be stored in the computer's memory.

DIMMs p. 90 Dual in-line memory modules.

direct connection p. 18 A dedicated, direct connection to the Internet through a LAN, with the computer having its own IP address.

directories p. 282 See directory.

directory p. 22 A logical container used to group files and other directories. Also called a folder.

dirty data p. 282 Data records with spelling mistakes, incorrect or obsolete values, or other errors.

disk drive p. 119 See diskette drive.

diskette (disk) drive p. 6 Device used to retrieve information from a disk and, in some cases, to transfer data to it.

diskettes (disks) p. 6 Small, magnetically sensitive, flexible plastic wafers housed in a plastic case, used as a storage device.

display p. 7 See monitor.

distributed computing p. 369 Integrating all kinds of computers, from mainframes to PCs, into a single, seamless system.

distributed database p. 281 Data strewn out across networks on several different computers.

distributed denial of service (DDoS) attack p. 394 A denial of service attack in which the flood of messages comes from many compromised systems distributed across the Net.

docking station p. 45 A device for expanding a laptop computer so that it has the power and flexibility of a desktop.

document p. 157 A file, such as a term paper or chart created with applications.

documentation p. 146 Instructions for installing the software on a computer's hard disk.

domain name registry p. 355 A company that provides its customers with domain names that are easier to remember and use.

domain name system (DNS) p. 345 A system that translates a computer's numerical IP address into an easy-to-remember string of names separated by dots.

domains p. 345 A class of Internet addresses indicated by a suffix such as .com, .gov, or .net.

dot-matrix printer p. 115 A type of impact printer, which forms images by physically striking paper, ribbon, and print hammer together, the way a typewriter does.

dots per inch (dpi) p. 225 A measurement of the density of pixels, defining the resolution of a graphic.

double-click p. 8 To click a mouse button twice in rapid succession.

download p. 317 To copy software from an online source to a local computer.

downloadable audio p. 357 Compressed sound files that you must download onto your computer's hard disk before the browser or some other application can play them.

downloadable video p. 357 Compressed video files that can be downloaded and viewed on a computer.

drag p. 8 To move the mouse while holding the mouse button down. Used for moving objects, selecting text, drawing, and other tasks.

drag-and-drop p. 9 A word processing program text editing tool that allows you to move a selected block of text from one location to another.

drawing software p. 229 Stores a picture as a collection of lines and shapes. Also stores shapes as shape formulas and text as text.

drive-by-download p. 392 A spyware download onto your computer that occurs simply by visiting certain Web sites.

drum scanners p. 108 Scanners used in publishing applications where image quality is critical.

DSL (digital subscriber line) p. 347 A type of broadband connection to the Internet offered by phone companies.

DVD drive p. 6, 124 An optical disk drive that can read high-capacity DVD disks.

DVD/CD-RW drive p. 124 A disk drive that combines the capabilities of a DVD-ROM drive and a CD-RW drive in a single unit.

DVD+MRW p. 124 An emerging new standard, also called Mt. Rainier, for rewritable media.

DVD+R p. 124 Recordable DVD disk.

DVD+RW p. 124 DVD disk that allows writing, erasing, and rewriting.

DVD-RAM p. 124 A type of optical disk with multigigabyte capacity that can be read, written, and erased.

DVD-ROM drive p. 124 An optical disk drive that can read high-capacity DVD disks.

dynamic HTML p. 358 A relatively new version of HTML that supports formatting and layout features that aren't supported in standard HTML.

E

electronic book (ebook) p. 194 A handheld device that displays digital representations of the contents of books.

electronic commerce (e-commerce) p. 369 Business transactions through electronic networks.

electronic data interchange (EDI) p. 369 A set of specifications for conducting basic business transactions over private networks.

electronic mail (email) p. 22 Allows Internet users to send mail messages, data files, and software programs to other Internet users and to users of most commercial networks and online services.

electronic paper (epaper) p. 195 A flexible, portable, paperlike material that can dynamically display black-and-white text and images on its surface, as well as erase itself and display new text and images as the reader "turns" the page.

electronic phone directory p. 273 A specialized database that can pack millions of names and phone numbers onto a single CD-ROM or Web site.

electronic street atlas p. 273 A specialized database that can pinpoint addresses and, with the aid of global positioning system (GPS) technology, locations.

electronica p. 246 Sequenced music that is designed from the ground up with digital technology.

email server p. 351 A specialized server that acts like a local post office for a particular Internet host.

email viruses p. 390 Viruses spread via email.

embedded computer p. 46 A computer that is embedded into a consumer product, such as a wristwatch or game machine, to enhance those products. Also used to control hardware devices.

emulation p. 161 A process that enables programs to run on a noncompatible operating system.

encryption key p. 397 A secret numerical code that can be used to scramble network transmissions; a matching key is needed to reconstruct the message.

encryption p. 397 Protects transmitted information by scrambling the transmissions. When a user encrypts a message by applying a secret numerical code (encryption key), the message can be transmitted or stored as an indecipherable garble of characters. The message can be read only after it's been reconstructed with a matching key.

end-user license agreement (EULA) p. 147 An agreement typically including specifications for how a program may be used, warranty disclaimers, and rules concerning the copying of the software.

Enter (enter key) p. 7 A keyboard key with a number of special functions, such as moving the cursor to the beginning of the next line, or activating a selected option.

enterprise network systems p. 306 Large, complex networks with hundreds of computers that are tracked and maintained with network management system software.

equation solver p. 200 A feature of some spreadsheet programs that determines data values.

ergonomic keyboard p. 103 A keyboard that places the keys at angles that allow your wrists to assume a more natural position while you type, potentially reducing the risk of repetitive-stress injuries.

ergonomics p. 120 The science of designing work environments that enable people and things to interact efficiently and safely.

Ethernet p. 309 A popular networking architecture developed in 1976 at Xerox.

Ethernet port p. 309 A network interface port that is included on main circuit boards in most newer PCs for easy connection to Ethernet networks.

ethics p. 407 Moral philosophy—philosophical thinking about right and wrong.

executable files p. 9 Files, such as applications, that contain instructions that can be executed by the computer.

expansion cards p. 90 Special-purpose circuit boards that can be inserted in a computer's expansion slots.

expansion slot p. 90 An area inside the computer's housing that holds special-purpose circuit boards.

export data p. 271 Transmitting records and fields from a database program to another program.

extension p. 15 A file name feature, usually three characters following a period at the end of the file name, that gives more information about the file's origin or use.

external drives p. 6 Disk drives, such as hard disks for additional storage, not included in a system unit but rather attached to it via cables.

external modem p. 309 A modem located in a box linked to a serial port or USB port, rather than being installed on a circuit board inside the computer's chassis.

extranets p. 369 Private TCP/IP networks designed for outside use by customers, clients, and business partners of an organization. These networks are typically for electronic commerce.

F

facsimile (fax) machine p. 116 An output device capable of sending, in effect, a photocopy through a telephone line, allowing for fast and convenient transmission of information stored on paper.

FAQs (frequently asked questions) p. 329 Posted lists of common queries and their answers.

favorites p. 21 See bookmarks.

fax modem p. 116 Hardware peripheral that enables a computer to send onscreen documents to a receiving fax machine by translating the document into signals that can be sent over phone wires and decoded by the receiving fax machine.

feedback loop p. 210 In a computer simulation, the user and the computer responding to data from each other.

fiber-optic cable p. 311 High-capacity cable that uses light waves to carry information at blinding speeds.

field p. 268 Each discrete chunk of information in a database record.

field type p. 269 The characteristic of a field that determines the kind of information that can be stored in that field.

file p. 9 An organized collection of related information stored in a computer-readable form.

file compression p. 16 The process of reducing the size of a file so that you can fit more files into the same amount of disk space.

file decompression p. 16 The process of restoring a compressed file back to its original state.

file manager p. 277 A program that enables users to manipulate files on their computers.

file server p. 317 In a LAN, a computer used as a storehouse for software and data that are shared by several users.

file transfer protocol (FTP) p. 351 A communications protocol that enables users to download files from remote servers to their computers and to upload files they want to share from their computers to these archives.

file-management utility p. 163 A program that allows you to view, rename, copy, move, and delete files and folders.

filtering software p. 372 Software that, for the most part, keeps offensive and otherwise inappropriate Web content from being viewed by children, on-duty workers, and others.

Find p. 16 A command used to locate a particular word, string of characters, or formatting in a document.

find-and-replace (search and replace) p. 9 A word processing program text editing tool that allows you to make repetitive changes throughout a document.

FireWire (IEEE 1394, FireWire 400, FireWire 800) p. 127 See IEEE 1394.

firmware p. 46 A program, usually for special-purpose computers, stored on a ROM chip so it cannot be altered.

flash memory p. 89 A type of erasable memory chip used in cell phones, pagers, portable computers, and handheld computers, among other things.

flatbed scanners p. 108 Scanners that look and work like a photocopy machine, except that they create computer files instead of paper copies.

floppy disk drive p. 6 A drive found mostly on older computers that enables them to store small amounts of information on pocket-sized plastic-covered diskettes. Also called diskette drive.

folder p. 15 A container for files and other folders. Also called a directory.

font p. 10 A size and style of typeface.

footer p. 179 Block of information that appears at the bottom of every page in a document, displaying repetitive information such as an automatically calculated page number.

force feedback joystick p. 118 A joystick that receives signals from a computer and gives tactile feedback, such as jolts and bumps, matching the visual output of the game or simulation, an example of an enhanced input device that delivers output.

form views p. 269 A view of the database that shows one record at a time.

format p. 9 The way that characters, words, and paragraphs appear in a word processing document.

formatting p. 165 The function of software, such as word processing software, that enables users to change the appearance of a document by specifying the font, point size, and style of any character in the document, as well as the overall layout of text and graphical elements in the document.

forms p. 357 On a Web site, pages that visitors can fill in to order goods and services, respond to questionnaires, express opinions, and the like.

formula p. 196 Step-by-step procedure for calculating a number on a spreadsheet.

fragmented file p. 165 A file allocated to noncontiguous clusters on a disk, thus degrading the disk's performance.

frame p. 236 In animation, one still picture in a video or animated sequence.

frames p. 357 Subdivisions of a Web browser's viewing area that enable visitors to scroll and view different parts of a page—or even multiple pages—simultaneously.

full-access dial-up connections p. 347 Enables a computer connected via modem and phone line to temporarily have full Internet access and a temporary IP address.

full-color p. 192 A desktop published document that uses a wide range of color. Contrast with spot color.

function p. 198 A predefined set of calculations, such as SUM and AVERAGE, in spreadsheet software.

function keys (f-keys) p. 7 Keyboard keys, often twelve lined along the top of the keyboard, that send special commands to the computer depending upon the program being run.

G

gateways p. 307 Computers connected to two networks that translate communication protocols and transfer information between the two.

GB (gigabyte) p. 81 Approximately 1000MB.

generation p. 402 One cycle of backups; many data-processing shops keep several generations of backups so they can, if necessary, go back several days, weeks, or years to reconstruct data files.

geographical information system (GIS) p. 273 A specialized database that combines tables of data with demographic information and displays geographic and demographic data on maps.

gigahertz p. 84 Billions of clock cycles per second, a measurement of a computer's clock speed.

GIGO (garbage in, garbage out) p. 202 Valid output requires valid input.

Global Positioning System (GPS) p. 307 A Defense Department system with 24 satellites that can pinpoint any location on the Earth.

GPS receiver p. 307 A device that can use Global Positioning System signals to determine its location and communicate that information to a person or a computer.

grammar and style checker p. 184 Component of word processing software that analyzes each word in context, checking for content errors, common grammatical errors, and stylistic problems.

graphical user interface (GUI) p. 157 A user interface based on graphical displays. With a mouse, the user points to icons that represent files, folders, and disks. Documents are displayed in windows. The user selects commands from menus.

graphics tablet p. 104 A pressure-sensitive touch tablet used as a pointing device. The user presses on the tablet with a stylus.

gray-scale graphics p. 224 Computerized imaging that allows each pixel to appear as black, white, or one of several shades of gray.

gray-scale monitors p. 115 Monitor that displays black, white, and shades of gray but no other colors.

grid computing p. 368 A form of distributed computing in which not files but processing power is shared between networked computers.

groupware p. 184 Software designed to be used by work groups rather than individuals.

H

hacker p. 394 Someone who uses computer skills to gain unauthorized access to computer systems. Also sometimes used to refer to a particularly talented, dedicated programmer.

hacking p. 394 Electronic trespassing and vandalism.

handheld computer p. 45 A portable computer small enough to be tucked into a jacket pocket.

handwriting recognition software p. 107 Software that translates the user's handwritten forms into ASCII characters.

hard disk p. 121 A rigid, magnetically sensitive disk that spins rapidly and continuously inside the computer chassis or in a separate box attached to the computer housing. Used as a storage device.

hardware p. 38 Physical parts of the computer system.

hardware compression p. 243 Compression using hardware rather than software.

header p. 179 Block that appears at the top of every page in a document, displaying repetitive information such as a chapter title.

help file p. 146 A documentation file that appears onscreen at the user's request.

helper application p. 357 A program designed to help users view particular types of graphics, animation, audio, or video that can't be played by the browser.

hierarchical menus p. 158 Menus that organize commands into compact, efficient submenus.

high-level language p. 143 A programming language that falls somewhere between natural human languages and precise machine languages, developed to streamline and simplify the programming process.

hits p. 22 Web pages containing requested key words, displayed in a list by a Web browser.

host name p. 23 The name of the host computer, network, or ISP address where the user receives email, contained in the part of an Internet email address that comes after the at sign (@).

host system p. 317 A computer that provides services to multiple users.

hot spots p. 330 Publicly accessible wireless access points.

hot swap p. 127 To remove and replace peripheral devices without powering down the computer and peripherals. Some modern interface standards such as USB and FireWire allow hot-swapping.

HTML (hypertext markup language) p. 181 An HTML document is a text file that includes codes that describe the format, layout, and logical structure of a hypermedia document. Most Web pages are created with HTML.

http (hypertext transfer protocol) p. 352 The Internet protocol used to transfer Web pages.

hubs p. 305 Devices that allow nodes on a local area network to communicate, though only a single message at a time can move across the network.

hyperlink p. 20 A word, phrase, or picture that acts as a button, enabling the user to explore the Web or a multimedia document with mouse clicks.

hypermedia p. 250 The combination of text, numbers, graphics, animation, sound effects, music, and other media in hyperlinked documents.

hypertext p. 250 An interactive cross-referenced system that allows textual information to be linked in nonsequential ways. A hypertext document contains links that lead quickly to other parts of the document or to related documents.

hypertext link p. 49 A Web connection to another document or site, like the many that loosely tie together millions of Web pages.

I

I-beam p. 8 The I-beam shaped pointer used to highlight text and move the cursor within a text document.

icon p. 157 In a graphical user interface, a picture that represents a file, folder, or disk.

identity (ID) theft p. 287 The crime, committed by hackers or other unscrupulous individuals, of obtaining enough information about a person to assume his or her identity, often as a prelude to illegally using the victim's credit cards.

IEEE 1394 p. 127 An industry standard for relatively new, extremely fast serial communications protocol, especially well suited for multimedia applications such as digital video. Apple, which developed the standard, refers to IEEE 1394 as FireWire.

image processing software p. 227 Software that enables the user to manipulate photographs and other high-resolution images.

impact printer p. 115 Printer that forms images by physically striking paper, ribbon, and print hammer together.

import data p. 269 To move data into a program from another program or source.

inbox p. 23 The place where email programs and services store recipients' incoming messages.

industrial age p. 51 The recent modern era, characterized by the shift from farms to factories.

Industrial Revolution p. 51 The era of rapid advances in machine technology that began at the end of the eighteenth century and ushered in the industrial age.

information p. 75 Anything that can be communicated.

information age p. 51 The current era, characterized by the shift from an industrial economy to an information economy and the convergence of computer and communication technology.

information appliance p. 50 Network computer or other Internet-capable device used in offices and homes.

infrared wireless p. 313 The use of invisible infrared radiation and infrared ports to send and receive digital information short distances, now possible on many laptops and handheld computers.

inkjet printer p. 115 A nonimpact printer that sprays ink directly onto paper to produce printed text and graphic images.

input p. 38 Information taken in by the computer.

input device p. 73 Device for accepting input, such as a keyboard.

instant messaging p. 325 A technology that enables users to create buddy lists, check for buddies who are logged in, and exchange typed messages and files with those who are.

instructions p. 86 Computer codes telling the CPU to perform a specific action.

integrated circuit p. 40 A chip containing hundreds, thousands, or even millions of transistors.

integrated software p. 149 Software packages that include several applications designed to work well together.

intellectual property p. 166 The results of intellectual activities in the arts, science, and industry.

interactive multimedia p. 251 Multimedia that enables the user to take an active part in the experience.

interactive processing p. 281 Interacting with data through terminals, viewing and changing values online in real time.

interface standards p. 126 Standards for ports and other connective technology agreed upon by the hardware industry so that devices made by one manufacturer can be attached to systems made by other companies.

internal drives p. 6 Disk drives that are included in a system unit.

internal modem p. 309 A modem that is built into the system unit.

Internet p. 18 A global interconnected network of thousands of networks linking academic, research, government, and commercial institutions, and other organizations and individuals. Also known as the Net.

Internet appliance p. 50 Non-PC devices such as set-top boxes that are connected to the Internet.

Internet service provider (ISP) p. 23 A business that provides its customers with connections to the Internet along with other services.

Internet telephony (IP telephony) p. 326 A combination of software and hardware technology that enables the Internet to, in effect, serve as a telephone network. Internet telephony systems can use standard telephones, computers, or both to send and receive voice messages.

Internet2 p. 371 An alternative Internet-style network that provides faster network communications for universities and research institutions.

internetworking p. 343 Connecting different types of networks and computer systems.

intranet p. 50 A self-contained intraorganizational network that is designed using the same technology as the Internet.

IP address p. 344 A unique string of four numbers separated by periods that serves as a unique address for a computer on the Internet. The IP address of the host computer and sending computer is included with every packet of information that traverses the Internet.

J

Java p. 161 A platform-neutral, object-oriented programming language developed by Sun Microsystems for use on multiplatform networks.

Java virtual machine p. 162 Software that gives a computer the capability to run Java programs.

JavaScript p. 359 A Web scripting language similar to, but otherwise unrelated to, Java.

joystick p. 104 A gearshift-like device used as a controller for arcade-style computer games.

justification p. 179 The alignment of text on a line: left justification (smooth left margin and ragged right margin), right justification, (smooth right margin and ragged left margin).

K

KB (kilobyte) p. 81 About 1000 bytes of information.

kerning p. 190 The spacing between letter pairs in a document.

key field p. 279 A field that contains data that uniquely identifies the record.

keyboard p. 103 Input device, similar to a typewriter keyboard, for entering data and commands into the computer.

keyboard/mouse ports p. 126 Ports for attaching keyboard and mouse to most older PCs.

keychain USB flash memory devices p. 125 Tiny devices that plug directly into the computer's USB port and are becoming popular for storing and transporting data files.

L

label p. 196 In a spreadsheet, a text entry that provides information on what a column or row represents.

laptop computer p. 45 A flat-screen, battery-powered portable computer that you can rest on your lap.48

laser printer p. 115 A nonimpact printer that uses a laser beam to create patterns of electrical charges on a rotating drum. The charged patterns attract black toner and transfer it to paper as the drum rotates.

leading p. 190 The spacing between lines of text.

legacy ports p. 126 The most common standard ports on PC system boards, including the serial port, parallel port, and keyboard/mouse port.

legacy-free PCs p. 127 PCs using USB ports.

Level 1 cache p. 87 Memory storage that can be quickly accessed by the CPU.

Level 2 cache (L2 cache) p. 87 Memory storage that is larger than a level 1 cache but not as quickly accessed by the CPU.

line chart p. 200 A chart that shows trends or relationships over time, or a relative distribution of one variable through another.

line printer p. 115 An impact printer used by mainframes to produce massive printouts. They print characters only, not graphics.

links p. 20 See hyperlink.

Linux p. 139 An operating system based on UNIX, maintained by volunteers, and distributed for free. Linux is used mostly in servers and embedded computers, but is growing in popularity as a PC operating system.

liquid crystal display (LCD) displays p. 115 Flat-panels displays, once primarily used for portable computers but now replacing bulkier CRT monitors for desktops.

list views p. 269 Showing data by displaying several records in lists similar to a spreadsheet.

local area network (LAN) p. 48 Multiple personal computers connected on a network.

logged in p. 158 Connected to a computer system or network.

logic bomb p. 392 A program designed to attack in response to a particular logical event or sequence of events. A type of software sabotage.

login name p. 23 See user name.

lossless compression p. 243 Systems allowing files to be compressed and later decompressed without a loss of data.

lossy compression p. 243 A type of compression in which some quality is lost in the process of compression and decompression.

M

Mac OS p. 157 The operating system for the Apple Macintosh computer.

machine language p. 143 The language that computers use to process instructions. Machine language uses numeric codes to represent basic computer operations.

macro p. 198 Custom-designed embedded procedure program that automates tasks in application programs.

macro viruses p. 390 Viruses that attach to and are transmitted through macros embedded in documents; usually spread via email.

magnetic disk p. 119 Storage medium with random-access capability, accessed by the computer's disk drive.

magnetic ink character reader p. 106 A device that reads numbers printed with magnetic ink on checks.

magnetic tape p. 119 A storage medium used with a tape drive to store large amounts of information in a small space at relatively low cost.

mail merge p. 184 A feature of a word processor or other program that enables it to merge names and addresses from a database mailing list into personalized form letters and mailings.

mailbox p. 23 A storage area for email messages.

mailing lists p. 322 Email discussion groups on special-interest topics. All subscribers receive messages sent to the group's mailing address.

mainframe computer p. 42 Expensive, room-size computer, used mostly for large computing jobs.

malware p. 390 Malicious software, especially destructive programs such as the viruses, worms, and Trojan horses devised and spread by computer saboteurs.

mathematics processing software p. 205 Software designed to deal with complex equations and calculations. A mathematics processor enables the user to create, manipulate, and solve equations easily.

MB (megabyte) p. 81 Approximately 1000K, or 1 million bytes.

megabits p. 81 Approximately 1000 bits.

memory p. 74 Stores programs and the data they need to be instantly accessible to the CPU.

menu p. 156 An onscreen list of command choices.

menu-driven interface p. 156 User interface that enables users to choose commands from onscreen lists called menus.

mesh networks p. 332 Decentralized alternatives to today's central-hub-based networks, allowing a message to hop from wireless device to wireless device until it finds its destination.

meta-search engines p. 366 A software tool that conducts parallel searches using several different search engines and directories.

metropolitan area network (MAN) p. 306 A service that links two or more LANs within a city.

microprocessor p. 41 Now known as a personal computer.

Microsoft Windows p. 157 The most popular and powerful PC operating system; uses a graphical user interface.

MIDI p. 244 Musical Instrument Digital Interface, a standard interface that allows electronic instruments and computers to communicate with each other and work together.

millisecond (ms) p. 89 A thousandth of a second.

modeling p. 208 The use of computers to create abstract models of objects, organisms, organizations, and processes.

modem p. 309 Modulator/demodulator. A hardware device that connects a computer to a telephone line.

Moderated group p. 322 An email discussion group in which a designated moderator acts as an editor, filtering out irrelevant and inappropriate messages and posting the rest.

Moderated newsgroup p. 323 An email newsgroup that contains only messages that have been filtered by designated moderators.

monitor p. 112 An output device that displays text and graphics onscreen.

monochrome monitors p. 113 Monitors, now dated, that can display only one color, such as green or white.

monospaced fonts p. 10 Fonts like those in the Courier family that mimic typewriters; characters, no matter how skinny or fat, always take up the same amount of space.

Moore's law p. 40 The prediction made in 1965 by Gordon Moore that the power of a silicon chip of the same price would double about every 18 months for at least two decades.

moral dilemma p. 407 A predicament for which rules and ethics don't seem to apply, or to contradict one another.

morph p. 240 Video clip in which one image metamorphoses into another.

motherboard p. 81 The circuit board that contains a computer's CPU. Also called a system board.

mouse p. 104 A handheld input device that, when moved around on a desktop or table, moves a pointer around the computer screen.

MP3 p. 244 A method of compression that can squeeze a music file to a fraction of its original CD file size with only slight loss of quality.

MS-DOS p. 156 Microsoft Disk Operating System, an operating system with character-based user interface; it was widely used in the 1980s and early 1990s but has been superceded by Windows.

multifunction printer (MFP) p. 116 An all-in-one output device that usually combines a scanner, a laser or inkjet printer, and a fax modem.

multimedia p. 251 Using some combination of text, graphics, animation, video, music, voice, and sound effects to communicate.

Multimedia-authoring software p. 252 Enables the creation and editing of multimedia documents.

multiprocessing p. 85 Employing two or more microprocessors in a computer in order to improve overall performance. Also known as symmetric multiprocessing.

multitasking p. 151 Concurrent processing for personal computers. The user can issue a command that initiates a process and continue working with other applications while the computer follows through on the command.

N

nanosecond (ns) p. 89 A billionth of a second; a common unit of measurement for read and write access time to RAM.

narrowband connections p. 347 Dial-up Internet connections; named because they don't offer much bandwidth when compared to other types of connections.

National Infrastructure Protection Center p. 412 A state-of-the-art command center created to fight the growing threat of system sabotage. The center includes representatives of various intelligence agencies (the departments of defense, transportation, energy, and treasury), and representatives of several major corporations.

natural language p. 146 Language that people speak and write every day.

Net p. 18 See Internet.

.NET p. 161 An operating system platform from Microsoft that blurs the line between the Web and Microsoft's operating systems and applications.

netiquette p. 328 Rules of etiquette that apply to Internet communication.

network p. 48 A computer system that links two or more computers.

network administrators p. 306 Workers who take care of the behind-the-scenes network details so others can focus on using the network.

network card p. 126 A network interface card that adds a LAN port to a PC.

network computer (NC) p. 50 A computer designed to function as part of a network rather than as a PC.

network interface card (NIC) p. 308 Card that adds an additional serial port to a computer. The port is especially designed for a direct network connection.

network license p. 320 License for multiple copies or removing restrictions on software copying and use at a network site.

network management system software p. 306 Software that helps network administrators maintain healthy networks, especially useful for managing large, complex networks with hundreds of computers.

network operating system (NOS) p. 315 Server operating system software for a local-area network.

newsgroups p. 323 Ongoing public discussions on a particular subject consisting of notes written to a central Internet site and redistributed through a worldwide newsgroup network called Usenet. You can check into and out of them whenever you want; all messages are posted on virtual bulletin boards for anyone to read anytime.

Next Generation Internet (NGI) p. 371 A future nationwide web of optical fiber integrated with intelligent management software to maintain high-speed connections.

node p. 305 Each computer and shared peripheral on a local-area network.

nonimpact printer p. 115 A printer that produces characters without physically striking the page.

nonlinear editing p. 239 A type of video editing in which audio and video clips are stored in digital form on hard disks for immediate access via video editing software.

nonsequential p. 250 Nonvolatile memory; memory for permanent storage of information.

nonvolatile memory p. 89 Memory that is not lost when the computer is turned off. An example is the read-only memory that contains start-up instructions and other critical information.

notebook computer p. 45 Another term for laptop computer.

notifications p. 367 Along with alerts a popular noncorporate type of push technology on the Web, notifying users about online auction status, fees due, and the like.

numeric field p. 269 A field containing only numbers.

O

object-oriented database p. 284 Instead of storing records in tables and hierarchies, stores software objects that contain procedures (or instructions) with data.

object-oriented graphics p. 229 The storage of pictures as collections of lines, shapes, and other objects.

objects p. 284 In object-oriented databases, a data structure defined according to its class.

online banking p. 204 Use of the Internet to conduct basic banking transactions.

online help p. 146 Documentation and help available through a software company's Web site.

online peer-to-peer (P2P) file sharing p. 244 See peer-to-peer file sharing.

online services p. 349 Internet access and a variety of other services in a privately controlled environment offered by gateway companies such as America Online (AOL).

Open p. 163 To load a file into an application program's workspace so it can be viewed and edited by the user.

open architecture p. 127 A design that allows expansion cards and peripherals to be added to a basic computer system.

open source software p. 139 Software that can be distributed and modified freely by users; Linux is the best-known example.

open standards p. 343 Standards not owned by any company.

operating system (OS) p. 151 A system of programs that performs a variety of technical operations, providing an additional layer of insulation between the user and the bits-and-bytes world of computer hardware.

optical character recognition (OCR) p. 106 Locating and identifying printed characters embedded in an image, allowing the text to be stored as an editable document. OCR can be performed by wand readers, pen scanners, and OCR software.

optical computer p. 92 A potential future alternative to silicon-based computing, in which information is transmitted in light waves rather than in electrical pulses.

optical disk drive p. 121 A disk drive that uses laser beams to read and write bits of information on the surface of an optical disk.

optical mark reader p. 106 A reading device that uses reflected light to determine the location of pencil marks on standardized test answer sheets and similar forms.

Outline view p. 181 The outliner option built into Microsoft Word, which enables you to examine and restructure the overall organization of a document, while showing each topic in as much detail as you need.

outliner p. 181 Software that facilitates the arrangement of information into hierarchies or levels of ideas. Some word processors include outline views that serve the same function as separate outliners.

output p. 38 Information given out by the computer.

output device p. 73 Device for sending information from the computer, such as a monitor or printer.

overhead projection panels p. 115 Equipment using LCDs to project computer screen images.

P

P2P model p. 316 See peer-to-peer model.

packet-switching p. 345 The standard technique used to send information over the Internet. A message is broken into packets that travel independently from network to network toward their common destination, where they are reunited.

page-description language p. 229 A language used by many drawing programs that describes text fonts, illustrations, and other elements of the printed page.

page-layout software p. 190 In desktop publishing, software used to combine various source documents into a coherent, visually appealing publication.

painting software p. 223 Enables you to paint pixels on the screen with a pointing device.

palette p. 223 A collection of colors available in drawing software.

paradigm shift p. 51 A change in thinking that results in a new way of seeing the world.

parallel port p. 126 A standard port on most PCs for attaching a printer or other device that communicates by sending or receiving bits in groups, rather than sequentially.

parallel processing p. 85 Using multiple processors to divide jobs into pieces and work simultaneously on the pieces.

parameter RAM p. 89 CMOS RAM, a special low-energy kind of RAM used to store the date, time, and calendar in Macintoshes.

Passport p. 370 A .NET-based user authentication service.

passwords p. 397 The most common security tools used to restrict access to computer systems.

paste p. 9 A word processing program text editing tool that allows you to cut or copy words from one part of a document and place the copy elsewhere in the same or a different document.

patent p. 166 A type of law that protects mechanical inventions.

path p. 352 The hierarchical nesting of directories (folders) that contain a Web resource, as described in the third part of the URL, following the dot address.

pathname p. 162 The unique location specification for every computer file and folder, describing the nesting of folders containing it.

PB (petabyte) p. 81 The equivalent of 1024 terabytes, or 1 quadrillion bytes.

PC card p. 91 A credit-card-size card that can be inserted into a slot to expand memory or add a peripheral to a computer; commonly used in portable computers. Sometimes called by its original name, PCMCIA.

PDF (portable document format) p. 193 Allows documents of all types to be stored, viewed, or modified on any Windows or Macintosh computer, making it possible for many organizations to reduce paper flow.

peer-to-peer (P2P) computing p. 367 See peer-to-peer model.

peer-to-peer file sharing p. 368 The online sharing of music or other computer files directly between individual computer users' hard drives, rather than through posting the files on central servers.

peer-to-peer model p. 316 A LAN model that allows every computer on the network to be both client and server.

pen-based computer p. 107 A keyboardless machine that accepts input from a stylus applied directly to a flat-panel screen.

peripheral p. 74 An external device, such as a keyboard or monitor, connected via cables to the system central processing unit.

Perl p. 361 Practical extraction and reporting language, a Web scripting language that is particularly well-suited for writing scripts to process text—for example, complex Web forms.

personal area network (PAN) p. 314 A network that links a variety of personal electronic devices, such as mobile phones, handheld computers, and PCs, so they can communicate with each other.

personal computer p. 42 A small, powerful, relatively low-cost microcomputer.

personal digital assistant (PDA) p. 107 A pocket-sized computer used to organize appointments, tasks, notes, contacts, and other personal information. Sometimes called handheld computer or palmtop computer. Many PDAs include additional software and hardware for wireless communication.

personal information manager (PIM) p. 273 A specialized database program that automates an address/phone book, an appointment calendar, a to-do list, and miscellaneous notes. Also called an electronic organizer.

personalization p. 357 Customization of a Web site's content, made possible because sites can use login names, passwords, and cookies to track and remember information about guests from visit to visit.

photo management software p. 227 Programs that simplify and automate common tasks associated with capturing, organizing, editing, and sharing digital images.

photo printer p. 115 A type of newer inkjet printer specially optimized to print high-quality photos captured with digital cameras and scanners.

pie chart p. 200 A round pie-shaped chart with slices that show the relative proportions of the parts to a whole.

pixel p. 112 A picture element (dot) on a computer screen or printout. Groups of pixels compose the images on the monitor and the output of a printout.

plagiarism p. 407 The act of presenting someone else's work as one's own.

Plain Old Telephone Service (POTS) p. 347 Used with a modem for narrowband dial-up Internet connections.

platform p. 161 The combination of hardware and operating system software upon which application software is built.

platform independent p. 127 The ability of a peripheral device to work on multiple platforms. For example, a USB disk drive could be used with both Macintosh and Windows computers.

platters p. 122 Flat discs that are the part of the hard disk that holds information.

plotter p. 116 An automated drawing tool that produces finely scaled drawings by moving pen and/or paper in response to computer commands.

plug-in p. 358 A software extension that adds new features.

point size p. 9 A measure of character size, with one point equal to 1/72 inch.

pointing stick (TrackPoint) p. 104 A tiny joystick-like device embedded in the keyboard of a laptop computer.

point-of-sale (POS) terminal p. 106 A terminal with a wand reader, barcode scanner, or other device that captures information at the check-out counter of a store.

pop-up menus p. 158 Menus that can appear anywhere on the screen.

port p. 90 Socket that allows information to pass in and out.

port replicator p. 45 A device that duplicates a laptop's ports, for ease of connection to monitors, printers, and other peripherals.

portable computers p. 45 Small, battery-powered computers such as laptops.

portal p. 367 A Web site designed as a Web entry station, offering quick and easy access to a variety of services.

PostScript p. 229 A standard page-description language.

PPP (point-to-point protocol) p. 347 A protocol that enables a computer to connect to the Internet via modem and temporarily have full Internet access and IP address.

prefetch unit p. 86 Part of the CPU that fetches the next several instructions from memory.

presentation graphics software p. 233 Automates the creation of visual aids for lectures, training sessions, and other presentations. Can include everything from spreadsheet charting programs to animation editing software, but most commonly used for creating and displaying a series of on-screen slides to serve as visual aids for presentations.

primary storage p. 119 A computer's main memory.

print server p. 317 A server that accepts, prioritizes, and processes print jobs.

printer p. 115 Output device that produces a paper copy of any information that can be displayed on the screen.

privacy p. 285 Freedom from unauthorized access to one's person, or to knowledge about one's person.

processor p. 74 Part of the computer that processes information, performs arithmetic calculations, and makes basic decisions based on information values.

program p. 38 Instructions that tell the hardware what to do to transform input into output.

proportionally spaced fonts p. 10 Fonts that enable more room for wide than for narrow characters.

protocol p. 315 A set of rules for the exchange of data between a terminal and a computer or between two computers.

public domain p. 228 Creative work or intellectual property that is freely usable by anyone, either because the copyright has expired or because the creator obtained a Creative Commons license for the work.

public domain software p. 148 Free software that is not copyrighted, offered through World Wide Web sites, electronic bulletin boards, user groups, and other sources.

pull technology p. 367 Technology in which browsers on client computers pull information from server machines. The browser needs to initiate a request before any information is delivered.

pull-down menus p. 157 In a graphical user interface, menus located at the top of the screen or window and accessed with a mouse or with keyboard shortcuts. Also called drop-down menus.

push technology p. 367 Technology in which information is delivered automatically to a client computer. The user subscribes to a service and the server delivers that information periodically and unobtrusively. Contrast with pull technology.

Q

query p. 269 An information request.

query language p. 271 A special language for performing queries, more precise than the English language.

QuickTime p. 358 An Apple program for delivering cross-platform streaming media in proprietary formats.

R

radio frequency identification (RFID) reader p. 106 A reading tool that uses radio waves to communicate with RFID tags.

radio frequency identification (RFID) tag p. 106 A device that, when energized by a nearby RFID reader, broadcasts information to the reader for input into a computer.

RAID (redundant array of independent disk) p. 402 A storage device that allows multiple hard disks to operate as a unit.

RAM (random access memory) p. 74 Memory that stores program instructions and data temporarily.

random access p. 119 Storage method that allows information retrieval without regard to the order in which it was recorded.

raster (bit-mapped) graphics p. 224 Painting programs create raster graphics that are, to the computer, simple maps showing how the pixels on the screen should be represented.

read/write head p. 122 The mechanism that reads information from, and writes information to, the spinning platter in a hard disk or disk drive.

real time p. 239 When a computer performs tasks immediately.

real-time communication p. 325 Internet communication that enables you to communicate with other users who are logged on at the same time.

Real-time streaming audio p. 358 Streaming transmission of radio broadcasts, concerts, news feeds, speeches, and other sound events as they happen.

Real-time streaming video p. 358 Similar to streaming audio Webcasts, but with video.

record p. 268 In a database, the information relating to one person, product, or event.

record matching p. 290 Compiling profiles by combining information from different database files by looking for a shared unique field.

relational database p. 279 A program that allows files to be related to each other so that changes in one file are reflected in other files automatically.

remote access p. 308 Network access via phone line, TV cable system, or wireless link.

removable cartridge media p. 121 See removable media.

removable media p. 6 Storage media designed to be removed and transported easily, including Zip, Jaz, and Orb disks.

repetitive-stress injuries p. 103 Conditions that result from repeating the same movements over long periods, such as keyboarding-induced carpal tunnel syndrome, a painful affliction of the wrist and hand.

replication p. 198 Automatic replication of values, labels, and formulas, a feature of spreadsheet software.

report p. 271 A database printout that is an ordered list of selected records and fields in an easy-to-read form.

resolution p. 112 Density of pixels, measured by the number of dots per inch.

retinal display p. 130 A device that works without a screen by drawing pixels directly on the user's retina with a focused beam of light.

right to privacy p. 291 Freedom from interference into the private sphere of a person's affairs.

right-click p. 8 Hitting the right-hand part of mouse button so that, for example, while pointing to an object the computer may display a menu of choices.

rip p. 244 Copy songs from a CD to a computer's hard drive.

rollover p. 358 A common use of Web scripting, used to make onscreen buttons visibly change when the pointer rolls over them.

ROM (read-only memory) p. 89 Memory that includes permanent information only. The computer can only read information from it; it can never write any new information on it.

root directory p. 162 The main folder on a computer's primary hard disk, containing all the other files and folders kept on the disk.

routers p. 307 Programs or devices that decide how to route Internet transmissions.

S

sabotage p. 390 A malicious attack on work, tools, or business.

sample p. 241 A digital sound file.

samplers p. 244 An electronic musical instrument that can sample digital sounds, turn them into notes, and play them back at any pitch.

sampling rate p. 241 The rate that a sound wave is sampled; the more samples per second, the more closely the digitized sound approximates the original.

sans-serif fonts p. 10 Typeface fonts in which the characters have plain and clean lines rather than embellishments at the ends of the main strokes.

satellite Internet connections p. 349 A broadband technology available through many of the same satellite dishes that provide television channels to viewers. For many rural homes and businesses, satellite Internet connections provide the only high-speed Internet access options available.

save p. 163 A basic file-management operation that writes the current state of the application as a disk file.

save as p. 163 A basic file-management operation that allows you to choose the location and name of the file you want to contain the current state of the application.

Scalable Vector Graphics (SVG) p. 238 An open standard of vector graphics format.

scanner p. 108 An input device that makes a digital representation of any printed image. See flatbed scanners, slide scanners, drum scanners, and sheetfed scanners.

scatter chart p. 200 Discovers a relationship between two variables.

scientific visualization software p. 206 Uses shape, location in space, color, brightness, and motion to help you understand invisible relationships, providing graphical representation of numerical data.

scripts p. 358 Short programs that can add interactivity, animation, and other dynamic features to a Web page or multimedia document.

SCSI p. 127 Small Computer Systems Interface, an interface design enabling several peripherals to be strung together and attached to a single port.

search p. 16 Looking for a specific record.

search engine p. 21 A program for locating information on the Web.

secondary storage p. 119 The category of computer storage found in peripherals such as tape and disk drives.

sectors p. 165 Units of data or memory on a hard disk, existing as parts of concentric tracks.

security patch p. 393 Software programs that plug potential security breaches in an operating system, often provided as free downloads or automatic updates to all owners of the OS.

security processors p. 416 Special-purpose hardware that allows every network message to be encrypted.

select (records) p. 269 Looking for all records that match a set of criteria.

selects p. 8 Chooses an object, by moving the pointer to a picture of a tool or object on the screen and clicking the mouse.

semiconductor p. 40 A device that packs hundreds of transistors into a single integrated circuit on a tiny silicon chip.

sensor p. 112 A device that enables digital machines to monitor a physical quantity of the analog world, such as temperature, humidity, or pressure, to provide data used in robotics, environmental climate control, and other applications.

sequencing software p. 244 Software that enables a computer to be used as a tool for musical composition, recording, and editing.

sequential p. 250 Linear in form, and designed to be read from beginning to end, as are conventional text media like books.

sequential access p. 119 Storage method that requires the user to retrieve information by zipping through it in the order in which it was recorded.

serial port p. 126 A standard port on most PCs for attaching a modem or other device that can send and receive messages one bit at a time.

serif fonts p. 10 Typeface fonts in which the characters are embellished with fine lines (serifs) at the ends of the main strokes.

server p. 44 A computer especially designed to provide software and other resources to other computers over a network.

set-top box p. 50 A special-purpose computer designed to provide Internet access and other services using a standard television set and (usually) a cable TV connection.

shareware p. 148 Software that is free for the trying, with a send-pay-ment-if-you-keep-it honor system.

sheetfed scanners p. 108 Small scanners that accept pages one at a time through a sheet feeder.

shell p. 157 A program layer that stands between the user and the operating system.

Shockwave Flash Format (SWF) p. 238 A popular form of vector graphics format associated with the Macromedia flash player.

Shockwave/Flash p. 357 Macromedia plug-ins that enable Web browsers to present compressed interactive multimedia documents and animations created with various authoring tools.

silicon chip p. 40 Hundreds of transistors packed into an integrated circuit on a piece of silicon.

Silicon Valley p. 41 The area around San Jose, California, that has become a hotbed of the computer industry since the 1970s, when dozens of micro-processor manufacturing companies sprouted and grew there.

SIMMs p. 90 Single in-line memory modules.

site license p. 320 License for multiple copies or removing restrictions on software copying and use at a network site.

slide scanners p. 108 Scanners for slides and negatives only.

slot p. 90 An area inside the computer's housing that holds special-pur-pose circuit boards.

smart badge p. 406 See active badge.

smart weapon p. 410 A missile that uses computerized guidance systems to locate its target.

smart whiteboard p. 108 A large electronic writing surface, as for use in a classroom, capable of sending its contents to a PC, where the informa-tion can be stored as digital information or turned into text files.

SMIL (synchronized multimedia integration language) p. 361 An HTML-like language designed to make it possible to link time-based streaming media so that, for example, sounds, video, and animation can be tightly integrated with each other.

social engineering p. 388 Slang for the use of deception to get individuals to reveal sensitive information.

software p. 38 Instructions that tell the hardware what to do to transform input into output.

software components p. 370 Pieces of existing software that can be used to assemble Web services quickly. Component technology can, for exam-ple, make it easy to plug a shopping-cart component into an existing Web site.

software license p. 148 An agreement allowing the use of a software pro-gram on a single machine.

software piracy p. 148 The illegal duplication of copyrighted software.

software-defined radio p. 322 A technology that allows a single wireless hardware device to be reprogrammed on the fly to serve a variety of functions.

solid-state storage p. 126 Storage, such as flash memory, with no moving parts. Solid-state storage is likely to replace disk storage in the future.

sort p. 271 Arrange records in alphabetic or numeric order based on val-ues in one or more fields.

sound card p. 117 A circuit board that allows the PC to accept micro-phone input, play music and other sound through speakers or headphones, and process sound in a variety of ways.

source document p. 190 In desktop publishing, the articles, chapters, drawings, maps, charts, and photographs that are to appear in the publica-tion. Usually produced with standard word processors and graphics programs.

spam p. 25 Internet junk mail.

spam filters p. 25 Tools found in most email programs whose purpose is to limit or control Internet junk mail.

speakers p. 7 The personal computer peripherals that emit music, voices, and other sounds.

speech recognition p. 112 The identification of spoken words and sen-tences by a computer, making it possible for voice input to be converted into text files.

speech-recognition software p. 186 See speech recognition.

spelling checker (batch or interactive) p. 183 A built-in component of a word processor or a separate program that compares words in a document with words in a disk-based dictionary and flags words not found in the dic-tionary. May operate in batch mode, checking all the words at once, or in-teractive mode, checking one word at a time.

spiders p. 366 See web crawlers.

spoofing p. 388 A process used to steal passwords online.

spot color p. 192 The relatively easy use of a single color (or sometimes two) to add interest to a desktop publishing product.

spreadsheet software p. 196 Enables the user to control numbers, manip-ulating them in various ways. The software can manage budgeting, invest-ment management, business projections, grade books, scientific simula-tions, checkbooks, financial planning and speculation, and other tasks involving numbers.

spybot p. 392 A spyware application program, also called tracking soft-ware, that gathers user information and communicates it to an outsider via the Internet.

spyware p. 392 Technology that collects information from computer users without their knowledge or consent.

stack chart p. 200 Stacked bars to show how proportions of a whole change over time.

statistical analysis software p. 206 Specialized software that tests the strength of data relationships, produces graphs showing how two or more variables relate to each other, uncovers trends, and performs other statisti-cal analyses.

statistics p. 205 The science of analyzing and collecting data.

storage device p. 74 Long-term repository for data. Disks and tape drives are examples.

stored query p. 271 A commonly used query recorded by a database so that it can be accessed quickly in the future. The ability to generate stored queries is a powerful feature that helps databases blur the line between ap-plication programs and development tools.

storyboard p. 239 The first step in a video project, a guide for shooting and editing scenes.

streaming audio p. 357 Sound files that play without being completely downloaded to the local hard disk.

streaming video p. 358 Video clip files that play while being downloaded.

Structured Query Language (SQL) p. 271 A query language available for many different database management systems. More than a query lan-guage, SQL also accesses databases from a wide variety of vendors.

stylesheet p. 179 Custom styles for each of the common elements in a document.

stylus p. 104 An input device, with much the same point-and-click func-tions as a mouse, used to send signals to a pressure sensitive graphics tablet.

subject tree p. 366 A hierarchical catalog of Web sites compiled by re-searchers, like that found at Yahoo!

subnotebooks p. 45 Portable computers, smaller than a notebook or lap-top, about the size of a hardbound book.

supercomputer p. 43 A super-fast, super-powerful, and super-expensive computer used for applications that demand maximum power.

switches p. 305 Hardware that decides how to route Internet transmis-sions. Switches are similar to software routers, but faster and less flexible.

symmetric multiprocessing p. 85 See multiprocessing.

synthesized p. 241 Synthetically generated computer sounds.

synthesizer p. 117 A device that can produce—synthesize—music and other sounds electronically. A synthesizer might be a stand-alone musical instrument or part of the circuitry on a computer's sound card.

system bus p. 90 A group of wires that transmits information between components on the motherboard.

system software p. 151 Software that handles the details of computing. Includes the operating system and utility programs.

system unit p. 6 The box that houses a personal computer's central processing unit—in other words, "the computer" or "the PC."

T

T1 p. 347 A direct connect digital line that can transmit voice, data, and video at roughly 1.5Mbps.

T3 p. 347 A direct connect digital line that transmits voice, data, and video even faster than a T1 connection.

table p. 268 A grid of rows and columns; on many Web pages tables with hidden grids are used to align graphical images.

tape drive p. 119 Storage device that uses magnetic tape to store information.

task bar p. 158 A button bar that provides one-click access to open applications and tools, making it easy to switch back and forth between different tasks.

tax preparation software p. 204 Provides a prefabricated worksheet where the user enters numbers into tax forms. Calculations are performed automatically, and the completed forms can be sent electronically to the IRS.

TB (terabyte) p. 81 Approximately 1 million megabytes.

TCP/IP (Transmission Control Protocol/Internet Protocol) p. 315 Protocols developed as an experiment in internetworking, now the language of the Internet, allowing cross-network communication for almost every type of computer and network.

telecommunication p. 304 Long-distance electronic communication in a variety of forms.

tele-immersion p. 256 The use of multiple cameras and high-speed networks to create an environment in which multiple remote users can interact with each other and with computer-generated objects.

telephony p. 326 Technology that enables computers to serve as speakerphones, answering machines, and complete voice mail systems.

templates p. 190 In desktop publishing, professionally designed empty documents that can be adapted to specific user needs. In spreadsheet software, worksheets that contain labels and formulas but no data values. The template produces instant answers when you fill in the blanks.

terminal emulation software p. 316 Software that allows a PC to act as a dumb terminal—an input/output device that enables the user to send commands to and view information on the host computer.

terminal p. 42 Combination keyboard and screen that transfers information to and from a mainframe computer.

thesaurus p. 182 A synonym finder; often included with a word processor.

time bomb p. 392 A logic bomb that is triggered by a time-related event.

timesharing p. 43 Technique by which mainframe computers communicate with several users simultaneously.

touch screen p. 104 Pointing device that responds when the user points to or touches different screen regions.

touchpad (trackpad) p. 104 A small flat-panel pointing device that is sensitive to light pressure. The user moves the pointer by dragging a finger across the pad.

trackball p. 104 Pointing device that remains stationary while the user moves a protruding ball to control the pointer on the screen.

tracking software p. 392 A spyware application program, also called a spybot, that gathers user information and communicates it to an outsider via the Internet.

tracks p. 165 A series of concentric units of data or memory on a hard disk.

trademark p. 166 Legal ownership protection for symbols, pictures, sounds, colors, and smells used by a business to identify goods.

transistor p. 40 An electronic device that performs the same function as the vacuum tube by transferring electricity across a tiny resistor.

Trojan horse p. 391 A program that performs a useful task while at the same time carrying out some secret destructive act. A form of software sabotage.

true color p. 113 Color that is 24-bit or greater, allowing more than 16 million color choices per pixel, creating photorealistic images.

tweening p. 238 The automatic creation of in-between frames in an animation.

twisted pair p. 305 A type of LAN cable that resembles the copper wires in standard telephone cables.

typeface p. 10 All type, including roman, bold, and italics, of a single design, such as Palatino or Helvetica.

U

ultrawideband p. 332 A low-power, short-range, wireless technology that transmits ultra-high-speed signals over a wide spectrum of frequencies.

Unicode p. 78 A 65,000-character set for making letters, digits, and special characters fit into the computer's binary circuitry.

uninterruptible power supply (UPS) p. 402 A hardware device that protects computers from data loss during power failures.

universal product codes (UPCs) p. 106 Codes created from patterns of variable-width bars that send scanned information to a mainframe computer.

UNIX p. 158 An operating system that allows a timesharing computer to communicate with several other computers or terminals at once. UNIX is the most widely available multi-user operating system in use. It is also widely used on Internet hosts.

upgrade p. 147 A new and improved version of a software program.

upload p. 317 To post software or documents to an online source so they're available for others.

URL (uniform resource locator) p. 352 The address of a Web site.

USB (universal serial bus) p. 127 A data path standard that theoretically allows up to 126 devices, such as keyboards, digital cameras, and scanners, to be chained together from a single port, allowing for data transmission that is much faster and more flexible than through traditional serial and parallel ports.

USB 2.0 p. 127 A new, high-speed version of USB that offers fast transfer rates of 480 megabits per second.

user identifier p. 403 A unique name or number assigned by the operating system to a particular computer user.

user interface p. 156 The look and feel of the computing experience from a human point of view.

user name p. 23 A one-word name that you type to identify yourself when connecting—logging in—to a secure computer system, network, or email account. Sometimes called login name or alias.

utility programs p. 154 Software that serves as tools for doing system maintenance and some repairs that are not automatically handled by the operating system.

V

value p. 196 The numbers that are the raw material used by spreadsheet software to perform calculations.

vector graphics p. 229 The storage of pictures as collections of lines, shapes, and other objects.

vertical portals (vortal) p. 367 Specialized portals that, like vertical market software, are targeted at members of a particular industry or economic sector.

vertical-market application p. 150 A computer application designed specifically for a particular business or industry.

video adapter p. 115 A circuit board installed inside the main system unit connecting the monitor to the computer.

video digitizer p. 108 A device that converts analog video signals into digital data.

video editing software p. 240 Software for editing digital video, including titles, sound, and special effects.

video port p. 126 A port for plugging a color monitor into a computer's video board.

video projector p. 115 A projector that can project computer screen images for meetings and classes.

video teleconference p. 325 Face-to-face communication over long distances using video and computer technology.

videoconferencing p. 108 Face-to-face communication over long distances using video and computer technology.

virtual instruments p. 246 Musical instruments that exist only in software; they are gradually replacing bulky, expensive hardware devices in the typical electronic music studio.

virtual memory p. 154 Use of part of a computer hard disk as a substitute for RAM.

virtual private networks p. 331 Networks that use encryption software to create secure "tunnels" through the public Internet.

virtual reality p. 168 Technology that creates the illusion that the user is immersed in a world that exists only inside the computer, an environment that contains both scenes and the controls to change those scenes.

virtual worlds p. 256 Computer-generated worlds that create the illusion of immersion.

viruses p. 390 Software that spreads from program to program, or from disk to disk, and uses each infected program or disk to make copies of itself. A form of software sabotage.

voice input p. 112 Use of a microphone to speak commands and text data to a computer, which uses speech recognition software to interpret the input.

voicemail p. 326 A telephone-based messaging system with many of the features of an email system.

volume licenses p. 148 Special license agreements for entire companies, schools, or government institutions to make use of a program.

VRAM p. 115 A special portion of RAM dedicated to holding video images.

W

warchalking p. 330 An unofficial grassroots movement to mark wireless hot spots by writing a symbol on a nearby sidewalk or wall.

waveform audio p. 241 Sound-editing software in which a visual image is manipulated using the sound's wave form.

wearable computers p. 294 Strap-on computer units for active information gatherers.

Web p. 20 See World Wide Web.

Web authoring software p. 355 Programs such as Macromedia's Dreamweaver that work like desktop publishing page layout programs to allow users to create, edit, and manage Web pages and sites without having to write HTML code.

Web browsers p. 49 Application programs that enable you to explore the Web by clicking hyperlinks in Web pages stored on Web sites.

Web bug p. 364 An invisible piece of code embedded in HTML-formatted email that is programmed to send information about its receiver's Web use back to its creator.

web crawlers p. 366 Software robots that systematically explore the Web, retrieve information about pages, and index the retrieved information in a database.

Web page p. 20 A single document on the World Wide Web (WWW), made up of text and images and interlinked with other documents.

Web server p. 352 A server that stores Web pages and sends them to client programs—Web browsers—that request them.

Web services p. 370 New kinds of Web-based applications that can be assembled quickly using existing software components.

Web site p. 20 A collection of related Web pages stored on the same server.

Webjacker p. 394 Someone who hijacks legitimate Web sites, redirecting unsuspecting visitors to bogus or offensive alternate sites.

Weblog (or blog) p. 355 See blog.

"what if?" questions p. 200 A feature of spreadsheet software that allows speculation by providing instant answers to hypothetical questions.

wide area network (WAN) p. 48 A network that extends over a long distance. Each network site is a node on the network.

Wi-Fi p. 313 A popular wireless LAN technology that allows multiple computers to connect to a LAN through a base station up to 150 feet away. Often referred to as 802.11b.

WiMax p. 332 A wireless alternative to cable or DSL service.

window p. 157 In a graphical user interface, a framed area that can be opened, closed, and rearranged with the mouse. Documents are displayed in windows.

Windows p. 157 See Microsoft Windows.

Windows Media Player p. 358 A Microsoft program for delivering streaming media in proprietary formats that are compatible with other players.

Wired equivalent privacy (WEP) p. 331 An encryption scheme that improves the security of wireless networks.

wireless keyboard p. 103 A keyboard that uses infrared signals rather than wires to communicate with a computer.

wireless network p. 305 A network in which a node has a tiny radio or infrared transmitter connected to its network port so it can send and receive data through the air rather than through cables.

wizard p. 181 A software help agent that walks the user through a complex process.

WMA p. 244 Windows Media Audio, one of a number of relatively new methods of audio compression than can squeeze music files to a fraction of their original CD-file sizes, often without perceptible loss of quality.

word size p. 84 The number of bits a CPU can process at one time, typically 8, 16, 32, or 64.

word wrap p. 9 A word processing program text editing feature that automatically moves any words that won't fit on the current line to the next line, along with the cursor.

worksheet p. 196 A spreadsheet document that appears on the screen as a grid of numbered rows and columns.

workstation p. 44 A high-end desktop computer with massive computing power, though less expensive than a minicomputer. Workstations are the most powerful of the desktop computers.

World Wide Web (WWW) p. 49 Part of the Internet, a collection of multimedia documents created by organizations and users worldwide. Documents are linked in a hypertext Web that allows users to explore them with simple mouse clicks.

worms p. 391 Programs that use computer hosts to reproduce themselves. Worm programs travel independently over computer networks, seeking out uninfected workstations to occupy. A form of software sabotage.

writeback p. 87 The final phase of execution, in which the bus unit writes the results of the instruction back into memory or some other device.

WYSIWYG p. 196 Short for "what you see is what you get," pronounced "wizzy-wig." With a word processor, the arrangement of the words on the screen represents a close approximation to the arrangement of words on the printed page.

X

XHTML p. 361 Markup language that combines features of HTML and XML; its advantage is its backward compatibility with HTML.

XML p. 282 Extensible Markup language, a language that enables Web developers to control and display data the way they control text and graphics. Forms, database queries, and other data-intensive operations that can't be completely constructed with standard HTML are much easier with XML.

Z

Zip disk p. 121 A popular type of removable cartridge storage media, developed by Iomega, that looks like a thicker version of a standard diskette and can hold up to 750MB of data.

Photo Credits

4.25	Courtesy of Microsoft Corp.	7.5	Courtesy of Microsoft Corp.		Apple Computer, Inc.
4.27	Courtesy of Microsoft Corp.	7.6	Courtesy of Microsoft Corp.	9.6	© CORBIS
4.28	Courtesy of Microsoft Corp.	7.7	Courtesy of Google Inc.	9.10	Courtesy of Microsoft Corp.
4.29	Apple Computers, Inc.	7.8	Hot-Air Balloon © Jan Butchofsky-	9.12	Screenshots Courtesy of Macromedia

4.25 Courtesy of Microsoft Corp.
4.27 Courtesy of Microsoft Corp.
4.28 Courtesy of Microsoft Corp.
4.29 Apple Computers, Inc.
4.31 Ivan Sekretarev/ AP/Wide World Photos
4.32 top: Argonne National Library
bottom: Bill Sherman/Paul J. Rajlich
5.1 AP/Wide World Photos
5.2 Bootstrap Institute
5.5 Courtesy of Microsoft Corp.
5.6 Courtesy of Microsoft Corp.
5.7 left: Internet Public Library
right: Bartleby.com
5.8 Courtesy of Microsoft Corp..
5.9 Courtesy of Microsoft Corp.
5.10 Courtesy of Microsoft Corp.
5.11 ScanSoft
5.13 Tobi Zausner
5.15 Screens courtesy of Adobe Systems, Inc.
5.16 Courtesy of Adobe Systems, Inc.
5.17 David Patryas/Index Stock Imagery, Inc.
5.18 Salon.com
5.20 Palo Alto Research Center, a subsidiary of Xerox Corporation
5.21 courtesy of Microsoft Corp.
5.22 Screen shots courtesy of Microsoft Corp.
5.23 courtesy of Microsoft Corp.
5.26 Courtesy of Intuit, Inc.
5.28 Argonne National Laboratory
5.29 University of California, Los Angeles
5.31 Screenshots courtesy of Microsoft Corp.
5.32 top: Courtesy of Laminar Research
bottom: www.X-Plane.com
6.1 © Sam Ogden
6.2 CERN/European Organization for Nuclear Research
6.3 Agence France Presse/Getty Images
6.4 Courtesy of Microsoft Corp.
6.5 Sanjay Kothari
6.7 Apple Computers, Inc.
6.9 MicroMedia
6.11 Eovia Corporation
6.12 AP/Wide World Photos
6.13 Photo Researchers, Inc.
6.14 Courtesy of Microsoft Corp.
6.15 Photo courtesy of Dream Works Pictures/Photofest
6.18 Apple Computers, Inc.
6.20 Images courtesy of Glyph/Image
6.21 RioPort
6.22 Apple Computers, Inc.
6.23 Comstock Royalty Free Division
6.24 top: Courtesy of Propellerhead Software
6.25 pg. 248 clockwise from top left: Siede Preis/Getty Images; Jules Frazier/Getty Images; Royalty-Free/CORBIS pg. 249 clockwise from the top: Apple Computers, Inc.; courtesy of JBL Professional; David Toase/Getty Images
6.26 top: Courtesy of Sienna Software
bottom: courtesy of World Book
6.29 Mark Richards/PhotoEdit
6.30 a. David Barry/ Corbis/Outline
7.2 Courtesy of Microsoft Corp.
7.3 COPYRIGHT © EBAY INC. ALL RIGHTS RESERVED

7.5 Courtesy of Microsoft Corp.
7.6 Courtesy of Microsoft Corp.
7.7 Courtesy of Google Inc.
7.8 Hot-Air Balloon © Jan Butchofsky-Houser/CORBIS
Airplane © Tecmap Corporation; Eric Curry/CORBIS
Helicopter © Royalty-Free/CORBIS
Sailboat © Royalty-Free/CORBIS
Hang Glider © David Cumming; Eye Ubiquitous/CORBIS
Canoe © Brand X Pictures/ PictureQuest Inc.
Cruise Ship © David Samuel Robbins/CORBIS
Bicycle © Brand X Pictures/ PictureQuest Inc.
Scooter © PhotoAlto/PictureQuest Inc.
Mini-Van © Photodisc/Getty Images
Automobile © Digital Vision/ PictureQuest Inc.
7.9 clockwise from the top: Courtesy of Microsoft Corp.; Motorola, Inc.; Nokia
7.13 James A. Folts Photography
7.15 www.askjeeves.com
7.16 Reason Foundation
7.17 Robert E. Daemmrich/Getty Images, Inc.
7.20 © Ralf-Finn Hestoft/CORBIS
7.21 © Royalty-Free/CORBIS
7.22 Spencer Platt/Getty Images
7.23 The Image Bank/Getty Images, Inc.
7.24 © James Leynse/CORBIS
8.1 Jeff Greenwald
8.2 © David Ducros/Photo Researchers, Inc.
8.6 Mark Richards/PhotoEdit
8.7 Jean Miele/CORBIS Stock Market
8.8 AP/Wide World Photos
8.10 left: Courtesy of Linksys
8.11 (top to bottom) Champlain Cable Corporation; Courtesy of Inmac; Optical Cable Corp.; Extended Systems; Proxim, Inc.
8.12 AP/Wide World Photos
8.14 Getty Images Inc. - Stone Allstock
8.15 Reprinted with permission from Microsoft Corp..
8.17 Courtesy of International Business Machines Corporation. Unauthorized use not permitted.
8.18 Screenshot courtesy of Microsoft Corp..
8.20 top: Courtesy of Microsoft Corp.
left: Courtesy of Microsoft Corp.
right: Courtesy of Apple Computers, Inc.
8.22 Courtesy of Google
8.24 top: Nick Koudis/Getty Images
8.25 Motorola
8.26 Qualcomm
8.28 Wi-Fi Alliance
9.1 © Clark Quinn
9.2 AP/Wide World Photos
9.4 school building: Courtesy of Yale University
office buildings: © Steve Allen/ Brand X Pictures/ PictureQuest
9.5 U.S. Robotics Corporation; Belken Components; Cisco Systems; Eicon Networks Inc.; NETGEAR, Inc.; Courtesy of Linksys; © CORBIS;

Apple Computer, Inc.
9.6 © CORBIS
9.10 Courtesy of Microsoft Corp.
9.12 Screenshots Courtesy of Macromedia
9.13 top: Microsoft Corp.
bottom: Apple Computers, Inc.
9.14 Courtesy of Shockwave.com
9.15 Amazon.com
9.17 Courtesy of Google
9.18 mysimon.com
9.19 Reproduced with permission of Yahoo! Inc.® 2003 by Yahoo! Inc. YAHOO! and the YAHOO! logo are trademarks of Yahoo! inc.
9.20 SETI@Home Project
9.21 COPYRIGHT © EBAY INC. ALL RIGHTS RESERVED
9.22 Tech Corps.
9.23 © ROB & SAS/CORBIS
9.24 Corbis/Sygma
9.25 a: Courtesy of NASA/JPL/Caltech
b: © The Electrolux Group
10.2 © CORBIS
10.3 Kensington Microware
10.4 PayPal
10.6 Symantec Corporation
10.7 © MARK POWELL/CORBIS SYGMA
10.8 Courtesy of Network Associates
10.9 Symantec Corporation
10.11 Symantec Corporation
10.14 American Power Conversion Corporation
10.17 © 2001Versus Technology, Inc.
10.18 Michelle D. Bridwell/PhotoEdit
10.19 © AFP/CORBIS
10.20 © Mark Leffingwell/ AFP/CORBIS
10.22 © Bill Varie/CORBIS

Images used in the following figures appear courtesy of:

0.21, 1.5, 2.4, 3.16, 4.24, 5.14, 6.17, 7.9, 7.12, 7.13, 8.4, 8.5, 8.9, 8.16, 9.3, 9.7, 9.9, 9.11, 10.10, 10.12, 10.13

Courtesy of Apple
Courtesy of Dell Inc.
Courtesy of HP
Courtesy Gateway Inc.
IBM Corporation
© Stephen Swintek/Getty Images
© Royalty-Free/CORBIS
Courtesy Imation Corporation
C.Borland/Photolink/Picturequest
© Agfa-Gevaert Group
© Epson America Inc.
Copyright © 2004 D-Link Systems, Inc.
Photo courtesy 3com Corporation
NASA/NSSDC
Photo courtesy Micron Technology, Inc.
© Edirol Corporation
NETGEAR is a registered trademark of NETGEAR, Inc.
© Photodisc/Getty Images

Images used in the following figures are courtesy of Scobel Wiggins: 3.19, 3.29, 5.19, 7.9, 9.10

Index